S0-CPR-771

DON PEDRO AND THE DEVIL

DON PEDRO and the DEVIL

A Novel of Chivalry Declining

by

EDGAR MAASS

PUBLISHERS

THE BOBBS-MERRILL COMPANY

INDIANAPOLIS NEW YORK

PRINTED IN THE UNITED STATES

First Edition

PRINTED AND BOUND BY THE
COUNTRY LIFE PRESS CORP.
GARDEN CITY, N. Y. U.S.A.

CONTENTS

The Past—the dark unfathom'd retrospect!
The teeming gulf—the sleepers and the shadows!
The past—the infinite greatness of the past!
For what is the present after all but a growth out of the past?
(As a projectile form'd impell'd, passing a certain line, still keeps on,
So the present, utterly form'd, impell'd by the past.)

—Walt Whitman: *Passage to India*

DON PEDRO AND THE DEVIL

1

A MIRACLE PLAY

I WAS born under the sign of Libra. In this circumstance is rooted a certain reluctance to come to a decision, a failing that has often worked to my disadvantage. It is hard for me to make up my mind even in the smallest matters. I weigh all the conditions, events, things, persons involved until finally yes and no come into equilibrium. With such a disposition I really should have been a jurist or a scholar and might have been, had not Mars on the night of my birth stood near his zenith, drawing me inevitably along his red path.

I, myself, do not understand much about the mysterious influence of the stars, but my teacher Agrippa once read me my horoscope, and he was a great philosopher, on intimate terms with all kinds of gifted men.

My mother came from a branch of the Sforza family which had great honor in Italy. My inclination to dream, they tell me, I inherited from her. Weeks and months on end I can remain alone without feeling the need of human society. As a matter of fact I can scarcely remember her. She died when I was only four years old. At times when I am sad and close my eyes I imagine I see a blonde woman with large blue eyes in a delicate face bending over me anxiously. But when I open my eyes again I am unable to keep the image of her features. The oval line of her white cheeks reminds me of the sorrowing young Holy Mary whom I saw as a youth in the Cathedral of Seville. Sancho assures me that my mother, too, was a holy woman. He says that she bore her difficult lot with humility and never besought her rich Italian relatives who cut themselves off from her after her marriage to my father, a poor Castilian nobleman.

One of my mother's great-aunts was the second wife of Don Maximiliano, the German Emperor and grandfather of our Don Carlos.

This Don Maximiliano is said to have been a lusty man who was always getting into the most fantastic money troubles. On the contrary our Don Carlos, they say, goes about with a hangdog air, and is quite unable to laugh from the chest. His father, Don Felipe, Duke of Burgundy and the Netherlands, had many love affairs with pretty burgher maidens. This simply broke the heart of his wife, poor Doña Juana, the mother of our Imperial master, and in the end drove her out of her mind. Well, Don Felipe is long since dead. May God forgive him his carnal sins. But Doña Juana, now an old woman, still lives on and shares the Crown of Spain with her son.

Since I have begun to talk about our ruling house I should like to mention Doña Juana's parents also, for it is quite possible that my words will fall into the hands of some ignorant person who might confront these exalted names as a bewildered ox a new city gate. Doña Juana's parents were Don Fernando of Aragon and Doña Isabella of Castile, under whose famous rule Spain was united and drove the unbelievers into Africa.

Now I must turn away from politics, come back to my own small life which, influenced by the great events of our time, moved along a strange and adventurous path. My father was a poor hidalgo. As a young man he participated in the renowned siege of Granada. It is still told how our blessed Queen, Doña Isabella, swore by all that is holy that she would never so much as change her skirt until Granada had fallen. The Moors gave in after eight months, if my memory serves me right, and for a while Doña Isabella took for her palace the castle Alhambra. The Alhambra, my steward Sancho assures me, when one considers its shadowed courtyards, innumerable fountains, alcoves and cunningly twisted columns, might easily be imagined the work of some Venetian glass blower who had turned his skill upon the whole top of the hill behind the city. In recognition of his services, my father some years later was sent as a member of a deputation to the court of our Holy Father, the Pope, in Rome.

It was there that he became acquainted with my mother. A long time passed before the wedding took place. For many months my mother tried to overcome the resistance of her prominent family, and my father struggled even longer to get his reward for the services he had rendered the Crown of Spain. In the end he was given, here in Cordova, a small house that previously had been the property of an Arab scholar. It was a well-built house. In the Moor's study it still smelled strong of sulphur. The former owner was said to be a great alchemist, and I well remember the pentagram on the threshold, and the great hearth with the sooted chimney-box through which on stormy nights the wind howled and moaned so loudly it made the hair rise on the back of my neck.

Sancho was of the opinion that this howling, like the smell of sulphur, came from some living thing which would have been able to enter the house through the flue were it not for the pentagram on the threshold. He said that the mysterious creature with horns and horse's hoofs let out such weird cries because below on the wall hung a great crucifix. This, at least, was Sancho's belief, and very often he would supplement it with a short but effective extemporaneous prayer to Saint Michael, conqueror of the Devil. But Teresa, my housekeeper, who was then a strapping peasant girl, used to cross first me and then herself, and afterward we would all go to bed.

I must admit that the creature of the chimney often came into my dreams. He wore a long red cloak and a cap with a red feather, and bore himself with the address of a hidalgo. He sat at my bedside and, shivering and blowing, rubbed his long skinny fingers. He talked to me very seriously, quite unlike the other grown-up people, then opened the leather pouch he carried at his belt and poured a heap of gold pieces on my coverlet. At first this pleased me very much, but the pouch seemed to have no bottom. A stream of gold piled up over me, pressing down heavily on my chest, legs and arms. I could not stir and when I wanted to cry out he would stop my mouth with gold. Everything ended when a light appeared above me, and I looked up into a round face with kindly eyes. It was my good Teresa. Bedded out of sight under the clothes against her warm girl's belly I soon slept sweetly, and dreaming I again heard the voice of Sancho from a distance, complaining that I had robbed him of his rightful place in bed.

Of my father I remember nothing at all. A few years after he had fetched my mother home to his small house he was sent by Don Fernando on an important mission to Naples. The galley never reached its destination. There was a terrible storm, and some days later the wreckage of a ship was cast up on the beach at Marina Piccola on the Island of Capri. In her anguish my mother betook herself with all haste to the island. Sancho has often told me how she sat on the cape days on end, looking out to sea, which stretched before her harmless and blue in the blinding summer sun. Many a sail bore slowly up over the horizon, ships from Sicily, Africa, and Spain, even from Portugal, but never did she see my father's vessel, the one carrying the arms of Aragon on her steep lateen sail. With a weary heart my mother gave up her search, traveled back to Rome with Sancho, there to seek comfort at the grave of the Holy Petrus and to pray for me, her small son, Pedro. She knew very well that her days on this earth were numbered.

Sancho used to tell me that in Rome, among the proud houses of the Colonna, Orsini and Farnese, among the castles of the Pope and the countless churches and holy places, there were huge gray walls of stone. These structures had been built by Julius Caesar, and his successors, the Roman emperors, had once lived in them. And there in Rome was a circus, with a wide arena, much similar to what we use for our bullfights. In this circus Emperor Nero, the same one spoken of in the Apocalypse, threw many Christians to the wild beasts. When I first saw the buildings of Tavanta-Suyu, the endless streets straight as a ferule and the aqueducts, I thought of my Sancho's stories.

A year after the shipwreck death closed my mother's eyes forever. I have not the slightest remembrance of this bitter event, but there still remains, I think, some of that ineffable, crippling sorrow, a feeling that so often overcomes me even in the liveliest company, and which must have been felt by the child I then was.

But I cannot say that my early childhood was an unhappy one. Besides the house, my father had gained a small piece of land which ran up the slope beyond the city gate. On it grew perhaps a dozen olive trees. I can still see in my mind's eye their silvery green foliage, and myself playing under them while Sancho tended the growing things after we had eaten a frugal midday meal together. No heavy Malaga or Burgundy will ever taste so sweet to me as that cool water out of our old stone pitcher. I can still see the bits of green grass afloat in it. A finer bread or a better cheese never graced the table of Emperor or Pope. And who was ever better entertained, were he a prince, than I by my Sancho, my chancellor, chamberlain, steward and jester all in one.

There I sat on the edge of the olive garden and watched Sancho as he grubbed about among our beans, lentils and gourds, sweating copiously, seemingly swollen by the sun, a red kerchief wound like a turban around his head. Or I looked down toward the city, bemused by the white walls, cupolas and minarets. Not far from our strip of land the highroad to Toledo passed by. On this road there were many curious sights to see, and there I got my first experience with the outside world. Blasphemous muleteers with their heavily laden animals were the commonest spectacle, and the peasant men and women driving their squealing, groaning two-wheeled carts, from out of the depths of which there often came the thin voice of an infant intermingled with the voice of the cart itself. The poorest carried their wares in high-piled baskets borne on their shoulders, and there were bizarre creatures all festooned with red earthen pots, garlands of onions or dried figs.

Now and then, led by outriders, there were long caravans of wagons carrying freight. The way over the Sierra led through rough, unfriendly heights where attacks on traveling merchants were not uncommon. And goatherds often passed by on the way to Cordova to sell at the market kids and mothers gone dry. These goatherds above all irritated Sancho, for their goats did not plod along circumspectly like a troop of old ladies but scattered incontinently in the fields to the detriment of our young bean shoots, which were especially attractive to their stomachs, so it seemed. Sancho cursed the animals, called them greedy Lucifers in animal form. He also cursed the mute, surly herdsmen, named them blockheads and vagabonds, let it be known that they were plastered with the filth of a thousand years. But he made an exception of one of these goatherds, old Manuel. This one he allowed to sit in the grass a respectful distance from us and watch us eat our meal. Once he bought a kid of him; another time a milk goat, whom we called Manuela. Teresa had found, it seemed, that I was growing up all too quickly in the grass, and had become as thin as a bounding skeleton. It was for this reason that Manuela was secured for her rich milk.

To and fro along the highway marched many a traveling student, scholars in torn black gowns. These fellows were often lively and talkative despite their sunburned skin, dusty shoes and the straw of last night's lodging clinging to their shabby clothes. They also enjoyed the particular favor of Sancho. They were almost all versed to some degree in the art of medicine, and would gladly cup Sancho of a little blood in return for a night's shelter. They varied their medical activities with long conversations interlarded with words of many foreign tongues. They knew their way around Spain as well as Sancho did about his patch of beans, and many of them coming from as far away as Cologne, Paris, Padua and Oxford, could tell strange tales of customs in these different centers of learning. Among other things they told of a sickness called the French disease, and said that it was most commonly found among the great nobles and the princes of the Church. One of them was very much enraged about a certain Paracelsus who had burned the writings of Galen in the market place of Basel. This Paracelsus, a heretic among doctors, should be dangled from the highest gibbet, he told us.

One of the finest sights on my highroad were the churchmen, who usually rode by on mules. Sancho would very likely bow and I follow suit. As a rule these people went by without any motion of recognition, but now and then one would raise his hand in blessing, which pleased us much. Best of all I liked the monks who came along on foot. The dark Dominicans, the warriors of the Holy Virgin who are still engaged in the task of cleaning the land of Spain of heretics, and the humble Franciscans, who waded through the dust on naked feet.

But one day something altogether extraordinary happened on our road. A great four-wheeled caravan hove into sight, which, so I thought, must belong to some merchant. But behind this wagon walked two angels, who I knew immediately were Gabriel and Michael. They had snow-white wings, fine robes and long yellow hair. These two children of light were biting into enormous slices of watermelon, spitting the seeds out merrily. On the spot I sank to my knees and folded my hands. Behind the angels came the Virgin Mary in her starry blue gown, a golden sickle of moon in her hair. Her dress was unbuttoned at the throat and a small child mouthed dribbling at her full white breast. After her marched two men. One was very stout, dressed in magnificent Flemish clothes, a turban embroidered with rows of feathers on his head and a fine gold chain about his neck. The other was piteously thin and starving, so it looked, his garb completely in rags, his toes sticking shamelessly out of the broken ends of his shoes. Still farther behind these two astonishingly disparate men came a person dressed in ancient Eastern costume. He had a white beard that almost swept the ground. I knew that this was God Himself, and prayed most fervently, for Teresa had told me that God always appeared just at the moment of one's death. Moreover, God led a camel by the halter, and on the camel there was perched a small ape. But who indeed could describe my terror when I saw that at the end of the procession there came the Prince of Hell in person?

I scarcely took time to give one more experimental glance at his fearsome cloven hoofs before setting up a tremendous cry that startled the melon-eating archangel almost out of his wits and brought Sancho from his beans running across the fields in frantic strides.

"Look there!" I bellowed.

Sancho looked out at the road, stood agape for a space, then smiled, made the sign of the cross at his breast and said, "But, Don Pedro, they are only actors who are going to give a miracle play in Cordova. If I'm not mistaken it's going to be the play of *Lazarus at the Rich Man's Table,* for I see both of them hand in hand. And the patriarch Abraham with his camel is there, too."

"Right you are, my son," said the Prince of Hell. "The little boy might well be frightened. Well, that's what comes of my excellent mask and, of course, my great art. For I must say, with all due modesty, I am the best Devil in all Spain. My appearance and my performance, which is both terrifying and true to fact, has scared many an errant soul back to the path of blessed righteousness, I can assure you."

I was very much confused and asked Sancho what actors were and what was a miracle play.

At this point the Holy Virgin entered the conversation. She pulled the child from her breast, tested the nipple between forefinger and thumb, and said, "He has drained me dry, the monster. He doesn't look like his father, that Devil, for nothing. Now your little blond boy there——"

"He is not my son," said Sancho curtly. "He is my master's son, and like his father is called Don Pedro de Cordova."

"Ah," remarked the Virgin Mary and observed me closely, "so he's a hidalgo. And you let the young knight grow up like a peasant boy among the beans and turnips. Don't you realize that nothing polishes anyone so much as art? How is he ever going to learn courtly manners if not from actors, such as ourselves who earned great praise on this score at the court of the Duke of Medina?"

"Too bad," replied Sancho and made a long face. "In our purse there's nothing but a vast nothingness."

"If it's nothing more than that," laughed the Virgin Mary, looking very beautiful, "come along anyway. It'd be impossible to squeeze a copper piece out of most of those who gawk at us, even if we used thumbscrews."

"For nothing? That's impossible," said Sancho. "That would be an insult to our honor. Entertainment for nothing! But I will say this to you. Don Pedro owns a house in Cordova. You might stay there for the night after your performance. I'll make you a supper, too, if you'll be satisfied with rabbit stew, some lentils, bread and red wine. On these conditions Don Pedro, Doña Teresa his housekeeper, and I would gladly attend your play."

"Done," said the poor Lazarus. This was the piteously thin man. "There's nothing pleases me more than a solid family meal. To fill up the stomach sack is still man's deepest delight. At least when he has reached a ripe old age."

"Words of wit," said the magnificent stout one with contempt, "mean nothing at all to my brother Juan. His belly is his God. And yet just because of a bulky constitution night after night I have to appear as a glutton and sot, while his soul is transported to Heaven as the angels chant. Such is justice in this world."

"Now don't start to fight," interposed the old man with the camel, walking up to us. "You had better thank this young knight for his hospitality than waste your time wrangling. Right away we are going to give a play in the outskirts of the city, naturally without Judgment Day and Hell Fire, for that would be too expensive for such miserable suburbs. But this evening, I promise you, there will be a play in the square which men will prate of a hundred years from now. Just be punctual, so as not to miss the prologue. A great Italian poet wrote it especially for my troupe."

We nodded assent. The players moved on, and soon all to be seen were the white dust-clouds that accompanied their passage. My heart was pulsing wildly and I nagged at Sancho to hurry on with his grubbing among the beans. But unmoved he worked on as composed and slow as ever, while I sent up prayers of thanks to the Holy Virgin and repeatedly watched the sun, which now seemed fixed in the sky as once happened over the field of Gideon.

At last Sancho gathered together his garden tools, untethered the goat who in her foolish beast's way had also kept a curious eye on the players, and the three of us went down the hill into the city.

Teresa scolded and stormed when Sancho told her that he had invited the actors, but broke off her tirade in the middle of a speech when she remarked my joyous excitement. Putting a pot over my head she cut the long hair sticking out under the rim of the vessel. She then dusted my jacket and pantaloons, ducked me into a tub of warm water and scrubbed until I shed great tears of protest. At last she dried me off, put on my clothes, stuck a piece of honey-smeared bread in my hand. "Well, now, Don Pedro," she said, completely satisfied with her handiwork, "behave like a hidalgo this evening. Don't shout, don't mix with those vermin, the common street boys, and don't laugh too loud even if something happens that makes you feel like it. In case anyone happens to look at you, and he is of your rank, then nod your head courteously. But if he's some sort of mule driver, or anything like that, pretend you don't see him at all."

When Sancho, Teresa and I went through the streets in the evening I was in festive spirits. The glittering stars had already come out in a sky of dark blue silk. A hushed stillness seemed to breathe forth from the houses, and here and there in an alcove burned a faint light. A big gray cat padded without a sound across the street, and Sancho noted with satisfaction that it was moving from left to right, a good sign.

Never had I been out of the house at such a late hour before, and I found the night much to my liking. The watchmen in their helmets and black cloaks enchanted me as they stalked by us carrying halberds. And so, too, did the sound of a guitar from some distance away, borne on a cool evening wind that came in gentle gusts from the Sierra. We walked past the broad, somber wall of the Cathedral, which looked quite different at this time of day. Like a massive fortress it crouched there, menacing and impregnable. In my secret heart I thought how good it was that it was no longer inhabited by the fearful devil, Mahomet, as Sancho had once told me, but by the Holy Ghost. But in my childish fancy this also seemed a little weird, as I imagined the cloudy being wandering through a forest of columns under the horseshoe arches.

The murmur of a great crowd drove all these thoughts from my mind for by now we had arrived at the Square of the Oranges, where the show was to take place. The broad space had its name from the many orange trees that bordered it and, in the month of May, sweetened it beyond description with the smell of many small flowers. Now, of course, it was midsummer and the trees, having long since been in bloom, were hung with countless small green fruit that were the property of the chapter house, even though the priests and monks seldom had the opportunity to eat them. They were usually picked green by me and my small kind long before they ripened.

The Square was bounded on the far side by a wall of the Cathedral, and a short way before this wall there was an ancient fountain, gray with time. Out of its mossy basin sprayed ice-cold water from the Sierra as plentifully in the height of summer as during the rainy season. At this spring the wives of Cordova did their washing, compiled a list of recent births, made up their own necrology.

Near by this spot a rectangular scaffold swathed in black had been set up, a stage exactly like the one from which I once heard a Dominican tell about the plenary indulgence of Pope Leo X. The worthy father moved us all to tears, I recall, as he pictured the frightful tortures that our unabsolved relatives, now deceased, were having to bear. For a very small sum, really, Sancho secured an indulgence of several years' duration for my father. It was not that he believed my father author of many sins but, as he said, in the excitement and terror of the shipwreck he had probably failed to obtain extreme unction. As a matter of fact my father wore an image of Our Lady of Sorrows on a silver chain hung about his neck and this, no doubt, Sancho comforted me, did much to ensure his status with the angels. So far as my mother was concerned, it was Sancho's belief, an indulgence was not necessary, for surely she must have entered directly into Heaven, if there were any justice at all.

The black platform, which had something sinister about it, was built with four long uprights at each corner. On the top of each a flaming torch burned red. Benches had been placed in front of the stage, and these were already filled for the most part. Behind the benches there pressed a still larger mass of people. It looked to me as if all Cordova had assembled here in the Square, which of course could not have been the case, since our city at that time had over fifty thousand inhabitants. I even recognized certain blind men and cripples who belonged to the Beggars' Guild. Among them were scattered apprentices of the different trades, carters, muleteers, hucksters, whereas in the front on the benches sat the masters, nobles and the members of the burgher class with their wives and countless children. Here and there a lance stuck up above the heads of the crowd, its point aglitter in the gusty light of the torches. These were the watchmen of our Alguazil Alcalde, whose duty it is to preserve order in large gatherings.

In the crowd could be felt, under the tense expectation, a tremor of earnestness, a strange, fearful, almost fanatic absorption, which despite my tender years I also immediately shared. My hands began to tremble and nothing would have pleased me better than to flee the spot, but Sancho kept pushing me forward by the shoulders until finally I found myself, bewildered, my heart beating wildly, on the second bench before the black stage. The first bench was occupied by officials. I saw some regidores sitting there in their long black mantles and black caps, next to several Dominicans, who talked to one another in soft but urgent voices. Every now and then one of these clerics would rise to his feet, face the crowd and examine it with what seemed to me a penetrating, almost contemptuous, glance.

"If the cursed he-goat ever turned up here," murmured one of the Dominicans, a tall, haggard man with sunken eyes which glittered like an animal's in the torchlight, "Castile would be able to rejoice in truth. My penitents would hang him up by the heels until the life had rotted out of him."

The others laughed softly. I shuddered at the cruelty of these strange men in black, although indeed Sancho was not very partial to goats himself. In this case, I thought, it must be an unusually bad goat.

Suddenly this same monk turned in my direction. I trembled inwardly, thinking that I had annoyed him in some fashion. Instead he addressed a buxom lady who sat near to me.

"Doña Catarina," he asked in a hoarse voice, "has the Corregidor come back yet from Coruña?"

"No, he hasn't, Father Pablo," she replied in a weak, worried voice. "We fear something must have detained him in Toledo."

"That's quite possible," he said with deep scorn. "The Toledans are the best swordsmiths in the world, and they know how to use their swords when it comes to defending the freedom of Castile."

"But Father Pablo," she objected, sniffing out her injury, "you know very well that Don Garcilaso is a stickler for carrying out every order of the Cortes of our King and Ruler, Don Carlos."

"Oh, we're convinced that as an old comrade-in-arms of our blessed King, Don Fernando of Aragon—may his soul rest in peace!—and as a true subject of our Queen, Doña Juana, he must side with the right-thinking people. But the cup is running over. And Cordova will not stand idly by when Toledo, Seville, Zamora, Salamanca, Valladolid and the other daughters of Castile reach for their weapons."

"Father Pablo!" the lady whispered, beside herself now. "How terrible!"

"On the contrary, it is the end of terror," retorted Father Pablo with evil pleasure. "That, as the people say, is much better than the terror without end which hangs over us at present." With that he returned to his ecclesiastic brethren. Some of the regidores had half turned their faces toward the monks to hear what was going on. And now they nodded knowingly and whispered together. But Doña Catarina, the stout lady, looked straight ahead, very much disconcerted.

"Doña Catarina," a voice broke in unexpectedly, a voice with a clear, light metallic sound in it like a little silver bell, "what does it mean what Father Pablo was saying about my father and the daughters of Castile?"

Doña Catarina sniffed loudly. "Nothing, my dear, nothing at all," she said, "nothing except what I have told you already a thousand times, that you are not to stick your nose into the conversation of grown people. It is not ladylike."

Twisting my head to one side I looked, full of curiosity. There, next to me, hitherto unnoticed, sat the owner of the metallic voice, a little girl perhaps a year or two younger than I. She had clasped her hands neatly out of sight in the folds of her dark silk dress. Her small feet, which did not reach the ground, dangled back and forth in bright red shoes. But the most beautiful thing about her in my first childish impression was her shining black hair, combed back sharply from her brow and hanging in two long plaits down her back. Over the hair glittered the meshes of a fine gold net. The pretty little girl noticed that I was watching her, and she returned the glance, her faintly slanting, almond-shaped eyes catching mine. Ashamed, I lowered my lids, observed my shoes, and saw how they contrasted with the elegance of hers.

"What's your name?" the lovely voice asked, and it was a few seconds before I realized it was I who was addressed.

"Pedro de Cordova," I stammered painfully.

"Pedro, that's a nice name," she answered. "Although really I like Juan or Carlos better. I'm called Isabella, after Queen Isabella the Catholic."

"That's a nice name," I answered, and I felt my face growing hot as if it had been flecked by the flame from the torches.

"Where do you live, Pedro?" she inquired, and hitched closer to me.

"I live in the Street of the Leather Merchants," I told her.

"It is pretty there?"

"Oh yes," I said. "It's very pretty there. But the trouble is the Devil is always coming into our house. He comes in through the chimney and wears a red cloak and gives me money that's gone when morning comes."

"How terrible!" she cried. "But how wonderful that must be! I wish the Devil came to our house and gave me dolls. Aren't you afraid of him?"

"Not at all," I said boldly. "Really, not at all. For my dead mother prays for me."

"My mother is dead, too," she said, "but my father, Don Garcilaso de Gómez,is the Corregidor of Cordova."

"And what is a corregidor?" I wanted to know, ashamed of my ignorance.

She clapped her hands. "A corregidor?" she said and put a finger over her lips in thought. "A corregidor is a friend of the King of Castile, Don Carlos. He sees to it that everything goes on in Cordova the way the King wants. He is very powerful, and even the Lords of Comares and De Priego look small when he is standing under the arms of Castile and gives orders."

Just at this moment a murmur went through the crowd. The brazen snarl of a horn rang out, and I saw the Archangel Gabriel standing on the stage, huge and red with the reflection, a being from another world. Despite his friendliness he frightened me so badly that I certainly should have crawled under the bench had I not feared more to disgrace myself before my new-found friend.

Gradually I calmed down, though my heart beat like a trapped bird's. I heard the angel tell how once he had been sent into the world to bring the holy tidings to the Virgin, whom he found sitting before a vase of lilies, her tender hands folded over a book of prayer. Then he said the "Ave Maria, Full of Grace."

To myself I sang with him, and greatly envied the angel who was permitted to act as messenger of God to his loved ones, always to be sweeping by the wheeling stars, eons through, from the creation of the world to the final day when eternity will swallow up all creation.

As the angel clearly spoke the word "poorest," a clamor arose in the rear of the crowd. Hoarse-voiced, the beggars sang *"gloria in excelsis*

Deo," until the heavenly being admonished them to silence with an outstretched arm.

He went on to tell in nicely fashioned phrases how the Lord wandered over the earth, how he had told the fisherman on the shores of Genesareth to be fishers of men, how he had said that man cannot serve both God and Mammon.

After these words he paused, turned, and told us, "Look, here comes Father Abraham with his camel."

Abraham, the long-bearded one, actually did come on the stage, tugging at the halter of the camel just as I had seen him the first time. This time, however, a cloth had been put over the camel's eyes, so that the burning torches would not alarm him. The black cloth gave the animal a supernatural appearance, as if he, like the angel, really did come from the beyond.

Gabriel felt around inside his robe, brought forth a large needle such as our saddlers use, held it aloft and bellowed, "Sooner shall a camel pass through the eye of this needle than a rich man enter the kingdom of Heaven."

A deep hush spread through the crowd when these words of our Saviour echoed through the Square. One could hear the fountains splashing, and the light wind among the orange trees. Suddenly the crowd broke forth in a tremendous cry of triumph. Certain words could be distinguished amid the roar. "Down with the Flemings!" "Hang the he-goat!" Father Pablo leaped to the bench on which he was sitting and yelled, "Long live Doña Juana, our rightful Queen of the House of Castile, and her son, Don Fernando, who was stolen from us."

The angel on the platform stood perplexed before the excited mob, then smiled slyly and said, "The words and parables of our Lord Jesus Christ have fallen like seeds on stony ground. For always the poor crowd Spanish earth, sucked dry by wealthy foreigners who come from Brabant, from Artois and Picardy...."

In the roar which now arose he could no longer make himself heard. He simply remained where he was, smiling and nodding. The confusion would have continued much longer had not the Archangel Michael suddenly appeared on the scene. He was helmeted, covered with shining armor, and wore gloves of light chain on his hands which were folded over the hilt of a heavy sword.

"The Day of Judgment is near," said the awesome angel. "Let us go down to earth, O Gabriel, to see how men are living there. Let us go to the city of Toledo, to the heart of Castile, which is beloved of God."

"So be it," answered the Archangel Gabriel, and the two celestial beings vanished from the stage. A table was now brought out, and upon it were placed heavy vessels of silver stuff, a silver beaker and a large wine carafe. Benches and chairs were drawn up to the table, comfortable red cushions with tassels as thick as one's fist were put on them. Out on the stage came the splendid fat one in the Flemish clothes, groaning with his own weight. He looked once in apprehension at the crowd, and with some hesitation sat down. A pair of young bloods, also in Flemish dress, sat down with him. The fat one began to pour out wine. A thick gold chain bobbed back and forth on his heavy chest. On it, as a charm, hung a little golden goat. The wine seemed to be very strong, perhaps Malaga, and they must have been drinking it unwatered, for soon they showed unmistakable signs of drunkenness. They bawled out a round, the first verse of which went:

"Let us bless Hell's depths and heights.
There we'll find some sturdy wights."

For some time the show went on in this manner. I listened to everything open-mouthed. I noticed that Doña Catarina carefully covered Doña Isabella's ears with her hands. Anger began to show on the faces in the audience.

After the song the young men started to throw dice. The splendid one laughed when he lost and gave the winner one of his golden chains. "Where this comes from, there's plenty more," he boomed, and banged his fist on the table.

"And where will it come from?" asked the winner.

"From the pockets of the Spanish people," laughed the fat one.

"The miserable beggar race is poor already," said one of the young blades.

"That means nothing," said the fat one with scorn. "I'll take their land and turn their fields into meadows for my sheep. Ypres, Bruges, Ghent and Arras will fill my empty pockets with gold. For where is wool going to come from, if not from England or Spain?"

"But who will care for the Spaniards when you have taken their fields?" asked the other.

"May they rot in Hell for all of me," roared the fat one and became purple in the face. "Am I the keeper and breadwinner for this rabble?"

I looked now at Sancho who sat on my left side. His glowering face took me aback. "What's the matter, Sancho?" I whispered in fear.

"Aren't you listening? Don't you hear?" he whispered back. "The Flemish dog is trying to rook us."

Again I turned my attention to the stage. There had reappeared the two archangels, whom I immediately recognized even though they had changed their wings for black cloaks. Gabriel, speaking very civilly, asked for quarters for the night.

"Have you got any money?" asked the fat one.

"A few maravedis," said Michael, his eyes flashing.

"Give them to me," ordered the fat one. Michael threw the maravedis on the table, and the young man picked them up.

"Now get out. Don't bother me any more! I'll set my mastiffs on you," shouted the fat one wrathfully, his fleshy face bursting with blood.

"Then give me my money back," said Michael, and put his hand on the hilt of his sword under the mantle. But Gabriel held him back, and the Archangel Michael stood there with death in his eyes, and did nothing.

"My money, my money," roared the fat one. "Everything that's yours is mine. We are the masters of Toledo. We'll show you some customs to your liking. The time for forbearance is over. Gallows and the sword are on the way."

"Enough," said Michael, grinding his teeth. "I have seen my fill of Castile. Let us be on our way, Gabriel."

But Gabriel pointed with his finger to the side of the stage. There came creeping over the floor poor Lazarus. Thin as a skeleton, he raised his hands in supplication to the rich man, whereupon the fat one reached into his plate, picked out a bone, hurled it at Lazarus and hit him on the head. The blow made Lazarus cry out in pain. Nevertheless he stretched out his hand to pick up the bone. As he did this a dog raised its head over the edge of the stage and snapped for the bone. Back and forth they chased the bone in great confusion until the dog stopped, bared his teeth and growled savagely. Poor Lazarus sank back on the boards.

Thereupon the archangels approached him. Lazarus folded his hands, looked up to them, and said, "Are you come to release me and my misery and my humiliation, you messengers of the All Highest?"

"Fear not," answered Gabriel, "for we bring peace."

And Michael spoke: "The day of judgment in Spain is very close at hand."

Then, from a great distance, it seemed, came the sound of thunder, as if there were a storm coming up in the Sierra. The magnificent fat one asked, "What was that?" and one of his companions answered, "Nothing, nothing at all."

Nearer and nearer the storm approached. The light of the torches sank, slowly died out altogether. A profound stillness descended on the Square; the crowd was now under the light of the stars. I became filled with apprehension; I felt the expectation of something awesome in the hearts of the people surrounding me.

Then suddenly, after some fearful moments, another light began to gleam, a supernatural and ghostly light. It was blood-red and dyed the faces of players and audience with an unearthly glow. At this point up rose Father Pablo, opened wide his arms, and spoke the Doomsday verses. All of us fell on our knees. The superior regidores, the pious Dominicans, the artisans and their apprentices, the leather workers, muleteers, thieves, beggars, all lifted folded hands on high and sang *Dies Irae, Dies Illa,* the song of the great day of anger come to purify the world with flame.

At the background of the stage a large painted canvas was unrolled and we saw God the Heavenly Father, sitting there, his Son at his side, the Sacred Dove hovering above him. About him, painted among clouds that resembled feather pillows, thronged the apostles and evangels, the martyrs and the patriarchs of Israel. A long-drawn-out, groaning "Aymé, aymé!" arose from the audience when they saw God in His glory. On the right side of the throne sat the Virgin Mary, looking very pretty. Before her knelt Father Abraham with his camel. In his arms he held the body of poor Lazarus and comforted him. Lazarus opened his eyes and smiled happily.

To the left stood the Prince of Hell, more fearsome and interesting than I had ever seen him in my dreams. With his mighty sword the Archangel Michael now drove the rich man and his companions, their teeth chattering, vainly imploring the Virgin Mary for help, over to the Prince of Darkness. His face twisted horribly, the Devil now clutched the rich man and throttled him so harshly that his tongue hung out and his eyes rolled in his head. Then like a sack of corn the Devil threw him to the boards, placed his cloven foot on his neck while the crowd shouted jubilantly. At my side Sancho clapped his hands in terrific excitement. Doña Catarina snorted wildly, her eyes damp with tears. But little Isabella jumped up, put her thin arm around my neck. I smelled the young perfume of her hair and felt the meshes of the gold net on my cheeks. She had begun to sob bitterly. Full of terror she whispered to me, "Save him, Pedro, save him. You're the only one who isn't afraid of the Devil."

I was very much upset. Such an undertaking seemed useless to me. I pointed at the archangel. "What can I do against Saint Michael, Isabella? Just look at his big sword!"

But she persisted, she kissed my cheek and whispered, "I'll love you all my life, Pedro, if you beat the Devil."

Moved by fright and childish despair I softly lifted Sancho's knife from its sheath, and actually started to clamber over the benches. But Father Pablo took hold of me by the collar, threw me back. "Sit down quietly, you little beast," he cried. "Don't you see that the Almighty sits in judgment!"

I tumbled back. Isabella put her arm about me, and said, "How terrible Father Pablo is!"

Up on the stage the rich one was groaning, "Father Abraham, have mercy on me and send Lazarus, that he may dip the tip of his finger in water, and cool my tongue; for I am tormented in this flame."

Abraham made an indifferent grimace and said, "Son, remember that thou didst receive good things in thy lifetime, and likewise Lazarus evil things, but now he is comforted; and thou art tormented. And besides all this, between us and you, there is fixed a great chaos: so that they who would pass from hence to you, cannot, nor from thence come hither."

The fat one moaned, worried grievously about his friends and his rich relatives, begged Abraham to warn them of the dread fate which he himself was having to endure.

Abraham answered that nothing would teach the rich, not even should a departed spirit appear from Hell itself to warn them.

Now the red glow was slowly extinguished. The torches were lighted again. The Archangel Michael stood before us, covered from head to foot in steel armor, his mailed hands on the pommel of his sword. "Take care, take care," he warned us. "It is inevitable that you shall do injury to others. But woe unto him who does not watch whom he injures. It would be better for him to tie a millstone around his neck and jump into the sea where it is deepest than to wreak the smallest hurt on these humble ones. Take care, then, take care."

The play was at an end. But the crowd was by no means satisfied. "Father Pablo!" they cried. "We want Father Pablo!" At first the Dominican sat still, made no attempt to move. Only when the shouts had swelled into a roar, had grown into a wild storm, did he rise slowly to his feet and step up on the stage. He nodded to another one of the Dominicans, who placed a torch near him. His face was lighted up from below. I saw the sunken cheeks, powerfully shadowed, the curved, Spaniard's nose, the glowing hawk eyes. Isabella was still huddled close to me, her arm about my shoulders, and I clenched my fist about Sancho's knife.

"Children of Cordova," said Father Pablo in his hoarse voice, "you have seen played before you a parable of our Lord. Although it is many hundreds of years ago since Christ preached this miracle to the listening crowd, it means the same today as it did then. For the words of our Lord are eternal. A great sorrow shrouds all Spain. Our Queen, Doña Juana, languishes in prison, and the enemies of Castile have spread the report that she has lost her mind through suffering and loss. Her son Don Carlos has feeling only for his Flemings, Frenchmen and Germans. From Coruña he has sailed away for Antwerp without bothering to give audience to the urgent presentations of the cities of Castile."

Once again a threatening mutter began, but Father Pablo had only to thrust out his arm to command silence. For a second he thought and then continued, "And how do things look in Spain? Enormous sums have been squeezed out of the cities to pay for costly tournaments. The festivities in Valladolid cost us no less than forty thousand gold ducats. The emperor's crown for Carlos will cost us a hundred thousand more. In vain did Doctor Juan Zumel of Burgos present a petition for audience to the King. Don Carlos has abandoned his country in the very moment when we don't know where our bread is coming from the next day, how we shall feed our children. He forsakes us in order to pursue a worthless phantom. For Spain's populous cities, strong castles, devout people are worth far, far more than the fat of Flanders, which nourishes Anabaptists and other heretics. And who has Don Carlos named the protector of golden Castile? I hardly dare say it! A miserable French

Archbishop of Toledo, Chièvres, chivo, a goat, rules Spain. He and his filthy hangers-on, Jean le Sauvage, Charles de Lannoy and a thousand other agents of misery. At our expense they fill the pockets of their Flemish garments. Oppressive taxes burden us. We know the shame of slavery. We are treated like slaves, like Moors, like Indians. They forget that the cities of Castile have the right to deny allegiance to the King himself should he not first swear with right hand raised to protect forever our freedom and manner of rule."

There were some outcries of approbation, but these were cut short when Father Pablo went on: "But the day of judgment is knocking at our doors. Already Antonio de Acuña, the revered Archbishop of Zamora, has gathered all right-thinking people about him. But it is not my responsibility, it is not for me, a servant of the Church, to pronounce judgment. That has been done by our Lord in Heaven, when he spoke this parable. Who is then this overweening man of gold, this sot, this gambler and unfeeling clod? It is Chièvres, the he-goat, the Knight of the Golden Fleece, he and his detestable followers. Who is poor Lazarus, who creeps in hunger over the floor and shares bones with the curs that bark on the highway? He is the enslaved and plundered people of Spain. But God stands by this people, the Ruler of All. He stands there in the form of the Holy Inquisition, which for all time will raise its sheltering hands."

Many in the crowd shouted, "Long live the Inquisition!"

Father Pablo did not stop here. His eyes burning, he raised both hands heavenward in supplication and cried, "Who lifts himself up, he shall be humbled." Then he bowed his head, pressed his hands to his eyes. By the movement of his shoulders, it was plain to see that he was sobbing.

"The Flemings!" the cry rang out. "Down with the Flemings!"

The huge crowd pressed forward, benches began to fall over. There was terrible confusion. Isabella held tightly to my shoulders. I remained where I was, wide-eyed with astonishment, thinking the day of judgment had actually arrived.

Some of the half-wild muleteers hauled the fat one off the stage. The actor defended himself violently. His face was shining with the sweat of fear, and he cried loudly, "I belong to the right-thinking ones of Zamora. Don't kill an innocent man!"

A hail of green oranges was the answer to this outcry. Isabella began to whimper, for one of these missiles had struck her on the forehead. I stood up and tried to shield her. At this moment we were both knocked down and men began to walk right over us, the edge of their cloaks brushing harshly across our faces. Somebody trod most painfully on my hand. I could see that Father Pablo with outspread arms was beseeching the crowd to hold back. I heard Lazarus bellowing as strongly as he could, "He's only a poor actor!" But the crowd's rage would not be appeased. They would have their sacrifice, cared nothing that he was entirely innocent. They shouted, "Hang him, string him up! To the gallows with the bag of guts!" And it would have gone badly indeed with the fat one had not something most unexpected happened. I heard the iron-shod hoofs of horses, the rattle of harness, and a deep, ringing voice shouting, "Halt! In the name of the King of Spain, I order quiet!"

I righted a bench, jumped up on it to see, pulling little Isabella with me. Some distance from me a man in gleaming armor sat on a rearing horse of dapple-gray. I could see him clearly in the torchlight. Loosely over his shoulders he wore a long scarlet cloak of silk. In his right hand he brandished a broadsword, while with his left he tried to hold in the excited horse. Behind him was massed a company of perhaps fifty men, their tall lances rested perpendicularly in their stirrups, so that the shafts of them were like a little forest under the stars. The knight raised his sword and with the flat of it whacked a beggar hard enough to make him squirm flat on the ground with pain.

I stared at the rider. He bore himself like some heavenly apparition. Never had I seen a man on horseback in such impressive and awesome dress.

Gradually the crowd calmed down, moved back, so that in a short while Isabella and I could edge almost directly up to the horsemen. Men with halberds and lances filled the Square. They were the watchmen of the Alguazil Alcalde, who by now had suddenly recalled the duties of their office.

"What's going on here?" the knight asked, looking at me, so I thought.

Open-mouthed I gaped at the wonderful man on the dapple-gray mount. But Father Pablo, who had moved back with the crowd, said contemptuously, "Have you ever heard of the Flemings, Don Garcilaso?"

Just then Isabella began to cry out, "Father, Father, take me on your horse!"

Don Garcilaso started, caught sight of Isabella, then looked at Father Pablo. Harshly he said, "This is your work. I know you're one of Antonio de Acuña's men."

Father Pablo replied defiantly, "It's the fault of the he-goat himself."

The crowd laughed. The rider shook his head, turned away. On the stage the fat one kneeled, no longer looking magnificent, praying fervently to the Virgin Mary. Garcilaso thrust his sword back into its sheath and trotted his horse up to the stage. "Why are you wearing Flemish clothes?" he asked.

The fat one stammered that the miracle play came from Bruges.

"And because of that you have to wear the insignia of the Golden Fleece?" asked Don Garcilaso angrily.

"It makes it look better," stuttered the fat one.

"You're still impudent, aren't you?" said Don Garcilaso. "Don't you know that your King is the Grand Master of this order? Are you aware you are committing high treason?"

"I didn't know anything about that," said the fat one. Once again the beads of sweat started on his brow.

"Arrest him," commanded Don Garcilaso. "Take him to the Alcazar. I'll have to see later whether he's sent to the galleys or gets off with a taste of the whip."

The fat one cried out to Father Pablo for help, but the somber monk stood by unmoved as the watchmen encircled the actor, bound his arms and with heavy fists rammed him on his way.

At this point Father Pablo turned to the absorbed crowd and shouted, "He is suffering for the freedom of Spain; he is like all of us!" And the crowd, which only a minute or two before had wanted to hang the fat one, murmured sympathy.

Don Garcilaso rode over to the benches, bent over from his horse and put Isabella on his saddle. "What's your name?" asked the rider, looking at me with forbidding mien.

"Pedro," I said, almost in tears.

"How does it happen my daughter is in this mob?" he asked.

"Doña Catarina——" I broke out, and actually began to weep.

"That's all right, my son," said Don Garcilaso. "Go home, now. Women are fantastic when they get along in years." He rode away. In my heart of hearts I wept most because I was young, without shining armor, with no mantle of silk and no sword. If I had had these, I felt, I should have confronted the Corregidor in a different fashion. I could have died of shame for bursting into tears before Isabella.

When I emerged from this fit of emotion I saw that the Square was emptying rapidly. I heard the soft rush of the fountain, and the stars glittered above my head. In this moment, I believe, the careless acceptance of childhood fell from me. During this night a world hitherto friendly had suddenly become a great mystery. Only years later, many years later, did I realize that then I had experienced a double revelation, that without Isabella I should never be whole, and that I belonged to a people whom I should love as flesh of my flesh until my mouth gaped in the earth, as all mouths will.

A heavy hand gripped my arm and looking up I stared into the broad face of my good Teresa. "So that heartless Sancho left you all by yourself in the night," she said angrily.

I took Sancho's part and told her nothing at all had happened to me, though at the same time I heard a voice telling me that it would be better to keep still than to lie at this particular moment. Teresa took my hand as if I were exactly the same child of a few hours ago. We walked homeward through the narrow streets, which were filled, I remember clearly, with the scent of geraniums. The walls of the white houses towered high, and above me I could glimpse a small strip of sky.

Soon we were home in our old house, and not long afterward Sancho came home, to get a warm reception from Teresa.

2

REVOLT

IT MUST have been almost midnight, but we still sat around the long, white-scrubbed table from which Teresa had just cleared the dishes and the remains of supper. In a state of overwakefulness I crouched in between the two angels, who by now had become everyday persons without wings, white robes or yellow wigs. With bated breath I listened to the wind from the Sierra Morena that from time to time groaned softly in the yawning flue. I looked at Juan, the Lazarus, who had laid his head on the table and was sobbing bitterly.

"The whole business is senseless," said the Archangel Michael. "We poor people are always in the wrong. If Alonso the splendid one hadn't listened to that abortion of Hell, Father Pablo, if he hadn't worn the Golden Fleece, they would have simply forbidden us to put on our morality in Cordova."

"It is for art's sake he is suffering," said Father Abraham. "He is also suffering for Spain."

Juan lifted his bleared face and said, "Oh, Alonso, my brother. That's what you get for your artistic standards! Now the rats are whistling so loud in your ears you can't get to sleep, I'll wager."

The man who played the Devil dandled the little baby on his knee, kissed it tenderly on the forehead. I still watched him with some shyness. He sat next to the Virgin, his right arm about her shoulders. When not fondling the baby he would make a sardonic face, so odd that I really did not know what the man was in all truth, a devoted father or the Prince of Hell. But I had already discovered that Father Abraham was the leader of the troupe, that the Virgin was his daughter and the Devil his son-in-law.

"The dead must be left in peace," said Father Abraham, and looked at me, so I fancied, in a threatening fashion. "Nothing good can come from opening and shutting the coffin lid."

These words frightened me terribly. But the Devil laughed and asked, "And what does my dear father-in-law mean with that riddle?"

"Oh, youth, youth!" mumbled the old man and shook his head. "They think everything began today, or at the most yesterday. Have you never heard of mortal sin, children? Don't you know about the sins of the fathers, and the mother's curse?"

"I've heard of the latter, in any case," the Devil replied mockingly, and kissed his child. "But I don't see how the caning which Alonso's rosy bottom is going to get tomorrow has any connection with these apothegms."

"Our mother never cursed us," said Juan, choking back a sob. "You must know that Alonso and I are twins. He came first and is the older, which I always granted him, even though I never did fall in with his opinion that the other world was preferable to this one."

"I'm not talking about the fleshly mother," cried Father Abraham loftily. "I'm speaking about our mother the Queen."

"About Doña Juana?" asked the Devil.

"Yes indeed, about Doña Juana," said Father Abraham with decision, and looked squarely at his son-in-law. "For, believe me, I can tell you a story which will raise the hair on your head. In the first place, you ought to know that Doña Juana was very unhappy in her marriage with Felipe the Handsome, the Duke of Burgundy. She loved him much too much. In Don Felipe's veins ran the blood of two rakes, the blood of his father, Emperor Maximiliano, and of his grandfather, Don Carlos of Burgundy, who was called the Bold. It was he, Carlos, who fell before the Swiss spears at Nancy. Now Doña Juana was thin and dark-haired. Don Felipe liked blonde, full-breasted women. He had a Flemish taste. You can just imagine the unhappiness. Doña Juana cried and ranted, and finally it got so bad that in Medina del Campo she went out of her mind with jealousy. The castellan raised the drawbridge, and Doña Juana was a prisoner in her own castle. All day she ran around with her hair wild and her clothes half falling from her shoulders. Night and day she coursed through the corridors and countless rooms of the huge building. And in order to quiet her down they had to fetch her mother, Doña Isabella, our Queen, God rest her soul. When Doña Juana had partly regained her senses, they put her aboard a ship at Coruña to bring her back to her husband who was holding a magnificent and merry court in Brussels." The old man sighed, looked up to see if his listeners were impressed, sighed, went on.

"Now there in Brussels was a lady-in-waiting of Doña Juana's who was called Doña Luisa, or some such name. While poor Doña Juana had been suffering so much in the Medina del Campo, Don Felipe had taken solace in this Luisa. Naturally his wife found out everything, for there are many busy tongues ready to wag at the court of any prince. And what did our Doña Juana do? In the midst of a large gathering she cried down Doña Luisa, boxed her ears so hard that the blows were heard all over the big room. Don Felipe stood there, red with guilt, swallowing his wrath. Our Doña Juana had a pair of shears brought and cut Doña Luisa's long gold blonde braids from her head. Snip, snap, and there they lay on the floor. Even then she wasn't satisfied, and so she called the court barber and had the unfortunate concubine's head shaved. For years this scandal was the talk of all the courts of Europe. Everyone was amazed that Doña Juana did not cast out the shorn Luisa. Instead she received her with a tender embrace back among her ladies-in-waiting after the shearing. Everywhere people whispered knowingly that Doña Juana was trying to find out certain secrets of the *ars amatoria* from Doña Luisa, matters which we could never discuss in our society."

"Ha, ha!" The Devil laughed, kissed the infant, and winked at his wife, who blushed and smiled.

"Well, now," said Father Abraham, thoughtfully stroking his whiskers, "Don Felipe and Doña Juana went back to Castile at the time that our beloved Queen, Doña Isabella, closed her eyes forever. They both wanted to take over their heritage, the Crown of Castile, though Doña Juana's father, Don Fernando of Aragon, made all sorts of trouble for them. For to his way of thinking the Crowns of Castile and Aragon, once united, should remain together forever. In any case, Doña Juana's behavior was hardly becoming for a daughter. Her love for her faithless husband was greater than her affection for her father. But the blessing of God was not on the couple's undertaking. Even on the way at sea there were terrible storms, and their ship was all but shipwrecked on the French coast. Then finally fortune seemed to smile on them. The Cortes of the Castilian cities accepted them as the rightful inheritors of the Crown, and overnight Don Fernando had to flee to the territory of Old Castile. In this way were the fruits of evil first sown, and Don Fernando cursed his daughter and her seed together with the cities of Castile which had worked his humiliation.

"One evening the glittering equipage of the young royal couple moved along a lonely, treeless road. There Doña Juana saw a haggard, gray-haired gypsy woman who stood humbly by the roadside. She was taken with a great curiosity to know the future and commanded the gypsy woman to read the days to come from the runes of her hand.

"But the gypsy woman said: 'Oh, Doña Juana, I don't need to read your palm, for you will be robbed of the Crown of Castile by your son just as you and your man would rob your father. Long, long years you will wander in the twilight, half among the living, half among the dead, and wish and want eternally for the day of release. And bitterness will also befall your son. In his lifetime Anti-christ will rear his head. The cities of Castile will reach for their weapons. I see blood flowing in the streets of Toledo, Zamora and Valladolid. In his lifetime your son will read the Mass of the Dead high up on the loneliest Sierra, burdened grievously by the many crowns of this world. And as for what is going to happen to your man, Don Felipe, I've no need to read his palm, either. For in two weeks from today he'll lie stiff as a rod in his coffin. But even then he will find no surcease from your overheated love. His soul will have much to atone for in the fires of purgatory, since for each sweet adventure he must pay one hundred years of torment. But in the end he will reach Heaven, since everything is possible in the sight of God.'

"And now when Doña Juana wanted to punish the gypsy woman for her shameless prophecies," Father Abraham went on to tell the company, who listened breathless, "and called for her bodyguard, behold, the gypsy had vanished and there stood an old tree. Doña Juana commenced to cry. Don Felipe comforted her, saying that she had imagined everything in the voice of the evening breeze which had sprung up with the sinking of the sun behind the Sierra."

Closer we moved in to the storyteller. For now he dropped his voice, as if about to impart some mystery that even the wind hissing and sucking gently in the chimney's throat might not overhear.

"Everything happened exactly as the strange gypsy woman foretold," continued Father Abraham. "Don Felipe was a dead man in less than two weeks. He died in the midst of a wild attack of fever, that shook him like a spirit out of Hell. Doña Juana's grief was startling to see. She could not tear herself away from the dead Don Felipe. It was late in the fall of the year. Slowly, with grim ceremony, the funeral procession began to move toward Valladolid over the plateau of Spain, which in that season was shrouded in cold, gray mist. The wagon bearing the coffin was drawn by twenty horses caparisoned in black, like horses from the afterworld. On the coffin lay scepter, crown and sword. In front of the dead man marched a mighty band of beggar monks, who filled the air with their songs. First behind the coffin walked the two court jesters of Don Felipe, decked out in gayest clothes, whips in their hands, their pied caps hung with little silver bells. On horseback behind them rode Doña Juana and Doña Luisa; then came the people of the Court, the nobility of Castile and Flanders and a great troop of knights in full harness, baggage trains, squires with tall lances, camp-followers, sutlers and their women. And still farther behind these walked the people. Rich and poor, merchants and beggars, artisans and goatherds, women and children, accompanying the corpse of the King from city to city, and village to village.

"Every evening the procession would halt in some lonely village or at a lonely castle. The coffin containing the dead man was lifted from the wagon and brought into a chapel, if there happened to be one on the spot. If there was none, it was simply brought into a room. Candles were lighted, and the Mass of the Dead sung. Then Doña Juana would order the coffin opened. She would kiss the hands and feet of the corpse. She tore at her hair in the great torment of her need, groaned in her desire for Don Felipe's caresses, so that even the Dominicans who held the death watch shuddered in terror. And Doña Juana commanded Doña Luisa also to kiss the corpse. She ordered this in contempt and wrath. No one dared to gainsay her. Then Doña Luisa, weeping in horror, would kiss the dead man. Thereupon Doña Juana would fly into an even worse rage. She scratched the face of the lovely concubine, spat at her full in the mouth, spat on the corpse, whose cheeks were now falling in like melting wax. In the next moment Doña Juana would rue her harshness, kiss Doña Luisa, and fall in a rush to her knees beside the coffin, begging her man's forgiveness as she had so often done in his lifetime.

"Often a kind of rigidity overcame her and she kneeled there as if cut out of wood or cast of bronze. And everything in the room seemed to become transfixed, as if touched by the curse of God, as once happened to Lot's wife before Sodom and Gomorrah. About midnight she would awaken from her trance. They gave her strong wine to keep her alive, for she was white as a ghost, with the child of Don Felipe even at the time kicking feebly in her womb. Under the influence of the fiery wine she would suddenly become wildly happy. She said that Don Felipe had always belonged among the happy ones. He should have it so once again. She ordered both the jesters to tell jokes, and commanded the Dominicans at the wake to laugh with their hands folded over their bellies, as is their style. This hollow laughter wearied her and finally she would fall asleep to the relief of the whole company. But sleep did not last long. Hardly had the first cock crowed before the Mass of the Dead was sung again, the coffin lid clapped shut, and the great funeral train once more was set in motion. The sinister murmurings of the Franciscans and the weeping of the people grayed the morning air.

"This misery lasted for six long weeks. You can imagine how the corpse of poor Don Felipe began to look. What had been at first a gently ironic smile widened into a fearful grin. The corpse could hardly be called beautiful any longer. From time to time Don Felipe's lower jaw dropped, flopped weakly, as if he were yawning, desperately eager for his eternal sleep. Day by day the lineaments of the face grew more blurred. The Dominicans had to be relieved every half-hour, for they were unable to bear the powerful sweet stink of Don Felipe's decayed flesh. But I'll spare you any more gruesome details. It's not very pleasant to think that our own bodies will encounter a similar decline, even though it may be in the kind obscurity of the grave.

"One evening came when Doña Luisa, her face streaming with tears, could no longer endure to kiss the face of her dead lover. 'See, see,' cried Doña Juana. 'Behold the constancy of a Fleming!' And with this she threw herself with open arms over Don Felipe. But she, too, had to draw back and broke out in terrible cries of anguish. For the first time she really saw the change that had come over the face of her husband. 'Oh, my sweet, my beloved Felipe,' she wept, 'why have you forsaken me? But I know who killed you. It was Castile, wild, wild Castile. My father's curse it was, and the evil Spanish people. The burning sun on its bare earth and the keen tooth of the wind on its people.' It was then that the catastrophe happened. Doña Juana uttered a curse on Castile, on the land that had born her and which she had loved dearly. She commanded the coffin to be closed, and never was it opened again. Don Felipe was buried in the chapel of La Mota. Often Doña Juana stands the night through at the window of her room and looks out over to the grated door of the vault. On each side of it four lamps are always kept burning. And it's this violation of the dead King and curse of the half-mad Queen, in my opinion, which has brought such bad luck to the cities of Castile."

All of us were silent. I wished fervently that Father Abraham had never told such a tale, at least not around midnight, for I had the feeling that in each of the four dark corners of the room stood a mad Doña Juana in mourning, looking at me with glittering eyes. I edged closer to the Archangel Michael, in whom I still felt unreserved confidence.

After a time the Devil cleared his throat, handed over the sleeping child to the Virgin, looked grave and said, "This may apply, what my excellent father-in-law has brought to the light, if I may so express myself. But on the other hand I don't take much stock in curses even when they come from royal mouths. So far as the dead go, on the gallows of Montfaucon in Paris I've seen no less than ten purple corpses dangling in the breeze. They were Christians, too. So far as I know they never caused the city of Paris any trouble. In fact, just the opposite, I suspect. That reminds me of some little Latin sayings I once heard in Salamanca, before jealous love overtook me in the form of the Holy Virgin and I had to take up the career of Devil. The first of these goes: *Austria est imperare orbem universo*. Or in good Castilian: It is Austria's destiny to rule the face of the earth.

"Now," the Devil, pleased with himself, went on, "that's just a prophecy like the rest. Of course there's madness in these words. It seems ridiculous that this Austria, an almost unheard-of place somewhere off near the borders of Turkey, should have such prospects. Why not Spain? Or at least Portugal? Has Austria ships, outside of those miserable rowboats the peasants use to paddle across that pathetic trickle, the Ister? Do they have men like Cristóbal and Diego Colón? Or even like Díaz or Vasco da Gama? Not at all, my friends. You can lay a bet that a Spanish swineherd knows more about what's going on in the world than all the Grand Dukes of Austria taken in a lump.

"But this shameless conviction ceases to be a vague possibility if we look the second little saying square in the eye. It goes:

Bella gerant alii, tu felix Austria,
Nam quae Mars aliis, dat tibi regna Venus.

And this means in good Castilian:

Let others wage wars, thou, oh happy Austria,
Lands given others by the god of war, Love will give thee.

In short, in order to make myself clear once and for all—" the Devil made a sudden grimace, swiftly eyed the puzzled listeners—"the house of Austria conquers the world in bed. Can you imagine anything more delightful? Off you pop with some hot wench into the feathers, and in the morning you wake up the owner of Flanders, Artois, Brabant, Holland, Cleves and Picardy. That's just what happened to Don Maximiliano with Doña Maria of Burgundy. Now something quite different happened to me, my friends. I went to bed with my better half as a student of law and woke up in the morning the Devil."

Both the Archangels laughed heartily at this quip and dutifully I laughed with them, until Teresa brought me sharply to book.

"The same can be said of the case of Don Felipe and Doña Juana," the Devil continued. "Were not Castile and Aragon and the lands across the sea worth an evening canter, even if the mare was thin and hairy? I know, sweet father-in-law, I ought not to talk in this fashion. But it's a fine state of affairs when the people's well-being and royal fornication are poured into the same chamber pot. Don Felipe may have been a good man. I won't quarrel about that. We're all of us good so long as a little silver jingles in our pouch and our stomachs are properly lined." By now he had his audience in the hollow of his hand. They listened even more closely than they had to Father Abraham.

"But what, tell me, what in the name of the Virgin Mary and all the Heavenly Hosts," said the Devil, "did this fat Fleming with his bowlegs understand about rich Leon, Castile, Catalonia, Valencia and Aragon? What did he understand of the soul and pride of the Spanish people? Of the freedom of the cities, yes even of our Moors, Gypsies, Jews, beggars, thieves and other assorted cut-throats? Nothing. Absolutely nothing.

"And do you think it's any different with this fine young man, Don Carlos? Of course, he's a hidalgo, I'll admit it. He knows his way with

Toledo swords, Augsburg harness and Italian helmets. He knows how to ride a horse, to strike with a lance and to bear himself with kingly dignity. But the young fellow needs far too much money. 'Give me four hundred thousand ducats,' he tells the procurators of the cities. And when they hesitate, he says in annoyance, 'Haven't got the time. I'll see you in Coruña.' All the while he's surrounded by his Flemings and Frenchmen.

"Father Pablo is exactly right. This Chièvres is a dirty cheat. Rumor has it that he casually slipped a hundred and sixty pounds of pearls assigned to the Crown from Hispaniola right into his own pocket. The Spanish people want their own King, without foreign hangers-on. They all but threw Don Carlos into the dungeon in Valladolid. He had to flee at night in a pouring rainstorm up to his neck in the soft mud of the fields. He went to mama and his little sister, the Infanta, at Tordesillas. In every city, village, yes, in all the streets of the Spanish kingdom they're muttering about the coming uprising against the foreigners.

"And so I close my *argumentum,* honored father-in-law and you other ladies and gentlemen, with the flat statement that unrest, hunger and everything else of the sort in Spain come from the fact that the King, himself half a foreigner, is continually mobbed round by strangers who are bent on nothing but making a good thing out of their royal connections. And if that isn't true, I, the best Devil in Spain, will eat my own grandmother—and she spiced only with garlic—on an empty stomach."

Both archangels burst into laughter at this irreligious observation, Father Abraham made a wry face, but Lazarus, wiping his dripping nose with a firm movement of the hand, said in a plaintive voice, "Oh, Alonso, my brother, you are sacrificed to tortured circumstance. For whether it was a violated corpse, widow's curses, the tournaments of Don Carlos, the pearls of that dog Chièvres, I don't know and I don't care.

"The trouble with you, Alonso, is that from youth on you were always too magnificent. It's your own fault. Oh, if you'd only gone around in sackcloth instead of brocade, penitently with a string about your neck instead of a gold chain, with peas in your shoes instead of pearls on your shirt! But worse than the pride of your dress was your pride of spirit. Your arrogant forehead stared down so long at that lovely stomach of yours that now you're in a fine mess, full of dark thoughts, your buttocks already trembling in prospect of blows to come. There you are, your exquisite guts filled with dirty water and pillowed on straw. Iron cuffs and collars won't give you much comfort! Ah, no.

"Oh, my beloved Alonso, it's not for simple people to mix in with high politics, or to ponder one's thoughts of the Immaculate Conception, as you did so often in private. If you'd only tried to learn instead how to soak lentils, to cook ham or how to grease the wheels of a squeaky wagon, it would have been far more sensible. But no, you would have your way. You had to listen to the advice of that hellish abortion Father Pablo. His words fell on rich ground, indeed. The tree of your vanity waxed great like the seed of the mustard, as our Lord says. You got yourself filled up with Father Pablo's lies as round as a peasant trollop with child. And now tomorrow, as soon as the first cock crows, you can bear your bastard in the travail of whipping. And you'll do it while the crowd looks on and laughs, the very same crowd that you insisted on reminding—against my better judgment—of their rights and freedom. Oh, Alonso, my second self, I'm at the end of the tether. I think it's time to go to bed. When a man's work is done and his supper digested it's time to rest."

It was indeed very late. We pushed back our benches and chairs, and were just about ready to seek our beds when the iron ring on the house door banged heavily. Sancho opened up. In the door frame stood a man, quite small, dressed in foreign clothes. He wore a scholar's mantle, the bright cap and broad sword of a *junker* and wide, dusty shoes, such as Swiss soldiers wear. The flickering light of Sancho's little thread in oil fell on the stranger's face. I was impressed by the deepset eyes, the mighty nose and the square forehead.

The stranger, speaking Spanish with a curious accent, begged forgiveness for disturbing us at such a late hour but he had seen our light and wished direction to the nearest inn.

But before Sancho could open his mouth, up sprang the Devil. He moved three dancing steps forward and bowed almost double, danced another three steps backward, and bowed again, as if he were confronting some very famous person. Then, really deferent, he raised his eyes, and said, "Who else do I see in our humble abode but the pride of Germania, Italia and Alsace and many other lands, the doctor *occultus* and *mirabilis,* the magician and philosopher, the friend of the spirits? Is it not the world-renowned Master Agrippa of Nettesheim who stands before us? The man, my friends, before whose fame the luminaries of

Salamanca and Coimbra grow pale and uncertain, like wax candles in the light of the sun. Greetings, Master, grace this house with your honored presence."

The stranger moved into the room. He seemed anything but pleased with this swollen speech. When the Devil spoke his name he even seemed visibly shaken.

"Please understand," he said to the Devil, "I'm here on private business. I don't want my name bandied about. Please show me the way to the inn."

"The farthest thing from our thoughts," insisted the Devil, and laid his hand on his heart. "Show the Master the door and relegate him to a nest of bedbugs! May it please you, rather, *doctissime doctorum,* to consider this house as your own. For this young man of tender years, Don Pedro de Cordova, our host, will never let you deny his hospitality."

The Devil pointed at me, and Master Agrippa observed me thoughtfully out of his sunken eyes. He smiled at me suddenly, like a friend, and the cockles of my heart grew warm. I reached for his hand and in modest words asked him to take his pleasure of my house.

Master Agrippa hesitated. Then his glance fell on the threshold, and I noticed that he had caught sight of the pentagram. A look of faint amazement came over his face. Critically he sized me up; half smiling he shook his head, then examined the room. The open fire held his gaze. "Well, all right then," he said unexpectedly. "I'll stay." Uncertainly he drew a silver piece from his pocket, and offered it to me.

"No, no," I said in confusion. "Be our honored guest, Master Agrippa."

"Good," he answered, and quickly thrust the silver out of sight. "Then I'll pay you in other coin."

After my good Teresa had given Master Agrippa a nightcap and had prepared him a place to rest his head, we sought our own beds. For a long time I could not sleep. The brilliant happenings of the day coursed through my excited brain in a train of images. Again I saw the Devil and the Archangel Michael, and it seemed to me as if they were struggling for the possession of my own soul. I heard Sancho and Teresa praying for me, and amid it all I heard the sound of little Doña Isabella's voice, beseeching me to conquer the Devil. I saw the Corregidor on his dapple gray, rearing and pawing. And through my dreams moved the Queen with the coffin of her husband, cursing me.

It was a very complicated dream, but at last within it I found myself sitting in a deep cellar. I recognized that I was not Don Pedro de Cordova at all, but Alonso the splendid one, the rich man. "I am your second self," said Alonso, and I became lost in his fat being as salt is lost in water. But suddenly at the threshold appeared the mysterious figure of Master Agrippa. Slowly, with his long staff, he drew a pentagram on the floor. "This will protect you," he said kindly. And I was taken aback; in the midst of the dream I determined in the morning to seek out bright and early Alonso the splendid one, and to bring him fresh water. Deep in my dream I still knew, curiously enough, that I was only dreaming.

I awoke early, as the sun was beginning to gild the earth with slanting gold. Without a sound I dressed, and went out into our little courtyard. On the step of the fountain I said my morning prayers. My heart became cool and clear, as if I too were filled to the brim with the cool spring water purling forth from the rude pipe of clay before me. I asked the blessing of God for my good friends. Then I filled my stone jug with water and took a crust of Teresa's bread, broke off a piece for myself, and chewed it on the way to succor Alonso the splendid one.

I had hardly proceeded a hundred steps down the Street of the Leather Merchants when I heard a dull boom and a rushing sound that cramped me with fear. Three, four more shots followed at brief intervals. I thought about the meaning of this shooting. The Feast of Corpus Christi was long over and done with. Ah, I said to myself, at last the King, Don Carlos, has come to Cordova—he has not sailed from Coruña to Antwerp after all as the people say. I was glad, for I believed now that I should see the son of Doña Juana with his beaked nose and his wetly hanging underlip. In a fit of excitement I burst out into a run, and paid no attention to the few passers-by who stared angrily after me as I bumped them out of the way. Running full tilt I raced past the Cathedral, and hardly noticed I was spilling water from my jug. In my eagerness I nearly forgot Alonso the splendid one.

Then, without warning, someone grabbed me by the shoulder and jerked me into a courtyard. I looked at the man in terror, for he was by no means a reassuring spectacle. He had red hair, his face was marred by many craters from the pox, his little eyes were black and piercing. "Little louse," he shouted at me, "what do you mean by tripping up the

Comuneros! Why aren't you sucking on your nurse's breast, you misbegotten bitch's pup?"

"Not so loud; easy, Frenero, my son," a rough voice said behind me. "That's not the way to talk to a fine young nobleman." I wheeled around. There stood Father Pablo and smiled sardonically at my fright.

"Father Pablo," I asked trembling, "what have I done?"

"You're too young, much too young to understand," he said, his eyes wild in his haggard face. "But in any case, remember this if you value your skinny neck. You have seen the Holy Junta of the Comunidades. Remember that it is bad to play with the freedom of Spain. . . ."

"Don Carlos?" I stammered.

"First the law, then the King," said Father Pablo with great passion.

Frenero, the man with the red hair, carefully looked around a corner of the wall. "The Comuneros are advancing again, Father Pablo," he said.

"Good," the monk replied. "The main thing is to get as close by the Alcazar as possible. Then their fire can have no particular effect. It will spray over our heads."

He turned to leave, but I hung to his coat, and asked: "What has our Alcazar to do with the Holy Junta?"

He looked at me gravely, and shook his head. "The Corregidor is defending the Alcazar and the Castle Calahorra for Don Carlos against the Junta. Besides, Don Garcilaso has thrown a right-thinking man into prison. We can't tolerate that."

"Do you mean Alonso the splendid one?" I asked.

"I believe that's his name," answered Father Pablo impatiently. "But so far as I can see there's nothing splendid about him. It isn't a question of his person. It's a matter of principle."

I was unable to understand his words. For in my mind's eye I could see Alonso sitting there in a dungeon, while Father Pablo's principle was a misty thing beyond my imagining. At that time I had yet to experience the fact that it is commonly ideas which move men most deeply, and things far less, least of all a man's flesh. I should have very much liked to question Father Pablo at greater length, but he moved off abruptly, followed by the terrifying Frenero.

For a moment I puzzled out what I should do. Outside the courtyard men dashed along waving swords, lances and clubs in their hands. There were, too, some screaming women, their hair streaming behind them, and a few scattered street children. In the end my curiosity won out, and I left the protection of the courtyard. I followed the roaring crowd. There, high above me, I saw the gray-white mass of the Alcazar, built long ago by the great Abdur Rahman, in the days when Cordova was the capital of the western caliphate. Grayish-white the Alcazar rose up: mighty walls, a wide four-sided tower and myriad spires.

The besieged had placed their cannon on the flat floors of the parapets. Again and again echoed the deep booms. Heavy round stones crashed onto the paved street and splintered into fragments. But they did no injury. For a moment the mob held back. Then the uproar grew even louder. We rushed onward. Another salvo came, sang through the air over our heads. But even here, directly in front of the steep walls of the fortress, there was some danger. By my ear an arrow whipped, made sparks as the steel head struck the paving stones. Unaware of the risk I was running I still clung to my jug of water and crust of bread. I saw the contorted faces of the crowd, the helmets of the city guard above on the parapets, and Father Pablo, who had lifted his black cross to the sky. Everything I saw in the white hard sunlight of early morning, as if I were looking at a woodcut showing the fall of Jericho.

Suddenly with an outcry the attackers began to fall back. I heard Frenero shouting, "They're going to make a sortie." But I stayed where I was, as if my legs had turned to lead. I stared in fascination as the immense door of the fort creaked slowly open. The tips of lances glittered in the sun. I was overwhelmed with fierce shouts of, "Long live Don Carlos!" of "Long live Doña Juana, the Queen, and the Holy Junta!"

Before I could fathom the sense of these cries I was gripped by iron hands, and someone threw me forward on my face. Then everything became dark and pleasantly cold. The cries died down, and at last I heard them no more. Cold water ran over my wrist, some that I must have spilled from the jug. Then I realized where I was. I stood under the powerful low arch of the gate. I was a prisoner in the Alcazar.

An armed man took me roughly by the collar, twisting it so hard I could scarcely breathe. He led me up through endless winding stairs. Suddenly we came into the open, where everything was bright and cooler. Far down below me lay the city of Cordova. There was the gray mystery of the mosque, the Cloister of the Augustines, the Guadalquivir with waters of amber and bridges arched thrice in Roman fashion. And beyond the white hills—terrace on terrace, where up climbed the vineyards and the olive gardens, transfixed in the sun. And in the distance dreamed the blue heights of the Sierra.

The armed man led me, more gently now, by the arm, to a knight who was sitting on the balustrade beneath the pinnacled wall. It was Don Garcilaso de Gómez. He looked at me with amazement, forced his face into sternness, and said, "You always seem to be around when the mob is loose."

"It was by accident, honored sir," I said, stumbling over the words. "I wanted only to bring Alonso the splendid one a little water. I didn't want him to drink bad water. I have a piece of bread for him." I showed him the crust I still held in my fist as proof.

"And who is this Alonso the splendid one?" asked Don Garcilaso.

"Oh, you know him well," I came back, surprised.

"Come, who is he?" he said with impatience.

"The same one you put in prison," I said, trembling. "He isn't to blame for anything."

"Not to blame!" said Don Garcilaso angrily. "Why, it was the fat lump who worked up the crowd into a temper. What have you got to do with this man-cow?"

"He isn't a cow," I cut in firmly. "He's a man who slaves for his art. His brother Don Juan told me so. At the table last night he cried for him, for they are twins, honored sir. And besides, he's not to blame."

Don Garcilaso smiled reluctantly, then asked, watching me closely, "He really isn't to blame, then?"

"No," I replied, "for it was Father Pablo who told him to put on the Golden Fleece."

"Where is Father Pablo now?" he asked quickly.

"He's down there with a man called Frenero."

"Who is Frenero?"

"He's an ugly man with red hair that everybody listens to, the Comuneros . . ."

"Where are the two of them keeping themselves, the reverend Father and his friend?"

"They dragged me into the courtyard of the Montesino House. It's under the arch door. I mean the door with the two wild men on it."

"Fine," said Don Garcilaso, rubbing his hands. "You're a good boy, Pedro." He stood up and patted me on the shoulder. The guard smiled as Don Garcilaso spoke to him quietly. I looked out over the city. The immense prospect excited and gladdened my heart. I looked along the river which now in high summer ran between sandy shoals and stony banks. I thought how the river must flow to the sea by the glorious city of Seville, the city of the Cathedral and of the Giralda, on out to the Bay of Cadiz, whence the ships of the conquistadors sailed into the west toward fabulous lands. And I must have felt the great pulse of the world. Within my heart there burned a wish that I, too, might sail in the name of the Holy Virgin, borne on white sails over the trackless sea. At last I remembered poor Alonso, and I thought of the task that I had set out to perform. "Could I take Alonso the water now?" I asked.

"Yes, go ahead," said Don Garcilaso, friendly enough. "Tell the jailer I've given the order. By the way I am indebted to you."

"To me?" I said.

"Yes, to you," he said, an ironic smile flickering about the corners of his lips. "You acted very gallantly with Doña Isabella, and protected her with your own hands."

"Oh," I said, in childish embarrassment.

"Is there any favor I could do you?" he asked.

I thought awhile. "Yes," I answered, not without hesitation. "There is something I would like you to do, Don Garcilaso."

"What?"

"Spare Alonso the splendid one the whip. The blessed Virgin will reward you for it."

"Granted," he said. "And more than that. As soon as I have driven the mob back into their holes, Alonso will be freed. I believe in his innocence, now he's found such an excellent witness."

I thanked him profusely and raced down the steps.

I found the jailer, a very old man. Grumbling, he rose to his feet and thrust a massive key into the lock. "There's always something new cropping up," he said darkly, while he shuffled before me, lighting with his lamp the way through a maze of stairs and narrow passages. "One time, I remember, prisoners were prisoners. Nobody came to see them but the hangman and the torturer. But in these God-forsaken times, old-fashioned customs don't count for much. It can only bring harm to everybody concerned, I can tell you that."

He opened a door reinforced with iron straps, and carefully I crept down a sort of chicken-run. So powerful was the stench of rotted straw and excrement that it almost took my breath away. From above a deep shaft allowed pale light into this unhealthy spot, but it was some time before my eyes became accustomed to the gloom. At last I made out Alonso, slumped down back to the wall. He was not alone. Across from him, chained down, was another fellow, thin as a spindle, who watched me with great curiosity.

"Honored Alonso," I said, "I'm awfully sorry to see you in this fix."

"Such are the princes of the world," said Alonso. "But perhaps heaven has chosen me for martyrdom, in order to purify my soul. . . . But who are you, young man, who shows such sympathy for a lonely twin?"

I was disappointed. "I am Pedro de Cordova. Don't you remember, the one you met on the highway, the one who put up your troupe for the night?"

"Don Pedro!" cried Alonso, placing his hand over his heart, making the chains clank briskly. "What an honor!" he said. "How's my brother Juan? I hope he hasn't overeaten himself again like the last time in Toledo. We had to fetch a doctor, and he gave him an enema."

I reassured him. "Nothing like that," I said. "But your brother Juan cried the whole night through. He looked awfully sad."

"Oh, Juan, my brother," said Alonso, and rattled his chains. "I know those tears which flow so easily and so copiously over your hollow cheeks. But within your heart nests a bird of a different feather. Really you think of nothing but roasts, soups and sauces. The deeper sense of suffering is denied you. You wander through the world looking for a fool's paradise, while in vain I labor to invest your carnal existence with a little godly content. What are you going to think when you teeter with a rattle in your throat on the grave's rim? Oh, Juan, what good are the fattest capons, the most luscious oysters and the sweetest wines going to do you then?"

"Enough of that twaddle," a scratchy voice said from the other side of the dungeon. "Don't start drawing such pictures on the empty slate of my fancy. Don't be joking like that, fat man, when the walls of my stomach are rubbing together like two millstones. Young sir, in the name of God stop listening to this bladder of wind and give me the piece of bread you've got in your hand."

I broke the bread, carefully dividing it, and gave Alonso and the stranger each a half. "Thanks," said the stranger, chewing busily. "Like St. Julian you share your all with the suffering. By the way, why were our brothers upstairs shooting so much?"

"The Comuneros attacked the Alcazar," I said. "And Father Pablo and Frenero . . ."

"What?" said the stranger, forgetting to chew. "Is that hellhound Frenero around yet? Hasn't he been hanged? And here I sit, practically innocent, just because a hen trailed after me wherever I went."

"What, a hen? How was that?" I asked, astonished.

"Don't ask me," said the stranger, glumly; "for who can see into the heart of a hen? I guarantee that even St. Thomas Aquinas or Duns Scotus or that equally savant fellow, Occam, would be staggered if you asked him such a question. Perhaps the hen loved me, or perhaps I aroused her bestial curiosity. I tried and tried to shoo her off. I aimed stones at her, trying to make her go back to her master, but she persisted in her unreasonable conduct. This finally made me so terribly angry that I wrung her neck and put an end to the whole damned business. Now you can't let a dead hen just lie out in the middle of the street. So what did I do? I stuck her in my pouch. It was there the guards found her. And it was they, those shameless monsters, who had the gall to accuse me, Diego de Vargas, a poet and a man of feeling, of a theft. Now here I sit in this dingy hole, much enriched in zoological knowledge, but stripped of honor."

Quite dazed by this tale, I expressed my sympathy, and the stranger asked me for a drink of water which I gave him. As I did this, Alonso drew me to one side and whispered in my ear, "Don Pedro, don't believe even the dying words of this disgusting creature, Diego de Vargas. He's the biggest liar in the whole kingdom of Spain. Not only that, he's a member of the Germania. He belongs among thieves, murderers, pimps and fences. It's true he's written many a ballad, some of which are almost worth listening to. But don't waste your sympathy on him. They tell a terrible story about this fellow." He crooked his forefinger, indicating that I should bend closer to him. "You know," he whispered, "they say that he's in love with a heretic."

Cold shivers ran up and down my back.

"You'll understand, Don Pedro," Alonso went on whispering, "that I, one of the most fervent devotees of Our Holy Lady of Guadalupe, a stickler in matters of the Immaculate Conception, can scarcely allow myself to become contaminated by a person threatened by eternal damnation. There are certain dangers in sheer propinquity, you know. You can easily see one wouldn't crowd into bed with a leper. At least, not unless one was that St. Julian whose name has just been fouled in Diego's mouth."

Very much confused, I nodded agreement. Diego de Vargas was, indeed, not entirely pleasing to me, for all his self-appointed charms. Then it occurred to me I had forgotten to tell Alonso he was going to be spared the whip and would soon be a free man. So I told him in great excitement.

With a cry of joy he threw himself on his knees, raised up his folded hands, chains and all, and, with a sob in his voice, said, "O Blessed Virgin of Guadalupe, with profound gratitude I thank thee for thy intervention in the affairs of thy humble servant Alonso. Thou canst be sure of two thick candles, for I know very well that you saints don't come down out of Heaven on the spur of the moment to soften the hearts of men for anyone like me. Thou hast chosen me for a great task. And I suspect it has something to do with my brother Juan, my thoroughly irreligious brother who's slipping deeper and deeper into a cesspool of gluttony. Help me, I implore thee, O Blessed Virgin of Guadalupe! Send my brother Juan a violent toothache or a rending cramp in his gut. For I have noticed that under such conditions he lends a more willing ear to whispers from above. But so far as this noble, albeit beardless knight, Don Pedro de Cordova, is concerned, send him a lovely and not too quarrelsome wife, bless him with progeny more numerous than the stars on your mantle, for he's a good boy."

Diego de Vargas let out a loud laugh at this, but Alonso barely hesitating, continued with gathering force, "So far as my prison colleague goes, Blessed Virgin, I beg you again to put your best foot forward. I implore you to have him beaten thin with willow rods, twisted by thumbscrews, impaled on a hot iron rod. Lead him, benign Lady of Guadalupe, out of the company of thieves and murderers up among the angels. And the quicker the better."

With that Alonso arose to his feet, groaning and moaning. I was much moved by his piety, but Diego de Vargas did not seem to share my enthusiasm. Angrily he said to Alonso, "Why, you hypocritical hog! When I get out of this place I'll know where to look you up, you shapeless sack of foul wind. I'll show you that a member of the Germania never forgets an insult!"

I took leave of Alonso and Diego, and again clambered up the incline into the light of day. After the jailer had let me out of the dungeon-keep—but not before I had pounded wildly on the heavy door for some minutes—I wandered off by myself through the intricate passages and many rooms. I was about to shout for help, when suddenly I heard voices. There, not far from me, I caught sight of the Corregidor and several armed men, standing in the shadow of some pillars. Before them stood Father Pablo and Frenero. Their feet were hobbled.

"I don't understand Your Excellency," Father Pablo was saying angrily. "Not even the Bishop, who is a church man, can call me to task. You know perfectly well I'm a member of the Holy Inquisition. It's only Antonio de Guevara, the Grand Inquisitor, who can trouble himself about my doings."

"What has this uprising to do with the Holy Inquisition?" asked Don Garcilaso coldly. "Was it part of your ecclesiastical office to lead the inhabitants of the Potro against the Alcazar?"

For a while Father Pablo said nothing, then he muttered grimly, "It is a part of the duties of the Inquisition to protect the Spanish people against anabaptists and parasites."

Don Garcilaso thought this over carefully. "That's quite true," he said at last.

Father Pablo smiled triumphantly. "And the Flemings are anabaptists," he said.

"And Don Carlos?" asked Don Garcilaso. "Do you consider him to be a heretic?"

"I consider the King to be the victim of his unfortunate circle of intimates," replied Father Pablo boldly.

"Which is an altogether personal opinion," said Don Garcilaso. "It gives you no right at all to lead the mob of Cordova against accepted worldly authority and the representatives of the King. Blood has flowed, I beg you to remember."

"Blood always flows," said Father Pablo, indifferent.

"What is it you want?" asked the Corregidor impatiently. "Do you want to depose the King? Why were you trying to storm the Alcazar and the Calahorra?"

Father Pablo thought carefully. "You have imprisoned a right-thinking man. We cannot put up with that."

"Do you mean the actor Alonso?" asked Don Garcilaso. He smiled ironically. "The splendid one?"

"Yes, that's it," retorted the Dominican. "For we can't endure . . ."

"He is free," Don Garcilaso broke in.

"Free!"

"As soon as everything has quieted down, he can go home."

"How is it you call him the 'splendid one'?" Father Pablo demanded suddenly.

"None of your business," said the Corregidor, stopping him short.

Father Pablo looked around the room. His glance trapped me, for I had stepped forward from behind the pillars the better to hear. A feeling of terror tightened my breast. For barely a moment the Dominican watched me, his eyes cold with hate; then he turned back to the Corregidor, saying contemptuously, "Don't imagine, Your Highborn Excellency, that any traitor however nondescript will ever escape the Holy Junta. As far as you are concerned, you will be answerable to the Queen, Doña Juana."

"Enough talk," said Don Garcilaso. "Throw Frenero into the dungeon. And you, Father Pablo, will be taken early tomorrow morning by my men to the Grand Inquisitor in Seville, to Antonio de Guevara himself. That is, if the crowd has quieted down by then. You'll answer to him for this uprising."

"That suits me," replied the Dominican.

Both prisoners were led away. Don Garcilaso remained standing in the middle of the room, thoughtfully watching their departure. He murmured something to himself, shook his head, and called to me. "Listen to me, Pedro," he said, bending down to look into my eyes; "I'm sorry that your name became mixed up in this affair. But whatever happens, don't forget you have a friend who will stand by you."

I nodded.

"And now . . . I have something to ask of you, Pedro. Run over to the Cloister of the Ladies of St. Ursula. There you'll find Doña Catarina, Doña Isabella and my son Miguel. Tell Doña Catarina that everything is over with and she must go home."

Very proud and happy I ran on the errand. At every corner of the city there were guards of the Alguazil Alcalde and sober burghers. These latter had put on coats of mail and in this uncomfortable attire were ceremoniously padding up and down the cobblestones. I knocked on the cloister door. The doorkeeper, one of the sisters, let me in, though not before she had questioned me at length about my business. She led me into a shadowy courtyard where I saw the plump Doña

Catarina strolling up and down with her two charges. Doña Isabella was wearing the same clothes that I had seen her in the night before, but she seemed far more beautiful in the light of day than I remembered her. The sight of her fine nose and her slanted dark eyes threw me into confusion.

"Oh," cried Doña Catarina when she saw me approaching, "he's dead, just as I suspected! This unlucky boy is bringing the news." And well she might misread into my awkward expression this suspicion, although it turned out that Doña Catarina, otherwise a rollicking woman, was only too given to premonitions of catastrophe.

"If you mean Don Garcilaso," I said, bowing deeply, "he's safe and sound. He asks me, his unworthy messenger, to bring his greetings. The Holy Junta has retreated, and Frenero of the red hair . . ."

"He's still alive?" asked Doña Catarina. "Is he badly wounded?"

"No, he's in a dungeon."

Doña Catarina shrieked terribly at this. She threw her arms about little Miguel, a child perhaps three years old, and said tragically, "You poor orphans!"

"But I mean Frenero," I said impatiently.

"Frenero, Frenero!" she wailed. "I'm talking about Don Garcilaso de Gómez. What do I care about Frenero? I never heard the man spoken of in my life."

"I told you already," I answered, somewhat vexed at all this misunderstanding, "that Don Garcilaso is safe and hasn't been wounded at all. He stopped the uprising and told me to tell you to leave the cloister and go home."

"That's another matter, then," she said, coming to her senses. "But how do I know you aren't being paid to say this by Father Pablo?"

"Doña Catarina," Isabella broke in, stamping her foot, "don't make fun of Don Pedro. Just because he isn't old, that doesn't mean he isn't a Christian knight who once fought the Devil."

"The Devil!" said Doña Catarina. "That is uncommonly amusing. We'll have to go into that story later on when we have more time. I couldn't sleep a wink all last night, you know. Well, let's go now. For I know, if anyone does, that Don Garcilaso is an impatient man." With this she brushed her way past me, dragging little Miguel by the hand.

But Doña Isabella hung back for a moment, looked at me and said, "Thank you, Don Pedro. Thank you for telling me about my father and helping me last night." I noticed that now she used the formal "usted" instead of the familiar "tú." And so I bowed my head ceremoniously, as Sancho had taught me.

Doña Isabella watched this proceeding thoughtfully, and pulled softly at the lobe of her white ear which stood out clean-cut against the dead-black hair drawn back from her temples. "Tell me something, Don Pedro," she said. "Do you love me?" She looked at me expectantly.

I grew red in the face with embarrassment, and scraped the gay tiles of the courtyard with my toe. "Yes, Doña Isabella," I stuttered, "I love you."

"I thought so," she said calmly. "I thought it all out last night. I think it's very nice."

"Thank you," I whispered throatily, and continued to keep my eyes fixed on the tiles under my feet.

"But," she went on, "you've got to understand that a lady asks wonderful deeds from a knight before she returns his love."

"Yes, I understand," I said miserably. "I could bring you some pretty stones from the river bed. They look like amber. Or I could write a ballad for you." I had remembered Diego de Vargas, who might possibly help me in this novel undertaking.

"Are you a poet?" she asked.

"No, I'm not," I replied, ashamed.

"Then you won't want to write ballads," she said decisively. "And stones are much too common for Doña Isabella de Gómez. There's something else you might do, though. Conquer a kingdom for me."

"A kingdom!" I was dismayed.

"Why, yes," she said. "It doesn't have to be a very big one, of course. It could be about the size of Leon or Valencia."

"Oh, yes," I stammered unhappily. "But even that isn't so easy, you see."

"You could send the captured knights to me," she said, her eyes shining eagerly. "And if you come yourself after the expedition is successful, I promise you on my word of honor that I shall become betrothed to you."

"Certainly," I said. "But . . ."

"I understand," she cut me off firmly. "What you want is a sign." She rummaged in her little brocade bag hanging at her girdle. "Here's a blue silk ribbon to fasten to your helmet. Later on I'll send you a lock of my hair. You'll have to wear that against your bare chest, next to your heart."

"I'll try to do everything," I promised, since I saw that any protest was quite useless. "In what direction do you think I ought to ride?"

"Ride into the west," she said, after thinking for a while. "Ride toward the setting sun."

"But they say there's a big sea in that direction," I objected. "Anyway, that's what people say."

"Well, then, ride over the sea," she persisted arrogantly. "That exactly is the right direction. The land of El Dorado lies that way, the land of giants and the fountain of eternal youth."

I kneeled down before her, and she fastened the blue ribbon on my doublet.

"May the Holy Virgin Mary keep you!" she cried, and laid her hand on my hair. "Protect the honor of gentle women, and bring to the unhappy people of El Dorado the blessing of our Mother the Church."

"I will," I murmured, "but it will have to be some years before I can start out."

"That doesn't make any difference," she said, a little disappointed. Then she turned away, picked up her train like a full-grown woman, and glided majestically over the tiles away from me. I stood and watched long after she had gone; watched the sun which was on the point of dipping out of sight behind the hills. Behind me the cloister fountain rippled and gurgled to itself. My heart grew suddenly heavy. But the resolve stuck fast.

The sister at the gate opened the way for me, and filled with conflicting thoughts I made my way homeward.

3

MASTER AGRIPPA

I HAVE often noticed that the most important events of my life occur together. For long periods the stream of my days flows evenly and with hardly more disturbance than the amber Guadalquivir. But suddenly it will become broken by rapids, and so plunge thunderously into new depths of experience. And I myself am forced to sit helplessly by as if I were lost in the stream without oars or rudder, with not enough time to watch the banks moving by as rapidly as the wind.

The emotions of the last twenty-four hours had filled me to overflowing. When I thought about what had happened, my mind grew dizzy with speculation. And even to this day, long, long years after, it has cost me no little effort to tell the story in proper sequence. I, a boy of twelve, in that short space had cemented new friendships; I had found a paternal protector in Don Garcilaso; and the image of Doña Isabella had become fixed in my soul like a vision from an Arabic legend. And she had given me a duty to perform which stirred me to the depths. I took the task of conquering a kingdom in complete earnest. From the beginning I decided never to share this secret with anyone. Such an ambitious adventure seemed scarcely fitting for anyone in my circumstances. In truth I was a peasant boy in training and knowledge. I did not know how to saddle a horse, to handle a sword. The art of reading and writing was beyond my scope, and I had great trouble managing any number over ten. I was ashamed of my presence among others, and hesitated over a choice of words so long that my slowness of speech was a painful embarrassment. My proposal to Doña Isabella to write her a ballad was sheer bravado of which I was secretly ashamed.

Nevertheless I did not lose heart. Hopelessness itself prodded me on.

Later, I recall, Diego de Vargas once told me about the knight Parsifal who grew up wild in the forest, but despite this became the flower of Christian knighthood. His example fired me. For this knight not only conquered innumerable kingdoms, but even became the guardian of the Holy Grail, that priceless vessel which caught the blood of our Lord when on Calvary he was wounded in the side by a soldier's lance. What would Doña Isabella say should I come to her in a long white mantle embroidered with a cross, as a guardian of some holy relic whose influence I had spread all over the world! It was simply not to be imagined, my success. But in secret I tried to imagine it, over and over again. And even today, as I write, I see these moving scenes before my eyes, and in my heart there is a gnawing bitterness that the future turned out so utterly different from my expectations. Indeed, I have conquered a kingdom, or at least part of a kingdom, and one in which all Spain would be lost ten times over. But where is my Holy Grail? Was it all only a childish fantasy? Or shall I yet venture forth into the world to seek out this treasure of treasures? When I hear these mysterious, teasing voices calling to me from afar, as so often happens of late, could it not be the urgent voice of some such precious jewel of God? I do not really know.

At that time my empty existence took a completely different turn. The circumstances of my household improved considerably. At supper we now had a roast, at least on Sunday, and during the weekdays we always ate *olla podrida,* the soup which is the chief nourishment of us Spaniards. Our bread became whiter, our wine heavier, our cheese richer. I suspect, of course, that Don Garcilaso was the enchanter who worked all these domestic wonders, although he once told me that he had never been able to get Sancho to accept as much as a maravedi. Neither friendly pressure nor the threat of a dagger in his middle would alter Sancho's stupid independence. My steward could never forget that he was in the service of Don Pedro de Cordova. So far as he was concerned this knight lorded it over a magnificent accumulation of land and buildings, presided at the head of a table which groaned with edibles, while Sancho and his dame, Doña Teresa de Trujillo, hovered about clothed in the most impressive raiment.

One day I said to Sancho that it was high time I was introduced to the knightly art of managing a horse and using the sword. He nodded thoughtfully, and scratched his scalp long and hard. On the following

Sunday he announced that the next day practice would begin. He had got hold of a fine steed, he informed me, a she-ass by the name of Pia. He admitted she was by no means a charger, but stubbornly pointed out that she had some rare qualities—obedience and steadiness—which would stand me in good stead in the heat of combat.

And so on that Monday I proudly rode through the streets shortly after sunup on my Pia, out through the city gate, past the vineyards and olive groves, to a stony open place. At the hip I wore a wooden sword, and on my left arm I bore a shield made of calfskin drawn taut. Sancho had armed himself with similar objects.

Several long hours went by and the sun burned the backs of our necks unmercifully, as Sancho exchanged parry and thrust with his small pupil, warded off my blows with his shield, showed me how to wheel my small mount this way and that. All my joints ached, but before my eyes floated the luring image of the towers and walls of my city yet to be conquered. I would not give up. In the end Sancho ordered me to attack him full tilt with my sword. Heroically I urged on my Pia and charged down on Sancho. But he struck off the blow with his shield, and there was a loud noise, just as if I had crashed a stick onto a big drum. This rumble frightened my mount, who in all her country days had never before heard such a startling commotion. With infinite stoicism she stopped dead in her tracks as if turned to stone. But I sailed out of the saddle and like lightning shot between the straining ears which grew out of her head like two enormous leaves. As I lay spent on the ground she observed me patiently with her sad, watchful eyes.

Sancho comforted me over this disaster and was of the opinion it was really a good sign. For even Alexander the Great, King of Macedon, had been thrown from his horse Bucephalus, which he broke to the saddle at a later date. Even the great Caesar had been hurled painfully to earth when his ship ran aground on the coast of Africa, and the queen of that country used him most tenderly, choosing him for her knight.

In the midst of this discourse I managed to drag myself erect and smile proudly for all my badly skinned hands. The omen pleased me greatly, salved my wounds and discomfiture. Then I told Sancho it was about time to get something solid to eat. We had each a chicken wing, the remnants of a fowl which had met its end the previous Saturday at the hands of our Teresa, and with it swallowed down some olives and figs, eased into our stomachs with wine that Sancho had kept cool in a stone jug covered with wet skins. Pia, now unsaddled, poked around among the thistles, choosing carefully, stripping off the tenderest morsels with an outstretched tongue and evilly yellow teeth. After a long siesta we again took up our exercises, and I was finally lucky enough to bowl over Sancho with a blow which, according to his opinion, would have done justice to a youthful Roland.

Chattering busily Sancho and I left the stony site of my first knightly maneuvers. My heart pounds in my breast when I think that then it was I took the first step toward realizing my bright dream in the rude and ghostly world of actuality.

But before I go on with the story of my knightly training I must mention my actor friends who, a few days after Alonso was freed, traveled on with their big wagon to Seville. I shall never forget the cry of joy which came from Juan when Alonso arrived unwhipped. Alonso told me that his jail companion, Diego, had also been let out, undoubtedly to the eternal sorrow of his own soul and the population of Cordova, especially the female element who would be once more exposed to the poet's sweet lies.

On taking leave the whole troupe threw their arms about me, and the Devil said, "Believe me, Don Pedro, my mind's miles away from this devilishness. For all my satanic arts, as superior as they may be, hardly bring me in my daily bread. It's a fine piece of irony that I should be called the Prince of the World. I beg you, then, when you're a grown man, think fondly of the best Devil in all Spain, of Alonso the splendid, and of Juan, his skinny twin." Alonso did not forget to implore the Virgin Mary to grant me all her blessings, while Juan wished me happy days.

Our other houseguest, Master Agrippa of Nettesheim, did me the great honor of accepting my continued hospitality. He settled down in what once had been the Moor's study. On account of the evil spirit lurking there it was little used by the household, in fact, deliberately avoided.

When Sancho was busy in the fields, and knightly exercises were impossible because of garden duties, I used to sit on the stone floor of Master Agrippa's room and watch him. Once in a while he would exchange a friendly word with me, but often in the pursuit of his studies and experiments he would entirely forget my presence. At such times he talked to himself, mumbling words in a foreign tongue that came more easily to him than Spanish.

Master Agrippa was very strange to see, with his long gray hair and his powerfully curved nose. He was small, rather thin and the big head with a furrowed brow contrasted strikingly with the inadequate body. Usually, for all the summer heat, he had a charcoal fire burning. On the hearth stood vessels of green glass, with oddly fashioned mouths, and twisted tubes which he blew himself. There were also large mortars, molded of bronze, and smaller vessels made of green stone or red clay. The cabinet in which the earlier owner of the house had stored his Arabic writings was still there, and this Master Agrippa kept filled with flasks of varying size marked with unintelligible symbols. In the flasks and in his stone jugs he kept the acids, metals, lyes and salts that he used in his work.

The low vaulted room was oftentimes filled with choking white or brown vapors. At such times I had the feeling that evil spirits were choking me, and had to cough deeply. At this Master Agrippa would laugh mockingly and say, "Look at the nice little boy! We'll have to distill some oil of violets for him to drink with honey, the sweet." At the beginning this persiflage annoyed me very much, but later I laughed too. In time Master Agrippa let me blow the bellows to make the charcoal fire glow a cherry red, and a spray of fine sparks would shower all over our clothing and hair. He would look sharply into the glass wherein there hissed a silvery molten fluid. "More, more," he would cry, "you lazy bungler! Do you think that the spirits give up their precious secrets without some effort? Nothing is more compelling than the force of fire. The little beings who live in water, earth and air fear nothing so much as the keen demon of fire. Work like a mule, little Spaniard!"

Once, when I was pumping away at the bellows with sweat streaming down my face, there was a terrific explosion; a heavy object struck me to the floor and made my ribs ache. Master Agrippa's face was smeared black and his eyebrows burned off. When I looked at him I was at a loss to know whether to laugh or cry. But he merely sat down before the fire, leaned his head on his propped hand and said in dejection, "In the art of alchemy one never learns." This made me deeply sorry for him.

On this particular day we worked no more. Master Agrippa said that he was lacking basic material. I asked him what was the basic material.

"Aurum," he said, "otherwise called gold."

"Well, then," I retorted boldly, "let's make some."

"Oh, yes," he mocked me, "that's easily said. This has kept me busy since the first hair sprouted on my milk-white cheeks. I have found an excellent way to make it. But now I discover I get less gold out of the process than I put in."

We fell silent, but after a while I got up the courage to ask him what really was the final goal of his great work, for that he had never told me.

He looked at me in astonishment; then he breathed deeply, and said, "I am looking for the prime stuff of which matter is made."

I did not dare to question him further, but merely gazed at him with a question in my eyes. He nodded and continued, "Science, my child, is not everybody's province. But in due time you will find out that there are four elements. These are called fire, water, air and earth. Everywhere we find them, in men, animals, metals, plants and stones. Plants are related to the earth by their roots, by the leaves to water, by the buds to air, by the seeds to air. With us human beings the bones are of an earthy nature. Our juices, spittle, gall and blood contain much water, and our flesh much air. Flesh rots like hay and vanishes at death into the air. And in our vitality, we have fire, a fire that burns much more brightly in a young boy like you than in me, an old man.

"Such are the different kinds of matter, the elements. But the prime element is a great and precious mystery, and one can crack his wits with thinking of it without ever glimpsing the meaning. I myself have studied until the sweat started from my brow, and I know many books."

In agitation he leaped to his feet, began to pace the room. After muttering to himself for a moment, he went on talking to me, or rather talking aloud to himself.

"But nevertheless I cannot really talk about the element of elements, which has been called the *quinta essentia,* for it is fifth in the series. You must understand, my son, that a great soul fills the world. Fine threads lead everywhere from God, the All Highest, to spirits and star worlds, connecting them with the whirling globe on which we pass our days. You and your knightly play with sword and shield, I with my books and parchments, Teresa stirring supper in the pot, your little donkey Pia eating thistles, the olive trees on the hillside, the stones in the street, the black waste of the Sierra, the yellow Guadalquivir—all of us are, live, breathe, because a forming strength is at work in us. God indeed is nearer to us than we to Him. When all life has been lived, as the noble poet says, it is He, God, who has lived it out. And if God no longer cared to live out our lives for us, we would sink to the ground in a heap, like puppets in a booth when the man who pulls the strings has gone home for the night. For this reason it is stupidity to say anyone is godless. God lives in fools, heretics, thieves, each in a different fashion, sometimes amusing, sometimes horrible...."

I looked at him startled. His mantle was flying as he stalked back and forth across the room. He cocked his eye at me impatiently. "Good enough, my boy. I won't frighten you. And I have also heard that in Spain the walls have ears. But one thing more. In the end God is the only form which has enduring motion and activity. It is this, the hand of God in the world, the energy, the deed, the eternal decision which is the prime element. It is that which I am searching for, why I sit nights through at this hearth, and extract, distill and sublimate metals. For this *quinta essentia* must be of a physical nature. We see its power everywhere. It is an ancient proposition, never contraverted since eternity, that like works only on like."

"Like on like?" I asked, still frightened at this flow of words.

"It is too much for you, my son," he said. "But so it is, in any case. If you want to awaken love in a woman, you must give her to eat the heart of a concupiscent animal, such as a dove or a sparrow. If you wish to become bold, eat the heart of a lion or of a cock. If you want a woman to tell you her secrets, lay on her breast the heart of an owl as she sleeps. She will then begin to speak, for the owl cries out only in the night. And if you want long life, and some fools do, eat the bowels of a snake, for the snake dies many deaths while slipping wisely out of its old skin. If you want to make a horse brave in battle and tireless, have him shod with shoes made from a hero's sword."

"Master Agrippa," I cried out, "you are teaching me wonderful things."

He eyed me mistrustfully, so I thought. Then he stroked his chin and said, "There are many mysteries in the world. I think you may sometime rue the day that you offered Agrippa your hospitality. But keep this always in mind: like affects like. Watch out for evil ones, for they emanate their wickedness and spread their infection. If a noble virgin looks into a mirror previously used by a vain woman, she will become vain and coquettish. A friend of mine in Dôle once had a barking dog who bothered him on moonlight nights. But he refused to part with the animal, for the dog kept good watch. One night when the moon was out I took the noisy hound and made him stand in the shadow of a civet cat which is a very silent animal. And never again did the dog let out the smallest sound."

I clapped my hands and said, "Oh, Master Agrippa, you are the wisest man in the whole world."

"Well," he said firmly, "there's no point in belittling oneself and hiding one's lights under a bushel. The Evangel himself forbids it. But even great scholars have their failings. I have them myself, as I am well aware, a certain melancholy and disposition to doubt. Strangely enough these feelings overcome me most often just when I have made my most exquisite deductions. But to return to the theme, boy: always keep company with the rich, the good and the pious, for then you, too, will become rich, good and pious."

"Thank you, Master Agrippa," I said, touched at this advice. "But I keep wondering just why like should affect like?"

"Oh!" cried Master Agrippa. "So you're a little philosopher yourself, are you! You pose questions like a seasoned scholar who is trying to put his magister in a hole. Not even Master Agrippa, the man of the last word in all discussions, the solver of all impossible questions, the worthy disciple of merry Democritus and of long-faced Heraclitus, not even he can answer that riddle. You must see, my son, that the effective in man is the power of imagination, the fancy. Stop, don't interrupt! I'll explain to you. See—if a pregnant woman looks long enough at an object, it forms in her womb, in the fruit of her love which she carries within her belly. In a certain sense we are all pregnant, pregnant with our own future. It is comforting to think only about that which is suited for us. On such things we turn the eyes of the spirit, and make them in fancy, fashion them in mind's womb."

"I don't understand," I said half in a whisper of disbelief.

"I might have seen that myself," said Master Agrippa and laughed to himself. "But don't doubt. No scholar leaves me without getting a heady draught of my knowledge. I'll give you a ladder to help your struggling thoughts climb up the wall. One night the great Cyppus dreamed a vivid dream of a bullfight, and to the horror of his acquaintances awoke in the morning with two enormous horns sticking from the side of his head. With the power of his fancy he by himself made this not altogether attractive ornament."

"Is the strength of the soul as great as all that?" I inquired anxiously.

"It is immense," said Master Agrippa, and struck his fist on the blackened hearth tiles so heavily the retorts jingled and danced. "I tell you, boy, the emanations of the soul are so strong that a man of parts by a single hateful look can kill a camel. For the soul, understand, is itself the whole world. And men's souls are not always trapped within their bodies. It says in the Koran, in the thirty-ninth Sura, if I'm not mistaken, 'God takes unto himself souls when they die, and souls which do not die he takes in sleep.'"

At this I breathed a sound of horror and put my hands to my face. For Teresa had told me when anyone quoted aloud from heretical books the demons of Hell would seize him and carry him away over land and sea. However, nothing of this sort occurred. Master Agrippa sat there calm and undisturbed. He smiled to himself and went on to say: "Man forms and imagines his own being by himself. Believe the magician, my son, when he tells you that the strength of imagination and belief allows man to accomplish anything. It allows him to enjoy the aid of spirits, to inhabit the elements and the stars, to have the help of the archangels who surround the throne of God, to receive the grace of God."

"Do you believe all that, Master Agrippa?" I said, and thought feverishly of my kingdom. "Do you believe that with my power of fancy I can get what I want?"

"Beyond the shadow of a doubt," the magician replied. "There's no question of it, if you wish deeply enough, and imagine constantly day and night. Be a man of fancy and a wisher like the famous Cristóbal Colón. For I tell you, boy, if those Indies had not lain there in the sea, with the sheer power of his fancy he would have raised them from the depth. And so you, too, will doubtless succeed in laying at the feet of your beloved, treasures and crowns."

"Master Agrippa," I said, blushing, "how did you know about that?"

He laughed at my outburst. "Don't forget that I'm a magician and know how to read men's souls."

"Oh, Master," I said, reaching for his hand, "you have made me feel so much better. Many times I've doubted that I was good for anything at all."

He observed me, became lost in thought, and his face grew sad. Sighing heavily, he said, "You're a happy child! The world still lies before you without limits, the seas are green and the woods sing. You have set yourself a life's task, you think? But do you know that this life imposes two tasks on men? The one comes from us, the other from God."

"From God?" I asked, thinking of the Holy Grail.

"God did not fashion man as a bauble," he said, more to himself than to me. I fancied that he was speaking someone else's words, some great authority, as in church the priest pronounces some saying of our Lord as recorded in the Evangels. But then his thoughts seemed to take another direction; again he turned toward me, and asked, "Does my philosophy please you, then?"

"Yes, it does, Master Agrippa," I answered. "It is wonderful. It seems just made for me."

He got up and poked around in a chest and threw a whole heap of papers on the hearth. I looked at them agog, and saw that all of them were covered with writing. "This," he said, and could not conceal the pride in his voice, "this is the manuscript of my three books *De occulta philosophia,* which are going to the presses soon in Antwerp. You won't understand much of it. But one or two ideas will get into your head, at least. Take them and read."

"I can't read, Master Agrippa," I said, fingering the hard sheets of paper.

"That's true," he said. "I forgot that the language of scholars, our sweet Latin, would be a book with seven seals for you."

"But, Master Agrippa," I stammered, "I can't read in any language."

"What!" he cried out, and actually shook me by the shoulder. "You can't read, you blockhead. Do you want to go through life as dense as a tanner, a charcoal burner or a swineherd! And you have the effrontery to discuss with me the *quinta essentia* and the strength of belief, instead of first asking about your ABC's! You clown, you have the unashamed gall to try the last step before you've even ventured the first!"

At this assault my eyes filled with tears. "But who's going to teach me, Master Agrippa?" I said. "Neither Sancho nor Teresa understands the art of reading." Trying to stifle my sobs, I began to move to the door. But Master Agrippa took me by the collar, and forced me back on the stool where I had been seated.

"So," he said, "you'd like to slip away like quicksilver from an unstoppered retort, would you! You don't know Master Agrippa, I see. I shall sublimate you until there is nothing left but the clearest metal. And first of all I shall show you the letters of the alphabet. Stop your idiotic whining. You ought to realize, boy, that the princes of Germany have vied to get me as tutor for their sons. For who, outside of Master Reuchlin who wrote the book on the wonder-working word, could hold a candle to me! Be consoled, my son. The difference between the most learned and a puddinghead like you is small indeed when one considers the gap separating me from most of my contemporaries."

On saying this he again rummaged in his chest and drew forth a copy of the Vulgate. He showed me the different letters and these I had to copy down on a piece of paper.

The art of reading and writing came to me rather quickly, partly because I was ashamed to bother Master Agrippa with such trivial matters. It was simply not suitable that one of his stature should spend his time instructing a child and thus waste precious hours of study. But curiously enough the whole affair seemed a kind of entertainment to him. Again and again he repeated to me the dissertations which had so puzzled me that first day, and I can recall the substance of his words still through having heard them so often. He did not content himself with giving me simplest words to copy, as do the monks, but forced me on to learn by heart difficult philosophical phrases, which gradually, despite my youth, I came to know in complete intimacy. He told me that it was important to write the words properly, letter by letter, not out of quill-driver's vanity, but because the essence of things lay in their names.

Indeed, it was his opinion that Adam on the behest of the Creator had named all things in Hebrew, and that these were the right names, as Master Reuchlin had also pointed out. But Greek and Latin were also holy tongues, for the Evangelists had spoken Greek, and long, long ago in the city of Alexandria seventy learned men had translated the Bible at once, and it was found that each man's translation tallied word for word. This miracle could only be explained, Master Agrippa declared, by the fact that the Holy Ghost himself had taken the trouble to transliterate the Hebraic text word for word into Greek and Latin, especially considering that each translator had his own axe to grind. From then on I regarded our dog-eared Vulgate with particular reverence. I all but saw the Holy Ghost standing before me embodied, chewing at a quill and wiping beads of sweat from His forehead. In any event, in this manner, almost casually and without the slightest trouble I learned the Latin tongue, and it was soon possible for me to carry on a conversation with Master Agrippa in this language, although I never succeeded in equaling his elegant diction, which he must have taken from heathen models. And when I made a very bad mistake, as so often happened when I used the *ablativus absolutus,* Master Agrippa would be moved to hilarity, and call me *vir obscurus,* a man fuddled with darkness.

Indeed, I derived much edification from my beloved Vulgate. Of course I had always gone to Mass, and had received many fine bits of wisdom from Sancho and Teresa that they had remembered from the Book of Books. But it was quite another matter to bring the thought, long since recorded and yet so alive, from the written page, word for word, with my finger following along each sentence, line after line. It was like digging for hidden treasure, and seeing it exposed all glittering in the light of day. But when I discussed what I had read with Master Agrippa, the words often took on an altogether different meaning from that given them by the Church—one might say, a worldly aspect.

For instance, the six days of creation posed some difficulties for me. I secretly thought it impossible. Even the Almighty could hardly account for all the size and variety of the world in such a brief time. When I voiced these doubts Master Agrippa would thumb through the leaves of the Book until he had found the place where it said that to God a thousand years are as one day. This dispersed my uncertainty, for in six thousand years anything is possible, especially if one is omnipotent!

Another thorny point was the Tower of Babel. I was simply unable to grasp such an undertaking, to reach Heaven by building a tower. To this Master Agrippa replied there was nothing hard to conceive. Were not the melancholy remains of this tower still to be seen in the land of Babel? And besides, the Egyptians, who were just as heathen, had attempted similar structures, in which they buried their kings and which they called pyramids. Moses himself had often vented his wrathful scorn on such heathen nonsense, had he not? And furthermore, every word in the Bible had a meaning beyond the mere literal, even though I, Pedro, did well enough to stick fast to that. For later on of its own accord the esoteric thought would blossom forth out of the exoteric. But since I had run hard aground on the riddle of Babel, Agrippa said, he might as well explain to me what the inner sense of the story is.

This monstrous scheme was simply an attempt by man to reach Heaven without the help of God. And such ambitious plans need not be limited to the godless instance of the Tower of Babel. There were the political ideas of the old Roman emperors, the dreams of phantasts who envisioned kingdoms enduring a thousand years and earthly paradise. There was a daemonic science, evil heretical magic, that had the same goal. But all such essays, said Master Agrippa, ended in the same fashion, in terrible strife, for the participants could never come to one accord on the best method to use. In the end there resulted tremendous chaos, wars, insurrections, famine and vast conflagrations. A great clamor of tongues broke loose. Men no longer understood one another, because every word meant one thing to one person, another to another, and therefore had no useful meaning. For a time God would endure such lamentable goings-on, but when He had decided that enough was enough He simply opened the sluices of Heaven and drowned the whole teeming mass of degeneration in a flood of water. When this happened the entire population of the world was condemned to the risk of a common death, except those few who had preserved tenaciously their faith, building it into an ark. In this ark they were able to float until the waters of heavenly retribution had subsided and the sun shone forth once more, and the skies cleared, becoming intensely blue and gold.

This explanation of Master Agrippa's made a deep impression on me, and it was indurated later in my career by similar stories which I heard from a heathen's lips, and which in due time I shall recount.

I must not forget to mention that Master Agrippa also taught me the rudiments of algebra and geometry. At the beginning he gave me nothing but simple arithmetical problems to solve. I soon became comparatively skilled in this naïve field. But I shall never forget the day when I solved a rather difficult equation and laid down my results before the Master, saying with not a little pride that I understood now practically all there was to know about number.

"Poor lout," said Master Agrippa, and to my horror the veins on his forehead swelled with wrath. "Why do you suppose that Plato, Proclus and Ptolemaeus drew back in trembling when they realized that the splendor of the idea outruns earthly powers of comprehension? Why did Hieronymus, Augustine, Origen, Ambrose and a hundred other fathers of the Holy Church hymn the insuperability of number? They knew, all of them, that our Heavenly Father created things with the help of number, the world's very totality, as godly Severinus Boethius has said in deep truth. And what has driven the wise men and the most zealous to despair, you grasp in entirety, you, a small weed in the garden of science! Your wit astounds me! Tell me what the number one means."

"One is a number," I stuttered, ashamed.

"You clown!" shouted Master Agrippa. "One is no number at all. It stands beyond all number. It is a unity, a fearsome mystery not to be probed by the minds of men. When God speaks to himself and says 'I,' then he has spoken the number one. Understand if you can, and enlighten me."

"Then one is no number, I see," I said in a low voice, crawling with embarrassment.

"How correct you are, my puffed-up little crackbrain," he said. "Look. There is only one spirit, one soul in the world, one sun, one philosopher's stone. And even in the bodies of men, in these ever fragmentary worlds, there beats but one solitary heart. And below there is but one Lucifer in the depths, not two, nor yet three, but one, who will defy God until the end."

"I am sorry for what I said. I had never thought of that at all."

"Then give your mind a chance before you loose your swiveled tongue," he said coldly. "For disregarding altogether the mystery of the number one, what do you know about the rest? Are you aware that two is the number of pity?"

"No," I said, "I did not know."

"But so it is, indeed," he went on, more calmly. "The 'I' and the 'you' are forever bound, like man and wife, like king and slave. But even unclean animals walked forth from Noah's ark in pairs. Two is the number of unfolding, the number in which good is separated from evil, light from dark, lies from truth.

"And not until the number three appears has the world completely unrolled into its triple kingdom, that of the earthly elements, of Heaven and of God. And the first kingdom is that of nature, the second that of law, and the third we call the kingdom of grace. Threefold, my son, is time, a division into past, present and future. Threefold is space, and threefold are the categories by which we measure the content of the universe—length, breadth and thickness. God has our heart, Heaven our brain, the earth the senses.

"And are you curious to know about the number four? Conceive, then, that the tetractys too is sacred. For there are four elements, with four properties, hot, cold, dry and wet. There are four regions of the world and four seasons of the year. This leaves out of account godly things. For has not the name of Lord four letters? Have not four Evangelists written about this very matter? And do not four animals bear the throne which conceals them?

"Boy, do not try me, or I shall indeed crush your smug certitude. All I want is to make certain you understand the way to science is long and stony. You're but a beardless wanderer, my son; you've scarcely taken the first step."

"Master Agrippa," I said, near tearful despair, "do you think there's any use of my going on if I am such a fool?"

"Now, now," he answered me, smiling gently. "I have heard that God loves fools. It is the same with Him as with a certain king who loved his fool. God stands all alone, and in His loneliness He created man. For a while it will amuse Him to see your capers, but in the end you must bear down and seek the place where you belong. Thus far you are safe, my child, for you were born an innocent, and such can do no real wrong. Never forget when in battle an enemy's sword cleaves your helm, when you faint in sorrow or in hunger, when a coarse deed smears your soul—even then you are close to God's breast. And now, though I suppose it's not really necessary, I have a special gift for you. I'll give you a demon, all for your own. But this will happen only when I see clearly that you have no further use for me, when my fate draws me away from you."

Fervently I thanked Master Agrippa for his advice. What boy ever had a finer teacher than I! O Master Agrippa, wherever you may be, you worker of wonders, only two other teachers have I ever heard of who can measure their keenness with yours. One is the wise Centaur, Chiron, who taught the boy Achilles. And the other is Socrates, that faunlike creature, that man with the broad brow, to whom came Alcibiades, drunk with his perfumed youth, borne along by two warm maidens, one on each arm. For it seems to me that even the very learned Aristotle, tutor of Alexander Magnus, I should not dare to compare with you, because that magister, grievously puckered with love's bloodroot, let the wanton maiden Phyllis ride on his back and like a common ass crawled on all fours about his garden, a peripatetic! But women have never touched in pique or sport as much as a damp fingertip to the cool mirror of your learning, Agrippa of Nettesheim, magister unsurpassed.

Quite often now I was invited to eat at the home of Don Garcilaso. There I improved my appearance and table manners. And there, too, I added to my knowledge of worldly affairs, for the hidalgos seated at the table spoke freely in my presence of Emperor and Pope, of King Henry of England, that corpulent, red-haired hunter of women, of King Francis the Magnificent. They talked also of his sister, Margaret of Navarre, under whose bed once hid a highborn noble, an admiral no less, who was discovered and thrown out of my lady's chamber with much scratching of eyes and buffets in the face. For it is said, even though this lady above all was enamored of her Boccaccio, she made no attempt to emulate, *privatissime,* the exploits so humorously described by the author. When I heard this story I laughed aloud and all the men laughed too, although I must confess that the admiral's plight moved my heart. It seemed to me that it was scarcely becoming for a man of such exalted station, one accustomed to stand on the quarter-deck scanning the uneasy waste of sea, to get into such a cramped position under a woman's bed.

At Don Garcilaso's table I also learned what became of the Comuneros. Since these affairs had an effect on the later course of my life I shall take the trouble to recount in brief the history of the rebels. It seems, then, that Don Fernando, the dead King of Aragon and the husband of Doña Isabella the Catholic, had cast our Queen, Doña Juana, into prison in the belief that the fate of her husband, Don Felipe, had jarred her loose from her senses. But, I noted, among the men at the table there was never any unanimity of opinion as to her madness. Some believed without reservation that the Queen was crazed. Others were of the opinion that so much unhappiness and frustrated love had merely made her odd and shy of her fellows. And still others held that she was completely in her senses, and had acquired some unusual mannerisms only because of long isolation.

Now, when Don Fernando died, the great Ximenes, Cardinal de Cisneros, became Regent of the united kingdoms, since Don Carlos, the elder son of Doña Juana, was in Flanders and in any case too young to rule in his own right.

But Doña Juana never heard at all of her father's death. Her jailer, so they said, a certain Don Bernardo de Sandoval y Rojas, Marquis de Denia, Conde de Lerma, in spite of his many titles and honors was a disagreeably coarse man, who handled the Queen roughly and generally behaved toward her as if she were a common slavey. Days on end, they said, she had to sit absolutely alone in her dark room with nothing but a candle light to warm her heart, and when she wished to perform the necessaries of her body he reproached her and called her a she-hog. At any time of the day or night the daughter of the Marquis walked in and out of the Queen's room without even bothering to announce herself or even to knock. And if the Queen wished to speak a word or two, the rude girl would tell her to close her mouth, since she could not stomach the conversation of a lunatic.

A few circumstances did, indeed, work to ameliorate the condition of the unfortunate Queen. One was the presence of her youngest daughter, the Infanta Doña Catarina, who had been born after the death of her father, Don Felipe, and whom her mother loved to distraction. Doña Juana, like her own mother, Isabella the Catholic, had always been a pious woman, and in her misery she derived profound consolation from the devoted presence of her confessor, Juan de Avila, who labored without ceasing to better the condition of the royal prisoner.

And even when Don Carlos returned to Spain Doña Juana remained incarcerated, though her son did visit her from time to time. The ticklish question on which Don Garcilaso's friends speculated ceaselessly was whether Don Carlos considered his mother to be insane. Or did he merely wish to prevent her from sharing with him the Crown of Spain, and for that reason preferred to maintain the fiction of her unbalance?

However that may be, the Spanish people and the Cortes of the cities of Castile did not consider her to be out of her mind. The only fault they could read into their Queen was she had always hearkened too closely to the voice of her heart. For this reason, they believed, she, the first heir of her great mother, had been misused, by those whom she loved most dearly, at the beginning by her father, Don Fernando, then by her husband, Don Felipe, and finally by her son, Don Carlos. Never before, it seemed to many, had a Queen been so consistently humiliated. Even among the muleteers and the goatherds and Moors the phrase was whispered: *"Juana la loca, loca de amor,"* Juana the mad, mad with love.

Now, when the uprising of the Comuneros occurred and the Spanish people took to arms, as I have previously described, there came into being two parties, the differences between which all hinged on a decision of Doña Juana. One word from the prisoner of Tordesillas would have sufficed to exalt the Comuneros into the right-thinking party, ready to free the Queen from her shame. Woe then to the Flemings, to Don Carlos himself! One word from the Queen would have robbed him of his crown, perhaps of the breath in his throat.

But the Flemings were quick to see. First they determined upon an appeal to the Queen, in actual fact in the person of Bishop Rogas, president of the Royal Council. With almost miraculous haste the Queen was treated with respect, and that abominable creature, the Marquis de Denia, was whisked out of sight and mind. The weeping woman was for the first time apprised of her father's death—never had Don Carlos told her the truth—and her help was implored. Spain was about to break forth into insurrection, they told her, and in the cities mobs were roaring their demands for weapons, while the clerics were themselves the most revolutionary elements of all, preaching at every chance a need for violent change. Her black eyes alight with horror, Doña Juana heard the anxious advices of the Bishop.

"This is what has become of Spain!" she cried. "The people have been enslaved—the same people freed by the Cid and all other heroes of the Cross."

This statement by the Queen did little to appease the fears of the Bishop. He begged the Queen to sign a public decree that all would be in order again under the Regency of the good Cardinal Adrian, the quondam rector of Loewen and the tutor of Don Carlos. It was he who had banished the he-goat Chièvres and who would restore neglected rights and laws. But the Queen denied him his request and said that she herself would find out firsthand what was going on in Spain. She was willing, however, to receive the Royal Council—to receive them standing while she remained seated, she, their rightful Queen. For thus had been her mother's custom, Doña Isabella's, may God rest her soul. To this the astonished Bishop pointed out that members of the Council were all elderly worthies, and that the meeting might last for hours. And so in the kindness of her heart Doña Juana did let him sit down on a comfortable chair, but forced the rest to squirm on unyielding benches. For six hours on end she listened to the urgent supplications and claims of these people. When it was all over she said she was tired, and retired to her room. It proved impossible to get her signature. It was Doña Juana's habit never to sign anything, whereas her son Don Carlos signed whatever anyone chanced to stick under his nose.

In the meanwhile the Comuneros had not been idle. They sent an army to Tordesillas, before which the Royal Council fled. Doña Juana gladly received the commander of the troops of the Holy Junta, Don Juan Lopez de Padilla. She looked benevolently at the young man in his shining armor as he kneeled at her feet, for she remembered perfectly that the youth's father, Don Pedro Lopez de Padilla, procurator of the city of Toledo and Captain General of Castile, had once held his influential tongue in consideration of her when her own father had not scrupled to let it be known she was mad. It was with horror that she heard from the lips of Don Juan about the humiliation of the cities and of the Spanish people by foreigners. She reached out her hand to the kneeling soldier and, in a voice veiled with tears, said, "Indeed I deeply love my people and everything that injures and drags down my children touches me as much as them."

And now the Comuneros awaited the decisive word from Doña Juana. But this word she never spoke. She preferred to endure imprisonment and humiliation, to be known as a lunatic, than to speak out—she, a loving mother—against her son Don Carlos. Not so much as a single word. Besides, the importunate tone of the Comuneros vexed her, the very appearance of the armed band. She recalled her mother's times, and how the nobility of Spain had stood around the throne. Should she, disloyal to her son and to the holy memory of her mother, surround herself with the city burghers of Spain, with merchants, artisans, peasants and the lower cleric elements?

The Comuneros waited month after month. Then they played their best trump. They had their own men pretend to storm the castle with loud war cries and clash of weapons, saying to Doña Juana that an army of enemies was approaching to seize the Queen and to carry her off by force from her people. At this Doña Juana fell on her knees before her private altar and with tears in her eyes begged the Holy Virgin to ameliorate the enmity between her son and the Spanish people so that she, a poor half-dazed widow, would not be driven to disastrous decision. For her heart was really torn between love for her son and a not less powerful love for her people. Grimly the leader of the

Comuneros heard the worried mother's prayers. From that day on they abandoned hope, no longer pressed their demands on Doña Juana.

However, Doña Juana heard from her father confessor that the attack had been nothing but a Comunero ruse to force her to give support to the rebellious cause. She thought of her anguish and of the prayer in which she had spoken untruths to the Queen of Heaven. No longer did she have a grain of faith in the integrity of the Comuneros.

It was in this fashion that the Holy Junta was robbed of its strongest prop. Now the Comuneros became nothing more than undisciplined rebels against the ancestral ruling house. Don Carlos, too, had become sly through repeated disasters. He had appointed more representatives of the high Spanish nobility as co-Regents with Cardinal Adrian. By means of this shrewd maneuver he drew the greater and more influential part of the Spanish nobility on his side. It so happened, in consequence, that the longer the rebellion lasted, the less feeble grew resistance to foreign rule in Spain and the more the rebels began to appear as an opposition to all rule and order whatsoever. In the end the richer burghers were bitten with fear and disaffection, and so withdrew their allegiance from the Holy Junta. The upshot of all this was that the German and Swiss mercenaries of Don Carlos smashed the soldiers of the association seven months after its inception at the battle of Villalar, and brought an end to popular insurrection.

We in Cordova were little affected by all these events. The prompt action of Don Garcilaso and the imprisonment of Father Pablo had put the matter, so far as we Cordovans were concerned, under lock and key. In any case, in the Potro, the criminal quarter of our city, there were not a few men who believed in the Junta and went to follow behind its banner. For this reason, Cordovans lost their lives at the battle of Villalar or spent many subsequent years in the galleys. But in the city itself everything remained peaceful, outside of the attempt to disrupt the guards of the Alguazil Alcalde. And this, in point of fact, occurred in the city of the Moors, and was blamed by the general populace of Cordova not so much on the Comuneros as on the heretics.

But even the successful repression of the great rebellion did not ingratiate Don Carlos in the hearts of his people. It was widely felt he was particularly reprehensible in the plundering and burning to the ground of Medina del Campo, during which uproar he permitted his mercenaries shameful liberties.

Don Garcilaso and his friends themselves were anything but charmed by Don Carlos' conduct, although at that time they remained loyal to him. I often heard them complaining that one after another the liberties of the Castilian cities were being stripped away. In place of proud and Christian Spain with its self-sufficient cities and powerful status, there was a country increasingly subject to the will of a single man, a man more often than not closeted with dubious and unpropertied advisers. More than once I heard the men around the table, the greater part of whom were advanced in years, express doubt about the future of the country. For, so they said, in the long run it was impossible to prevent the morality and customs of Spain from sinking into oblivion along with Spanish freedom and honor.

Many a time when I have been eating at the home of Don Garcilaso I took the opportunity to let Doña Isabella know of my presence. But according to the custom of the time it was forbidden me to speak of my love before I had fulfilled my lady's commands. It was permitted me, nevertheless, to give circuitous praise to Doña Isabella's beauty and to communicate my ardor to her as best I could. I therefore spoke very poetically of the color of her hair, which I called "dark as the robe of night"; her eyes I called "the inviolable watchers of her virginal soul"; her teeth I compared to mother-of-pearl, her cheeks to the alabaster cheeks of the goddess Venus, and her feet to tender swallows. Unfortunately I made not the slightest impression on her with all these childish images and similes. Quite the contrary. She would draw her dark brows together and look at me angrily as if I had been making poor jokes. Still I had one very much interested audience for these high-flown conversations. This was Doña Catarina, who marveled at my choice language and considered it the last word in politeness of address. She said that undoubtedly I should become a poet, for in the Song of Songs that King Solomon wrote for his many wives, there were found similar things. Doña Catarina's approval, I must admit, took the wind out of my sails rather than encouraged me. Once I told Doña Isabella about Master Agrippa, how he was a great savant and would surely find sooner or later the philosopher's stone. This information gave her great pleasure, and from then on I had to tell her everything the Master had told me while it was still fresh in my mind. All this Doña Catarina also enjoyed.

But when I used to speak of the arts of alchemy and about the different spirits and sephira she grew uneasy and made the sign of the cross over her enormous bosom, while Doña Isabella clapped her hands in glee and asked when the next spirit was due to make his appearance. As for me, after the mishap with the bellows I placed no particular value on improved acquaintance with the spirits, for I was afraid that in the future they might behave in an even more abrupt fashion. I made no mention of my private doubts, however, and only said that unfortunately we no longer had any experimental material—that is, gold—as Master Agrippa had told me.

Doña Isabella, it seems, must have told her father of the incident, for one day Don Garcilaso took me to one side and questioned me at length about Master Agrippa. He listened to my story with a half-smile on his lips and inquired whether my Master was versed in the mundane writings of antiquity. With explosive importance I began to count off the names of many famous men and women whom Agrippa knew forward and backward. But Don Garcilaso broke me off and said he was of a mind to get Master Agrippa to teach his daughter and perhaps some of her young friends a few things about such matters. On the one hand by so doing Master Agrippa would be able to procure the gold for his alchemistic experiments; on the other he would be able to render him, Don Garcilaso, a great service. A girl was considered ill-bred and vulgar if she did not know a few poems by Ovid, Horace or Catullus, or had not shed a few discreet tears over the tragedies of Seneca. Beyond this a well-born girl had to know something about the background of the different Phyllises, Phrynes, Diotimas and Helens of antiquity, and be able to keep them properly separated in conversation.

Said and done. It must be told that when Master Agrippa heard of the proposal he grew beside himself with rage. "What in the name of the seven thousand and seven Virgins of Spain," he roared, "does this overweening Don Gasco want of me? So he wants to make me preceptor of a school for little girls, does he, an arbiter of maidenheads! Think of it! Me, a Prince in the kingdom of the spirit, before whom this Don with straw-stuffed ears ought to crawl on his belly in awe. Well, it's plain to see that women are behind the whole foul business. . . ."

"But, Master Agrippa," I interrupted, "even the learned Centaur Chiron carried little Helen on his back over the dark river of Peneus."

"Yes, yes, yes, so he did," said Agrippa. "I see they've snared you to begin with. But let me tell you one thing, my son, and that isn't two. Women are as untractable as matter itself, as the wise men have often said. For they are the *peccati causa,* the *instrumentum diaboli* in person. I call women a chaos. They are made up of pure contradictions, a hyle, a bottomless pit, that's what they are indeed. For they cannot be satisfied; with ease they can accommodate the entire world in more ways than one. Women as I see them are a *silva,* a primeval forest. And woe to him who wanders into this dark wood, for never will he get out again! What do you say about Helen, answer me that—the slut for whom the great towers of Ilium crashed to the ground? Who ruined Samson, when he was well on the way to being something of an emperor with his lion's skin? Who caught great Hannibal in Capua? Who proved to be the damnation of Hercules, the tamer of lions? Who gave him the Nessean robe? Who betrayed Emperor Claudius with mercenary seamen and a ring? A woman, my son, always a woman, once, twice, thrice,always. So watch your step, little soft brain, and don't step into Father Adam's shoes. *Mulier, quam dedisti mihi, ipsa, ipsa me defecit!"*

This tirade went on for some time. I merely stood listening with my inner thoughts on Doña Isabella, on her lovely face and gracious bearing. My Master's words were sown on sterile earth. In the end he quieted, began to pace back and forth in the room stroking his squarish beard. "Well, son, the day after tomorrow in the morning we can start the comedy," he agreed in bitterness. "Sheer necessity, vile Mammon, presses my face in the dirt. What do you say? Should I start this young Doña Isabella off right by giving her a good caning?"

"No," I shouted. "You can't do that. Doña Isabella is a lady. I wouldn't let you do that!"

"Tut, tut, what a frightful pity," he said, laughing with pleasure at my concern. "An English friend of mine once told me that a sound thrashing not only softens the ground but plows it up just enough so that the seeds of knowledge take hold and flourish better."

I saw that he was in one of his sardonic moods, did not bother further to expostulate, and considered the matter settled.

4

THE CITY OF THE MOORS

MASTER AGRIPPA had lived with us for several years and I might have been around fifteen years old when he told me one day to come along for a walk with him. He had to take some books, so he told me, to a learned acquaintance of his and it would be a great help if I carried part of the load.

Early in the morning we set out laden with our books. Talking cheerfully, we moved slowly through the streets. Master Agrippa pointed out the mosque which even in the clear morning light had something dark and worn gray about it. He told me that Abdur Rahman the Great, of the tribe of the Omayyads, a descendant of Mohammed, had begun the great structure, one of the wonders of the world. The famous Caliph had wanted to make another Bagdad out of the chief city of his caliphate, perhaps even another Mecca. The pulpit he had made out of ebony, richly inlaid with ivory, with sandalwood, aloe, lemon wood and other aromatic timbers which are found in the hot faraway land of the Yemeni. The Koran, the Moorish Bible, he had kept in a golden casket, which was so heavily overlaid with pearls, rubies and emeralds that at night amid the gloom of the interlaced columns it glowed like another sun, or like the treasure which Aladdin with the help of his magic lamp found in the depths of the mountain.

And not without justice, Master Agrippa added, was the Koran preserved in such a costly, strange reliquary, for God is the life of the soul, as the soul is the life of the body. This was said by none other than Saint Augustine, a very pious and learned man, who in his youth had strayed into the paths of gnosis, but in his old age had returned to the Fold, the Church alone blessed, the successor of Peter and Paul.

I should have liked to ask Master Agrippa what gnosis meant, but I saw he was completely immersed in his thoughts. He said to me, "Oh, the deep splendor of Almansor. They came here from all directions, the wise ones, the ones enamored of God, the astronomers and alchemists.

"It was at that time that El-Makkari cried out when he first saw the capital of the Western caliphate, 'Praise be to Allah, for I am come to Cordova, the seat of learning and the throne of the caliphs!' But where, my son, has all this vanished, all this splendor? Where are the baths, the palaces, the mosques? Where is the tumultuous crowd? Where the songs of the poets, the laughter of the women? Where is the deep thinker Ibn Roshd Averrhoës, who tried to peel from pure being the rind of mere chance as one takes a walnut from its shell? Where is this man now, whom the strict believers of Fez spat on full in the face as they left the mosque?"

Master Agrippa dropped his head to his chest wearily. In order to distract him I tugged at his sleeves, pointed at the old Roman arch and asked him what the letters carved into it—SPQR—could mean.

"They mean *'Senatus populusque Romanus,'"* he told me, "for you know long before the time of the Arabs this old Cordova was a great city. Here ruled the Iberian kings. And after them the men of Carthage from the great Phoenician merchant city. It is thousands of years since men first used iron. But in those days they made everything out of copper, and if they wanted to harden the blades of their plows or swords they melted tin into the copper as do the brass founders today. You see, my son, Spain has much of these metals, and what more was needed was brought from Britannia, which was called the Island of Tin. The Phoenicians' ships sailed all over the earth, as do the Spanish and Portuguese ships today. They rounded Cape Vasco da Gama and some of the boldest of them ran out from Tartessus westward into the sea toward the setting sun and reached the land called Atlantis."

"Atlantis!" I cried. "But in the west there is nothing but the sea, the Canary Islands, the Azores, and again the open sea."

"And?" he asked me watchfully. "And what besides?"

"And the Indies that Admiral Cristóbal Colón discovered."

"Wrong," he said in triumph. "Absolutely wrong. I won't go into your error. The great Admiral himself believed he had found the Indies."

"But tell me then, how is it that Atlantis lies there and not the Indies?"

"The seaman Ulysses," he said to me, smiling, "left behind him a logbook full of lies. Of course, it may be that it fell into the hands of a blind poet who turned it into hexameters and so improved on it in many a way. In any case, my boy, this seaman sailed to the cliffs of Tarek, which then had another name. From there out he moved into the wide sea and finally landed at another island that he called Ogygia. We, today, call it Teneriffe. After many adventures with a loose woman by the name of Calypso like any sailor he grew bored and remembered his own wife, who while he was gone was earning her living by weaving cloth. And so he sailed east again, until a terrible storm pushed him off in the opposite direction. He was shipwrecked on a strange coast and escaped death by swimming ashore through the heavy seas. This land was inhabited by the Phaeacians, as he called them. They were a lazy people, given to dancing, eating and singing the whole day through. In short, they behaved much the same as do our own Indians today. Ulysses had landed in Atlantis without even realizing it."

"I don't understand that," I said doubtfully.

"Patience, have a little patience. I'm not through yet," he retorted. "You can't understand everything in the first breath."

"I beg your pardon, Master Agrippa," I told him.

"Well, then," he went on, "many hundred years later when the sailor Ulysses had dissolved into dust there was another man in this land of Greece called Solon. He traveled a great deal and once found himself in Egypt, the same country mentioned in the Bible. The Egyptians knew many things about the ancient past. Their priests had a secret knowledge that the common people knew nothing at all about. Solon wanted to measure his wits with the priests' and so talked at great length about the Deucalion flood, which is something like our own. But the priests just laughed him down, called him a child, and told him about their giant island, Atlantis, which lay in the Western Sea."

"And what did Solon say to that?" I asked.

"He didn't even know there was a Western Sea. All that he knew of was the Mediterranean. He made a wry face when he learned that the Atlantides inhabited a mighty city surrounded by seven concentric walls and seven canals in the center of which the shrine of Poseidon rose up in a seven-terraced pyramid. This island of Atlantis, as the Egyptians had it, was destroyed in one day. Earthquakes shook the earth and ashes rained from the sky. After the great flood coming in from the sea the island of Atlantis again arose from the waters. But no news of this even reached the Mediterranean world, for neither the Greeks nor the Romans ever ventured outside their inland lake. Only in our own day, in 1492, on a fine October morning, did Admiral Cristóbal Colón set foot on one of the little islands which were once part of the continent of Atlantis."

"And was there nothing left at all of the great kingdom and the cities?" I inquired, seething with excited interest.

He looked at me thoughtfully. "It's curious," he said, "but only the other day did I get a piece of news from my friend Pietro Martire de Angleria. It is going to set the learned men on their ears. It seems that a certain conquistador by the name of Hernando Cortés wrote the Emperor a long letter in which he said that in the Indies, which I call Atlantis, he had discovered a great kingdom and almost conquered it. The capital of this kingdom is called Tenochtitlan. It lies in a broad lake and is connected with the land only by long dikes. The buildings are splendid to see and everywhere tower mighty pyramids of stone on the top of which burns fire, night and day. The emperor of this country lives in a huge palace surrounded by hanging gardens like those once owned by the Princess Semiramis. Yet the inhabitants of Tenochtitlan do not know how to use iron. They make their tools either out of stone or of bronze, which I've just this moment told you about. And they also are ignorant of our letters. They write in picture words, as the Egyptians once did. They have neither horses nor mules. Nor are there any sheep or cattle there. They do not raise wheat or any other fruits of Ceres. But they do have their own kind of grass, which they call maize. They also raise little dogs, which they eat."

"How disgusting!" I said.

"Well, my boy, other lands, other customs," said Master Agrippa indifferently. "On the biggest pyramid that stands exactly in the center of the city—they call it Teocalli—is built the temple of their god, another Baal. All the walls of this temple are inlaid with gold and everywhere the air reeks with the smell of human blood. For every day of the year the priests of Tenochtitlan offer human sacrifice. Sometimes on feast days thousands are killed. They lay the sacrifice on a large slab of jasper, carve open his breast with a stone knife and rip out his heart. The heart, still beating and warm, they lay at the feet of their terrible god. When they do this they beat a monstrous drum that is covered with the skin of a snake."

I walked beside him, fascinated by the stories; my mouth hung open and I hardly knew whether I was awake or dreaming.

"And this place, my child," continued Master Agrippa decisively, "this Tenochtitlan must indeed be the descendant of that city of Atlantis which the Egyptians spoke of to the wondering Solon. For everything—the lake, the dikes, the pyramids, the picture-writing—everything indicates that in Tenochtitlan still lives much that we knew long before the days of Egypt, before Assyria and Babel. Of course, this depends on whether Hernando Cortés has lied or not. But I hardly expect he has. His letter was sent directly to the Emperor, and he would hardly deceive him for no reason. Besides, accompanying the letter were remarkable objects fashioned of gold and silver, of blue and green stone. Pietro Martire has seen them with his own eyes. He wrote me that never did he see such things as the Indian hands have made. For he was struck not only by their rudeness and barbarity. He experienced an odd feeling of the primeval past as he toyed with the smoothly polished stone, slippery in his palm."

"If Don Hernando Cortés has conquered this land," I said, bitterly thinking of my vow, "then there aren't any more kingdoms in the Indies left to win, are there?"

"Who can say!" he replied ironically. "Atlantis stretches immeasurable distances to the north and south. I am sure there is yet to be a discoverer of the greatest kingdom. We'll call it Petriterra, the Land of Pedro."

And the two of us imagined for a little just how Petriterra would look, for the sport of it. We fancied it would have rivers of milk and honey. Its cities would be made of gold and silver, its mountains of solid precious crystals. And its people would be kindly Indians with feathers.

At last we arrived at a massive archway built into the white wall. The portcullis was drawn up. Beneath it a watchman leaned against the wall, his halberd hanging loosely. Yawning, he eyed us up and down, but we paid no attention to him and continued into the cool semidarkness of the interior.

On the other side of the door there was a strange new world such as I had never known before. Today I know, of course, that I had entered into the City of the Moors, but then it seemed to me I was seeing another and less gruesome Tenochtitlan, or perhaps a less impressive Petriterra. The streets along which we walked were narrow clefts between the high walls of the houses. It was very dark in these alleyways. When I looked up I saw that white awnings had been spread between the upper stories of the houses. Some of the buildings had low arches, and higher up the walls were broken by little windows, covered with a finely laced grating. Now and then we ran into men with long beards. These people were dressed either in white or white with dark robes on top, and their heads were covered with turbans.

We had to step to one side to let donkeys laden with leathern bottles pass, or mules piled high with rolled stuffs. There was a brooding quiet in this City of the Moors, and it was some time before I noticed that in behind the arched ways of the houses many men were hard at work. There was the light silvery hammering of the smiths, the tapping of the cobbler. When my eyes had become accustomed to the twilight in one alcove I saw a big loom. Back and forth, as quick as an arrow, shot the shuttle. In another place a potter's wheel whirred, and from under the potter's hands as if by magic grew a lovely clay vessel. In the alleys there was a strange, sweet and somehow acrid odor in which there was strongly intermingled the smell of sizzling sheep fat.

And then we came to the bazaar. Master Agrippa led me under the vaulting arches and I stared in wonder at the multiplicity and fineness of the wares. In our market in the Christian city there were only fruits and other products of the countryside to see and buy, everyday utensils like earthen pots, knives, glasses and brooms. But here everything under the sun seemed to be collected, everything the human brain ever devised or the artists created. Deep in my heart I had always despised the Moors, because Sancho had told me they were little better than heathens and knew nothing except the satanic arts. But there seemed nothing satanic to me in these beautiful tapestries, glazed ceramics and Damascene swords. I noticed, too, that the unfaithful bore themselves with each other exactly like ourselves, only with fewer curses and livelier gestures.

I told Master Agrippa of my astonishment. He laughed and nodded his head.

"Never think, my son," he told me, "that all the evil men speak about strangers is for a moment true. Most of these tales spring from the great weakness of mankind, pure envy. Each people has its special virtues and faults. The people who consider themselves the most exalted more often than not are the least, certainly the least renowned in wit. But really the Spaniards cannot bear the Moors and Arabs for different reasons. In the first place, they cannot forget that the Moors once ruled all the way to the Pyrenees. And in the second place they are also aware that the unfaithful are much more industrious, skillful and generally wiser than they are themselves. And that is a mortal injury, is it not?

"Certainly the Spaniard has his points. He is brave, resourceful, honorable, pious. He is true to his God and his King. But I tell you, my boy, it will be a bad day for Spain when there are no more Moors. For look around you. See the colored pots from Badajoz, wonderful needlepoint and crocheting from Beja, pillows from Calatrava. Look at these woolen goods from Cuenca, the glazed plates and dishes from Denia, the silks and satins of Granada. There you see bolts of fine linen and the finest paper which the artist and the scholar would sadly miss. They come from Jativa. Over there are guitars and horns inlaid with pearl, flutes and kettle-drums from Seville. Moorish hands in Almería have made that heavy brocade and blown glass. Look at the bazaar of food, both common food and luxuries. Look at those oranges, lemons and cucumbers, the vessels of wine and oil. Here are figs from Malaga, honey from Lisbon, sweetmeats from Zaragoza, muscatel raisins and pears from Valencia, which has been called the perfume-flask of Andalusia. For there, too, grow the most beautiful flowers out of which the Arabs press sweet oils that are worth far more than their weight in gold.

"And yet, my boy, these bazaars can give you no full idea of the industry and knowledge in handiwork of the unfaithful. For the ships built in Almería, the iron and copper from the mountains brought out to be smelted—for all that are they responsible. What would become of Cordova itself if you did not have the leather workers, jewelers and silversmiths who live in this quarter? These people support you, yes, pay your taxes. Your highborn regidores would shamble about in rags, barefooted, if the Moors' hands should lie idle in their laps."

Ashamed, I nodded my head, for it was plain to see Agrippa was right.

We now left the bazaar and turned into a narrow passageway. We had walked some short distance when we heard a shout of warning. A sedan chair was being carried by, and we had to press close to the wall to give it room. The chair brushed by my body, and at this moment a girl's slender hand pulled aside the red silk hangings, so that I was able to look into two dark, almond-shaped eyes that gazed into mine with curiosity and impishness. The lower part of the girl's head was covered with a thin veil, but I was able clearly to see the delicately aquiline nose and the long ovals of the cheeks. It was a lovely face. Then the curtain fell and the sedan chair passed on.

Not long after this meeting Master Agrippa abruptly turned into a doorway. He knocked on the door, and slowly it opened for us. An old man stood just within the threshold. He bowed and murmured to us to follow him. The house was very simply, almost barely furnished, and the corridor down which we walked had an arched ceiling and white-washed walls. And then the door of a room opened, a room so different that I all but dropped my books in astonishment. It was the most beautiful room I had ever seen. From the walls hung tapestries with in-worked figures of lions, dragons, deer and birds, and the floor was covered with a very soft rug. Along the long side of the room were arranged ebony tables inlaid with mother-of-pearl, and on them lay many rolls of paper and parchment. The light streamed into the room through panes of gaily colored glass and threw red and blue rings on a giant beaten copper gong suspended at the wall. Out of the midst of a heap of cushions piled on the floor a little thin man arose.

This man's face was deeply lined and brown as leather, and his beard, reaching nearly to his belt, was snow-white. He looked at me out of two light-brown eyes. To my surprise he placed both hands on his forehead, bowed first before Agrippa, then before me. "Praised be Allah," he said in a light, slow voice, "who in his goodness has granted me such worthy and honorable guests in my abode. Greetings to you, a king of Western knowledge, a prince of magic, a wise man."

Master Agrippa bowed and said: "I greet you, Abu Amru ibn Al-Jad, ornament of alchemistic rose, who pleases the heart of knowing men. The boy at my side is Don Pedro de Cordova, my beloved pupil. On his father's side he is a noble Castilian; on his mother's side a nephew of the Sforza, prince of Italy."

"Indeed a proud race," answered Abu Amru. "May he consider my unworthy home his own."

"Thank you, honored sir," I said discreetly. "It is kind of you to welcome me despite my age."

"And why should I not?" he answered. "There has been friendship between the men of Castile and of Yemen since San Fernando and Al-Ahmar fell into each other's arms in the battle tents before Jaén and swore ever to love and tolerate each other."

I did not understand what he meant by these words. But without saying any more in explanation, he clapped his hands, and a servant brought two chairs on which we sat while Abu Amru, in the manner of his race, squatted on the pillows. Then another servant fetched three rosy red goblets. We put them to our lips and drank the orange liquid, cooled with snow. I looked at Abu Amru over the rim of my glass and found his leathery skin and his brown, friendly eyes much to my liking.

Without delay Master Agrippa plunged into conversation, saying, "I've come to you because I've encountered terrible difficulties in my search for the prime element. I've pulverized masses of gold and I'm farther from the goal than I was at the beginning."

"The prime element?" asked Abu Amru thoughtfully. "And is this young man looking for it, too?"

"No, he's not," answered Agrippa. "At least not in our alchemist's fashion. Don Pedro wants to be a knight."

"When he becomes a knight," said Abu Amru, "I suppose then he, too, will seek the prime element, at least with sword and lance if not with retort and crucible. Let us hope he doesn't stop at mere gold."

"But gold is the first step," said Master Agrippa. "Or do you think otherwise?"

Abu Amru bent his head to one side and replied, "Alchemy is something that requires a long time to learn."

"What do you mean by that?" asked Master Agrippa, taken aback.

"I mean that the adept must be intimately adjusted to the prime element before he can find it. If he thinks about gold, he can never succeed. For the prime element is not any alum, metal, salt, acid or earth. It is a great al-iksir, the krates, which was seen by the heathen and priest of Serapis in Alexandria in the house of Venus. Consider that well, Master Agrippa—in the house of Venus."

Master Agrippa sighed but had no comment to make.

"Is there anything you need?" inquired Abu Amru. "Can I be of any help to you?"

"My knowledge of Arabic is faulty," answered Master Agrippa to this. "I should like you to talk with me about some troublesome passages in the *Book of Perfection* by Jabir ibn Hajjan. I've heard also about the *Book of the Sublime Porte,* and assume it's in your possession."

"Kitab albab alazam," murmured Abu Amru. "Indeed, I do have it. It can be of further use to you." He pointed to the scrolls on the tables. "I have the *kitab alhazarat,* the *Book of Levels of Warmth,* and the

kitab alsahifa, the *Book of Scrolls,* which also contains much interesting information."

Master Agrippa looked hungrily at the parchments and papers. His hands actually began to tremble.

With patent satisfaction Abu Amru stroked his long white beard and said softly, "Disregarding these writings I have all kinds of formulas and secret information which in part come down from Chalid ibn Jazid, the son of the race of Omayyads, in part from the monk Istifanus, who was a great sage. You must know, worthy Master, that with us the most important matters are never set down on paper or scroll, but pass on in whispers from mouth to mouth. We consider it dangerous for our knowledge to lodge in heads not fit to contain it, for who can tell how they may misuse their power? There's nothing worse than an educated fool. And I must warn you that our talks may go on for weeks and months on end."

"If they last for years," answered Agrippa quickly, "it would be only too pleasing to me. My life is dedicated to the investigation of truth, and to nothing else."

"So be it, then," said Abu Amru. "But I hardly believe that my young guest would find much amusement in endless conversation on the properties of quicksilver and of copper. I have a lovely garden where he can while away the time."

I thanked him. He clapped his hands, a servant appeared, and I was led through long passageways into an inner courtyard where a fountain was playing. There were many flowering shrubs and trees planted there which filled the air with a delightful scent. The courtyard abutted at the city wall, and I saw that a little door let out into the street.

Seating myself on the edge of the fountain's cool basin I dipped my hands in the water. There were golden fish swimming about, their strange fins undulating. Now and then they would come to the top opening their carp mouths to catch a floating crumb. I had sat here for some time when I heard a rather scratchy voice singing:

"Reach out thy dear arms,
Sweet fairy child—
Give the kiss that warms,
Make my sorrow mild."

I listened, and thought I heard the sound of splashing water intermingled with the words. Curious I walked quietly up to a little hut from which the sounds seemed to emerge. And I was right. There sat a man in the middle of a large basin made of black and white lime that was built into the floor of the hut. He was taking a bath. To all appearances he was a Spaniard. I could tell by the color of his skin and his little brown pointed beard. He was amusing himself by pouring water from his cupped hands over his head and face. Now and then he would burst out laughing to himself and, keeping time by smacking the water with his hand, would sing another strophe; very melancholy, in the hollowest voice imaginable: "O Sobeya, cruel Sultana, who reigns with terror in my heart, O Sobeya!" This he repeated over and over, but I noticed easily enough he was merely making believe, and in fact was in an excellent humor.

I coughed to make my presence known, for it embarrassed me to keep on watching him in such an attitude. He twisted his body around, looked at me sharply, laughed and cried, "Well, see who's here. St. Julian himself, by the grace of God! Come here, Don Pedro, my dove. There's plenty of room for both of us. I mean right here in this tub." He hitched over to make room for me. Then it dawned on me that it was none other than Diego de Vargas, poet and mortal enemy of all fowl.

I greeted him and said, "I'm not an unbeliever to bathe that way." There was a shade of censure in my voice.

"Unbeliever or not," said Diego tranquilly, "you're hot and dusty, aren't you? And isn't the water cool and clean? What do you want, anyway? Why, even our Lord and Master took his pleasure splashing around in the Jordan and called it his baptism. Be so good, anyway, as to hand me that woolen shirt hanging over there. Then I shall cease to be a water sprite, my exalted sir, and become your dutiful servant, ready to do or die at a moment's notice."

I reached it to him and sat down on the edge of the fountain. In a moment or two Diego came out of the hut. I was astonished by the change that had come over him since I saw him last. He wore a doublet of blue silk and hose of the same color with long slits of brilliant carmine let into them. On a finely tooled belt he had hung a saffron yellow pouch and a dagger in a golden sheath. His brown hair and brown beard were trimmed to a nicety and brushed with meticulous care. On his head was rakishly perched a black beret with a gay white ostrich feather.

He saw my amazement and said, "My worldly circumstances have altered for the better, Don Pedro, as you may have noticed. I have my honored patroness, Doña Sobeya, to thank for much, and then again there is the royal dignity which of late has descended on my careworn brow."

"Royal?" I asked. "Are you a rival of Don Carlos?"

He shook his head and made a magniloquently negative gesture with his hand. "Nothing of the sort, my esteemed young friend," he said. "We get along nicely together, he and I. Our rights, fiefs, prerogatives and provinces scarcely impinge on each other. My kingdom is not of this world, I can say, although it does extend all over Spain. I am the King of the Germania."

"King of the beggars, swindlers and thieves?" I asked contemptuously.

"Your tongue is too quick, Don Pedro," he said evenly. "Let us say, rather, king of the unhappy ones, of the publicans and sinners so beloved of our Lord. Yes, publicans, tax collectors. In a sense we, too, are tax collectors. For along the highroads we levy a small toll on travelers in order to introduce a little more equity into this sordid world of goods."

"So you're a highway robber, then?" I said coldly.

"Quite the contrary, my little dove," he said with mock pride. "For a certain minimum compensation we ensure the traveler against injury to his person and property. The Germania is a deeply feared gang. But no one would dare molest anyone protected by our letter of marque and seal no matter what deserted road he took through the Sierra. But if the traveler, by some regrettable contingency, should be burdened with ambition and a stony heart, then he is smitten down by the wrath of God. And out of honor we naturally participate in this celestial retribution."

"I understand," I replied curtly to this. "And I thought you were a poet."

"That, too, my noble friend, that above everything else," he cried. "But it was scarcely possible for me to live in the style to which I am accustomed by inditing ballads. Neither the lovely clouds of my fancy nor the ambrosia which delights my soul suffice to provide this earthly carcass of mine with a warm bed and coarse nourishment. I saw clearly that I must renounce the service to a half worldly, half other-worldly master. Perhaps three months ago, then, amid acclamation from my dubious subjects assembled in the inn of Fat Pascuala, I was elevated to a throne still warm from the contact of my predecessor's buttocks. He, I loathe to say it, was hanged in the very prime of life by the Alguazil Alcalde."

"Is that so!" I said. "Anyway, I wish you health and a long reign."

"A very sensible thing, indeed, young honored sir," commented Diego. "For I must say we kings succeed each other with the rapidity of Popes in Rome. They at least are commonly old men when the fisherman's ring is slipped on their finger. Yes, our mortality is grievous. But what's the use of getting lost in such a thicket of dismal prospects. Let's go into the garden, for if I'm not mistaken you're expected there with considerable impatience."

"I?" I said in surprise.

"Yes, you," he replied. "The fame of your nobility has preceded you in the City of the Moors. It has flown before you in the form of a poem from the powerful hand of Diego de Vargas, baccalaureate of the free arts. It is entitled "The Soul of a Feathered Fowl."

We walked out into the garden. The land sloped gently upward, and off in the distance before me there rose up the blue hills of the Sierra. On each side of us stretched out long beds of herbs. On the wall were espalier-fruit, pears, apricots and cherries. In the middle of them grew a great old walnut tree, which made a wonderfully shady spot. A bench of dark stone girdled the trunk of the tree. Down below us in one direction stretched out the City of the Moors, looking almost like a single tremendous house of white stone for the alleys and footpaths could not be distinguished so narrow were they. Beyond I saw the great mosque, the Alcazar, the Roman city gate, the brown river with its old bridges, and farther along on the opposite side, the Castle Calahorra. And still farther to the left, was the part of the city in which I lived. The warm air was so clear that I imagined I could see Sancho working in our olive garden on the steeps of the hill. But under the tree it was shadowy and cool. Now and then the big leaves rustled, although we could not feel the slightest breath of wind.

"What do you think of women, Don Pedro?" asked Diego suddenly, as if the thought had come into his head from nowhere.

I looked at him in surprise, moved my lips, but was unable to find any words to say.

"The women of the East are famous for their cruelty," said Diego, without waiting for a reply. "If you remember, Salome asked for the head of John the Baptist in a trencher, Delilah tore out her husband's hair, and Esther was delighted when Haman was done away with. But of the Calipha Sobeya it is told that she could not tolerate her husband Al-Hakem because he was a poet and a friend of poets. So for that reason she preferred warlike Almansor to him. . . ."

"Don't believe what he says. Not a word!" said a laughing voice behind me. "He's telling lies."

I turned around and looked toward the latticed window of a kiosk. From behind the screened window there peered two girls' faces. One of them I recognized immediately as the face of the lovely stranger who had passed me in the street. I remember that I turned very red, jumped to my feet and bowed.

Diego also turned around. "This critical girl who is making sport of my love," he said, "is Doña Sobeya, Abu Amru's niece. And the young one, if I'm not very much mistaken, is Doña Tamila, the daughter of Abu Gadar of Seville."

"We're very happy," said Doña Sobeya, "to have Don Pedro's company. We're sure he's a man of honor, not a good-for-nothing in a blue silk doublet like some people I know."

All this confused me greatly. Diego sighed and said, "Couldn't you come outside for a little while? Both the old witch doctors are very, very busy and I have something very important to tell you."

Sobeya blushed and said angrily, "Now, it isn't right to call my uncle and a learned German scholar witch doctors. Besides, I don't trust you and it wouldn't be proper."

Diego made a despairing face and let his head sink into his hands without a word.

"Oh," cried Sobeya, "I didn't mean to hurt your feelings, Diego. Are you angry with me?"

"No, not at all," he said. "But I'm terribly sad to think what your opinion of me must be. Of course, you're always free to call for Don Pedro if I should attempt the smallest familiarity."

Sobeya looked thoughtfully at Diego for some time, whispered in consultation with Tamila, who nodded her head. The door of the kiosk opened softly, and the two girls tiptoed out. Each wore billowing trousers of silk, a beautifully embroidered vest of the same material and a short loose overgarment of linen.

Tamila came over to me, took my hand, and to my amazement pulled me gently to the other side of the kiosk. I sat there motionless, my heart pounding so strongly that I thought Tamila must surely be able to hear it beat. I did not dare so much as glance at her, but stared rigidly at the heights of the Sierra where in the terraced gardens many peasants were hard at work. From the other side came sounds of laughter from Sobeya and Diego. Then all was still, and even the rustle in the crown of the walnut tree stopped.

I looked at Tamila. In her black eyes I saw a faint amusement. That vexed me and I said with some heat, "I'm not so terribly young, you know. I'm nearly sixteen years old. I know how to handle a sword and shield and how to ride Don Garcilaso's Andalusian horse to attack. And besides that I know how both high and low born people act. I know Latin, Spanish spelling, the art of musical harmony and of the starry firmament. And not only that"—I lowered my voice to a whisper—"I'm on pretty good footing with the spirits." At this I reddened, the moment the words were out of my mouth, for other than the spirit that had hurled me to the floor I had never come in contact with a single one.

"Well, that kind of experience isn't everything," said Tamila indifferently.

"Well, what is?" I asked boldly.

"There isn't much use talking about that," she said, seemingly irritated. "But if you've a mind we can talk about the spirits."

"Fine," I replied, quite master of the situation by now, and immediately drew a pentagram in the ground with my toe.

"Is that a geometric figure?" she asked.

"That's a pentagram," I answered, happy to be instructive. "The spirits are so frightened of it they don't dare to step over its edges, if one of the five points happens to be heading in their direction."

"Is that why you pointed one of the corners at me?" she said, all smiles at my erudition. "Do you think I'm a ghost?"

"No, you're a kobold," I said, almost without thinking.

"Oh," she cried, amazed and flattered both. "I take it all back. You're deep, aren't you? How did you see that I was a kobold?"

"I saw it in your eyes," I answered. "They're big and sad and bright all at once. And behind the veil I can see a line in your forehead, which means you're sarcastic if you want to be. That shows you're a kobold."

"You don't miss anything, do you?" she said.

At this moment Diego and Sobeya appeared again, and sat down beside us. "Look, Tamila," Sobeya said, "I can't make this popinjay in his blue clothes see that I'd rather have him in woolen rags with a carving knife at his belt and an old felt hat on his head if he would only do some honest work instead of wasting his time showing off in the Fat Pascuala."

"Doña Sobeya talks very persuasively, doesn't she!" said Diego. "But she has never warmed her hands in the wintertime over a candle flame, she has never been bent double with hunger cramps, she has never chewed on a quill and tried to think while children, dogs and seamy old women were making Hell's own racket all around. How can I paint the splendor of Indian kings if my bedroom is a hole that even mice and bedbugs wouldn't consider inhabiting, if my bed is a mound of dry dung which even a self-respecting leper wouldn't dream of burrowing his weary bones into!"

"I don't care," said Sobeya stubbornly. "I say he ought to finish his epic describing the discovery of the Indies and then put it in the bookseller's hands."

"It can't, in the name of the milk-white Virgin of Guadalupe, it can't be done, my Sobeya," cried Diego, and in his voice there was genuine feeling. "I swear to you on my mother's name it can't be done. The world is meaningless to me, corrupt. I am always the stranger, the homeless one, the one who is tolerated. In the sweet name of Christ, Sobeya, don't grudge me my mood, don't grudge me a few friends, even if they do cut throats for a livelihood. Why can't I have a little glass of wine in the Fat Pascuala and a good time once in a while? All this eternal struggle for goods, this mad running around, this monstrous business—what, dear lamb of God, does it mean? What point, I ask you, in poems when the poet himself sees the world as a joke in cruelly bad taste, a scene that needs more ultimate distraction than to be caught in a few frail verses?"

"I thought you were a Christian," said Sobeya.

"Indeed, you're right," said Diego to this. "But prayers, Masses and confessions mean about as much to me as scratching my skull or snipping my whiskers."

I was horrified and looked in terror at Diego, whose eyes had grown wide with passion. "Then you're no Christian at all," I said with not a little stiffness.

"By the bowels of Christ!" Diego threw down his fine beret and ground it under his heel. "Tell me, I beg you, what is this, anyway?

Is it a hearing of the condemned? Go on, send me to Jerusalem! Or shall I crawl backward up the holy steps at Rome ten thousand and ten times! My boy, grow up, grow up. Then, and not until then, can I listen to the drool that drips from your chin."

"Don't intimidate our guest, if you please," said Sobeya calmly. "Wisdom isn't always confined to graybeards, as anyone can plainly see. Furthermore, I promised my uncle I would entertain Don Pedro, and Tamila is supposed to help me."

"Well, then, entertain him," said Diego sourly. He worked the beret nearer to him with his toe, picked it up, brushed it off vigorously and clapped it back on his brown hair. "I'll be out of the mood now for days."

"Calm yourself," said Doña Sobeya.

"Ah, Sobeya," broke in Tamila in a soft voice, "tell Don Pedro a fairy tale, one about those spirits he likes so much."

"What do you mean, Diego?" said Sobeya, not listening to the interruption.

"I'm not supposed to open my mouth," he replied darkly.

"You can say yes or no, Diego. I give you permission." She laid her hand on his shoulder.

"Well, yes." He began to laugh wildly, turned to me and said, "I didn't mean to offend you, Don Pedro. Forgive my gross manners."

"Of course," I said firmly, and reached him my hand.

"That's better," said Tamila, evident relief in her tone. "Now everything's all right again. You ought to know, if you don't, that Sobeya is the best teller of fairy tales in the whole of Cordova."

"If not the best, certainly the dearest," said Diego loudly.

"Now stop, that's enough," cried Sobeya. "You're making my head whirl. The very best was my nurse, Habiba. You don't find any like her these days. At night, when the charcoal glowed in the iron tube and I was already under the covers . . . and the rugs with the woven animal pictures . . . in the firelight they used to come to life and I could even hear them talking to me in their strange way. The lion, the jackal, the mule and the owl. Habiba was a very pious woman. She herself had been to Mecca and had seen the holy black Kaaba. She had heard the prayers of the believers and seen the Dervishes dance. And when I envied her, she used to say, 'If you have Allah, why covet the Kaaba?' Wait now! I've just thought of the nicest story. I believe I can tell it word for word, just the way Habiba told it to me. It's called "The Men and the Animals Before the Spirit King."

"Tell it," I said.

And Sobeya, her warm eyes turned from the teasing softness of Diego's, told us of how, long ago, men and animals had warred against each other, the latter refusing to serve men, and how through the goodness of Allah the omniscient finally the hostile parties had agreed to submit themselves to the judgment of the wise and just King of the Spirits. Impartially, King Bivarasp heard the plaints and the defenses as each beast stepped up to exalt the endowments of his fellows and to belittle man and expose his wanton cruelties, while on each animal's heels a man sought to refute his accuser.

The mule first, bent on his hard knees before the throne, told of the indignities and cruelties too numerous to mention that man had heaped on him and on his cousin the horse, on the camels of the desert, and on cattle, sheep and goats. In one fashion or another man injured all the animals. Even the fish were caught and eaten with fantastic prodigality on Fridays and other fast days. And as for men themselves they were the ugliest, most helpless and commonest of creatures, inordinately proud of all sorts of ridiculous things.

Kalila the Jackal echoed the charges of his four-legged brother and further pointed out the stupid vanity of man in robbing the beasts of their skins to cover his own white nakedness "that brought to mind the damp bellies of lizards. Among us," he said, "it would be considered simply absurd to see an ass wearing the garments of a butterfly, or an oyster sporting the clothes of a leopard."

King Bivarasp seemed swayed. But quickly a Moor pressed forward to extol man's tireless industry, his heavily laden caravans wending to the market places, his galleys straining over the deepest seas.

A roar filled the room as the speaker finished. Abu-el-Harith the Lion lifted his mighty voice to decry man's gluttony for gold, that false god whose glitter blinds him to the true splendors of the earthly kingdom. "Nothing does man know of the majestic freedom of the eagle who sweeps like a dark angel over icy peaks."

A great cry of acclamation arose out of all the animals' throats for their fine king. But from among the men one from Flanders came forward and spoke: "Oh, worthy King of the Spirits, the last word hasn't been uttered. This last and deciding word must necessarily be of man's knowledge. Man alone is the most learned of creatures. Only man wants to know the reason for everything, to investigate the constituent parts of reality, to pry into celestial motion, separate soul from spirit. Man alone has knowledge, which he uses to generate reason and wisdom. Is this inestimable gift possessed by animals?"

Bivarasp thought weightily and seemed about to pass judgment. But a commotion again sprang up among the animals as they parted to let pass a large drab bird whose bushy brows hung over round yellow eyes that seemed unable to bear the light of day. "Whoo-hoo," spoke the funereal voice of Abu Mahu the Owl. "The knowledge of mankind creates no wise men at all. It produces only dilettantes and educated fools, great in debauchery, gaming, dagger thrusts and tupping. And moreover, of what avails man's knowledge when his proud cities must go down in the gray grit of centuries, when every brain that reared them must rot within its limey skull? For men, great King, even as the beasts, must die!"

King Bivarasp spoke out of the awaiting silence. "In my opinion, this settles it. Men are beaten in their discourse." But an old man's thin treble cried out, "Hold on a moment, O mighty King," and forward crept an ancient from Mecca, silvery-maned, bent double, supported by his staff. "No one," he said, "has yet mentioned the great diamond which Allah bestowed on mankind alone."

I still see Sobeya leaning forward, the eagerness of her lambent eyes concentrated to her tale, and I think I can tell it from this point in her own rapt words.

"'The owl,' said the ancient, 'spoke the truth. Impermanence is the inmost essence of the world. Death, which each one of us carries in his body, men and animals alike, cannot be supervened. And so the lot of mankind would indeed be intolerably hopeless had not Allah said: *I have not created man to die, and after death will take him unto me!* The name of the diamond, the crowning glory of mankind, is immortality. Man stands between visible and invisible things, midway between heaven and earth. Like the bee that flies from flower to flower, so man touches things as things, creatures as creatures, envelops all within himself and keeps it within his treasure house of invisible space. And in this fashion men rebuild the world in the realm of the spirit. In this inner kingdom Babylon and Palmyra rise up forever, and people long dead roam amid the antique pillars. Everything, O King of the Spirits, which was once is restored by mankind. Thus the believer has conquered death, that death which animals know only as a melancholy dream. The believer is a wanderer, sent out by Allah the only God to imbibe the world for Him, the All Highest. And so, returning to God, man carries with him a heavy burden, back to the final resting place of all created.'

"King Bivarasp sprang to his feet and cried out, 'This old man has spoken the truth.' Even the animals gave assent. And then the wise King pronounced his judgment, decreeing that the animals should continue to serve man. For man alone of all the beings under the moon of Allah has been blessed with the gift of Eternity."

Sobeya sighed, trembling with the passion of her faith, and looked long at Diego. It was then I saw that she loved him and he loved her. And suddenly I no longer saw any sin in this love between Christian and Moor. What Alonso, the splendid twin, had told me in prison now seemed vague nonsense. Sobeya was more of a believer than Diego, yes, even than Alonso himself, in spite of his knowledge of the Immaculate Conception.

Sobeya said, "I never thought that a fairy tale would entertain a baccalaureate, one dressed all in blue."

Diego laughed. "I thought you'd have to bring forward some little morality sooner or later. But don't trouble your head, Sobeya; you'll never make a man from Mecca out of me."

By now evening had fallen, the vineyards and olive groves were empty of people. Night came creeping down from the Sierra, and its cool breath stirred about us. The silken blue dome of the sky slowly darkened. The world seemed to grow much more vast. Behind us the city and all its houses, which here and there showed a yellow light, were as unreal as something in a half-remembered dream.

"My Diego," said Sobeya softly, "whether you know it or not, you too are called to build mosques and churches within the spirit, places with high windows and flaming panes of glass, peopled with men, carvings and angels."

"Later on, Sobeya, perhaps later," he said, sad and lost. "And maybe never. For the winds of the spirit blow contrariwise, where they will. They are not easily steered and held within bounds."

"Still," Sobeya persisted, "they can be controlled through renunciation and composure. But I don't want to make you sad. Tell me, do you think my fairy tale had any moral in it for our young guest Don Pedro de Cordova, as it did for you?"

"Not in the least," said Diego and laughed heartily. For it was his way to become astonishingly happy in the midst of dejection. "Whom do you think you see present before you in the form of Don Pedro?"

At this Tamila began to laugh. She clapped her hands and said, "I know who it is! I'm sure I do!"

I sat still without saying a word, for I half felt I was being made a fool of. But Diego, still chuckling, said, "Speak up, Tamila. Tell us who he is."

"He's Abu-el-Harith," cried Tamila, and shook with glee. "He's a young Abu-el-Harith. Look, he has on desert-brown clothes, even if his hair is blond instead of brown. And his eyes look bold, his gait is noble and measured and he has a generous heart."

"Long live Abu-el-Harith!" shouted Diego. "Long live the desert-tinted, blond-haired knight!"

"Long life to him!" both the girls shouted. I rose to my feet, not knowing whether to laugh with them or not, bowed and felt both ashamed and flattered.

"And whom do you think you're like yourself, Diego?" asked Sobeya.

"I? Oh, I'm Kalila the Jackal. I've been kicked around and I'm wise; I've got a pointed meddler's nose and a scratchy voice. Yes, I'm Kalila." He looked down at his light-blue hose. "I'm Kalila dressed like a parrot, the talkative poet-bird of your Persians."

"Don't you want to go along with Abu-el-Harith?" asked Tamila mockingly.

"Why not?" said Diego. "When our Abu-el-Harith looks for his kingdom I'll accompany him. All I hope is that it won't be a desert waste. For as it is, I'm a man with a consuming thirst. Yes, in all truth, Don Pedro, sometime you'll become a councilor, and then you'll need a vizier or a secretary. Don't forget Diego de Vargas, the one forever spurned."

"But you are a king yourself," I answered quickly, getting into the sport as best I could.

"Ah, yes, but my crown is made of fool's gold and tinsel, just as this young lady told you. My crown jewels are cat's eyes, the scepter a jester's whip, my earth a rotten apple and my royal sword a nicked breadknife. My palace smells of sour wine and my subjects have lost their ears and had their cheeks branded. All my battles are against night watchmen, and my kingly bier is an airy one, I'll tell you. Oh yes, particularly the last. I can see myself swinging with the wind, back and forth, my bones rattling and frightening off that prophetic raven of yours who has just been making a delectable meal out of my eyeballs. . . ."

"Enough, that's enough of that," said Sobeya.

"As a matter of fact," continued Diego irrepressibly, "the only kingly thing about me is my queen and my feeling for her. Nothing else is genuine. But you, Don Pedro, will indeed become a master of men. I can see it written on your forehead, even though this young girl thinks she is twitting you by calling you Abu-el-Harith. You can as little escape your destiny as I mine."

At this point voices from the courtyard interrupted our lively conversation. It was the worthy Abu Amru and Master Agrippa. I thanked my host and Sobeya for their kindness. After we had exchanged some polite commonplaces my Master and I took our leave. Carrying a lantern I preceded my teacher through the narrow alleyways, which by now were deserted. Only occasionally did we hear a soft silvery hammering or the hum of a spinning wheel in one of the arched places. Up above our heads a weak light streamed out of the latticed windows, and now and then we heard laughing voices or the notes of a flute. The great bazaar was empty and all the goods were covered over for the night with cloths.

I walked along as in a dream, for I could not tell whether I was little Pedro or Abu-el-Harith, king and knight. At last we arrived at the huge gate separating the City of the Moors from the larger Christian section of Cordova, and the iron grille was drawn up for us. The watchmen were tired and surly, and raised the portcullis only high enough for us to duck our heads and get out as best we could from the land of the unbelievers. "You're out late, aren't you?" growled one of them, and to this Master Agrippa replied, "Knowledge is timeless, my friend."

Once again we passed by the Roman gate, by the huge mass of the mosque and through the Court of the Oranges. Young people sat talking and whispering at the rim of the fountain. And at last we arrived in the Street of the Leather Merchants. I sat down at the table tired to the marrow, and Teresa gave me my supper. I saw that she was looking at me curiously, and it was clear enough that she had something on her mind.

When Master Agrippa had left—he was a very rapid eater who hardly noticed his food—Teresa said to me privately, "Don Pedro, your mother was a very pious Christian and your father fought in the wars against the unbelievers. You must never forget that!"

"No, I'll never forget it, Teresa," I said, yawning, without bothering to think of what she was really getting at. Then, having eaten my supper, I kissed Teresa's forehead as I always did, and ready for bed climbed up the stairs, wondering whether Abu-el-Harith, Kalila and Abu Mahu would appear in my dreams as they had in Sobeya's.

5

THE GRAND INQUISITOR

VERY often from then on I accompanied my Master on his trips to Abu Amru, and I became bosom friends with Diego de Vargas, Sobeya and Tamila. I had many beautiful times in the garden of Abu Amru. I even became bold enough to bathe in the sunken lime bath. At first this unchristian practice caused me some pangs of conscience, but gradually I became used to it, and on hot days even found distinct pleasure in splashing around in the water for hours on end. Diego often stopped there with me, and his conversations broadened my knowledge of the world in their way as much as Agrippa's in another, or the polite discourse around Don Garcilaso's table.

"It's very strange," I said to him one day, "that there are two different peoples in Spain who each have contempt for the other. Even my good Teresa, who's really another mother to me, doesn't like to see me going into the City of the Moors. And Sancho's face gets black every time he hears the name Abu Amru spoken."

Diego laughed aloud, then grew pensive and sighed. "You're broaching a ticklish subject now. You're looking at a gravelly stone the poor Spaniards' stomachs will never digest in a thousand years."

"There shouldn't be two beliefs in one country," I said.

"Ah, this comedy of believing, my friend," answered Diego. "It would be easy enough to come to an agreement about God, if men could only rid their hearts of envy and ambition to rule. The God that people are always prating about is only a filthy lie. The true God makes a man silent, not full of mouth. And, if you recall, the purest and noblest king of Spain came to such a good understanding with Allah and his followers that Arabs as well as Christians hailed him as a saint."

"You mean King Fernando of Castile?" I asked. "Abu Amru mentioned him the first day that I stepped through his door, but then I had no idea what he was talking about."

"There isn't much to understand," said Diego, observing me closely. "King Fernando, who conquered Cordova and Seville, had many Arab friends and comrades-in-arms. But his closest friend of all, so it happened, was a certain Al-Ahmar, the king of Granada. It's now three hundred years since there was a war between Castile and Granada. Al-Ahmar, at that time, looked over his blooming kingdom, saw the fields and orchards, the vineyards and olive groves. He saw his people, too, busy at work, laughing at play. And, by chance, Allah had given him the great gift of insight. He realized that whether he won or lost a war there would be great misery in his land. He thought it far better to humble his kingly pride than to make innocent children into orphans, active men into decaying corpses, and his countryside into a shambles.

"Accordingly he went in person to see King Fernando who was waiting in his camp before the fortress of Jaén. He bent his knee to the Christian and begged for peace. Because King Fernando was really a king, he did not feel any triumph at all. On the contrary, he was overcome with shame. As a Christian he could not help but feel that Al-Ahmar had won the battle which was never fought. Rising to his feet he put his arms around Al-Ahmar, and tears ran down his face. Such a man was Fernando, whom we now call a saint."

"And what happened then?" I asked eagerly.

"Then?" Diego was lost in thought. "Oh yes, then. The two great kings became like brothers. They made a covenant that neither Christian nor Moor should ever persecute the other, neither they nor their children, nor their children's children. And they said that whoever should break this agreement would suffer the vengeance of God, and be overtaken by the fate of Judas. There was peace between Christians and Moors, and the land prospered.

"When Fernando felt that he was dying he called Al-Ahmar to his bedside. In his last battle the Moor held the hand of this Christian friend who had put a halter around his neck to show that he considered himself but a common man who like anyone else could only hope for his Lord's grace. When Fernando was dead they wrapped him in a shroud made by an Arab artisan. It was decorated with rampant lions and golden castles. The catafalque was set up in the open square before the cathedral, and the people moved about the black candles burning feebly in the sunlight. Men and women, Christians and Moslems, poor and rich, peasants and lords cried in tears, 'Santo! Santo!' And so Fernando has always been called the Saint by the people, and later on the Church recognized him by canonization."

"Tell me more, Diego," I asked, for now he had turned within himself to his own meditations.

"Yes, there is a little more to tell," he said slowly. "Every anniversary of his death the silver coffin in the Cathedral of Seville is opened up, the brocade coverings are pulled to one side, and great crowds march by to take a look at the holy king. I myself have seen him. He rests peacefully on his red satin cushion. His face has not changed at all. Only the skin has become brown and leathery, almost like an African's. At each side of the coffin with straddled legs are the guard of honor, leaning on their halberds, dressed in silver harness and helmets. The guards wear long mantles of green silk which are embroidered in gold threads with lions and castles. Their gloves are also green. This is in memory of Al-Ahmar and the Arab watch which encircled the king on his deathbed. For the banner of the Prophet is green, you know. The holy man's corpse is put there to remind the Spanish people and their rulers that once a sacred oath was sworn, and to break it means to endure the fate of Judas the archtraitor. But, my friend, I'm afraid that most of the people who go to look are there for the sake of curiosity, and pay little heed to the warning itself."

"And how did it happen that you fell in love with Sobeya?" I asked, irrelevantly, before I could hold back the words. The blood rushed to my cheeks and I mumbled a plea for forgiveness.

But Diego merely smiled and said, "That's another story entirely, young Abu-el-Harith. It's just as well you asked me now, though, for you would have some time, I suppose.

"When I left Salamanca I found myself without any means of making a living in this none too friendly world. I have an old mother. Did I ever tell you? She lives near a women's cloister about halfway to Seville and scrapes along by doing this and that for the devout ladies of wealth. Well, I tried all sorts of things. I worked as a scribe for a lawyer, wrote love poems for fat burghers' sons, figured out for a hidalgo the wealth of his holdings and argued with the clerics about mortal sin and other such theological matters. I am not precisely a reticent fellow and by sheer gift of gab I got me many a maravedi, many a draught of wine, a meal and a place to sleep.

"But one night on the highroad I was set on by robbers. I might tell you first that I know how to use a dagger to take care of myself, for I consider fighting, love and drinking as the main ends of knowledge. Why these thieves ever picked on such a barebones as me I can't say, when the road was swarming with pot-gutted priests, rich wool merchants and arrogant rug dealers. I drew my dagger and slashed one of the brothers in the mouth; he fell into the grass swallowing his own blood. And again I drew back as quickly as my long legs could move against a big rock, which protected me from the rear.

"The rest of the band of cut-throats hesitated to move in, merely held back and made threatening gestures. I fancied myself a real hero; I actually sat down on a shelf in the rock and began to compose aloud a long ballad, called 'The Wandering Scholar and the Robbers.' Even today you'll hear many a pretty girl singing it behind latticed windows. My mood grew gay and I began a conversation with my besiegers. It all ended, to make a long story short, in their inviting me to come down from my stony perch and make their closer acquaintance. Which I did. We ate and drank together.

"When I awoke the next morning to my amazement I discovered the band had chosen me as their leader. The whole crew of assassins placed all their hope for the future in me. The man whose face I had cut open was their former chief. I checkmated him permanently at a later date, but there's no point in going into that story right now, nor will I burden you with the details of our daily existence. In any case, from then on I lived comfortably, if not without considerable effort for the life of a highwayman isn't quite the bed of roses a layman thinks. It's a calling fraught with as much danger as navigating the open sea. Many a candle have I dedicated to Santo Jacopo in Santiago, many a prayer to the Mother of our Lord to save me from gallows, rack, sword and similar devices. And the saints have not been reluctant to lend an ear to my pleadings, as you plainly see."

"Oh, Diego," I said, completely disillusioned, "then you really are a robber, just as Alonso the splendid one said."

"I was, my dear friend, I was. But in the meantime I've raised myself to a much higher station. At present I'm on good footing with the Holy Brotherhood of the Highway and the Alguazil Alcalde of the cities.

They both often need my help. And anyway, don't scorn my sins. If you had ever lived as I have among genuine burghers, you'd know well enough how wonderful is the free wind of the Sierra after the physical and spiritual stench which fills men's houses, hearts and brains. You would then understand the pleasure of our Lord in sitting at the table of a thief or in talking to a whore, all of which was horrible to the mealy-mouthed righteous."

"You're fooling yourself, Diego," I said critically.

"That may be," he answered. "We all fool ourselves in some degree or other. But a full-fledged sinner has nothing left but God. Death is always just around the corner for him. He is separated from eternity by a thin hair's-breadth. The burghers have their houses, their land, horses, mules, workshops, goods and all sorts of worldly clutter which they pile up as a barricade against God and death. Is it a wonder then that at last God gets tired of the ridiculous business and says, 'Let them go to the Devil, for they certainly don't want me'?"

"You are a fearful sophist," I said, laughing. "If you keep on talking you'll have me believing that black's white."

"Everything's relative, of course," admitted Diego. "And what does the whole complicated hodgepodge mean, I ask you, if He, the Absolute, isn't present?"

"You want me to believe that you became a highway robber in order to serve God?" I inquired ironically.

"No, I don't mean that. I did it out of sheer necessity, to keep alive. But I have personally met the absolute on the highway, even though it was not God Almighty. One day when the sun had already sunk out of sight and the tops of the Sierra were blood-red, a sedan fastened to two mules chanced along. It was guarded by two or three Moorish riders. We lay in wait, for as I could see we had a nice fat catch in hand. The idea flashed through my mind of capturing one rider as the other two took to their heels. I got close to the sedan, looked inside. You could have knocked me flat on my back with a soupspoon. Instead of the fat merchant I had expected to see, there leaning back asleep against the cushions was a girl. Her right hand was under her cheek and her dark hair hung down over her face. I bent over, and before I knew what I was doing I had kissed her face, still warm from sleep. She stretched and yawned and with her eyes half open asked, 'Are we there yet, Juan?'

" 'Not yet, lovely mistress,' I replied.

"Her eyes widened, she put her hand to her mouth, and said, 'Who are you? What are you doing here?'

" 'I'm a robber, mistress,' I replied.

" 'You are!' she said. 'I must say you're a very polite one.

" 'One does what one can in this world,' I said in turn. 'Many travelers haven't got the slightest bit of sympathy for us.'

" 'What is it you want of me?'

" 'Just a small subsidy, mistress mine. For here we are without a maravedi to our names in the middle of a bare plateau.'

"She examined the little bag she carried, which was filled with gold pesetas. I stowed it in my pouch.

" 'Isn't that enough?' she wanted to know. 'Do you want my jewels, too?'

" 'Are you very fond of them, mistress?' I inquired.

" 'Well, you know how we women are,' she said, and looked at me with her dark eyes.

" 'Of course, of course,' I said hastily. 'Keep them, by all means. I'd only have a lot of trouble with the fences, anyway. They're as crooked a lot as you find between here and Rome.'

"She looked out through the curtains. The twilight by now was deepening into night and the whole landscape was gray and cold. Not far behind me were my men, looking on openmouthed at all this diplomacy. Their wild clothes, swords and daggers scarcely gave them a trustworthy appearance, as you can well imagine.

" 'What's going to become of me?' she inquired.

" 'Oh, you can ride on,' I said, 'and may God keep you, my dear.'

" 'I'd like very much to have some protection along the way,' she said to this, and looked at me pleadingly. 'This neighborhood seems to be anything but safe.'

" 'You won't be bothered again,' I assured her. 'We're like a herd of lions. We don't like to see anyone else hunting in our territory.'

" 'Just the same . . .' she objected.

" 'As you will,' I told her, yielding after all. I got up on the outrider's horse, my gang of cut-throats moved on, ahead and behind the sedan. By now it was pitch-dark. I rode beside the sedan.

" 'Tell me something, Don Diego . . .' she said, after a time.

" 'How did you know my name was Diego?' I asked her.

" 'Your friends called you that. But tell me, how did you ever get into this affair, if I may ask?'

" 'It was like this . . .' I replied, and went on to tell her the whole story. She smiled in genuine amusement, and said laughingly, 'Then it isn't really your calling at all?'

" 'No,' I admitted. 'But when I followed my real calling I grew as thin as a skeleton. I looked like Death himself riding on this dun horse.'

" 'And what was this calling?' she insisted.

" 'Well, I've been through the trivium and the quadrivium at Salamanca. And I'm not bad at making up a little song or a ballad.'

" 'So, you're a poet!' she cried. 'In the name of Allah, a poet!'

" 'You might say so,' I said, half ashamed.

"She shook her head and went *tsk, tsk* with her tongue. It was very quiet and I could hear nothing but my men talking in undertones, and the sound of horses' and mules' clopping hoofs. A cool wind came from nowhere and struck sharply against my forehead, which had suddenly become hot.

" 'Don Diego,' she inquired softly, 'why did you kiss me?'

"I was so surprised I dropped the reins, but quickly gathered them together and said, 'Why, weren't you asleep, then?'

" 'Why?' she persisted.

" 'Because you're so beautiful,' I told her in confusion.

"For a time she kept still in thought, then said, 'You can't get off that easily. I'm called Sobeya and I'm the niece of Abu Amru of Cordova and live in his house. If a man kisses a Yemenite, do you know what that means?'

" 'I didn't know that girls from Yemen who're so lovely and so wise could ask such questions!' I said in evasion.

" 'That doesn't help you at all,' she sighed. 'A man kisses an Arab girl not just to pass the time until he can find a better one. He does it, well, because . . .'

"I looked up at the sky which by now was sown thickly with stars. I rode so close to the sedan I all but brushed the door.

" 'Give me your hand, Doña Sobeya,' I said. "I want to give you back the money.'

" 'Keep the pesetas, keep them for good,' she said. 'Share them with your men for accompanying me.' But just the same she did reach out her hand, and I found it to be long-fingered and slender. I could smell her strange sweet perfume coming from behind the drawn-back curtain, and see her eyes glitter faintly in the dark.

" 'Doña Sobeya,' I told her, 'I'm the worst lump on the face of the earth, perhaps, and you're the prettiest and wisest girl I've ever seen. You're brave and kind. I love you, Sobeya.'

"Her hand rested in mine. I felt with my thumb the lovely veins in her thin wrist, and almost in a dream I felt the pulse of her blood and the distant beat of her heart. It seemed to me at the moment that her blood and mine were intermingled. The night was big with stars. There was no moon out at all. We rode over the Sierra, not saying another word. And the men, too, said no more after a time, and there was nothing to hear but the horses' feet, the creak of leather, the jingle of the bits. And perhaps the wind, sighing over the barren heights as if seeking a dark wood.

"To this music, Don Pedro, the whole world changed for me and took on a new meaning. She was everything, I felt. And, mind you, I was no longer a silly boy. Or was I, really? Anyway, it was like this in that one night of my life. I loved everything, just as I loved Sobeya. Not the wandering stars alone and the great mass of the Sierra behind us. More than the heights. The wind, too, the horse I rode on, the mouse that ran squeaking from under his hoofs. Everything, even things I could not see, things in the distance. I loved the alleys of Salamanca, the rug merchants, the priests, the stupid hidalgos, the goatherds. And I loved, too, what had long since passed away. My own childhood and youth, for instance. The piece of dry bread, the well, the splashing water from it, the folds in my mother's face. Even evil things, sickness, misery, hunger, fear and death. Oh, dearest, dearest Sobeya! Bow down always before Allah. You yourself are expiation and eternal peace.

"Yes! To come an end, my young friend, soon the lights of Cordova blinked in the distance below us. It seemed to me as if I were looking upon a foreign land, as if I had been born again into another world. I shook my head and looked over the city, peacefully asleep. Then I got down from the dun horse, gave it back to its owner, and bowed before Sobeya.

" 'The way to Abu Amru's house is easy to find,' she said.

" 'I'll find my way there,' I told her. I stood on the hilltop and watched after the sedan chair, which swayed this way and that on the mules' backs. Some few days later I presented myself at the house of Abu Amru, who thanked me for saving his niece from harm. Since that time I have come here often."

Such was Diego's history of his love's beginning, and like Sobeya's fairy tale I have recorded it here because both these stories often run through my mind during the sleepless nights when I sit at the window sill and look over my courtyard.

In the meanwhile Master Agrippa had accepted Don Garcilaso's offer. We visited the Don's house three or four times a week. In the summer when the weather was fine the lessons were given in the garden. In the winter, during the cool, rainy months, we met inside the house.

I remember hot summer days sitting in the shadow of the trees while Master Agrippa told stories about gods, beautiful ladies, heroes, wise men and evildoers of antiquity. Isabella hung on every word that Agrippa said. Plump Doña Catarina would often let her crocheting fall into her lap the better to listen when unhappy Leander sank to his death in the Hellespont, or when Master Agrippa told about the fortunes of Psyche who, in her search for her love, Eros, wandered through the realm of the envious gods jealously pursued by Venus, only in the end to fulfill her need. In his instruction for the young girls Agrippa left out of account all difficult themes, and from the events of nature and history sought out only those which had a nice moral for his sheltered pupils. He talked about Saint Elizabeth, the Countess of Thuringia, who gave bread to the poor which unaccountably turned into roses when the jealous Count looked into the basket. He spoke also of Tristan and the beautiful Isolde, told how she drank dry the love potion, betrayed King Mark and came to a bitter end. And, too, he used from time to time to quote from the poets of the day whose words were on all learned men's tongues. Sometimes it was Petrarch and his Laura.

But it was really wonderful when he discussed the poet of poets, Dante. In the middle of his discourse he would leap to his feet, strain his arms upward, quite beside himself with a rush of feeling, and orate magnificent terzinas in the Italian language. We sensed rather than really understood the meaning of the words. When he spoke of Hell the Master's forehead became deeply creased with wrinkles, his tone rough and bass. Glaring about him he would cry, "And I, too, was created by eternal Love." By that he did not mean himself, but Hell, over the portals of which was inscribed this phrase. This would alarm Doña Catarina so greatly that the crochet needle would fall from her hand to the tiles, and she would stare in horror at his exalted face.

Some years later I heard these awesome words from another's mouth, from Antonio de Guevara. And it is solely for that reason I mention them at this moment, because as it chanced they affected my whole life.

When the Master spoke of Paolo and Francesca, how forever they wandered through twilit space borne hither and yon by contrary winds, we all grew sad and moved by sympathy. The girls reached for their handkerchiefs and wiped the corners of their eyes. Still, how wonderful it was when the blessed Beatrice met the tired wanderer through the kingdom of eternity and led him, higher and higher, up the mountain of light, until at last he caught sight of Empyrean and the Heavenly Rose, in which were the saints, angels and God himself. At such time, when recounting these verses, Master Agrippa's voice would soften, he would smile at us almost dreamily, and we, taken by the moment, would fold our hands and bow our heads. For so great indeed is the incomparable Dante that the willing hearer imagines he is actually glimpsing eternal blessedness when he listens to the poet's rhymes.

Master Agrippa's illustrations from the works of the great Florentine were also not without influence on my love for Doña Isabella. Whereas formerly I had seen in her all the women of knightly romances embodied, so to speak, she now took on some of the spiritual qualities of Beatrice. I imagined firmly that without her consent and help I should never reach Heaven.

But it must be admitted that the fourteen-year-old Doña Isabella was anything but another Madonna such as Dante saw coming across the bridge over the Arno, which sight made him say to himself, *Incipit vita nova*. Doña Isabella actually was in those difficult years between childhood and womanhood, the years of sweet and sometimes vexing indiscretion. Sometimes she would be very quiet and self-contained, quite adult in manner. And then again she would behave badly, quarrel easily, act like a spoiled princess. Again she would be lost in a pathetic dejection, hard to fathom. She was changeable, in short, as an April day. The spring of life, like the spring of the year, is not only gay, eager and full of the promise of flowers but is shot through with the burden of life, with lightly fearful questioning of what is to come, of premonition of that time when the vague paradise of childhood will forever sink into the past.

Now everything is clear to me about those days when we all studied under Master Agrippa. But then the moods, willfulness and strange caprices of Isabella were simply unintelligible to me. If we happened to be in the house together she would open Doña Catarina's chest and take out Arab sweets hidden there in a blue-glazed pot. She longed for honey, too, and forced me to eat some with her, even though I had a natural dislike of all sweet things. If I hesitated she would throw herself across a chair and begin to cry loudly. When Doña Catarina hastened to her side she would tell her duenna that I had pulled her hair and pushed her around the room. And if I helped her to steal she did not shame to lie and say that I had made her eat the candied dates and figs. As a caballero and lover there was little else I could do except hold my tongue, even though I felt completely humiliated and miserable. So I would stand there, my ears crimson, and let the scoldings of Doña Catarina fly about me.

At other times she pestered her little brother Miguel, pricked him with her crocheting needle as if it had happened by mere accident. In Don Garcilaso's garden there were many springs and lovely cool grottoes. In these lived green and brown frogs, who hopped merrily around under the dark bushes. Miguel was fearful of these damp, soft-bellied creatures, and Doña Isabella seemed to take pleasure in suddenly putting one of them down his neck or on the back of his hand.

In brief, she behaved in a manner totally foreign to anything ever recorded of the Florentine Beatrice. Yet I do her injustice if I forget to mention that after these tantrums she would become conciliatory and kind. At such times she would give little Miguel some pretty toy or a soft fruit to suck on, and present me with a silk ribbon or perhaps stroke my hand gently.

Once when I crossed her she flew into such a horrible temper that she picked up a stone and threw it at my head. A thin trickle of blood began to run down into my eyes from the wound. I looked at her in reproach and anger, whereupon she burst into tears, threw herself on the ground, clutched me about the knees and said, "Oh, Pedro, Pedro! Please forgive me. I didn't know what I was doing." I then picked her up and told her it was nothing to cry about.

As I did this she pushed me away, stamped her feet and cried, "Why don't you see I'm not a little girl any more?" And then she came very close to me so that I could feel her tear-warm breath on my face. I saw that her eyes rolled a little, as if the muscles about the iris had lost their power of control. She gripped my shoulders, clung to me with many kisses, so strong that they hurt my mouth, and at last in her curious transport bit my lips. She tore my hair and cried, "And I am not a child, you blond fool. You bore me with your humility and easy, forgiving ways. Why don't you strike me in the face and show me who's the stronger! Why don't you make me kneel in the dirt before you for hours on end, until my knees bleed. Then I'd hate you! But when I was hating you I'd love you, too. You could put your foot on my hair, and grind my head in the earth. I might cry, but I'd know then that you loved me, just me, and not the sickly saint you have in your mind."

Her shoulders trembled with emotion, her young breast rose and fell. She threatened me with her small fist and shrieked, "I know what you want. You want to humiliate me. 'See how mean you are in comparison with my goodness'—that's what's in the back of your mind. That's why you do everything I tell you to; that's why you don't open your mouth when I tell lies. Right now you have a long face. Oh, Pedro, Pedro ..." and with that she covered her face with her hands. "I'm so ashamed," she said, "I feel as if I don't have any clothes on when you're looking at me now."

"What are you talking about, Isabella—my kindness! . . . and saying that I want to humiliate you! I haven't done anything that amounts to a maravedi yet, either good or bad. But anyway, the years haven't been wasted. I've learned all the knightly arts, and the day isn't far off when I'll go out to seek my kingdom. I know already where to find it. It's near Tenochtitlan on Atlantis."

She looked at me wide-eyed. "You took me seriously, Pedro!" she said.

I was shocked, but quickly I concealed my dismay and stiltedly answered, "There was nothing childish in your longing at all. Many men find and conquer kingdoms."

"Oh, I know," she said. "But I don't think I can let you go now." Her voice was sad. I sensed that somehow, like everyone else, I would go despite her wishes, one way or the other. For at that time all women were taking leave of their husbands. The cities were being emptied of men, I often heard the complaint at Don Garcilaso's table. In the country the peasant women could often be seen plowing, barefoot and with billowing skirts tied up around the waist, because their men had shipped out from Seville or Cadiz in order to find lands and riches among the Indians across the sea.

Not long after this incident with Doña Isabella—it must have been some time in the year 1527—it became clear that a great change was coming over Don Garcilaso. He was now always serious and moody, and very often for hours he would pace back and forth in his garden. At such times he was so completely lost in himself that he would not notice my greeting, but looked through me as if he did not know who I was. At the beginning I thought it was worry over his large estate, for he owned extensive lands in Old Castile. Later I came to believe that it must have something to do with Don Carlos and Doña Juana, for I noticed that his table friends were also in a bad temper. Once, I recall, one of them said, "Don Carlos has broken his oath again . . ." and the others pricked up their ears as he murmured something into his beard and was thereafter silent.

One day Don Garcilaso sent for Master Agrippa. When my master left the house several hours later he carried a carefully rolled parchment in his hand. He was very grave and nodded at me to accompany him. We went home without bothering at all with lessons, which astonished me, for Agrippa was very punctual as a usual thing.

We went directly into the study and Master Agrippa told me to sit down. He himself walked restlessly up and down the room, like an imprisoned animal, as was his custom when he was excited.

"My child," he said, "the hour has come at last when I must take leave of you."

I jumped up, looked at him in terror. I had come to believe that my Master would always be with me. Tears came to my eyes.

"My child," Master Agrippa continued, "so it always goes in this world of change. It is a constant meeting and parting which we must live out. When you grow older you will learn that everything in this life adds up to one enormous renunciation. Today duty calls me to Flanders. There, in Doña Margarita, the Emperor's aunt, I have a powerful protector. But I'm sorry to inform you it isn't merely to improve my lot I'm leaving your house. I'd have liked only too well to stay here longer with you and Abu Amru and tell Doña Isabella pretty fairy tales. I've liked it here and my experiments were going along well." He pointed to the blackened hearth where stood the mortars and distillation alembics.

"But, Master Agrippa," I said, "if you want to, why don't you stay? When you're gone . . ." I began to sob in earnest.

"Yes, yes," he admonished me roughly, and put his hand on my shoulder. "You're grown up pretty much now, even though you are young in years. If God grants me long life, we shall see each other again, even though years may go by."

"But why must you go?" I insisted.

Master Agrippa came over closer to me, and whispered, "Whatever you do, don't repeat what I am going to tell you. Walls and chimney flues have grown ears in this country in the last few years. I sometimes wish that the Holy Junta had won during the insurrection, for then we might have somehow escaped the terror that hangs over our heads at the moment.

"You must know that in all Spain persecution of the Moors and the Moriscos has broken out. And not only are the believers and half-believers spied on, lied about, hated and murdered, but all those as well who believe in the freedom of living and thought. It's because of this I never go any more into the City of the Moors. And you must never go, either, for by so doing you will only endanger both Abu Amru and yourself. Don't take any more Moorish baths; don't talk about elements and the three kingdoms. Be tight-mouthed and sly. The unholy Inquisition is lurking in the streets of Cordova.

"This young man who has cost Spain so much heartache, this fine-born Don Carlos, the grandson of the tyrants of Burgundy, wants to purify Spain until it is as white as the driven snow. And backing him is the land and gold-hungry nobility of Castile and Flanders. The mob's lust for revenge on anything, anyone, is part of it too. For a long time they have looked enviously on the fruits of Moorish industry. Evil times are surely hard upon us, such days as have been prophesied in the Holy Book. Brother will betray brother, and son the father, friend the friend.

"The Church has tried in vain to avoid the issue, until at last that miserable Clement VII—may God pry the soul from his poxy carcass!—has given in to Don Carlos' wishes. I have often told you that in the German city of Wittenberg there has appeared a man by the name of Martin

Luther, who six years ago before the Diet of Worms maintained his freedom of conscience against all the dictates of spiritual and worldly power. And now this man, long believed dead, has translated the Bible into his own German language. Many princes and a great number of common people have come over to his side and renounced their obligations to the Catholic Church. All through German lands there have been riots and quarrels. They are tearing statues, paintings, eucharistic vestments and altars out of the churches. Old people are being baptized again and want to share all their worldly goods, thinking the Day of Judgment is near. For if you stop to think, nearly one thousand and five hundred years have passed since the death of our Lord. They are saying that the time is ripe. But the time is always ripe, my son. The Day of Judgment is always at hand. But all these acts of violence are opposed to clerical authority in the world.

"Don Carlos sits there, his conscience badly bitten, wondering why it should be in his time that chaos troubles the earth. The eyes of the world are turned on Spain, not only because it is the inherited possession of Don Carlos but because many expect it is from this land that the salvation of the crumbling Church will spring. This unhappy country is to serve as example for the rest, and schism will be attacked here first. Nonbelievers must either come into the fold or leave the land. But what has begun in blood and terror will end in blood and terror, my child. The hand of God will rest heavily on this land.

"And so far as I personally am concerned, I too am in some danger. For the evil minds of these Dominicans peer into all forms of knowledge and see in it nothing but witchcraft and magic. In Cologne two of them have smeared together a monstrous book of nonsense, the so-called *Witches' Hammer.* I know that so far as these two black puddles of corruption are concerned, experimenting with metals and minerals and acids is nothing but witchcraft—not to mention philosophy. To them philosophy is more disgusting than Luther's phrase when he calls the Church the whore of Rome. The most stupid peasant trull is superior to such people. Even a simple goatherd would be hard put to it to swallow the foul ragout which these black apes have cooked during the past fifteen hundred years.

"Never let on, then, that you have helped me with my little kitchen work. When some wise fellow begins to talk about the *quinta essentia* or the world soul with you, look dumb, as if you considered such stuff so much twiddle-twaddle. I don't like to tell you to lie. But God himself has said, Be wise as the serpent. You'll have to do exactly that in these topsy-turvy times. They're out to get every hide they can strip off unwitting victims.

"I'm not merely trying to assure my own safety, though. It's really in the hope that Doña Margarita of Savoy will listen to my argument. Everybody knows that her nephew often follows her advice. But I have little hope. In Don Carlos' veins runs the blood of maniacs, tyrants and murderers. The voice of knightliness and reason, which he ought to have inherited from his grandfather Maximilian, as Doña Margarita did, seems to be lost. But one has to try everything. Don Garcilaso has given me a very influential letter of introduction to different people. He carries a great deal of weight, you know. Tonight, when it's dark, he's sending me a mule, a servant and supplies. And you must arm yourself with your father's sword, and lead me to the beginning of the Sierra."

I assented silently. The day slipped away heavily. It was very dark when we rode out through the city gates. I sat morose and disconsolate on Pia. We passed by the olive groves and I remembered clearly how here I had made the acquaintance of the players. I thought of that evening when Master Agrippa had first come to my home. And now he was leaving me, perhaps forever.

When we arrived at the wasteland where I had first practiced knightly exercises with Sancho, the Master drew up his reins and looked around. He gave the bridle to the servant, told him to wait by the side of the road. We clattered up the cliffs and slopes of the place. Thistles and burs stuck to our clothes. At last we arrived at a hollow in the hills which was walled round with steep rocks. The wind rustled in the dry weeds, for it was in the fall of the year. The sky was black as the pit, and the stars stood out in it like the heads of golden nails. It must have been around midnight. The immense loneliness of the country weighed down on my spirit.

Master Agrippa took his staff and with it, as he mumbled to himself, described a circle in the ground into the center of which we moved. "Unsheathe your sword, my son," he commanded, "and hold it toward that reddish star. Whatever you see or hear, say nothing, and never leave the protection of the circle. And never talk again to anyone of what is going to happen, for loose talk will spoil the strongest magic."

I obeyed him, took out my sword and raised it aloft. A strange fire began to play over the steel blade.

"In the name of Clio," Master Agrippa incanted, "you, bitter Muse, who rule over the fate of men and inscribe with iron style their deeds, good and bad indifferently, in the ledger! In your name, snaky-locked goddesses of revenge who are the daughters of Dikë, before whose will the sun himself moves subject! In your name, great fire, which swells and wanes, now visible now invisible, the breath of life in men! Look down, red star, on this youth, strengthen him with your rays and bless his sword which is consecrated to Dionysos Christos, the ever martyred, the shamefully murdered, him who was buried in the night and him who rose again. This sword will be ever raised for those who believe, for the Church and the Blessed Virgin, for the poor and suffering and the oppressed. Take it, O red star spirit, and let it cut through iron helmet and armor as through water, let it wallow in the blood of the unjust and the oppressor, let it be a terrible weapon for him who wears it!"

After chanting this invocation Agrippa took the sword lightly from my hand, and etched in the blade with his ring a small and curious sign. As he did this I heard a gentle lisping and sighing, and the dry thistles rattled hoarsely. The breath of the night blew coldly on me, and far off one star fell, was lost.

"See," said Master Agrippa, "I have scratched the sign of your daimon into this steel. May the daimon be ever at the side of this youth when he is in danger!" After pronouncing these last words he fell on his knees and prayed. I did likewise. The wind fell, and no longer sucked loudly through the creviced rocks. . . .

We clambered over the rocky place back to the road. Master Agrippa put his arms around me and said, "Now go back, my son, and don't be down in the mouth. We shall see each other again."

"May you have a safe journey!" I said. "May the Virgin Mary watch over you!"

"So be it, indeed," he replied, and made the sign of the cross. He poked the mule with his staff and rode slowly away followed by the servant. I remained standing in the road as if rooted to the spot. I saw my beloved teacher disappear over the next rise, his small, thickset figure bent forward over the mule's ears. I heard the hollow clop of the hoofs becoming fainter and fainter. And at last all was still. I got on my Pia and with heavy heart returned to the city.

Three days after this leave-taking, early in the morning I was awakened by a clamor of voices. Startled I sprang out of bed. It seemed as if the voices were muffled and threatening, as if the clank of armor and weapons mingled with the words. Hurriedly I dressed and ran downstairs.

Several men were assembled in our study. They wore helmets, and swords were slung from their belts. Among them I recognized the ominously morose face of Frenero. By him stood a certain Bernal, who had a black patch over his right eye. I knew him, too, for at one time he used to run errands for Diego de Vargas. My Sancho was there, stubborn-faced, and behind him hid Teresa, weeping and wringing her hands. Over the hearth was crouched the black form of a Dominican as he carefully inspected the flasks and alembics scattered there.

"Here he is, Reverend Father," said Frenero. Out of that pocked face his little eyes bored into me.

The Dominican wheeled around. It was Father Pablo. He had aged, was thinner than I had ever known him. Silvery threads gleamed in the thick black hair that ran down to a sharp point on his forehead. His eyes were deep-set in his head, evilly alive as I remembered them from childhood, burning with some consuming inner fire.

"What does this mean, Father Pablo?" I asked. "Why these armed men? What are you doing with my master's alembics? What's behind all these knowing looks?"

"I mean this," shouted Father Pablo, and dashed the alembics to the floor, shattering them to tinkling bits.

"Hold on there," I cried, and would have grappled him had not Bernal held me back.

"Miserable heretic!" said Father Pablo, menace in his tone. "Don't play the fool. These men are my familiars, my trusted servants in the great task of restoring lost souls to the paths of righteousness. I've come to you for a double reason. You stand twice accused. *Ad primum:* You have dealings with a certain Agrippa of Nettesheim, a Lutheran dog, a magician and a sorcerer who owes allegiance to the Prince of Darkness. *Ad secundum:* In the City of the Moors you have had intercourse with an unbeliever called Abu Amru, and have listened with great satisfaction to his heathen doctrines. My people have seen you in the garden with the women of this Moor. You have also experimented with ablutions in the godless manner of these heretics. . . . I haven't much time to waste on you, my fine young man, so sign this paper at once and admit everything in full and with contrition. Then we'll see to it you escape the worst—I mean, the fire. As I said before, there is little time. It's hard enough for us as it is to weed out the thistles from the corn. Therefore I caution you to make haste. I mean you no harm. Long ago I forgave you your miserable betrayal of me and my cause, for I'm a Christian."

Father Pablo smiled. He unfolded a scroll, which he laid with care on the table, first sending the little flasks crashing to the floor with a wide sweep of his arm.

"It is quite true," I said, "that I know Master Agrippa well, but he is neither a Lutheran nor a magician. I know also Abu Amru, and hold him for a very learned man. But he has never spoken to me of his arts. I am also acquainted with Doña Sobeya and Doña Tamila. . . ."

"Yes, that complicates matters," said Father Pablo. "You won't slide out of this so easily. We need a detailed confession of guilt."

"It's the truth I'm telling you," I said.

"Maybe," retorted Father Pablo. "Your truth, not ours. We need a deposition that has but one meaning."

"What are you driving at, Father Pablo?" I asked.

"You must sign the following and confirm it with your oath. *Ad primum:* In your presence the said Agrippa has declared that the Lutheran heresy is the only true faith. In his sorcery he has besought and sold his soul to the Devil, also called Satan and Lucifer, and afterward nourished the thought of doing away with Their Most Catholic Majesties, the King and Queen, with poison."

"No," I stammered, "no . . . no . . . that's sheer madness."

"Ad secundum:" Father Pablo continued unruffled, "the said Abu Amru has attempted to beguile you into his false faith. In order to achieve this purpose he has offered you women and counseled heretical ablutions. Beyond this, in your presence he has soiled with spittle from his mouth the image of our Lord and of His Mother, and threatened them in the most frightful imprecations."

"But such things he has simply never done," I remonstrated. "That would be a lie."

"Consider carefully," said Father Pablo, his words dark with warning, "that with this confession you may expect to be accorded clemency. Perhaps a small loss of worldly goods, a pilgrimage to Santiago or

Guadalupe. The Church rejoices over the contrite sinner. But if you are obstinate, I can guarantee you nothing."

"I shall never perjure myself," I said, enraged.

"Don't make any difficulties," urged Father Pablo. "I'll dispense with the oath. Sign it without any oath."

Of themselves my fists clenched, and I assuredly should have struck the terrible Dominican in the face had he not suddenly bent again over Master Agrippa's apparatus. As he turned his back Frenero took me by the arm. "Watch out!" he whispered, and pressed a bit of dirty paper in my hand. I stole a glance at it and read, "The King watches." I eyed Frenero. Almost imperceptibly he nodded, his eyes cold and piercing in the pocked face. Bernal, too, stared at me with hostility in his solitary eye.

"Now then," said Father Pablo. "Ready?"

"I shall never sign the paper," I said. "It would be the most infamous of lies."

"You shall indeed sign it," returned Father Pablo curtly, "for the Holy Inquisition needs this evidence. But do as you want. As far as I'm concerned, I've done my best. And now I'll have to ask you this very day to go to Seville to the Palace of the Inquisition, and present yourself there. They will take up the matter from this point."

"Good enough," I rejoined. "I'll go."

"On your word?" asked Father Pablo hastily.

"Yes, on my honor," I agreed, disgusted and cold.

My good Teresa began to shed tears loudly. Sancho regarded his shoes, livid with anger. Smiling secretly to himself Father Pablo said, "Godspeed, my son." He turned, left the room, his armed men following after. Only Frenero hung back a little, moved close to me, and whispered, "I'd never go to Seville. Go to El Potro. They'll show you the way to Fat Pascuala's."

"I'm going to Seville," I replied shortly.

Frenero shrugged his shoulders. "I've carried out my orders," he muttered. "You're a little too stubborn for your own good."

Then he joined the others. They moved down the Street of the Leather Merchants, the Dominican in the lead.

Teresa was inconsolable. "Oh, you poor child," she sobbed. "If the Mistress ever knew that I'd neglected my duties this way! O Blessed Virgin Mary, take pity on your child; see to it he does the right thing."

Sancho saddled my Pia, and after eating a hurried meal I made a start. Sancho went with me as far as the city gate. There I bade him to return, and rode away accompanied by his fervent good wishes. When I strained round in the saddle to see, there he still stood motionless before the gate.

Late at night I arrived at Seville and announced myself at the Palace of the Inquisition which stood like a mighty fortress on the banks of the Guadalquivir in the suburb of Triana. A Dominican greeted me cordially, led me through long corridors, up steps and down, into a room. I was taken aback, for I had expected to be thrown into a dungeon. The room was very simple, but comfortably enough furnished. I waited to hear him slide the bolt or turn the key but nothing of the kind occurred. I might have been a guest in a monastery. Thoughtfully I walked over to the window and saw that it was barred. The prospect gave out over the river which was much broader here than in Cordova. I saw the lights of a boat slowly moving downstream. Everything looked unreal to me. I pressed my forehead against the cold iron bars.

I had stood thus for some time when suddenly I heard a shriek. It was almost like the howl of a wolf in the loneliness of the mountains, but more human and so more sinister. I listened. Once again the cry came. My hands shook; sweat ran from my pores. I kneeled before the image of the Holy Virgin Mary and begged her to protect me. Again I listened intently. All was still as the tomb. Only now from the direction of the river I heard voices. I became powerfully disturbed. The flame of the little oil lamp burned steadily, without motion. Sweet Christ, I thought, what shall I do! I must not be afraid. I stepped over to the table and ran my fingers through the pages of *Lives of the Saints.* I closed my eyes and told myself I would take my cue from whatever words I chanced to hit upon. My finger wandered over the hard paper. I opened my eyes and read: Thou shalt not bear false witness against thy neighbour.

This commandment solaced me to the roots. I felt myself out of danger, protected by a power invincible. No longer was I alone. I threw myself on the pallet, shut my eyes and prayed. I prayed for Master Agrippa and Diego, for Doña Isabella, for Sancho and Teresa. I named all of them by name, even Abu Amru and Sobeya. Toward the end with some reluctance I mentioned also Father Pablo, Frenero and Bernal. At the very last came the King, Don Carlos.

For a long time I was unable to get to sleep. I saw the little flame of the oil lamp which I had left burning. I pondered, thinking it might be that souls were like flames kindled by God, that we must tend them, keep them burning clear and bright instead of aflicker with smudge. And even when I closed my eyes, the flame stood burning before my gaze and it seemed almost as if it were burning within me. Not until it was getting toward morning and the night was beginning to gray, did I blow out the lamp and go to sleep.

In these early morning hours I was visited by a dream. I shall tell about it here because at the time it seemed fraught with premonition, and upon my awakening—even later when I was on trial before Antonio de Guevara—it gave me a good heart, though it was but a simple dream. I dreamed, then, that I was walking along the bank of a river. The water of this river had all but dried up, the worn rocks stood out naked to the view and the banks were barren and stony. Then I heard, very soft from afar, a rustling. The water began to rise. The rocky bed vanished, the meadows and fields which had been waste and arid commenced to green. Wider and mightier swelled the flood until the waters lapped round my feet. Deeper and deeper into the cooling wetness the ancient willows on the banks dipped their branches. On the green boughs of the willows little silver fish sported. Merrily they capered about, opened their round mouths and sang a joyous song.

The sight of this so lifted up my spirits that I awoke and jumped from my bed. I went to the window and saw the river bathed in the silvery morning light. Beyond rose a round hill. Then I noticed, to my amazement, that I had not merely dreamed the singing. Below, not far from the wall of the Palace of the Inquisition which dropped precipitously into the river, a fisherman was busy with his nets. At the same time his voice gave forth in song. Involuntarily I hummed the song after him, and the refrain ran:

"Abu Harith, sweet gallant knight,
List well the song by fool indite,
If from dungeon dank and dour
To sunlight free it would thee lure."

Tensely I glanced downward. I noticed the fisherman looking, with great caution, up at my window. I nodded him furtive recognition. In a little while the man in the boat sang another melody:

"At midnight's stroke, when all it still,
The keeper sleeps, if so God will,
My boat is dark, all lights burn low.
Within the house creep soft below.

"If owl doth hoot, hold fast and steady,
For sudden journey be thou ready,
Fear neither groans nor thievish rags,
The hour has struck, and no man lags."

Over and over I repeated the words until I could say them by heart. Again I nodded. The fisherman went on:

"From King Diego am I boldly come,
To save thee from a churlish doom.
Live out my words with every nerve,
Keen soul and body to preserve."

I nodded for the third time. Thereupon the fisherman drew his nets from the water, bent over them, and let out a sustained cry that rang out over stream and land. It seemed to me that an echo came from somewhere. The man rowed into the middle of the stream, where he busied himself further with his fishing.

Not long after this interlude breakfast was brought to me. When I had eaten, the silent and friendly Dominican appeared and commanded me to follow him. I walked behind, carefully noting the direction of the steps. We came to a door. Two guards stood beside it who regarded me suspiciously. The brother opened this door and we entered a magnificent anteroom. Along the walls ran tall bookshelves decorated with gold and silver and filled with volumes of all sizes. The Dominican indicated that I should wait here. I sat down in a chair covered with red damask. My glance rested on the titles of the books, and to my surprise I saw that all of them were worldly works, mostly by the authors of antiquity. This discovery gave me some courage.

After a little time the Dominican returned and pointed to a door finished off in tooled leather, saying, "His Eminence is expecting you." My heart pulsed heavily in my throat. With a trembling hand I opened the door, which noiselessly closed after me. I stood in a high arched room the walls of which had been washed with white lime. Its simplicity contrasted strongly with the splendor of the anteroom. Seated behind a writing desk roughly knocked together out of unfinished pine there was an oldish man who wore a three-cornered biretta on his silvery hair. As the only ornament on the unpainted table stood a black cross to which was nailed the body of our Saviour. The old man looked at me. I saw his eyes were dark and quick, his brows very black and heavy. His nose was long, his lips narrow and the chin round and strongly sculptured. He wore spectacles rimmed in black and secured to his ears by dull red ribbons of silk. These two wide strips of crimson were the only bits of color in his whole dress or, indeed, in the whole room.

"My son," the man said severely, but without hostility, "complaints have come to us from Cordova, and we have taken pains to summon you to us to be our guest for a time under our roof. Does your room satisfy you?"

"Most certainly, Your Eminence," I answered, surprised.

"Have you noticed the book in your room?"

"I have, Your Eminence."

"Did you look into it?"

"I did, Your Eminence."

"And what did you read?"

" 'Thou shalt not bear false witness against thy neighbour.' "

The man's face clouded. He examined me searchingly, smiled with some effort and asked, "Do you know who I am?"

"No, Your Eminence, but I think you are the Grand Inquisitor, Antonio Cardinal de Guevara."

"A good guess. Now, to come back to what you read in the book—who are your neighbors?"

"My neighbors . . . they are my fellow men, Your Eminence."

"Are the Indians your neighbors?"

"No . . . I suppose not . . . they aren't," I stammered in great confusion.

"You see, my son," he said evenly, "your answer was false. But do not be dismayed. It is a common error, the seed of many a heresy. Your neighbors, as understood in the text, are neither your fellow men—a vague concept in any case—nor yet the people who live next door to you, as the crude mind of the peasant would perhaps interpret it. Your neighbors are other members of the same Church to which you yourself belong. If I were a layman," he continued with a faint smirk of contempt, "I should say: My neighbors are the other members of the state and the people from which I am sprung. You are a Catholic and a Spaniard, are you not?"

"I am, Your Eminence," I said, quite shocked by this.

"It would grieve me deeply," he went on, staring at me coldly, "if Father Pablo, who is a great zealot of our faith, should have so pressed his passion to serve good ends that he demanded from you false testimony against pious Catholics and good Spaniards. Has he done that?"

"Yes," I said hastily. "Or no, no . . . perhaps."

"Your words are not clear, my son," said the Cardinal, smiling softly. "Your answers must be either yes or no. Anything more is extraneous."

"I mean," I managed to say, at a loss, "that Master Agrippa is a Catholic, but not a Spaniard. Abu Amru is a Spaniard, but not a Catholic."

"You are mistaken, my son. Master Agrippa is not a Catholic but a Lutheran and a heathen magician. Abu Amru is not a Spaniard but a Moor. Both are followers of Antichrist. The commands found in the Holy Bible do not apply to them, and Father Pablo has dealt justly. Do you see now?"

"I don't know," I mumbled. "I cannot gainsay Your Eminence, but I feel it is a great injustice to make false accusations even against followers of Antichrist."

The Cardinal bowed his head and in deep thought inspected his slender right hand on the middle finger of which I noticed he wore a heavy gold ring. "It would lead too far afield," he said, emphasizing each word with precision, "to instruct you on the nature of justice and injustice, to demonstrate to you that these concepts are significant only within the frame of Church and State. I am afraid, too, you are too young and inexperienced to understand my words. You must trust me, my son. For see, I am a Cardinal and a servant in the world of the Church and of the Corpus Christi"—he looked at the crucifix and nodded—"and nothing could be more alien to my purpose than to wreak injury on others. Ecclesiasticus writes of our Holy Mother, the Church, *Ego mater pulchrae dilectionis et agnitionis et sanctae spei*—I am the Mother of perfect peace, of understanding and of blessed hope. And that also means there is neither peace, nor understanding nor blessed hope outside the Church. For this reason hearken to my voice, which gives tongue to this understanding, and ignore the voice of your heart, where no doubt the Evil Spirit has made his abode."

I looked at him horrified.

"Perhaps you hate the Holy Inquisition?" he inquired grimly.

"No," I replied.

"That is good," he said slowly, "for the Inquisition, as serious and terrible as it may be—and it is just that, my son—says of itself: 'I, too, am born of eternal love.' A great unrest, a chaos, an ignorance of whither one goes and whence one comes, a profound doubt, insane bloodshed and martyrdom would desolate Spain and all Christianity were it not for the Inquisition. Perhaps already it is too late, for even on the throne of St. Peter itself, on the throne of Charlemagne, sit milksops in these latter days. It is better that thousands and hundreds of thousands, yes millions, should die like flies, than that earthly existence be stripped of all meaning and goal, that the humblest of the humble who love our dear Lord should come to doubt their lives and God.

"You hear, my son, I speak with gravity. I, too, bear Master Agrippa and Abu Amru no ill will. But it is necessary for the welfare of the Church and Christianity that both these antichrists be rendered innocuous. We know that Agrippa carries letters from the Spanish nobility and the State which are to help him hinder, through Doña Margarita of Savoy, the work of redemption. So far as Abu Amru goes, he is very influential among his people. In his case, it so happens, the matter has already been brought to a close, and we no longer need your testimony. As a rule my subordinates would conduct this trial. But you, my son, I must examine personally, for it is a question of saving Spain. The deliverance of Christianity is at stake."

The Cardinal gazed at me fixedly. Great drops of sweat ran down my brow. I felt as if Antonio de Guevara had shaken a tremendous burden from his shoulders, removing it to my own. Yes, it seemed to me as if tens of thousands were listening hollow-eyed to our conversation—monks, nobles, merchants, learned men, artisans, muleteers, beggars and thieves. The matter touched them all.

I fell to my knees, in supplication folded my hands, and sobbed, "Oh, great Cardinal, have mercy on me. Whether I talk or hold my tongue I commit a great injustice. Oh, why has God cast the weight of the world on my shoulders!"

"Such is the greatness of mankind," said the Cardinal. "This responsibility is spared no one. Neither today nor in a hundred thousand years. A certain One decided the fate of the world. But you, you must not shrink from your charge. Do not forget that a Third One stands between us."

"Who?" I moaned. "Who?" The tears ran down my face.

"He!" With astonishingly youthful energy the Cardinal sprang to his feet, snatched the black crucifix and thrust it at me at arm's length. "Do you see, my son, that he is dead? Do you see the pierced feet and hands, the wounds in his side running blood? The head sagging on his thin breast?"

"Dear Christ," I implored, "do not forsake me. Give me a sign. A miracle!"

"Signs and miracles are not necessary." He crashed the crucifix onto the table. "Did I not tell you that God is dead? His martyr's body long since vanished in corruption, his meager bones at one with the earth? Cling to the Resurrected!"

"Where?" I cried. "How?"

"Cleave fast to the Church, which speaks to you through my lips. The community of the faithful is the Corpus Christi. This body must never rot, must not suffer pain like that flesh which more than fifteen hundred years ago was lowered into the grave. If one of its limbs becomes gangrenous and foul, then off it must be lopped. Never will the Kingdom of God vanish from the earth. Men will live side by side in peace, I say. No one will hunger again; no one will wander astray. Life will flow onward like a lovely dream in the happy isles. There will be no more thorny mysteries. Everything will be open, drenched with light. But this way is feasible only through strictest obedience of each member to the dictates of the whole. You understand me?"

"Yes, I understand you," I said quietly, and rose to my feet weak and shaking. "But within me I clearly hear a voice that admonishes me . . ."

I fell silent. The Cardinal, too, said nothing for some time. Then, as quietly as I myself had spoken, he continued, "We all hear this voice of which you speak. I, too, have heard it. I, too, have thought that it was the Voice of God. Yes, even I have thought this, my son. Do not look at me so apprehensively. Shall I tell you what this voice says to you? It says, Any heaven on earth which shows the smallest crack in its foundations is not Heaven, but the kingdom of lies. It is Hell itself."

"Your Eminence," I murmured, shuddering, "you read the souls of men as if they were an open book."

"Because I am also a man," he retorted, again smiling gently. "Being a man I can read men's thoughts. We are all of us brothers under the skin, whether we wear purple, silk, a coarse habit or are clothed in tatters. All the same substance, my son. Mere flesh. But that voice which all men hear, above all those in whose veins the blood runs red, is the voice of the serpent. It whips up the pride and says to the children of Adam, You shall be as God, knowing good and evil."

"Yes," I cried, "yes, that is true; it is true."

The Cardinal thinned his lips in triumph. "Decide for yourself, my son," he said solemnly, "to whom you will hearken. To the Voice of God, who speaks through our Holy Mother the Roman Catholic Church and through the Holy Inquisition, or to the voice whispering within your own heart. I know that you, as a Spanish knight, will choose correctly. There is no haste. Come nearer, and let me bless you."

I drew closer and again dropped to my knees. Very slowly he made the sign of the cross over me. "Now go," he said. "Tell the brother in the anteroom to lead you back to your retreat. In three days I shall have you brought to me once more. May the Lord make easier your proper choice."

I bowed and left the room. Behind me the leather-padded door shut noiselessly. In my room I sank into the chair, bent my face to my hands. It seemed to me that in the last half-hour the very contours of my face had altered. Now it has really happened, I thought. Now God has come into my life.

Hour after hour I sat motionless. Food and a glass of wine were put on the table for me, but I did not touch them. I noticed that the Dominican attendant stopped to watch me, and shook his head. He said nothing, however, and departed with scarcely a sound.

To the right outside the fortress I could hear the guard being changed every two hours. They laughed and talked among themselves. I wondered whatever there could be to laugh about in this world. And when all became still again, down below I could hear the little waves of the river caressing the wall of the Palace. Thereupon I thought again of my dream, and of the song which the fisherman in the boat had sung:

"At midnight's stroke, when all is still . . ."

The evening crept in, a light wind blew. I looked out the window. The sun was just sinking into the river, enormous and blood-red. Despite the present peace there was a feeling of foreboding in the air, as of an approaching storm. Downstream lay anchored several caravels, and one of them labored slowly and clumsily into the middle of the current. The crew was trying to catch the evening breeze to make the mouth of the river and the open sea by midnight.

Midnight? The open sea? My heart wavered; I was helpless with doubt. And yet, should I leave Antonio de Guevara like a coward? Should I avoid the decision imposed on me by God? "But you, you must not writhe out of your charge." The words rang in my ears.

I made a final decision not to run away. But I also concluded I ought to creep down the steps at midnight to let Diego and his friends know what was going on, for I feared they might press even right up to my room, running the direst risks. This resolve lightened my heart, and to my amazement I was able to eat my supper with great pleasure. The wine tasted like nectar. . . .

6

THE GERMANIA

WHEN it grew dark again the silent Dominican appeared and lighted my candle with a resinous pine splinter. For a while I read in the *Lives of the Saints,* but my thoughts were not with the book and at last the letters danced before my eyes. I extinguished the light and drew my chair over to the window.

It was a dark windy night. The storm howled mournfully about the walls and towers. Somewhere on the building a chain swung and a weathervane squeaked as the wind tossed it about. A blast of wind threw open the window, brushed sweetly through my hair and the rain whipped my face. Big drops ran like tears down my cheeks. I looked downward at the empty stream, dark as ink in the night. I could hear the waves slapping heavily against the walls when the wind slackened now and then. And then, out in the middle of the stream, or at least where I imagined the middle to be, I caught sight of a flickering light. At times it would disappear altogether, lost in the wind and the rain. Then again it would appear. It comforted me deeply.

I knew that the call to Mass would be sounded about midnight. But I was afraid that the storm would swallow up the tinkling of the bell, for no longer could I hear the watch changing every two hours outside the fortress. I looked anxiously out over the river. And suddenly a great weariness overcame me. I leaned my arm on the sill and rested my head.

How long a time passed I cannot say, but without inner warning I jumped in horror to my feet. I was sure that I had heard the sound of bells, very faint, but certainly nothing else. The light in the river had seemingly disappeared for good. I strained my eyes to see, but it did not shine any more.

I got up as quietly as possible and stood near the door. There was not a sound. Carefully I opened the heavy door and looked down the corridor. The long arched space was empty, full of shadows, illuminated by a single torch whose flame wavered and guttered in the draught. I moved out bodily into the hallway and closed the door behind me. Gently, on tiptoe, I crept along the wall. Once I hesitated. My heart beat wildly. I imagined that my own shadow had taken a great leap, as if it beckoned me back like a fearful ghost. I thought of many evil things. But it was only the light faggot. Outside the storm moaned and soughed, sweeping in through the open window in the corridor.

At last I reached the steps. Carefully I bent down over the stone balustrade and looked down the well. The winding steps were swallowed up in a pit of darkness. Trembling with excitement I edged my way down, back hugged to the wall. I could smell the damp lime. The building, in the night, seemed to have grown much larger. Each step that I took was an ordeal, and I was resigned to rack, thumbscrews and death at the end of my venture. But at the same time the thought of Diego urged me on relentlessly.

In this fashion I came to the second floor, and there heard footsteps, shuffling sandal steps, not the tread of an armed man. I knew, of course, that it must be some of the friars. On tiptoe I ran down a second-floor corridor. Half crazed with anxiety I opened one of the doors which led into the passageway. The room was dark and empty. I leaned against the door and listened. One of the Dominicans said to the other, "Did you hear somebody running?" and the others replied calmly, "No, it was only the storm." They went farther along and the steps grew fainter and fainter. Then behind me a weak quavering voice asked, "Is someone there?" I pressed myself against the door and had to hold my mouth in order not to cry aloud.

Then I heard deep groans, and the same weak voice sobbed, "Allah, God of my fathers, you will forgive me my lies. I can't stand any more. . . ." The unseen person drew in a heavy breath, said, "Whoever you may be, an angel of Allah or a murderer, answer me!"

"Keep still!" I whispered. "In the name of the Virgin, keep still!"

"Who are you!"

I moved away from the door, and gradually my eyes became accustomed to the darkness of the room. I thought I saw a white form lying in one corner on a plank bed. "I am called Pedro," I said.

"You, too! They're even torturing children!" he whispered back.

"And you?" I asked. I thought I remembered the voice from somewhere. "Who are you?"

"I am called Abu Amru. Do you know me?"

I let out a low cry, walked softly over to the pallet.

"My child," he whispered fearfully, "don't come too close. However little you shake the boards it hurts me so much I can scarcely breathe. My limbs are broken and pulled out of the sockets. I am dying. But Allah has surely sent you. . . ."

"What is it?" I asked in terror.

"You shall hear," he said, sobbing. "But now reach under the cushion of the chair. You'll find a little round pill. And give me the water. The jug is on the table."

I did as I was told. I felt his skinny fingers clutching for the pill. "Praise be unto Allah," he said. "It is finished."

"What do you mean by that?" I asked, cold with apprehension, still holding the pill in my hand.

"The pill will bring me deep sleep," he said. Strangely, his voice grew stronger, and he no longer sobbed. Outside I heard an owl screeching eerily.

"Hear, Don Pedro," he said. "They have tortured me—I won't tell you how—until I told the lies they wanted to hear me say. I have spit on Miriam, the virgin, and cursed her. They then wanted me to indict your Master Agrippa, but I held my tongue, even though the torturer racked my legs and broke my shinbones with iron rods. I am only a man. I don't know how I can stand it tomorrow, or the day after tomorrow. And besides, I am an old man. My time has come. It is better that I go. . . ."

"What?" I asked. "Do you want to escape?"

"No, not in the way you mean, Don Pedro. For I'm chained to the floor, and couldn't get away. I am escaping to Allah."

"It is a great sin," I began fearfully.

"Be quiet," he whispered. "You're still a child. Otherwise you would know that to die is better than to betray. Now listen closely to what I have to say. Tell my niece Sobeya that she must go to Africa. I have close friends in Fez. And even there she must only rest, then go on to the land of Yemen, her home. Tell Diego de Vargas to help her. He can have half the jewels. . . ."

"I'll do it," I said tensely.

"Now for you . . ." he began. His voice was becoming noticeably weaker. "I do hope you get away." Again the owl screeched.

"I'm not going to run away, though," I told him, and explained my plans as hurriedly as I could.

"But you must, you must," he groaned. "Give me your word. Otherwise they'll just torture you the same way they've tortured me. Oh, Allah, I can't stand it. Give me the powder, the powder, boy."

He groaned once more. Then all was still in the room. And, curiously, at this moment the owl outside cried out again, slowly, unmistakably. Every limb atremble I stood over the dead Abu Amru, reached in terror and made myself try to close the lids of his eyes. But again and again they sprang wide open. Suddenly, with a terrible shock, horror possessed me. With a muffled scream in my throat I sprang to the door, tore it open, crashed it shut behind me and ran as if chased by the devil down the stairs. I took three and four steps at a time. I began to stumble and would have pitched headlong in full flight if I had not bumped into a man. The apparition gripped me around the waist, pressed a big, calloused hand over my mouth. His breath stank of garlic and wine intermingled powerfully.

"You're late," he whispered hoarsely into my ear. I struggled wildly in his arms, but to no avail. He held me as in a vice. "Be quiet, you fool," he muttered. "I'm Frenero." And with that he threw a gray cloth over my shoulders and put a pointed cap on my head. He splashed something wet on my face and hands. "Here," he went on, "here is a rattle. Outside you'll find Bernal. Go with him; he'll take you to Diego. Don't forget you're in Triana. Get busy with that thing."

I took the rattle. A small door opened in the wall. Frenero shoved me outside and the door closed behind. It was absolutely dark and the slanting rain blinded my eyes and streamed down my face. Gradually I realized that I was in an alley in a poor quarter of the suburbs. On the one side of the narrow street was the wall of the fortress and on the other shabby, dilapidated houses. The air reeked of offal, and there was a smell in the air as if someone near by were boiling soap. I came to a full stop. Creeping along the wall toward me was a crumpled figure. Slowly it came nearer and nearer. Then I saw it was a leper. So frightened was I that I could not move as the man lunged toward me. His face was white as chalk in the rainy murk. He laid a finger over his mouth, which was twisted. I stared in a transport of fear.

Close to me he came, and said, "I'm Bernal. We've got to get out of here in a hurry. Didn't you hear the owl?"

"Yes, I heard it," I told him.

"We've got to get out of Triana," he whispered in my ear. "We've got enough friends here. But most of them believe in the Inquisition with soul and body. That's why we have to be disguised. Everybody will give us a wide berth."

"Disguised?"

"Yes. We've got to act like lepers. Follow me." He began to hunch his way along, and I behind him. It was a miserable night. I stole a glance up at the steep walls of the Palace of the Inquisition. Like a threatening giant the enormous gray fortress towered over the foul suburb of the city. For the first time I realized what mortal dangers I had just escaped. My knees knocked together at the mere thought of it, and I had trouble forcing myself along. We met no one. Once a big dog came trotting up boldly and smelled of my mantle. Then he growled in his throat and loped away to creep back into the ruined house from which he had emerged.

Bernal began to shake his rattle and I followed suit. We walked along close to the walls of the houses. Some riders came upon us. Behind them rode a churchman on a mule. He wore glasses, and said in a voice like Antonio de Guevara's, "Poor devils . . . they ought to be put on an island somewhere." He fumbled at his belt and threw us a small gold piece which fell with a tinkle on the cobbles. Bernal bent down, picked it up, and spat thoughtfully into the road. He went on, and the horses' hoofs clattered into nothingness behind us, lost in the driving rain.

"That was the Grand Inquisitor," said Bernal. "He gave us a gold piece. Did you see?"

I nodded.

"He's a great man," said Bernal. "He's a pious Christian, may God keep him! He always has something for the poor. He's a friend of the people. He's driving out the Moor bitches, the bloodsuckers of our land. I find myself that an act of faith is a pleasant change after a bullfight."

My heart was so heavy that I lacked the energy to contradict him. I was soaked through to the skin. The heavy wet cloak burdened my shoulders as if made of soft lead. One minute my teeth chattered with cold and the next I was burning with fever. Knowing that I was ill with a heavy cold my thoughts yet wandered as I grew light-headed.

Bernal walked down some cellar stairs. I followed him, heavily, clumping down step after step as if each were the last I could navigate. I was completely indifferent to everything now. Impatiently I realized that certain things in my surroundings were impressing themselves relentlessly against my unwilling brain. The hollow chute of the cellar stairs, the terrible weight of my rain-sodden cloak, the cruel surface of the wall over which I slid my hands as I descended—all these sensations I could not suppress nor bring into perspective. Somewhere water was dripping steadily. I felt the dripping, drop by drop, coming down with iron regularity. It seemed as if the drops were falling within my being, not on the cellar steps.

We had to bend deep. The passageway grew narrower and narrower. My cloak rubbed against the wall. There was a choking smell of limed walls and plaster, of the rotten wood and packed earth that never feels the sun. "Bernal," I said faintly, holding my hand to my forehead, "something is happening to me. What can it be?"

"I don't know," he replied, and I saw that, after peering into my face, he made the sign of the cross over me. "Pull yourself together. Say a prayer to the Virgin. We've got only a couple of steps more."

I prayed. But the prayer gave me no comfort. I felt, to my horror, that the Virgin meant no more to me at the moment than a statue of stone.

We crept on, bending lower all the time. Then Bernal opened a door that squealed loudly on its hinges. The air suddenly became purer. There was the rain again on my face and hands. We stood under the crippled boughs of an ancient olive tree. We might have been suddenly transplanted into the Holy Land, standing in the Garden of Gethsemane. We sat down in the wet grass and leaned our backs against the trunk.

I cannot say how long we remained in that position. I looked at Bernal. I saw the white flakes on his cheeks and the black plaster over the empty eye socket. Yet he seemed completely lovable and friendly to me, in God's truth. I asked him, my voice thin with fatigue, "How is it, Bernal, that you risked so much to save me?"

"It's nothing. Just forget it," he told me gruffly. "Life is just one endless risk in any case. It's all the same to me whether I lead you through Triana, search houses with Father Pablo or waylay a wagon train in the Sierra."

"Can't we go now?" I asked, after we had sat for another few minutes in the shower that came through the branches of the tree.

"Yes, lean on me," he said.

We labored to our feet and walked slowly over the ground, which was as soft as a carpet. Through olive groves and terraced vineyards we arrived at the bank of the river, which coiled by us with hardly a sound. A boat lay moored at the end of a painter fastened to a stake. Men's voices urged us to make haste. Then I found myself lying down among some sacks. There were big cheeses in the sacks, half a ham, a pile of coarse bread and many flasks of wine. Over the mound a tarpaulin had been stretched to protect the cargo from the falling rain, which had now lightened into a mizzle.

The boat cast off. I heard the oars bite into the water and strain squealing against the locks. The men talked to one another loudly, in laughing voices. Though my head was splitting, I realized that I was not sick, and could have wept with relief and gratitude. I fell into a restless sleep from which every now and then I would start, cramped with fright. The boat moved steadily on, the water hissed as it parted at the bow, and little waves slapped against the strakes of the waist. There was a pleasant domestic smell of cheese, fresh bread and cold mutton fat.

After a while one of the seamen came aft in the little boat, dug into the pile and with his long knife cut a thick slice of dark bread and a massive piece of cheese. With it he gave me a handful of olives and a beaker of wine. I ate and drank. I began to take heart again, although fear still choked my throat.

The men also ate and drank while they leaned on their oars. Then they sang some verses to a gay but monotonous tune. Bernal kept time by banging the bailing scoop on the thwart where he sat. They sang:

"Ho, ho, you brothers! . . .
Watch out for your oars,
Ho, ho, you brothers! . . .
Keep an eye on the whores. . . .
Or a chance child will pop.
Ho, ho, you brothers, ho, ho!"

And now Bernal sprang up on the thwart and improvised in his roaring baritone:

"Ho, ho! you brothers! . . .
Steal no gold, filch no stones,
Or you'll swing in the sky,
All rain-rotted bones.
Ho, ho, you brothers, ho, ho!"

In turn he gave way to a thickset man, who growled out in a jovial bass:

"Ho, ho, you brothers . . .
Priestly fleshpots let lie,
Or grim old Saint Peter
Will ne'er let you by.
Ho, ho, you brothers, ho, ho!"

This jollity continued for a long time. Now and then the crew would burst out into a loud clamor of laughter and voices, all speaking at once. The merriment echoed over the water and raised wild ducks from their rest among the reeds of the banks. But always the boat moved swiftly upstream, steadily into the graying dawn. The rain-drenched willows along the shores of the river gradually took shape in the gloom before morning, and I could distinguish single houses and, slowly, the blurred outlines of the vineyards steaming in the mist.

Bernal crept over the thwarts to where I lay under the tarpaulin and handed me a cloth and a basin of water. "Bestir yourself, young fellow," he said. "Wash off your face. We're almost there."

"In Cordova? Is that where we stop?" I asked, looking out over the empty river.

"No," he said, smiling grimly, "you can't go back to Cordova now. We're going to land at the Carmelite Cloister. All these provisions are going there."

"Is anyone expecting me there?" I inquired anxiously.

"We'll see," he said cryptically.

Slowly a large white structure on the left bank of the river hove into view. It looked well cared for and freshly washed. As we neared the place I saw landing steps dipping down into the water. A man stood there all alone and waved to us. In a few moments I discovered it was Diego, who greeted me warmly.

"Welcome," he said, "welcome to the Casa Blanca de Santa Catarina."

"How can I ever repay you, Diego?" I said. "I'll never be able to now that I'm a penniless runaway without a home."

"Never mind that," he assured me. "You can keep my mother company and another lady who happens to be there."

The men began to unload the sacks of foodstuffs from the boat and carry them into the cloister. Diego drew me to one side. "Did they question you?" he wanted to know.

"Antonio de Guevara had me up before him," I said. "It was terrible. I really began to wonder what was right and what was wrong. I don't think I'll ever be sure again."

"I hope you didn't let out anything," he said gravely.

"No, not a thing. They gave me three days to think things over," I explained. "But . . ."

"But what?"

"But Abu Amru is dead."

"No!" Diego gripped my arm.

I nodded, told him how I had stumbled on Abu Amru, and how he had found swift release.

Diego listened to the whole story without comment. He led me, even as I was telling him what had happened, to a small white house. "You know, Don Pedro," he said, "perhaps I shouldn't say it so bluntly, but it's really better that Abu Amru is dead. He was a good man, and God will take up his soul. On this earth he faced nothing but a great suffering and a painful death. It would have been very bad if he had been forced to condemn Master Agrippa. They may burn his corpse now. These black vultures even go so far as to disinter the dead from their graves. But he can't feel the heat of the flames, and may even look at the whole affair from the beyond as an amusing spectacle. So far as Sobeya is concerned, I'll have to tell her Abu Amru's instructions and start moving as quickly as I can."

We entered the house. Before the open fire, over which many pots were suspended by sooted chains, two women were seated. One had gray hair and a very finely cut nose. She looked so much like Diego that at once I knew it was his mother. The other woman was dressed like an Andalusian peasant girl in a billowing red dress and a white, gaily decorated blouse. Over her black hair was a red and black cloth. I looked at her. "Doña Sobeya," I cried in quick recognition.

We embraced warmly. Diego threw a quick glance at his mother.

The aging woman took my hand in hers and said, "My dear Don Pedro—if you will permit this familiarity—you must be dead tired. I've made a bed for you in Diego's room."

I thanked her, and without any more words she showed me to my resting place. I noticed that she limped. Upstairs in the attic she opened a door and showed me a small room with whitewashed walls.

"Things are bad these days," she told me, as she busied herself with the bed covers. "I've seen times like these before. I remember Tomás de Torquemada when he first began his killings in Seville and Cordova, and later continued in Valladolid, Toledo and Saragossa. It was just the same then as now. Whoever got trapped in Triana . . . well, that was the signal to begin saying the Mass of the Dead. Poor Sobeya! But you'll be all right here in Casa Blanca. The abbess is a friend of reason and has already helped many learned men and artists when the Dominicans began to reach out to seize them. You can sleep easily tonight." She nodded to me, and left the room.

I threw myself on the bed and in a few seconds was sound asleep. When I woke, the rain had stopped altogether, my cold had left me, but the gray clouds still scudded across the sky. Across from the house lay the wide, low buildings of the cloister. It was a very peaceful landscape. The air smelled strongly of cow dung and freshly plowed earth. Mules grazed in the green fields, at the moment still dark and lush with rain. The busy sound of hammers came from the workshops. Up the lane which the morning before Diego and I had traversed on our way to the house toiled a cart drawn by two dirty white oxen.

But strangely enough, despite the peace and the fruitfulness of the earth round about, there was no calm within me. I still had the smell of the Sevillian suburb strong in my nostrils. The short distance I had come did not suffice to drive it away. As the evening came to veil the earth in low gray shrouds of mist, I heard crows cawing in the fields. I threw myself on my knees before my couch and tried to compose my thoughts in God. But always before my eyes stood Antonio de Guevara, barring the way. Horrible as it may sound, I could not banish his monstrous presence from my mind.

As I knelt there the door opened, Diego walked in, and started to withdraw when he saw I was at prayer, but I bade him remain.

"Everything has been decided on," he said. "Doña Sobeya is going to leave as soon as I can find a passage for her. Tonight I am going to

Cordova. We'll have to act quickly before we're trapped in the net. It's taking in more of Spain every day."

"Take me with you," I said. "You've got to. I don't want to stay here all by myself."

"Are you as badly hit as that?" asked Diego. "Is the spirit of Abu-el-Harith broken already?"

"I don't believe in God any more," I said grimly. "When I think I hear his voice as I used to in the old days, to me it sounds like the voice of the serpent."

"I don't understand that," said Diego, and shook his head in slow disbelief. "What did they do to you there in Triana, anyway?"

"Not much," I admitted. "Really nothing at all. But they taught me a good deal about the ways of the world." And from out of nowhere a deep anger overcame me, uncontrollable anger. I rushed to the window and brandished my fist in the direction of the Triana which lay somewhere in the distance, beyond the mist shrouds.

"God is dead," I shouted wildly. "He died of His wounds, long, long ago. It's so long ago the smell of His poor corpse is forgotten! But go on singing *Te Deums* and *Glorias in Excelsis!* The Holy Inquisition is taking His place. Everything's going to be wonderful on earth, my Diego; everything will be fine and peaceful. People will go about kissing one another. We'll all die of boredom, it will be so calm. If there are enough of us left . . ."

"Don't shout like that," said Diego.

"Diego," I said, in a transport of despair, "the end of the world can't be far off. It must come. I've looked on Antichrist with my own eyes. He wore a Dominican's habit and blessed me. Since I faced him, I know he's stronger than Christ, who is dead."

"Get hold of yourself," cut in Diego, coldly, taking me by the arm. "Are you forgetting you have knightly blood in your veins? Are you letting a ghost become your master!"

"A ghost!" I said. "It's real enough, what I saw. It's so strong a part of this racking of bodies, breaking of bones, blinding of eyes and burning alive that there's nothing ghostly about it. For think you: all the hateful murmuring, the base informing, lying evidence, this Kingdom of God and earthly paradise—the whole thing presses on my heart. I just can't stand aside any more and wail: Brother, this is too bad indeed, but what has it got to do with me? I tell you, Diego, it came over me last night when Bernal and I were crawling along the wall of Triana. It struck home. I thought I should bleed slowly to death from it. That filthy place with its lepers, murderers, beggars, gypsies and whores is alive within me. And in the very center in the Moorish fortress, the prison. It's the Golgotha of Spain."

"Listen, Don Pedro," said Diego, turning the issue. "I know well enough what you mean. All you say is true in a way. And in another it's not. In any case, there's not much point in your sitting here and grumbling about it. I'll take you with me to Malaga when Sobeya leaves."

He took his leave of me, and went out.

From now on I lived all the time in the little white room. Day after day I waited anxiously for Diego's return. Sobeya was even more depressed than I. Hours on end she sat before the fire and looked into the glimmering coals. Now and then she would nod to herself, as if to be reassured that her uncle really was dead and gone. When with some hesitancy I began to talk to her, she cried softly, and bowed her face in her hands. And then I would get up quickly, leave the room and go outdoors.

I saw the plowman treading slowly in the furrow turned over by his span of oxen. I saw the peasants with harrow and spade, the women in the lemon and orange groves, and the children who tended the sheep and cattle of the cloister. I smelled the damp earth, breathed in the mist from the river, and now and then caressed the rough bark of a tree trunk. After this I would feel somewhat consoled. The thought often came to me that the peasant's life is the only one, a life close to the earth and its creatures. I regretted that more men could not spend their time toiling on the land, caring for tree and plant, nurturing the beasts of the field. It was at that time I learned first how dangerous it is to lose touch with the soil. The opening words of a poem I knew would run through my mind, "Legends, now from the earth uprooted . . ."

The unnatural legend of which the poet spoke seemed to me to be the Inquisition in Triana. Everything that Antonio de Guevara had told me seemed worlds away. Finally my longing became so intense that I begged the plowman to instruct me in his art. He agreed, smiling, and I took the handle of the plow in my right hand, the rude rope reins in my left. The furrows which I made in the fat earth were uneven, shallow and very crooked. The sweat ran from my forehead. Yet after a time things went better, for my patient teacher persisted in showing me how to handle the heavy tool and how to force the sluggish oxen to do my bidding. Soon the clods rose up smooth and shining on the side of the share, fell over to one side in pleasing order, steaming gently in the damp air. When the vesper bells rang out at the cloister the peasant and I kneeled together on the heavy earth, folded our hands, and softly said our Hail Marys.

Once in a while I would go into the cloister chapel. It was a very simple place, quite lacking in any kind of impressive ornament. The light of day came through the uncolored panes of the small window in the high-ceilinged, arched room, the walls all white with fresh lime. In the middle stood the high altar with the cross, the Lord pinned to its arms, John in a red robe and the Mother of God weeping bitterly.

I would sit down on the steps leading into a tiny side-chapel. The north side of the nave was cut off from the rest of the room by a tall, gilded screen, and through the arabesques, leaves and branches with singing birds I could glimpse the rustling, white veiled figures of the nuns. I heard them talking to each other in whispers, and occasionally they would sing in clear voices.

In the church there were two murals. One of them showed Paradise, with angels playing on harps and flutes, and broad-branched, thick-crowned fairy-tale trees under which the blessed ones wandered hand in hand. The other mural to the left depicted Hell. The wicked in the picture were being boiled and roasted, some spitted on glowing skewers. This made them cry out in soundless anguish, and the yawning jaws of the underworld were sown with snake's teeth, on the barbed points of which sinners had become impaled.

When the nuns sang I felt as if transported into Paradise. I fancied myself strolling with Isabella under those trees which were the trees of life. When everything in the church was silent, especially in the evening when only two candles were burning at the altar, the shadows once more would fall across my soul, and the Hell within me awoke.

One evening when my thoughts were particularly depressed, Diego's mother came into the church. She kneeled down, said her prayers, then came over to my side.

"Don Pedro," she whispered to me, "you mustn't stay by yourself too much."

"I need loneliness," I said awkwardly. "I must think things out, and find my way back to the place that Antonio de Guevara blotted out for me."

For a time she said nothing, and then went on softly, "Once I knew a woman who when she was young got in trouble with the Inquisition. It happened a long time ago, nearly forty-five years to be exact, but the story sticks out clearly in my memory as if it happened only yesterday. At that time in Saragossa—for that was the city where the girl lived in a wealthy home—there were many enlightened and genial people. They called themselves the Friends of Light. They lived more in the Athens of Plato and in the Rome of Scipio than in King Fernando's Saragossa. They preferred the words of Homer, Virgil and Seneca to the Saints'.

"But then the Inquisition came to Saragossa. For a time it raged like a wild beast. The Jews suffered especially from its zeal. Whoever wore clean clothes on Sunday, whoever ate fish and olives out of respect for the dead, read his children's horoscope, or murmured a prayer while slaughtering a calf was considered a Jew to be burned at the stake. His property was confiscated, his family driven into exile. People of substance were particularly suspected, for both King and Church needed money. The Inquisitors did not stop with the Jews. The persecution struck at everyone who believed in freedom and civilian rights. They even went so far as to drag Don Jaime of Navarre, the King's nephew, out of La Seo Cathedral because he was a freethinker.

"But this girl, and it is she I really want to talk about, worked in a noble house in which the sons and daughters had been educated by Italian scholars. They threw the children into a dungeon, and tried to force them into evil deeds. They put the girl's foot in the iron boot and crushed the bones. . . ."

I recalled at this moment that Diego's mother limped, and stole a glance at her foot.

She reddened, drew back her foot, and quickly went on to say, "But finally through the intervention of the Franciscans, who at that time were stronger than the adherents of the Order of Saint Domingo de Guzman, she was allowed to go free. She never forgot this kindness, and became a lay sister of Saint Francis of Assisi, wore the gray robe of the order over her dress. . . ."

I looked at her in astonishment. She smiled to herself, gave up all pretense, and went on, half bemused, "Yes, and for a long time I couldn't get over what they had done to me. It was brute injustice, I told myself. This idea burrowed into my heart. It was like a hidden ulcer. Why does God tolerate this violence, why should innocent people be martyred? Why, above all, does He allow all this to be done in His name? Those were the questions I asked myself. I became very shy and withdrawn. I was ashamed because I limped. For it seemed to me there could be no greater disfigurement than a lame foot. I treated people curtly, was quarrelsome and arrogant. It was small wonder that in the end they began to leave me completely to myself. True, I wore the garments of the Poverello. But in my heart there was only hate and pride. It was hard for anyone to put up with my company. And for me hardest of all."

I nodded my head, my curiosity conquering my embarrassment.

"In the house where I worked every morning there came a young man, a student who instructed the daughters in the Latin tongue. He was a carefree young man with thick brown hair and a hawk nose. There was nothing he liked better than to laugh it seemed. His pupils, their parents and all the servants merely had to see him coming to feel in a good humor. But I could not bear the sight of this young man. I felt that nobody in the world had a right to laugh so loudly or to feel good so much of the time.

"I began to quarrel with him, and torment him as best I could. I asked him stupid questions. I sent him to fetch objects which didn't exist. But he did everything I told him with a good will. The idea came into my head to do him out of his breakfast. It had become the custom of the house when he showed up in the morning—telling jokes in his scratchy voice—to give him a glass of wine, some bread and cheese. He was always very glad to get these scraps. I carried out my scheme. I noticed that the young man was indeed taken aback by the bare table. Now and then he would look at me in amazement. In my heart I felt triumph, a sensation of exquisite power.

"One day I happened to be in the room while he was teaching the girls. As he talked I watched him from one side. I saw his thin neck under the thick hair, the white cheeks and the thin shoulders. I noticed his clothes were worn and often mended. There was a patch on his right elbow, put on so clumsily I knew he must have done it himself. But he was unaware of all these things it seemed, and went on talking brightly, so brightly that I felt a pang in my breast. So severely did my conscience bother me that I dropped the sewing I had in my hands. The air in the room became too warm, unbearable.

"When the lesson was finished and the children had left the place, I went up to him. I told him it was on my account that he had no longer had his breakfast. He nodded understanding wearily, then with a smile said, 'Did it make you feel any better?' He might quite as well have thrust a knife into my breast.

" 'No, no!' I cried. 'It's made things worse. I wanted to ask your forgiveness. But I see now you're making fun of me . . . making fun of me because I limp. When you laugh, you're probably really laughing at me. I've seen you do it. I'd spit in your face, but for . . .'

" 'Why do we make life so miserable for each other?' he said quietly, always watching me. I gripped the back of a chair with my trembling hands as he talked. 'You're right. I'm hungry most of the time. And it's true, too, that your foot has been injured, and that you limp a little.'

" 'Make fun of me!' I shouted at him. 'Go on! Keep it up! Make more jokes!' And then I began to weep with my misery.

" 'I'm only telling facts,' he said sadly. 'I don't see anything amusing if someone is hungry or lame. The only disgraceful thing is to inflate those matters so much out of proportion that they make a clear outlook on the world impossible.'

" 'Well, then,' I said, filled with hatred, 'if you're so wise and understanding, perhaps you can tell me why innocent people suffer and are tortured.'

"He looked at me thoughtfully, and said, 'Suffering may well be a token of distinction. Man cannot always stay as a child; he can't endure in a condition of passive innocence like an animal or a flower. Suffering may mean nothing else than that we have stepped out from a state of ignorance into a larger, more dangerous, possibly far more beautiful world. All pain is the travail of birth.'

" 'And the stupid crippling of my foot? My lameness! Is all that travail?' I insisted.

" 'A new self awaits you, if you only knew it,' he told me sharply. 'You have wrapped yourself in that gray robe like a caterpillar in a cocoon.'

" 'But I'm crippled,' I repeated again and again.

"I tried to force my way back into the familiar despair, in which I had found solace. But try as I might I found the ashen garments no longer suited me. The real despair had disappeared, and now I could only play the game. We looked at each other, the young man and I. Suddenly I began to laugh and cry all at once. I could hardly control myself. He came nearer to me, patted my shoulders, stroked my hair and did what he could to bring me to my senses. He even kissed me. I kissed him back. I called the servants and had them prepare a fine meal, game and fruit, white bread and the best wine. I sat with my elbows on the table and watched him devour the food. I could not help laughing, and at times the tears would spring into my eyes. The servants shook their heads incredulously. I could not help noticing.

"Some weeks later I heard the master and mistress of the house saying, 'If Inez is so much in love with Diego, she ought to marry him. He's a good boy.' And so it actually happened, less than a year later. Our marriage was a very happy one, and you know my son who is more like his father than like me. I blessed my lame foot, and still do, though I confess I'm still a little awkward about others looking at it. After all, because of it a stupid, self-willed girl became a happy woman."

And now as I looked at Diego's mother I saw that she was, indeed, still beautiful. Her white hair was smooth and her forehead clear. It was a kind of beauty more spiritual than physical, even I could see, and so would endure.

She took my hand in hers and said, "Don't stare at that stupid picture of Hell any more, Don Pedro! You're not in Hell. Hell isn't in you, either. You have left childhood behind you. You have lived through your first experience with reality. Because your first opponents were the Inquisition and Antonio Cardinal de Guevara you may be sure that destiny has even greater experiences in store for you. You will overcome the Inquisition and the Cardinal, just as I conquered my crippled foot. You mustn't think our country and these times are especially terrible and godless. Lands and times are always wicked, for men are always wicked. It is the same with you as with my son Diego. You are a part of the times, still fettered to their bitter confusion."

"And how shall I become unfettered?" I asked in a murmur.

"Oh, it's quite possible," she said. "My husband used to say that man becomes free through creation."

"But not all men are creative," I objected.

"No, you are wrong. All men are creative, all without exception. It's only that most of them are afraid and hesitate to face what lies hidden within."

This conversation comforted me and I often turned it over in my mind, wondering whether the conquering of a kingdom was also a creative act. But before my eyes moved the heroes of the past, and I dreamed again of Amadís and Tancred, of King Arthur, of the magician Merlin and the iron-shod knights, Lancelot and Galahad. The greatest of all of them still seemed to me to be Parsifal. Trudging slowly behind my plow I envisioned Montserrat and the Holy Grail.

I was jolted out of these day-dreams by the arrival of Diego. With him came Bernal and Frenero, and my good Sancho with them. When Sancho saw me he burst into tears. "Oh, Don Pedro! Terrible things have happened to us. Father Pablo and his men have seized your house in the Street of the Leather Merchants. The Inquisition has taken all your land. We're as poor as church mice now. Teresa and I were thrown out of the house overnight without a word of warning. I made bold to save your helmet, sword and woolen mantle. Your father's heritage! Teresa saved the ass Pia, and I rode her here to see you. Teresa went to Trujillo, where a brother of hers owns a little farm. But for myself, I've made up my mind to stick with you wherever you go. It was hard enough to leave Teresa. And now here we are, scattered all over God's wide earth, with nothing between us and beggary but Pia, an aged ass."

I threw my arms around Sancho and gave him what solace I could. "My good Sancho," I told him, "the time has come when I'm going to take up my career in earnest. First of all we must escort Doña Sobeya to the coast. After that's done, we'll board ship ourselves and sail out into the setting sun to conquer a kingdom in the Indies." Such were my swollen words.

Sancho looked at me in perplexity and said, "But, Don Pedro! We'll need plenty of money to do all that. We can't go without something to eat. The ship's captain certainly won't take us unless we can pay our passage."

"Indeed, you're quite right, Sancho," I admitted. "I'll have to give the matter some thought."

And true enough, at the beginning the solution of these practical riddles puzzled me not a little. Then I recalled how the heroes of the ballads lived on their long journeys. "We might live on wild fruits, berries and roots if the worst came to the worst," I told Sancho.

"That's pretty scanty fodder," Sancho pointed out. "Why, it would hardly hold body and soul together. But I've saved a few gold pieces which will take us to Malaga and back to Cordova."

A few days later our little caravan drew out of the Casa Blanca. Doña Sobeya rode on a mule that we borrowed from the cloister. Another mule and small Pia were loaded with what we had managed to rescue of her property. Diego and I, Bernal, Frenero and Sancho proceeded on foot. Doña Sobeya continued to wear the costume of an Andalusian peasant girl. The rest of us put on broad-brimmed hats with leather thongs passing under the chin, and long cloaks. Diego had the foresight to pack onions on the top of the sack containing Sobeya's worldly goods. In face we appeared like a troop of country people on the way to the marketplace.

Every day we made short marches, and at night found shelter in some obscure courtyard. All the time the weather stayed cool and cloudy. The roads were deserted. Diego and Sobeya were both very silent. Frenero and Bernal were also down in the mouth, for running away little accorded with their sanguine temperaments. And so the lot of us moved forward, each enveloped in his own cloud of dismal prospects.

Often we passed through abandoned villages in which many of the empty peasant homes yawned wide to the elements. The fields had gone to seed, the olive and wine-gardens were untended. On the steep mountain slopes now and then we saw great flocks of sheep grazing quietly. Otherwise the landscape was barren and lifeless as if all God's creatures had perished in some frightful plague. This was the land King Fernando of Aragon had conquered some forty years ago. Many of its people had been sold into slavery; others had fled to Africa. What was left of the Moorish population had now taken flight before the Inquisition, or lived a life of terror in lonely crofts or high up in the mountains. The land looked as if it had been visited by a curse. It seemed incredible that we were moving through what once had been one of the richest and happiest regions of Spain.

On the sixth day of our journey, quite without untoward incident, we reached the sea coast some miles to the east of Malaga. We made camp on a little-frequented inlet. A warm wind blew from the east; the weather was tending to clear. When evening came we built a fire, wrapped ourselves in our cloaks and tried to sleep.

Doña Sobeya and Diego talked to each other in undertones, but I could not help but overhear, since I was stretched out so close by.

Sobeya said, "I shall never go to Yemen. That would mean we'd be separated forever. I'm going to stay in Fez with my uncle's friend and wait there until you come for me."

"If I didn't have to stay here without a maravedi, I'd have found a way for us before now."

"The jewels! Don't forget that half of them are yours," Sobeya reminded him.

"No, I don't want them," said Diego. "You may find yourself without anything as it is. What a pity that our bodies aren't made of some finer substance, which wouldn't be subject to hunger, thirst, heat and cold at every turn. Curse the luck!"

"Sh-sh!" Sobeya cautioned him. "Speak quietly and don't let your temper ride you. Some time you'll have money enough. And just now let's look up at the stars. We can listen to the sound of the sea and the wind. The night is beautiful. And that's something we have, at least."

They both said no more. I, too, opened my eyes. The skies were sprinkled with golden sparks; the warm east wind was salty on my lips, rich with the smell of the sea. On it was borne, I imagined, the perfume of strange lands, of the far-off Nile, of the oases and palms of the East, of the unbounded deserts and white cities.

Diego spoke again. "When this trouble has blown over, Sobeya, I'll write to you. Perhaps we'll find a new home in Portugal, or France maybe, or in the Netherlands."

Then the night closed in on us, the rush of the wind and the sea. My tired eyes blinked as I stared into the fire, which crackled softly, sometimes showering sparks. I fell asleep.

As morning neared and I awoke, a light mist shut us in. We brought Sobeya's belongings to the beach. It had become cool, so chill that it made us shiver. The rolling bank of fog floated around us in clinging wisps, and more than once I thought I saw a sail moving in close to shore. But every time it was only blurred misty shapes, constantly balling into grotesque forms that vanished without a trace. The appointed hour had already passed by some considerable time when, as if by magic, a galley loomed up in the gray murk. The lateen sail hanging lifeless and wet against the mast, was dropped without a sound. A boat was lowered over the side and was quickly rowed to the spot where we stood on the beach. The hour of parting had come.

The oarsmen had red kerchiefs wrapped about their heads. Cutlasses were stuck in their broad leathern belts. They had round beards, and their skin was very swart. Their leader greeted Sobeya with deference, paid almost no attention to us, and scarcely nodded his head to Diego. I felt plainly that he had nothing but hate for our whole breed.

When everything had been put aboard the pinnace and Sobeya had taken sad leave of us, the leader of the boatsmen said, "We thank the Christians for saving this virgin of the house of Jad. I have been commissioned by the elder of her line to parcel out the ransom money."

Frenero began to mutter and look black. But Diego smoothed matters over by saying, "We are men of honor, not jailers. Divide the money up among your own men, as a favor to Doña Sobeya and us."

At this Frenero made a wry face, for all his earlier touchiness. The leader of the Moors bowed deeply before Diego and said in a different tune, "I regret my error. I see in truth that I am dealing with a knight whose presence would do honor to the court of our Caliph, the Sultan Bjadiz."

The seamen laughed among themselves at this ceremony and nodded to each other. Only Doña Sobeya, sitting forlorn in the stern sheets, was openly moved by the leave-taking. Huddled in a heap, she cried into her handkerchief. Tears came into my own eyes but I felt it unmanly to wipe them away, and so stared hard after the pinnace as it disappeared into the drifting fog like a shapeless ghost.

We caught sight of the pinnace again as it drew alongside the galley. The sail was hoisted, billowed out in a breath of land breeze, a little white foam hissed under the bow, and the vessel came halfway about as the sail flapped again. On her mast we could make out a long pennon with a silver half-moon. The vessel disappeared, heading into the thinning mists to the southwest.

The sea lapped idly about our feet. We turned away in silence, returned to our camp. It was amazing how bare everything seemed, of a sudden—the half-extinguished fire, the copper kettle with soot-blackened bottom and sides, the empty sacks and scattered heaps of onions.

Diego and I together rode the mule, while Sancho led Pia by her halter. In this fashion we retraced our footsteps to Casa Blanca. The third night of the return trip we passed in a deserted barn. Scarcely had we settled ourselves as comfortably as we could on the straw-covered floor of one of the stalls when we felt the earth shake with the weight of horses' hoofs. We blew out our light. Nearer and nearer drew the sound of cantering horses, and we could hear men shout to one another. To our dismay they came directly to the barn and began to rattle the door which Frenero had had the good sense to bar. After a while they gave up their banging and pounding and moved on to the main building, which was pretty much in ruins. We took counsel. Finally Frenero offered to steal over and investigate the strangers. In this mountainous country it paid to exercise every caution, we all agreed.

It was not long before he was back. He said the travelers were a Dominican, two merchants and two armed men. The merchants had some wares with them, Frenero said. And the Dominican, to whom the two guards were attached, had a heavy chest reinforced with iron. Even now he was sitting on it as he ate his supper.

Diego, Frenero and Bernal whispered together, and at last told Sancho and me that the opportunity had come to better our impoverished lot. I asked him how we were going to go about it. He informed me that by some sheer stroke of luck the very people had fallen into our hands who could get us out of our misery; that it would assuredly never happen again. In short, he had decided to rob the travelers.

Sancho and I, completely taken aback by this violent decision, stood to one side and told Diego we could never consent to have part in any such maneuver. Diego shrugged his shoulders, and said, "My dear boy, it's a question of our lives now. Shall we go abegging, as long as we have weapons in our hands? Do you really prefer to starve to death?"

In disgust he turned his back to me and followed Frenero and Bernal out of the barn into the night.

Sancho and I sat in the straw, our faces drawn tight with fear. We strained our ears to listen. There was nothing to hear—only the wind moaning softly through the cracks.

After what seemed to me to be a very long time Diego came in and whispered to follow him. "Come with me," he said. "You can't miss this. It appears we've picked out a very choice offering indeed."

"I'll never change my opinion of this business," I warned him.

"Listen anyway," he ordered me roughly.

The door of the barn opened without a creak, and on tiptoe we crept over to the larger building. Hugging the wall close I peeked in through the small window.

The travelers had made a fire on the hearth and the flame of the burning log cast a red, flickering light on their faces. The two merchants and the monk were deep in conversation. Both the armed men were stretched out on the floor, apparently fast asleep.

"Listen to what they're saying," whispered Diego.

One of the merchants was boasting. "In Canterbury we have the biggest collection of relics in the world. Haven't you ever heard of it?"

"No, I must say I never have," replied the monk sourly. "But I have heard that there are more heretics in England than in Turkey, ever since this Wycliffe interfered with the priests."

"Why, what do you mean!" said the second merchant. "Wycliffe was a pious man."

But the first merchant forced him out of the discussion, and, returning to his subject, went on, "In Canterbury we have some tatters from Christ's shift, three thorns from the Crown, a lock of the Virgin's hair, one of John the Baptist's back teeth, a flask filled with the blood of John the Evangelist, a finger of Saint Stephen the Martyr, the hair of Mary Magdalen, Thomas à Becket's head, the bowels of Saint Lauritius, the bones of Saint Clement and the right leg of the Virgin Recordia. I don't believe that anywhere in the world, perhaps with the exception of Rome, you'll find such a heartwarming collection of precious objects."

"Those are just trifles," said the monk haughtily. "Why, in one city, in Saragossa, we have two miracle-working statues. The statue of the Virgin Mary in La Seo Cathedral, you know, talks every once in a while. Now and then the statue of the Blessed Virgin which stands over the door there steps down and walks around. But even these miracles are nothing compared with those wrought by the Blessed Virgin of Guadalupe. Occasionally she restores unclaimed bodies to new life. Or what about those wrought by Saint James in Santiago, our Lord's brother, who often appears to us Spaniards in the heat of battle, high above the clouds, and leads our side to victory?"

Now the second merchant interposed. "We Englishmen have Saint George the dragon-killer who does the same thing for us."

The monk stretched, yawned, and said, "Well, that may be. But just the same, Spain is the most Christian country of all. Why, anyone can see that the Inquisition has more real power among us than anywhere else. It would be impossible to have a Huss, Wycliffe, Luther, Zwingli, and all those other Devil's henchmen in Spain."

The merchants laughed, and one of them said, "At home where we come from there are no infidels, praying to Allah. We know only Christians."

This observation seemed to irritate the monk. "In any case," he said sarcastically, "in Spain we don't have a fat redhead on the throne like your wife-murdering Henry. We're blessed with a pious man who keeps his eyes looking straight ahead. And as for the Moors—we'll soon dispose of them."

"How will you do that?" asked the first merchant. "Even when you've had them baptized, they'll keep right on praying to Allah. You can't look into the Moors' brains, you know, worthy father."

The monk tapped with his forefinger on the ironbound chest on which he sat. "In this chest there are enough documents and depositions to bring hundreds of Moors to the stake, not to mention many costly rings and ornaments on the way to Seville, whence they will be sent to Brussels."

Diego pulled me away from the window, muttered in my ear, "Did you hear that, Don Pedro? Have your honest ears heard that black pig say that in his box he's carrying complaints, libels and false testimony? What does your conscience have to say now?"

"I'm with you," I said, "if you'll only spare the merchants and the guards . . ."

"Of course," said Diego, "I wouldn't harm a hair of their heads. After all, we aren't cut-throats. I'll have to speak to Frenero first. He's inclined to be a little hasty."

"Well, do that," I said. "But I wouldn't like to see the monk injured, either, for that matter."

"He won't be. But I can't say as much for his chest," Diego laughed gently.

In a low curt voice, Diego gave his orders to the men. We saddled our mules and Pia, and decided to take the strangers' mounts along with us. When we opened the door to the house we saw that the company had all fallen asleep. We fell on them, bound their hands and feet, and drew empty sacks over their heads. They offered little resistance. Both the merchants cried out in their own language for mercy, and the priest called down on us God's curse. Disregarding his clamor we took the key to the chest out of his pocket. We threw all the documents into the fire, and there they blazed away brightly. The rings, which the monk had greatly overvalued, we divided among ourselves. We also split up equally among us the gold pieces in the monk's pouch. We did not touch either the merchants' belongings or their purses. The whole affair was carried off with great expedition.

When we were ready to leave Diego made a parting speech. "Worthy father, honorable merchants, and brave guards! It makes us desperately unhappy to disturb your sleep in this precipitate fashion. I'm sure, quite sure indeed, that you know the cramps of hunger, the pangs of thirst, the abject misery of cold. It's because of all that, really, that we are taking the rings and the gold of this servant of God, for it's for just such eleemosynary wretches as we that these treasures are devised. Don't think harshly of us when we've gone. In retrospect, when deep in prayer, dwell lovingly upon this humble assembly of God's birds. The papers which filled your chest we threw into the fire to thaw out our frosted marrow. For you must admit that the night is chill. We're going to take your mules and horses along with us for a way, for, as we look at it, it will improve your health to exercise your legs a little after lying there bound so long."

From under his sack the priest said in a muffled voice, "Holy Santiago! Thou, above the clouds, visit Thy wrath upon these misbegotten rabble. Let them be boiled in oil, let them fry eternally in Hell's fire. Amen!"

"Shall I pluck out his tripes?" Frenero shouted, beside himself at this celestial challenge, and slipping his long knife out of its sheath.

"No," said Diego.

"Priest-killer!" roared the monk hollowly. "Help, help!"

"He's going to curse us some more," said one-eyed Bernal, with considerable anxiety. "I'm going to kill him. I'll feel better when his mouth's stopped."

"My friend, sweet friend!" said the monk with alacrity, his hands fumbling piteously at the strings which bound the sack about his throat. "Whoever you may be, save me from these murderers. What you found in the chest isn't my property anyway. It belongs to the Inquisition."

"You see," said Diego, "if you only behave properly nothing will happen to you. But if you persist in cursing us and showering disaster on our heads . . ."

"Hold on, just a minute!" choked out the monk. "Dear Santiago! Use some discretion. Just forget what I was saying a minute ago. Protect these brave fellows who've taken nothing from me, a poor monk. They've merely relieved a very rich man of some of his pelf. Grant them a long and happy life!"

"Well, now, that's better," said Frenero, mollified. "I think you like us after all, worthy father!"

"Yes, yes, I do!" The voice was getting weaker within the sack.

"Are you sure?" Bernal asked.

"Yes, yes, I'm sure, I'm sure! May the Holy Santiago bless you all, my beloved sons!" The monk had begun to whimper.

"Well, I suppose we can let him live now," growled Bernal, while Frenero nodded grave assent.

We went out into the yard, swung into our saddles and rode off at a trot. I was rather depressed, and Sancho hung his head over the saddle-horn in shame.

"I never thought that a knight would start this way," I said to Diego.

"It all depends how you look at it," said Diego, laughing shortly. "In our fancy everything may seem gay enough. It's like looking at a tapestry from Brabant. But reality has more substance. There's a bitter kernel to it. It is edged with mockery. Today you have reinherited a small part of the goods taken from you by the Church. Think of yourself as Saint George! Is not the Inquisition a dragon? You have tickled his shin, my little lion."

"You're not afraid, Diego, of robbing people?" I was miserable.

"Why do you choose such ugly words?" asked Diego, reining his horse closer to me and laying his hand on my arm. Don't you know that everyone glosses over his deeds and misdeeds with fine words? Merchants buy and sell goods to further commerce, not to fill their pockets. Emperors conquer kingdoms to introduce justice, not to sate their ambition. Seamen endure the hardships of stormy weather, never out of greed for gold and fame, but to explore the face of the world. It's always the same song."

"But isn't that living a lie?" I asked, and made Diego groan.

"Ah, my contrary lion," he said, "appearance is still everything, prod me as you will. Thorny truth is not for this world. It cannot flourish. Life itself is but a dream, and a dream is only a lie."

I was mystified and troubled. I thought of Master Agrippa, who once told me he had given his life to the search for truth.

We reached the Casa Blanca de Santa Catalina without further incident. Diego's mother gave us a friendly welcome. We rested one night in the little house with the white walls. Then we boarded a small boat which took us to Cordova, where we arrived as night was falling.

7

A MEETING

IT WAS strange to return to the city of my birth. Although I had been away scarcely a month from Cordova everything looked different. The mighty gray mosque was the same, and the Roman bridge with the three arches, the Square of the Oranges, the Alcazar and all the cloisters, churches and streets. But it all seemed much smaller and shabbier. It was I, of course, who had changed. I no longer belonged in this world. The thin walls of my childhood were shattered as when a bird breaks through its shell.

I felt myself very much alone and forsaken as I wandered through the familiar ways of the city. My aloneness filled me with fear, fear for the future and my place in the world. Indeed I thought of Doña Isabella, but Sancho had told me that Don Garcilaso had followed in the train of Master Agrippa and departed for Brussels. In my confusion I lacked the courage to present myself before my beloved. I feared that she would inquire what had happened to me and how I had lived during my absence from her.

In any event it was dangerous for me to remain for any length of time in Cordova. I dared not show my face during the daytime. For this reason we went into the Potro, where the Fat Pascuala was situated. The Potro of Cordova was like Triana, the suburb of Seville. The only difference was that the Potro quarter was much less extensive, and it did not have quite so many cut-throats and thieves. Actually it was not nearly such an evil place. And there was no Palace of the Inquisition there.

But there was the Fat Pascuala. This large building dated back to the days of the Knights Templar. When the order was driven underground throughout all Europe and many of its adherents killed by fire and sword, the castlelike structure, with its high Gothic windows and pillars before the door, had been abandoned. Nobody wanted to inhabit it, for the saying went the rounds that the ghosts of the murdered Templars, wrapped in their blood-soaked garments, wandered through the many rooms. But finally the city, which owned the property, had managed to rent it to a man who made it over into a hostelry for the poor. The wife of this innkeeper, a certain Pascuala, was a very corpulent woman who, after a lusty and none too savory youth, had grown into a sly, thievish yet kindhearted hostess. The inn was called after her by all who frequented it though its real name was "At the Sign of the Three Rings." These three rings were plain for all to see on a blue shield which hung over the door.

On the day of our arrival there was a meeting of the Germania in the big hall. Sancho and I took no part in this gathering of Cordova's lost men and women. All real members of the band had brushed at least once with the law of the land. We waited in our room for Diego to come back.

The session lasted for quite a time and was very noisy. Diego's forehead was covered with sweat when he came back to the room. He looked very tired, his sharp nose thrust forward, creases about his mouth I had never noticed before. He sat down on a stool and breathed deeply. In time he gathered himself together.

"The filthy cattle thought up a masterpiece today," he said at last, with much laughter, bitter and overwrought. "I'm their king no longer. In truth, I'm not even a full-fledged brother any more. They've been discussing the matter among themselves. They've decided I must be banned."

"Banned! Why should they do that?" I asked. And, secretly, I was glad.

"They say they aren't able to carry it off if they get mixed up with the Holy Inquisition. As it is the Inquisition gives many of them a good living as armed guards and familiars. The Church has taken good care to protect herself against secular authority. And, I must admit, even if the Church isn't particularly discriminating in many respects, at least she has a sense of honor. Spaniards always get first call. It's considered unworthy by these pure Spanish cut-throats of ours to do anything against people who want to rid Spain of its Moorish bloodsuckers. And furthermore, it would be too dangerous to flout the Church. Her hand is everywhere, everywhere you can think of. It's an old law of the Germania, you know, never to rob holy places and churches. At the most they'll grab a potbellied cleric. Very gently, of course, if the risk of discovery isn't too great.

"And I, the king, was foolish enough to set myself up against precedent! In the first place I freed a prisoner of the Inquisition from Triana. In the second, I waylaid a monk who was carrying important papers and other Church property. And, worst of all, I forced this monk on the pain of death to bless my companions and me. They consider that to be on a par with desecration, like having a good laugh at the Sacraments. There was a terrible quarrel about the whole matter. It almost ended in bloodletting. But anyway, adding it all up, it finished with the withdrawal of Frenero, Bernal and me from the Guild. We were thrown out, to tell the God's truth. And so you see me once again as a wandering student out of his time."

"What Sobeya wanted to happen has happened, after all," I reminded him.

"Yes, yes, have your way," he said wearily. "My crown has gone to Hell in a leathern bucket down a well. Of course, my mealymouthed lion, you are aware what that means. It means an empty belly. It means no more Malaga, no more meat. And all the rest."

"Well, after all," I said, "we're all in the same fix."

"Wipe the mother's milk off your face, boy," said Diego, in irritation. "Does it make it any better that five men go hungry instead of one!"

"But we aren't pinned down here," I objected, and in my eagerness to restore his self-confidence began to walk up and down. "The world is big enough for five of us. We'll go somewhere else and find a new life."

"I know where we'll land," said Diego. "We'll land on the gallows. There are enough of them in Spain to take care of the lot of us, I can tell you that."

"Don't you think, Diego," Sancho said timidly, "it would be the most sensible thing to go to Trujillo. At least we have a crust of bread there. Teresa . . ."

"Trujillo! Don't be a fool," said Diego. "The day has yet to dawn when I'll rot away my days in an Estremaduran village. There's the whole world to choose from. Our lion has the right idea."

As we were talking the door swung open and in walked Bernal and

Frenero. Frenero looked ironically at Diego. His pocked face was alight with pleasure. "I've just heard a good piece of news," he said in his deep voice. "Tomorrow morning a group of merchants leave for Toledo. They haven't been able to get themselves any guards. We could trap them on the Sierra. They say they've got some expensive goods along with them."

Bernal nodded approval solemnly. "God himself has sent them into our hands," he said piously. "Why, the fools have asked us to sit on the coach box and protect them!"

Sancho looked at me apprehensively and I cleared my throat to protest, but before I could get out a word Diego said, "You're going to have your wish fulfilled, Don Pedro. We'll travel toward Toledo and take a look at the wide world."

And we actually left the following night by the city gate. I sat next to the driver of the first wagon, bundled up in my father's woolen mantle, with his sword banging between my knees. Diego was on the second wagon, Sancho on the third, and Bernal and Frenero brought up the van of the column. They rode on rickety old nags reluctantly provided by our charges.

It was a clear, cool night. All the stars were out. The wheels creaked heavily, the axles squeaked in time. I sat on the high seat and dreamed away the hours. It was not long before the moon came out. From my high seat I could get a good view of the treeless waste of the landscape. Now and then I caught sight of a campfire in the distance, where some shepherd or goatherd was sleeping for the night. Once in a while there was the light of an isolated house far below in the valley. Before me there were the rhythmically nodding heads of the four horses as they labored forward, steam rising from their sweating bodies. The air was strong with the acrid smell of the stable. I huddled deeper in my mantle and gripped the pommel of my sword. I felt I was keeping the first watch of my knighthood.

Sometimes the cliffs would suddenly glitter as they caught the moonlight. Or a storm-stripped tree would suddenly loom against the lighter sky, like a wild spirit with crooked outstretched arms. At times the road would drop through deep canyons and again it would rise sharply upward. An air of expectation seemed to hang over mountain and valley. The world had never seemed so enormous to me before.

One of the merchants rode up to my wagon on his mule and offered me a drink of wine from his flask. I thanked him and took a draught. It ran like fire through my young veins.

O great and wonderful night! So sang my heart, and I was glad. There was really nothing to justify my exaltation. But I have often found that joy or sadness arises without visible cause, that as if in some earthquake of the soul new layers of my being become exposed while old ones disappear from view. Perhaps it is the unseen powers who occasion these moods, and the spirits and angels which are all about us put their light hands on the shoulders of the quick.

So it was with me this moonlit night on the wagon seat. A powerful joy carried me along, and within I cried aloud in delight, and answered all life's challenges with a bold affirmation. The groaning of the heavy wheels, the clear impact of the iron hoofs on the stony road, the screeching of the brakes—all this was sweet music to my ears. The irregular swaying of the laden wagon lulled me and freed my thoughts. Like the vision of a saint, all Spain was clear before my eyes. Beautiful and boldly limned, the moonlit country spread into infinite distance. Even the gentle moonlight could not soften the jagged insolence of the peaks against the sky, nor the sheer drop of rocky cliff face. It was then that I first began to see that we Spaniards can never be as other people. Our very landscape, the earth on which we are bred, is austere and fashioned in extremes. This is also true of us. We do not understand half-measures. We must pray either to God or to the Devil. We must die in violence, or be consumed in love.

On this night for the first time I realized that in some fashion not easy to explain, I must confront eternity and sustain it—or perish.

Again—though it is laboring the matter—I repeat that nothing extraordinary happened to justify this apotheosis. That is the strangest part. In life there are catastrophic events. Kings fall, battlefields are covered with thousands of dead, great cities disappear in flame, destroying the work of generations. And yet our hearts may very well live through all this without being touched. Often such magnitude of occurrence seems like a play, something to be stared at, not lived in. But then comes a summer morning, we see mist over a valley, a horse looks at us with the white in his eye twisted large. Or we see a girl in the distance, looking out over the sea, or we smell fire in the brown autumn, or we watch the moonlight on the Sierra. Then we know ourselves, feel whatever meaning is in us.

Indeed on that night it was my turn to take stock of myself. Too long, I saw in a flash, had I been dependent on Sancho and Diego, yes, even on Bernal and Frenero. Enough of that, I thought. After all, was I not a Sforza, even though only seventeen years old? Did I not hold in my hands my father's sword, the sword of a man who had conquered the Moors, and was not his soft soldier's mantle of wool warming my narrow shoulders?

Toward morning we arrived at a small farm. The mules and horses were unharnessed and led into the stalls. Since I had not closed my eyes once during the night, I was overwrought. I went to the spring and freshened my face. A brightly feathered cock was perched atop the dung heap, and below his flock of hens scratched busily for their morning meal. A high wall made of field stone separated the orchard from the barnyard. My friends winked at me to come with them, and I went with them behind the wall amid the fruit trees, while the merchants and their servants sought rest on beds of straw in the stalls.

"About an hour more to wait, Don Pedro, my noble friend," said Diego, yawning. "Then, with the aid of Morpheus we'll empty the pockets of these solemn fellows and take whatever we need of their goods."

"No," I said, "the time has come right now to decide whether we're going to live as vagabonds or as knights."

"Hercules at the crossroads," said Diego, still yawning.

"So far as Sancho and I go," I went on, "we've made up our minds. We'll never allow people who trust us to be robbed."

"You think so!" said Frenero, and began to finger his dagger. "My crop is getting pretty well filled with your old-woman's saws, greenguts." He looked significantly at Bernal.

Diego shrugged his shoulders. "Don't forget, little lion," he said to me, "we've simply got to live. And I don't know why God ever created merchants if not to take care of us in our need."

"We'll live all right without them," I persisted. "We'll live somehow."

"You talk like a girl," he said, irritated into contempt as in retrospect I can well understand, for I was an overweening fool at times in my callowness. "You might be Doña Sobeya herself."

His words stung me, and I looked into his eyes. He stared back at me coldly, but at last his glance fell in shame. A mere slip of his tongue had won the day for me, the mention of Sobeya.

"We'll call it off, then," he said sadly.

But at this moment Frenero sprang between us, very evidently not so susceptible to the pressure of sentiment as the poet Diego. Drawing back and half remembering all my knightly instruction from Sancho, I drew my father's sword from its scabbard. But it would have been all up for me if Frenero in his eagerness had not stubbed over the root of a tree and landed right at my feet. I took the opportunity, not without much inner concern, to place the point of my sword below his Adam's apple.

Speaking very carefully, in order not to provoke my nervous hand, Frenero said, "Mercy, mercy, Don Pedro! I swear to be your slave. Don't push that sword any farther."

In the meantime Sancho, also very much beside himself, was telling me to shove the sword through his throat and have it over with once and for all.

I drew away my sword, and Frenero got to his feet shamefaced.

"Let's stop this quarreling, all of us," said Diego sharply, taking charge of the situation. "We're forgetting that neither the Inquisition nor the Guild protects us any more. We're outlaws, the pack of us. Perhaps Pedro is right, whether he knows it or not. We'll suck the hammer for a while."

"That's all right with me," agreed Bernal, and added, laughing aloud, "But don't forget that this young strawfoot here is a Spanish nobleman. He's supposed to take care of his faithful servants before he stuffs his own belly. What's he going to do for us?"

By now I had lost all my zeal for combat and indeed was white and trembling with fatigue. "You're right, Bernal," said Diego. "It looks as if he were going to pose us some fine riddles before he's through, this noble colleague of ours. I shouldn't be surprised if our bones bleached in some far-off land before he's through with us."

"That's all the same to me," said Bernal, in a better humor. "I'm not looking for any long life, but a merry one while it lasts. To tell the truth I'd like to get on the right side of the Inquisition again. I can still hear those curses in my ears. I still think we should have cut his fat throat. Up to that moment I was on the best of terms with the Blessed Virgin."

And so, through my intervention, they abandoned the scheme of filching money and goods from the merchants. Instead we accompanied them, as we had contracted, to Toledo, and so for the first time in my life I visited this high city. A storm was coming up as we creaked our slow way over the bridge which spans the Tagus. The gray walls of the city rose up before us, sharply vertical against a lead-gray sky. There was lightning flashing in the somber distance. My spirits had rallied again, calmed by the splendid sight, it may have been, of man's work against the works of God.

In the Toledo inn we found another caravan of merchants about to start on their way to Valladolid. We offered our services, which were gratefully accepted. Our company could not speak highly enough of our loyalty and watchfulness.

And so in a like manner we came to Valladolid. We examined the marketplace, peopled by a teeming throng. We wandered through the Great Square, where our King Don Carlos once gave a glittering tournament before the insurrection of the burghers drove him out of the city. But sad to say, our worldly fortunes continued to be unsatisfactory, for no sooner had Diego, Frenero and Bernal been paid off than they gambled away their substance. I noticed immediately that the dry air of this city did my friends much good. So spirited did they become that the whole day was spent in bibbing, throwing dice and coursing with women. It was plain that if they remained indefinitely at stud their backs would be broken and their eyes lost in the sockets. Secretly, then, I planned to lead them out of the wilderness, like another Moses. And even more secretly I hoped to find other adventures of a more knightly variety in the mountain defiles, such as those spoken of at great length by Amadís de Gaula, Orlando and other knights.

Unfortunately I had chosen the very worst season of the year for such an undertaking. To my sorrow I was soon to learn that northern Spain in winter makes an altogether different face from my own gentle Andalusia. Our feet in the stirrups lost all feeling, and might have been so many blocks of wood, our noses dripped without surcease onto our upper lips, and our ears became red and as stiff as if made of glass. In time our supplies were dangerously depleted. Our stomachs grumbling, our cheeks miserably hollow, we rode aimlessly on the high plateau, over mountain passes, through scattered snowy woods. Not a single errant knight, fairy or giant did we encounter. This, however, did not shake my stubborn resolve.

Nights we customarily spent with the goatherds, if we came across any, in their sod huts. These places were very warm, but sad to relate, also alive with vermin. The heat made the lice strong as tigers. All night long they busied themselves on our meager flesh, biting furiously and skipping about with incontinent ardor. Because of them we could not sleep soundly, and were forever coming half awake to find ourselves scratching industriously at the most choicely itching spots on our carcasses. I soon knew that these ordeals were the true test of a knight, and wondered why I had never been told the truth in all the books I had read at the behest of my Master. In time, too, our clothes took on the color of the earth. Sancho carefully mended all tears and holes for us as best he could with his clumsy fingers. We looked like men who earned their living cutting brush in a hidalgo's forest.

One day an ice-cold rain began to leak out of the skies. We rode along with our heads bent on our chests, only occasionally troubling to wrack our necks sidewise for a furtive glance to see where we were heading. Nowhere in sight was there a barn, a hut or a sign of fire. Under the slanting rain the great plateau rolled off into misty distance, as hard as an iron plate. Toward evening the rain stopped, but then a stiff breeze sprang up which struck home to our marrow. Our teeth chattered, and the wind whipped tears into our eyes as we stopped to watch the sun, a giant angrily glowing orb of red, as it swiftly plummeted out of sight over the rim of the horizon.

Suddenly, as if in a dream, wonderful colors began to play in the sky not far above the spot on the horizon where the sun had just disappeared.

They trembled and flared so beautifully that we were all bemused into forgetting our evil state. They shimmered in great strata of light, shifting ceaselessly one above the other. At times the colors were fiery reds, like the glow of hot iron. Again they would become a deep orange, like nothing else on earth, then a light, light green, which would suddenly melt into a curious violet, the most exciting of all, the nearest to our inner being, if one can say such things to the inexperienced. For we were contemptuous, perforce, of our weakness of nerve and blood, and this made us free of all those querulous needs that blur ordinary days.

As we watched, the play of color stopped as suddenly as it had commenced. Only one great stripe of pure lightness sprang up from the brooding earth into the mighty sky. We saw this, agape with astonishment.

Whether lightheaded with exhaustion or not I cannot remember, but

I know that I let the reins fall and pointed toward the west. "I can see the West Land," I shouted. "Look! Quick! Look at the mountains. They're covered with snow. Look at the forests!"

"Those are only clouds," Diego said half in impatience, half in sadness. He kneaded his worn face with his hand. "But I did think I saw a smoking chimney, as God stands judge over my soul. We'll not freeze tonight after all."

I was stung into resentment, for what was a smoking chimney to me compared with the West Land. I said in pique and obstinacy, "It's Tenochtitlan that I see, whatever you think. Don't I know! Do you think I'm going to give up Tenochtitlan for a smoking chimney?" This last was nothing less than youthful pride, for then I was still dewy behind my ears and full of quick feeling.

"And I, little mouth," retorted Diego, now cruel and no longer considerate of my fancies, "say that it is a smoking chimney. Wipe the mist from your eyes, noble lion. For me I would give all Cathay and its pearls, all Arabia, all the island kingdoms of the East and West for a hot soup and dry shelter. We must live, my child, we must live. I say it is a chimney. There it is, as sure as if it lay on the palm of my hand."

Again the curious shaft of light shot up into the sky and momentarily illuminated the barren landscape. Our pale wasted faces were white and small in the midst of an insuperable loneliness. When the light was gone the night settled on us like a great tent, still sodden damp with the rain. The wind began to ease off as the hours of darkness crawled along.

"Perhaps it was a sign from heaven," I said hopefully, thinking of what my Master had once told me of such strange affairs.

"Yes, the boy is right," broke in Bernal. "It was a sign from the Blessed Virgin. I saw one once before in Flanders."

We stumbled along in dismal silence, saving our wind. The beasts which carried us were almost as far gone as we ourselves, and we listened to their laboring breath with numb anxiety,for if they collapsed we were done. It was so pitch dark that we sensed rather than saw each other as we rode along. The ground under us grew flatter and the animals got their courage again as the going became easier. We found—or better the beasts discovered—a road, and this we pursued without knowing or much caring where it led. It moved steadily downward at an easy pitch.

"By God, Diego," Frenero said in a low voice, "this time I really see something below us."

We all drew rein and strained our eyes to see. Sure enough, in the valley beneath we saw flickering lights. Or so we imagined, I least of all. I was shaking like a wet dog with the cold, and I could have vomited with misery.

In time it became apparent that what we saw was indeed some kind of fire. It turned out to be torches borne by mounted men. We heard hoofs clattering on the stony road winding up to meet us. A great host of riders wound into view, the fiery glow of the torches lighting up their dark forms. In the midst of them a coach rolled along slowly, swaying with the ruts and holes in the road. At that time, it must be remembered, we did not have many coaches in Spain. All of us knew instantly that it must be some fine lady or nobleman who was traveling with a strong escort. The golden trimmings of the coach glittered now and then in the fiery light as the entourage, a mass of black silhouettes, moved upward in our direction.

With courage born of despair, only half knowing what I was doing, in foolhardiness I moved to meet the first rider and drew my sword. I shouted at him, "In the name of the King and Queen of Spain, who goes there!" as I had heard was always done in such cases.

"Who are you?" the rider bellowed at me in a bass voice. "Who dares to stop peaceful travelers?"

"We want to know the name of your master, and where you're headed for," I retorted like a puppet on a string.

"Get out of the way, beggar," said the rider, as he drew his dagger and gave his horse the knee to set him in motion.

"Shall I do it?" Frenero asked me hoarsely.

But like magic, it seemed, we were surrounded by men, many men, as quickly as in a dream. Servants came up, bearing torches. A deep laugh rose from the mounted soldiers—for such they were—which echoed from the rocky walls hemming in one side of the road. I had forgotten I was sitting on Pia, the little droop-eared ass. She, in her unhappiness, had let her tired head fall between her knobby knees, careless of the dignity of the knight who straddled her. My father's long white mantle, now the color of clay of course, trailed around my legs on the ground, and I was unable to lift the heavy sword above the pommel of the saddle. My cheeks were hollowed out, and my hair was long enough for a girl's, yet matted and filthy.

"Who are you?" the first rider asked, laughing heartily.

"I am Don Pedro de Cordova, a knight of Castile who owns land in Andalusia," I told him in a high voice.

At this they all broke into hearty laughter. "By God, he talks like an actor," the first rider told the others. "Why aren't you sitting on your property in Andalusia, boy? Why are you out so late at night with these bandits? Do you know what you're doing, stopping us?"

"You'll laugh once too often," I shrilled at him. "My honor! I'll break your peasant skull like an eggshell."

"Yah-ee!" shouted the crowd of men, and the first rider, turning half away from me, said, choking with amusement, "By the bowels of Christ, he's a mummer lost in the mountains!"

At this my courage welled up in me, and I felt anger restoring the strength to my arms. I swung my sword behind me, ready to whirl it forward against the lot of them. But out of the riders who pressed on all sides of me, their horses lathered at the bits and tugging to get on out of the chill of the night, a little man came forward. Like me, he was riding an ass. He wore a high pointed cap, and when he moved his head, the bells strung on it tinkled softly. His clothes were gay in the torchlight, all stripes which did not match.

"Now, my young man," he squeaked, "I'm the one here who's the professor of laughter. You're straying into my pasture. I don't see anything funny about this young nobleman. He just wants to know our names. Anyway I wouldn't dare laugh at anyone who carries such a sword as that. Not I, in this cold and windy world. Let's talk to him softly, friends; let's give him a gentle answer. Who can tell what he's got under that cloak of his. Maybe he's the Cid, a Cid from the North where the mountains are covered with snow."

"Noble sir," I told him, "whoever you are, God has given you more wits than these other lumps. You see before you Don Pedro de Cordova, on his way to conquer a kingdom."

At this the company roared with amusement, worse than before. Their horses' bellies dwarfed my tiny Pia. They took turns inspecting me by torchlight, bending forward the better to see. I saw their soldiers' faces, their beards and glittering eyes. I saw now that their horses were all of the Andalusian breed, and their bridles and saddles made by Moorish hands, their shields and helmets ornamented with the silverwork of my homeland. The sheaths of their daggers were richly inlaid. I could no longer conceal from myself my complete indigence. My pride gagged in my throat. The contrast between my impoverished state and my fine words struck me, despite my tender years, and I could have perished of simple gall. I began to tremble with frustration.

"Just a minute, my sirs, just a minute," said the little man, with a warning wave of his hand aloft. "You ought to get acquainted with our leader, Don Pedro, my boy. He's a man after your own heart. Why, he has conquered a bigger kingdom than Caesar himself. Let me tell you about us. Our master's richer than Croesus, why he's . . ."

"That's right, he's right!" the riders roared as one, and encouraged the jester to go on with his recitation.

"The lady of his heart is called Doña Juana de Zuñiga," he chanted, "and she comes from the house of Arellan, which stems from the house of the Queen of Navarre. Her father is the Count of Aguilar, and her uncle is the Duke of Béjar. When she walks into the great hall of the King's palaces in Valladolid, Toledo or Brussels all other feminine beauty fades into nothingness, just as the stars pale before the sun."

"The fool speaks true words," one rider broke in wildly, and they all yelled their approval.

"Now do you know whom you have met, boy?" the little man asked in the expectant silence that followed.

"No," I answered, dazed by the strain of so many words and so much uproar.

"Then look over there," he said.

My eye followed his outstretched arm. To one side stood three men, shivering and huddled together. Their skin was red, and in their straight black hair they wore gay feathers. Feathered cloaks covered their broad shoulders, and the muscles of their naked arms shone like polished wood in the flicker of the torches. In their broad belts were thrust stone axes.

As soon as I saw these men I knew who was the leader of the company. "I know, I know now," I said eagerly.

"Tell us who it is, son," squeaked the jester.

"Don Hernando Cortés," I replied with more confidence.

The men laughed again, but no longer mockingly, it seemed to me. The little man went on in a professional tone, "Watch out you don't disturb our master. For he is trapped in his thoughts and full of sadness. It has been the same since he lost in Palos the friend of his boyhood and his comrade-in-arms, Don Gonzalo de Sandoval. But death spares neither the loveliest virgin nor the bravest knight. We buried Don Gonzalo in La Rábida, in the cloister garden. It is there that a grove of pines soughs its sorrow in the west wind which blows in from the open sea. My friends, my comrades, were I not a fool I should bemoan the lot of man, instead of mocking it. And now we are traveling to Guadalupe, praying that the Mother of God, the Blessed Virgin, will take into her loving arms Don Gonzalo, conqueror of the heathens, noble knight. And you too, Don Pedro on the she-ass, pray for this lion-hearted man. For the dead are many, a host invisible. Time is short, and eternity long."

"I'll do what you say," I told the jester. "We'll all do what you say. We have nothing but respect for any man who was the friend of Don Hernando Cortés."

A murmur of approval arose among the riders at my stiff boy's words. One of them whispered loudly, "The boy isn't so bad, after all." The rest voiced agreement, and many of them crowded round me to clap me on the shoulder or to give poor Pia's ears a rough tweak. And the rider who had threatened me came up with much show of courtesy, and said, "I beg your humble pardon, Don Pedro. In the darkness of night I had trouble seeing that I had a caballero to deal with."

After this some of them, including the fool, encouraged me, half in malice, half in pity, to ride for a while beside the big coach. My companions nodded me to go ahead, and this I did.

When I rode up to the equipage my spirits rose as if I were hearing Mass. My heart sang with excitement and my fancy pictured distant lands, pennoned caravels, great cavalry engagements and native kings with crowns of feathers and bronze-skinned daughters.

As I jogged along with some difficulty, since my Pia was reluctant to force herself forward at the common pace, I was awakened from these excited fancies by a voice asking me how late it was. Unwillingly recalled to myself, I answered that it must be somewhere about midnight. Out of the window of the coach a man leaned and beckoned me to come closer. He wore a cloak over his shoulders, and beneath it a simple leather breastplate. His long, squarely trimmed hair and his pointed beard were thick and brown, and at first sight he appeared to be very young. But as I peered more closely at him I saw this was an illusion. I saw that little folds lay under his eyes, and the corners of his mouth, as if in easy contempt, were drawn down and wrinkled. Again he made a questioning gesture with his gloved hand and asked me, "How far is it now to Toledo?"

"It's still two or three nights away, Don Hernando," I told him.

He nodded his assent wearily, then recalled the strangeness of my voice and looked closer.

"Why are you riding on an ass?" he asked me sharply.

"A horse costs too much."

"What do you mean, costs too much!" he shouted at me harshly. "Do you want people to think I'm a skinflint?"

"No, I don't," I told him. "I don't belong with your people."

"You don't!" he said. "How is it you're riding alongside my coach like a page?" He looked at me so angrily that my knees grew weak.

"Because I wanted to look at you," I told him. "I've wanted to see you ever since Master Pietro Martire told my Master Agrippa about your expedition to Tenochtitlan."

"So that's it," he said, mollified I thought. "How old are you?"

"I'm eighteen."

"What's your name? Where do you come from?"

"My name is Don Pedro de Cordova; on my father's side I come from Old Castile and on my mother's side from the house of Sforza," I said like a parrot.

"What! You are part Italian?" he said, leaning closer to look at me, and I could hear irony in his voice.

"Yes," I said, ashamed.

"And how are you related to Don Gonzalo de Cordova?" he asked me persistently.

"Only distantly," I told him. "My father and the Captain were only second cousins."

"Then in the name of all that is holy, why are you riding on an ass?" shouted Don Hernando, banging on the window frame. "Are you a monk or a peasant? Aren't you ashamed of yourself, boy? Or are you a simple?"

"A what?" I asked, astonished.

"A fool, a village idiot, a clod-pate!"

I swallowed hard, said nothing and looked down at the ears of my struggling Pia, who had drawn down on me the wrath of the great Don Hernando Cortés.

"Don't be stubborn with me, boy," said Don Hernando. "Come closer here. Let me take a look at that beast you're riding."

"It's a she-ass," I informed him.

"Beast or she-ass, it's all the same to me," he said. "There's something wrong here. It's a personal insult to me. I can't tolerate it. How in the name of all the saints of Spain did you ever land in such ridiculous circumstances?"

"I got in trouble with the Inquisition," I told him.

"The Inquisition?" said Don Hernando, and fell still for a moment. "Come in here with me for a minute where I can see what kind of a caballero you are," he went on. "Give your she-ass to that rider behind you."

I did as I was told, ran along with the coach, and clambered aboard as Don Hernando opened the door. He peered at me in the darkness of the interior as we swayed forward.

"You look as if you're speaking the truth," he said at last. "Your generation is something to marvel at. What were you doing? Sleeping with some Jewish whore, I suppose! Did she teach you the way the world goes round, boy?"

"No, it wasn't that," I said, half embarrassed and half frightened by his directness. I told him briefly what had happened to me, and he let me tell my tale without interruption.

At last he began to nod his head. "Stupid, very stupid," he grumbled. "The best thing for you would be to go to the Indies and let some grass grow over the whole affair." He thought for a while then went on, as if talking to himself, "Listen to me, my son. In Estremadura there is a small town called Trujillo . . ."

"I know the place," I broke in eagerly, "that's where my housekeeper lives, Teresa . . ."

"Shut your mouth, boy," said Don Hernando, "and give your betters a chance. You talk a little too much for my liking. Let me do the bellowing for a change, if it pleases Your Majesty."

"Yes, Don Hernando," I said, terrified anew at his captiousness.

"Well, then," he went on, leaning back comfortably on the cushions, and stretching out his legs, "in this city there lives a family by the name of Pizarro. They're some of my distant relations—very distant, praise God's infinite mercy. There was old Don Gonzalo Pizarro, who fought not without courage at Cerignola. His blasphemous mouth is now filled with earth, I'm happy to say. But he certainly left a troop of sons behind him. And not all from the one womb either. Don Gonzalo was a great man for the women, my little cock. They tumbled into his lap like ripe peaches on a late summer day. He was built like an ox. You should have seen his shoulders—you could have built a bridge on them. And what a nose! Do you know what goes with a big nose, Don Pedro what's-your-name? Well, he had what goes with a big nose, unless history lies. You know, he was a poor devil, yet within his limits as big-hearted as any man that drew in a breath of morning air. But on the whole he was crude. He had the manners of a peasant. He drank until it ran out of his ears. He loved dice and had a leaning for coarse company, especially for women with fine bellies like a cask. Ss-sh, my son. Don't look so horrified. He was a man you'd like to have around when you're far from home."

He roared with laughter, pleased with himself. I could smell wine on his breath, and suddenly understood his excessive language.

"Yes, Don Hernando," I said.

"My blond son," he said, puffing sourly into my face, "with me you're as safe as in the arms of Jesus. Breathe easy, the wind is fair. I don't see a cloud in the sky, my onion. Where was I? Yes, give me time. Don Gonzalo has a son, a bastard by the name of Francisco Pizarro. How do you like the name?"

"I like it," I said, numbly.

"You'd better," threatened Don Hernando. "Well, this Francisco Pizarro I'm talking about has knocked around Hispaniola, Darien and Panama for some time. He's just got back to Spain, I hear. He has big plans in the back of his head, enough to give any man a headache. He claims to have discovered a great kingdom to the south of Panama, on the coast of the sea which no man has as yet explored. They told me in Cadiz, in the Casa de la Contratación de las Indias, that Pizarro brought back with him a lot of strange Indians. He brought back with him, too, they said, gold things, emeralds and other precious stones. And he had some fine clothes woven out of a very fine wool. But the strangest things of all were two little camels. They were covered with wool, I heard. They say these little camels are just like gypsies. When you bother them they spit at you."

"There is everything in the Indies!" I said, beside myself with delight and excitement, my fatigue forgotten for the moment.

"Yes, everything," agreed Don Hernando. "It's enough to make a man's hair stand up straight on his head. But let me do the talking, my pippin. Anyway, they threw this Francisco Pizarro into jail in Cadiz.

Something to do with old debts, as I understand it. They were never really his, as I heard it. But that's not to the point. Now Don Carlos our noble King, if I may be so expressive, was gripped with an extraordinary curiosity to see these little camels. He also wanted to hear all about the adventures and travels of our brave Pizarro. So he had him released from jail and promised him all kinds of help. Of course, he didn't promise him any money so that Pizarro could travel to Toledo to the court."

"Why didn't he?" I inquired.

"Don't ask foolish questions, my son," said Don Hernando, and laughed in his throat until he almost choked. "Anyway, things are getting better for my distant relative, that distant caballero. And, when you look at it, what does he really want? He merely wants to conquer another kingdom for Don Carlos, even though he may want to stuff his pockets the meanwhile. You can't blame him for that. When Pizarro finally managed to get to court he behaved himself like a hidalgo. It opened Don Carlos' eyes, for he'd expected him to keep his hat on like a peasant with hay sticking out of his ears. He spoke up like a man, and told the King everything that had happened to him on the coast of the South Sea. He talked about mighty cliffs and swamps hot with fever, enough to shake six men out of a single pair of boots. He talked about his dead comrades: how their last wish had been to carry out a crusade against the red-skinned heathens."

"I suppose the King liked that, didn't he?" I asked hopefully.

"He certainly did; nothing could have pleased him better," and again Don Hernando broke out into a gale of laughter so disproportionate that it confused me. Without waiting for further cues he went on, "And above all he liked the little camels. They just suited a man of his delicate tastes. The camels acted like a virgin's prayer breathed into a pillow scented with drops of balsam from Cathay, if you know what I'm talking about, my slim dove. Oh, those precious camels with their soft wool. How the ladies liked them! Enough tears ran down their cheeks to put out a bonfire. Do you follow me, Don Pedro?"

"Yes, yes, I understand," I said, but really did not.

"Well, so far so good. Now, I'm going to give you a fine piece of advice, something worth a cargo of gold to a young colt like yourself. Get as fast as you can to Trujillo. You'll hear more about the brothers of this Francisco Pizarro when you get there. But, by the sweet bowels of

Christ, don't ride into the city on that miserable she-ass of yours. That animal is a disgrace to the nobility of Spain."

He fumbled around his legs, drew up a flask and drank long and hard. "What was I saying?" he went on. "Yes, and get your hair cut. You look like a bad painting of Mary Magdalen. You've got enough hair to dry the feet of our Lord if He'd been out in a rainstorm for three days on end." Again he laughed at his own wit, seemingly not aware of my horror at this blasphemy. He kept still for a moment, collecting his thoughts, perhaps taken aback at his own boldness, and then went on with great gravity to salve his previous rashness.

"I'm no Jew," he continued, slowly. "I'm not a Fleming or a Lombard. I'm a Spaniard, Don Pedro de Cordova what's-your-name, and what I got, I paid for. And you, little blond, are a Spaniard of sorts. I'll make a bargain with you."

He fumbled at his neck, unhooked his leather breastplate and exposed the white collar of his shirt beneath.

"Look here. Do you see that?" He pulled out a pearl which hung about his throat loosely.

"That's a pearl," I said uneasily, wondering what was coming next. "I've never seen one so big before. Doña Catarina had ..."

"This pearl," said Don Hernando, yawning impressively, "is worth about four hundred florins on the market. But you're going to pay me five hundred for it."

"Five hundred!" I said, astonished. "I don't..."

"I said you'd pay me five hundred for it," he went on severely. "But you don't have to pay me until you're loaded with the treasure you're going to bring back from this Southland of Pizarro's. I leave it to your honor. And God help you if you don't keep to the bargain. But right now you've got to ride down to Tordesillas and get yourself a horse. From there you can go to Trujillo and scrape an acquaintance with my distant relative, the pearl of the Indies, Don Francisco Pizarro."

After saying this he tore the pearl from his neck and put it in my hand. He began to mumble to himself as the wine took hold of his brain and he lay back on the cushions. Once in a while he would chuckle to himself.

With the pearl in my hand I waited, and at last summoned enough courage to open the door and jump out. I slammed the creaking door, and quickly got on my Pia, who was worrying her way along as the rider inexorably tugged at her bridle. I told the man that Don Hernando had fallen asleep, and this satisfied him after he had cautiously peered through the window to make sure I had committed no violence.

I made my way to the rest of my company, and motioned them to follow me away from the cavalcade. We moved to one side and let Don Hernando's men ride by us until we were left alone in the chilly darkness of the night.

"And where to now, little lion?" asked Diego stiffly, for he wondered what had been happening all the time I had been gone.

"To Tordesillas. We've found a way," I told him, and then explained at length. They were all overjoyed, and we started on the journey without delaying to rest our aching bones. So great was our joy that we sang together, Diego, Frenero, Bernal, and I with my light voice. We sang this song:

"Our leader is Fernando,
The invincible Fernando.
Our leaders are Fernando
And his matchless Queen,
For she too's a soldier,
A soldier, a soldier
Of courage and renown."

So, we rode on.

8

THE PRISONER

IT WAS already morning when we reached the rim of the Sierra. Below us spread the great valley of the Duero. We could see fields and meadows, white farmhouses and countless orchards in a pattern, and the shining river, which ran into the distance between reedy banks and lush meadows.

We got down from our animals, fell on our knees, and in our morning prayers thanked God for the lovely Duero which blesses the Spanish earth. On its banks far down below lay a small town—gray walls crowned with battlements and watchtowers, the roofs of the houses huddled together like sheep in a fold.

The Alcazar, the point of its Gothic main tower rising from behind the piled masonry, was built very close to the water. I saw a great flight of crows rise up from one of the other towers of the fortress. Suddenly the valley and the river no longer seemed so idyllic and harmless. Something evil, menacing, hung over the meadows, the poplars and the roofs of the town, a mist of doubt. Far off I could hear the cawing of the crows. They moved like painted birds on a painted landscape, and suddenly vanished as in a dream. It was very strange and out of key.

In Tordesillas, for that was the town, our first way was to an old Jew, pointed out to me by the burghers as a money lender and jeweller. The haggard old man eyed us distrustfully, fearing perhaps that we had committed murder to come into the possession of the pearl. But then he seemed to decide that this was not part of his business, and he paid us reluctantly four hundred shining florins. At that time the Jews were eager to buy pearls and precious stones because these they could hide better from the hawk's eyes of the Inquisition than other investments of like value.

Then we found a good inn, and bought ourselves some nourishing hot soup in which swam thick pieces of ham, some freshly baked bread and a strong wine. It rather bothered me, to be sure, that while we were eating, the thick-necked host always stood behind our chairs and observed with sorrow in his eyes every morsel that we stuffed into our mouths. In the market we bought ourselves new clothes, two breastplates for Bernal and Frenero and a sword for Sancho. The little pearl that Don Hernando had given me was inexhaustible, to our impoverished way of thinking.

Then we went to the horse dealer's, where we became chance witnesses of a lively conversation. A man dressed in peasant clothes was saying to the horse dealer, who stood before him with averted eyes, "You louse-ridden cheat, you tried to sell me a nag not fit for a bull to bury his horns in. He's as crazed as you are."

The peasant pointed to a big piebald animal, tethered to a stake around which it danced uneasily as if possessed. He began then to talk to us as we lent a curious ear to his troubles. "It isn't only that this hell-horse threw me so hard that every bone in my body cracks when I move. This blockhead of an animal has been kicking the sides of his stall to pieces. And what else did he do? He bit a piece out of the neck of my old mare. She never did anyone any harm in her life. Now she won't touch her fodder. Just hangs her head over the manger. But that isn't all. My young wife took sides with the horse. We got into an argument about him. I lost my temper and gave her a few slaps in the face to quiet her. What did she do? Why, she picked up a new earthen pot, threw it square at my head, and split my cheek open. It was the talk of the neighborhood. Every old hag for miles around joined the crowd in front of my door. They were all gossiping about the affair. This disgusting nag has ruined my marriage. And he kept me away from Mass. I can't very well go there with this mark on my face. He may even have ruined my chances of getting into Heaven, for all I know, with all these doings. Yes, and I'm not taking the broken pot into account. It was painted with red roses. I never saw a nicer one in all my life."

"My good man," the horse dealer broke in with heat, "you asked me to sell you a good, sound animal worthy of a soldier. You wanted something your wife would be proud to ride on; you asked for a horse that would look good with a saddle with silver inlay and red leather snaffles. So I sold you this full-blooded Andalusian. I told you the horse needed a good rider."

"That's what you say," the peasant came back at him. "But how in Christ's name was I to know that some Moorish dog had taught him to stop dead in his tracks and start rearing, as if he wanted to fly through the air on wings? Why, you cheat! How was I to know that this flayer was going to kick my whole married life to pieces? Give me my two hundred florins back. If you don't, by God as sure as I'm a Christian, some fine morning you'll wake up with a knife in your back. Your children and wife will have to go abegging like the gypsies, while your lying carcass rots in some forgotten corner of the graveyard. . . ."

The peasant continued to talk in this fashion, his speech becoming wilder all the time as the thought of his two hundred florins possessed him. A big crowd gathered round to listen to the fight. Some took the side of the peasant, others of the horse dealer. A great cry arose from the quarreling throng. The men cursed and the women screamed imprecations at one another. Eyes flashed and it would surely have ended in a free-for-all with drawn knives if Diego had not suddenly nudged me and pointed to the cause of the fracas. His lips bared, the stallion was biting at his chain and pawing the earth with his forefoot. Diego said, "Two hundred florins is cheap enough for such a fine beast."

"Just a minute!" I shouted at the peasant, and worked myself closer to him. "Let me try the horse. If he suits me, I'll pay your price."

"Noble knight," the peasant cried in astonishment at such a piece of luck, "you'll buy yourself a wonderful horse if you decide to get him. He'll carry you faster than an arrow from the bow. You can ride him in the Toledo tournaments. You'll have all the women looking at you. A finer horse . . ."

Meanwhile he untethered the stallion and with the help of the horse dealer held him in while I climbed into the saddle. My heart was beating violently.

"Grip him with your knees," Diego told me. "He's not a she-ass. Watch what you're up to, now!"

"Let him go!" I shouted as loudly and bravely as I could, and took the reins in one hand.

In an instant the horse lurched forward, and I threw myself forward on his neck to keep my balance. He took a few tremendous leaps and made off. To me it seemed as if the whole world had suddenly lost its focus. A fat peasant woman fled before me across the street, her skirts picked up the better to run. I caught a glimpse of her huge thighs and wobbling buttocks. Pots and spilled onions were crushed underfoot as I knocked over a vegetable stand. Suddenly a hanging shield with three golden lilies on it came straight for my head. I ducked, but too late. It cracked me solidly on the skull so that I saw stars, but I hung on in desperation. The city gate sped by me with a sharp whistle, and as I shot through the narrow space the guards scattered like sheep and one fellow tripped over his lance so that I just missed his prostrate body.

Open country now lay before me, and I ventured to sit fairly upright. The horse suddenly veered, and with horror in my throat I felt the branches of trees brushing my head. We were headed directly for the river. But instead the wild animal bore up a narrow stony path. At my right was the high wall of the city, and behind it rose up the Alcazar. I heard a piercing cry. Someone was trying to get my attention. Out of the corner of my eye I saw above me a woman standing on the stone balustrade of a balcony. I caught a brief view of her gray hair, hanging in strings over her forehead and down her shoulders. Her clothes were gray, I saw. In my excitement she seemed like a gypsy, the personification of some ominous fate. In looking at her I all but fell off my perch in the saddle, and lost one stirrup.

Far down below me now ran the river, and I shuddered at the thought of what would happen if my steed should trip and hurtle the pair of us down into the rocky river bed. By luck I caught my stirrup, and managed to look back over my shoulder at the woman on the balcony. I waved to her, for she screamed at me again. I could hear it clearly above the stallion's pounding hoofs. A man and woman appeared beside her, and led her off, I thought.

The Alcazar and the city walls left behind, the ground became soft and springy. Before me in the soft haze of afternoon stretched a lovely countryside. Fat cattle raised their heavy heads to watch me sadly in my violent flight through space. Indeed, as the peasant had promised, I was all but flying. It was a strange feeling, this being divested of all bodily weight. Damp air streamed into my half-open mouth and filled my chest. Carefully I raised myself into a more comfortable position in the saddle, gradually felt how the horse and I became as one.

Like a centaur of old I galloped through the heroic landscape. It was the happiest thing on earth to be on a horse's back, I thought. I should not have been surprised to see dryads run forth from the trunks of the poplars along the way. It was as if the great piebald were carrying me restlessly out of the familiar world into another, much larger in all proportions and yet even more human than the one I knew.

In time the horse under me had his will. I could feel him ease his pace a little, and so I decided to try to control him. Firmly I drew in the reins. He fell into a long, rocking trot, then into an easy walk, and at last stopped stock still as if molded from bronze. Triumph filled my heart, although I had really played no greater part in taming this Bucephalus than to stick as best I could to his back, certainly not in the approved fashion.

I dismounted, clinging shakily to the bridle. The horse stood before me with his head raised proudly although he was badly blown. I could see into the lovely trembling nostrils, and the dark godlike eyes did not look at me but beyond into some space which a noble animal alone can perceive. The badly trimmed mane lay disheveled on his muscular neck, of which the skin was like silk. There was nothing coarse or heavy about this beast. But although everything about him, legs, chest and head from ears to fetlocks, was elegantly formed, the whole frame was of a splendid balance of enduring strength.

I climbed into the saddle and rode slowly back to the city. My friends greeted me in the marketplace with cries of joy and laughter. The little girls clapped their hands. When Diego had paid off the peasant, the man all but kissed the cheating horse dealer, so great was his relief at recouping a cruel loss. The crowd followed us to our lodgings, and cried "Bravo!" when Sancho held bridle and stirrup for me to dismount and my horse stood as still as a statue. I ordered the host of the inn, who watched the proceedings open-mouthed, to pour out some wine for the people. This gesture was loudly cheered, understandably enough. Some men moved forward with tufts of straw in their hands and offered to rub down my fine piebald, but Sancho made a stern face of refusal, threatened to kick them away, and led the horse into a stall behind the inn.

I then ordered the host to have a barber sent to me, for I felt it would be unbecoming to ride on such a horse with hair more unkempt and longer than his own. While waiting I asked my friends about the strange woman on the balcony at the river. I said it appeared as if she were in great need, and I thought that we should do something about it. Diego, however, felt it would be much more reasonable to sound out some of the townspeople in order first to get an idea of what was going on in the Alcazar. The woman might very well be a criminal, he said, perhaps even a heretic thrown to rot away her life in the great palace.

The barber was a long thin redhead. He talked incessantly.

"How do you want your hair cut, my young nobleman?" he asked. "Do you want it cut square across your forehead in the Flemish style? Or in the Italian style, combed back over the ears? Which way would you like?"

"Cut it Spanish style," I told him.

"Your wish is my command," said the barber, and bowed low. The snip of the shears seemed to set his tongue loose. "I was just about to tell you that we barbers are in favor again. We haven't enjoyed it very long, to be sure. It wasn't so long ago that we were regarded as dishonorable cut-throats."

He paused for a moment, took a powerful snip with his shears and went steadily to work, pressing me back gently in the chair. "Yes, my young knight, right now we are very much the cynosure of all eyes. We understand how to let blood, to straighten crooked bones, to use quicksilver, and mix love potions for sick animals. Yes, it can be said without exaggeration that the future is rosy for us barbers. Some in our trade have become court doctors. We stand by the King's throne like ministers, no less. Even Don Carlos listens to us with attention when we tell him what to do for the gout in his fingers and toes. He suffers from the disease, you know, like a rich grandfather. If he were wise, to tell the truth, he'd get out of the swamps of Flanders and come back to dry Spain. And you—are you by any chance on the way to Toledo? Are you going there to see Don Hernando Cortés receive the crown of Viceroy of New Spain?"

"You know Don Hernando?" I asked in amazement.

"I know them all," said the barber contemptuously. "In this respect I am like the sun. Nothing is hidden from my glance. I know every nook and corner of Spanish politics. I know exactly what's going on in the Indies. I can describe to a nicety the battlefield of Pavia, the galleys of Andrea Doria now lying in the harbor of Barcelona ready to carry Don Carlos to Italy. I even know what the Pope, Clement, the seventh of that name I believe, is thinking. And I assure you they're not pretty sentiments, either, which throb in his brainpan. You mustn't forget he was sitting in his angelic stronghold when they plundered Rome. Furthermore, I have unusual gifts for seeing far into the future."

"Astonishing, worthy friend," Diego cut in. "And since you are omniscient, you might tell us who that old prisoner in the Alcazar is."

At this the barber sprang back, and the shears hung limp in his hand. His face under the red hair looked the color of cheese, his eyes began to stare and his eyebrows rise in a parody of caution.

"My dear noblemen," he whispered loudly, "kindly refrain from making jest of me."

"Come on, out with it. Who is she?" said Diego.

"I can't tell you. I don't know anything about it," stuttered the barber, forgetting to go on with his work. "Everyone knows, but nobody talks about it. Don't ask me any more about it, if you please, my dear . . ."

"Shall I cut the liar's throat?" asked Frenero, winking at me.

"Cut off his thumbs, the big mouth," said Bernal evenly.

"My dear, dear friends," the barber broke in, his voice trembling in genuine fear, for both Frenero and Bernal were enough to discourage the hardiest souls, "if you must know, step closer. Closer, closer, I beg you. It's high treason to do it, and it might cost me my trade, my living and even my neck. But I'll do it, if you'll promise to keep your mouths shut. It's Doña Juana, the rightful Queen of Spain, who is imprisoned in the Alcazar. God, they say, has robbed her of her wits."

"Is that true?" asked Diego.

"I beg you not to ask me any more," the barber pleaded. "But if you must know, the godless rumor is going about that she really does have her full share of sense. It's only the greed of her son to rule, our beloved Don Carlos, and the baseness of the head jailer, the Marquis de Denia, which keep her there. If she were free the Holy Inquisition would collapse, they say. For we know from the servants that right now she refuses to say her prayers or attend Mass. The story goes that Denia has even suggested to Don Carlos that he put his mother to torture. But so far Don Carlos has been afraid to do it. As it is Denia scarcely dares show his face in the city. Everybody hates him. Even the merchants in the marketplace don't like to sell him their wares—provisions for the prison are brought from another town."

"That's more like it," I said. "We thank you kindly for your information."

"And for the sweet love of Christ our Lord," the barber implored, "don't let anybody know I've been talking."

"Don't worry about that," Diego assured him. "And keep still yourself. Or you can depend on getting paid for your pains in double coin."

When the barber had finished with me, we took stock of what we should do. I argued that at least we must see the Queen, and measure with our own eyes the extent of her need. Diego was anything but pleased with the whole undertaking. He gnawed at his underlip with his long teeth and was of the opinion that we would land in hot water with a vengeance if we got caught mixing in the domestic politics of Don Carlos. But I persisted. I even threatened to go alone, for it was to me, after all, that she had shouted for help. But my friends would not hear of anything so foolhardy.

When darkness had fallen and the new moon was up in the sky, we moved out through a side door Bernal had ferreted out in the city wall. A cool night wind murmured in the poplar tops, and below us we could hear the delicate splashing of the river current. In time we became accustomed to the darkness and could make out the towers of the castle and the white balcony. At first sight the high city wall cutting us off from the Alcazar appeared to be an insurmountable obstacle. But Frenero, who was skilled in dealing with such situations, discovered a poplar which had a strong branch leaning out over it. Like lynxes we clambered up the bole, crept out on the limb and swung down onto the top of the wall. Below us in the courtyard of the castle not a thing was stirring, and not a single watchman on guard was to be seen. Only a few steps separated us from the balcony, but now we discovered a new hindrance. The heavy wooden door leading into the interior of the castle was barred from the inside. Bernal worked the point of his knife through a crack in the planking, and thus managed to edge back the bolt. The door gave suddenly and, as if of its own accord, swung back noiselessly on its hinges. It was a ghostly thing, and all of us were chill with apprehension.

We now found ourselves in the main corridor. All the while I could not help thinking of the Palace of the Inquisition in Seville. In this building there was the same atmosphere of danger and cruelty. I cannot remember precisely how long we stumbled through the dark passageways of the Alcazar. I only know that it seemed a very long time. At last by experiment we found a windowless, high-ceilinged room in which there were two candles in silver sconces. Between the candles, which burned with a motionless flame, hung a very old picture, darkened with time. It represented the Mother of Christ, in great sorrow, with the body of her Son across her knees. The left arm of Christ dangled white and crushed, the eyes rolled up like those of a slaughtered beast, and the beard was thrust forward as if made of iron wires. The Mother of God, Holy Mary, with an aureole about her head, was painted in the Byzantine style. Her lineaments were as if carved out of wood, and only the over-large black eyes were alive. A soft glow seemed to emanate from them, as if the painter had fashioned the pupils from mother-of-pearl rather than from pigment. I felt, like all the rest, that she was watching us, our every move. All of us at once removed the covering from our heads and bent one knee. The tears which were coursing down the sunken cheeks of Mary for a moment seemed to be genuine, and not made of dead paint.

"So you have come, then, you angels of the Lord," a voice said, a remarkably clear, plangent voice. At the moment I could have sworn that the image on the wall had spoken. A shiver of fear ran down my back and robbed my knees of their strength. But almost at once I saw that an old woman sat in the shadows, stiff and straight on her high-backed chair. She was looking at us quietly, fixedly, with a curious pride and casual acceptance in her manner.

"Oh, I know what you've come for," she said, and laughed gently to herself. "You're angry because I didn't go to Mass last Christmas Eve. My confessor has been worrying about it. He's such a good man. But foolish, horribly foolish. To tell you the honest truth I don't feel the Son of God at work in my heart. And in my youth I once heard—or did I read it somewhere in Ruysbroeck?—that God must be born in the hearts of men. Anyway, nothing has been born there of late." She laughed again, softly, sadly.

"Gracious lady," I said, deep embarrassment having overcome my terror, "we are not angels—we're Spanish men, that's all."

"What!" she cried out sharply and got to her feet. "You intrude in my room? Did that Denia send you? Just because I'm not eating or drinking? Because I won't wash my body tomorrow morning or the morning after? Because I won't sleep in my bed tonight? Or perhaps you're a pack of murderers! What are you? What do you want of me?"

"No, no," we said in unison, and then I got up the courage to explain. "We've come to help you. You are our Queen, you are the mother of Spain."

"Mother of Spain!" The woman's voice grew strong, was cold with command. "My friends, I need no help. I am alone. I shall stay alone, and what comes I shall support alone."

"We want to help you," I broke in, half in fear again.

"All my children have deserted me," she went on, oblivious of my interruption, intoning the words to herself. "Last of all it was Catarina. Little Catarina. I heard the hoofs of her horses grow fainter as I stood on the balcony. I saw the hills swallow up the light of the torches. Yes. I'm through with love. It's the greatest unhappiness of a mother, to love so much. Do you follow me, my friends? The world tears our children from our breasts. They belong to us only when we feel them kicking in the womb in the quiet of the night. Come closer, my dear Spaniards. Come under the candles. Let me feed on your wild faces. Closer, close to me, closer to your mother, my great sons. Bend your knees. How exciting it is to have you all before me. It's so long since I was at Court, I had all but forgotten. What's your name, young man, and what do you want of your Queen and your mother?" She now sat down again and folded her arms across her sunken breast.

"Pedro de Cordova is my name," I said, as in a dream. "And on your call to me for help as I rode by the castle, my good friends and I have come to the Alcazar to do your bidding."

"You would know my will," said the Queen, catching up the ritual, "and my will is this. Take this cold man who inhabits my home, the Alcazar—this man called Denia, this half-man. Cut off his head. Cut it off as Judith, whom I love as my own sister, cut off the head of Holofernes sleeping in his tent. Beyond this, tell the men of my lovely city Tordesillas to arm themselves, and imprison the black cat who has so often spoiled my rest."

"What do you mean, black cat?" I asked.

"Yes, I suppose you, too, like all the rest, are cowards when it comes to the black cat!" she shouted. Her voice had grown in power, and now she truly sounded like a queen, inexorably decided to follow her own counsel. "I say this animal must be driven out and destroyed. The beast disgusts me. He makes me doubt myself. He sits in every dark corner and stares at me. I get tired of the show. At night he sits on my bed, looking at my throat. It is all I can do to breathe the night through. I know all about ghosts. Dozens of them keep pestering me. Thin ones, fat ones, tall and short. All kinds. But they drop their eyes when they look at me, the mother of Spain. Their courage is sapped when they think of my sons, my many sons."

The Queen fell silent, closed her eyes like a man in his cups who has talked out all he has to say. Her head inclined toward her breast, and it seemed almost as if she had fallen asleep. Her body was delicate and slender, not much different from the body of a young girl. Her white hands were long and small. Her feet were small in her dark shoes of brocade. It was only the thin gray hair tumbling in disorder over her forehead that betrayed her age.

She belonged to the breed of women who cannot be seen without arousing a deep emotion of tenderness. And the most lovely thing about her was her voice. It seemed to arise from some great depth. Her words rang out clearly, like bells on a frosty night. And yet over the sound there was a light hoarseness, an implacable harshness, not at first perceptible. Or so it all seems in retrospect. And everything she said, which everyday people would pronounce mad at first hearing, on second thought was full of sense. Not once did I feel I was talking to a lunatic. Even now as I write, I shame to use the word. Rather, if I must commit myself, I felt as if I were listening to an oracle, a sibyl, a day-dreamer speaking of what she sees.

And now she spoke again, looking up and directly at us. "Get to your feet, my Spaniards," she told us. She spoke with ease and accompanied the order with a wave of her hand. We did as we were told.

She looked at me thoughtfully. "I remember this boy who was galloping along on a piebald horse. What did you say your name was? I remember. Wait." She began to stroke her cheeks. "Let me try. Let me remember. Was it at Granada, Cordova or Ghent? No. It was somewhere else. . . . You were not there, Don Felipe. Please don't be angry with me. You see, I'm a Queen after all. I have to talk with these men who have sought me out. They are my people and yours. Now I know! It was so beautiful. I'll have to tell you about it."

The old woman on the chair smiled to herself. She had forgotten we were in the room, and went on talking steadily to herself. We listened now almost comfortably, and not without curiosity if the truth be told.

"My grandmother sat there, and my father near her, under the baldachin. And next to my father, as thin as a reed, was my brother Juan. Poor little Juan! But we girls stood behind a curtain, my sister Catarina beside me, the same one who's now in England. We peeked through the curtain. A man was standing in front of our parents, talking. He had a high forehead, and bore himself like a king.

"He was saying: 'On the seventh of October, Your Most Christian Majesty, I found I was in 52 degrees 30 minutes latitude north. And I was very much concerned,' he said, 'for according to my reckoning the coast of Cipangu should lie two hundred miles more to the east. However, there was nothing to see but open water. Night was soon to fall.

"'My captain, Martin Alonso Pinzón, came to me from his caravel, the *Pinta,* in the ship's boat. He told me that his man on the masthead had seen a flock of parrots in flight toward the southwest!' That was what the man said. I remember it all because the man astonished me with his calm.

"All of them—Their Majesties, my brother Juan, the lords and ladies of the Court—were craning their necks forward to listen. And then the man talked like this, 'Thereupon I turned the rudder of my ship and made off on a southwest course. For I assumed the birds were seeking their homes on land for the night.'

"At this everybody began to murmur. One clerical person said aloud, 'It's almost like Noah's dove above the waters of the flood.' But the Queen, my mother, asked, 'And so, my Admiral, did you find the western passage to Cipangu, to the land of Cathay, and the island of Taprobane?'

"'Your Majesty,' the admiral answered, 'five days later the island of Guanahani rose out of the sea before our eyes. We went ashore on the sandy beach, which was shadowed by palm trees. We kneeled down and thanked God and the Virgin Mary for leading us safely to the Indies. Red men and women gathered around us. They stood off at some distance, as if they were afraid of us. In the meanwhile we made a big cross. I had the flags of Castile and Aragon brought ashore, and in the name of Your Majesties, took possession of this land.'

"'That was well done, Lord Admiral,' the King, my father, said to the man. And my mother nodded her head at the servants and they brought a chair. She asked the admiral to sit down. Up to that moment this had only happened to dukes and cardinals. The Court began to whisper loudly. But the admiral declined to accept the offer. He remained standing, and said, 'I've brought home with me two people from Guanahani for Your Majesties, a male and a female.'

"The two red people knelt down on the carpet. They had a wreath of parrot's feathers about their heads, and in their ears they wore heavy golden rings. The upper part of their bodies was naked, but they wore clothes over their privates. Their sandals were ornamented with mussel shells. The man's face and chest were painted. The crowd pressed in closer to get a better look at the two strangers. My brother Juan jumped from his stool, ran down the steps of the throne and out of childish curiosity touched the breast of the man, who smiled at him in a friendly way.

"I said to Catarina, 'Just look how they kneel down as innocent as can be, those two Indians.' My sister said, 'They're like Adam and Eve. The admiral must have discovered the Garden of Eden.' My sister's words often run though my mind, though I haven't seen her for years. When they come to me I think of the happy isles under the hot sun. I think of the blue sea and the palm trees. Sometimes I ask myself if there really are such things. I think about Spain, Flanders, France and Italy. I see every country doomed to war and uproar. But there, across the western sea, there's a wonderful world."

The Queen slumped into silence. She said nothing for many minutes. We began to think she had forgotten us entirely. Then she began to mumble to herself. It was some time still before she formed the words clearly.

"I love them all, all my people, and I fold my hands to pray for them. Just as long as I can keep on sitting here thinking of all my people, there will never be any curse afflicting Spain. For I protect them. I promised to do that once on my oath. I raised two fingers for the sun to see, and kissed the Book with my lips. I am the Queen. I could not break my oath. It is true they have imprisoned me here. They have taken my crown, my queenly clothes. They even feed me poor food these days. That man-bitch, Denia, pesters me. Those whorish daughters of his come in and out of my room at their pleasure. But that makes no difference. I'm still a queen. I must stay where I am, at the post for which God ordained me. It's impossible for me to go with you."

"Yes," murmured Diego, and I was with him in thought. "Your wish must be carried out."

"It isn't my wish, not mine at all," she cried sharply. "Something higher is at work here. Kneel down, all you Spaniards, and receive my command."

We drew closer, and did as she ordered. She got to her feet and said loudly, in a sonorous voice: "We, Juana, by the grace of God and the will of the people Queen of the United Kingdom of Spain, Queen of Sardinia, Sicily and Calabria, Duchess of Burgundy and of the Netherlands, ruler of all lands across the sea, we command you to do this: Go with your men to your ships, well-armed and well-provisioned, and sail into the west. There you will find the country discovered by that admiral who served my mother, Queen Isabella, now at rest in God, the Admiral Cristóbal Colón. There carry the cross of Jesus Christ."

She paused, then continued slowly, "I see dark drawing over the earth. Brothers will murder one another. Parents will deny their children, children their elders. They will throw themselves down before Baal and pray to false gods. I see uprisings, war, hunger and misery. The waters will rise. Neither the suckling asleep in his cradle, nor the virgin at her spinning wheel will be spared. But you Spaniards must prepare for a new earth. O joy, joy! I see Mount Ararat, arched over with the rainbow. Men and animals walk in pairs on the damp ground. The elephants are standing on patches of dry ground and the cranes are flying overhead. The seven-colored rainbow binds Heaven and earth, as God promised."

The Queen's shoulders trembled with her passion, her black eyes blazed like the eyes of the Mother of God in the image. She stood tall and slender. On the middle finger of her right hand she wore a thick old-fashioned gold ring, on which two rampant lions were engraved. I saw them plainly. I bent down over her hand and kissed the ring. Diego, Sancho, Bernal and Frenero also bent their heads and kissed it. We cried softly, "Long live Doña Juana, our Queen!"

At this point we heard voices and steps outside in the corridor. The Queen listened. As she strained forward to hear, her face changed. The corners of her mouth fell in, and magically she became an old woman. Quickly she told us, "Go now, Spaniards. Your Queen is tired. Never forget my words. Behind that picture is a door. It leads out to the balcony overlooking the Duero." She sat down, pressed her chin in her hand and closed her eyes. With a weary sigh she let her head fall against the back of the chair. To our amazement in almost the time it takes to tell it she was asleep.

I nodded to my companions. We left the room on tiptoe; soundlessly the door closed behind us, and we were on the balcony. High up in the sky hung the thin sickle of a new moon. An unforgettable earthy perfume arose from the dewy loam, and the night air came welling up from the river in cool gusts which I could feel passing over my face. An owl flew above us, a shadow in the night. It struck me that the world now stood in the sign of the Ram. Strength was brewing everywhere.

"Perhaps the earth keeps its place in the sky," I said aloud, "only because there are people like our Queen. If she should give in, there would be nothing to prevent God from letting everything fall to destruction out of His hands."

"That's true, true," said Sancho, to himself.

9

THE STRANGER FROM LOYOLA

WE STAYED a few more days in Tordesillas. I busied myself with learning to ride my piebald horse. We bought new clothes for Sancho, Bernal and Frenero, and gave them swords and crossbows. Diego de Vargas, however, fitted himself out with a pair of blue hose the color of the sky. This was his favorite color, light blue, and it looked well on him. He chose also a light green jerkin and a red cap, and at last looked like the parrot to which Doña Sobeya had once likened him.

The day of leave-taking finally wore round. On a lovely spring morning we filed out through the city gate into the country. Our animals' hoofs clattered gay on the cobbles, and behind one grated window I saw a girl peeping at us, curious to know whether among us she could find some future lover. I thought I must cut a pretty figure.

I was in the most brilliant spirits. Beside me Diego rode on a fine mule. He was now my secretary by official agreement, for my holding the purse strings had consolidated my superior position—that and my inherited name. Behind me walked the two crossbowmen Bernal and Frenero. Even the beautiful spring day, the bright sun, the young foliage and the colorful flowers could not disperse the air of evil hovering about these two. Bernal looked appraisingly with his one eye at every traveler who crossed our path, and to all appearances seemed to be calculating just how to snatch a purse or slit a throat. Two jet eyes glittered in Frenero's pocked face and his rough red hair did little to soften the picture. My worthy Sancho brought up the rear of the procession. He rode on Pia, his countenance rigid with conceit. He now considered himself to be marshal, officer of the commissariat and page all in one.

In this fashion we moved across country. Men and girls working in the fields ran to the edge of the road, and stood gawking, idly working the soil from between their toes as they watched us approach. The nearer we drew to them, the farther their mouths dropped open. The girls giggled and whispered to one another, quite loud enough for us to hear, "Surely he's a prince. Perhaps he's the chance child of the King. Maybe he's a duke's son, perhaps the Duke of Béjar's."

This kind of comment both flattered and injured me. But soon the girls forgot to look at me in their delight at the spectacle of Diego. They poked one another and said without lowering their voices, "Just look at that cockatoo. I'd bet my shift he'd plow a deep furrow if he ever got you into bed, even if he is thin." And another added, "A good rooster is seldom fat." Diego had no dignity and winked boldly at these peasant girls, calling to them in his scratchy way, "Good morning, my blushing virgins." At this the girls would burst into a tumult of laughter. This made me angry, and it was I who blushed until I was red as the evening sun. The men behaved quite differently, however. They stood mute, looking at us critically, and at the most one of them would venture to remark, "A good horse; he has Andalusian blood." This pleased me to the roots of my heart, and I wondered how the Lord in his wisdom could have granted such little intelligence to womenfolk.

From time to time we chanced upon beggars. In rags and stinking sourly, these unhappy creatures would lurch into my path, try to kiss my hand and, if I pulled it away in time, kiss my horse. At the same time they would whine piteously, "Have mercy, knight, mercy in the name of Christ, who sat at the same table with the beggars!" Thereupon Sancho, as I had instructed him, would reluctantly dig into his pouch, extract a few coins and throw them disdainfully at their feet.

Out of the valley of the Duero we rode up into the mountains. The road was very bad and we seldom met any other travelers. Along the way grew great oaks. Many jays stormed out of their branches as we moved into their view, and flew about screaming their dislike at being disturbed.

Now and then we had to get down from our animals, so stony, pitted and tortuous was the road. Little streams, ice cold, trickled down the bald face of the rocky cliff. An old pine now and again would bend a twisted head over the canyon below. At a turn in the road we got a fine prospect of the valley of the Duero. Everything had become tiny again.

We bade this world good-by, and steadily climbed on toward the pass, a chill wind on our heated bodies.

Very often we would pass by old gray watchtowers. For in this land at the time of the Arab rule there had been great wars between the kingdoms of Aragon and Leon on one side and the Saracens in the south on the other. Now and then we chanced on a watchtower which was inhabited. Long-haired men with sharp faces came out and eyed us mistrustfully. They did not greet us at all. Most of them were people who had come into difficulties either with civil or clerical justice. A few had their wives with them, and dirty children played about the door of an occasional home in exile. We rode by without saying a word.

One night we found shelter in one of these towers. We lighted a big fire which drove out the many bats and owls. Now and then a bat, in his frenzy to escape, would fall into the fire. The sparks rose to the ceiling; the smoke burned in our eyes and made our throats dry and rasping. Whenever we spoke in full voice an echo came from the arched roof, as if someone were concealed in the lofty darkness. But we ate of our provisions with good heart, commended our souls to God and slept peacefully, far better in our weariness than many a prince under soft coverlets of damask.

Some few nights later we found that the tower we had counted on to keep out of the weather for the night was inhabited by an old man. He was as emaciated as a skeleton, and he kept on shaking his head as he watched us devouring our supper. My Sancho gave him a mutton bone, and the old man fell on it like a wild beast. Then we broke bread and drank wine. I commanded the old man to draw closer to us. But he continued to sit in his corner, as still and anxious as a partridge under a tussock of grass. Frenero then got up, took him by the nape of the neck and threw him toward the fire.

"Can't you hear when you're spoken to, you bag of bones?" he said roughly.

"Mercy, mercy, honorable knight!" the man sobbed. "Let me live! Don't kill me."

We all laughed at this, but in my inner mind I really wondered what he had to live for anyway. To me his life seemed almost worse than death itself. I told the men to give him wine, which they did. Thereupon he sobbed more loudly, and stretched his arm out in stubborn refusal.

"I'll fix you once and for all, you Moorish dog," Frenero growled, "if you don't drink this dry."

At this point I intervened. "Sit down by the fire, old man. Take some bread. Never mind what they say. Frenero wouldn't harm a hair of your head."

At this the old man became easier and began to eat. Once in a while he would cast a terrified glance at Frenero and Bernal, who sat and stared at him with open hostility in their ugly faces. But he would drink nothing but water with the bread.

When we had finished our meal and had drunk the wine, Diego said to the man, "How is it, old fellow, that you live here all by yourself like an owl? Did you commit some crime or other? A murder, maybe?"

The old man drew back in fear and shook his head violently.

"Speak up," said my Sancho, "for these people mean you no harm, on my honor."

The old man began to cry. He buried his face in his dirty hands. It was very still in the tower. The bats flew about soundlessly, sometimes brushing our hair. Only the fire crackled, and the soft spring wind sighed at the doorway.

Finally the man pulled himself together, wiped the tears from his eyes with the back of his hand and looked at me questioningly. He had very dark eyes under bushy brows.

"You're very young, my lord," he said, addressing me, "and you cannot know how much bad luck there is in the world. I'm a tinsmith from Seville. My trade was good and I lived well. I made kettles and pans with the best of them. By the grace of God I had reached the ripe age of seventy-one. It was not until then that misfortune made me into a second Job."

The old man watched me carefully. As a genuine interest showed in my face he gained confidence, and even seemed to take pleasure in his confession. He went on, garrulously, "You must understand I was born and raised in the faith of Allah and his prophets. Then when Antonio Cardinal de Guevara came to Seville and settled in the Triana, I called my sons to me. We became apostates and prayed to the Virgin Miriam and her son. But I never could bring myself to eat the meat of that filthy animal the pig. Nor could I force myself to drink wine. And I did not stop washing myself according to the ritual of Gesezu. My sons kept to my example.

"It wasn't long before the neighbors heard about this. They all envied me my security. They complained about me in Triana. They accused me of disloyalty to the Church. For a whole year I sat in prison until one day armed men came to my cell. They undid my chains and put a yellow robe on my back. The robe was covered with red laughing devils and black crosses. On my head they put a tall pointed cap. They fastened my hands and led me out into the courtyard. There were many hundred people gathered there, all of them dressed just like me. Among them I saw one of my sons. At the same time life-sized dolls were brought out, and dead persons on biers, all dressed in the same fashion.

"The soldiers made us form in line two abreast, and in a procession we marched out through the gate. At the head of the line walked the Cardinal. Behind him came a standard-bearer, then the monks and ourselves. At the end were the dolls and the corpses. A huge crowd had gathered in the street to watch the sport. The monks sang the *Misericordia Dei*. Many of us wept. Some were so weak they had to be dragged along by the soldiers. The people in the street—they were mostly the poorest of the poor—were full of rage. They threw horse droppings and stones at us. One man who had more daring than the rest rushed up to me and struck me heavily on the chest. 'You miserable kettle-mender,' he shouted at me; 'they'll put you into flames now, and smoke you until you're as black as one of your own pots.' Everybody laughed at this. I saw some of my neighbors who owed me money for work standing all together.

"At last we came into the big square in front of the Cathedral. It's the same place, you know, where the great King Don Fernando made his vow years ago. They formed us in long rows this time. One Dominican I heard say to a foot soldier, 'Let the whole family of them have a good time together now.' And so they brought two of the dolls and put them beside me, and brought my sons besides. They brought a coffin, too. When I looked into it I saw the naked body of my wife. I fainted at the sight. Though I was only partly in my senses I felt two men jerk me to my feet. In the far distance I heard a voice condemning one after the other either to life imprisonment or to the fire. They condemned my wife to the fire, even though her soul was already with Allah. And they also turned over my youngest, the son I liked best, to the civil authorities for death by fire. The other two were sentenced to the galleys.

"But these two had fled. It was for that reason they had given me two dolls for company. They had to be satisfied with such substitutes. My youngest stood near me. He said coldly—I was amazed to hear how hard his voice had become—'There is only one God, and he is Allah, and Mohammed is his prophet. The Son of Miriam is a liar. He betrays men.'

"I said to my son, 'Boy, it is wrong to leave the world with your heart full of hate. Think of their own saying, Love your enemies and do good to those who hate you.'

"But he would have none of it. I could feel his breath hot on my face. He said that the days of San Fernando were over. He said he would again follow the green silk banner of the Prophet, that even if he were only a tinsmith he would act like a warrior. He told me I should perish of shame at the thought of standing up for these whirling dervishes."

At this Bernal jumped to his feet, tore his knife from out the sheath at his belt. Frenero sat and stared at the Moor like a starved cat at a mouse. Sancho kept his eyes on the floor, and Diego shook his head warningly. "Calm yourself, Bernal. He's out of his mind, crazy. . . ."

But before he could end his admonition a knife hissed by my head. As if entering green melon it sank into the breast of the old man, who collapsed with his face in the fire. The sparks flew and the stink of burning hair arose. We pulled him away, and saw that Frenero's knife was stuck deep in his chest, a little left of the breastbone. We had to hold him down with one knee to pull it out, for it had split its way through a bone. The blood pumped rhythmically out of the wound, the old man lay like a stricken child and could say nothing. He died in a spreading pool of blood which got on our hands and smeared our clothes.

I stood there speechless and sick at my stomach. "What in Christ's name are you thinking of, you son of a dog?" Diego said evenly to Frenero. "The man meant us no harm."

And I said, trembling, "He was a Christian. He believed in the word of God. You have committed a murder, Frenero. . . ."

"He insulted God," Frenero complained, and looked around uneasily.

That night we had little rest. We carried the old man's body outdoors and buried it in a shallow grave before it was properly cold. It was a hard task for we had no shovels.

We then lay down near the fire. I was unable to get to sleep. My thoughts were as anxious as the bats that hovered all about us in the dying light of the fire. Puffs of smoke kept rising from the fire as if evil spirits were at work in its glowing heart. Long shadows played on the walls of the bare room as the smoke billowed first thickly then in a thin cloud. Some of these shadows looked to my fearful eyes like Dominicans with long noses, others like mounted Saracens racing by with their long mantles flowing around them. When my horse outside neighed on hearing a night sound, I would break into an icy sweat.

In the morning I told Frenero that he must part from us. I bade Sancho give him a florin and enough food for one day, turned away and left him standing like a whipped dog, his shoulders hunched up foolishly.

Around noontime I happened to look back. We had already covered some miles. There behind us a half-mile or so trudged Frenero, small in the distance. We all stopped to look and Diego said, "Now we've got a rearguard, like Charlemagne when he crossed the Pyrenees."

"He's not our rearguard," I objected. "He's nothing but a murderer in cold blood."

"Orlando Furioso!" said Diego to this, and laughed. "He's like anyone else, our Frenero. He suffers from the faults of his virtues."

But I was unable to force out a smile at this old saw.

In a short time we came to a crossroads. There stood an image of the Virgin Mary. We got down from our mounts and kneeled to pray. As we were busied in this fashion a rider came upon us from the other road, going in the same direction as we. He rode a mule and carried no weapons. He was very oddly dressed, in half-worldly, half-clerical garments. He was of good height, skinny but very wiry. The cheekbones stuck out prominently above hollow cheeks. His high forehead was creased deeply with wrinkles. Bringing the mule to a halt, he seemed about to strike up a conversation with us. But first he limped over to the image and suddenly threw himself prostrate in the dust. He lay there for some time. Then he got up and limped back to his steed.

When he had settled himself in the saddle he said, "It's always a profound delight to me to see men who find time in the press of the day to turn to our Protector."

I had no answer for this courtly observation, and could only nod my head in acquiescence. But the stranger did not need an answer, and went on to say, "I see we're going to follow the same route for a while. Permit me to accompany you. I do like to meet good men and exchange words with them. Allow me to tell you my name. I am Iñigo López de Recalde. I'm going home to the castle of Loyola, to the Basque country, to the Province of Guipúzcoa."

"Your company is more than welcome, Don Iñigo," I told him, with equal ceremony.

"You mustn't call me Don," he said, plucking sharply on the reins. "I'm neither knight, nor priest, leaseholder, merchant, nor anything so important. I'm simply a learner."

"You don't look like a student," I remarked.

He smiled, a little sadly, and said, "You mean, I look too old for it. Indeed, I'm nearly forty. But I was already thirty before I made the acquaintance of my true teacher."

"I had different luck," I retorted, not without some conceit. "When I was a boy I found a great teacher. His name is Agrippa of Nettesheim."

The stranger regarded me closely. "My teachers have been war, sickness, death and despair," he said mildly. The words embarrassed me greatly, and his eyes troubled me even more. For they were green as glass, and knife-sharp. I felt as if they were cutting through my being and examining what was within my soul. The man had something commanding about him, as if he were used to leading a company of warlike men. His language was temperate and measured, his words were perfectly chosen.

"What do you mean by that riddle?" I asked, more respectfully than I had intended.

He did not answer my question at once, but first asked my name and where I was going. I explained that I was on the way to Trujillo, and from there, with God's help, I would go to the Indies.

"I see," he said to this. "Yes, I see you're a true Spaniard. You are going to the West for the very same reason I went toward the East. But when we get older we realize that the true crusade is not a question of geographical length and width, but of spiritual depth. Dark forests lie in our own hearts. Man himself is a Nova Terra. He himself is a Jerusalem with wailing wall and olive gardens. And he is God's grave."

"I don't know what you mean!" I objected.

"You'll learn by yourself, in time. There's no doubt about that." He measured me with his icy green eyes and I felt a tremor in the pit of my stomach. "All things come in due time, each in its place. Every step of being must be arduously scaled. You want to conquer a kingdom, to make great discoveries. Once I did, too. I believed just as you do now. I wrote romances in honor of Saint Peter, who drew his sword to defend our Lord in the olive groves and lopped off the ear of the soldier Malchus. For I loved above all the martial saints and angels, George the dragon-slayer, and Michael, the conqueror of Satan. . . . But then one May day when we were defending Pamplona I was badly wounded. A bullet splintered my right shinbone, and a fragment of masonry blown from a wall crushed my left foot."

"You were at Pamplona?" Diego broke in.

"Yes, I was there," the stranger said. "I saw plainly that henceforth I should be a cripple." He smiled at me coolly, and a curious feeling possessed me. I had to avert my own glance in some unreasonable fit of shame.

"I noticed you had some trouble walking," I told him hastily.

"Speak out," he said coldly. "Say that I limp and can scarcely walk. It is of small consequence to me, my friends. In any case my servants brought me to my father's castle. My pain was severe. The doctors broke my shinbone twice in order to reset it. The leg was shortened, and some of them tried to restore it to its proper length by the use of an iron apparatus. This gave me more pain, as you can well understand. I lay in bed, week after week, month after month. All my dreams of martial fame and honor and the love of women had vanished. I had an endless time to consider my life. Most of us, lusting for gain of one kind or another, never enjoy this privilege.

"So now I know what really matters in the lives of men," the stranger went on, and thoughtfully tapped his mule's skull to emphasize his point. "The differences separating men are small indeed. What does it matter that one is rich and another poor? It is pathetic nonsense to squander our given span in hunting gold and property. How small, too, is the difference between the stupid and the wise, for at the bottom the wise man is only a little less inadequate than his fellow. What do we know, really? What can we know?"

He made a deprecatory gesture and said evenly, "Not that I scorn knowledge. In dealing with my friends I have always struggled to use insight and decorum. I loathe those Dominicans who want to gain their ends with fire and sword. Those are the weapons of fools. Has not our Lord said, Be wise as serpents and simple as doves? And again, the difference between the just and the unjust is hardly worth discussion. In actual fact there is only one difference setting one man off from another. But this difference is in the nature of a bottomless canyon. On the one side stand those who believe. On the other, those who do not. My friend, without belief there is nothing. No kingdom, no knowledge, no happiness. And what is more, no reality. We are real only insofar as we share in God."

About us lay the Spanish highland, bright in the spring sun. The stones were heavy on the ground, packed with their own weight. The tender twigs of the yet leafless trees made lacework against the sweet blue sky.

"And those stones there? Do they, too, get their reality from God?" I asked.

"They do," said the stranger, lifting his right hand on high. "Do not look with contempt at stones. Like the stars they are among the first-born of Creation. I love this hard world. See how it overcomes its heaviness, this stony heath, and lifts itself up in eager peaks, seeking heaven. I understand. Once I rose from my bed and climbed up into the heights of Montserrat."

"Why, that's the mountain where Parsifal found the Holy Grail," I said eagerly.

"I found the Grail, too," the stranger said.

"Then it's true!" both Diego and I shouted as with the one voice.

"Yes, it is true," said Iñigo. "But the Holy Grail appears to every person in a different form. You must know that today on the top of the mountain there is a chapel with a miracle-working image of the Mother of God. Near this image there hang countless arms, hands, legs and other human parts, all fashioned out of wax. Pilgrims who long to have their sickness cured have brought these gifts.

"I hung my sword, my shield and my armor under the image. Armed only with the lance I kept vigil, for my wish was to become a Soldier of the Virgin Mary, to ride among her hosts. Yet in the dark I was overcome with black doubts. It was hard for me to believe that I was worthy of the honor. It was very cold and dark. The wind moaned as if some great animal were crying out over the whole world. Damp clouds of mists enveloped me, and water ran down my cheeks in icy drops. I stood there the whole night, leaning on my lance. Toward morning the world became gray. In the fog about me there was commotion as if I were witnessing the first day of creation out of chaos. Then doubt again grew within my breast. I begged the Blessed Virgin to give me a sign that she had taken me into her hand. And behold, my friends, suddenly I saw myself standing in the mist clouds, in the very center of billowing chaos. I was like a giant, a titan. The lance in my hand reached into eternity, higher than the tallest mast of the greatest ship afloat on the sea, stronger than the mightiest oak that grows in the stony soil of my homeland."

"A miracle!" Bernal shouted. He rushed forward, bent one knee and kissed the stranger's hand. It was only then I became fully aware that Frenero had been standing behind Bernal all the while. I said nothing, let him remain there, as he averted his eyes from my gaze.

"When I had received this sign," Iñigo continued, "it became bright and transparent within me. I was filled with joy. The sun now came up out of the eastern sea. The long rays gleamed about the sun's head like swords made of light. In my soul I heard how God the Father said, Let there be light. For the words of God are eternal. They are here today as well as yesterday, and will be here tomorrow and forever. In tumbling haste the thick air welled skyward, opened up, and soon all about me was a flood of pure silver. The mountains sprang up in the light, bathed with a sweet-smelling morning wind. Only here and there were memories of the night in some as yet unlighted strip of deep valley, far, far below. But this did not last for long. The woods awoke, and the streams of the plains glistened. Thereupon I hung my lance under the image of the Mother of God. And so I, a cripple, was knighted a soldier of God.

"I was a newcomer to the arts of battle against the enemies of the human soul. I descended from the mountain in order to acquire better, deadlier weapons in the Universities of Alcalá and Salamanca. Now I am on my way home, and from there will move on to Paris. Like San Domingo de Guzman, like San Francisco de Assisi, I want to gather round me a band of warriors. This band must be small, select and armed with knowledge. Nothing annoys me so much as four-cornered, crude stupidity and the dirt of barefoot monks and the rheum of the mendicant orders."

"What?" I cried. "You, too? How can that be!"

"Do you know something of these things?" he inquired.

I told him my experience with the Inquisition. He listened attentively and nodded from time to time in understanding. "Your refusal to give an oath does you honor," he admitted, "but I cannot see that Antonio Cardinal de Guevara was entirely in the wrong. In the interests of belief, honor must occasionally be abandoned."

"But that is impossible for me," I said, and my eyes grew hot with angry disappointment at his response. "It is hard for me to see how you can think that way. All you have said makes you out to be a just and deep-thinking man."

"Sometimes the way to truth winds among lies," he answered thoughtfully and quite indifferent to my criticism. "Sometimes the way to power can be accomplished only by cunning, and the way to justice often demands the exercise of violence and injury. The end justifies the means, my friend."

The stranger, despite his fundamental lack of sympathy, attracted me. From the first time I set eyes on him he captured my trust. His tales of his wounds and his vigil moved me almost to tears, for though I could not talk coherently the same needs burned within me. And Diego was also touched. The others, Sancho, Bernal and Frenero, looked open-mouthed at the man with the glass-green eyes.

"In the world of the spirit," Iñigo went on slowly, "the straight way is preferable to all others. For a straight line, so the mathematicians tell us, is indeed the shortest distance between two points. But the world, my sons, is in nature crooked and curved. It is necessary, at times, therefore, that men on earth follow the crooked path. Anything so long as the line within their souls remains straight and unsullied.

"It would not be polite of me"—he was now addressing me alone—"to take advantage of your youthful inexperience. But think on your own skill in combat as you have learned it. Is not the art of battle a matter of concealing one's own strength from the enemy? And then, at the proper moment, of felling him suddenly by striking home at his weakest spot? Or do you think that a good soldier runs headlong into the culverins of the enemy? Such a war as that now being pursued by the Dominicans is doomed to failure from the start. They must always withdraw, however terrible the slaughter they may inflict on the front ranks of the enemy. Position after position has been lost to the Church. But I shall place my cannon upon an unconquerable height, and my light cavalry will threaten their flanks until eternity. My spies will sit at the council table of the enemy. I shall know their intentions, and like a chess player I shall foresee the moves to come, and prepare for them long in advance. Yet life is short, short, too short. There is much to learn and much first to unlearn. I can see no other way out than to found a school."

He lowered his head, possessed by inner thoughts, and tested with forefinger and thumb the roughness of his mule's scrubby mane. To himself he muttered, "Everything can fall into ruins. But the fortress of the Church will not be stormed."

When he said this there came to mind an old saying which I had once read in the Alcazar at Cordova. It was engraved in a broad sword, and ran, *Fiat justitia, pereat mundus*—Let there be justice though the earth perish. It seemed curious to me, beyond understanding, that the stranger did not put justice in the place of the Church. I said to him, "Then you don't believe in justice?"

To this he replied obliquely, "The greatest mistake of mankind is that they are forever changing means and goals. By so doing they lose their sense of reality. The last goal, the final reality, is God. It is toward this end that man must strive. Justice is only a means, just as the state is but a device. Some make the state or justice their final aim. They might as well pray to the iron furnace of the Phoenicians. Justice and belief complement each other as do the Old Testament and the Evangels, as the blind synagogue and the clear-seeing Church, as the state of Israel and the *civitas Dei* of Saint Augustine, as law and grace."

In the meanwhile we had come some distance from our dead stop, and now had reached another crossroad. The stranger drew in his mule and told us he must head toward the north.

"It is my hope," I said politely as he was taking leave of us, "that you have a good journey, Iñigo López, and that soon you reach your goal."

"My goal will keep for a few days," he answered with a sigh. His eyes followed the road to the north, a white line over hill and dale. "My father's castle—it has been called Loyola since time immemorial—lies far in the Pyrenees, where the Basques live." He stared at me attentively with his almost unnatural eyes, and added slowly, "Don't forget, my son: convince yourself that at times injustice is the working of a higher justice. Consider it as necessity."

Thus we parted.* For a long time the stranger's words rang in my

* In after years I was to realize that my chance acquaintance was the great Ignatius—the name the Church gave him.

ears. I looked down on Frenero's bushy red hair as he trudged along beside me. I decided to let him stay with us after all. The distinction between right and wrong which before had been as sharp to me as the edge of a knife had been blurred by the words of the man of Loyola. Who knows, I told myself, perhaps Frenero had acted justly after all? He had murdered out of zeal, out of anger at sacrilege.

With a sigh I turned from such onerous thoughts. I really had but little desire for them, for it was spring. The wind was soft as a child's lips and was honeysweet in my nostrils. On the slopes along the way grew thick clumps of narcissus.

We now arrived at a stony declivity, at which place people lived in dark caves in the mountainside. The sun had lured them from dark abodes. Half-naked men, their uncut hair hanging below their shoulders, and slatternly women loitered on the mountain meadow. About them tumbled many brown-skinned children, all without a stitch of clothing on their backs. They wore crowns of narcissus in their hair and greeted our little cavalcade with shouts of glee.

"Where are you riding? Where are you going, great duke?" the children cried. "Are you on the way to the Holy Land?" And even the grownups got to their feet and came toward us in curiosity.

"Let's crown your horse," one comely girl said, and rushed toward me. The horse was startled and began to dance. Bernal took hold of the child and threw her to one side. In a trice she had turned on him and bitten him severely in the hand. "Why, you dirty little bitch!" Bernal roared. "You she-goat, I'll flay the hide off your body."

He tried to catch her, but she dodged him with skill like a creature of the woods. He persisted, and it was a strange sight to watch him galloping uncertainly over the stony ground and peering wrathfully behind every bush. It was like a heavy faun chasing a dryad. Everybody, including ourselves, burst into laughteer.

"They live like wild people," Diego said. "Spring is bubbling in their blood. It has turned it to wine, and as sure as the sun rises tonight more of these little brown babies will be conceived. They grow and decline in innocence, like trees or flowers." He smiled at my face, full of wonder.

"Yes, Pedro, our Spain is a curious land," he declaimed. "We have a king and a court filled with ladies, and we have our burghers. And here lives a lost people who have no idea at all of what is going on in the cities. Why, our Lord's name has scarcely echoed in their ears. In forgotten times they lived here. Nights in the firelight they have always painted the walls of their caves with drawings, showing bears, buffalo and hairy elephants."

After more days of journey we came to the land of Estremadura. It was a broad, rolling, hilly country. On the hills grew groves of oaks. Their gnarled limbs stood out clearly in the light spring sky. Outside the villages we often met droves of swine. The swineherd walked along clothed in a torn, clay-colored cloak; in his hand he had a long staff with an iron point, and slung from his shoulder was a twisted horn. If a hog strayed from the herd to get a special bit of mast, the herder took the horn and blew melancholy tones at the erring beast, not unlike the grunts of the animal himself.

But we liked this swinish music. And the swineherds, mostly bearded men, usually tall and very thin, seemed to be equally pleased with our presence. They carried themselves with unexpected dignity. They often told us that some of their own relatives had just left for the Indies. We ate many a suckling pig beside a smoky fire, and here we learned many a curious bit of news.

Among these people we often heard the name of Pizarro, for years ago he had been a swineherd, and not so good at his work at that, according to common report. Yet despite a poor standing in his early calling, his former colleagues seemed very proud of him and were of the opinion that it was this initial disciplining of his courage that lay behind his success in arms. For these swineherds are much given to fighting among themselves, usually over the ownership of a pig which has wandered into the wrong drove. They all carry long knives in their broad leathern belts.

An old man told me that Pizarro was a bastard who had been found on the church steps, and had been adopted into the home of a swineherd. Since the family had neither a cow nor a goat to provide milk for the infant, he was put with the sucklings to slake his need at the dugs of a prize sow. Fed in this uncommon fashion he grew up into a strong, well-made and knowing child, since from the start he had had to struggle desperately with his squealing foster brothers to keep his belly full.

We all enjoyed this story, and laughed together, although the old herder sat there like a graven image, unsmiling, from time to time spitting carefully into the fire.

10

CAMPEADOR

LATE one afternoon, as we wound our way along the road, we saw before us a church built atop a low hill. This church had a gray, square tower, and walls built out of field stones. Though it was not a feast day, the bells were ringing and the deep sound echoed far and wide over the land. This aroused our curiosity, and at first we concluded that somewhere near by there must be a fire. Yet there was no sign of fire anywhere when we stopped and carefully looked in all directions. We decided to inquire of the sexton about the alarm, and also of our whereabouts, for we calculated that we were getting very close to Trujillo.

As we drew nearer to the church we saw an excited crowd of peasants milling about the front door. We smelled a very fine odor of meat roasting and of newly baked bread, and to our amazement lively music of anything but ecclesiastic spirit.

The crowd was gathered in the graveyard. Men and women sat on the gravestones and the children were playing games near the crosses that leaned against the church wall. Not far away stood a huge white baker's kiln. Out of it a man was drawing roasted pig and mutton and many loaves of bread, while the gathering cheered lustily.

The tumult in the belfry grew louder as heavy men took turns swinging with all their strength on the rope. Suddenly a thickset man jumped up on a tablelike marker over a tomb and cried out in a mighty voice, "Food's on the way!" To which all said in loud antiphony, "It's coming, it's coming!"

Diego laughed. "By the dear bowels of Christ," he remarked, "we've come at the opportune moment."

The pork and mutton were piled up on two handbarrows and carried into the cemetery along with the bread in a tremendous wicker basket.

Now they all pressed round the food, laughing and joking, the children screaming fiendishly under their parents' legs. This confusion lasted a few minutes, the crowd miraculously parted, and the barrows were stripped. Sancho, watching the procedure with covetous eyes, sighed, and a feeling of disappointment gripped me, too, I confess. Everyone but ourselves had a huge, dripping piece of freshly roasted meat in one hand and a fistful of bread in the other. The rich food was devoured gluttonously. Even the small children who as yet could not chew sucked busily on a bone. Soon more men came up with casks of wine and filled the beakers which were offered on all sides.

Faces grew red, men spoke wildly and the young girls tittered into their hands, forgetting the howling babies consigned to their charge. Many a beaker was spilled, and all about were dark patches where the wasted wine had stained the dry earth. Many of the revelers had eaten and drunk far too much and too quickly. I saw one woman of middle age, her hair disheveled and her face pale, rush to the church wall, lean eagerly against it, and vomit until the tears ran down her face, forced out by the violence of her retching.

We had stood watching this feast for perhaps half an hour before anyone paid much attention to us, but at last an old man approached, removed his cap, and said, "Please join us, worthy caballeros. We've got another ovenful of food. You're welcome to share it with us."

"What is this feast?" I asked politely. "Is it in honor of someone who died? Is it a wedding?"

"Anyone would think so," replied the old man with great satisfaction. "But it isn't anything like that. A certain man by the name of Don Francisco Pizarro—bless him and his brothers—has just come back home to Trujillo from Toledo. He has been visiting the King at the court. He set up this feast for us. He's going to tell us an important piece of news when he gets here."

My heart came into my throat. "He's coming here?" I asked.

"Of course," said the old man sharply. "Why shouldn't he! He lives here."

"We are very glad to accept your invitation," I mumbled hastily, and beckoned the rest to come along. Diego and I dismounted. As I was handing over the bridle of my horse to a peasant boy to hold for me—for now many of the feasters, having had their fill, were coming to find out who the strangers were—someone threw her arms about me, and began to kiss me in the most extravagant manner. I struggled free and discovered to my amazement it was Teresa!

"My Pedro," she said to me as Sancho watched, beaming with excitement, "how glad I am to see you again! What a great lord you've become! What a horse! And where did you get all those beautiful clothes? And look at my Sancho. He's a marshal!" She laughed and cried at the same time, and I was embarrassed at all the attention.

"Yes, Teresa," I said, "things have changed a little on the surface. This is my secretary, Diego de Vargas. These are my bodyguards, Bernal and Frenero."

In the midst of this reunion, to make matters more distracting, two men, one thin, the other very fat, came hurrying up.

"By God, it's him, all right," said the fat one.

"Look at him! He's grown up!" the thin one added.

It was Alonso the splendid that I recognized first. "Can it be you, Alonso?" I asked him, genuinely amazed at so much coincidence.

"It's me, as sure as ears sprout from the skull of a mule," shouted Alonso, almost beside himself. "Before you stands the very lump of flesh you once saved from the whip. It's me, Alonso, the man who lives always for an idea." He turned and pointed to his thin brother, Juan, who stood by grinning and grimacing with delight. "Yes, and I suppose you know who that beanpole is. There he stands, that half-starved, riotous whoremongering sliver, fresh from a night's sleep in the pigpen." I took Juan's hand and we laughed merrily together.

In a moment Rodrigo, the Devil, came up. He still had the same sardonic manner, and after kissing me on the forehead, said:

"Sweet knight, that's not the kiss of Judas, either. It's a sign of reverence, as sure as I'm a Devil." He cackled at his own wit, then neighed loudly, like a horse.

I learned that Father Abraham was still alive, but that his camel had died of old age. It was not long before the Devil, whose loquacity had not diminished in the slightest, was in the middle of an elaborate dissertation on the passage of the years.

"My son, everything has its time, I've discovered," said the Devil. "Love, too, you can include in the list. Did I tell you? I didn't, of course, for I didn't have a chance, but I shall in a moment. Well, my wife ran off with the Archangel Michael. She was a fine woman. I revere her memory. I never did get to the bottom of the matter. But, my son, take away his angel's sword, that silver breastplate he used to carry around on his chest and his wings, and what have you? A sod. His appearance, his address and his brains cannot compare with my own. Am I right?" he wound up, and belched like a cannon.

"I grant you that," I told him in all honesty; yet not wishing to encourage more revelations of domestic catastrophe, I purposely concealed my sympathy.

"Grant it or not, I know it to be true by actual experience," he continued, undismayed. "But women, you see, after having my demonic person around them for a while long for a heavenly change. Women, including my wife, like to see their men generally admired and sought after. Why, every mud-hut village we'd come to, that pudding-brained Archangel would create a stir. They all flocked around him—the women, I mean. They couldn't do enough for him. They thought he really was Michael, the fools. And they must have thought I was really the Devil."

"What a shame," I said. "I really don't know what..."

"Never mind, Don Pedro, I'm not looking for sympathy. I just like to talk about it. It's the wine I've been drinking," Rodrigo assured me. "You see, my son, I've been sacrificed to my profession. I've sent my boy—he was four years old when he left—to live with my mother in Salamanca. I gave her instructions never to let that boy get a peep at a stage. He's going to be a notary or a licentiate if I have my way. He's going to enjoy a well-ordered life, and not have to cock his leg at every pillar and post to amuse the yokels. He'll never be hated and reviled as I am. For I am, you know. I'm tired of all forms of deviltry. It's become a mountainous bore, my son. My reputation has always preceded me. I'm a belled cat. And the harder I run to do the right thing, the more noise I make.

"Yes, I wandered through the whole of Spain half crazed, like this belled cat I'm speaking about, after my wife left me. I could play the role of disappointed Devil, but the role of cheated husband was too much for my powers. But now it's all over, dead and gone. This Pizarro, I heard, needs men. The three of us, the two brothers and I, thought we'd try it out. I'd like to have a large expanse of salt water between me and my devilish past."

He chuckled to himself, and winked at me horribly. "Alonso, you see, feels he's cut out for a crusade. He's yearning to experience torments, hunger. He spends most of his time imagining himself pulling Indian arrows out of his brother's hide. But that Juan—look at him!" He pointed at the thin one, who was just holding out his beaker for a refilling. "He'll never get to the Indies if he keeps it up. It's a wonder his guts don't burst."

In the graveyard, Diego and his gay clothes were attracting a great deal of interest. Little barefoot girls were gathered around him as he reached his beaker for wine, and older ones as well. I noticed that many a young swain was looking at him blackly out of hate-filled eyes and I was suddenly afraid of murder. For we Spaniards are only too ready to draw the knife when a stranger interferes in our affairs with women, something that Diego, if overheated with wine, would not hesitate to do. The old man who had invited us to partake of the food inquired about Diego. "Who's that man?" he said.

"That's Diego de Vargas, baccalaureate from Salamanca, and a poet," I replied, putting Diego's best foot forward for him.

"A poet!" the old man cried, his suspicious face lighting up. "Why, that's just what we've been lacking. Excuse me, my lord." He hastened over to Diego, and left me to my devices.

Bowing low to Diego, he said with ceremony, "My lord poet, would you be so kind as to favor us with a song?"

"A song?" said Diego, now grand with wine. "A song? Not at all. I'm as hoarse as a crow in the stubble. But I'll go that one better," he reassured the old man loudly, so that everyone could hear. "Get somebody to pluck out a suitable melody at the right place and I'll tell you a story which covers the tragic, the sentimental, the romantic and every other intermediate phase of love."

"Just a minute," said the old man, and nodded urgently to the young men who not a moment ago had been slaying Diego with evil looks but who were now as eager as the women, having discovered Diego was a poet and so apart from them. Everyone cheered when a pretty girl stroked his hair and an old beldam planted a dry kiss on his cheeks. Someone came forward with a lute.

"Is there anything you'd like?" shouted Diego. He had leaped onto a flat tombstone. "Speak up, good people. Name your choice and you shall have it!"

Amid shouts and cries a variety of suggestions was shouted out. "Tell us about Boabdil el Chico de Granada!" "Tell us about the three Sanchos!" "The battle in the Cloister of Saint George in Cordova!" "About the Moorish treasures and the spirits of Solomon!" Finally someone overruled the rest with his selection. Over and over he bellowed, "Tell us about the Cid Campeador!"

"Am I right?" said Diego, putting a hand behind his ear. "Is it the Cid Campeador you want to hear about?"

"Yes, yes!" everyone shouted in unison, and the children screamed so shrilly that it made the hair rise on the nape of my neck.

"Well, then, good people, draw closer, all of you. I'll tell you about the Cid when he was a boy, when he was only about five feet tall, about like you over there." He pointed to a peasant boy who looked at him with his lower lip sagging down in wonder and anticipation.

And so Diego told them the story in this fashion, as well as I can remember it:

"In the year 1000 after the birth of our Lord Jesus Christ, the head of a noble Gothic house, Diego Laynez by name, went into the country on the feast day of Santiago. He was in his middle years and wanton; he liked to play with love. He saw a miller's young wife who was carrying food to her man on a trencher. The young wife defended her virtue a little, for it was the seemly thing to do, when Diego Laynez tried to drag her into the bushes. In the end she had to give in, for more than anything else she was afraid of spilling her husband's food and wished to get the matter over with as quickly as possible. And so it was done, in but a few minutes, for Diego Laynez was a warm man.

"So there sat the broad-cheeked miller, chewing like a bull in the pen, and his spouse in her shame told him how Diego Laynez, the nobleman, had laid hands on her. But the miller shook his head, and said, 'Forget about it. He's just another nobleman, and has a weakness for women.'

"The wife sat still. Her head lowered, and her long black lashes brushed her cheeks. She thought to herself: 'Ah, yes, he is a hot man, indeed,' and did not know what else to think. A few tears stole down her face, and she sobbed gently, for she was upset by Diego's love-making. This moved the miller who loved his young wife in his way. He kissed the little dark-haired woman, and stroked her hair tenderly.

"And so it happened that ten moons after this feast day the miller's wife bore two sons. The miller reckoned it out on his fingers and came to the conclusion that the oldest of the twins was the son of Diego Laynez. For in those days the nobles always walked out the house first, with the common people following after. The older boy he named Rodrigo Diaz. The younger one, his own, he named Fernando Diaz.

"Rodrigo Diaz grew up with the friendly miller. At an early age he was remarkable for his knightly accomplishments. With his wooden sword he could whip off the head of a tough thistle better than any boy for miles around. And when the boys from the next village set on him, he beat them all off with ease.

"When Rodrigo Diaz was older, he helped the miller at his trade. He threw the heavy sacks onto the asses' backs. By himself he lifted the heavy millstone into place, while his father and his brother stood by. Sometimes Diego Laynez would come riding along to inquire about his son. He was always friendly with the boy, and every time left a present behind. But the nobleman's wife, Doña Teresa, the daughter of Count Nuño Alvarez de Amaya, wondered about this, and said, 'I sense a dark mystery. What is it, my husband?'

"He merely laughed at her and replied, 'There's no mystery to it at all.'

"And now it happened that Diego Laynez was publicly boxed on the ears and kicked by his arch enemy, the Count of Gormaz, who was known as the Proud. At this time Diego Laynez was no longer so young, and was unable to revenge himself on the Count. He suffered terribly from the insult. He could no longer sleep, eat or drink. He walked around with his head hanging, never speaking a word to his friends when they tried to get him to talk.

"Finally he assembled all his sons about him, including Rodrigo Diaz. In order to test their honor, Diego Laynez had each one put a finger in his mouth. Then he bit on it, harder and harder, to see how long it would take before they cried out. The sons of Doña Teresa were horrified, and said: 'Father, what is it you want! Let us go. You're hurting us.'

"But the son born of the miller's wife, who stood last in line, took the nobleman by his beard and threw him into the corner like a sack of corn. He said, in his anger, 'You miserable old man, get down on your knees and thank God that by luck you are my father.'

"The father then got to his feet. His limbs were sore but his heart was glad, and he threw his arms about his son. 'Oh, my true, my finest son,' he said, 'you will avenge my honor just as you would your own!'

"And so it happened. When Rodrigo Diaz appeared before the castle of the Count of Gormaz, him whom they called the Proud, the Count shouted, 'What do you want, you lump? Get out of here before I lose my temper and have you beaten with rods until the blood spurts out of you like a Moorish fountain.'

"To this Rodrigo Diaz cried, 'Noble Count of Gormaz, you may be very proud. You may be able to kick old men around, and drag women up and down by the hair of the head, and pick the pockets of the Jews. But when a man stands before you, your heart drops into your boots. You're no better than a cutter of whiskers.'

" 'That's far too much,' said the Count, his eyes bloody with rage. He raced to get his sword, and rushed out to the castle gate where Rodrigo Diaz was waiting for him. A terrible fight now began.

"On the balcony of the castle stood the beautiful Doña Jimena Gómez, the Count's daughter, surrounded by her women. She cried out for all to hear, 'Teach that bumpkin a lesson, Father!'

"At that very moment with a mighty sweep Rodrigo Diaz lopped off the Count's head. He picked up the bleeding head by its black beard as David once did Goliath's. He held it up in the air for the daughter to see. She cried out in fearful anguish at the sight.

"Diego Laynez was satisfied completely with his son's success. From then on he could talk out loud with his friends and laugh at will. No longer was his breath contaminating. But Doña Jimena Gómez sought an audience with Don Fernando, the King of Castile. She tore out her beautiful hair in handfuls, and implored, 'O Don Fernando, O Christian King, behead my father's murderer, and pay like with like in all justice.'

" 'I cannot do that,' said the King, 'for I'm in need of brave men. There are too few of them in this world. One of them, your father, has been taken away from me. Would you have me take still another one?'

" 'But who will protect and shelter me now?' asked Doña Jimena Gómez with the sparkling eyes. 'Not that I really need protecting, for I can do that myself. But custom demands it. I cannot go about alone. Women's tongues will gabble about me.'

"Don Fernando thought for a time, a very long time, with his great white head buried in his hands. At last he pronounced judgment like Solomon, and said: 'Doña Jimena Gómez, my beloved daughter and vassal, I give you the life of Rodrigo Diaz who slew your father in mortal combat. But I do not give it to you to throw it away. He must not sprawl lifeless like a slaughtered calf. You must take him, the living man, to you, into your warm bed, as your husband. May he give you many sons and daughters.'

"On hearing this, Doña Jimena cried aloud and her hair almost stood on end. Yet in her heart she thought, amid sobs and tears, 'Don Fernando the King has indeed spoken wisely. For Rodrigo Diaz has dark locks like mine, and is well-built and very strong. I can scarcely find a better man. His life will be mine and should be. And so I shall avenge my father.'

"When they had pledged their troth in Burgos, Doña Jimena threw back the veil from her face and said this to Rodrigo Diaz, 'You cannot be my man, Rodrigo Diaz, and I shall never take you with me to my bed until you have become a knight whose fame is celebrated by every singer and teller of tales in Castile. The women and girls must whisper together and wonder at the happiness and pride of Doña Jimena.'

"At this Rodrigo Diaz had to hang his head, for he loved her dearly. He rode out through the city gate of Burgos, taking some armed men with him. In this fashion he pursued justice as a master of the knife and the gallows. When the peasants saw the corpse of some wicked man dangling from the limb of a tree, they said, 'Rodrigo Diaz has been here and brought justice.' In time he achieved great fame among the tillers of the fields, the keepers of the flocks, the hewers and burners of wood, the fishers on the rivers' banks. His name carried from village to village, from house to house. And the singers of the people praised him in the flickering torchlight.

"It happened that five Moorish kings came into Castile from the lands of Aragon. They stormed and sacked the good cities of Logrono and Nájera. When they were returning over the mountain passes with their booty and prisoners, Rodrigo Diaz fell upon them on his horse Babieca. It was like an avalanche of stone from the heights. He seized the rich booty, freed the prisoners and encircled the five kings with his men. In their fear the Moorish kings said, 'Worthy master, let us return to our homes in Aragon. We promise never to come here again so long as you keep watch over this land.'

"Rodrigo Diaz bowed courteously, and said, 'Send for a rich ransom by messenger. Give me gold, silver, pearls, precious stones, fine tapestries and cloths, all ornamented with images; send me myrrh and other incense, weapons, helmets and some good horses. Then I will let you go free, you kings. But he who fails to meet my demands will feel the edge of the sword hanging in my scabbard.'

"Everything happened just as Rodrigo Diaz asked. In a few days the son of the miller's wife became a rich man through the strength of his arm and the quickness of his wits. His great bravery, wisdom and mildness became a byword among the Moors. But since they did not know his name, they called him by a simple word in their own language, the Cid. And this means the great leader, the prince. Because the Moors had popular minstrels and their bards wandered all over Spain from city to city, it was not long before Rodrigo Diaz was called the Cid everywhere from the mountains of the North to the warm valleys of Andalusia.

"And now I wish that one of my listeners would give me a full beaker of wine," Diego said. "I must drink it up. It will make my tongue lighter and quicker. For now I am coming to a deed of my master the great Cid which needs high praise."

The peasants did as they were told. Without exception they hung on Diego's words, not even whispering to one another. From time to time they would murmur their approval, for all Spaniards feel a mighty pride in their veins when they hear of the Cid. After Diego had drunk solemnly, draining his beaker dry in a few gulps, he went on. The interruption was hardly noticeable, and the lute-player continued to strum his instrument.

"There are many men," Diego said, resuming the story, "who fear neither bloody wounds nor death itself. For what is death but a long sleep? But there are few men who dare stand up to the prospect of sickness and homelessness and persecution. The wine is good and fiery. But since I don't have the tongue of an angel I can only say that my heart is full of love for the man of my people, whom I revere—the Cid. For if my heart were not filled with this love, my friends, all that I said would be empty tinkling, a groaning and moaning of the wind.

"And so know, then, people of Trujillo, that in those times a war broke out between the King of Castile and the King of Aragon over who should possess the city fortress of Calahorra. Civil war is a great scourge, from which even the winner can hope to gain nothing. And, knowing this, it was decided by the kings and their councilors that instead of a battle between the armies of Castile and Aragon there should be a single combat between two champions, one from each side. Whoever was the victor, to his side would belong the city of Calahorra. The King of Aragon chose the knight Don Martin Gonzalez as his champion. The King of Castile, Don Fernando, chose Rodrigo Diaz the Cid. He advised him urgently to make a pilgrimage to Santiago de Compostela before the mortal fray, in order that his soul should be composed and he could enjoy the protection of the saint.

"The Cid rode away with twenty knights for a company. He held his head down in deep thought. To himself he meditated on the uncertainty of men's lives and the gossamer of happiness. For like the shifting shadows on the broken waters of the sea, mankind comes and goes eternally. The Cid saw it might well be that Don Martin Gonzalez would slay him. At this his heart trembled in his breast. For even the bravest of men know fear, though they may be able to conquer it. The Cid looked out over the countryside and said to himself, 'The dream of our life is spun tightly. But where lies reality?'

"He saw himself lying stricken on the field, with a gaping wound in his breast. He heard his Babieca neighing piteously. He saw them burying his own corpse while his soul stood by now homeless and confused. His heart cried out and asked, 'Where then is reality?'

"At this, our master the Cid broke out into a rage. He cried out so loudly that his escort drew aside in fear, and Babieca jumped in terror. The Cid shouted, 'I will tell you something, you craven heart! God is reality—He and none else.'

" 'Yes, but God is in Heaven,' the heart complained, 'and Heaven is far away, so far away.'

"Then He must come down from Heaven!" roared the Cid. At this the men of his retinue drew their horses together in great anxiety, for they began to believe the master had lost his mind. They looked at one another with a question in their eyes.

" 'But you cannot make Him do that,' sobbed the heart. 'Never can you make Him bend to your will.'

"Suddenly the Cid laughed long and loud. He sprang down from his horse, and said, 'I'm not talking about forcing Him to come. But behold, my heart, I shall give to the poor who wander in hunger through the land. I shall comfort the unhappy who tend the sick. The innocent shall find in me a father, and the wavering spirits a staff. For such was God on earth. I shall ride no longer in arrogance on Babieca, but wade barefoot through the dust. For God is love, and love is God for our earthly eyes. It is as love that we know His splendor. What God may be beyond love is known to the saints, the apostles and the angels. But not to me, for I am but a simple man. My head is already afire with this purpose.'

"Thereupon the Cid's heart moved back into its accustomed place in his breast and said, 'Your simple understanding speaks well, great Cid. Our life is no dream. We do not move aimlessly through a country of dreams when we love. Then we stand on firm ground. It is as if we had granite underfoot. When we love, we are protected better than if a breastplate of three thicknesses covered us, one touched by the magic wand of Merlin.'

"And now our master the Cid, who was once Rodrigo Diaz, did many good deeds. He cheered many who wept. No beggar was too poor, too hideous, that he did not have him ride on Babieca, while he himself led his horse along by the bridle. Babieca was amazed at all this.

"One evening, as the shadows were lengthening over the countryside, the Cid heard someone crying bitterly for help. It was a leper, who stood deep in the water of a swamp into which he had fallen. He was waving his rattle in a transport of fear. Up to the hips he was embedded in the black quag. His face was not unlike a skull, his skin was covered with white scales like the body of a carp, and some of his fingers had fallen away from his hands. When they saw this man the Cid's companions said quickly, 'Let us ride quickly from this creature, for nothing can be done to help him.'

" 'That is not so,' retorted our master the Cid. He reached out far into the quagmire and drew the suffering leper back to safety. He then placed him on his horse Babieca, and let him ride along, while the rest held off at a good distance, looking at each other with anxious faces. For the sickness of the leper is worse than death itself and they feared contamination.

"When they got to an inn, the Cid had mutton stew brought out, and sat down next to the leper. They ate out of the same dish which stood in the middle of the table. And when the leper reached out his spoon the flakes of dry flesh fell like snow into the dish. This distressed the companions of the Cid, so that they jumped to their feet and left the inn.

"When they both had eaten their fill, the Cid had a bed prepared. He lay down with the leper at his side, both under the same cover. About midnight he awoke, as if a chill draught had struck him. He felt about him, and saw that the place at his side was empty. The Cid called for a candle. He looked under the bed and in all corners of the room. But the leper could be found nowhere at all. The Cid, giving up the search, again lay down and went to sleep. Suddenly he awakened out of a deep sleep. At the side of his bed stood a huge man in long white robes. About his head there was a halo of fire.

" 'Who are you?' asked my master the Cid, 'and why have you a halo of fire about your head? Are you a ghost?' As he said these words he yawned loudly, for he was very tired.

" 'I am Lazarus, the resurrected,' replied the man with the halo. 'I am Lazarus, whom the Lord loved dearly, and for whom he once shed tears in Bethany which is in the Holy Land. And know, my child, that I came to you as a leper in order to prove your courage and compassion. For in Heaven I had heard others talking about your spirit. And you did show me love and respect. This shall be repaid you a thousandfold. You shall become a great knight, a fortress of belief. At the very sound of your name, your enemies, Moors and Christians alike, shall tremble as stricken with the ague. But your friends shall find joy in you. Your praises shall be sung by the minstrels to the end of time. And when you have spun out your days, as all men must, you shall die peacefully, on your own land among those who love you. But now I must leave you, my child, though I shall see you again. Rejoice that your sword and shield are blessed.'

"Now the man vanished, and the Cid left his bed to spend the rest of the night in prayer, until the sky reddened and the cocks crowed.

"At last the day came when the fate of Calahorra was to be decided. Two mighty armies came down from the mountains amid the wonder of the morning sun. On one side was the banner of Castile with a three-towered castle and a lion rampant. On the other side fluttered in the fresh breeze the arms of Aragon, a red cross on a striped field. Behind the long ranks of knights, of attendants with their lances, the women rode on their palfreys. Behind all these, farther still, was a great throng of common people. For everyone wanted to see the battle, and witness how God would decide the fate of the city of Calahorra.

"At the appointed hour the heralds gave voice to their trumpets. As the brazen throats rang out, two small companies of knights rode to the front of the armies, very slowly, and met face to face in the middle of the field of combat. At this all the knights and ladies got down from their steeds, threw themselves on their knees and prayed to God for victory on their side. Then the women began to weep and the people to shout. All over the countryside there was an indescribable clamor in which intermingled the ruffle of drums and the blare of trumpets. It became still suddenly, as if a curtain had been dropped. Nothing could be heard but the hushed voices of the seconds giving last-minute advice to the champions from each side. Then these, too, drew back to their places in the armies, and on their great horses Don Martin and Rodrigo Diaz the Cid measured each other alone.

"They placed their lances and charged. The crash of their meeting was so powerful that they both fell off their horses wounded. They could barely climb back into the saddle.

"Thereupon Don Martin Gonzalez said to Rodrigo Diaz the Cid in order to unsettle his purpose, 'It was an evil hour for you, O Rodrigo Diaz, when you agreed to meet me here on this field. For Doña Jimena will never be your woman, nor will you ever go back to your home in Castile when I am through with you.'

"To this the Cid replied, 'Don Martin Gonzalez, you are a good knight. For this reason, such talk ill becomes you. Our battle will not be decided by the strength of our words, but by the strength of our hands. And God gives strength to whom He will.'

"Saying this, the Cid smote Don Martin Gonzalez so hard on his helmet that blood ran out of his mouth and trickled onto his breast. In return Martin Gonzalez, the knight of Aragon, struck the Cid's shield so hard that it broke in two and was rendered useless. When they saw this, the men of Castile let out a great cry of horror for the battle now seemed to be decided with the Cid defenseless against his adversary.

"But God had not so judged. For the Cid caught his opponent a blow on the cheek and cut him so badly that he choked on his own blood and had often to turn his head to spit. But Don Martin Gonzalez continued the fight. The sun was already midway in the sky before he fell from his saddle, weak from the loss of so much blood. Thereupon, the Cid dismounted from Babieca and killed the brave Don Martin. Stumbling along, using his sword as a staff, he walked up to the judges, and asked, 'What else do you ask of me to win Calahorra for Don Fernando?'

"They told him they expected no more. In the ranks of the Castilians there arose a tremendous shout of joy. They waved the banner with the three-towered castle and the rampant lion. But the men of Aragon lowered their pennant with the red cross and the barred field, and admitted the judgment given by God through the arm of the Cid who was born of a miller's wife.

"Now Don Fernando the King rode out onto the field. He commanded Rodrigo Diaz to kneel before him. He slapped him across the cheek and then gave him three blows, one on the head, and one on each shoulder, with his sword. He told him to stand up, and said, 'My Cid, Rodrigo Diaz, you are a knight of Castile. Your coat of arms shall have my own, the castle and the lion rampant. But beside that, your arms shall bear three lilies because you have innocence and kindness, the blooms of the Blessed Virgin. Furthermore, you shall have two flying griffons with ruffled feathers, because like that fierce bird you fall with knife-edged claws on the enemies of Castile. I, therefore, name you, my Rodrigo Diaz, the Cid Campeador. For like a champion you have borne yourself today.'

"The King, Don Fernando himself, now helped the Cid to his feet, put his arms around his shoulders and kissed him tenderly on both cheeks. When this happened, the throng cheered wildly in a paean of joy. The lance-bearers hammered on their shields and sang songs in honor of the Campeador. The ladies on their palfreys waved their handkerchiefs, and their knights were jealous.

"When the Cid came to Burgos, the people crowded the way, even standing on the walls. The heralds blew him a welcome just as if the King himself had come to visit. They opened the city gate wide, laid down carpets and strewed flowers in his path. And even the boys and girls of the street knew enough to shout, 'See, there comes the Cid, the Campeador of Castile.'

"Now Doña Jimena came out of her house. She had removed the mourning garments she had worn since the death of her father, the Count of Gormaz who was called the Proud. Her face turned red when she looked into the face of her man, Rodrigo Diaz. She said softly, in a hesitant voice, 'Welcome to your home, my master, and to the home of your servant.'

"But the Cid told her not to talk in such a manner, and his own cheeks were red. She was perhaps seventeen, and he twenty at the most. And he had killed her father.

"But she clung to him and loved him, forgetting the past. She thought to herself, as women always think, 'The singers and the tellers of tales in the castles will spread the news of his deeds, and the women and young girls will whisper to one another, saying, 'Oh, how happy must be this Doña Jimena!'

"There is much more to tell, my friends. I could tell you how Doña Jimena bore the Cid two daughters, Elvira and Sol, and how the Cid kneeled at the coffin of King Sancho. I could tell you how he threw his iron glove so hard against the city gate of Zamora that even the dead in their graves shivered with fear. I could tell you, too, how the Cid wandered through the mountains, an exile, and took cities from the Moors. For as inexhaustible as wondrous things from the sea are the deeds of the Cid."

The crowd sighed with pleasure and delight, and said not a word in their enchantment at Diego's tale-spinning. More softly he went on, bringing them back to earth:

"But now I feel the cool evening wind. And soon—I think I see him now in the distance—our host will come, to whom we are all beholden, the friend of our King Don Carlos. I could but tell of another's deeds. But now before us comes a man and a conquistador who will tell you of many strange things that he himself has seen and done. The minstrel must make way for the hero himself. . . ."

11

THE MAN IN THE WHITE MANTLE

LIKE the rest of the spectators I turned toward the little group just arrived at the chapel gate. Diego de Vargas had drawn our attention to them with a wave of his hand. A few paces ahead of the rest was a tall man clothed in white. A long mantle brushed his shoes, and he wore a broad-brimmed hat of white felt held on his head with a leather chin-strap.

This man looked not much better than a swineherd, though his companions were dressed either in military costume or in the style of the court. Since I was one of those fairly close by the entourage I was able to see, despite the twilight and the uncertain flaring of the torches, that on his face were written most extraordinary contradictions.

In the first place, he was both old and young. The iron-gray pointed beard and the deep folds at the corners of the mouth belonged to a man of fifty. When he swept off his hat he revealed a powerful forehead, deeply creased. The nose was strong, but if anything too generous in length, and rather drooping. The outer creases at the hollows of the eyes ran upward, giving his expression a quality of pride, almost disdain.

In spite of the arrogant set of the eyes the upper part of the face was strikingly pleasant, although on closer inspection it betrayed a certain caution which might even have been thought cunning. The big ugly mouth stuck out clearly above the tuft of hair. The shape of the chin was masked by the beard. But today I know, of course, that Pizarro's chin was round and strong, just as one might expect in a man given to a life of action.

Two knights in gold-plated breastplates stood behind Pizarro. One of these I immediately recognized as his brother. The man in the white mantle—Don Francisco Pizarro, I neglected to say—was broad-shouldered. a fine figure of a man not lacking in stature. But his brother

Hernando was a giant. He held himself very erect and stared down his nose at the world of ordinary men with a pride that was both physical and spiritual.

It was a remarkable thing about the Pizarro brothers that in each of them some particular trait of Don Francisco their leader had come to have the upper hand. In Francisco himself these diverse characteristics were in continual flux, sometimes in conflict, with first one and then the other in evidence. He was continually calling to mind the actions of this or that brother.

Hernando Pizarro was the oldest of the lot, and the only legitimate son of his lewd father who, as Don Hernando Cortés correctly painted him, had in his day shown great aptitude for coursing with the women. This eldest son seemed fully aware both of his primogenital advantages and of his responsibilities. It was his habit to look out beyond his brothers when something annoyed him, a trick which invariably abashed his audience. Even Francisco Pizarro became confused on such occasions, and he as well as the rest of the brothers in this case would take pains to act after that with special consideration of the injured giant's feelings. They would straighten out his stirrups, pretend to brush imaginary dust from his clothes, or offer him sweetmeats if any chanced to be at hand. To these conciliatory attentions Don Hernando would say, "Thank you, my son." Thereupon there would be great relief, all out of proportion.

But when Don Hernando was genuinely irritated he seemed to freeze into an image of stone. He would sit on his horse as stiff as a ramrod. Not a word would he utter, and nothing would move him. His lower lip would hang down like a Hapsburg's, and the pupils of his eyes would turn upward in an amazing fashion so that a great deal of the whites showed, though indeed they were much more yellow than white and shot through with blood. This stony withdrawal and the upward twisted eyeballs, as if he were trying to see into his own brain, always made his brothers visibly uneasy and very often afraid. It was like a sinister calm, this rigidity, the calm which precedes a tropical storm.

At times Don Hernando would suddenly spring to his feet, the veins in his temples swollen into little blue snakes. In his bass voice he would roar formidably, cry out in tones and words which left no doubt of his inexorable contempt for the world at large. In a breath he would whip out his sword and offer to slay his brothers and even himself along with them. As he said, he would like to brand with eternal shame the cowardly, lying toads in whose bodies ran the blood of a nobleman commingled with the poison of both Flemish and Spanish whores. This calumniation of their various mothers always aroused the remaining Pizarros to violence. All at once they would shriek at each other, brandishing their swords like madmen and tearing at their beards in a transport of choler. Those unacquainted with their natures expected murder any moment. In reality it was largely a show to be played every month or so. At the bottom they were profoundly attached to one another, and nothing was farther from their intention than to let each other's blood.

The knight behind the older Pizarro was called Pedro de Candía. This man was a lover of pomp who hailed from the isle of Candía. There was a story about him that once, having landed in an infidel prison, he had passed the enforced stay in Byzantium by seducing a pasha's daughter. On this account, at least it was so rumored, it had been decreed that he part with the pendant bag containing his manhood. However, I have reason to believe, judging from his actions when I knew him, that he safely escaped this dismal fate.

The most notable feature of this nobleman was his long and narrow skull. It looked as if a strong pair of hands had tried to press the cheeks together. A thin beard sprouted haphazard from his chin. Diego de Vargas used to say of this beard that it looked as if mice were nesting in it. For although Pedro de Candía combed out and forever caressed this ornament it somehow managed always to appear unkempt.

Pedro de Candía wore a gold-plated breastplate and a very high helmet decorated with dyed ostrich feathers. He cast a melancholy glance over the assembled country folk, and from the first time I laid eyes on him I dubbed him *philosophus*. He was an excellent artilleryman and today I often think that the lives of our small band depended greatly on his incredible speed in handling our culverins and four-pounders.

The rest of the Pizarros were arrayed behind these two knights. Because they have played an important role in my story I shall go to some brief pains to describe them.

Gonzalo Pizarro was always distinguished from the others by his superior cunning. His hair was as blue-black as a raven's feather and glistened as if steeped in oil. He was very comely, oval-faced, with a fine forehead and darkly bright eyes under beautifully arched brows. He was the only one of the Pizarros who showed any friendliness at all in his demeanor. When talking he often laid his hand on the other person's shoulder and, if in a lively mood, sometimes went so far as to tweak the man's ear or give him a light buffet with his open palm on the cheek. The soldiers were always fond of him. They called him "Handsome Gonzalo."

The youngest of the brothers was Juan Pizarro. Unlike the rest he easily lost his self-possession and flushed again and again when caught off balance. His face was round, almost like a peasant's in contour, and his cheeks were red like a healthy child's. In council little attention was ever paid to him. But if any undertaking required courage to the point of foolhardiness, every eye was turned in his direction. The others disliked to see him throw himself into needless danger, which it was his wont to do at every opportunity. Accordingly Juan always behaved with almost unnatural composure when in his brothers' presence, especially so if Don Hernando were around. But when he was free to act as he pleased, it was all most of us could do to persuade him from deeds bordering on sure suicide. Juan Pizarro was indeed the boldest of the crew. But he had none of Francisco's foresight and experience, or the cold pride of Hernando, or the slyness of Gonzalo, to give it fruitful meaning.

Francisco's last brother was Francisco Martín de Alcántara. This man was very pious and it had been his father's original intention for him to enter the Church. As it happened, sad to relate, he proved to be not very intelligent, and seemed to understand sword and plow far better than psalter or quill. Up to the time I now speak of he had acted as steward for Hernando Pizarro's small properties, since the proud one considered it beneath his given station to trouble himself with material things. The animals for the feast had been slaughtered and dressed by Francisco Martín's own hands. He himself had mixed and rolled out the dough for the bread, no doubt to the accompaniment of many pious exhortations to Heaven.

Next to this Francisco Martín stood Pedro, a cousin to all the brothers. Very much unlike any of them, Francisco in particular, Pedro was a good scribe and loved books.

Don Francisco, who had waited for Diego de Vargas to finish his tale of the Cid, now walked forward, reached out his hand, and said, "My friend, thank you for your flattering words. You couldn't have chosen a better spot to tell your tale. All our forefathers' bones lie buried in this place. Their bravery deserves to be commemorated by stories of the Cid. But there are men today who are both brave and not without brains, just as there were in the days of the Moorish wars. It's to them I have come, with my brother Hernando and the rest. I'm going to talk to my countrymen about a great task. For, so I tell myself day in and day out, why should a fighting breed live like peasants? Why should a man fit to be a hidalgo endure a serf's lot? Why should my countrymen, I ask you, always bend to the plow, load pack-mules and eat barley soup until they gag? Where I've just come from, any Spaniard is a king. There all Spaniards, great and small, are champions of the Blessed Virgin, warriors of God and His saintly hosts.

"And I don't need to ask my close friends and advisers, the Dominicans, to know that across the sea the worst thief's sins are forgiven. There, should a man die, his soul is guaranteed admission to the throne of God. Why, it would be as easy as knocking on a neighbor's door right here in Trujillo to pass the time, getting into paradise from that land. At the same time a Spaniard is assured some recompense for his services while he's still on earth. Any poor devil without a maravedi to his name can go there and become rich. When he comes back home to Spain, with him he'll bring chests filled with gold and precious stones. Fruits grow there by the thousandfold, and there is the sweet cane from which sugar and fine brandy are made. There's the Indian corn. Its ears are thicker than a hundred ears of wheat taken together. There is even a plant on which wool grows."

A murmur of astonishment passed through the crowd on hearing these glowing words. The peasants edged closer to the speaker the better to hear. By now twilight had given way to night. The torches' red flame smoked and guttered in the dark wind.

"I'm no teller of fairy tales," Francisco said, taking up his discourse. "My words, every one that falls from my lips, are true. I intended to bring an Indian camel with me to show you, but when I was talking to the King in Toledo he took such a fancy to the animal that I gave it to him. He was delighted with the soft wool that grew on its back. I told him the day would come when the weavers of Flanders would buy all their material in Spain. Don Carlos was grateful, as no doubt you've already heard. He has made me Governor and Captain-General of New Castile. He has given me the title of Adelantado and Alguazil Major for life, with a stipend of 725,000 maravedis. Such are the fruits of the new land."

At this there arose cries of wonder. I saw that Pizarro was anything but displeased at the intense interest he had aroused. He stood motionless in the light from the burning faggots, his head inclined toward his left shoulder, listening greedily to the massed response.

"But perhaps," he said thoughtfully, light contempt wrinkling the corner folds of his slanting eyes, "perhaps you are too thoroughly satisfied with your present lives to be amused by my proposals. Perhaps you're thinking of our old proverb, Stick to the land and make an honest living. But this honesty in your case means poverty. It means sweat and boredom. Neither today nor tomorrow nor the next day will anything be different. But if that's what you want, tell me, good people of Trujillo. It's all the same to me. I can find plenty of men in Seville or Palos. Why, they'd pay me in gold to take them along."

"No, no!" came scattered cries. "Tell us more, Captain-General! Let's have the whole story."

"Well, if that's the way you feel about it," said Pizarro, with much apparent hesitation. "But you must understand that with me time is money. My brother Hernando has got plenty on his mind, too, and enough engagements to keep him busy from now till Doomsday. Only today the Marquis Don Hernando Cortés, the friend of our King Don Carlos, arrived at his house to talk things over with us."

I poked Diego de Vargas, who was at my right hand, and whispered, "Everything will be all right for us now."

"Yes," he replied, but without the enthusiasm I had expected. "The stone has begun to roll. At least that's the way it looks to me. This Francisco Pizarro has got the whole village in his pocket. He's a dangerous man, or I miss my guess."

"He's a soldier of the Blessed Virgin," echoed Alonso the splendid. He was captivated with Pizarro's speech. "He makes my heart turn over in my chest. He makes me long to get my hand on the hilt of a sword. I'd like to start fighting the Indians right now. What do you say, Brother Juan?"

"I was just thinking about those ears of corn," Juan said irrelevantly. "If sweetmeats grow on bushes in New Castile, Cockaigne can't be far off. They say in Cockaigne broiled squab fly about in the air, right into a man's mouth if he keeps it open. I'm all for going. When Pizarro talked about that barley soup I had to think how there's always a bubble of grease floating in it. It always looked to me like a sick eye. It seemed to say, How in the name of the saints can you down this swill?"

"Why, you're nothing but a bladder of lard, a fart-filled great-guts," Alonso complained loudly, and turning to us continued his diatribe: "Military fame, honor—why, they mean nothing to this curious hog. All that interests him is the kind of bay leaves they use in cooking. I remember once showing him a picture of the Virgin Mary stroking a unicorn. You know what he asked me? How does roast unicorn taste? Roast unicorn! It makes me vomit to think of it."

But once again Francisco Pizarro claimed our attention. He had now removed his broad-brimmed hat, and stood bareheaded confronting the crowd, whom he admonished into silence by a showing of his upturned palm. He went on to say:

"Ever since our Admiral discovered the New World, since Vasco Núñez de Balboa forced his way across the Isthmus and planted the flag of Castile on the shores of the Southern Ocean, we have heard reports of a mighty kingdom far to the south. There, the story goes, Indians drink out of golden goblets. The roofs of the houses are tiled with gold, and precious stones are as common as gravel in the river beds of Spain.

"Now, I settled down in Panama, the new city on the Southern Ocean. I had had many battles and explored far and wide. It wasn't bad there. I had a roof over my head and plenty to eat. But I couldn't rest in peace thinking that just over the horizon was this other richer land. Many a day I've sat on the beach and looked toward the south. I've sat there far into the night watching the stars and the sea. There were some who wondered why I found so little time for talk, or dice, drinking and women. That land fascinated me far more. I couldn't stop thinking about it. It seemed as if fate were calling to me from far off.

"But all this talk, my friends, is a personal affair. It has nothing to do with you. But I'll admit that I began to talk aloud of my vision, in full daylight. It's just such people as myself among you that I'm interested in, the unsatisfied ones, the restless, the ones who refuse to countenance the present prospect. Such people as I talk of are the salt of the earth. They are cut out for great things.

"But to get on with my story. With the help of friends I fitted out two vessels—miserable little ones they were. I set sail for the south. So it happened that one morning after a long voyage we made a landfall under an enormous headland. The cliffs here fell down steeply into the sea. Mountains rose up behind this cape as far as the eye could see. Higher and higher endless peaks towered, one behind the other, rank on rank. When the shadows of night had already shut in our craft we still could watch the snowy mountain tops glittering rose and gold as they caught the light of the sun. When I circumnavigated this cape, which I named Saint Helena after the holy woman of Egypt—for it was her day when I first beheld it—before us stretched a great sunny bay. It lay there like a lake, smooth as glass. We saw many small islands. Our vessel slipped by them without a murmur. We saw the treetops mirrored in the silvery waters. Everywhere on the slopes of the mountains herds of little Indian camels were grazing, and still farther below were fields of Indian corn, sugarcane and cotton. We stood on the forward deck, hardly able to trust our eyes. For months on end we had stared at nothing but the empty sea, or at best at stony islands and mangrove swamps. Our hearts trembled with joy, as you can understand. It was like seeing the mighty gates of Paradise yawn wide for us.

"The next day we hove to before the city of Tumbez. Indians came out to greet us in dozens of rafts. Men and women craned their necks to see us. They watched our every move. A great crowd of people gathered on the shore. But I felt no fear. It was plain they were friendly people, easy-going. It wasn't long before the Alcalde of Tumbez came out to pay us his respects. With him he brought corn, yams, cocoanuts, bananas and other fruits of the land which on the outside looked like pine cones, but had flesh sweeter and juicier than peaches. The brown men who swarmed onto our ship brought game with them, wild birds and fish. There was enough to feed the whole village of Trujillo for a week.

"It was then I noticed a man standing beside the Alcalde. Everyone treated him with great respect. One of his ears was so laden with golden ornaments that the lobe had been dragged down nearly to the shoulder. We called him 'Orejon,' big ear, in jest. We struck up a conversation with this man through one of the native seamen Ruiz had found who acted as interpreter. I showed him our ship, the forward and after decks, the rudder, compass and our maps. He looked at all these things in amazement, but the one thing that caught his eyes above all else was a small axe. He had never before seen anything made of iron. He called it 'hard silver.'

"I made him a present of the axe and he was so pleased he burst into tears of gratitude. He considered it a kingly present worth its weight in gold. I let him partake of our meal. When he had drunk some of our Spanish wine he said he understood where we got all our wonderful powers. He knew now, he told us, how we were able to build floating cities, and to trap the demon who always pointed his finger north, and to harden silver.

"This moment I considered proper to tell him about our Lord Jesus Christ. I told him that God had come to earth, had instructed mankind and died on the cross. He listened carefully, but made no comment. When I told him about eternal salvation he was amazed. I told him also about Don Carlos our King, how he was an emperor, the ruler of Christendom before whom all must bow the neck. But I think now his understanding was unequal to my arguments. Anyway I let him go with good grace, and bade him carry greetings from our King to his own monarch.

"You can all see that diplomatic relations with the South Land have already been established. All that remains now is the task of occupying the country in order to convert its inhabitants and to teach the King his obligations as vassal of Don Carlos. Nothing else stands in the way of our enjoying the riches and fruitfulness of the land. Indeed I maintain that the South Land is a present from God and the Blessed Virgin to their favorite children, the people of Spain. It would be sinful for us not to rejoice over this gift and make use of it. But now I must beg you to listen to what my friend and comrade-in-arms, Don Pedro de Candía, has to say. It was he alone who actually trod the streets of Tumbez. The duties of a commander did not allow me to leave my vessel. Don Pedro, I ask you to assure my friends and kinsfolk of Trujillo that I've spoken nothing but the gospel truth."

Don Pedro de Candía, as he was told, stepped forward in his gold-plated armor. The ostrich feathers on his helmet waved languidly. He sighed, and cast a thoughtful and melancholy look over the crowd, stroking his beard the meanwhile as if milking a goat.

"My friends," he began in a solemn tone, just as the throng was on the verge of open restlessness at his reluctance, "when I came into Tumbez I thought I was moving in a dream. I found a great crowd of people, men and women with reddish-colored skin and black stringy hair. They pressed around me, feeling my breastplate, my sword, my hands and hair, as if they doubted I was really a human being. Without praising myself I may say to you that to them I looked like a god. It was a mighty sensation, to be thought half a god. Almost at once they asked me to make my weapon speak, as they are wont to say, and I aimed at a piece of wood and pulled the trigger. When the report rang out and the splinters flew, they all cried out in terror. The women wailed aloud, and the men raised their hands in supplication to the sky. But I calmed them as best I could. I saw at once that we should never have the slightest trouble making these simple people our subjects.

"Later they led me into a girls' cloister. In the cloister garden there were plants and bushes fashioned out of silver and gold skillfully hammered. The flowers were made of jewels. Even the butterflies, birds and beetles were of costly metals. I saw this and gaped with wonder. Then they took me to the workshops where their artists make these precious works.

"As we walked through the cloister more than a hundred young girls swarmed about me, laughing and murmuring like doves. They circled about me and led me through the rooms. I could not look enough at their rounded brown shoulders, their shining hair, the small firm breasts and swinging hips. They trusted me as if we were old friends. They brought me fruits, sweets and cool drinks, while I chaffed them lightly, making them laugh aloud with pleasure. It made no difference that they were unable to follow exactly what I said.

"The dignitaries of the city insisted on my staying in Tumbez. They said I could choose the best of the cloister girls and keep them for myself. In brief they offered me an infidel paradise, such as that the Moors tell of. I must publicly confess that it took several prayers to Santiago before I was able to master my inclinations. Indeed, as a man of honor I will admit that later on board the ship I often regretted not tarrying at least for a short while. And even at this moment as I stand before you, you men of Trujillo, I can feel my heart hammering in my breast at the thought of the delights of Tumbez.

"But to get back to more serious things, I want to tell you how the men of Tumbez led me through a temple dedicated to the sun god. The tiles on the roof of this building were made of silver and the walls plated solid with gold. Here, too, I saw many precious objects and ornamental tapestries. I can say in God's truth that even the cathedrals of Burgos and Seville are poor in comparison with this heathen splendor. At once my heart spoke and told me what a good work it would be to get this kingdom for God and our ruler, Don Carlos, and at the same time for a man to get his own due. They showed me their Alcazar, which rises up from the crest of a hill in the city, like our own. According to their style of building, the fortress was made entirely of huge blocks of stone. It commands the whole city. Three great walls protect the inner castle. I took careful note of all these details as I stood on top of the walls and looked out into the bay at our ship, which was surrounded by the Indian rafts. To myself I thought that such a brave man as our own captain, Don Francisco Pizarro, could easily seize the fortress with two cannon and a hundred men. And then the city of Tumbez would be his. All its gold, silver, precious stones and sweet-shouldered maidens.

"Yet I am sure, too, that my captain, Don Francisco Pizarro, is aiming at higher goals. He is planning great things. Why should we Spaniards content ourselves with a single city in the southern kingdom if we can make ourselves masters of the whole? I have heard that at the court of the ruler, a man called the Inca, everything is made of gold, even the palace floors and the chairs on which he sits. Yes, I assure you that the wealth of the capital city, which lies up in the high mountains—they call it the navel of the world—puts to shame the wonder of Tenochtitlan itself. I say this without any intention of belittling the efforts of the Marquis de Oaxaca, Don Hernando Cortés, and especially of my friend and former comrade-in-arms, Don Pedro de Alvarado. For every man's steps are subject to the direction of Divine Providence. They found the city of the teocallis on the great lake. You have all heard about it. But we found the Kingdom of the South, the land of sun and gold.

"So now listen to the call. Fetch out your sword and crossbow from behind the hearth where they lie forgotten. Patch up your uniforms with wool. Sole your shoes with iron. That is—if you want to get on in the world and become masters instead of peasants. But perhaps you are satisfied with your lot. Perhaps you think it is God's greatest pleasure to split melon seeds on the ground and have a mutton bone for the Sunday pot. In that case, stay where you are till death overtakes you. For all of me the pack-masters can hoist your scrawny asses with a broad-toed boot until Hell becomes a lake of ice. Sleep away on your lousy straw-sacks and breed your feeble children. I shall never weep for you. For now you have your chance. If you fail to take it you are cowards, born to the yoke, slow fools. Never forget in your misery that I, Pedro de

Candía, have spoken to you of escape, and proved the riches which lie within your grasp.

"Let us hope there are some among you who see things my way. Let us hope that some of you have hearts under your ribs where men's hearts belong. Remember: Luck has but one golden forelock. Behind, his head is as bare as a eunuch's shaved pate."

With this the nobleman fell silent, stared out over the crowd with gloomy eyes. During his long discourse the crowd had become powerfully excited. The faces gleaming in the torchlight were now scarcely to be recognized. Cries of wonder had come out of every throat when he described the city of Tumbez. And laughter was mixed with resentment when at the end he had spoken of their village lives with such contempt.

"He's right enough," said Juan the thin one. "Only a man with a slave's spirit would be satisfied with a mutton bone. That is, when he could as well have lamb. It makes me weak in the bowels just to think of it."

"Yes, he's right a thousand times over," agreed Alonso the splendid. "He's more right than you can possibly dream of, you miserable skeleton. We have heard the call of a new apostle. We'll save those lovely maidens from the fires of Hell if it's the last thing we ever do. Yes, my gluttonous brother, I can picture it. Right now I can see you bound down to a martyr's stake while the red men shoot burning arrows into your flesh. It reminds me of St. Sebastian as I picture you, the way their copper axes are cleaving your hungry carcass. But when you are finally martyred, praise God the true meaning of life will come to you. It will be like the rising sun on a hot midsummer morning. How Heaven's angels will rejoice!"

"Not for me!" Juan objected violently. "No you don't. I don't care whether the angels rejoice or not. I want to stick close to those brown girls. I'm going to make love to them on those beautiful carpets until I can't raise my hand to my head. Then I'll eat a bunch of that fruit that looks like pine cones, and have a nice long sleep."

"Nothing is sweeter than the fruits of suffering," retorted Alonso harshly.

"Did you hear what that fellow with the ostrich feathers called me?" asked Frenero of one-eyed Bernal. "He called me a coward. I never took that kind of talk from any man!"

"He didn't mean you in particular," Bernal said impatiently. "He meant the whole lot of us."

"All of us? Well, that's different," said Frenero.

"But don't you belong with all of us?" inquired Rodrigo, the crafty Devil.

"Why! What? Why not? Of course I do," agreed Frenero, bethinking himself.

"But don't you want to go to the South Land just the same?" Rodrigo asked.

"Of course. Why not? What do you think—when the streets are paved with gold!"

"Don Pedro only called the stay-at-homes cowards," Rodrigo persisted thoughtfully.

"He did!" said Frenero loudly. "Where am I now, anyway? Did he mean all of us? Did he mean me? Me along with the rest? Or was he talking about me when he named everybody? Well, whatever he meant, I know how to avenge my honor, let me tell you that. And when I'm in doubt about an insult I act accordingly."

"Act accordingly?" inquired Rodrigo. "What does that mean?"

"What does that mean?" bellowed Frenero. "I give up! Pretty soon I won't know whether I'm standing on my feet or on my head. It's as bad listening to you as to those doctors at the University of Salamanca. It's like being up before a judge. When I think of all the times I've had to pay for other peoples' crimes just because I got twisted up on the stand..."

"Yes, you are a shorn lamb," Bernal said, fixing Frenero with his single eye.

But this kind of conversation was cut short by Don Hernando Pizarro. He strode forward, stood there immense and stony, seemingly gazing into the air at some invisible flight of night birds.

"You have heard, you people of Trujillo," he began in his bass voice, "you have heard all that my brother, Francisco, Governor-General of New Castile, had to tell you. You heard the story of a brave knight, Don Pedro de Candía. I have nothing to add to these words, for personally I have no knowledge at all of the South Country. Up to now I have never left the soil of Estremadura, as you all know. But I stand as guarantee for the truth of these stories and the honor of the Pizarros.

"I am the first and the oldest of my family. And any man who doubts our words, who dares to spit on my honor or on my brothers' honor, shall reckon with me. I shall cut him down as sure as the scythe reaps the grain. But if any man feels otherwise and wishes to cast his lot with ours, I have this much to say. We are going to fit out three caravels in Seville and sail with them across the sea. We shall conquer the Kingdom of the South. This will be done at the command of His Majesty Don Carlos, under the approval of the Council for the Indies. We shall be well provided with provisions, cannon and all kind of implements. We shall not lack the support of the Church.

"All that I ask of any knight is that he be well armed and fitted with a good horse. He must have harness, helmet, vizor and a young horse sound in wind. Beyond this he must come equipped with a secretary and a steward. His soldiers, in case he has any with him, ought to have swords and muskets, or at least lances or crossbows. As you see, any well-armed man is welcome to join us. Anyone who is not a knight and who is not from the city streets can fall in behind the banner of my brother Don Francisco. We Pizarros have decided to follow our brother and our cousin.

"You people of Trujillo know me and my brothers. We are no fools. When we set our minds on something, we follow through to the end. Now we have aimed our strength at something that will bring honor, respect, fame. And riches. Today, with open heart, I offer you a share in our undertakings and the fruits which will accrue from it. Whoever decides to join us can come to my house and see Master Pérez, my brother's secretary, who will take his name and tell him when to appear in Seville. I thank you for your attention. Now I must leave you for we are all overburdened with duties."

With this Don Hernando made a curt bow, wheeled around, and strode heavily back to the waiting group of Pizarros. His departure seemed to disperse an oppressive nightmare which had possessed the crowd during his solemn lecture. While he talked the people had hearkened silently, not breathing a sound. Now scattered cries of approbation arose. Someone shouted, "Long live the house of Pizarro!"

The Pizarros, the knight from Candía and the rest of their company swung up on their horses. I especially noticed Don Francisco in his long white mantle, how he sat erect yet careless in the saddle. His powerful roan stood stiffly as if hewn from stone under the arch of the churchyard gate. The torchlight played on the silver snaffle chain and the inlaid work of the rich saddle. Now and then the light caught Don Francisco's face. As the light flickered across the features they were never twice the same. This I remember clearly, and have good cause not to forget.

It was almost as if some great Italian painter were making rapid sketches for a portrait in order to catch the real being of this extraordinary man. At one time the heavy peasant lines of the face would stand out, almost coarsely. At another, the face became sly and mysterious. And yet again it would be bold and oversize, seemingly a lonely face among men. Indeed, among the hundreds of men I have known Don Francisco Pizarro was the only one to have as many facets to his soul as circumstance dictated.

Now the Pizarros were all ready to leave, their horses pawing about in eagerness to be on the way. It was Juan, the youngest, who took up the rear. He waved in parting with his gloved hand, and called out in laughter, "God be with you until we meet in Seville, you topers!"

Everyone roared with laughter at this and many cried, "Stay a while with us, Don Juan. We've got some nice gypsies coming. They're going to dance!"

And one voice in the crowd shouted boldly, "They'll do something else beside dance for you, Don Juan!"

But Juan, simulating regret, pointed to the broad backs of his brothers, shook his head and rode after the rest.

There was a great clamor when the Pizarros had disappeared. Men and women like magic formed into little groups and circles, everyone talking at once. Others gathered round the open space before the church door where the gypsies were going to dance.

Soon there actually were sounds from stringed musical instruments, and in a short time the revelry was in full swing, with the men clapping time sharply with their hands. But I sat down on a gravestone. My thoughts were far from dancing and music. My spirit was heavy with a question, a question whose answer would be decisive for all my plans and all my future.

12

TONIATUH

SITTING there on the gravestone the gypsy music beat at my ears but not my heart. There rose up before the eyes of my fancy the golden South Country which the words of Don Francisco Pizarro and Pedro de Candía had brought to life for me. I had the feeling I could reach out and touch the great blocks of stone which made the palace. I could all but smell the strange air of aromatic trees, the flowers and fruits. I could smell the damp sea tang of the hot coast, swooning with the sun's heat reflected from naked cliff. I saw the snowy peaks hemming in the port of Tumbez.

The fulfillment of all my knightly dreams seemed near at hand. And yet between me and the South Country lay a vast abyss. The thought of bridging it cramped my heart. I do not mean the sea separating Spain from the Indies, nor the endless Western Ocean which at that time I could only vaguely imagine. I knew, of course, that it took the caravels weeks and months to sail across these waters. These physical concerns, however, appeared trivial compared with others that beset me.

The first obstacle was simply that I had no breastplate. A good suit of armor was very expensive. It cost several thousand maravedis, and the money from the sale of Don Hernando's pearl had shrunk to less than a hundred. Again, man is so made that he must ever eat and drink. Not only propriety but the exigencies of Spanish weather force him to clothe his body. But my lack of armor and equipment was not the only basis for doubting that I should ever really arrive at the shimmering goal.

It was hard for me to believe that men like the Pizarros and the Knight of Candía would accept the company of such an untried youth as I. For in truth I had never engaged in pursuits any more desperate than the attack on the seedy monk and the brace of merchants while they slept, a deed of which I was still profoundly ashamed. Beyond that, I was a fugitive from the Inquisition. The words uttered by the stranger from Loyola haunted me. I was not really sure whether I had done the right thing in fleeing Seville. In any case it seemed impossible that I should take part in a crusade against unbelievers with such pious men as the Pizarros, and live at odds with my Mother the Church.

Today, of course, I see that I was merely multiplying excuses in order to evade the real issue. Now I can admit that neither armor nor Inquisition was the main stumbling block. The foremost cause of my hesitation was personal.

In my wanderings I had not forgotten Doña Isabella de Gómez, however long it may be since I have mentioned her name in these writings. It was she, at the bottom, who was the occasion for all my seeking after kingdoms. It was her I wished to delight with knightly deeds of valor. How often during the night had I looked at the bit of ribbon and kissed the black lock of hair she had given me, while my companions snored, oblivious to my sweet torment.

I was on the brink of taking ship over the Western Ocean. Many years would assuredly elapse before I could ever see her again. For I had always heard it said that men who once trod the soil of the Indies were held by invisible hands. I had heard it told that the magic strength of those mountains and virgin forests was stronger than the prayers of an old mother pining away for her son, stronger than any need for a woman left behind. All this confusion weighed on me. The image of Doña Isabella stood clear before my soul. I almost wished we were children again,reading poetry in the garden. So great was the turmoil that I rose to my feet unable to control an impulse to be on the move. I took my horse's bridle in my hand, and left the cemetery with the animal ambling along after me. I hardly knew what I was doing, so strong was the passion which rose from nowhere to grip me in its vise.

The night wind blew gently against my face. I thought of Isabella's blue-black hair, caught in a golden net, and I thought of her slanting eyes. Above all I saw clearly her forehead and the pure line where the hair met the brow. For the first time it came upon me that there was more in this sweet brow than childish trust and an intimation of womanly wisdom. There was anxiety, I thought, and already light resignation as well. It touched me to think that through my Isabella there should be humility and submission on this same earth's crust where rode the Pizarros, swords unsheathed, where Dominicans whispered strange words into their breviaries, where merchants fingered their gold and the poor—may God have mercy on their souls—groaned aloud in misery. At this exalted moment I was caught up by the greatness of the world and trembled at its wondrous beauty.

Leading my horse I walked heedless through the night, my heart both sad and joyous at once. At last I found myself entering the main gate in the wall surrounding the little town. The entire population, including the watch, were up at the churchyard enjoying the festivities. About me the village lay dark and deserted. In the air was a country smell of manure piles and pigsties. Some of the villagers had gone off without even so much as bothering to shut their doors. Apparently here was no fear of thieves, doubtless because no one had anything worth the trouble of taking.

I came to a house that was bigger than the rest and stank more violently of sour-smelling pigs. At the door several horses were tethered to an iron ring in the masonry. One of them was a roan, Francisco Pizarro's mount. I likewise tethered my animal and opened the door. The vestibule was lighted by candles, and the beams of the ceiling were so low that men of the Pizarros' stature would have to bend their necks low to navigate the room.

When my eyes had become accustomed to the soft shadows I noticed I was not alone. Against the wall sat a very old woman with a cat on her lap which she stroked absent-mindedly. She paid no attention to me at all.

"Is Don Francisco Pizarro here?" I asked.

She stopped stroking the cat only long enough to say, "Look around for yourself, young man."

This rude answer upset me, but I insisted, "You don't know whether he's here, then?"

"No, no, for the love of God, no!" the old crone shrilled at me. "I've already told you to look for yourself."

Without further ado I walked by her, hesitated, chose a door and opened it. By good luck it was the right one. In the middle of a long room a large table had been placed. Sitting at it and standing around was a group of men. Opposite me stood two Indians, as immobile as if cut from wood. Only the glittering whites of their eyes betrayed that they were alive.

A man with his back to me—he was dressed in a tight-fitting leather jerkin—was saying in a level voice, "According to the way I look at it, we ought to head in a northwesterly direction. We ought to hit the seven golden cities up that way. The coast of the South Sea is practically unexplored in that region."

At this another man, whose shining black hair identified him as Gonzalo Pizarro, laughed heartily. "Why, we're parceling out the New World like cutting up a melon! Popes couldn't do it better."

"That's right," said a third, Francisco Pizarro himself. "I wonder what that old bastard of a Guzmán's going to say to all this. And I don't imagine Don Pedro de los Ríos is going to be exactly pleased. It's been some time now since he wished to God he were anywhere but in Panama. With that bloated carcass of his he'll never be able to stand the heat."

"That's all right," said the man in the leather jerkin. "But all that interests me is that right now Don Carlos is backing me up. I've got to capitalize on his mood before it fizzles out. Nobody I ever knew yet got fat on court favors. My gold mines in Tehuantepec, the silver mines in Zacatecas can't support everything, you know. I've been looking around while the sun shines. And I've been making plans between times. As I see it, it would be a good idea to take sugarcane from Cuba and transplant it in the *tierra caliente*. I might plant mulberry trees for silkworms. I thought of Merino sheep for the uplands.

"I want to tell you something, cousin. You may think the worst is over when the country has been won. But that isn't the case at all. Your troubles will have just begun when you begin to take charge of things. All that conquering the land takes is courage and persistence. But it takes knowledge to rule it. We simple soldiers will have to accustom ourselves to dealing with a thousand and one mysterious affairs in this unknown land."

"I understand you well enough," agreed Francisco Pizarro. "Would you believe it?—since my youth I've always had it in the back of my mind to found a city. For a city with walls, an alcazar and cathedral is the finest offspring a man could ever leave behind him. Why, centuries later people will look about them and say, Pizarro built this."

As these last words were leaving his lips one of the Indians pointed a hand at me as I stood agape in the door frame. He spoke one word, "Toniatuh!"

Startled, some of the men at the table jumped to their feet. The one in the leather jerkin let fall the quill from his fingers. He looked at me with hostility which almost immediately dissolved into a smile. As I recognized at the first sound of his voice, it was Don Hernando Cortés. I imagined that somehow since our meeting in the night he had grown much younger. Quietly he stroked his short pointed beard. His eyes rested on me with the ironic amusement of a much-traveled and widely experienced man. It was plain that he was deriving a mild enjoyment from my discomfiture. I was unable to bring out a single syllable, and looked at him with the moon-eyed gaze of a sickly calf, my mouth all but hanging open with bewilderment.

"Young man," said Gonzalo Pizarro in a voice so icy that it quickly brought me to my senses, "you might at least have knocked on the door. Don't you know you have broken into a private meeting? You've been listening to conversation never intended for your ears."

"Just a minute," intervened Cortés. "I know the boy. He's a friend of mine. He's called Don Pedro de Cordova, a soldier like Don Gonzalvo, pretty near a Sforza."

"He is!" said Gonzalo incredulously. His ominous appraisal vanished, and he was the usual easy-going Gonzalo. This swift change of countenance was most uncomfortable. He walked over to me, took me by the arm, and led me to the table on which, I now saw, was spread out a large map showing land and sea.

Don Francisco Pizarro, gray-bearded, looked at me critically. "Toniatuh?" he inquired. "How does the young man happen to have an Indian name?"

"All that Xicotencatl meant was that Don Pedro is blond and blue-eyed. Toniatuh means child of the sun. But really, the fellow gave me a fright. I thought I was looking at Pedro de Alvarado. The Aztecs and Tlascalans always used to call him Toniatuh. He was just as blond as this Pedro. Of course so far as I know Alvarado never did much riding on sway-backed asses! But if you take my advice you'll have this green shoot along with you. He'll be worth more to you than a hundred men or two cannon."

Don Hernando smiled to himself, slyly. The handsome Gonzalo put his chin in his hand and examined my features with as little personal interest in his black eyes as if he were sizing up a horse in the market or a slave from the Portuguese Gold Coast.

"I don't follow you at all," Don Francisco objected almost irritably. "Supposing this young fellow has got the spirit. What use is such an unexperienced boy to us?"

Don Hernando hardly acknowledged the objection. He was looking hard at the gentle flame of the candle in its stick. He seemed far off, preoccupied with things that had nothing to do with the business at hand. A dreamy look possessed him, and it was several seconds before he came back to earth. Looking at me curiously, he said:

"In the land of Tenochtitlan and in many other regions of the Terra Firma, but above all in Tezcuco, there is the legend that many hundreds of years ago blond-haired and blue-eyed men came from over the sea. They taught the inhabitants many new arts, none of which had ever been heard of before. And it must be admitted that there are many things to be found that can't be very well explained otherwise. Everywhere you run into crosses and the Virgin Mary with her Child. Even our Lord himself is not unknown to them. They call Him Quetzalcoatl. He is called that because He is supposed to have risen out of the western part of the ocean. His sacrificial death is said to have come when of his own will he plunged into the bloody path of the rising sun in the southern sea.

"Perhaps the whole matter is foolishness, heresy. Everything they believe is twisted around and has no clear meaning. I've often talked it over with my Dominicans. Some think it is all an invention of the Devil, just to trouble the faithful. But others, on the contrary, say it might be possible that the Apostle Thomas came to the land on one of his journeys. Others think it might have been an Irish monk, driven westward by great storms. Or these white-skins might have been Icelanders. They say that the Northmen used to make great voyages long ago on ships with dragon bows."

Don Francisco and Gonzalo both were amazed at this. I, too, became uneasy. I looked cautiously from time to time at the Indian Xicotencatl. But he remained backed up against the whitewashed wall as motionless as his fellow red man. They both might have been basalt statues.

"Well, that may all be so, or it may not," Don Hernando continued. "In any case the people of those lands consider blond hair, blue eyes and a light skin to be sure signs of a godly ancestry. But if the blond man is also brave and behaves himself like a knight, they will never doubt for an instant that he is a god. They'll think of him as highly as the Indians I know thought of Alvarado. A man like me with brown hair could never in a lifetime impress them as much, not if I rode a winged horse. And, my dear cousin, remember that we can never control these people through military means alone. For after all, what do we count even with our two or three hundred men, even with horses, cannon and muskets against tens and hundreds of thousands of warriors?

"I tell you I learned something on that nightmare retreat. I know what happens when the mystery is lost. Many of my men and thousands of my Indian fighters paid with their lives after Alvarado and Sandoval became known as just the ordinary men they really are. I can still hear the human offerings shrieking out their last hours, my dear cousin. All I have to do is to close my eyes to see my men drowning in the great lake. The Indians should never have known that we thirsted and hungered like common men, that the heat of the sun made us dizzy and the cold of the mountains set our limbs to trembling. Only as the immortal children of the sun could we be conquistadors.

"That's why I'm advising you most seriously to take this Don Pedro de Cordova on your crusade. For as Xicotencatl just said, he is Toniatuh, a child of the sun."

All this depressed me bitterly. I had imagined my reception by the Pizarros to be something quite different from what it turned out. Now I was acceptable to them because this heathen Xicotencatl saw in me some pagan superstition embodied. I even feared, at the moment, that my future comrades would treat me with contempt because of it. Surely Diego de Vargas would laugh heartily at such nonsense. No doubt he would make a satirical ballad out of the story. They might call me Toniatuh the Tit-brain, or some such thing, on account of it.

"No, look here a minute," I stuttered. "I don't want to do anything like that. I think it's a deadly sin, Don Hernando, and another way of keeping up heathen lies. I don't want to make more heretics. Furthermore it isn't like a knight to make himself out to be something he isn't."

"My dovelet," said Don Hernando to this, laughing into his whiskers, "what have you got to do with the superstitions of the Indians? Did you bleach your hair and color your eyes blue just to play the mummer? Not at all. If you want to, tell them you're not a child of the sun. They won't believe you. They'll believe all the more, thinking it's some kind of trick."

"Why, of course," said Gonzalo, laying his hand on my shoulder. "Your conscience is all a-twitter, my son. By the bowels of Christ, you're as finicky as a nun with her head newly shaved. Can't you see that wisdom and imagination are as good as swords in converting the heathen? We have to get them in hand before we can do anything with them."

"Get somebody else," I said stubbornly. "If I have to go on those terms, I don't want to go at all."

"Well, my son, if you don't want to, you don't. Let's drop the matter entirely," Don Francisco broke in. "Nobody meant any disrespect, my boy. Perhaps the Indians of Tumbez will think my Pedro de Candía a god because of that bush of whisker he sports on his chin. There's no telling what they're going to think next. I remember one time we were hard put to it in a skirmish. One of my riders was thrown from his horse. When this happened the Indians let out a terrific howl. They were terrified and rushed away. Come to find out, they had been thinking horse and rider were all of a piece. When the two came apart they took it for another one of the white man's mysteries, as when a crab breaks off a claw that's caught in a rock."

As always, Pizarro was speaking with gravity. Laughing was foreign to his nature. But this story of Spanish centaurs tickled me. I had to bite my lips to keep from laughing in his face. Gonzalo noticed immediately. Quickly he came up to me and said, "It's settled then that you go with us?"

Before I could answer yes or no, Don Francisco had gripped my hand; he shook it ceremoniously. Gonzalo gripped my other hand, came close, kissed me on both cheeks and said loudly, "Welcome to a knightly friend, a comrade in adventure, in battle and in victory!" To this everyone murmured rumbling approval. But my need to laugh was gone. I had become a conquistador without even knowing what was going on. Gonzalo opened the door and called his brother.

All the Pizarros grouped about me, and I stood in the middle with my senses whirling. They were all enormous men, broad-shouldered. Their hands were as big as the blades of shovels; their heads scraped the beams of the ceiling. All of them spoke at once, slapped me on the back. It was a fearful ordeal. Don Hernando Cortés did not move from his seat, and I clearly saw he was laughing. Even the old crone who had been sitting at the door came into the room. She carried the cat by the scruff of his neck, which made him mew piteously. When she stood up, it became clear that the old woman was just as large of limb and powerfully built as the Pizarros. The passage of the years had crooked her back a little, but that was all. She looked at them angrily and shouted, "What's going on in here, you bulls of Bashan. Behave yourselves. Listen to what Hernando says. He's the master in this house."

"Bring us some wine, mother Teresa," Don Hernando Pizarro commanded.

"Yes, bring on the wine," they all echoed.

"Hurry up, *chiquita,*" said Francisco. "Our guests are perishing of thirst."

The old woman paid them off each with a baleful glance. "What! More wine! Another jag already?" But she shuffled off, and in a short time was back with a metal vessel full to the brim. It was as large as a kettle in which peasants cook their olla.

The oversize goblet was first handed to Don Hernando Cortés, who carefully raised it to his lips with both hands and cried, "A good journey!" He took a mighty swallow. The beaker was then handed over to me. Out of politeness I wanted Don Hernando Pizarro to drink first, but neither he nor his brothers would hear of it. They whacked me painfully on the shoulders and shoved the pot back to me with the wine slopping over the sides. And so I said as loudly as I could, "To a prosperous journey!" and drank a draught.

"Bravo!" bellowed Juan Pizarro. "Spoken like a man."

So it went, round after round, with all talking wildly. They toasted New Castile, Don Carlos the King, the golden treasures of the South Country, the red-skinned maidens, themselves, and Martín de Alcántara even drank to the health of his little camel. The old crone had her turn, too, and she drank with astonishing power, saying each time, "Come back home rich men or don't come back at all!"

"Spoken like a man, chiquita mama," they chorused, and gave the old lady a slap of approval on the shoulder that might easily have knocked the wind out of a young mule.

After these preliminaries, with the wine burning like fire in their bellies, they turned their attention to the future. For a long time they discussed plans with Don Hernando Cortés. There is no point in retelling this conversation in detail. But I must mention one point which later in the South Country proved to be of the greatest importance.

Today I do not entertain the smallest doubt that Francisco Pizarro marked every word that Don Hernando Cortés said. Indeed, I believe now that the words of Cortés burned themselves so clearly in Pizarro's mind that all he had to do later was turn within and read them off the scroll of his memory. Already on that first occasion, before he had had any chance to think over what Cortés had spoken, I can remember as I look back that absent look of concentration. It is by no means easy to turn another man's experience to one's own account.

It was perhaps Pizarro's greatest talent to be able to hearken to all good advices, to remember them and have them at hand to weigh in balance when the situation arose demanding most reasonable decision. Such was his genius. He had colossal patience. And he forgot nothing. His way to final decision was a slow and tortuous one. It was like a peasant trudging across a rain-sodden field newly plowed. But decision once reached, he pursued his course without wavering as much as a hair's breadth, even under the greatest trials.

Don Hernando Cortés, though he was a statesman, was also a knight. It is because of his knightly, open character that we hear so much of swift surprises, bloody frays, gay meetings—always the unexpected in the story of the conquest of Tenochtitlan. Francisco Pizarro was no such man. Despite his peculiar courage, his audacity, he was more like a politician of a new breed. He was not a conquistador of the old school. His rules of the game were political rules. One could easily believe that he knew by heart the writings of the Florentine, Messer Niccolò Machiavelli. As a matter of fact it must be noted that Don Francisco Pizarro could not read a single word of Spanish or any other tongue. Although I have seen him busily inspecting some document or other as if he were reading it with great attention, actually his secretary, Master Pérez, had previously read him off the contents and Don Francisco, who like so many illiterate people had a perfect memory, simply repeated what he had memorized. Even if such documents were long and written in fine print, even if they bristled with columns of figures, he was able to play this little ruse.

Don Francisco could not write either, of course. Master Pérez signed all papers, after which Pizarro would draw a circle at the tail of the signature and affix within it a cross. He was always annoyed when anyone chanced across him while engaged in this labor. For the sweat would be rolling down his forehead with the effort. At times he would seize the quill in both hands and jam it down on the parchment in a fit of rage.

Considering his extraordinary skill in matters of state, it might be thought that Don Francisco knew everything about the lives and opinions of the great statesmen of recent history. One might have thought that he had chosen a list of them as exemplars, perhaps the tricky Don Fernando, King of Aragon, Louis of France, eleventh of that name, or the Fleming Comines. But he knew nothing of them. For him accounts of the past were books sealed with seven seals. His view of world history was founded on Scripture alone. Like all of us he believed in the Creation, Paradise, the fall into sin, the confusion of tongues, the deluge, the coming of the Lord and Judgment Day. Beyond these common beliefs he did not care to go, or particularize in any fashion.

For Don Francisco the crusade on earth was a mere preliminary for larger exploits in afterlife, in what Master Agrippa might well have called the metaphysical battle between good and evil. It is true, on a little reflection, that all of us have intimations that life on earth is but a prologue to the real play that begins only when death raises the curtain. But few among us have the cold courage to express just what he thinks will happen in afterlife, at least as clearly as Don Francisco. For somehow men are fearful, or ashamed, of biting into the kernel of things, much preferring to nibble on the rind.

But to return to Don Francisco as a man talented in handling affairs of state: in this arena he acted entirely according to his own inner bent. The true Pizarro was really a peasant who, caught in the mighty wave of the times, was made over into a *condottiere,* a duke, in truth a king and founder of cities.

Whoever understands the toughness of our Spanish peasants, their piety, pride and their ambition, will understand Don Francisco Pizarro. Who was it, in retrospect, that during the long centuries under the Moorish yoke remained Christian and Gothic in temper? It was not the city dwellers, who opened their eyes with almost painful celerity to the refined ways of living and the material luxuries of the Arabs. The peasants stayed where they have always been, on their fields, their eyes fixed on the earth. They were the ones who stuck fast. Many of them were driven to live like wild beasts in the forests and the mountains. But only those who live a life of struggle can hold the future in their hands.

So it has always been. Heroes and saints are born in straw more often than on fine sheets.

In those days the battles between single villages were of unparalled ferocity. Many a man lost an eye, had an ear bitten off, or met his end through repeated dagger thrusts into his soft middle. Through these village feuds the swineherds became the leaders, like Diomedes and Ajax among the Achaeans. It was their lot to defend the most valuable property of the place. They banded together, and different bands fought one another. Not only did they measure the strength of their muscles, but the strength of their cunning and martial resource. There has been many a Spanish Ulysses sitting scheming about the campfire never exalted by a Homer. Many a Thersites has been smacked on the ears and driven from the company without having his fate preserved in shining hexameters. The heroes of Estremadura carried no harness, no shield. They wore mantles of skin, broad-brimmed fur hats and they stank of swine. Their only weapons were their oak staves and slings, which they used with equal skill against wolves and their fellow men from alien villages.

This was the school of knighthood and experience, the Valladolid and Salamanca, of my captain Don Francisco Pizarro. In this school he won great honors when hardly dry behind the ears. Others may laugh at this. But I say it in all seriousness. For I cannot help but observe that in our times those who arrive at great influence on men and events more often than not spring from the lowest classes, the very dregs of the populations, the nameless sediment, the yeast. What are the English Tudors, the Florentine Medicis, the Spanish Borgias, the German Frundsberg and Luther except the offspring of petty merchants, poverty-rotted squires, bush-cutters and mountain goatherds?

The beer of the time was flat and thin. God—or the Devil it might have been—threw common yeast into the brew. Now it foams and ferments as if crazed.

It really seems as if all mildness and sweetness have now disappeared from the earth. Where are the times when there were only a handful of dead in great battles, and these only because certain unfortunates were thrown from their horses to break their necks, arousing consternation among enemy and friend alike? When we Spaniards first came into contact with the Italians they used to say, Spaniards are mad; they kill and let themselves be killed! In statecraft, theology, the sciences and the arts there is also a new inexorability. No longer do men think in terms of knightliness, virtue and love. They speculate on the strength of armies, weapons, ships and the riches of cities as if they were sitting in a counting house totting up so many maravedis spread out on a green cloth.

In any case, that evening, with the candles burning in silver candlesticks, Don Francisco Pizarro said to his guest, Don Hernando Cortés, "It strikes me you describe the conquest of Tenochtitlan as a rather simple matter. Am I right?"

At this Don Hernando, as was his manner, leaned far back in his chair with his hands spread out flat on the arms. As Don Francisco spoke to him I saw weariness creep into his eyes. When he answered, his voice was tired and listless, almost bored. At the time this puzzled me. Today, however, now that I know many successful men, am in fact one myself, I know that he who has arrived more often than not feels a carking mockery in his success. I myself have discovered that gnawing discontent is closely bound up with ambition. There is a tremendous fear that one false move, one adverse mood of fortune, and everything will be lost. How quickly we become the slaves of our own projects for advancement! Like the sea coral, we build a dead monument over the living self, a kind of grave shutting in life.

When Don Francisco asked his question of Don Hernando, this was the answer he received, "You must understand, dear cousin, that the people of Tenochtitlan, Tezcuco and Tlascala are different from us. When a king dies in Spain, his son takes his place. If Don Carlos should die today, which God forbid, tomorrow little Don Felipe would sit on the throne of all the Spains. Without thinking twice we should all bear him allegiance. With us, then, the king never really dies. But supposing that some pest killed off every member of the House of Hapsburg now scattered all over Europe. The people of Castile, Aragon and Leon would then meet and choose a new king. There are many noblemen among us Spaniards whose heads could easily bear the weight of a crown, the Dukes of Béjar or of Alva, for example.

"Among the Indians there is nothing of this sort. With them, kingliness has nothing to do with crown and scepter. They think the king of godly origin. In their eyes the king is of a different nature from themselves. No Indian Alva could ever substitute for him, no warrior however brave, no councilor however wise. For all of these would lack the essential quality—descent from god.

"Perhaps at some time or other, my cousin, you have watched a swarm of bees. The glistening mass hangs fast on the limb where the queen rests. The queen is the real life of the swarm. That is why the beekeeper tries to catch her, since with her once caught her whole realm of subjects follows blindly after. But if the queen escapes him, all is lost! He could spend months running around with his net without capturing as much as a single bee. On the other hand the beekeeper may have the bad luck to have the queen die in the hive. In such case the bee kingdom drops into ruin. The workers refuse to work, the soldiers fight among themselves, the drones are no longer nourished and so must die. No honey is made. The bee kingdom falls to pieces and in this decline all constituent bees are lost."

Don Hernando had become lost in his own discourse, half smiling to himself at the aptness of his own images. Pausing for a moment, indifferent to the bewilderment of his audience, he went on to say:

"The Indians are like these insects. Each one of them is much less a person than we are. Each Indian is much more a part of the state. I felt this clearly the moment I set foot in Tenochtitlan. Not only do they greet their king with great reverence, throwing themselves on their knees and approaching him only in the poorest of clothing. They love him as well. Tears of joy flow down their painted cheeks at the sight of him, and their voices tremble with emotion. We met their king, Montezuma. Four tall noblemen bore him on their shoulders on a bier decorated with feathers and gold. His robe was made of fine cotton with pearls and other jewels sewn into it. The soles of his shoes were of pure gold. On his hand he wore a long green feather, the sign of superiority on the battlefield. All this made the crowd murmur with delight."

Again Don Hernando Cortés stopped, and looked inquiringly at Don Hernando Pizarro. "Am I boring you?" he said absently.

"Go on, go on. Tell the whole story," said Pizarro, and the others joined in, impatient to hear more of wonders they themselves would perhaps experience.

"Well, then," Cortés went on, beginning slowly as he enumerated his memories, but gradually speaking with rapid authority.

"These people were always busy. Each craftsman worked unceasingly at his trade. They were all like bees in a hive so long as Montezuma lived. The fishermen were hard at work on the waters of the lake, and the makers of salt on its shores. Canoes were everywhere in the lagoons, filled with food, with jars of liquid and flowers. In the marketplace I saw the goldsmiths of Azcapozalco, the potters of Cholula, the Tezcuco painters, stonemasons from Tenayucan, hunters from Xilotepec, fishermen with their catch taken from Cuitlahuc, flower-dealers and weavers of bast from Quatilan. There was as much business being transacted as in the markets of Salamanca or of Cordova.

"There were all sorts of strange wares. There was the *escaupil,* a breastplate made of cotton. There were feathered clothes, lances, spears and pointed arrows. Their broadsword was called the maquahuitl and had a stone handle. They sold a curious kind of paper made from agave fiber. Food of all kinds was piled high. There were fish, wild flesh and fowl, and the fat little dogs Indians like to eat. The heaps of fruit and vegetables were beyond counting. Everywhere Indian maize was for sale. It is the Indian staple all through the New World. Curious drinks could be bought. There was the foamy chocolatl, which tastes very sweet. They also have pulque, which is like beer made of the fleshy leaves of the aloe.

"In cages there were all kinds of wild animals kept for amusement. I saw a beast they call the puma which is like the lion of our world, and a big striped cat that lives in mountainous country. They had hawks and great eagles, little songbirds with red feathers, green parrots and red pheasants. But what took my eye more than anything else was a medium-sized snake that looked harmless enough, but was not. It had castanets on its tail and rattled them like a gypsy. They told us that this snake's bite, however gay the tail may sound, is always fatal to man or beast.

"There was always a great hubbub in the marketplace. Without exaggerating I believe that sometimes fifty thousand people must have been busy buying and selling, at least that many counting those just looking on. Tenochtitlan was like a giant beehive so long as Montezuma sat in the palace. And these bees of Tenochtitlan were by no means lacking in sting. Many a night I've paced up and down my room in the Palace of the Axayacatl, with my footsteps ringing back from the heavy stone walls. There I was, with only four hundred soldiers in a populous city. I was hardly more than a prisoner. One word from Montezuma would have been enough for the Indians to reach for their weapons. Even if they were only stone weapons, sheer numbers would have easily won the day for them.

"I was in constant fear of just that possibility. I knew well enough that the Aztecs were a fighting people, a cruel lot. Already they were looking at our guns, crossbows, breastplates and helmets with greed in their eyes. Besides that, they hated us. We had made an alliance with their traditional enemies, the Tlascalans. And so, thinking it all over I decided there was nothing for us to do but to seize the king, Montezuma. He was the king of the bees.

"I put a plan into effect without delay. The plan succeeded, partly because of its suddenness, partly because Montezuma considered me a half-god whom it would be useless to resist. When this was done I was safe. I was protected against any attack. In one blow I secured all the riches and power of Tenochtitlan. I had the whole city, pyramids and all, in the hollow of my hand. That one trick really completed the conquest of Mexico. From then on all that I and my men had to do was to divide up the spoils, and we should certainly have done that but for an unforeseen accident.

"Our King Don Carlos gave my old enemy, Velazquez, the title of Adelantado. It was done through a mistake and the crookedness of the Bishop of Burgos. Two of the emissaries I had sent home to Spain were scarcely given an audience. All this happened at the time that the people of Castile rose up to demand their rights and the King rushed out to sea from Coruña in order not to lose his imperial crown. This Velazquez wasted no time taking advantage of the situation. He sent out an armada to rob me and my comrades of all we had gained, both honor and gold. His subordinate, Don Pánfilo de Narváez, set sail from Cuba with eighteen caravels and nine hundred men. He coasted along the island of Yucatan and landed his army on the mainland, not far from a place called San Juan de Ulúa. I got this bad piece of news from Gonzalo de Sandoval, who stuck by me. I'd left him behind with a small detachment in Villa Rica to cover our rear.

"There was nothing left for me to do but to take arms against Don Pánfilo de Narváez. I left Tenochtitlan with seventy picked men and two thousand Indians.

"It would bore you to have to listen to all the details of my little campaign against Narváez, my dear cousin. I'll sum it all up by saying that one stormy night I overcame the enemy at Cempoalla. I remember how the rain whipped us in the face. The thunder was so loud it almost drowned out the cannon. Our battle cry was *Espirítu Santo!* The lightning kept flashing blue. For a second or two the pyramids and temples would stand out clear whenever the heavens split open. The Indians yelled and called on their own gods, while we stuck to the Holy Ghost as I've just told you. If anything, I imagine the Indians' gods had the upper hand on this particular occasion. We fought right on the steps of their pyramids. It ended when one of my men rammed his spear into the face of Narváez. He let out a shriek you could hear for miles. I remember how he bellowed, 'Blessed Virgin Mary, he's got my eye. I'm done for, I'm done for!' We knew we had them then.

"In the meantime I had left the force occupying Tenochtitlan, some two-thirds of my whole army, under the command of my old friend, Don Pedro de Alvarado. He was the one the Aztecs used to call Toniatuh, the child of the sun, because he was blond and blue-eyed. They liked his style. He was an open fellow, a good soldier, and afraid of no one. But, dear cousin, though the spring sun in Estremadura may bring forth wood violets, in Tenochtitlan at the same time of the year it burns on the plateau like the fires of Hell. There it brings forth nothing but agave and cactus. It breeds fever in the brain and fills the mind of the thirsty with fanatical thoughts. That is exactly what happened to my Alvarado. He turned from a Castilian lion into a native puma. Making my Toniatuh into the commander of the occupying force was the worst mistake I've ever made in my life. He cost countless men their lives. We just saved our own necks by the width of a red hair.

"You may not know it, my dear cousin, but the foremost god, demon and devil of the Tenochtitlan people is called Uitzilopochtli. He is a monster. His temple reeks of blood. On high feast days the number of human sacrifices made to him runs into the thousands. One May day a priest of this god came to Don Pedro de Alvarado. He was dressed in black and wore his hair long, as is their custom. He asked Alvarado to let him hold a feast in honor of Uitzilopochtli. Not only that, but to hold it next door to the Spanish quarter. Don Pedro hesitated at first. Finally he gave in. He stipulated that there should be no human sacrifices, and the high priest agreed.

"This celebration was called the 'Kindling of the Fire.' The brands on top of the pyramids were turned into bonfires. They looked like volcanoes in eruption when this was going on, like so many small Popocatepetls. The priests, nobles and captains of the soldiery gathered, then, in the 'Court of the Winged Snake' as they called the plaza before the temple.

"Everyone attending the ritual was dressed up in barbaric fashion. They wore garments made out of brightly colored feathers—that is, all but the priests,who were dressed in black robes. They began to sing and dance and cry out, always in the same rhythm. Don Pedro and the rest of the Spaniards left behind were scared out of their wits by this devil's feast. The faces of the dancers grew twisted with excitement, and the priests were dripping foam at the mouth. The dance speeded up gradually. It became wilder all the time. It looked as if the pack of them had been taken with St. Vitus' dance.

"Don Pedro was seriously concerned. He felt sure the Indians were possessed of the Devil. They were feeling a contempt for their own lives which would be hard to cope with. It looked as if they would turn on the Spaniards at the least excuse. The dance, to all appearances, was the first step in preparing for a pitched battle. At this point Alvarado asked a Tlascalan what the words meant that the dancers were screaming in their ecstasy. The spectators shouted them back, clapping their hands in chorus. He said they were the words of a song to their Moloch as he rose up in the morning sky. They went something like this:

"'I am the warrior; nobody is like me.
I am the Sun God in the Kingdom of the Morning.
I have put on my yellow feathers.
The Heaven of sacrifice has opened up.
From the man in the country, dying from cold,
From the man in the cloudland, I have taken a foot.
Who conquers for the Sun, earns an offering.
The God of War has come to hold you in thrall!
Before me fear flies. The white chalk,
The white feathers which consecrate to death,
Have been parceled out. Dust whirls on the plain.
Mankind has been blessed with battle.'

"When Don Pedro heard these words, his heart began to quake. His suspicions now seemed to be a certainty. He expected the Aztecs to fall on the Spaniards and use the prisoners as victims to sacrifice to the god of war. Unfortunately it never occurred to him that he still had Montezuma in his power, and that without Montezuma the dancers were helpless. Yet he had some excuse. The smell of blood and death is in the air whenever the Indians hold these feasts. It's all part of the Devil's plan to delude mankind. Don Pedro himself was half beside himself with all the noise and dancing. He completely lost his head. He commanded his men to mow down the dancers. The Court of the Winged Snake was soon turned into a shambles. The wounded cried out to Moloch. It must have sounded like sweet music to him. There was a terrible blood bath. The Indians died like flies.

"But we Spaniards had to pay for this folly. Moloch and the Devil must have been thirsting for a little Spanish blood, too. The Aztecs turned on Alvarado, and bottled him up in the palace. They cleared out the marketplace to make sure he had no food. It was a ticklish situation, to put it mildly, my dear cousin.

"When I returned from my campaign against Narváez I found the whole city in an uproar. I lost my temper with Alvarado and relieved him of his command. I still hoped to make good the mistake and begged Montezuma to speak to his people in an effort to calm them. But Alvarado had pulled the bowstring one notch too tight, and the bow broke under my hands. When we murdered the nobility of Tenochtitlan and the priests of Uitzilopochtli, we had done more than alienate the Aztecs. They went beyond us and turned against their own king. He was really our prisoner. But for all the public knew he was staying with us as our guest. And so, naturally, they thought he had deliberately countenanced the slaughter, which to them could only mean he had repudiated his gods. Of course, this was anything but true. To the very last he absolutely refused to become a Christian.

"That day, in any case, Montezuma went up on the roof of the Palace of Axayacatl in which we were living. He had put on his robe of office, the tilmatli, which has white and blue stripes. He pinned on his green stone brooch, and wore a crown, the copilli, that looks something like the Pope's tiara. We saw to it that the golden shield which marked his kingly power was raised up high over his head behind him for everyone to see. We stood about like humble vassals, playing the game as best we could.

"He bore himself like a king. For some time he said nothing, his arms folded on his breast. I saw awe and fear running through the crowd assembled below. The Aztec soldiers dropped their lances, heads bent down like ears of wheat in the wind before a storm, Montezuma began to talk in a quiet voice. The silence was so great that every word he said was audible. It seemed as if these words were standing out in the air, chiseled out of stone, crystal clear.

"He told his people that we Spaniards were his guests, and that the gods always protect guests. He said we would soon withdraw from the city and everything would be as it was before, in the time of their forefathers. And so everyone must go home to his house, take off his war-paint, lay aside his weapons and pay homage to the will of the gods, and to him the king, so that he need not redden with shame before strangers.

"At this faces began to look up, faces painted in bright stripes and patches. One of the Devil's priests shouted, 'Miserable Aztec, you understand the will of the gods poorly. White feathers for these white men!'

"The crowd began to moan and cry in anger like a great beast. They cried in unison, 'The white feathers!' Others cursed the king and shouted, 'You coward. You can weave and spin, but you'll have nothing to do with fighting.'

"Then, before we knew what was happening, a hail of stones, arrows and spears struck us. They bounced off our bronze helmets and armor. But the king himself was caught by the three stones on the head. We weren't quick enough to protect him with the shield. He was knocked out, bleeding from the skull.

"When the people saw the king fall, an amazing change came over them. They howled and groaned. Tears ran down over their painted cheeks. They raised their arms in despair. Suddenly a fear too strong to bear overcame them. They ran away, shrieking in horror. The great plaza became as still as death under the blazing sun. We Spaniards up on the roof took the king and brought him into his father's house. We gave him cool drinks and put damp cloths on his wounds. It was then I saw that his red breast was thin and his arms skinny, as if already he had been ailing for a long time. I looked at his torn face and remembered something he had said to me when we first met. 'Perhaps, my Malinche,' he said, 'perhaps they've been telling you that I'm a god, that I come from the Sun up there. But look, I'm a man like the rest. I have bones and sinews. The blood runs in my veins as in the veins of any man in the marketplace.' Then he said a little song to me, smiling. Marina translated it for me.

"'Let us seek the lord of life,
For some time we all must go,
And our happy home is there,
In the land of the dead,
Where life has no end at all.'

"He had chanted these words to me while showing me his bare arm. As he lay dying now, I had to think of what he had told me then. It was hard to stomach the fact I had brought him into such a dirty piece of luck. But what will you do? There can be no conscience in the man who acts. And are we not Christians? Confession will free us of these slips.

"I saw in his face the shadow of death, the shadow that comes into the hollows of the cheeks, under the eyes, under the loosened lip and beneath the nostril holes. He began to look like a mask of himself.

"But why go on with this morality. I asked Father Olmedo to speak to the dying king. But Montezuma turned his eyes away as best he could from the man of God. With his last words he recommended his children to the protection of our King Don Carlos, who on my request has promised to rear the girls and to give them a fitting dowry.

"When Montezuma died he became a free man. The nobles among the Aztecs carried him away on their shoulders out of his ancestors' house. They took him to the people of Tenochtitlan, who received him with woeful singing and moaning.

"Well, cousin Francisco, the past seems to have got the better of me. I'm losing sight of the point of this meeting. What I do want to say flatly is this: Hold fast to the queen bee! All the beekeeper's strategy will be wasted unless he has the queen safe in his net—or the Inca, if you want to put it that way. Make him your friend and the game's half won. I'd wager it won't be much different in the South Country from what it was in Tenochtitlan.

"When Montezuma died I lost my last pawn. The whole country broke out into an uproar. The priests cried for Spanish blood day and night. War stepped down from the teocallis. Many a Spaniard, and many of our Indian allies as well, learned what the Aztec white feathers meant. They hadn't forgotten how to use their obsidian knives. They knew how to carve out their victims' hearts steaming hot and to smear their mouths with blood in honor of the feathered snake they worshipped. War! Yes, war is indeed a Uitzilopochtli! And whoever heard of a beekeeper that deliberately smashed the hive, threw his jars of honey against the wall, burned up his bees? Would he destroy his own livelihood? And wasn't Tenochtitlan mine, taken without drawing my sword? Everything was mine, cousin, everything, so long as I held the queen bee captive. Alvarado, that fool, has cost me and Spain millions upon millions of pesetas. I wish to God his sword had rusted away in its sheath. With one stroke of it he cut away the bonds I had knotted with such care.

"In the end I had to destroy what had belonged to me, Tenochtitlan, the loveliest treasure I've ever laid eyes on in all my life. I had to raze the houses and palaces, the temples and the teocallis. I had to fill in whole sections of the lake. It was a cruel labor. Sixty-two of my men were killed by the barbarians during the siege. Among them was my best of comrades, Guzmán. We had to stand by helpless as they carried him to his death at the top of a pyramid. I, myself, almost met the same fate, and would have if Cristóbal de Olivas hadn't saved my life by sacrificing his own.

"What did I have when the story was ended! At the end of all my pains! Nothing more than a heap of smoking ruins, alive with foul odors and pestilence. The corpses were scattered around by the thousands. Everywhere amid the ruins lay wounded Aztecs, who were all slaughtered, against my orders, by the bloodthirsty Tlascalans. Half-crazed women dragging children by the hand wandered about. Many of them carried dead ones at their breasts, breasts that now gave no milk. The entire booty from all this was only three hundred thousand Castilian thalers in gold.

"That was the result of war. Ruins, death and misery. And a trickle of gold. When the survivors left the city under the order of Guatemotzin, Montezuma's successor, I got a clear picture of what had happened. I never saw such misery. For three days and three nights they straggled out over the dikes. So far as I know they had nowhere to go. The wounded had to be helped along. There were old men and children who died by the wayside. That was the end of Tenochtitlan.

"That was my experience, dear cousin. I know we learn slowly from the experience of others. It's hard on the pride to be the pupil. It's almost better to fail, and have one's own way. But, anyway, my advice is good. It was bought dearly enough."

The room was very still. Peacefully the candles burned away in yellow flame. Against the white wall were the two Indian soldiers whom I now saw with altogether different eyes. The huge Pizarros sat engrossed in thought.

It was Don Francisco Pizarro who spoke first. "Thanks very much for your council, my cousin," he said. "You can be sure your words haven't fallen on deaf ears." I saw immediately that he really meant what he said. There was no doubt in my mind that everything Don Hernando Cortés had told him had been swallowed up as if it had fallen into a dark well.

"How is it, my dear Marquis," the handsome Gonzalo inquired, "that on the one hand you warn us against the blunt methods of your Toniatuh, and in almost the same breath advise us above all to take another one along with us? I mean this Don Pedro de Cordova?"

The weariness disappeared from Don Hernando Cortés' face. Once again he was a slim young man. He looked at me in amusement and said, "Just a minute, now. You mustn't get a false impression. In my whole company I had only two men who were absolutely indispensable. One of them was Pedro de Alvarado and the other Sandoval whom I called my son. But Sandoval is dead. And Alvarado is going his own way. At the moment his fancy has led him into Guatemala. The point is, if I couldn't have either of these I would choose Don Pedro de Cordova."

At this I grew hot all over with embarrassment. It was hard for me to know whether Don Hernando was joking or speaking in earnest.

"I don't follow you," objected Gonzalo. "For as it stands Don Pedro has had experience neither in fighting nor in dealing with the Indians."

"That may be," said Don Hernando. "But he can learn. And there are some qualities in a man which cannot be bought with a hundred years' experience."

"Yes?" said Gonzalo. "And what may they be?"

"Nobility," said Don Hernando. Carefully he measured the handsome Gonzalo from head to foot as he said this, paying him off for his incredulity.

Gonzalo was taken aback. In his powerful black eyes hate flamed up. Don Francisco sucked in his lower lip and bit on it, and the folds about his mouth grew into deep furrows. The rest of the Pizarros kept a heavy silence. Only Juan nodded slowly. The oldest Pizarro, Don Hernando, now spoke up.

"How true! Fairly said!" he agreed eagerly. "I've always told you, haven't I? But you'd never listen to me. You'd never listen to my advice. At the bottom you all know who's the born nobleman among you. I'm the only one who doesn't measure everything in terms of gold or success. I measure things in terms of how much honor or dishonor they'll bring to my name."

"Very good, brother," Don Francisco cut in. "We're all fully aware of your opinions on the matter."

"See! What did I tell you!" said the mighty Hernando. "He's touchy about it. He doesn't like it. And he knows it's a mortal sin to bear a grievance against his own brother. It says so in the Bible. Jesus Christ himself said so. Seventy times seven shall the oldest brother be forgiven."

"We have already exhausted the number," said Gonzalo dryly.

"Hold your mouth, Gonzalo, or I shall clamp it for you," roared Hernando, now thoroughly aroused. "Do you dare to mock the Scripture in front of me! Because you have a pretty face? There are lovely whores who will lie with any man in the straw. And there are pretty men, who squander on these whores money that others have earned."

"Yes, and there are ancient tight-cods and penny-pinching eunuchs," said Gonzalo, rising from his chair.

"I beg your leave!" interposed Francisco Pizarro. "Let's call it quits. Kindly remember, all of you, that we have guests. Do you think they enjoy listening to these remarks?"

"It's his fault; he began it," said Gonzalo stubbornly.

"He has no respect," Hernando flung back, also rising.

"Yes, yes, yes, my brothers," agreed Don Francisco, himself nettled with the evil turn of spirits. "We can straighten this out later among ourselves." He looked around the room, as if seeking something and finally let his eyes rest on me. He spoke quickly, "The agreement stands, then. We'll meet in Seville. And in case you have any followers, Don Pedro, make sure to bring them along."

"I have seven men," I told him.

"Seven!" said Gonzalo. "In the name of the Virgin Mary, how did you ever do it?"

Francisco eyed me incredulously. He sighed and said bitterly, "We've spilled wine like water and spread out a feast of mutton and pork for the fools. Don Pedro and I have talked ourselves hoarse just to get a couple of vagabonds from Trujillo. And this boy without whiskers has seven of them."

"Of course; he knows how to do it," said Don Hernando Cortés, catching my eye. "Everything is in order."

"Not everything," I corrected him. "I haven't got any armor."

"Seven followers and no armor!" Gonzalo laughed. "He certainly is showing us the way."

"We could give you armor," said Juan Pizarro, as they all smiled. "But you'd disappear inside it."

"What Don Pedro means," said Cortés, helping me out, "is that he hasn't got any armor fitted for an expedition to the Indies. It has to be light, simple and without decoration—yet made from the best steel. I still have Sandoval's armor with me. Just by luck. He had about your same build, Don Pedro. I'm sure you'll bring it no dishonor. Take it if you want."

I rushed over to Don Hernando Cortés and shook his hand. I was deeply moved. And yet I had a sour taste on my tongue, not from wine alone. I felt like the runner of Marathon who, his laurel wreath in his hand, saw before him the white walls of the city, the many-columned Acropolis, the mountain of the gods. For it seemed to me that after a long course I stood near the goal of my wishes, a goal which had danced before my eyes as long as I could remember. "Doña Isabella," I cried thickly, "I am armed and ready. The caravels are going to sail. Only the sea lies between me and the kingdom."

The Pizarros looked at me in amazement, thinking at first that I had suddenly lost my senses. But Don Hernando Cortés, unperturbed, had the armor brought, and his servant helped me on with it. They buckled on the cuirass for me, the armlets and greaves. They set the heavy casque on my head, and girdled me round with the belt for my sword. Everything fitted well. With pride I saw the candlelight reflected blue in the glittering steel. Only my father's sword was still rather too big for me.

At the wall the two Indians watched all these maneuvers. Their dark eyes glowed with interest as the armor was brought in. Suddenly, without warning Xicotencatl moved over to me. In his hand he held a green feather, which he rubbed on the breastplate just over my heart, the meanwhile hoarsely mumbling some words. Then with great dignity he returned to his place against the wall. There was a sinister air about this gesture, in his slow, careful manners, in his guttural voice. My heart beat against the steel that covered it over. I clearly saw that beneath the stoic expression of Xicotencatl there was passion and bloodlust, that the red man must be terrifying when he rages with stone knife among his enemies. This ritual of the feather was my first contact with any Indian.

Much later I understood that Xicotencatl had endowed me with the magic of the war god to whom the snake and the humming bird are sacred. But Don Hernando Cortés immediately understood the significance of the Indian's gesture. Startled and withdrawn, he watched me, saying nothing. All this was mostly beyond me at the time, and even now it is not easy to explain the symbol. Perhaps I shall be considered a heretic if I confess I am inclined to believe there is such a devil with a feather-crowned forehead. Who will believe me when I say that we sailed to the Indies to prepare the way for our Lord Jesus Christ, and instead of that welcomed into our hearts the demons of the New World, the Indian gods of earth, mist and war. On our tongues was the word of the Saviour and of His Mother the Blessed Virgin. But in our hearts lodged Indian demons. Unless this be known it will be impossible to understand the things I have yet to tell.

All the rest of the long evening I was trembling with excitement and joy. Everything that happened afterward is blurred in my memory, almost unreal. I was drunk with joy and anticipation, and so remained. Like a drunken man, too, I am to this day able to recall only snatches of what happened in making the mosaic of the story.

I do remember Gonzalo Pizarro telling stories about women and the fiery brood of Sevillian mares, as he politely put it. Juan said something over and over about the sword being the true cross, and Cortés agreed there was something to that idea. But today, outside of these scraps, I have completely forgotten where the conversation led us.

I do recall perfectly, however, that Master Pérez was called in, and that he slid a parchment on the table. Don Francisco seemingly read this parchment (he knew it by heart and repeated it easily from memory, though I was unaware of this at the time). The document concerned the responsibilities of each member of the expedition. At the end was an account of how the spoils were to be divided. This part of the text received the closest attention from the Pizarros. They listened carefully, their heads bowed forward. At the beginning of these paragraphs our King Don Carlos was mentioned. The tenth part of all gold, precious stones and tapestries was promised to him. Beyond this to him would accrue all works of art in case any should fall into our hands. The division continued on to include Don Francisco Pizarro and his followers. Then a certain Don Diego de Almagro was mentioned, and a man of the Church, Father Hernando de Luque. Both of these names were totally unknown to me. But even then I knew they must be of considerable importance, for they got nearly as much as the Captain and Adelantado himself. After these came the rest of the Pizarros, with Don Hernando ranked first and Francisco Martín last. Then followed the rest of the caballeros. My name was added directly to this list by Pérez on Don Francisco's command. The names of my people were also inscribed. I was astonished to see what an imposing rank these homeless fellows made when set down in ink as soldiers. For the account ran:

Don Pedro de Cordova, caballero from the house of the Great Captain, at the special command of the Captain-General
Master Diego de Vargas, also mounted, knight's secretary
Sancho de Trujillo, also mounted (on an ass), marshal
Bernal, a man with crossbow and sword
Frenero, another man with crossbow and sword
Rodrigo, named the Devil, a man with lance and sword
Alonso, named the Splendid, another man with lance and sword.
Juan, named the Thin, a third man with lance and sword.

I marveled, too, at the precision and coldbloodedness with which the Pizarros divided up treasure which as yet they had not even seen. For the gold here in question still rested, of course, in the coffers of a far-distant king. But the Pizarros doubted themselves not in the slightest. I heard later that in making up the list there had been endless quarrels. Don Hernando Pizarro in particular had demanded the same share as Almagro and Luque. Since this was not possible, because of certain circumstances, Don Hernando was wounded to the quick, both in pride and greed, and forthwith began to hate both these men who at that time were complete strangers to him. I mention these things because they led at a later date to further—and bloody—arguments.

After signing the parchment I took my leave amid a great deal of ceremony. I had begun to think it was about time I sought out my friends, who certainly must have been concerned about my mysterious departure from the feasting at Trujillo.

Half in a dream I walked out through the big vestibule, where the old woman still sat with the cat on her lap, both of them lost in the bad light. She looked at me ironically and said, "A child clothed in metal—like the rest." This might have hurt me, but so exalted was my mood that I simply dismissed the old woman as half cracked. Besides, I thought, she is Francisco Pizarro's mother, just a peasant woman.

I was surprised to see my companions waiting for me when I opened the door. They were all sitting on the wall, Alonso the splendid excepted. He had slumped down in sleep and was snoring loudly.

Diego de Vargas bowed to me, and asked in a strange voice, "Could you tell me, sir, if a certain Don Pedro de Cordova has left the house?"

"What!" I said. "Don't you recognize me? I'm standing right in front of you, Diego."

"Sweet Virgin of the Rocks!" exclaimed Diego. "Have you been robbing somebody all this time! In the bowels of Christ, where did you get loaded with all that iron?"

"Iron!" I objected. "Why, it's the best steel I'm wearing. Everything is settled, Diego. Signed and sealed. This breastplate, you see, Sandoval . . . Cortés, you know . . ."

They all crowded about, talking at once, examining my armor. Alonso, however, snored on.

"I don't understand," said Diego. "I feel as if someone had hit me over the head with the trunk of an oak tree."

"And Montezuma," I rambled on incoherently. "Tenochtitlan, the god of war and the green feather. You've got enough material for a whole coffer full of epics. You're going to outstrip Homer and Virgil. But how did you ever find me?"

"The apple never falls very far from the bough," Rodrigo the Devil replied. "This horse, which only a blind man could ever mistake—well, you see him tethered there as big as a house."

"But what do you mean . . . signed and sealed?" Diego de Vargas asked.

"We're going to the Indies. The way stands open as that road. We're going to the South Country. There's no more turning back now."

There was a little silence, and then Diego de Vargas solemnly declaimed, "Farewell, my Spain! Farewell, old earth. Streets I have coursed, merchants and dealers I have robbed, I shall never forget you. Farewell, Cordova, and you, too, Casa Blanca, Seville, Valladolid and all you other daughters of Spain. Farewell, for we're headed for a new realm, a new earth, a new world."

And Rodrigo took up the refrain, "Let's make something better out of this new life we're going to. Let's cast off the old one like a snake's skin. To Hell with the Devil! I'm all for becoming a man of substance!"

Then all of them talked at once again. The piebald was brought over to me, and we set out to find quarters for the night. The little town was still empty and dark, still smelling powerfully of hogs.

I took Diego by the arm and whispered in his ear, "Diego, they're men for you, these Pizarros and Cortés. It's like reading *Amadís de Gaula* just listening to them." In my pleasure I attempted a little leap. But my armor was too heavy, and I would have stumbled had not Diego caught my arm.

13

LEAVE-TAKING

I BELIEVE I have already mentioned that the Guadalquivir, where it runs past my city of Cordova, is not very deep. In high summer gray stones and rubble stick up from the river floor. In many places are beds of whitish gravel under the shallow pools. Long sandbanks run out into the water, like the spines of monsters buried deep. Here and there in deeper pools live fish which the poorest of the poor in Cordova prize very much during Lent.

The banks of the stream are very stony. In place of fields and meadows at the water's edge are marshes and willows, much used by basket makers, and acres of a reedy grass. Under the tangle the earth is damp and fertile. In this little wilderness live wild ducks and geese. No hunting is allowed because the land, which in the spring of the year stands deep under water, is owned by the Church, and the priests allow hunting only when they have important guests. In earlier times the land had belonged to the mosque. The story has it that once teachers and their pupils used to wander among the willows talking about Allah and his dealings with men.

In my time a little pavilion, built out of black and white field stone but half in ruins, stood atop a low hill. From a distance it looked almost like a tent. It was very pleasant to sit in front of this tent of stone, for it was shadowy under the willows and there was an outlook over the green marshy place toward the river and the walls of the city. Evenings, when the sun had gone down and a cool wind began to blow off the water, the nightingales would sing. When I was a child it seemed to me as if the dark wilderness of reeds and willows below me were alive with sweet song, as if they were singing rather than the little gray bird itself which is not so much to look at. I loved this sobbing melody, the song of the night in Cordova. Even now, as I sit with my quill on the paper, my heart beats faster at the memory of it.

This place was where I met Doña Isabella when I returned to Cordova. I chose this unfrequented spot because the city itself was much too dangerous for me, with Father Pablo and the Inquisition still hard on my tracks. It was not exactly to my liking to cower hidden in the rushes like a scared waterfowl, but I had no alternative. Both Diego and Rodrigo had warned me earnestly to keep out of sight, for my own sake as well as for Doña Isabella's and her family's. The Inquisition, they reminded me, had long been casting covetous eyes in the direction of their property. The two of them promised to find Doña Isabella and tell her where I was waiting. My other men I had left behind in Trujillo. They stayed in a stall of Teresa's barn, and earned their keep by working in the fields under her relentless eye.

I sat in the trysting place waiting and watched the sun drop out of sight in the west. The shadows of the willows grew longer, and pointed like giant fingers at the city. It was very still. Now and then the river splashed or something moved in the reeds, whereupon the stillness grew deeper and my expectation more tremulous.

Just about when I had made up my mind to wait no longer, but to go right in to Cordova to seek out Doña Isabella whatever the danger, I heard someone cry softly, 'Abu-el-Harith!' In a moment or two I recognized the shadowy figures of Diego and Rodrigo climbing up the hill. They led a horse by the bridle. On its back were perched two people, a slender person and a fat one. It was Doña Isabella and her duenna, Doña Catarina.

I ran toward them. I saw a stranger in a billowing hunting dress of green sitting on the sidesaddle. Her mouth was parted and her cheeks dark with blood as she stared at me. I stared back in disbelief. Then I realized that my childish Doña Isabella had grown into a young lady. It was hard for me to know whether I should rejoice over this beautiful woman, or give way to the pang of losing the trusted friend of my boyhood.

Who does not know what it means to see a beloved face again after long absence? Who does not know the tentative looks, to see if the familiar manner and smile are still there? Who has not felt the strange pang of bitterness, the hidden qualms? For this meeting the past again is the greatest mystery and the greatest pain of love. Like a breath from the grave, time sweeps softly over the coming and going of lovers, time and its eternal flow. From day to day the flood seems to stand still, almost, and is as clear as a mountain water. But then something may happen which whips up the surface of the mighty stream to make it into a thundering, foaming torrent. The incident may be simple enough. The day comes when we suddenly begin asking ourselves where that wrinkle about the mouth has come from, that fold under the eye, that droop of the shoulders. We ourselves can never answer these questions. Our being is a mystery. Mysteries look at us in muteness from all sides. But we live out our lives with them as if they were old friends, as commonplace as the chair in our room, the coat covering our shoulders, the staff in our hand.

It was the duenna's voice that awakened me from this impasse, for Isabella and I had been staring at each other like two statues. She said, "You've grown very big, Don Pedro. But you've used us very badly, I'd say. You might at least have let us know how things were going with you. Out of sight, out of mind, I suppose."

Doña Isabella smiled almost imperceptibly and shook her head. She closed her eyes.

"Why don't you speak to each other? Why don't you greet him, Doña Isabella? Open your mouth!" continued Doña Catarina impatiently. "Diego, tell the young man to hold the stirrup while the lady gets down from her mount."

"I beg your pardon," I said, and quickly took hold of the reins to hold the horse while she dismounted. I kept my eyes downward, and saw her slender foot, covered with green leather. I thought how Diego had once told me that the troubadours of times past had drunk the wine of Provence out of their ladies' slippers. When I heard this I laughed, but at this moment it no longer seemed so improbable to me.

She rested her left hand on my shoulder as she got down. Her breath brushed my cheek, and then she was standing there on the soft ground amid the rushes.

"Good God in Heaven," Doña Catarina cried out, "did anyone ever see anything like it? You're both standing there like a couple of deaf mutes."

"Your pardon," I said. "I'm so glad, Doña Isabella . . . I should say . . . I don't mean any rudeness . . ."

"I know," said Doña Isabella, "I know exactly." She reached out and took my hand.

"My gracious lady," said Diego, breaking in, to Doña Catarina, "not far from here I know a lovely spot. You can get the finest view of the city you ever saw. And of the river, too. Permit me to show it to you."

Doña Catarina looked at him suspiciously, an ironic smile on her lips. She sighed and said, "I suppose so, if there's nothing else to do. But you look to me like a very dangerous man, my dear fellow."

"A man does what he can," said Diego coolly. He winked at me, and added, "You can hardly blame men, you know, if the women are so lovely they rob him of all sense of discretion. My knees are quaking this very minute."

"Flatterer! Liar!" said Doña Catarina, dryly. She slapped Diego lightly on the cheek, and took his proffered arm. Rodrigo followed slowly behind.

We stood alone. In the tops of the willows there was a silvery whispering and sighing of the night wind.

"The wind is coming in from the sea," I said aimlessly.

"Yes, it's from the sea," said Doña Isabella. "It comes from far off, doesn't it?"

"Yes. But I've given Don Francisco Pizarro my word," I told her. "I've signed my name. It's all settled that I'm to go along with them."

"I know," she said. "Master Diego told us all about it. He told us everything—about the Cardinal and all the trouble you got into, about the winter days in La Mancha, Cortés and the Pizarros."

"He did?" I said, rather disappointed. I looked at her closely. There was no sign of the pleasure I had expected. Something was wrong.

She saw my disappointment, and shrugged her shoulders. "I'm stupid," she said, "terribly stupid. I know I ought to be glad of your success. But can't you see I don't want you running off to the other side of the world? And then . . . no, I can't tell you."

"What can't you tell me?" I insisted.

"The Devil," she murmured.

"The Devil? What are you talking about!" I said, smiling. "I suppose you found out Rodrigo is called the devil. But he's really the best of men. Believe me, he is. He just lost his wife to an angel, to tell the truth. No wonder he's a little melancholy."

"Don Pedro," she interrupted sharply, "I beg you, stay in Spain. Or at least for my sake go to Italy, to the Emperor's court in Bologna. Or go to Germany and fight the heretics, or to Hungary and fight the Turks. But not to the Indies. You can find just as much of a name

somewhere else. And that kingdom—do you still take that childish promise seriously? We're grown up now, you know. We know that crowns don't hang on trees like apples for anyone to reach up and pluck."

"I'm aware of that," I assured her. "I don't imagine it's going to be simple. But after all, there really are some kingdoms and crowns left, waiting for conquistadors to claim them. There will always be crowns on the earth for those who can take them. Think of Cortés, of King Juan and the rest."

"Maybe," she said slowly, and half turned away. "There's no use trying to persuade you, I can see that plainly enough. You're obsessed with the idea. I can see the Indies shining in your eyes. And I've helped make it."

"I don't really know what you're talking about," I said.

"Don't you?" she asked almost bitterly. "Don't you really know? I'm talking about what is real. About what does not have cloven hoofs. There may be no devil with a fiery mantle, any more than there's a man who throws sand in children's eyes to make them sleep. But there is sleep. And there is evil, too."

"Yes, I know," I said, in utter confusion. "But how does that affect me? What have I got to do with it?"

"I'm afraid, I'm terribly afraid," she went on, unheeding. "I've been afraid of it in you since that day when we were children at the miracle play. Do you remember how you took your Sancho's knife and wanted to attack the player on the stage? You'd have done it, too, if Father Pablo hadn't held you back."

I smiled and shook my head. "That's not quite right," I told her. "Actually I was trembling with fear. I was only too glad to have Father Pablo hold me back."

"Well, you ought to be just as afraid now," she said, not to be beguiled from her belief. "It isn't some actor that's threatening you now."

Involuntarily I wheeled around. But behind me there was nothing except the ruins of the pavilion and evening quiet. I began to feel irritated that Doña Isabella should spoil the meeting with her fancies. Yet there was no doubt she was really concerned, for she was atremble. . . . How much older she had grown, how much more mature!

"I swear to you," I told her, taking her hand, "whatever it is you're afraid of, it will never have any power over me."

With these words we both fell silent. In the undergrowth beyond the pavilion the first nightingale began his song. Tentatively, like someone lightly running his hands over the strings, the nightingale sang and seemed to ask a question beyond the reach of words. The darkness slowly rose up from the earth, enveloping everything, closing us in. There was a deep hush. All that could be heard was the flight of some unseen insect, a soft rustling in the reeds, and from far off a light sobbing of the river's waters.

This first seeking melody was suddenly answered, and from near by. The liquid sounds poured out into the night not far from us, then as suddenly stopped. I could smell the brackish smell of fresh water and damp earth. My expectation was so tremendous that I felt the mute things of the earth, the very plants and stones, were struggling to vent their pent-up strength. Release came. The whole taut place was alive with the song of the nightingale.

The strangest thing of all happened to me then. I felt that I was no longer Pedro de Cordova, no longer the anxious young man with a thousand small cares and plans. The girl was no longer Doña Isabella, a proud and difficult girl from a family much concerned with its status. Against our will the paean of the nightingale carried us away as it gave tongue to some ancient dumbness. The human in us dissolved. In us moved trees, stones and river-flow and the stars. The world and ourselves became one. Things around us no longer were stiff and dead, but as alive and breathing as we were.

Which kissed the other I cannot say, for we moved together impelled by a common impulse. No longer did we feel any shyness or hesitation. A power outside ourselves seemed to act for us. I remember that I put my arms around her and drank from her lips as if they were the fountain of life. I kissed her hair and breathed deep of its cool perfume. I kissed her temples and traced with my lips the bony structure of her face under the soft skin. And as I did this she turned her mouth nearer to mine, with her lips parted slightly to allow mine to enter.

"I wonder how it is," I asked her in a whisper, "that even when we were little children we knew that we loved each other, and always would." It was easier to talk to her now. We moved toward the pavilion, and finally sat down.

"Yes, I knew, too," she told me. "But now I can't understand why you should still love me. My forehead is much too high, and my eyes are almond-shaped like a Moor's. It's simply ridiculous." She laughed at her own objections and pressed her cheek against mine.

"That isn't true," I said. "And what about me? It's much worse with me, as you can see. My hair is as yellow as straw. Besides that I'm too shy and not very bright. If Master Agrippa hadn't helped me, I wouldn't know anything at all. It frightened me to see how clever Cortés and Pizarro are. Diego knows more than I do. And I couldn't answer Guevara, the Cardinal, once."

"You should be glad," she said to this. "You don't need to know. Haven't I seen that just being what you are is enough? You walk straight along without swerving. Everything petty falls out of your way. That's one reason why I love you. That's why they all love you—my father, my brother, Doña Catarina, Diego and your Sancho. All of them. Even a murderer like Frenero is fond of you, and that fanatic Father Pablo has his weakness when it comes to you. I can understand. Why, I believe that even the Great Inquisitor must have liked you secretly."

"You do! The Cardinal!" I exclaimed. "He tried hard to get me to see his way, if that's what you mean."

"That's it, that's it," she said, gripping my arm. "That's what I'm so afraid of. Some day some Guevara will get you on his side. And I know why a man like the Cardinal wants you on his side. For if you should recognize him it would be all the self-justification he would need. He wants you as his good conscience. He told my father you were free, that the Inquisition was only determined to speak a serious word with you. He said, 'I know a Spanish nobleman when I see one, and the Inquisition is not out to injure such people. On the contrary, it means to help them.' Then he said, 'I wish the young man had stayed with us. I would have shown him the right path. I'm no monster. Loayza, the King's confessor, and Don Carlos himself depend a great deal on my advice.' "

"I know I shouldn't have run away," I said, shame reddening my face unseen. "It was a cowardly thing to do. But when I saw Abu Amru dying I lost heart. I had to get out. . . ."

"You did right," said Doña Isabella, slowly. "You did right to do what your feeling told you. But I fear the day will come when you will stay to listen to the endless arguments. I don't know what will happen to you then."

"And yet that isn't it," I objected thoughtfully. "There will come a day. But on the day I'll have to give the Cardinal my answer with no stammering. He is more than an old man who knows a great deal. I can't forget how he held out the crucifix to me, right in front of my eyes, and how he smashed his fist on the table. He said that God was dead. . . ."

"What did he mean by that?"

"It was terrible," I went on. "But Iñigo de Loyola said about the same. It upset me more than I can say."

"Who is this Iñigo?" As she asked this, Doña Isabella moved closer to me, for the nightingales had stopped singing and an oppressive silence hemmed us in. I had the feeling someone was listening to us.

"Iñigo de Loyola," I said. "He's a strange man with green eyes. He is crippled from the wars. He seems to be almost a saint."

"I don't like him," said Doña Isabella, childishly. "I don't like any of them, these saints. Saint Francis himself had something sinister about him even if he did preach to the birds. Besides, he had stigmata on his palms and holes in his cheeks. And Santo Domingo, the Spaniard, reminds me of a bullfighter out for the kill. They're all importunate, these saints. They lock up God in their teachings, all their rules and cloisters. They don't have common politeness; they're plebeians. I like the madonnas alongside the road, the ones the peasants take their caps off to. I like the kind of prayers my mother taught me. I remember best one that began:

" 'Small maiden demure, of heart so pure
That none but God shall e'er immure.' "

Almost foolishly I repeated her little prayer, and suddenly felt very happy. It was hard for me not to laugh aloud. Too eagerly, perhaps, I said, "Everything's really very simple, isn't it? I don't see why people make such a to-do about everything. The priests and saints, I mean. I don't understand."

"But don't you know that the simplest things are always hardest to understand, little dolt?" said Isabella, laughing and kissing me. She grew very wise and old again. "That's just why people spend so much time on complicated matters. Everybody wants to be sure of something as a question of pride. How simple our Lord's word is, Love thy neighbor. Just think how that word has been twisted around, just because it's hard to love thy neighbor. They say, I can't love that fellow because he has black hair. I can't love him because he speaks Arabic, while I speak Spanish. He calls God Allah, which is a terrible sacrilege.

"They say, That one I couldn't love because he's a thief, or a fence, or a murderer. Let's cut off his ears instead, let's put him on the rack, let's lop off his head. That's justice. But they forget that God said, Vengeance is *mine,* I shall repay. Some retort that justice is necessary in order to curb evil. There would be no necessity of justice, as they call it, if men loved one another. How could there be thieves, fences and murderers then? How could there be hungry people and revelers at the same time? People in rags and others in silks. Would it be possible? But because people have erected this maze of mutual distrust there are rich and poor, masters and subjects. Instead of the kingdom of love we have the kingdom of fear, of complications. For it is out of this fear that wars and hate arise. Men fear everything. Except the one thing they should fear, God."

"What is all this you're saying, Isabella?" I protested. "You make me worry when you talk like that."

"Yes, but I know, I tell you," she insisted, trembling with conviction. "He'll come back, he told me, my Pedro. He said so; he promised it. But he'll be different from now, my Pedro. He will be clothed in steel, a soldier, a master of the sword. Time will unroll before him like a carpet, and then we'll stand in the midst of eternity. Eternity is terribly near, my Pedro . . . but no, I won't talk to you like that. It's so long since I've seen you. It's not right to make you sad. Just keep on being as you are now. But come back—you must come back!"

With that she reached into her breast, drew out a little silver cross. "Here," she said, and kissed the cross. I took it and kissed it, too. It was still warm from pressing against her flesh. I opened up my doublet and she hung it round my neck. It was like plighting our troth forever, as if the cross bound us together far more strongly than the golden ring which the priests say is without end, like real love.

I took her hand and we moved nearer to the pavilion. The light from a full moon bathed the milky leaves of the willows, shaking gently in the soft breeze. The night was like a fairyland. We could smell the orange blossoms from the city gardens, borne to us in soft gusts.

Far away there were faint voices crying out, the rolling of a wagon wheel over the cobbles, the clang of hoofs.

We said nothing now, just looked out over the black and silver river down below beyond the reedy space. I held her hands. Our silence was filled with questions and answers. But it was not Isabella and Pedro who spoke to each other in this sweet silence. It was man and woman, reed and willow, river and hill who talked. I was filled with exaltation. I knew that we had spoken to each other like this thousands of years ago, long before Caesar ever came to Spain. I knew that we would speak to each other again thousands of years hence, among men for whom our own times would be no more than legendary. The little tentlike pavilion near which we sat might to me have been the hub of a great wheel about which the spokes whirled endlessly, like the fixed point in the restless flow of appearance.

I cannot say how long we sat there. But suddenly we were startled by voices and laughter very close by. Before I came back to earth Doña Catarina and Diego and Rodrigo were confronting us.

"Look at them! Sitting on wet stones. They'll surely catch their death of cold," she scolded. "They aren't worrying much about me, that's certain. If these two caballeros hadn't entertained me with one ballad after another I'd have been sound asleep long ago. It must be very late. Who knows what kind of gypsies and murderers are lurking in these marshes?"

"Don't worry in the slightest," said Diego de Vargas. "Nobody would ever think of coming here. Don't you know that in that pavilion the wicked Averroes used to wait for a nightly visit from the Devil? They say he still comes to see if his old friend is waiting there for him."

"I beg you, sirs, talk no more about it," pleaded Doña Catarina. "Let's have no more jokes if you don't mind."

We helped the women on their horse, and my friends made ready to accompany them. At the last moment Doña Catarina, bethinking herself, said, "Just a minute. I've forgotten something. A letter came for you a few days ago, or some sort of writing."

"For me!" I said.

"Yes, it's for you," she replied tartly, eager to be off. "It's from your Master, the one who read to us from Dante."

I was so overjoyed at this double pleasure that I kissed Doña Catarina full on her fat cheeks. She, who was so tender-hearted beneath the thorny exterior, immediately began to leak tears, and said, "You ingrate! Going off like this and leaving us all behind!"

"But I'll come back," I protested.

"Perhaps! Perhaps you will," she agreed sorrowfully. "Now you're here, right in front of our noses. But tomorrow God knows where our thoughts will have to gallop to catch up with you."

In a moment my love was gone from sight. I was alone, and again sank to my seat on the stones. The magic of the hour had vanished. The landscape was as beautiful as ever and the full moon still shone. Yet now everything was lifeless, indifferent to my feelings.

Out of the willow shadows I walked into the full light of the moon. I opened the seal, rolled out the parchment and began to read. Master Agrippa had printed rather than written his letters, as was his custom. He used to tell me that no one really knew whether his writings might have some value for posterity. The letter, then, looked more like a court document than an ordinary communication between two friends. At first glance, as I rapidly scanned the page, I saw that its contents were of more than everyday significance. Although through reading and re-reading I could repeat his long letter almost literally, I am glad now that I preserved his scroll through everything. It is here beside me as I write. Translated from his Latin into our own language it ran:

"To Don Pedro de Cordova, a Noble and Knight of Castile, Master Agrippa of Nettesheim, magician and investigator of all the world under the moon, sends his greetings.

"Worthy Sir and Dear Son:

"As Saint Paul the Apostle wrote to his son Titus, may the grace, pity and peace of the Lord God and of His only son, Jesus Christ, be with you! May you never forsake the hope for eternal life! For this hope the Lord God has promised us, and He cannot lie. This He promised us when He shaped chaos into the world, when He placed the stars in the firmament, when He peopled the forests, the rivers and the seas with His creatures, when He created man in His own image in the land of the four streams, of the living waters, in Paradise.

"Think well, my dear son, and dwell on thoughts of God. Then dwell on the deeds of man, the created, and what he has made from the works of the Master. For to man alone has God given the fearful gift of freedom. The stars wander eternally in their given paths through the heavens, and the sea rises and falls according to ancient command. The seasons come and go in order. The plants unfold their leaves and blooms and bear fruit as always ordained. Birds nest and feed their young and the animals of prey roam as it has always been given them to do. But as lovely as the stars may be, the luminous masses of great mystery on high, as lovely as may be the cobalt ocean, mighty trees, tender buds, gay birds and the multiple animals of the woods, yet all of them lack the unique sign of mankind. And this quality is freedom.

"For the stars, my son, can be nothing except what they are. They must stick to their courses in the sky. The oceans of the earth and the icy peaks are subject to the same eternal law as the tiny songbirds and the beasts of prey. Only with man is it different. Even to him God has shown His will. Yet man is free. He can move hither and yon, as he pleases. He can think this or that. He can cling to God, or he can fall into darkness. He is free.

"This freedom of choice, my son, is the very kernel and the innermost content of life. On this very account, God created the world. He was weary of hearing over and over the eternal yea and yea of the angels. Just because of it He removed himself from the world of men and retreated out of time into eternity, sitting on His throne. I shall see, He said to Himself, whether of themselves men feel my strength from the swooning depths of eternity, whether they will fly to me like splinters of iron to the mountain of lode.

"But when the Lord God quit the earth the great Negator believed that his hour had come, and he emerged from darkness into time. Indeed, the angelic doctor Saint Thomas Aquinas says that there never was any creator of evil, that evil is only separation from God. Yet where do we go when we are separated from God? Perhaps we wander from being into not-being, into nowhere. *Ignoramus et ignorabimus.*

"We do not need to know, however. Often of late it has occurred to me that all metaphysics is useless. For it seems to me that it lures man away from what is truly essential in the order of things. They say that Saint Thomas himself shortly before his death was similarly overcome with the thought that all knowledge might be pure vanity. His bright spirit was all clouded and from this he suffered grievously. But he overcame his spiritual illness by sinking himself into the contemplation of trees, flowers and herbs in the cloister garden. In the cloister itself he undertook duties which, in fact, poorly suited his rank and time of life.

"In me, too, my son, there has evolved a similar change of heart since I took it upon myself to mix in the life of the court at Brussels. It is very hard to penetrate this net of intrigue and jealousy in order to get my words to the Emperor. You must know that in the interim since I last saw you my patroness, Doña Margarita of Savoy, has left this earth. The good lady's death has been a heavy blow for me to bear. It has not only complicated my political task a thousandfold—my personal life was closely bound up with hers. Doña Margarita was a woman of good understanding. Although she was born into advantage she saw beyond the pettiness and hedging of court existence into the caldron of life itself.

"Now I have no idea what will become of the Netherlands. At times I am sorely afraid. Trouble is brewing everywhere. Cities, provinces and bishoprics are clamoring for their rights. Preachers are wandering through the land stirring up the common people. They carry the Bible in their hands and say that baptism is a sin, for the child is unable to decide for himself, which makes the ritual a satanic mockery. It is their practice to baptize only adults. These people are called Anabaptists. But what horrifies me most about Anabaptists is their iconoclastic spirit. Fire burns in their eyes and flashes from their tongues. They love to dwell on images depicting hunger, war, the pest and destruction. It is exactly as if they would as soon see the Four Horsemen abroad as not, would rejoice in the spectacle. Many right-thinking burghers turn away from them. But there are enough poor, dissatisfied or simple people to give them a hearing. The women especially are set on them. I have seen women whose limbs were shaking, their mouths dripping lather, when some rude fellow, his stringy hair flying, spoke crazily of Judgment Day as if it were the coming Saturday.

"These Anabaptists also believe that everything belongs to everybody, and that the rich should divide their goods with the poor. They argue that such was the custom among the early Christians, who also lived in daily expectation of Millennium. The women believe that every man should have several wives, and that it is a great sin for a man to copulate with a pregnant woman. For if a man does this, coitus loses its God-given intention, namely, to create life, and becomes no more than the fulfillment of bestial lust.

"Unfortunately, these religious maniacs do not themselves practice what they preach. They gorge themselves with whores and drink worse than peasants at Kermesse, even if they do contrive an elaborate apologetic for their excesses. In fact, there are some among them who say that a knotty log of wood can be split asunder only with a mighty wedge, and that likewise Satan can be banished only with the forces of Beelzebub. This the Lord himself taught, they contend, when he said, Turn not away from evil. They try to atone for sin by committing more sin, just as many doctors try to cure the diarrhea by application of a powerful clyster, believing that by so doing the patient will part intestinally with his disease, providing he is not killed in the process.

"I should not be so fearful of the harm these brothers may cause, were it not that even among the sensible Flemings there is deep unrest. These rich merchants, weavers and brewers of ale in Antwerp, Ghent, Bruges and Ypres watch events in Spain with infinite care. They see that, since the uprising, Spanish cities have had to endure the imposition of one tax after the other. They note the doings of the Holy Inquisition, which is certainly as much concerned with the property of heretics as with their souls. From refugees, especially from the many who have found sanctuary in Holland, they hear terrible reports of imprisonment, the rack and executions, as likely as not of their own friends.

"For this reason it is very bad that Doña Margarita is no longer alive. She understood these Flemings and was liked by them, as the niece of the last Duke of Burgundy. Don Carlos also grew up among these people. He, too, knows perfectly well that Spanish political customs cannot be applied in Flanders without causing uprisings as numerous as the snakes on Medusa's head. So I ask myself how it will be when Don Carlos is no longer here. What will happen when a stranger sits on the throne of the Count of Flanders and the Duke of Burgundy?

"You will understand, my son, that it is difficult, practically impossible these days, to undertake any course of action against the Inquisition. All devotees of the *status quo* and all the Emperor's friends are of necessity intimately in league with the one institution claiming to promulgate spiritual justice. It sounds like madness to Flemish ears to level the dikes and open the sluices just when the land is threatened by flood. Yet I am far from convinced that the Inquisition is a secure dike. It is not my opinion that the subterranean powers now threatening mankind can be held down by inquisitorial means.

"Nothing remains within my scope to do but give a helping hand to some oppressed victim, and ameliorate as best I can the worse miscarriages of justice. It is seldom I can do even as much as this. My influence is very much limited these miserable days. It often fills me with hopelessness and tires out my will to have to force every step I propose. This fatigue follows me into my study. More and more I see that everything in the world, in the life of action and in the sciences both, is at the bottom noxious vanity. My pen scratches industriously forward across the paper almost against my inner intention, and one vanity after the other falls to pieces. I pray God may at least grant me that my embittered reflections are but a dark frame accenting the brightness of the final picture of man's salvation.

"Not so long ago I talked with His Eminence, Cardinal Loayza, the Emperor's confessor. It moved me to hear that he, the statesman, is hounded by the same cares as I. After all, I am only a scholar, and approach worldly matters with no little diffidence. 'What is wrong with mankind?' the Cardinal asked me. 'I see nothing but persecution, revolution and war on all sides,' he told me. 'Is the whole Western World collapsing as Rome did under the last Caesars?' he wanted to know. 'Or is the Day of Judgment really coming, as the fanatics shout in the streets? But,' he added thoughtfully, 'for some time now I have busied myself with Indian affairs, for I have been named successor to Fonseca as chief in the Council for the Indies. There I find that the same violence obtains in virgin lands as in Europe. We still have a long and weary road to travel before we find the Kingdom of Christ here on earth. And then,' he added, 'if there were only more heralds like Brother Bartolomé de las Casas!'

"I looked questioningly at His Eminence, for never before had I heard this name. His Eminence shook his head and to my surprise suddenly burst into laughter. Usually the Cardinal is a very grave man whose shoulders are bowed down with the burden of affairs attaching to his many offices. Now he laughed in full voice, quite contrary to his court manner.

" 'Our Brother Bartolomé is going to give us some hard nuts to crack before he is through,' the Cardinal said, 'as soon as he hears that I have taken Fonseca's place. He is a very excitable and impatient man. He thinks the Kingdom of Christ must come to earth right now, with not an instant's delay. He will grant no one a moment's respite. Some years ago he appeared before His Majesty and harangued him as some ancient prophet might have castigated Herod. All the courtiers and I with them stood listening aghast. But our Brother Bartolomé's blunt address seemed to please the King, may God keep him, and he granted all that was asked. Thereupon Brother Bartolomé, the Cardinal explained, established a colony in the Terra Firma in which life would run as smooth as oil. His pearl fisheries were so successful, however, that all kinds of adventurers were attracted to the place, and trouble began forthwith. The godly state was a complete fiasco.

"'Brother Bartolomé is now living in the house of Santo Domingo in Hispaniola, from which vantage point he issues occasional diatribes against worldliness. I should not be surprised,' the Cardinal said, 'if he soon quit his retreat and began to preach a new crusade. Our Brother Bartolomé can be silenced only by death, and perhaps not even then,' he said, 'for there is assuredly something immortal in him; I love him very much.'

"You may wonder, my child, why I talk at such great length of Brother Bartolomé, whom I know no better than you do. Yet I could not help but get the impression from the Cardinal's discourse that Bartolomé is a genuinely great man. Since such men are rare in the world, rare as diamonds as big as my fist, I do not begrudge the time spent in discussing him. Did not our Lord Jesus Christ once promise us, according to the legend, that we were not forsaken so long as one good man remained on earth? Perhaps Father Bartolomé de las Casas is this man among men.

"It also came to me that one fine day you yourself might depart for the Indies, for this kingdom you seek will give you no rest until you have found it. I always remarked that your eyes lighted up when I told you about strange lands. If you should go, then, I think it would be good for you to seek our Father Bartolomé. Him I recommend as your teacher and guide. It is possible that now you will smile at me, already considering yourself a Master like myself and so no longer in need of advice, especially gratuitous advice.

"Yet think, my son, life is hard to know and to subdue still harder. Even we, we old ones, have our hours when we behave like striplings and are at a loss. The majority never learn to master their lives. Their heads are muddled. Their thoughts are like so many onions held loosely in a sack. But he who would be a Master must bring his house in order. It is easy to perform martial deeds, to learn a trade, to acquire gold and even fame. All these things can be done with health, ordinary wit and will. But it is infinitely harder to build up the inner cosmos.

"Man, my son, is a world in little, as I have so often told you heretofore, a reflection of the larger one in which we all live. For this reason long not too strenuously for success and women, but thirst for purity of soul. There are, believe me, beggars in the street who are greater than kings. As such a humble man our Lord appeared on earth. He sought Heaven's light, not purple robes.

"The dawn is already graying my room. Outside in the linden trees early spring birds are singing. Farewell, and grow into a good knight. Your old crow, your Master Agrippa, will take pride in the eagle that has taken flight from the nest. *Vale.*"

I rolled the scroll together and looked out over the silvery river. Before me the future and all life loomed large, an endless adventure, a brilliant tapestry of promise. Without thinking I let forth a cry of joy. The echo came back, now a question, from far away, from over the river, where the hills and valleys of my Spanish earth were lost in the misty moonlit night.

14

SEA JOURNEY

AT LAST came the open sea and the oaken planks of a ship underfoot. The east wind was filling the sails of the *Espíritu Santo,* as our vessel was piously named. She was an old craft, severely battered from the trials of many, many years afloat. So nail-sick, indeed, was she that we had slipped like thieves out of Seville harbor about midnight. Our Captain-General, Don Francisco Pizarro, had been afraid that the *Espíritu Santo's* crew would desert if they ever suspected how close to unseaworthy was the vessel they had blithely contracted to work across the broad wastes of ocean.

At the bow of the *Espíritu Santo* was nailed the image of a gaily colored dove, carved out of wood. Whenever I looked down on this plump bird from the forward deck it was easy to imagine that we were being helped along on our passage by the steady beat of its wings. And so, in time, the white roofs and towers of Cadiz sank from sight behind us. In good time the hills disappeared, and on the morning of the third we could see nothing more of land but a bluish mist. All of us, with the exception of the seamen working the vessel, stood on the poop deck gazing landward. We watched the flight of the gulls, saw them tossed aloft on a sudden wind squall, followed them as they were driven into the seething wake. Ever complaining and screaming they trailed along behind, sometimes pausing to rest on the tumbling waves, small specks of white. But this spectacle did not endure for long. After a few days the last of them headed back in the direction of the shore, and we were left solitary on the immense plain of sea under a lowering gray sky.

At the horizon, however, where cloud and water were separated by a thin clear line of light, the waves rose into hills which some of the landlubbers aboard mistook for solid ground. Only when the very last intimation of land had failed us did we commit ourselves completely to life aboard ship. We had very little to do other than eat, drink, sleep and engage in protracted conversations. Sometimes, when the wind blew up strong, so that the ship rolled and groaned in every strake, we did lend a hand to the seamen taking in sail, or hard at work at the pumps. We ran about ineptly, buckets in our hands, unaccustomed as yet to the violent tossing of the deck beneath our feet. Now and then one of us would be thrown with a crash into the scuppers, as the ship slid with dizzy speed down the side of a big comber.

Several of us quickly became victims of seasickness, and Alonso the splendid was especially hard hit. Frenero had scarcely strength enough left to roll out his brutal curses. The seamen let Frenero lie in his own filth and vomit, fearing that he would run a knife into their ribs if disturbed, but our two monks, Father Vicente de Valverde and Father Juan, were not loath to take charge of him. Father Vicente jogged him with the toe of his boot and said curtly, "Enough of that kind of talk, you hairy hog. Another word out of you and over the side you go."

But Father Juan merely smiled at Frenero's misery and gave him his rosary to while away the swooning hours. "The poor animal doesn't know what he's doing, brother," he said. "I'll make a prayer for his soul."

"A waste of time, as I see it," said Father Vicente to this, while he stroked his chin with a hand as big and brown as a smoked ham. "But what's the difference? Try it anyway. With God anything is possible." So saying he shuffled away, leaning this way and that to meet the motion of the vessel, and his colleague, Father Juan, followed after him, now and then stopping to look backward commiseratively at the stricken bravo.

All during this period our Captain-General did not once leave his cabin aft. Yet all of us enjoyed a sense of security in the simple knowledge that he was there on hand should occasion for his manifest resources arise. Even that early in the expedition Pizarro had a quiet and pervasive hold on the spirits of his followers. Everyone depended seriously on his presence aboard, and attended the day when he would come on deck as if awaiting an omen of good fortune. Among themselves they nicknamed him the "Old Boy," but aloud no one was rash enough to use this epithet rather than "Captain-General."

Francisco Pizarro sat day in and day out before the little table in his cramped quarters. On it was spread out the same map the leaders had consulted at the Pizarro homestead in Trujillo. But our leader paid no attention to what was drawn on the map, so his brother Gonzalo informed me. Instead he stared out through the latticed port cut into the high counter, forever watching the curling seas that slipped away behind us. During the night he would sit in this fashion for hours on end, his cabin dark, and assuredly unable to see more than the foaming crests of the rollers gleaming in the feeble light of the stern lantern. The servant would tiptoe in in good time, place candles on the table, and draw a dark green curtain over the leaded panes. Yet even then Pizarro continued to peer out into space, as if neither curtain nor the darkness of night could hinder him from sweeping the reaches of the sea. He hardly touched the food and drink regularly placed before him.

Another curious passenger was Don Pedro de Candía. This glittering knight had taken off his golden harness, and now went about in a Franciscan's cowl. During the day he kept mostly to his cabin, which he shared with Gonzalo, the two priests and me. On the wall one of the brothers had hung an old-fashioned image of the Virgin Mary, under which, swinging at the end of a thin silver chain, was suspended a little oil lamp. Don Pedro, his legs curled under him Turkish style, sat beneath this image for hours on end. He swayed back and forth, like a Jew at his devotions in a synagogue, and mumbled to himself constantly. Occasionally he would be overcome with some terrible excitement, and cry out so loudly that his mad words rang throughout the ship. At these moments of spiritual seizure he would crash his long head against the side of the cabin.

He did this, so Father Juan informed me, after contemplating the sins of his youth, after recalling all the tender-thighed virgins he had raped, including among this interesting number the famous pasha's daughter. He, speaking for himself, said that he was in mortal combat with the devils of the flesh during these penitential transports.

When night fell, however, Don Pedro girt himself with sword and scabbard and came out on deck. He was always concerned, so he told us, lest we should be beset by corsairs during the hours of darkness, or should become prey to some sea-monster who, sweeping the vessel with a thousand tentacles, might very well drag us down to death in the deeps. And so Don Pedro was a kind of nightwatchman for us. All that he lacked was a halberd to make him look like a Cordovan alcalde.

I might mention, incidentally, that during this epoch of penance Don

Pedro wore neither shoes nor sandals. He went about with his enormously long-toed feet, yellow as a duck's, bare for all to marvel at. He often sneaked up without warning upon some seaman at work who, suddenly finding this long gray apparition, drip-nosed and wild of beard, immediately behind him would nearly fall overboard in his fright.

To my astonishment the crew and soldiers both took a great fancy to Don Pedro and his manifold eccentricities. And as a matter of fact the time did come when he saved the lives of the lot of us, not in truth by battling any sea-monster, but by being the first to discover a burning candle that had fallen over and set afire some littered straw bedding in the foc'sle.

The horses and mules were a great burden during the first leg of the journey. They were sicker by far than the human beings and showed no signs of recovery until the sea became very calm. Only my old she-ass seemed equal to supporting the rigors of life at sea. This caused my good Sancho to be inordinately proud of her, and so continuously did he bruit her constitution that she became a symbol of good luck for the whole company. "That's the way things go," was Diego de Vargas' comment. "They don't place the slightest reliance on Caesar and his luck, but count on an old she-ass whose stomach happens to be so toughened by eating thousands of thistles she could make a nice meal out of gravel and crushed stone."

The day finally arrived when the lookout shouted "Land ho!" We all rushed out on deck. Straining our eyes we could make out a mountain rising above the western horizon. This was Gomera, one of the Canary Islands. It was not long before the awesome peak came into full view. We could see green woods on its slopes. Soon fields and orchards in a great pattern of light and dark greens became visible, and at last the white walls of houses. A sweet-smelling wind, free of salt, blew across our vessel as we drew nearer into the bay. It was scented with flowers and fruits, and now and then was sharp with the smell of sun-seared rock.

I recalled how Master Agrippa had once told me that this Gomera and the ancient isle of Ogygia were perhaps one, the island where the nymph Calypso lived in her grotto, combing her golden hair.

Soon many small boats were swarming about our ship as we slipped into our anchorage. The men and women in them were singing and shouting as they offered their wares for sale. The girls wore billowing shirtwaists, brilliantly scarlet, and had gay kerchiefs about their heads.

Pedro de Candía stood on the poop deck in full armor, shouting out gallant greetings in his ringing voice and kissing his hand to the pretty girls, all of which caused much merriment. The glass-green water was alive with shrill voices and laughter. No one seemed to mind the terrific swell. Men, women and children alike moved with perfect confidence over the piles of goods and food in the little skiffs, even when they were all but standing on end, and no one fell overboard or capsized his craft.

Now and then a stark-naked youngster, brown as a nut, would dive headlong into the billowing waters to swim to some neighboring boat, or simply to float on his back as comfortably as if lying on a feather bed. Some of these youngsters made their way on board by clambering up the anchor chain, and drew after them beautifully woven baskets filled with fruits of all kinds. Both soldiers and seamen bought these offerings with alacrity, and soon all of us were busy eating and drinking—for on some of the bumboats there was wine or fresh mountain water carried in leather skins.

Looking over the side I could see white sand wavering beneath the glossy water. The surf was breaking heavily on the beach. It looked like the embroidered hem of a Spanish dancer's skirt, flashing white in quick time. As regularly as the breathing of a slumbering giant was the deep music of the breakers and the hard clacking of the shale as water swept it forward only to suck it back again. It was there in Gomera that for the first time I learned to love the sea, even though I feared it, as one might fear the angels who once sat around the throne of God singing the song of Creation.

We lay to in Gomera for several days and refreshed our foul-tasting mouths with the fruits of the island and also took on a supply of fresh water.

At last there appeared on the horizon two more sails. These were under the command of Don Hernando Pizarro. Our little fleet and armed force were now united. Don Hernando came on board the *Espíritu Santo,* and for a long time was closeted with his brother, our Captain-General. It was decided—we did not find this out till later—to sail by Hispaniola to the southwest, and so make for the southern part of the New World, running down the coast.

As is well known, the Indies consist of two great areas of earth, held together only by a small strip of land between Nombre de Dios and Panama. Our attention was claimed by the southernmost of these two halves. To get there we would have to leave our own vessels in Nombre de Dios and take ship again in Panama after crossing the difficult Isthmus. In Panama it would not be easy to find men to build ships, and even with these once found, the expense would be enormous. Any vessel had to be built on the spot, and other than wood, all the material had to be carried across the mountains of the Isthmus on the backs of Indians from Nombre de Dios to Panama.

In any event, our Captain-General had other more serious difficulties complicating his plans. I was to learn this at Nombre de Dios, in the most startling circumstances.

On the morning of our departure from Gomera High Mass was celebrated aboard the *Espíritu Santo.* Afterward our Captain-General's standard was raised under the flag of Castile. It had a large black eagle and two arrows, and in the foreground stood a bemused Indian camel, which caused much astonishment among the people of Gomera. They pointed at it with long forefingers, making ribald comments and laughing gaily at the odd spectacle. After Mass we weighed anchor, bore heavily about to the west, and were off.

To the west of Gomera the sea was notably calmer, and our journey slowed down to a marked degree. Once we ran into a school of whales, and to our surprise saw that some of these leviathans were fully as large as our vessels. Some of us were overcome with fright, and Alonso, along with many others, fell on his knees to pray for deliverance from the fate of Jonah.

Father Juan stood near me at this time. "We're coming to the green meadows of the ocean very soon," he said. "These animals graze there like the cattle of Guadalquivir. Over there, beyond, is the middle of the Western Ocean, of which Jonah said to the Lord, Thou hast cast me forth into the deep in the heart of the sea, and a flood hath compassed me: all thy billows, and thy waves have passed over me."

I nodded and said nothing, having perceived that Father Juan was in a pensive mood. He had prophesied correctly. One morning when we went up on deck we thought we could never again trust our own eyes. For all about us, as far as the watery horizon, there was a great meadow of floating green. If this meadow had not heaved up and down in great flat waves, it might have been thought we were traversing a narrow canal which ran through verdant lowlands. We were in the grazing grounds of the leviathans.

We learned to amuse ourselves by throwing overboard buckets attached to lines, with which we drew up curious sea creatures. They were the strangest fish I had ever seen. One had a body like the clearest glass. Plain to view, its heart beat wildly and the tripes were filled with green matter. There were other odd creatures, shaped like bells, bright in color, and we were hard put to it to decide whether these were fish or flowers. Their veil-like wings moved in a slow rhythm, and in the grass they looked like butterflies on the summer turf. There were big-eyed fish, their orbs the size of a man's and these had horns on their noses. On the long arms of the seaweed, which in part was covered with air bubbles as big as a man's fist, crept little red thread eels among pretty little mussels that opened and closed their valves like Sevillian fans. In the depths we could see great shoals of fish darting about. Many of these were as gay in color as a parrot, others as drab as a thrush.

The floating weed piled up at our bow and impeded our progress seriously. Seamen had to be dispatched to cut free the sluggish, dripping mass of green. Every morning, and often several times a day, this task was performed. Some attempt was made also to scrape free the shellfish which had attached themselves to the strakes of the vessel. The planking was almost obscured by a mass of mussels and green slime. Some said that more than one ship had sunk, like a cart sinking into a bog, with the weight of the slowly accumulated watery growth on its sides.

All this while it was very hot. Anything made of iron after lying for a time in the sun became searing to the touch. The deck planking completely dried out, and it became necessary to soak it frequently with sea water to keep it from cracking altogether out of shape. The strakes and rigging dripped tar, and its pungent smell intermingled with the salt rasp of the sea.

Slowly and heavily the vessel wallowed under that brazen sun. All day long we lay in our bunks, sweating without surcease, groaning aloud with intense discomfort and boredom. I had the sensation of being consigned to living forever in an enormous oven. It often occurred to me that if I had been Admiral Don Cristóbal Colón I surely should have turned back and renounced all hope of ever seeing the Indies. At that time I was not yet aware that such men as he are maniacal in their steadfastness, that they would wade through the molten fires of Hell itself in order to find the land of their dreams.

Sickness came with the great heat. Our breath became a loathesome stench, our teeth loosened in the spongy gums as we tried to bite into the hard bread, and many of us were shaken to the roots of our being by mysterious fevers that came and went. All of us grew ghostly thin, and could barely crawl around. It was only toward nightfall that a light wind would spring up. Then the rigging slatted softly and in between sails and yards we could see enormous trembling stars in the dark blue sky.

At this time of the day we would all go up on the high forward deck. Sometimes we would carry up there two or three of the most grievously ill, and lay them down to stare into the night sky. The planks never really cooled off during the night, but the soft wind played comfortingly on our hot cheeks and with gentle fingers dried our matted hair.

In my fancy it seemed that the airy coolness was coming from the stars immeasurably far above, which I gazed at hard through the long night. Over us the whole brilliant firmament rocked and rolled, and we seemed still. Far down on the horizon, just above the rim of the soundless waters, hung Polaris the star. Swiftly the planets sped among the great constellations. I watched ruddy Mars and ice-blue Saturn, but did not bear long with this last, for according to Master Agrippa it was Saturn that stood between me and my love. When I looked at this mysterious planet I reached into my blouse, drew forth my little silver cross, raised it to my lips and kissed it, vowing that the archons of the heavens would never conquer my soul.

At this time I felt free in my love and in Christ. I did not experience any laming fears of fiery demons, or of the temporal rulers of this world. I was free and unafraid. But when the ship lurched suddenly, a light dizziness would blur my senses, and I heard a buzzing in my ears. I realized dimly how finite was my life as under me swelled depths teeming with leviathans and over me arched the mighty vault of sky, nailed in eternal place with stars that have a strange power over man's destiny. Yet it was not hard for me to take comfort in the knowledge that our vessel was named after the Holy Ghost, and that on her bow was carved an image of a dove. The mood sometimes would suddenly shift as life welled up in me, and then I became proud and bold quite without particular cause. Once I recall how I jumped to my feet, rushed to the rail, beaded with nightly damp, and gripped it with all my strength, straining upward and muttering imprecations against a sky and sea that heard me not at all. It was a childish thing to do, and in retrospect I blush to think of it. But still, it was in those days that I first undersood the fragility of mankind.

Throughout all this doldrum period the Captain-General had not once stepped up on deck. Gradually I had lost all interest in his whereabouts, or in what he might be doing. Gonzalo Pizarro, who was really very ill, remarked in deep chagrin, "My brother can't bear to have the captain and the navigator know more about the sea than he does. That's why he's sticking out of sight like a mole until he can come out and be a man of might." He laughed sarcastically at his own words, and added: "What do you think he wants, the great Captain-General! Does he want us to rot until we spit all our teeth over the rail!" His beautiful features were twisted with hatred.

"But we are all suffering," I said, uneasily. "Isn't he suffering like the rest of us?"

"That man!" Gonzalo laughed, supporting himself with difficulty on the rail. "He never suffers. He's made of stone, that man. He has an Indian's heart. We could all melt into pus, and he'd keep right on with his maps."

What Gonzalo spoke aloud was thought in secret by nearly everyone aboard. But no one dared speak, and no one except his brother ever mentioned the Captain-General's name aloud in public hearing. Instead the ship's evil humor expended itself in practical joking and savage quarrels. Once there would have been a serious knifing but for the weakness of the two bickerers. We were able to separate them with only a few light scratches to show as damage. By now we had lived a whole month crowded together in unbelievably narrow quarters. We rubbed against each other morning, noon and night; we became irritated over the slightest trifle, as always when a crowd of men with nothing in common are thrown together by a whim of fate.

There were men from all classes aboard the *Espíritu Santo,* drawn from every walk of Spanish life. But there were more vagabonds and cut-throats than any other kind of man—adventurers by the kindest definition, who had neither a manual trade nor any profession. Among these belonged Bernal and Frenero and the actors, all of whom had spent their lives under one strange roof after another, and a good deal of the time simply out in the open. Apparently these fellows were best suited for the wild task at hand, for they bore up well. Yet any semblance of soldierly discipline under the conditions of the voyage was out of the question.

Beyond the murderous heat and the absence of life-giving wind, beyond the profound boredom of being forced to live with those whom we cared not a pin about, there was a steady decline in the quality of food and water. The water in the casks now stank strongly, so that when they drank the men held their noses in order to keep it down. The beans, our only real staple, were little more than shells filled with white worms.

One noontime when, as usual, a soup of mutton bones and beans was ladled out from the iron kettle on the deck near the galley, Frenero stepped forward, took the big wooden spoon, filled it brimming full and deliberately poured its contents over the cook's head. The cook stood by helpless and dripping, while Frenero wrestled the pot to the side, and spilled the filthy brew overboard. "See if the sharks can live on it," he said. "Ten to one they puke it up."

Everyone now raised his voice in anger, threatened the cook Tafur, and demanded more and better rations. Even Alonso, the one who despised such earthly concerns as food, joined in. Above all, the aroused men wanted the cook to slaughter the boar he had in his safekeeping, though they all knew it was destined to be used at stud in Panama. The cook, sorely alarmed, defended himself as best he could with his cleaver. But one of the menacing crowd knocked this weapon out of his hand from behind, and then with one accord they fell on him. "Throw him overboard with his swill," the cry went.

I saw clearly that now or never was the time to interfere if our one and only cook was to serve another meal. I began by getting a good grip on Juan the thin. I gave him a blow in the belly, and he collapsed to the deck, struggling for air. A belaying pin came to hand, and with this I belabored the maddened Frenero, who was hissing like a snake, the corners of his lips white with spittle. His eyes turned in his head, and he, too, crumpled to the deck. As I turned to quell Alonso's temper the crowd sought to prevent this. They all tore at my arms, legs and hair. I saw one man, a certain Belalcázar, in a transport of anger set his teeth into my boot and ineffectually try to bite me. At this point Diego and Rodrigo and my good Sancho attempted to rescue me. But it would assuredly have gone hard with me and my rescuers if at that moment Don Pedro de Candía had not rushed onto the scene.

As was his wont on shipboard, this odd noble had on his long, gray hairy mantle, and his feet were naked and fearsomely yellow. But with two bony hands he gripped his enormous sword in a terrible grip, and brandished it so that it flashed in the sun, a bolt of lightning. Like a charging unicorn he ran down the deck toward the milling throng, yelling in a high voice, his face contorted with anger, his long skull seemingly even more bony and compressed than usual, his whiskers flying. There appeared to be nothing left to his eyes but the whites, and this above everything invested him with a most terrifying aspect. With fearful alacrity the coil of men unraveled, each desperate to get out of the way of Don Pedro's avenging sword. As they scrambled to all sides, I fell hard with my head against a stanchion, near by the sobbing Tafur, who was both frightened out of his poor wits and hurt as well. Some of my assailants swung up into the shrouds as quick as monkeys, the others scrambled onto the foredeck.

To the terror of the ship's company, who thought him crazed, Don Pedro de Candía rammed his sword into the cabin wall again and again, gouging out white slivers, shrieking to himself.

"There must be order on this vessel," he screamed. "I, I, I demand it! I ask peace. I will have peace. Hogs! I was thinking about the resurrection. Hell-hogs, you have disturbed my thought! Let it happen again, let it happen once, and I'll draw blood. I'll gut you and tie your bowels around your necks in ribbons, you whoresons!" With this he wheeled about, drawn up to his full height, and padded slowly to his musty quarters aft.

This incident, strangely enough, shamed the lot of us. Vainly we tried to avoid contact, and looked at each other with mutual distrust. That same evening we all lay down in a lump on the deck above the foc'sle, but spoke no words of mutual commiseration. Frenero, I remember, was bathing his injured head with a damp cloth. He kept glancing at me anxiously, finally summoned the courage to crawl close and whisper:

"Shall I strangle that bastard?"

"Who?" I wanted to know, not much troubling to approve his contrition.

"Who! That Belalcázar, the fellow who bit your foot."

"No, let him alone," I said wearily. I was weak and tired to death. For the first time I was engulfed with the need to be home in my small house in Cordova, eating good food prepared by my Teresa.

The hours crept slowly on. I slept for a few hours and awoke with a heavy ache in my back. I heard Sancho snoring beside me. Most of the men were awake though they lay there inert like so many corpses. By the stars I could tell it must be shortly past midnight. Despite the late hour it was sticky and very warm. The water splashed lazily against the sides of the vessel. Suddenly I raised myself on one arm. Like a specter Don Francisco Pizarro was stalking on deck. He wore his broad-brimmed white felt hat, and his long white mantle was thrown loosely over his shoulders. Others, too, saw the Captain-General, and also rose quietly on their elbows the better to watch what was going on. I remembered, with a twinge of horror, that lately Juan the thin had told me it was generally whispered among the men that the Captain-General had died of fever, that in the depths of a dark night his body had been cast into the sea in order not to create panic. But I soon realized it was no ghost I was staring at.

"We are out of the Sea of Grass," said Don Francisco clearly, but as if to himself. He wet his finger at his lips and held it aloft as if by so doing to call the wind to life.

And now I, too, noticed that indeed the atmosphere had changed. The foul smell of the floating weed was no longer in the air.

Our Captain-General sat down on a barrel top. Every face was riveted in his direction. Everyone saw his white forehead, untouched by the sun, his deeply hollowed cheeks, the glittering wide-set eyes, round and feverishly glaring.

"From now on we'll have a good voyage," he said, when he finally addressed us. We were all on tenterhooks, trembling with excitement, weak as women for the need of his decision. "A storm is coming, and that will be good," he said.

Without thinking I nodded assent to myself, though I had not noticed the faintest sign that weather was breeding. The sea stretched out infinitely, as calm as a mill pond. Even the soft lapping of the water against the ship as it rolled out of tune with the swell had stopped. Our vessel lay as still as if afloat on a sea of molten lead.

"You have borne yourselves much like men," Don Francisco said absently. "You've put up with heat and sickness. You've drunk bad water and eaten bad meat. I've been keeping out of the way to see whether you could hold on without my help. You appear to have done this." He fell silent, and was lost in meditation.

"I am quite aware," he continued, "that you have become dissatisfied.

I know you tried to throw the cook overboard. That, of course, was stupid. The cook did not rot the beans. It wasn't Tafur who put cockroaches in the meal. Those things always happen on a long voyage, my friends. Don Carlos the King, himself, would have to drink foul water and eat rotten meat like us if he traveled the great sea. It would be hard for him. It is hard for you. I myself do not find it charming.

"But let me tell you something, my children. I do not forget that there have been times in my life when the food you have been eating would have tasted better to me than wheat flour sifted seven times. For my part, I have been delighted to gnaw palm sprouts, to stop the ache in my belly with the slime of shellfish dug from the beach. After all, my little sons, do you not live in comfort and safety on board this stout craft? At night you have a bed of straw to ease your bones. The wind rocks you all to sleep when it blows, and blow it soon will. But there have been times when I had no such eunuch comforts.

"I remember when I had to lie down at night on damp swamp earth, tormented by flies and mosquitoes. And behind me was the forest, an endless forest. The nights were indeed the worst, my little ones. Think of it. The heavens would open and the rain come down in solid sheets, so that all of us lay in puddles. Bugs, flies and crawling beasts ate into our flesh. They crawled over our faces, they made their homes in the folds of our garments; they played hide-and-seek in the crevices of our armor. Then our clothes would steam when day broke and the sun came out. We fell to our knees and thanked God for the gift of seeing bright day once again. For that much, consider."

Don Francisco paused in his slow oration, letting the words sink in. All the time the sea was becoming uneasy, the ship began to creak and whisper in a hundred places and we felt the grain of the planks pull against the grip of our damp limbs as the roll increased.

"Yes, my sons, those were harder times than any you have dreamed of. Our ship would not come. Not at all. Not this day, nor the next, nor the next. Fever took off many of my close companions, and we buried them on the beach above the high water mark. Not a single day went by that someone did not abandon the fight. There were some who toyed with the idea of suicide, for we had nothing to live for, so far as anyone could see. But to this day I believe, as I believed then, that the saints were trying us, and that in good course we would be requited for our pain.

"We are chosen for great triumphs, my sons. Never forget that. All of you, all of you men aboard this vessel, have the chance to share in these coming victories, in the golden inheritance of those who died on the shores of the Biru. And how do I know that, you ask? How do I know so much? Well, I will tell you. Those were trials that few men have ever endured since the Creation. And never did I falter. Not as much as a hair's breadth. That lived through, anything is possible.

"Yes, my little ones, it was in the dark time on the Biru that I got my first real knowledge of the South Country. It was then we stumbled on an Indian village, and for the first time saw the yellow gold of the South Country. The natives ran away. But we captured the head men, one way or another. No one spoke the Indians' language. By signs we learned that many days' journey away to the south lay a mountainous land. Its king, we found, was thought by his subjects to be a child of the sun. The Indian who told us first pointed to the sun then to a baby strapped on a native woman's back. That was how we knew. It was simple enough."

Here the Captain-General stopped and wheeled around, for Don Pedro de Candía in his penitential robes had come up behind him.

"Why waste your time on this mob," he said abruptly, addressing us, and not Pizarro himself. "I wouldn't take the trouble to give this poxy lot of whoresons last year's sweat from my armpits. Not I! Not if I could kiss the breasts of the Virgin Mary. Hang a few of them from the yardarm. Give them something substantial to whine about. Put the rest of them in irons. You're forgetting they're guilty. They laid hands on my namesake and cousin, Don Pedro de Cordova."

The silence grew oppressive. Everyone hung on the Captain-General's words as he continued, turning to the knight from Candía, "Don Pedro, my old friend, I'd like you to tell us about the days on Gallo and Gorgona. Then they can see that our present difficulties are child's play, and that we paved the way for them in the wilderness with blood and pain."

"On my soul's honor," said Don Pedro, needing no further solicitation, "I cannot believe that any one of these sneak thieves here could stand up under the punishment as we did in that hell. We were all as thin as skeletons. Our hair was matted and hung down our shoulders. Our clothes hung in rags, scarcely covering our nakedness. The knobs of our backbones could be counted with ease from the front, and my stomach shrunk to the size of a baby's fist.

"My body was so thoroughly covered with boils and sores that at night I dared not stretch out on the ground. Often I have spent the whole night propped up between two stones on the beach, looking out toward the sea. But I did not see the water, nor did I see lightning, nor hear thunder. For my misery was so profound that it drowned out the cries of my senses. My strength was no greater than a grain of sand. If anyone had pointed a finger at me I should have toppled to the ground, and risen again only on Judgment Day.

"But as we suffered thus, with the rain pouring down on us in endless torrents, our Captain-General did not forget to have morning prayers, and in the evening we sang *Ave Maria*. We had Mass on Sunday and observed holy days. And so we were preserved, like the hermit saints in the wilderness, like John the Baptist and Saint Anthony.

"There were weak spirits among us, of course. In fact, these were in the majority. They spent the day complaining, mewling about their bad luck. They could not understand that God was letting us feel the weight of his wrath in order to try us, and see if we were made of the stuff out of which conquistadors are fashioned. But I knew. I always knew. I knew that each one of us must drain his cup of bitterness dry as a bone. And this we did, some of us willingly, more with infinite reluctance. So after some months of denial on the Isle of Gallo two ships sent by the Governor of Panama arrived to fetch us away, to balk us in our task. At that moment even the strongest spirits wavered. I admit that I, too, almost succumbed in this ultimate trial. I thought of the wine, the white bread, the soft bed all waiting me in Panama.

"But our Captain-General, understand, you whimpering dogs, did not waver. With his sword he drew a line in the sand of the beach. I have not forgotten his words. To this day they ring in my ears. He said, 'My friends and comrades-in-arms! To the south of this line is suffering and ceaseless privation. To the north comfort. To the south lie Peru and its riches. To the north Panama and its poverty. Choose as befits a Spaniard. So far as I am concerned, I go south. Even if I go alone.' Saying this our Captain-General stepped to the south of the line."

Don Francisco nodded solemn approval. "You were the first to step over to my side, Don Pedro," he said gravely.

"Fourteen of us assembled on the south side of the line," Don Pedro went on. "But understand, we were men, not small Jeremiahs, howling like a bitch with the mange just because the water was foul. From that day on the die was cast. Things began to improve when the cowards no longer contaminated the men of good heart. As we marched over the quaking marshland toward Gorgona at least we had the pleasure of the hunt. No birds ever tasted better than those we brought down with our crossbows on the way to Gorgona. The water in the springs was sweet and cool. I should have been completely satisfied if there had been fewer mosquitoes and not so much fever.

"Never shall I forget the day when that small white sail appeared on the heaving waters, nor how we argued whether or not it was a boat or a sea bird on the wing. After seven months, what a great day of deliverance! As the wings of the distant bird spread wider and higher there was no more doubt that it was a ship, the one sent to us by Father Luque. Do you know, do you understand, that I left Gorgona with some regret?

"Then, safe on the deck of our vessel, some days later the cordillera opened its stone gates for us, and we entered. There was the South Country. There spread out the blue waters of the bay, the wooded islands, the cliffs on which the sea lions bellowed defiance, the green fields, fruit orchards, the villages, the viaducts, the city and the enormous mountains beyond, all glittering rosy ice at the summits. So God led us through adversity into Paradise."

Pizarro now stepped in front of Don Pedro de Candía and by this silent action put a period to any more telling of tales. With long, heavy strides he moved to the very bow of the vessel, stood there staring out over the dove on the cutwater into the darkness. He remained there saying nothing for some time, and in his long mantle billowed by the rising wind he looked like a pilgrim. One by one the men had risen to their feet. They were ashamed and felt small. In truth our Captain-General was never more dangerous than when he was soft and tolerant. There were few among his followers who did not see him as a sort of father. Yet he would have sacrificed any one of them without a qualm if it suited his purpose, I was to learn.

While Pizarro was standing at the bow a wind came up. First there was a light breath that filled out his mantle like a sail. It grew stronger, and all but tore the garment from his shoulders in a sudden gust. Then he wrapped his mantle closely about him, so that his sword in its hilt showed through the downy cloth.

The wind grew into a steady breeze. The rigging began to sing and moan. The boatswain's shrill whistle pierced the darkness. Seamen clambered into the rigging and set all sail to catch the life-giving wind. Our Captain-General turned, walked through the company without a word. His features, dim in the night, were set and his lips moved gently. The masts began to groan with the strain of the breeze and the ship quickened.

15

THE MONK

AFTER a voyage of twenty-four days we reached the shores of the great Southern Continent and landed at a place called Santa Marta. This settlement consisted of a handful of mud huts roofed with reeds. The entire population of Santa Marta had assembled on the beach to greet us. They broke into a loud shout of welcome as the ship's boats grated on the sand of the beach.

This first glimpse of the New World was not especially entrancing. All around were swamp and reedy wasteland. Some distance behind the dirty huts reared the primeval forest, a dark wall. Still, we were all joyous once again to feel earth under our feet. The land, in spite of its forbidding aspect, was not without a certain attraction, which was no doubt largely rooted in our common wishfulness rather than in the landscape itself. The endless beaches where the forest met the sea were ineffably lonely. Never did the surf cease its thundering. With the majestic sound of breaking surf was intermingled the lighter sounds of grinding stones and sucking sand, forever washed back and forth by the motion of the sea.

It was a world in which the primitive powers of Creation, wind, wave and earth, held unrivaled sway. Man's purpose had left not a solitary mark on this land. I felt myself forced by the steady wind and the marching breakers inland into the dark jungle, into an impervious world, given over to extravagant growth of rooted and crawling things. There seemed no place for man at all.

This sensation of littleness was even stronger at night. Then the roaring of the surf grew louder, and the wall of forest became a screaming demon world in which all manner of dread beasts lurked to do us harm. I soon comprehended the anxiety and gravity in the faces of the white men, and the impenetrable remoteness of the Indian features. For the relentless pressure of the wilderness, its indifference to the spirit of man, is not easily borne. One either becomes resigned, and so a wild part of the untamed, or a sort of collapse occurs, and one lives as a living ruin, forever dreaming of the past.

The white men, in rags, their faces bearded, were always inquiring about the homeland. They wanted to know such foolish things as whether the orange trees behind the mosque in Cordova were still blooming, whether vespers were still rung in the Giralda in Seville, whether cattle still grazed among the rushes of the Guadalquivir—and asked many questions of the same obvious sort.

At first I laughed at these queries, but later, after I had been some time in the Indies, I fully grasped their meaning. These men were afraid of losing touch with the homeland. They wanted reaffirmed what they saw in their dreams. For it is very bad when man loses the familiar ground under his feet, when the springs of home and youth no longer flow, the springs from which we drink all our life long. Not every man is a Pizarro; not everyone is fitted to be a conqueror of strange peoples. Hundreds, perhaps thousands of years will pass before the white man can say of Indian earth, This is my home. For the new world is titanic and empty.

A man, even as I did, in time feels within himself the silence of the forest, the barren heights of the cordillera, the pounding of the surf. It is too much to put up with, it cracks the heart with its weight. Even now I have just had to get up from my paper and pen to look out over the courtyard, in order to make sure that the fountain is murmuring in the night, that the orange trees perfume the air, that the grapevines are fast to the wall. For merely to talk of these matters overwhelms my senses with the grinding sand of the beach, the bitter smell of guano on the cliffs. I see once again the pyramids made out of great blocks of stone, the shrunken brown skulls and the shinbones scattered about in the cities of the dead, while the sea wind blows the red dust of finely ground porphyry.

Never did Father Vicente with his wisdom and Father Juan with his simplicity have more thoughtful listeners than there on the beach before those dilapidated hovels. When night fell, we raised our voices with all our might to sing the *Ave Maria,* and thus tried to drown out the sound of the breaking waves. Though we had to shout ourselves hoarse to do it, at least so long as it lasted we had the satisfaction of bringing one inimical force to heel. Before prayers, the Captain-General made it a practice to sound a loud fanfare of trumpets, in order to remind us that we were here in the capacity of soldiers. But it seemed to me that we were blowing a brazen challenge to sea, wind, waves and forest, indeed to the whole New World and the mysterious powers of Creation.

This sound of music made a deep impression on the Indians. They gathered on the beach as soon as the first rays of the sun reddened the east. When the drums began to roll, and the sun rose up a red ball out of the sea, they let forth wild cries, and began to dance and jump about like persons possessed of the devil. Seemingly they thought that our drums and trumpets had brought forth the sun itself.

The Indians were much taken too by the man Frenero. It was his red hair that they found entrancing. They had never seen hair of such a carroty, bright color before, and were of the mind that Frenero was a kind of fire god. They stared at him wide-eyed with amazement when he played a long tattoo on the drum, for Frenero, I neglected to say, had taught himself the art. He was very proud of his accomplishment and never parted with his drum, carrying it about slung over his shoulder. Frenero's pockmarks also attracted the Indians. They thought they were the scars of self-inflicted wounds dating back to some time of severe penance. Once in a while one of the bolder among them would creep up to him and touch a finger to his red hair, only to shrink back in delighted terror as if he had touched red-hot metal.

A council of war was now held, after the men had lost their sea legs. The Captain-General proposed to strike out directly west, and so avoid altogether going to Panama. The piteous inhabitants of Santa Marta argued against this, and warned that the great forests were filled with alligators and snakes, that beyond the forest there were impassable mountains. The Captain-General dropped his eyes and thought. He seemed undecided, and concern grayed his face.

"By the grace of Heaven, Don Francisco," said Father Vicente de Valverde, "we can't be expected to ride alligators like St. Pacomo crossing the Nile. Our horses and mules will certainly be lost in the swamps."

"Let me take care of these alligators!" bellowed Don Hernando Pizarro.

His brother looked beyond him, unimpressed. He addressed Father Vicente. "As you wish, father. But don't forget that you have it written down in black and white." What he meant by this I did not learn until we had arrived at Nombre de Dios.

Dismayed by the prospect of swamps and alligators, two men from Toledo deserted. The Captain-General gave up his plan completely. We went aboard the *Espíritu Santo,* and set sail for Nombre de Dios. This was a much larger settlement though it, too, consisted of nothing more than a collection of mud huts. There were several caravels at anchor in the harbor, prepared to cross the sea to Spain.

Hardly had we cast anchor than a ship's boat came over to us. In it sat a short, fat man in shining armor. With him was an elderly cleric, and several Indians worked the oars. The little fat fellow climbed up the rope ladder with unexpected agility, with the priest following slowly in his wake. The man in the armor had only one eye. With this one eye he cast a baleful glance at all of us. His fleshy cheeks and his huge nose were netted with bluish-red veins, like a drunkard's.

Taking a ship's boy by the collar, he shouted, to everyone's astonishment, "Where is he? Come on now, where is he?"

"Just a minute, just a minute. Peace!" interposed the priest, who in the meantime had labored on deck, and stood wiping the sweat from his brow.

"Peace? What the hell are you talking about! Peace—I'll give him peace! I'll cut him down like a mad dog, the traitor, the envious bastard. He has stolen my gold and my honor."

"Softly, softly," the priest replied. "You won't get anywhere carrying on in this fashion. Be reasonable. Remember you're talking of Pizarro. He was your oldest friend, you know."

"And what a friend he turned out to be!" said the fat man. "What a friend he is, I must say. Why, he'd draw the bowels out of my body with his own hands and hang them on a limb."

At this point the Pizarros all came out of the afterquarters together. The Captain-General hastened over to the fat man.

"Why, my dear Diego," he said pleasantly. "At last!" With a cry of delight he bent down, swiftly embraced the fat man, and kissed him on both cheeks. The fat man shook with anger like a wet dog. "Father Luque!" Pizarro went on, and reached the cleric his hand, who took it limply, meanwhile regarding him with an ironic eye.

"Brothers, friends," the Captain-General said heartily, "here are at last the two men to whom I owe everything. My good friend, Don

Diego de Almagro and and worthy Father Luque of the Panama Cathedral."

This seemed to be the signal for us all to bow low before these worthies, which we did. Hernando Pizarro alone was reluctant, and merely nodded briefly in response to his brother's zealous greeting. He began to stare at the fat man as a farmer might size up a prize porker.

"Is it true?" De Almagro asked sharply.

"Is what true, my dear Don Diego?" Pizarro inquired. Anyone could see that he was uneasy.

"Who's that long-legged bull glaring at me?" asked De Almagro, pointing with his finger at Hernando. "Do we have to have him taking in every word we say?"

"Sweet Virgin Mary!" Gonzalo Pizarro was heard to whisper loudly.

The oldest Pizarro's face turned dark, his brows gathered together at the bridge of his nose, then his eyes opened wide like a crazy man's. He bared his lips, standing like a stone image. Then, with no more warning, he emitted a piercing yell, whipped his sword from its sheath and raised it aloft.

"Brother, Hernando——" shouted the Captain-General, seizing the arm that brandished the sword. "Wait, hold on, just a minute. He didn't mean you. He wasn't talking about you. Wait . . ."

By this time the rest of the Pizarros had formed a circle around the enraged head of the family. They took away his sword by force. Diego de Almagro watched the performance open-mouthed.

"Who is that man, anyway?" he persisted, his voice thin with fright, and when told with only too much eagerness, commented, "Oh, so that's who it is! Pardon, pardon. But that's got nothing to do with my rights."

He turned accusingly to Francisco Pizarro, and went on, "It is true, Pizarro, that you've been made Captain-General of Peru and Adelantado and Alguazil Major for life? Is it true they gave you over seven hundred thousand maravedis in gold? And have I heard correctly that you were so kind as to have me made Governor of Tumbez with a stipend of three hundred thousand maravedis? Your inferior? With not one-half your returns? Is it true that Father Luque has been made Bishop of Tumbez? And that you were so wonderfully thoughtful as to give him a thousand ducats? What have you got to say, Pizarro?"

"You have not been misinformed, my dear Diego," said Pizarro, his eyes narrowing perceptibly.

"So! You heard that, Father Luque! You heard what he said!" squeaked the fat man powerfully. He was as red as a lobster freshly boiled. "Why, this man has deliberately cheated us, he has broken his word. But I'm not going to endure it. I know how to ensure my prerogatives. I know how to deal with men who break their oaths. Was it not sworn to and sealed that everything—gold, treasure and offices—would be equally divided? Was it not? Did we not make a compact? Haven't you fitted out ship after ship for this man, Father Luque? Tell me, haven't you? And haven't you poured out sacks full of gold into his pockets? Didn't I go to sea again just on his account, and didn't I go tramping around swamps and all but give him my eyeteeth? Why, it's monstrous, the deceit! Aren't we the people who saved you from the gate of hunger, from Gorgona?

"Listen everyone! Open your ears while I make an announcement! Here stands a man who broke his word, who sinned against God the Father and the apostles, who disdained the sign of the cross, the martyrdom of our Lord Jesus Christ. Francisco Pizarro, I predict you will come to a bloody end."

"Let us have a little less wind," said Pizarro to this tirade. "I didn't break any compact. I can explain everything."

"I don't want any explanations. I want my due; I will have my rights!" shrieked the little fat man.

"You are tampering with the will of the King," warned Pizarro calmly. "In Toledo, Don Carlos decided . . ."

"My rights!" Don Diego interposed. "What do I care about the will of Don Carlos! Has he given you his eyeteeth? Has he been raddled by fevers until he thought his hour had come? What does Don Carlos know about the Indies? He knows as much about Peru or Panama as a block of stone."

"Drippings of a she-dog," panted Don Hernando Pizarro, struggling with giant strength to get away from the men pinning him down. "One more word about my King, you bastard, you son of a whore, and I'll gut you with my hands. Dare you insult the Pizarros and God!" He swayed back and forth, dragging the sweating peacemakers about the deck. But the effect on Don Diego was unexpected. Far from becoming pale with fright, he grew more angry, turned purple, looked exactly as if he were about to give way to a mortal stroke. He had to hold on to Father Luque.

"Just a minute," said Father Luque calmly. He raised his hand to command silence. "Both of you, Hernando Pizarro and Diego de Almagro, must come to terms and find peace. In word and deed. Otherwise I'll have the pair of you thrown into irons in Panama. I'll have you sent back on the next ship to Spain, Don Hernando. We brook no troublemakers in the Indies."

"He is the troublemaker, that fat pig," roared Don Hernando. "He insults His Majesty, the Emperor and King."

"And you, Diego," continued Father Luque, without paying further attention to the sweating Pizarro, "you should be covered with shame, taking part in such a brawl. Look at these men staring at you."

And in fact the whole ship's company, soldiers and seamen both, had crowded close around the two opponents. On the outer edge of the circle little groups had formed, each one engaged in excited conversation.

"This is a very bad beginning," said Father Luque. Then, obviously seeking to distract the interest of all from the combatants, he turned to me. "You don't belong to any party, do you, young man? What do you think ought to be done? Speak out your opinion."

All eyes were turned on me, to my profound confusion. I felt myself growing red.

"Worthy father," I stuttered, "I don't know anything about the agreement between our Captain-General and Don Diego de Almagro and you. But it seems clear to me that Don Diego isn't satisfied with the King's judgment. I believe that our Captain-General has done all he could to hold to the compact . . ."

"Well, now, do you!" commented the fat man slowly.

"As it looks to me, there's no sense arguing about the King's command," I said more clearly, now that my argument had been questioned. "Nobody can change that but the King himself."

"That's quite true," agreed Father Luque.

"It certainly is, by the Father, the Son and the Holy Ghost; truer words never fell from a man's lips," said Don Hernando solemnly.

"Wait till he's done. Give him a chance," interposed the Captain-General.

"For my part, then," I went on more shakily, "I think that Don Francisco Pizarro and Don Diego de Almagro should write a joint petition to His Majesty asking that the title of Adelantado be transferred to Don Diego . . ."

"That suits me," said the fat man hurriedly.

"And it suits me," agreed Don Francisco with some hesitation.

". . . but never forget that the decision rests with Don Carlos the King."

"No. Let me say something," objected Don Hernando in his bass roar. "That advice is no good at all. The honor of the Pizarros is at stake. I, I am the oldest. I could not tolerate it." But Don Gonzalo stopped this by whispering swiftly into his brother's ear. I saw Don Hernando look at me in astonishment. "Did he mean it that way?" he inquired, a half-smile on his rugged face.

"Furthermore," I went on, considerably encouraged, and now beginning to plume myself on my role, "words have been uttered which in Spain mean a duel. Therefore to wipe out these mutual stains, I say that Don Hernando and Don Diego must shake hands, as a sign that they regret their hasty language, and are willing to forgive each other."

"A good idea," said Father Luque, "an excellent idea."

Diego de Almagro held back a moment, then waddled slowly over to the Captain-General, embraced him and kissed him quickly on both cheeks. After this he said, "Good luck, my Francisco, and may the saints be with you." He smiled slyly at his own change of face.

"Thank you, my brother," said Don Francisco, also smiling coldly.

This done, Don Diego reached his hand to Juan Pizarro, to Pedro, Francisco de Alcántara and Gonzalo, and finally to Don Hernando, who accepted the dimpled pinkish lump with ill grace, his eyes downcast.

In this simple manner peace was restored, at least on the surface. Of course the seeds of hatred did not lie on sterile ground within the hearts of Don Hernando and Don Diego de Almagro. These seeds grew in silence, and at last bore bloody fruit, to the deep sorrow of Peru.

After a few days we assembled men and supplies and began the march across the Isthmus. This region is mountainous and covered with a thick low growth. In small knots we forced our way through the thorny undergrowth. I was alone with my own people. We had an Indian guide who led us on the way in utter silence. From time to time we passed by little swamps. The trees were mirrored blackly in these evil waters; gray moss hung down like hair on an old crone's skull. It was a miserable, barren landscape. During the day an incredibly hot sun burned on our heads. Our clothes were dark with sweat. At night a thick white mist arose from the boggy land. It stank of rot, and we had difficulty drawing a deep breath The heat was worst just at sundown. There was no fresh evening breeze as in Cordova, where the cool wind comes at this time from the heights of the Sierra Morena and people sit talking in the orange groves. Later, when the sun had dropped like a plummet into darkness, we shivered with the penetrating damp that shut us in.

Occasionally we ran across wanderers from Panama, for this Isthmus was the most populous road in the New World. This strip of land both separated and provided a means of transit to the two great seas that belong to the King of Spain, on which our caravels sail as easily as the galleys of Venice on the Mediterranean. The road from Nombre de Dios to Panama is an indispensable artery in the great body of the Spanish possessions. And important it will always be until that Western Passage is found for which so many brave men search arduously these very days in which I write.

Considering its importance I was amazed at the poor condition of this highway across the Isthmus. Not only was it full of deep holes like the roads in Spain, but at times disappeared entirely and became a patch of swamp through which we should assuredly never have found our way had it not been for the guide.

Quite often we ran into long files of Indians. They marched one behind the other like so many geese. Each one wore an iron ring about his neck, these fastened together by chains and making the slightest chance of escape impossible. A handful of Spaniards was quite sufficient to guard hundreds of enslaved natives. At first I thought the Indians were criminals, but later I was surprised to learn they had simply been removed from their villages like cattle and condemned to perform hard labor. The greater number of these unhappy creatures bore heavy burdens, bundles of skins, and pandora sacks or chests. Among them were some women, but men were preferred. For ordinarily women bore up no more than a few months whereas the men were often good for years of service.

One evening on our journey across the Isthmus we came, very late, just before darkness had shut out the world, upon a gang of Indians transporting ship timber. The loads were so heavy that the men moved forward slowly, bent almost double. Even in the bad half-light I could see that they were half dead from lack of food. Their emaciated bodies were covered with evil sores, and about them buzzed clouds of flies feeding on the blood running from chafed spots on their necks.

Our party cleared off to one side to let them pass, and mutely straining beneath their cruel loads, the Indians began to file by us, some of them obviously at the very end of their powers and too exhausted to move their eyes our way. The rough voices of the guards never for a moment stopped sounding imprecations, madly persistent and no longer aware of the living object. But the Indians appeared not to hear. Their heads hung low like jaded horses. From time to time a guard prodded the thin buttocks of some laggard, or belabored him with a leather cat-o'-nine-tails, or the flat of his sword. In short, it might have been because of the lateness of the day with its accumulated irritation, the guards treated the Indians far worse than any Cordovan muleteer his four-legged beasts.

As I sat on my horse, leaning on the pommel of the saddle watching the spectacle, I could hardly believe my eyes. I thought how Doña Juana had talked about the red-skinned Adam and Eve from Paradise, the pair brought back from the Happy Isles by our Admiral.

My indignation suddenly found a definite object when one of the Indians collapsed under his load and, struggle as he might, was unable to rise again. The two brothers, Alonso and Juan, rushed over to help the man up by lightening his load, but they could do nothing, for evidently when he had given way the timber had come down full force on his leg, breaking it. No sooner did he manage to stand on his feet than the pain forced him to sink again prostrate on the ground. In the meantime, of course, the whole company, chained together as they were, had come to a halt.

Up strode the guard, a tall, thin man, and like one possessed he fell on Alonso, thrust him to one side shouting, "Keep your nose out of our business, bag of guts."

"But I was just looking to give him a hand," Alonso came back in anger.

"Help him! Help him, did you say!" screamed the guard now out of control. "I'll show you how to help him."

With these words he turned to the unfortunate native and rained blows upon him until there was no more sound. Foam stood at the corners of the guard's mouth.

"He doesn't feel anything, my friend," said Frenero, laughing coldly. "You might as well be thrashing a sack of grain."

Frenero's words seemed to add fuel to the flames of the guard's mad rage. Drawing his sword he plunged it into the Indian's limp belly, sliced it open and exposed the hot guts. "Red dogs! Red devils! I'll kill them all! They ought to be wiped out!"

And now, the moment I saw the Indian's blood flowing down his groins in dark rivulets, an exalted anger overcame me. Never before in Spain had I experienced such a transport of quick hate. My teeth chattered like castanets. Yet finally I controlled myself enough to say in a high even voice, foreign to my own ears, "Brother, that's enough. The man is dead. And he had broken his leg in any case."

"You, too!" shouted the guard, taking my interference in turn. "You fine flower of Castile. Do you know what we do with the lazy ones in the Indies?" With that he again raised his sword to strike.

"Let him lie," I commanded tonelessly, and felt the hilt of my sword in my fist.

"No!" shouted the guard, in a voice loud and long drawn out, as if I were miles away.

"Shall I get him, master?" whispered Frenero, never taking his eyes off the man. "He's dangerous, out of his mind. . . ."

"No, I'll take care of him," I said and turning to the guard added, "Unloose the man."

"Such sweet, sweet feelings," the guard mocked me, and deliberately kicked the broken leg. Then with even more evil resistance, he raised his sword and lopped off the Indian's head. "Now he's unchained," he growled. "How do you like that!"

But as he stared at me I saw his face change, and grow taut with fear. From afar I heard him whimper, "Have mercy, my lord, in the name of the Virgin."

Without thinking I rose in the saddle, stiffened my legs, bracing them against the horse's belly, and raised my sword. I brought it down with all my strength, and edgewise it struck the guard's head slicing through the leather helmet and into the skull as easily as through a chestnut rind. The guard tumbled over the Indian's body and lay still. With an immense effort I sheathed my sword, feeling dizzy on my living perch, so that with my free hand I had to take a grip on the horse's mane.

"Don Pedro," my good Sancho encouraged me, "take hold. There was no way out."

"You think I had to?" I inquired foolishly. "I did, didn't I?" All the Indians were looking at me. I could see the whites of their eyes gleaming in the dim forest light.

"He was crazy," Frenero assured me. "He was trying to make a fool of you."

He reached up, slipped my sword from its sheath, wiped it off on his shirt and slipped it back into place.

"I must tell you, Don Pedro," he said, "that was a good blow. You have a wrist like Saint George himself."

"Indeed, that he has," Bernal chimed in. "There's nothing better to see than a young man with noble blood in his veins killing with a clean stroke."

Now the other guards came up, and turned to us with threatening looks, which disappeared as soon as Bernal and Frenero began to draw back on their crossbows.

When we finally collected our wits and were about to set off again, we discovered that our guide had silently stolen away without being noticed by any of us. It is quite probable the man feared that we would replace the dead slave with him, or he might have thought that we white people were going to come to blows among ourselves. There was nothing for it but to grope our way forward through the wilderness, which was no easy task. For in the meanwhile it had grown pitch-dark, and the night was moonless and heavy with mist.

It happened, then, that we strayed off the main road, if road a dim trail can be called, and onto a side path. Careless of where I was going I slumped over the neck of my horse, oppressed with thought, disturbed to the roots with the full realization of what it meant to bear oneself in true knightly fashion in our predatory age. I could not forbear recalling that I had launched my career with assault and thievery, that for many long months I had played the vagabond around the back country of Spain like any gypsy, and that now I had reached the culmination of all this dirty-necked adventuring with a murder. I lost all interest in keeping to the path, paid no attention to the mosquitoes that swarmed eagerly over my face and hands. My people moved behind me wordlessly, stumbling over branch and tussock. The smell of rotten mold was strong in the wet night air.

We must have progressed in this dazed fashion for several hours when the narrow path gave out into a wide clearing. Barely discernible in the night were the ruins of several huts, their dark outlines standing out against the flickering light from a little fire. Near the fire, with his back to an adobe wall, crouched a monk. It was a strange sight. All about, the luxuriant jungle growth sent out fingers and tendrils to cover the ruined settlement, appearing alive and growing even in the darkness. And in this wilderness a Christian monk alone. Stranger still, he spoke to us without surprise at our coming.

"My evening blessing on you, brothers," he chanted sonorously, in a beautiful accent.

Near him, we saw a big traveler's pack on the ground. His staff was stuck upright in the soft earth. It had a crook like a bishop's staff. So far as we could see he carried no weapons. And we noticed that farther off an Indian squatted. The monk threw him a piece of the loaf which he himself was chewing with powerful teeth. The traveler was a huge man with a thick torso. His head was round, his face broad, and his tonsure had long since grown unkempt.

"Sit down, my children," said the monk in his resonant voice. It was like a dream, hearing this bell-like human tone in the steaming forest. Its magic dispelled the terrors of nature and the profound melancholy of the night.

The Indian sprang to his feet, rekindled the fire, and started a fine blaze.

"The ground is dry enough here," the monk informed us, "and there are no snakes. You can pick off the leeches in the light. We don't want to strain to see each other like so many ghosts."

We did as we were told, and listened to the monk's clear voice.

"I feel better now," he went on without invitation, as he stretched out on his back, resting the base of his heavy head on his clasped hands. "Jacob, here, has told me the whole story." He indicated the Indian with a roll of his eyes, and it was then we saw that it was our guide.

"Don't take offense at him," he said. "There's no use getting angry at him for running away. For whenever white men begin to fight among themselves it's always the Indians who are the losers. He'll take you to Panama. It isn't far now, anyway. But you, young man, I must warn you you've acted very rashly. One death was quite enough, don't you think? Not that I don't appreciate your feelings. But look! You'll notice I don't wear a sword. So not having any I never use one, no matter how wild my temper may become. I personally prefer to carry a heavy stick."

"Aren't you afraid of the Indians, father?" Alonso asked in wonder.

"Afraid? Not at all. Why should I be afraid?" the monk returned. "I live by the grace of God. In such case fear is superfluous."

"Yes, but when you wander about all alone, father?" said Diego de Vargas.

"Alone? But I do not walk alone," the monk explained, and stretched out a long arm. "At night there are the stars. The soft bats amuse me. In the daytime there is the sun, there are the birds, the butterflies and plants. I can even pick up a stone from the ground and contemplate its being, feel its weight and its lovely roundness, filled to the skin with pity and humility."

Our Indian guide kept close to the monk, watching his lips form the curious words.

"Of course, father," said Diego de Vargas, smiling quietly, "but I was referring to men, not animals or things of the wilderness."

"Men! That's a different thing," the monk replied hastily. "You're right if you think I become lonely among men. Quite right. You appear to be an intelligent man. And you know that men talk too much. They are much too busy for their own good. The Indians, however, are quite otherwise. You may have noticed. They sit saying nothing. They neither think nor dream. They simply exist. And for that they are content."

"But, father," said Alonso, stung into argument, "Indians are heathens, infidels. You must admit the truth of that. And that upsets some people. It disturbs me, for instance, for I'm a great champion of the Immaculate Conception."

"The Immaculate Conception! Nonsense!" the monk objected resonantly, so that all the wilderness rang with his words. "What is immaculate! Nothing. Nothing at all, my son. Where would children come from if they were not industriously conceived? Yes, you talk like a stupid man. But nevertheless, I like you very much. For I, too, in my way, am a stupid man.

"Would you believe that in my youth, when I was in Salamanca, I had an Indian servant that my father gave me? When I went to the University the red man followed behind, carrying my books. I always had him keep three paces to the rear. It was a strict command, if you can imagine it. I fancied this little conceit most tremendously, my sons. Can you conceive it? Three paces always! When I came along everything in the street simply stopped. The market women, the muleteers, the beggars, the asses themselves watched my triumphal march to the halls of learning. This public interest was as sweet as honey to my vanity. And so you see I was outrageously stupid. Yet my Indian servant was not so thick between the ears. He was tolerant and he loved me and so held his peace. Otherwise, I suppose, he would have waited his chance and jolted the conceit out of my head. This he never did. I have had to perform the sorry task myself."

Friendliness and love radiated from the monk's fleshy countenance like heat from an oven, but had no soothing effect on Alonso. Jumping to his feet the latter shouted wildly, "Without the Immaculate Conception the world means nothing to me. And I shall cry it out here in the wilderness, in mountains or wood. Our Virgin Mother never slept with any man and the Lord Jesus Christ was conceived by pure spirit. Whoever says different is a heretic and worse than an Indian who prays to a lump of wood." So powerful was Alonso's emotion that tears rolled down his cheeks.

This filled the monk with pity, and he said, "Now, my dear friend, pray sit down again. Calm yourself. I don't doubt you believe every word you say. But as for me, these matters are too subtle. I'm no student of dogma, nor do I want to be. I can see that your belief fills every cranny of your heart. That is good. I'd be the last person in the world to decry your faith. Yet so far as lumps of wood are concerned, you are laboring in grievous error, my friend. With quite as much justification I could say that Spaniards pray to a wooden thing when they bow down to an image of the Virgin Mary, or are enraptured by the Holy Ghost portrayed in a stained-glass window. No, not at all, my son. God's red children know perfectly well that the Almighty sits on his throne in Heaven. They know He is the true keeper of souls. They have forgotten much, perhaps, and daemons have come between them and God in the form of frogs, feathered snakes, pumas and little butterflies that have jeweled wings.

"I don't like that, I admit. But who are we to be puffed up? Do we not pray to the Golden Calf? Do we not kindle the iron Moloch of war and render him offerings numbering into the thousands? The daemons of blood lust, of cruelty, vanity and pride—do they not lurk in our hearts like vile worms in an apple's core? The very ships flying Christ's banner from the masthead have brought a thousand new miseries to this land.

"Do you want to know why these huts all around us here have fallen to pieces? They were sacked by Spaniards, my sons. The people who lived in them were carried off into slavery. When God looks down at the earth from his loftiness—and that he surely does—and sees this waste land, then it is our turn—I refer to us men of Castile—to step forward and say, We did this, we, we are responsible. We have made free men into slaves. We have forced them into toil without feeding them. And so they have died. We have raped their wives, burned their huts to the ground, leveled their fields, murdered their elders—for the old people could neither tickle our lusts nor work for us."

The monk stopped his exegisis, gave all his attention to brushing away a cloud of mosquitoes that had landed on his forehead. We all sat still, not saying a word. I had listened to the monk's discourse with sickness in my heart, and my thoughts were fixed on the violence that I had committed. Everything was strangely in keeping with the impenetrable darkness of the forest; everything he said was fearfully invested with the torpor of the night and the melancholy of the ruins amid which we sat morose.

"Well, my friends, I must go now," the monk said, and rose to his feet, fumbling for his staff. He stood over the fire. The shadow of his mighty frame danced slowly on the black wall of forest. As he prepared to leave he brought to mind Saint Christopher, crook in hand, his great pouch hung by a leathern strap over his left shoulder.

"What? Are you going now? In the middle of the night?" asked Diego de Vargas.

"Night is as good as day," the monk said loudly. "The poor Indians are afraid of the spirits but they never seem to bother me."

"But the animals, the snakes!" protested Diego de Vargas.

"Snakes? I'm fond of them," the monk said evenly. "It pleases me to think that they shed their skin, and become new and glistening, born all over. I only wish that men could do likewise. I wish they could cast off their wickedness for a Christian skin. Besides, snakes have lovely eyes, lovely golden eyes. So far as animals go, the only ones that trouble me are the mosquitoes. But I have blood enough for them and to spare. Anyway, in the night I find it interesting to while away the time with song."

Abruptly changing the subject, the monk leaned over me, took me by the arm and forced me to my feet. Slowly he examined me in the firelight.

"I see, my son," he observed, "that the deathblow you've just dealt is weighing heavily on your conscience. I recommend strongly that you present yourself to the secular authorities. You ought to tell your story to the Governor of Panama. It's true the man you killed was bad, a murderer. But it is scarcely right to outreach the arm of justice, my friend. Sooner or later the man you killed would have found his way by himself to the gallows. Beyond that he was probably a doubter. Panama is teeming with doubters. When you get to the city, then, you must say a prayer for his soul's rest. Your act of violence denied him the guidance of the Church."

"But I don't know his name," I said, forgetting to ask how he read me so quickly.

"No. But God does," the monk replied. "He knows the whole story."

"Then I'll do it."

"I am glad, then," said the monk, and pressed my hand in parting. "You must remember, too, to treat the Indians with kindness and to watch out for them. You must become their protector. I am counting on you."

He stopped, again looked into my face. "It is one thing to conquer and plunder a country. It is quite another task to spread the Gospel. The world would be a paradise if every one believed spontaneously and practiced this belief at every opportunity, never counting on limiting it to the hours spent at Mass and Confession. But more and more the Catholic faith has become a matter of Sunday contrition. We are forever slipping in and out of our warm cloak. In everyday life—in trade, in the council chamber, on the battlefield—it is always something quite different we believe in. Only when by luck we find ourselves alone, alone in the forest, or on a mountain-top, or on the shore of the sea at night, do we become Christians again. All our talk, our rushing around, our eternal scribbling is for the sake of the *consensus omnium*. We try to drown God in confusion. For mankind is weak and fears the face of the Lord.

"I cannot take your deed on my conscience, my son, though I might for a weaker one. You have a brave face. You must learn to break a lance with evil. Bear in mind the young nobleman who met Satan on a long road. Instead of running away, he took his glove and flung it in Satan's face"—the monk laughed aloud at his own thoughts. "Lord, lead us into temptation that we may find you! Let us sink up to our necks in evil, so that we may know you! Let us suck dry the gall of disbelief, that we may learn faith!"

With the strange words, which to me—at that callow time—seemed perilously close to blasphemy, the monk turned away. His broad bulk vanished into the blackness of the forest. He was gone. And suddenly the place was crawling with loneliness, intolerably empty. I consoled myself with the light of the fire and with the sight of my companions cowered about it.

When I finally arrived at Panama, I had myself announced to the Governor, Don Pedro de Los Ríos, who like myself was native to Cordova. Don Pedro received me squatted in his bath tub, in which it was his custom to spend the greater part of the day. He could think better in water, he used to say, and disdained more polite explanation.

And so there he sat, Don Pedro, a fat man of fine birth who ruled Panama—sat in a wooden butt in the fly-ridden courtyard of his estate. The house was the most pretentious in the country and was built entirely of white stone. In the courtyard stood some tall palms and on the walls grew hibiscus, brilliant with red bloom. At the time of my visit Don Pedro was busy drinking wine. Making rich noises, his fleshy lips apart, he drank greedily from the brim of a silver goblet, while his quick black eyes, hard with malice, sought my countenance.

About him were ranged several Indians, wearing feathered headdresses. They were to all appearances chieftains. Other Indians, half-naked creatures curiously bronze of body to my inexperienced eyes, constantly poured water from the tub over Don Pedro's heavy carcass. Behind him hovered a muscular Negro who steadily waved a palm fan to stir the heavy air over Don Pedro's dripping flesh. Our Father Vicente de Valverde lurked in the background, morose and ill at ease.

"Give the man of God some wine," Don Pedro squeaked irritably at one of the Indians, and pointed a stubby finger at Father Vicente, but the priest shook his head. "What! You don't drink wine!" shouted Don Pedro. "Then give it to the young man there," and in turn pointed at me.

"Your Excellency appreciates that we are all anxious to get aboard ship and carry out His Majesty's commands," said Father Vicente. "Every little delay merely means that the heathen remain that much longer in benightedness. So many more souls in consequence will be lost to Heaven. All that die in this interval are ripe for Hell fire."

"Did Pizarro tell you that?" inquired Don Pedro and scratched his hairy chest noisily.

"He did not," said Father Vicente. "I say it. As a servant of the Church."

"Pizarro is a liar," Don Pedro went on without hearkening to the priest's objections. He slapped the water furiously. "But don't worry, Your Reverence. I'll keep you informed. Ah! this dismal heat. More, Nero! More!"

The big black man worked harder, the sweat trickling over his chin and down his neck.

"What the muleteers, swineherds, beggars and generally assorted bastards are driving at escapes me quite," said Don Pedro. "From the very beginning this foul Pizarro has caused me nothing but trouble. Trying to lure my colonists away from me! His fancies have already cost plenty of men their sweet lives. Peru! Perhaps there is such a land. But what of it? I can easily picture the place. There stands Peru—mud huts roofed with reeds, a few straggly fields of Indian corn and some natives with gold rings hanging from their ears and noses. And of course the famous camel, the one they all broke their necks wondering at. But what in the name of God is so exciting about that! Is it worth making a cheat into a captain-general and adelantado? God only knows that if it weren't our own King who has been bewitched by this humorless adventurer I'd say only a fool would believe such a vagabond profession.

"Yet let us suppose the man is telling the truth. Let us imagine what that means. Suppose Peru is all that he says it is, with streets of gold. Even then it would be sheer madness to send a Pizarro there. What can this moth-eaten middle-aged squire and his handful of rowdies accomplish in such a place? The lot of them will end in disaster. And this time, on my honor as a Spaniard, there'll be no ships sent to retrieve them. Not so much as a raft. Let them all rot on a hot cliff among the droppings for all of me, my dear Father. I've got plenty of troubles of my own to keep my mind occupied."

The fat man paused to get his wind, took another deep draught of wine, and fumbled about in a basket of fruit one of the Indians offered him. The juice shone on his mouth and chin, and impatiently he washed it off as the flies gathered.

"Yes, my enormous responsibilities!" he said. "Take some fruit, my lords. It comes from Don Pedro Arias de Ávila's plantation. He was my esteemed predecessor. He had the same trouble with Balboa as I'm having with Pizarro. They're both too big for the space around them. But in those days things were run in a reasonable fashion. Balboa, you perhaps recall, Father Vicente, had his head chopped off. My hands are tied, I regret . . ."

"His Majesty the King," Father Vicente broke in, "is counting on your giving every assistance to the Pizarro expedition. For it is really an expedition of the Crown. But what are you doing? Holding us here on account of a ridiculous scuffle."

"Scuffle! I call it murder, my precious bishop in the making." Don Pedro waggled an admonitory forefinger at the nettled priest. "What an odd way for a man of God to be talking!"

"According to what our men say," Father Vicente objected coldly, "the dead man had previously struck down an Indian and killed him. As I see it he got his measure."

Hearing these words I flushed with shame, then opened my mouth to speak, but in the end decided to hold my tongue.

"Measure? Where's the justice in that," objected Don Pedro, and began meticulously to peel a banana, parodying his argument. "My dear worthy, you make me wonder. No one in Panama would give a lead maravedi for his life if everybody decided to become his own judge and decree acts at will. If matters came to such a pass, I'd simply get an Indian to plant an arrow in Pizarro's neck, and he might very well do me the same disservice. Where would justice be then in Panama? Furthermore, don't forget that the first man to be murdered was only an Indian. The man killed by one of your party was a servant of the Crown however small. . . ."

"I, it was . . ." I blurted out.

Don Pedro and Father Vicente both turned to me. "You were saying something?" Don Pedro asked.

"Yes, I killed the man," I said.

Father Vicente clasped his hands and looked up in irritated resignation at the sky. Don Pedro stared at me with undisguised interest. Even the Indians began to watch me attentively, and the huge Negro stopped his fanning.

"Sweet Virgin Mary!" said Don Pedro, slapping his forehead, "we've got the murderer, at last. Unless he's making a bad joke . . ."

"No," I said. "I killed him."

"You did!" screamed Don Pedro in inexplicable rage. His piggy eyes sparkled with malice and forcefully he pounded on the rim of the tub. "Nero, you black African ape, move faster or I'll have you caponized. Get out, you Indians! Get out! And what were you thinking of, young man? Did you think you were in Triana where differences are settled with a knife? What was in your mind, I'd like to know? Why didn't you report the matter to me and let me take care of it? It is I, Don Pedro de Los Ríos, who looks out for injured parties. I am the representative of Don Carlos our King. I am like a father to the Indians. Day and night I have to worry about these red dogs. It's bad enough as things stand without having such hotheads as you to complicate affairs. The Dominicans, especially this Father Bartolomé, this enormous boor, are buzzing in my ears from morning till night. Nothing will satisfy the Dominicans, Father Bartolomé at least, short of an uprising. When every Spaniard in Panama is roasting over a slow fire, then they'll be satisfied. How they'll crow then, the dears! What in God's sweet name Don Carlos sees in Bartolomé I fail to understand. Bartolomé! These whiskery, swilly Pizarros! It can't go on forever.

"By the tender bowels of Christ, I'm a man when all's said and done. The time will come when I'll cut them all down by the legs. I'll mow them down like a ripe field of grain. What is it, pray tell me, sirs, that the Council of the Indies is driving at? I'd like to be informed, for I'm the Governor of Panama, in case anyone is interested. Who's going to cut cane if the Indians don't do it? Who's going to haul mahogany? Who else, kind sirs, can do any work in this Godforsaken land? And Don Carlos wants gold. Gold, gold, gold! That's all I hear.

"I'd be the last one to complain about this tremendous hypocrisy of conversion and the milk of human kindness. I'd let the Indians run off to their wives and breed more hideous specimens than there are flies in Panama. For all of me fornication can be the order of the day. But, my dear worthies, believe me, I have to show results. Save for that I'd clap a crown of feathers on my pate and demonstrate to the Indians how a Cordovan can pirouette under the moon. Yes, that would be a merry, merry day for me, my solemn brothers. But I can't conjure cane out of the earth, and gold still less. Animals just don't walk up to me and say, my omnipotent Don Pedro de Los Ríos, please accept this fine skin as a token of esteem and homage. Trees don't come walking into my dooryard from the forests, then fall apart into convenient stacks. Work, sirs, miserable, disgusting, sweaty work—that's the watchword.

"If Panama is queen of the Southern Ocean, as the Council of the Indies so eloquently puts it, she's queen because of my incessant labors. The New World is no place for sluggards. And so either the Indians work, which prospect they abhor with passion, or Spain must do without Panama's riches. There you have the brutal choice, my nobles, and which way the scale will tip I leave it to you to figure out for yourselves."

Exhausted by this tirade Don Pedro let his melon head droop down onto the hairy chest. Slowly he worked back his matted hair, and began to knead his eyes viciously.

"Now, my young man," he continued sternly, "I'm gradually coming round to you. Are you aware, my caballero, that you come to me warmly recommended by Don Garcilaso de Gómez? Do you understand that I actually looked forward to your arrival? That I wanted to—really wanted to talk again with a young person of noble blood? You must see that here in Panama there is no one to pass the time of day with except swineherds like your Pizarros, the Alcons, the Cuéllars. All of them are not worth a man's sour breath on a rainy morning. They're fanatics, thieves, and they are liars to boot. They can neither read nor write. They gibber about nothing but gold and slaves and the women they'll rape when the raping's good. To cut it short, they bore me. I was thinking I might talk to you about the world, about Bembo and Castiglione. There are people who have courage and spirit besides these roughnecks. And now look. What a profound disappointment! Here you come, apparently as innocent as an unborn babe nestled in the womb, and on practically the first day in Panama you hack out the brains of a Crown servant. What a ghastly absence of tact! My dear boy, you have distressed me beyond words. Haven't you the faintest idea of good manners? Are you aware that some of us have sensibilities, an eye for decorum?"

"I did wrong, my lord," I said, and dropped my eyes. "I wronged the Crown. I wish I could undo it."

"At least you're contrite," said Don Pedro, thoughtfully, again scratching his hairy breast. "You don't beat around the bush. I'll tell you without mincing words that I don't care in the slightest about the pig you killed. But justice, my friend, justice! Think what chaos there would be in Panama if this sort of thing were allowed to go on every day. I've talked about it enough already for even a numskull to catch the point. The only extenuating circumstance in this case, as I see it, is that it happened outside the city limits. But however that may be, you'll have to give yourself up to the alcalde."

Don Pedro meditated further, his forehead creased into three deep parallels. Pearls of sweat ran down his cheeks like tears. "I suppose actually it was a matter of self-defense. Wasn't it?" he inquired.

"No, it was not," I told him.

"It wasn't!"

"Indeed it was," Father Vicente said sharply. "The man had a drawn sword in his hand when he was found."

"But he hadn't drawn it on my account," I explained stubbornly.

At this recalcitrance Don Pedro laughed loudly, his belly so strenuously shaken with amusement that waves slopped wildly against the tub's side. Nodding his head, he looked at Father Vicente, who smiled fixedly, then as quickly resumed his cautious gravity.

"But wouldn't the man have used his sword if he'd known what was in your mind?" Father Vicente asked gently.

"Perhaps . . ."

"And wasn't he out of his head with anger, a raving maniac?" Father Vicente went on. "What he did to the Indian was proof of that. Who can tell whom a madman will turn on next."

"You've dissolved my last doubt, reverend father," said Don Pedro. "You missed your calling, sir. You should have been a lawyer. But that's beside the point. For disturbing the peace, young man, you'll have to pay a fine of one hundred ducats to the Crown."

"I haven't got a hundred ducats," I told him.

"Then get them, my boy, get them; earn them, steal them, find El Dorado. Anything you like. But get them!" Don Pedro was now in much better humor, having settled the matter with honor and dispatch. "I'll give you time to make good the debt. At least until you return from the South Country, if return you do. Mark my words, my son, you cannot toy with the law, no matter how pure your blood or how influential your connections. Indeed, even knowing me is no guarantee of protection."

"There are no more obstacles, then?" asked Father Vicente. "We can leave when we want?"

"The Pizarros can leave," agreed Don Pedro de Los Ríos ceremoniously. "They can leave with the Governor's blessing, and the quicker they leave the better I'll like it. The farther away they go, the easier I'll breathe. All that I hope is I have a few men left after Pizarro finishes luring them away with his herdsman's horn. I hope he bursts a lung blowing the horrid thing. And there's just one more matter, Father Vicente. See to it that the compact is kept. Otherwise the Almagros and the Pizarros are going to shed each other's blood in buckets full."

"Secular power is not my concern," retorted the priest dryly. "My task is to augment the Kingdom of the Lord." Having made this thrust he began to bow his way out, and I followed his example. But Don Pedro de Los Ríos would have none of this.

"A moment, young man," he said, "I want to talk to you. I'd like you to meet my wife, Doña Elena. She'll want to know how things are with Doña Isabella, and whether Doña Juana is still the talk of the land. She has been pestering me for weeks trying to find out whether sleeves are wide or not, whether dresses are long or short. She'll like to know whether Don Carlos has one mistress or a dozen. Ah, these Burgundians! How well I remember our dead king. Ah, when Don Felipe first came to Coruña. He brought with him fifty horses and a hundred concubines on a specially outfitted ship. The vessel foundered in the Bay of Biscay. Did you ever hear the story? Some of the horses were saved but every one of the girls was drowned. It was a tragedy of antique proportions. A hundred at one stroke! We young people were very much moved by the affair. They said at the time that Don Felipe, who wasn't precisely a sentimentalist, made no attempt to hide his tears. Ah, well, here I sit in my tub, talking, talking, talking. And you must be hungry."

Don Pedro with a great heave stood up in his bath, a wide paunchy man covered with hair. He clapped his hands like an emperor, quite oblivious to the ridiculousness of the situation, and squeaked portentously, "Come here, you idiots! Wake up, wake up. My towel! My shift! My shirt! My hose!"

This was the signal for a wild scurrying about in the courtyard as Indians, Negroes, mestizos and whites all began to carry out their multifariously prescribed duties. It was precisely as if Don Pedro de Los Ríos had casually dug with his sword into an anthill. Some Indian maidens carefully dried his body with woolen towels; others oiled and combed his black hair. Then men came with his shoes, clothes and dagger.

They assisted their corpulent master to a bench where he was hidden from my eyes by the many zealots busy about him. When he emerged he stood forth in black silk, a Flemish ruff about his throat. The silver handle of his dagger was set in jewels. He bent low in my direction, velvet biretta held elegantly in one hand, the other clasping the hilt of his dagger.

"An amusing transformation, my son?" he asked. "You mustn't forget that Panama is the queen of the Southern Ocean, the bright eye of the world. I simply have to play the peacock, don't you know. But confidentially"—he drew me abruptly toward him, gripping my doublet with an arrogant hand—"many a pretty lady who became acquainted with me in court dress thought she'd popped into bed with a monkey when my furry hide tickled her white bosom. Never mind that, though, don't give it a second thought. I soon give them all something pleasanter to take up their time. As a matter of fact, I'm something of an artist in this particular field of man's endeavor. Thick and short, makes the ladies snort. Ah, my son, you should see the lovely beads of sweat dampening their brows when I'm in the proper humor for dalliance!"

He laughed with unconcealed pleasure, winked at me evilly and pinched me under the arm. "Of course, we can't talk about these matters at the table," he said, and laughed some more at his own wit. His vast pod bobbled up and down like a keg of jelly.

In this extraordinary fashion I made the acquaintance of Pedro de Los Ríos, Governor of Panama. Both he and his wife, Doña Elena, later did me many kindnesses at a time when I wanted to return with all possible haste to Spain. That evening, amid the chatter of Don Pedro and the endless queries of his wife, both natives of Cordova like myself, I completely forgot the crime which but a few hours before had seared my conscience.

On the day of Saint John the Baptist our banners were blessed by Father Juan in the Cathedral of Panama. The brilliant morning sun streamed in through the high windows and the golden tips of the standards bowed with slow pomp toward the altar in the direction of the great crucifix. "Lord Jesus Christ, bless the banners of Castile!" implored Father Juan as the whole population of the city bent laboriously to its knees on the hard tiles. In front, hard before the main altar, the Governor and his spouse kneeled on two velvet cushions. Arrayed behind them in order of rank were long rows of caballeros and occasional ladies of family, soldiers and planters, and far back a solid mass of Indians. The crowd was large and the Cathedral none too roomy so that some of the onlookers spilled out onto the steps and even into the street. Suddenly a puff of morning breeze came through the open door of a chapel in the apse, and the banners fluttered briskly. It looked as if the lions moved, as if they were drawn back to spring. A deep sigh of relief rose from the crowd, and a clear child's voice was heard to say, "Mother, was it God who blew into the flags?"

This occurrence was generally taken to be a most propitious omen, and members of the expedition began to whisper excitedly to each other. Then silence came over everyone in the Cathedral as the ancient wonder of the Mass was once again enacted for all to see and the Lord became substantially present among us. The little silver bell tinkled, and like two cherubim the altar boys kneeled in their white robes.

Father Juan stepped down from the altar, deftly divided the bread among the Pizarros, their caballeros and men, the while repeating, "May the body of our Lord Jesus Christ preserve thy soul to life everlasting."

Even with the Lord's body still dry-sweet on my lips I saw the gloomy preoccupied face of the Captain-General, and the tears of fanatic passion that unashamed rolled down the cheeks of Don Pedro de Candía. Out of nowhere at this ecstatic moment a memory possessed my mind, possessed it so strongly that I felt as if some invisible person were speaking in my ear, and forcing the violent attention of my whole being. Once with my Master Agrippa I had studied the Scripture of Saint Luke, though we were both aware that the Mother Church does not readily countenance such activities, since the mysteries of the Gospel are difficult to fathom, and in plumbing their depths the common mind may easily be lost forever. In the book of Luke, however, it may be, I read of the Last Supper of our Lord, and of what he spoke when he raised the beaker of wine: "Behold, the hand of him that betrayeth me is with me on the table."

Now these words came back to me, like a soundless clap of thunder, jarring the body even though unheard. Anxiously I looked about. Who can it be, I asked myself. Who can it be? There in his pride kneeled Don Hernando Pizarro, Don Gonzalo in his cunning, candid Don Juan, young Don Pedro Pizarro, Don Pedro de Candía in his fanatic belief. I felt clearly that any one of these was quite capable of betrayal, not so much through his vices as through his virtues, not out of any deficiency, but rather out of an excess of zeal.

For the first time—I was only a boy then, it cannot be forgotten—I had the feeling that in the Deity there is something terrible, impossibly remote. I envisioned how the Great Judge of the World must appear in all his dread brazen majesty when, amid the angels' trumpetings, the graves open for the great day. I considered in my mind's eye the time when the mild voice loses its softness, when miracles of compassion come to an end, when there are no more parables to bring tears to the eyes, for even God's forbearance has its limits in time. I saw the white mantle fall from the mighty shoulders, and caught sight of the diamantine heart, which no white mantle, loving kindness and compassion can permanently conceal. But woe unto him who betrays Me!

With the bread dry on my tongue, I stared at the altar. But the Man of God on the Crucifix, crowned with dark thorns, great ruby drops of blood on His forehead, the cheeks hollow and the cheekbones gauntly carved, gave no sign. His head was sunk low in the bitter travail of death. What a strange drama, I thought. The Lord in His final agony, and spread before Him on the gay tiles all the vanity and pride of the world. The Governor in black silk; his lady in a magnificent wine-red dress with shimmering pearls about her throat. The secretaries, all in black; the young women, some with raven hair caught in golden nets. The deeply breathing bosoms, the wonderfully smooth cheeks, the dimples and round tender limbs. And the knights in silver harness, casting back light on the motes of dust dancing about them, the soldiers in many-colored doublets with my Diego the brightest of them all. Then the Indians, red-skinned and covered with rustling feathers, much more enraptured by the ceremony than their white masters, their eyes glistening with excited delight. The native women, holding aloft their pot-bellied sucklings the better to see God and perhaps profit by contact with His omnipotence, or perhaps as unaccepted offerings to a different Quetzalcoatl. All this I saw.

And seeing, I folded my hands, and let myself sink deep into the purple depths of the sacrament, which may perhaps be better gauged by the simple than by the wise. Earnestly, my lips moving without making a sound, I prayed to God to take me to His breast and there let me lie, like John the beloved disciple, John of the long lock and red mantle.

16

TOWARD THE SOUTH

WE BOARDED our ships one sunny day in January. The wind was favorable and we set a course southward. Soon the many islets in the bay of Panama had dropped from view and by nightfall the last faint outline of palm tree had disappeared behind the horizon. Under the keel of our vessel now heaved the great Southern Ocean, whose limits were unknown to man. Many people said that at the farthermost western limit it washed the shores of Cathay and Cipangu, that its waves rolled on the beaches of the Spice Islands, those rich lands which the Portuguese found when they rounded the Cape of Storms at the tip of Africa. Others maintained that Heaven alone bounded the Southern Ocean, and that it ended only where the bowl of sky dipped down into the vast flood. But this is a question to be discussed only by such men as my Master Agrippa and the lately deceased Abu Amru ibn Al-Jad. Such a common mortal as I can only grow dizzy with speculation when trying to imagine the earth with its snowy mountains and endless seas as a whirling ball, which is Master Agrippa's contention.

But whatever shape the earth may be, the Southern Ocean is the greatest body of water, though by no means the stormiest. For storms are far more numerous on the Western Ocean, indeed on the little Bay of Biscay. It is the same with oceans as with men. Big, strong men are usually pleasant-tempered and avoid quarrels at all cost. It is the small and weak who open their mouths at every opportunity and are ever ready with fist and knife. Similarly the Southern Ocean is usually peaceful, as if the rolling waters were aware of their gigantic extent and power. And yet anyone who has had the experience will verify my opinion that nothing is more awesome than the rare storms on the Southern Ocean. The waves are high as houses, living walls of dark water threatening to engulf the vessel cowering in their trough, the wind howls like all the madness of the world over the torn wastes of foam and scud, and the lonely ship is driven from its course toward lonely isles, mountainous places where strange gods with long noses and slant eyes look down upon the sea.

The people of Peru say that it is faraway amid these isles where lives the Lord of Waters, Pachacamac, in the isles of the dead where abide all departed spirits. To us, however, the Southern Ocean revealed only its smiling countenance. Our trip was as quiet as if we were sailing on a summer afternoon over an inland lake. The only bad aspect of our situation was the cramped quarters aboard our vessel. In Panama, seeking ships to transport his company, our Captain-General had announced if someone would take the risk he would later repay the investment a thousandfold, once the gold of the land he sought was safely in his grasp. That is why he fared so badly in dickering for means of transport.

Everything that we took with us had been bought on credit at exorbitant terms. This is the usual custom in outfitting an expedition in the Indies. For the conquistadors are like poets. They have little money but many lively ideas. The merchants who advance ships, horses and arms reckon a thousand per cent interest, or a total loss. And the latter contingency is realized far oftener than the former. Already many a conquistador has been swallowed up in the dark maw of the forest or has foundered in the sea, never to appear again. In the New World fortune is like nature itself, immense, overwhelming and pitiless. Luck lifts one to the pinnacle of fame, makes him the master of great lands and peoples, smothers him in a heap of gold and its attendant horrors. But more likely it casts him down with no recourse except to draw his last breath in a brutal end, either under the lonely sky or in a debtor's prison.

Because our two ships were very small and incommodious, and we were forced to sit tight in them like salt herrings in a keg, great dissatisfaction arose among the soldiers. There were continual quarrels. The men whom we had taken on in Panama in order to augment our scanty numbers were very lazy. If one of them was told to help man the pumps he would set up a terrific protest, threaten his superiors, and argue that labors of this sort were not for a free Spaniard. Some pointed out that in Nicaragua every Spaniard had ten or fifteen Indians to carry his weapons, helmet and other paraphernalia, and even to carry the lordly warrior himself if he grew fatigued, or if the way were swampy. They proposed that the Captain-General should take Indians on board in order to have these red toads, as they called them, perform menial tasks. But this expedient was, of course, out of the question. The vessels were already overburdened; they were leaking at every seam so badly that we were leading an amphibian existence. Furthermore, the coasts that we skirted showed not the smallest sign of human habitation. For league after league we could see nothing but great tongues of brooding mangrove forest thrusting darkly into the sea. Only once did we see smoke from a great wood fire, far inland, but Don Pedro de Candía was of the opinion that a bolt of lightning had set the forest on fire.

On and on we crept, over placid expanse of what might as well have been sweet water, and always hugged the coast. For had any serious storm blown up, it is certain that both ancient craft would have sunk to the bottom like two leaden ducks. Now and then we sailed by the mouths of great rivers, the waters of which yellowed the sea into the color of bean soup. One day we turned up one of these estuaries in order to take on fresh water and to look around for Indian villages. Great alligators plowed quietly through the water like heavy logs, and among the thick reeds along the shore we could see long-legged swamp birds with rosy feathers.

In this narrow estuary it was heavy, hot and intolerably close. Dragonflies with metallically glistening wings as broad as a man's hand shot over the smooth surface of the river in which near the banks swam white and yellow blossoms as big as a dish plate. As our ship plowed her way through this monstrous patch of posies they began to tremble and sway from one end to the other.

The river narrowed quickly and on each side the dark forest walls hemmed us in closely. But where the sun was able to shine down on the primeval earth we noticed that huge flesh-colored flowers had sprung up, looking almost like animals. In the matted crowns of foliage there were countless birds of bright plumage. Many of them were parrots, and yet some were no longer than butterflies. Others were like our sparrows and swallows, only much more gaily plumed, and with a hood of feathers on their crowns resembling what we put on falcons to blind them before setting them loose on the prey.

All these birds took to flight as soon as they spied us, and let out ear-splitting shrieks of alarm. The tumult was so great that we actually had to shout to one another to make ourselves understood and we were greatly relieved when the Captain-General gave orders to head back downstream.

We saw no native villages, not one. I did not doubt that this stream had been barren of humanity since the day of Creation, but this idea was not shared by the Captain-General who thought it quite possible that watchful eyes had noted our coming and going, and that this news would be passed on and on until it reached the throne of the King of Peru. For, he said, these people have the gift of becoming one with the forest, like a deer or a fox. A native, he told us, can be standing only two steps away from a Spaniard as motionless as a tree-trunk, and not be discovered until his arrow has skewered its victim through the heart.

On account of the unrest among the men stirred up by the newcomers, and also because of the dangerous overloading, when we arrived at a bay that we named after Saint Matthew, our Captain-General gave orders to disembark. He had decided to make the rest of the trip southward to Peru on foot. Don Francisco Pizarro was always glad to feel solid earth underneath his feet. The water was not his element. Even the sight of the sea made him moody and unsure of himself, perhaps because on the shores of the New World he had lost so many brave men. I, too, was of the same temper. I am always at my best when I hear horses' hoofs ringing on stones, the soft squeak of saddle leather, and the clank of steel weapons, instead of the monotonous splash of the waves and the melancholy groaning of the ship as it rises and falls.

And yet it would be a gross miscalculation of our Captain-General's character to assume that his personal dislike of the sea or any fear of disturbance aboard ship influenced his decision to proceed southward on foot. In good times and in bad our leader was a reasonable man. Never did he allow his passing emotions to overrule his purpose as was frequently the case with his brother Don Hernando, who was often the dupe of his own arrogance. Yet Don Francisco was proud, too, like all the Pizarros, though the difference was that he knew enough to give way when this furthered his larger aim. He was greedy, but he could relinquish all thought of gold for the moment if this were to some ultimate advantage. He was infinitely jealous of his status as commander of the expedition, yet even on this ticklish score he would hearken and follow the youngest soldier's advice if he thought it better than anything within his own power to devise.

Everything he did was considered over and over again a hundred times. Today I can see that the whole plan for conquering the great South Country, a gigantic undertaking with the means at our disposal, was clear in this man's head to the last detail, like one of Behaim's maps. And nevertheless he was willing and patient enough to make constant adjustments as experience dictated, as step by step we drew nearer to the goal and he became directly acquainted with the nature of the land, the customs and government of its inhabitants.

When the decision to march south was generally announced, Don Francisco told the soldiers that he wanted to become acquainted with the nature of the land and to seek out Indian villages that promised booty. Almost every day he sent out patrols to explore the country on each side of our line of march. I soon noticed, through comments I overheard Don Francisco exchanging with his brother Don Hernando, that the Captain-General was worried about the mixed composition of his company. He was eager to submit the mob to the final discipline of battle and harsh physical trials in order to mold them into a group that understood the necessity of taking orders and of subordinating the personal will to the common good.

Physical difficulties, at least, were not long in coming. We were especially troubled by the countless rivers which, at this season, were swollen to overflowing with melted snow from the mountains. Often we found ourselves neck-deep in thick slimy water at which the horses and mules balked, necessitating their being laboriously led across by halter ropes. But no sooner were we all on the other side, many of the men chattering with the cold and upset by so much swallowed water, than without a moment's rest the march was resumed. Our wet clothes and the animals' hides steamed in the sun, attracting clouds of flies that, without exaggeration, blackened our faces. Often by midday we reached open places burning hot, and thirsting mightily for the water which a few hours before had nearly turned our stomachs. Every piece of armor, the smallest dagger, hung on our protesting carcasses like lead, and our feet burned furiously, like the feet of sinners on Judgment Day, who must traverse hot iron plates.

At such times some of the company began to wail and openly implored that their breath might stop in their throats. But on marched Don Francisco at the head of the procession, as deaf as a stone to the outcries. He proceeded briskly, impervious to flies and heat, sweating like a mad bull in his full armor, the heavy leathern battle helmet set squarely on his head. His weary horse—for in truth we wore down our animals to skin and bone—he led by the bridle. His thin beard and thick brows were matted with gray dust and dirt but he paid not the slightest attention to these minor discomforts.

From time to time a member of the company would collapse, his knees buckling as if he had been struck by a cannon shot. The Captain-General gave orders that everybody at all times should wear his helmet, since there was a poison in the sunlight that robbed men of their senses. The half-conscious and those completely prostrated were helped along by their friends and the company stretched out longer and longer every day. When this came to such a pitch that the danger threatened of the company's head parting completely from the body, Don Francisco would stop, an evil smile of contempt playing about his lips, raise his hand for silence and shout, "You milksops can't even bear up under a little sun. Do you want me to get you all veils so you won't get your skin red?" This put everybody in a passion of anger. We all responded to the taunt exactly like children. There was much grinding of teeth and threatening words were muttered. But the Captain-General heard nothing. Abruptly he would turn his back, and plod on.

And yet at times it seemed as if he must have eyes in his forbidding back, for he seemed to be able to calculate to a nicety the amount of endurance among his men. If things came to such a pass that a man was actually about to be abandoned to his fate because his fellows were too feeble to hold up under the added burden, the leader would stop and in silence let the whole straggling line pass by him. Every man he examined critically, like a horse dealer looking over so many geldings. At each one he would either nod approvingly or shake his head in concern. When the man who was about to give up finally staggered along on his comrades' arms, Don Francisco would have him hoisted onto his own horse and let him ride until he had recovered his strength. This naturally made a profound impression on the soldiers, particularly since he uttered not a single word of reproof or disappointment. He was also very careful about the horses' hoofs and fetlocks, which he had bound round with cloths as protection against the sharp stones that covered the country.

Another grievous difficulty was the thickness of the forests, above all at the rivers' edges where they grew most densely, so tangled indeed that at times we had to hew our way through with axe and sword. The men were forever tumbling heavily to the earth as their feet became entangled with roots and creeping vines, and many of them were so weak that once down they could not rise again unaided. For it must be recorded that our food was none too good. Our small stores melted away steadily, day after day, and strangely enough there was little game either in the forests or in the stony upland country. Occasionally we shot a swamp bird, but the flesh was fatty and rank. On the other hand the rivers teemed with fish, but unfortunately we had neither nets nor hooks and lines so that perforce we had to stand by in helpless longing as these plump creatures splashed and sported in the sun.

But taking all these disadvantages into account the Holy Virgin Mary was good to us and at last led us straight to an Indian village. She allowed us also the good fortune that the Indians, for all their superior numbers, offered no resistance. As we stormed the settlement with swords drawn there was a great outcry and all the inhabitants fled their homes into the forest. And indeed our appearance must have been unsettling to these untutored heathen, for our small detachment of mounted men, about fifty knights all told, made the earth thunder as they led the way. At the same time the troops on foot blew their horns mightily and rolled the drums with all power, while the musketeers for the first time discharged their weapons. They hit nothing, of course, but the moral effect of the explosion, the general appearance, and the belching fire from the arquebuses' belled mouths were all so tremendous that one might have thought Jupiter had visited the earth to deploy himself on our side.

It is understandable, then, that the Indians ran for their lives, the mothers dragging along the children by the hand, infants bobbing and wailing on their backs. Of course, the Dominicans let out a terrific protest and maintained we should capture the Indians, for they wanted to convert them since that was the true purpose of the attack—namely, to teach them the wonders of our Church and true Christian piety. We might easily have captured some of the natives, especially the women, hindered as they were by their children, but in all the uproar no one gave this a thought. At least not I. Most of us, including myself, jumped down from our lathered horses and raced into the huts.

I know that I, quite unaware of what I was doing, followed the lead of Don Juan Pizarro. For our horses were the swiftest of the lot and we were the very first to get into the middle of the village where there was a rather broad square of stamped earth and a big campfire. Here we spied a building somewhat larger and more elaborate than the rest that must have been the chieftain's home. Inside there were gaily colored reed mats, which in our overeagerness we tore to pieces with our spurs. Juan Pizarro found a large piece of dried meat and threw me a piece of it. Chewing greedily, we both searched for the coveted treasures. To our great joy we found several golden masks, hammered out of the precious metal, and several more ornaments made of gold and silver.

There fell into my hands a double mask, which I mention particularly not because of its value but rather because it is linked with a superstition that to my mind recalls the story of Ulysses and the Sirens. One part of the mask represents a man's face with round bulging eyes and a fleshy mouth puckered ready to whistle. The other part portrays the visage of a corpse, with cheeks collapsed, eyelids tight shut and helplessly dangling lower jaw.

Now, the Indians say that the first section of the mask shows the "Man of the Forest," an evil spirit and enchanter who goes through the woods whistling mysteriously bewitching tunes. If an Indian crosses his path and is addled by the sweet music, the evil spirit falls on him, sucks the blood out of his cheeks, and leaves him lying a dead man. When the Indians celebrate their feast days, the priests devoted to this daemon put on this double mask, with the evil spirit's face looking forward and the mask of the dead man to the back. I have seen this ceremony with my own eyes. And on my oath it is a chilling spectacle, since the feast of the evil spirit takes place at night, amid moaning song by the assembled Indians, hollow drum beats and great leapings and sneakings about the fire by the priests. Finally, after the dancing and singing have gone on for some long time, each priest remains on one spot and begins to whirl like a half-stunned dog, round and round dizzily, so that the two faces of the daemon and the dead appear mingled into one.

Among the spectators the excitement is so great that they all begin to dance, men, women and children. They leap about taking little springing steps. I must mention that actually not all dance, but only those who are possessed of the daemon, who is doubtless the Devil himself. In time this one or that one tumbles out of the circle, to lie on the ground apparently lifeless and stiff. In this condition, I was told, the spirit of the man is carried as quick as thought to the Islands of the Dead far away in the Western Sea, of which I have spoken before. The dead are awaiting the arrival of the man's spirit, all met together on the beach. They lead the living spirit, bring him among his ancestors, and they talk with him, telling him many awesome homilies similar to those told by the great Florentine when he discusses the world with departed friends and enemies both.

They believe, these Indians, that a lover can thus again find his dead beloved and take her back with him, providing that the other spirits are willing, just as Orpheus is said to have done with Eurydice. But they add that good fortune seldom attends such a strained union, for the maid forever longs to return to the Isles of the Dead as her true home.

Yet all this is dark superstition, and I am recounting it merely because I chanced to find the mask. It has occurred to me that Dante, too, went into the depths, led by his dead love Doña Beatrice. But never did he think of taking her out of the realm of the blessed to share with him a hard crust during his banishment in Verona, the castle of Casa Grande.

After we had searched out all the huts in the village we gathered the booty together in the central square and piled it up into two big heaps. For it was agreed that on pain of death no one should keep what he had found. Otherwise some of us, for example Juan Pizarro and I, would have far outstripped the others in spoils, and so have bred a later dissatisfaction, whereas Juan the thin, who had found nothing but the shank of a deer on which to polish his yellow teeth, would have had every cause to nurse his disappointment. All night long we worked over the fires, and melted down the masks, ornaments and utensils into ingots. After the Crown's tenth had been taken away, eighteen thousand ducats were left for us.

The Captain-General, his officers and the knights received more than the common soldiers. No man received less than fifty Castilian ducats, though at the time, of course, he was only credited for that amount by Master Pérez. It had been previously agreed, I must make clear, that all gold and silver was to be sent back to Panama, this with double intent—first to amortize our huge indebtedness for ships, and second to attract more people to the standard of our Captain-General.

Our company submitted to this proposition, though there were many doleful faces, for everyone of us in his heart felt that we were much too small in numbers ever to conquer the great South Country, and yet, curiously enough, everyone of us likewise hoped, in his still more secret heart, that in the end he would have not fifty, but fifty thousand ducats. As everyone knows, we Spaniards are great gamblers, and all of us by nature would disdain to clutch the sparrow in his hand if there were the remotest chance of snaring the pheasant in the copse. For in those days, be it understood, fifty ducats was a small fortune; there were few farms in the fat Estremadura which would command such a price.

In the short interlude between those exalted days and the present, gold has fallen drastically in value, this largely because of the great quantities of precious metal which we sent to Spain and again because of the rich yields of the mines of Potosí which fell into the hands of Gonzalo Pizarro.

Apart from the metals, stores of food were seized by us, and were more than welcome. We found also many precious stones. Because we were uncertain whether they really were gems of value, and not another example of the Devil's treachery which infests that land, Father Reginaldo de Pedraza, a very pious and acute man, advised us to test them with a hammer, since, so he said, a genuinely precious stone would resist the impact. Sad to tell, we smashed the stones into powder in our earnestness, but Father Reginaldo did not fail to collect the larger bits and preserve them carefully in his leather pouch. In this fashion, as from time to time our forays were repeated, this man of God became rich, since the stones, though in flinders, were still easily marketable in Spain.

Our ships had followed us down the coast, from harbor to harbor, from one river mouth to the next. When they finally caught up with us, and we had stowed the gold away and carefully instructed the captains what news they must carry back with them to Panama, once again we marched off through the South Country.

From now on we traversed a barren landscape, great reaches of sand and cruel stones which tried us bitterly. Tugging at the balky mules, nearly blinded by the swirling sand, we struggled forward, till the grit worked its way into our flesh and through our garments. The sun turned to darkness and the Day of Judgment seemed to have come, so said Father Juan. These were not healthy thoughts, and one man after another eased his conscience in full confession. We were indeed a mixed company. But sooner or later all of us, thief or murderer, whoreson or adulterer, fingered our rosaries plaintively as we waded through the moving sand. When the spirit moved them our ecclesiastics would begin a melancholy song, and it was strange to hear the supplication intermingled with the rush of the wind, the swirl of the fine sand and the distant beat of the surf.

And once it happened that we heard a mighty grumbling which shortly ceased and was succeeded by an even more terrifying event. To our horror the mountain to our left began to shake, and the earth under us, as if we were aboard a heaving vessel about to break up in a storm. The sand dunes became fluid, and flowing like rivers, while immense clouds of dust rose into the air.

All of us fell to our knees. With trembling hands the Dominicans held their black crosses high over their heads and cried out *"Maran atha,"* which is the same as "Come, O Lord!" In every limb we trembled and were sick with horror. Sweat covered our bodies, and cowering in the dust we feebly sang the old song:

Dies irae, dies illa
solvet saeclum in familla.

Finally the terror passed, and we were grateful that God had let us off with a simple warning, for none of us felt himself worthy of eternity at such an early date.

We discovered, as a matter of fact, that in this part of the world the earth quaked regularly, perhaps on account of the great sins that have been committed here in ages past. It may be that the commotion is caused by the old daemons of the Indies, Viracocha and Pachacamac, who are said to move about in the depths of the sea, wild with anguish at having their great powers usurped by an even greater one. I know it struck me that the heaving ground began to grow quiet when the Dominicans raised up their crosses.

But if the Lord aided us in escaping the elements, another trial visited the struggling company. We were stricken by a remarkable sickness. What caused it I am unable to say, for I am a poor *medicus* and can no more than bind a wound in the crudest fashion. I know nothing about the philosophy of medicine, although Master Agrippa once did read aloud to me from the *Paramirum* of the great Swiss doctor Paracelsus. I recall that this learned man spoke of the five origins of sickness, but of these five I can remember only the astral reason, because it happens that I love the stars and am always curious about their powers. It is a certainty that all the great events in the history of man, all the wars, sieges and crusades, have been bound up with the appearance of some fearful malady. The discovery of the Indies brought the scourge of syphilis, which spread like wildfire over all Europe. The Crusades and the trade with the East introduced the Asiatic pest, the black death which almost depopulated the continent, and which is accurately pictured in the works of Master Giovanni Boccaccio.

I do not know whether our sickness came from the stars, or was caused by the flying grit that constantly ground into our flesh. In any case, our bodies were covered with immense and horribly painful boils, which looked something like huge warts. The sufferers became very weak and feverish when they were stricken. For this reason day by day our marches diminished.

Among those who succumbed to this curious malady was Rodrigo the actor, whom we always knew as the Devil. I let him ride on my piebald, but one night his pain became so great he said he could ride no farther, and he begged me to leave him behind the following morning. I turned to Father Vicente de Valverde, who had some medical knowledge, and asked him whether he could help the sick man. Father Vicente looked over the patient, and concluded that if he could open the boils with a knife the pain would ultimately be somewhat eased.

The sick Rodrigo agreed to endure this operation, and Father Vicente dug around in his sack until he had found a very long lancet. I begged him in a whisper not to cut too deep, but Father Vicente informed me that it was necessary to get at the root of the evil. We had to hold down Rodrigo during the operation. Father Vicente went directly to work and cut open the boils. Rodrigo groaned softly, and we could feel his emaciated body trembling beneath our hands. Out of the boils streamed blood, so much that we had trouble finding enough bindings to stem the many little floods. But the relief Father Vicente had promised ensued. In a moment the sick man was eased of his pain, and said that he was better except for feeling a little dizzy and cold. This was strange, for it was a very warm night. We pulled his pallet nearer the fire, and comforted him as best we could. He professed to be satisfied and suddenly became very talkative. For more than an hour he rambled on, speaking clearly enough about women, their libidinous disposition, their natural alliance with the Devil, and other cynical notions.

I sat listening to him, not altogether pleased when his opinions crossed my own more delicate ones, but at last he fell asleep. I remember that just before this happened Rodrigo told me that this illness was a mortal one, that it was so great he had lost all relationship with his own body, from which he seemed to be standing off to one side, as if he were a ghost.

Thinking this a good deal sheer nonsense I pulled a cover over him, and myself fell asleep by the fire. When I opened my eyes again the sky was gray with morning and the fire had gone out. We let the sick man lie quiet as we fed and watered our animals and prepared the morning meal. We cooked him some broth, and pulled the covers aside to wake him up, for the day's march had to be carried out at any cost. Then we saw that he had died during the night. He looked peaceful enough, his hands folded over his chest, with all trace of the Devil's mask gone from his face.

We dug a shallow grave, that is, with our shovels and branches we scraped aside a little dry earth, and laid Rodrigo's corpse in the trough. Father Juan spoke some words, blessed the dead, and then we all prayed for the soul's rest of the first white man ever to be buried in this land. We then closed the grave and rolled heavy stones over it to protect the body from wild animals.

This was all finished shortly after sunup, and we moved on, away from the blackened embers of the campfires, away from the grave at the edge of the forest. In the next weeks more of the company were struck down by these boils, and there was scarcely a morning when we did not leave a grave behind us. The Captain-General was very much concerned about these repeated misfortunes, and the spirits of all of us were at a low ebb. We dragged along like tired animals, our heads drooping, with not a word spoken. It was really very much like a bad dream. We seemed at times to be tramping through the silent land of death, a land of lonely, shifting dunes, of thorny weeds, black forest's rim and the eternal moaning of the sea. I thought the day was assuredly not far off when the Captain-General would ride on alone, the only one left fit to see realized the vision which had sprung from his own brain.

And yet the day did come, after interminable marching, when we tottered over the crest of a high dune to see mirror-smooth waters stretched out before us, the Bay of Tumbez. Xenophon himself could not have experienced greater exaltation than we at the sight of these black and silver waters. We, too, threw ourselves to our knees, and with joyous hearts we thanked the Virgin Mary and her heavenly host for having led us safely to the South Country.

The prospect was overwhelming. Islands swam in the land-locked sea, thickly wooded in antique fashion. To the south and west towered up immense mountains, the like of which I had never seen before for there is nothing to compare with them in Spain. Their peaks were covered with snow; they strained upward heavily, shoulder to shoulder, giants with white and rosily glistening helmets. If we had not been under the protection of God and our beloved Virgin Mary there is no doubt that this spectacle would have given us pause forever. For as far as the eye could strain the immense expanse of gray sea, mountain and woods hemmed us. On the fantastically broken earth our horses, weapons and standards were entirely lost, mere pinpricks.

In the direction of the open sea lay curiously formed islands, round masses of stone which gleamed palely gray in the sun. From that quarter we could hear the distant roar of the surf, broken now and then by the hoarse barking and bellowing of sea lions and the screaming of the terns, miles and miles off. The clear air, which seemed to have some strange luminous power like Venetian glass, carried the sound perfectly. I have never seen such an atmosphere, such intense clarity, except perhaps in the High Sierras on an autumn afternoon.

Toward the east, amid the mountains, there were great canyons, their declivities covered with a tough, dark bushy growth. On the massy slopes were little plateaus of cultivated land dotted with huts, and in the tortuous valleys strips of green fields were visible, winding out of sight, appearing again in the tremendous inner reaches of the range.

We saw, too, a broad, shining river that ran from the mountains into a reedy delta. And to the south the black band of the stony shore delimiting the bay was lost in a haze of bluish mountain and water. In that part of the country only the peaks of the mountains were sharply defined, so that everything below them was fused into an unearthly Fata Morgana in the land of Orplid. There lay Tumbez, the city itself.

Only when we were thus face to face with our goal did I come to the full realization of the boldness of our undertaking. I felt that the mysterious compulsion of our purpose matched the sublimity of this New World. I should have liked to stretch out my arms as an eagle strains out its wings. My heart hammered against my ribs. It was as if I had drunk a magic potion distilled of mountain air, clear sea water and virgin foliage, a potion that smelled bitter, like the guano high on the cliffs, like the sun-drenched rock of the canyons.

And so we all stood on the high dunes and looked off toward the South Country. I thought of the dying Moses, and how by the grace of God he was permitted a glimpse of the promised land. I turned to Diego de Vargas, who stood behind me, his cheeks sunken, his eyes burning with fever, the skin a dirty, unhealthy yellow through his rags. "How strange, Diego!"

He smiled his habitually ironic smile and said nothing.

I walked far along to the head of the line where Don Francisco Pizarro was standing, and saw that three Indians had come up the dunes to meet us. They wore long, gaily decorated robes, into which were worked the figures of birds with human faces. I particularly remember this because the ornaments reminded me of harpies or sphinxes. I remember, too, how much I was struck by the dark mystery, the greed and cold calculation in these aboriginal features. For, be it understood, no one should make the mistake of thinking that the Indians are childlike and trusting people. They are superior to us Spaniards, if anything, in cunning and scheming. Better than we they know how to conceal their intentions, to hide behind the wooden mask and the monosyllabic utterance. Their natural stoicism gives them a distinct advantage in matters of guile.

These Indians had very dark copper skins. Their faces were framed by long, coarse straight hair, blue-black. About their necks they wore strings of mussel shells. What they were discussing must have been of great importance. For the Spanish leaders stood looking at them open-mouthed. Only our interpreter Felipillo could make out the sense of their words, and he was deeply moved by what he heard as anyone could plainly see. He interrupted them with sharp cries. Sometimes he spoke as if he were about to burst forth in tears. More than once our Captain-General had to prod him to bring over the conversation into Spanish so that all could catch the drift of what was going on.

Gradually we were able to piece together a mosaic out of the wild cries and jumbled gutturals. These three Indians, we discovered, were inhabitants of a big island named Puná, which lay at our very feet in the bay. They told Felipillo, scowling evilly, that for years they had been waging war against the Kingdom of the Four Corners of the Earth, especially with the city of Tumbez, at the northernmost periphery of which their sphere of power began. They had their own customs, their own sea-gods, they told us, and they had no intention of submitting to the dictates of the children of the sun.

They told us at great length about two Indian kingdoms which long ago had risen up on the coast of the South Sea only to come at last under the yoke of the children of the sun. These conversations lasted for hours. The Indians seemed to be tireless in their forensic zeal. On and on they chattered and grunted, and we unable to understand a word, except through the sweating Felipillo. At last the Captain-General, unable to stand any longer, sat down on the sand, and both we and the Indians followed suit, making a circle with the indispensable Felipillo in the middle.

We finally learned this from the Indians of Puná: Through their spies and couriers in the mountains they knew there was a war being waged between the two descendants of the Inca Huayna Capac. This Inca Huayna Capac had been the mightiest of them all. He had turned northward from the navel of the world, and had conquered the great kingdom of Quito, that lies among the high mountains. (When they told us this, the Indians of Puná pointed in a northeasterly direction).

It was a custom among the Inca race that each new Inca should add to the kingdom. Now they ruled the world to the very limits of the earth. (At this point we had to smile at the Indians' ignorance, and Don Pedro de Candía became very angry, for he considered such opinions to be an insult to our Christian Majesty Don Carlos. However, Don Francisco nodded at him, bidding him hold his peace and let the Indians continue with their story). It seems that the son of Huayna Capac, and his rightful heir, was called Huáscar. Huáscar was a mild man more loved than feared by his subjects. This Inca, Huáscar, had a brother called Atahualpa, whose mien caused the blood to run cold. Atahualpa was wild, cruel, warlike, and given to fits of anger, as could be seen in his bloodshot eyes. When Huayna Capac had conquered the kingdom of Quito, he had taken the daughter of the king as his second wife. Whether he really loved this girl from the first, or whether he professed to in order to control that much the better the new kingdom, no one could say. But it was well-known that his last years were spent mostly in Quito, and that he always kept this second wife by his side. It might well be supposed that the wild, stubborn, precipitate manner of this woman from the race of mountain kings pleased him more than the gentleness of his first wife, who was his own sister and some years older than himself. His doting had known no bounds when the girl from Quito bore him a son, this Atahualpa.

It had seemed to him that Atahualpa was more his son than the legal heir to the crown, Huáscar. For even as a child Atahualpa had been skillful in the hunt, and was most at home among the soldiers and officers of the royal army. The mild Huáscar, on the other hand, preferred to linger in the gardens of Cuzco, to look at the goldsmiths at work, and above all liked the company of women. When Huayna Capac felt death drawing near he began to suffer from great anxiety over the future of his realm. He felt that it was much too large to place in Huáscar's tender hands.

Besides he had also heard that the true children of the sun—the Indians pointed at us as they told us this—had landed on the shores of the South Sea. He had learned about the fearful animals, which carried the children of the sun into battle, and he had heard of the hard silver which covered the newcomers' bodies, making them impervious to lance and arrow thrust.

All this had given him profound concern, a concern fortified by a tale current among the Inca people that some day a great host of children of the sun would appear on the shores of the South Sea. Then the kingdom of the Incas would come to a sudden end.

So Huayna Capac had divided up the kingdom between his two sons, the rightful heir, Huáscar, and Atahualpa, the son of his best-loved wife. It was his desire that the attributes of the two half-brothers should combine and complement each other, that together they would amount to what he himself had been during his reign. He gave the kingdom of Quito to his son Atahualpa, and the old kingdom and capital to his first son, Huáscar. After this he had died and his body was taken to the navel of the world, far over the mountain passes, through snowstorms and hot sun. There in the temple he now sat on a golden stool among his ancestors, male and female. But his spirit was with the sun, the origin of his race.

The story, of course, was by no means as fluent as I have written it down here. Many times Felipillo, struggling to bring the Indian ideas over into a strange tongue, would mass whole rows of substantives together. Then he would curse and shout in his own Indian language, and get tied into a hopeless knot and it took some time for the sense of the discourse to emerge.

It was atop this dune, then, that we first learned about the kingdom of the Incas. As I looked over toward the mountains, which had become a stone reality instead of the dream compounded of light, tender color, horizon blur and drifting cloud that they had been before, it occurred to me that it was strange and moving that here in this weird fairyland—for I had always regarded the Indies as such—the relations among men should be much the same as at home in Spain. For this story of the two brothers, the mild and the bold, is nothing else but the story of Jacob and Esau, and is as old as mankind itself. Too, the love of the aging king for a strange girl who made his blood run hot in his veins once again—this common delusion that bright September days promise another summer—and the inevitable falling away from the oldest son, whose years are an index of his own, all this can be discovered without rummaging about in old chronicles. It can be observed anywhere, among peasants and among kings.

And it was not the events in themselves which moved me so much, but the fact that the Indians were just men like ourselves, however much their strange speech, clothes, the necklaces of mussels, the straight, blue-black hair, the dark-red, stony faces might distort the similarity at first sight. Their strangeness seemed to arise particularly out of their language. This language had something in it of the sharp salt smell investing the bay and islands, a quality of harsh difference. It was natural to speak of sea-gods, children of the sun and pyramids in this tongue, and to have gods mingle in the affairs of men as casually as crossing the road.

Atahualpa—the very name attracted me from the start. It was partly the sound of the word, which was pronounced something like At-a-ba-li-pa. This sonorous, broad tone recalled the resounding names of the kings of Persia and Assyria which as a boy I had often secretly used as magic words. As a child I had thought that this richness of sound must mean gigantic kingdoms, populous cities, immense columned palaces and temples, and hosts of warriors thundering over a dusty plain. Any man whom the Indians called Atabalipa must certainly be a great man,

I thought to myself, especially when the Indians themselves uttered the name with patent awe, their eyes alight.

But it was not only the name's sound, the face of the name, which attracted me to Atahualpa. It was something else, something that later on was to have a powerful influence on my life. The name and the early life of this Atabalipa recalled the life of a Roman emperor to whom I had always secretly been attracted. The emperor's marble bust stood in the outer hallway of Don Garcilaso's house in Cordova. It showed the face and finely formed neck and upper breast of a beautiful young man. His hair, unlike the hair of most Romans, was smooth and straight. It fell down over the forehead, making a line above the proud eyes. The cheeks were oval in shape under high cheekbones. This was a youth from the family of Julius, named by the soldiers Caligula, or the "little boot," for already as a child he went about in small imitations of the boots of the legionaries, and was very much at home in their tents.

Most people let out a cry of horror at the mere mention of the name Caligula, for the old court gossip Suetonius has told the most horrible tales about the boy. All these rumors and lies—though no doubt they did contain a modicum of truth—were recounted to me by Master Agrippa, who strenuously advised me to take up my time with the heroes of Plutarch and Cornelius Nepos. But I could not lose the childish fascination this dubious hero had for me.

Now Atahualpa was for me an Indian Caligula, the reincarnation of a childhood memory. It is almost incredible how such memories out of a man's youth, things sunk far out of sight—the shimmer of light on a marble cheek, the odor of a blooming bush, the morning call of a bird, the smell of the earth after a storm—color our adult sympathies. It is almost as if we pick and choose among the objects of a newly discovered world just those which will lead us back into the world of our youth.

But I must return once again to that stream of occurrences which, like an impetuous mountain brook swollen in the spring, carried me to the real Atahualpa, to the greatest triumph—and perhaps to the greatest humiliation—of my life.

The Indians of Puná went on with their story. There was peace in the kingdom of Quito and in the kingdom of the Four Corners of the World for nearly five years. But then the two brothers quarreled. The immediate cause for the differences was a dispute over who should rule the city of Toumebamba. Both brothers claimed this right, neither would give way. Huáscar said that it was the apple of his father's eye, and since he was his father's first son, it should come under his control. Atahualpa said that it was part of the old kingdom of Quito. But the real reason for the war was the fact that the two kingdoms and the two brothers could not live independently of each other since the Incas from time immemorial, as children of the sun, had claimed dominance over the whole world. To each of the brothers it seemed impossible that another equally important kingdom should exist removed from his will, just as impossible as that there should be two suns in the sky.

Although Huáscar, as described before, was a mild and peace-loving man, nevertheless the power of ancient belief was so great that it forced him into conflict with his brother. As far as Atahualpa was concerned, his spirit was so warlike, and the blood of the rude mountain people ran so strongly in his veins, that it was unthinkable he should ever live as a vassal of his weaker brother. Beyond that he hated Huáscar for having had the irreparable good fortune to be born first.

Unfortunately he was abetted in these hatreds by his chieftains, the men of the army, who promised their master an extension of his power, a rise in rank and greater possessions. Their greedy eyes swept downward toward golden Cuzco, the navel of the world. And, too, they thirsted for revenge on the proud nobles of the Inca house, the so-called lop-ears. They wanted retribution for the humiliations visited on them by the great Huayna Capac. Atahualpa they did not consider to be a true branch of the Inca tree, but rather a rightful heir and scion of the old kings of Quito, which he was indeed from his mother's side.

And so it was that the great Huayna Capac had begot a being who was destined to undo his great accomplishments, to destroy his carefully realized handiwork. Atahualpa struck down the armies of his brother Huáscar, on the plain of Ambato, which lies three days' journey to the south of the city of Quito. It is notable that Huáscar did not personally take part in the fighting, but passed the time while death was being sown among his men in the gardens of Cuzco, dallying with women and picking all manner of flowers; whereas Atahualpa, covered with dust and heavily armored, fought bitterly in the front ranks of his hosts who spilled down over the land like a mountain torrent, killing everything in their path. They overran the Gañari land, killed all the able-bodied men, and did in fact not even spare women, children or old men. The women of the city of Toumebamba in vain came out bearing green branches as a token of conciliation. They were done away with, and the city was burned level with the ground. Some thought that the great sun-god had gone over to the side of the enemy, shamed at having such an unworthy protagonist as Huáscar.

Atahualpa's army pressed on down to the coast. The men of Puná took counsel and determined to resist them. The shell horns were blown, a tattoo was played on the drum of Pachacamac, and as Atahualpa's warriors moved toward the isle on rafts, they were met with a hail of spears and poisoned arrows. The battle was terrible. The cries of the wounded, the shrieks of the drowning, echoed across the bay. The echo came back from the mountain, and the men of Puná saw that the sea-god was on their side. His surf-voice came back from the iron cliffs, and heartened them.

When evening came the children of the sea-god, thousands and tens of thousands of scythe-winged sea birds, descended, so that the twilight was shattered by a tumult of wings and of harsh screamings. The sea birds shot down upon the milling corpses, upon the riven carcasses stranded mid the shale, and with cruel bills picked out the eyes of the dead, leaving bony hollows, picking clean the flesh from the rosy bones. This pleased the men of Puná, this demonstration of godly concern. Therefore, they built smoky bonfires, and to their ally, the deity of Puná, they sacrificed as burnt offerings the most notable prisoners.

On hearing these words, our Dominican showed signs of uneasiness, and Father Vicente plucked forth his crucifix and loudly began to pray. The Indians watched the kneeling clerics with earnest impassive faces. I later learned that the Indians considered Father Vicente weak-minded, and learned, too, that they believed such people enjoyed the special solicitude of the gods. But Don Francisco nodded impatiently at Felipillo, annoyed that the Dominicans had interrupted the narrative.

By next morning, the Indians went on to say, Atahualpa's hosts had disappeared, going on to the city of Tumbez where Atahualpa was welcomed as master. But the people of Puná had no love either for Huáscar or for Atahualpa. They did not want to carry the lop-ears about their island in palanquins, nor did they want to be told when they should marry, when they should have feasts, when they should creep next their wives in bed. There was one thing that the men of Puná knew better than the haughty children of the sun-god. They knew that Atahualpa would take grim revenge upon them, once he had succeeded in annihilating his brother Huáscar. They feared that once his passion was consummated, he would drive them out of the bay, out of the sea, and up into the stony, barren mountains. For such was the custom of the Incas in dealing with rebellious folk—to transplant them from their homeland and set them down amid bitterly unfamiliar surroundings.

The men of Puná knew nothing about hewing terraces from the mighty steeps, nor did they know how to care for little gardens. They knew nothing about raising llamas, protecting their young from the condor's swoop. They hated the glittering snow, the blue ice, the breathless air, and they feared the tumbling masses of stone which crash thunderously into the resounding valleys.

They loved, the men of Puná, the heavy, salt sea air, they loved the monotonous sound of the surf, and in their reed huts, they loved to gorge on feast days on the flesh of fish and sea-birds' eggs. When they planted their corn, their tobacco and cotton, they merely had to scratch furrows in the earth and throw in the seed. The first task was performed by the women, and the latter by the men. For the earth would be insulted if the men of Puná did otherwise, and the women of Puná would be barren.

In the spring of the year, the priests would walk over the fields of Puná, walk to the shore and pray to the sea-god. When this was done, the sea-god would send forth thick fogs and command great rains to come down so that the sprouts would be protected from the envious gaze of the sun-god. But up there in the mountains only with infinite labor could the soil be brought together in handfuls and taken to the terraces that had been hewn from the living rock. Up there on the heights, where it scarcely ever rained, all living things would have to be carefully tended, and their thirst assiduously quenched with water carried in huge jugs of clay. Over and over again the sun-god would have to be propitiated, for in one day, should the wind sweep down from the snowy peaks, a whole summer's struggle could come to naught.

But what dismayed the men of Puná most was that from this harsh toil they would not gain as much as a solitary jot. All the corn that they would harvest, all the wool that they sheared from the llama's back, all the fish caught in their nets, all the vicuñas that they slew, all the yams that they prized from the earth would not belong to them in the smallest fraction, but would be heaped together in the storehouses of the Incas to be used only according to their reluctant disposition. It is true that from these stores they would receive enough to preserve the spark of life within their frames. And yet the most of this arduously cultivated provender would be eaten up by the countless warriors, the workers in the mines, the builders of fortresses, palaces, temples and streets, by the lop-ears and the daughters of the sun.

And now the men of Puná stood ready to defend their island, even to make forays against the city of Tumbez on the mainland. They did not want to render up their sons to the Inca, to have them thirst to death on the salt deserts of Chile, to be impressed into battle against the wild folk of the distant forests far across the mountains, to have their heads lopped off, cured, and hung up to blacken in the smoke of nameless huts. They did not want their sons and their sons' sons to grub forever beneath the earth, groping in darkness, crouched in cramped tunnels, for the silver by which the Incas set such greedy store. They did not want their daughters to be carried off among strangers, to take strangers for husbands, to bc taken off to the houses of the sun, their bodies there to be used at the idle dictates of the Inca.

The Indians now reminded us that we were the true children of the sun, that our skins were much whiter even than the Incas, and that some of us had hair—they now pointed to me and to Frenero—which was far lighter than anything ever seen in the memory of man. With this in mind, and in consideration of the evil fortunes threatening them, they invited the wise chieftain—here they pointed to Don Francisco Pizarro—to unite with them against Atahualpa, to come as guests to their island, bringing along all the magic animals and the thunder weapons. They told Pizarro that they had heard of his exploits in Coaque and knew that even the great Huayna Capac at that time had feared him.

"Come, be our friends," they said, "for the period of the great rains is about to commence. With us you will have maize, you will have sweet potatoes, fine mussels and fish, you will have game, fowl, and eggs, cool water and liquorous drinks, and you can live in our dwellings just as if they were your own, restoring yourself after the vicissitudes of the long march and the countless deeds of valor, countless as the hairs"—here they pointed a finger at Don Francisco Pizarro—"of your graying head. Then, as soon as the rains are over, when the storms have blown themselves out, when Pachacamac has returned home to the bottom of the sea, then we will blast a martial trumpet call on our conches, and tens of thousands of warriors of Puná will assemble on the strand in order to await the word of command from the great leader, the glad word to follow him to the city of Tumbez, that haughty citadel, to raze, to plunder, to erase it from the face of the earth."

Hearing this proposal, our Captain-General leaped to his feet. His eyes glittered with eagerness. With difficulty he controlled his pleasure, ceremoniously turned to the three Indians, then to Felipillo, and made this speech:

"Men of Puná, in the name of my master and my King Don Carlos, to whom all peoples are subject, I accept your invitation to come to your island as a guest. But it must be understood that we have come to this country not as the enemy of that king whom you call the Inca, Atahualpa. We have not come here to destroy cities. Rather we have come here to collect fitting tribute for his Most Catholic Majesty, and to instruct the ruler of the land and his subjects in the beneficent truths of Christianity.

"But if this great Inca kingdom is as you say divided against itself, that is something we cannot tolerate. We shall summon both kings, Atahualpa and Huáscar, to appear before us to have their differences properly adjudicated in the name of the Lord God. We shall send them back into their rightfully inherited kingdoms, to carry out the will of the dead king Huayna Capac who, in our opinion, was a wise man. For it is plain that the whole kingdom is much too large to be ruled by one vassal."

The Indians showed signs of discomfiture as Felipillo gradually translated the Captain-General's words. They whispered together, smiled slyly and professed to read an ulterior sense into the flowery language.

Their smiles irritated our Felipillo very much, and once again he began to hop about in excitement, making no attempt to conceal his hatred of the men of Puná. "I warn you, Don Francisco," he cried, "I warn you these Indians will betray you! They never keep their word. I can see that they've got their eyes on our horses and arms. I've known these Puná people for a long time. They killed my father. They'll kill you and all your men while you're asleep!"

This outburst had an odd effect. It was almost as if the Indians understood Spanish. Hatred gleamed in their eyes as they looked at Felipillo. They laughed aloud at him which put Felipillo in a worse temper and finally reduced him to a state of trembling frustration.

With gestures of disgust the Captain-General commanded Felipillo to silence, and himself took up the conversation in sign language. He made no mistake about letting the Indians know where they stood in Felipillo's estimation. The Indians were taken aback at this and made a great show of pointing to heaven, earth and sea, in attestation of their integrity.

We were inclined to believe the Indians. But Felipillo, turning directly to us, cried out like a stricken animal, "Look out! Look out! They'll cut the towlines. You will all drown in the sea. And they will burn me alive as they burned my father."

We paid no more attention to his whining. Soon afterward, moved along by many red men paddling in time to monotonous songs, there came several rafts from the wooded shores of the island. Our Captain-General arranged it so that only two rafts at a time were utilized. Because of this, no more than a small fraction of our total company was on the water at one time, while the rest of us stayed on the mainland or on the island shore.

My people and I were the first to embark. The sudden night of Birú was ready to fall by the time we had reached the middle of the waters. The mountain peaks were aflame, great torches shining out over the mainland, over the darkling mirror of the bay. Our little craft crept slowly on. The feeling of uneasiness which had always troubled me in this new world grew stronger than ever before. Looking shoreward I fancied that with the eventide the rose-flecked mountains huddled together like a flock of sheep before the shepherd's crook. To my eyes the landscape appeared to grow smaller, or rather to crowd nearer to me, and the immense bastions, sheer sable heights, began to topple seaward. And yet, the universe other than this now vertical surface, the world above and behind the wall of rock, took on an infinitely increased depth, valley beyond valley, violet and purple, golden interstices, flakes of light, and a calm infinity above. The sea beneath me, so I felt, for my eye could not penetrate the surface, had grown bottomless, the roar of the surf was louder, and the Indians' cries more solitary.

Then there was the stillness of Birú, the void in the heart. This stillness infected the great curtain of the dark mountain, and it rang louder than the surf. The lowered voices of the Indians, the softly groaning timbers of our raft, the splashing of a water bird's wing as it flicked the glassy water—all these night sounds deepened the unutterable loneliness of the world.

17

PUNA AND TUMBEZ

NIGHT had fallen by the time we disembarked. Our Indian guides led us up through the forest. Even though our way was lighted only by torches, it was easy to see that this wood was quite different from the swampy jungles of the mainland in which we had so grievously suffered. There was a complete absence of undergrowth and the clutching lianas which had so tediously impeded our progress. The trees appeared to be giant cedars such as those the Scriptures describe in the mountains of Lebanon. Their trunks were as thick through as watchtowers, their branches festooned with moss, and the clear ground was heavily carpeted with needles. Through the splotches of foliage brushed outward against the sky, we could discern an occasional twinkling star, and the air was keen with the bitter smell of resin.

It was like riding over a great soft carpet, soft enough to muffle the footsteps of infidels in their mosques. To me it seemed that I was moving through some sacred grove, through a greater mosque than the one in Cordova, through a forest of columns which God himself had privately chosen for His retreat. Strewn about in this wood lay large blocks of stone, strangely formed. They looked like dwarfs carrying humped burdens, like limping giants, like ships turned to stone, like dragons; in some places these stones leaned against each other as if carrying on a whispered conversation like so many petrified monks in heavy cowls, like so many whispering witch-women, in grossly disordered dress.

It dawned on me that these woods were enchanted, exactly like the woods through which knights of old once rode. I expected any time to hear magic voices ringing and mocking in the night. And so, I was not at all surprised to hear later on that this was a grove of the great daemon Pachacamac. Here he tarried when he rose up out of the sea, and, on occasion, assumed the face of a night bird. In the daylight, however, the Indian legend had it, he looked just like any other simple old man who laughed long and merrily when an Indian spoke to him, and no one would have been aware of the deception did he not suddenly vanish while the sea wind moaned in the branches of the cedars, betraying the passage of Pachacamac, ruler of the waters and of the dead. When this happened to an Indian, he would run home as fast as his legs could carry him, lie down, and fast for three days, for it is not good for men to have intercourse even with beneficent daemons, since their moods are incalculable. Today they will overwhelm a favored person with their blessings; tomorrow they will cut his throat.

When we came out of this wood, which our guides led us through as rapidly as possible, there before us stretched out the Indians' fields, and beyond were the many reed-covered houses of a large village. In all the squares and alleyways of this village, the Indians had lashed torches to poles, and at first I had the false impression that the village was afire. The entire population was out to greet us, all of them chattering, shrieking and singing together. Hundreds of half-grown boys and girls ran toward us bearing green boughs in their hands, but when they got a good look at me they were seized with terror, flung themselves flat on their faces as if struck by lightning, and later rose to their knees holding out the palms of their hands in obeisance. Among the crowd there were many women with large eyes. Most of them seemed to have impassive little sucklings strapped to their backs. Some of these women snatched forth their infants and held them, quietly dribbling, to my face as if I were a cannibal.

I could not fathom this novel behavior and the tumultuous welcome confused me. To make matters worse, my great piebald cared as little for the general clamor as I myself and whinnying madly, he reared up on his hind legs, his nostrils fluttering, his forepaws flashing. When this happened, the crowd melted away with a concerted shriek of horror, and the younger Punás swiftly clambered into the trees like monkeys. And, as usual, my Frenero had to endure the most alarming advances, for the Indians, like wild things, would suddenly rush up to him and with squeals of amazement, touch his red hair, his fiery beard and his pitted face. When I took off my helmet and they saw my blond hair, the

Indian women rushed to surround me like flies around a bull on a hot summer's day.

It soon turned out that the Puná Indians' invitation was a blessing to us, an instance of God's grace, as Father Juan so aptly phrased it. For we had been no more than three days on the island when the rains began to fall, rains the like of which I had never seen. I must confess there were times when I was gripped by the fear that another Deluge had commenced. The little alleys of the village became muddy brooks, and day in and all the night through, the rain drummed ceaselessly on the wattled huts in which we had found refuge. A man had but to step outdoors and he was soaked to his skin. Behind these gray sheets of rain the mountains in the mainland were hidden, and only by straining could one make out the shapes of the near-by cedars. In the night, the wind blew, and the great sanctuary of Pachacamac was alive with sound, a deep soughing, a crashing of torn limbs, an endless moaning. The Indians said that it was only the daemon of Pachacamac hard at work germinating their corn, but it was notable that they never left their huts and carefully avoided even looking toward the woods. They had no desire to confront their deity, however much they might profess belief in his good will.

I often wondered how it would have been with us had we been trapped in the swamps during this rainy season, for it seemed as if every tiny rivulet which we had bridged with a single leap must surely by now be a mighty river, and every river a sea. Merely to imagine our company freezing and soaked to the marrow, our bellies flush against our backbones, increased by contemporary sense of comfort to such a degree that our wattled abode had greater charms than any palace of Castile.

Hours on end, whole afternoons, I sat at the entrance to our hut and looked out over our streaming roofs, the gullied fields, while the rushing, the prattling, the gusty sighing, and the liquid gulpings of the rain merged into a sweet music that evoked within my young head the gayest dreams, wrapping me in fancy. With my legs stretched out full-length before me, with my head leaned up against the doorpost, I fell into a relaxing slumber, while on and on and on the rain thrummed, steeping body and soul in tender melodies.

As the weeks wore on, I began to notice that a tense expectation hung over the woods, the dunes, over the barren cliffs, which moved inexorably to fulfillment. Like a persistent lover, a lover often disillusioned and half despairing, the earth awaited the coming of Pachacamac. Now he had risen up out of the endless sea, had come through the wild foam of the surf on the wings of the salt sea wind to hover over the land. His fertile waters fell without halt, soaking into the very womb of the earth, nourishing the mysterious shoots. Lying there in the Puná hut—it must involve some risk of displeasing our Lord Jesus Christ to say this—I thought of how great a god was the daemon, Pachacamac, how much closer he was to the earth, and how much mightier than the saints and angels of our creed. They lurk in the brightly colored cathedral windows, softly smiling; they are like gentle women within the safe walls of their palaces, like women gesturing among themselves behind high walls. They know nothing about mingling without a single qualm in the brutal, windswept, tormented scenes of creation like the god Pachacamac, intent on balancing the eternal scales of the seasons in the far South Country.

To our sorrow we soon had an opportunity to feel the power of Pachacamac, an experience that cost many lives in our company and all but put an end to our expedition. While we had gladly accepted the chance to sit around doing nothing, the Dominicans had busily set about collecting souls. Not a day passed but that a gang of Punás underwent coercive baptism, a ritual which at the beginning they greatly fancied. They liked exceedingly to be given new names such as Carlos, Miguel, or Felipe, leaving the barbaric epithet behind them as a larva leaves behind its dessicated shell upon emerging, so to speak, as a butterfly. Carefully they listened to the sacred parables and were enthralled by the wonders and the mysteries which they were now for the first time hearing. But in spite of this attention, the Dominicans to their disgust soon learned that the Indians had not the slightest desire to disown Pachacamac. In almost every other utterance they speculated about how many men from the city of Tumbez they would soon sacrifice to the horrible daemon.

In short and in sum, for them our Lord Jesus Christ was but another daemon. In cold fact, they compared our tender Shepherd with a certain magic entity, Pachacamac's son, whom they call Coniraya Viracocha. Coniraya Viracocha, they said, had once come to the earth clothed in rags, had seduced many pretty maidens, and had distinguished himself in the most flagrant fashion by his thrilling on the flute and other multiple stupidities.

When Father Vicente heard this he burst out in tears and begged our Captain-General to burn the authors of such tales at the stake as an example to the other Indians of the superior urgency of our credo. But Don Francisco refused him this concession because, as he said, he did not feel his forces to be quite numerous enough to risk such active reproof, and begged the good Dominican to have a grain of patience. Furthermore, at first he gave express orders not to disturb the sacred grove of Pachacamac. These orders he subsequently countermanded.

So far as the holy objects within this grove went, they were only a row of old stones. Sad to relate, even when we tried, it was impossible to throw these monuments of the Devil to the ground. Even when we hitched our horses to them, the leather traces broke like woolen threads, and the fervent prayers of the Dominicans helped not at all. For the stones continued to stand, their calm, immovable stony selves. In the end, I remember, we had to satisfy ourselves with the construction of a massive wooden cross. This, we hoped, would turn Pachacamac's taste for this particular spot sour as bile within his pagan gullet. For daemons, as we Spaniards know, will have little truck with the cross, which always reminds them of their deepest humiliation: namely, our Lord's descent into Hell to pluck souls from their very hands.

This cross proved to be the drop which caused the bucket to overflow. For some time past the Indians had become pretty much fed up with our Christian extravagances. They had various grounds. The main cause for their disaffection was that several of the company, among them my carrot-topped Frenero, had tampered freely with the Puná womenfolk, who were considered by the masculine elements to be the oxen and mules of the agricultural activity. Very naturally they did not fancy seeing their beasts of burden incapacitated during the time of sowing, so soon to come.

To us Spaniards all this was ridiculous. But, be that as it may, the Puná believed that work and pleasure both should be carefully divided among the sexes, with the men getting the lion's share of the latter, and a man of Puná would as soon think of working in the fields as a Spaniard would of snatching off his shift and sitting in the middle of a spider's web. On the other hand, the women do not hunt and fish; indeed, if they as much as see a fish-spear, or a balsa, or a raft of reeds, with sudden modesty they squeeze their eyes far tighter than a dead pig's. This modesty by no means extends to their relations with the owners of these spears, balsas and rafts. As Diego observed, they dote on copulation as much as any bag-bellied trull who ever scratched her buttocks against the city wall of Cordova. In this carnal respect they offered no resistance to Spanish advances. In fact, they threw themselves upon us. In these men this spectacle seemed only to prick that vanity which the Puná possesses in full measure, and which, no doubt, nourishes the seeds of jealousy.

Another ground for Indian dissatisfaction was the fact that the provisioning of so many strangers imposed a heavy burden on the Indians. Actually, they had only as much as they needed for themselves, and were as content with this imprudent arrangement as wild animals. At certain times, I noted, they stuff themselves even though they know full well that before another harvest comes they must in consequence go hungry.

And beyond all this it must be admitted that many Spaniards were intolerably overbearing toward the Indians. But it was the cross, thrust within their sacred grove, that was the sore point. After its erection the Indians went about with menacing faces, and their chiefs avoided us with ominous care. The priests and magicians dedicated to the daemon did their best to nag their charges on to reprisal.

One day, out of the blue, there appeared in the village a number of men from the city of Tumbez. No sooner did they see us than they rushed to place themselves under our protection. The men of Puná were beside themselves with excitement. On the spot they wanted to dispatch these emissaries from the enemy's stronghold. The men of Tumbez dissembled, saying that they were not inimically disposed to Spaniards, and that their master Atahualpa was extending his most cordial greetings. He was most curious, they said, to have a first-hand glimpse of the white men, to ask questions of those people about whom his father Huayna Capac had so often discoursed in his venerable lifetime. Our Captain-General kept these plenipotentiaries under his wing, much to the displeasure of the Puná.

One evening, Felipillo, our interpreter, rushed up as we sat in council with the Captain-General. The whole situation and the relation between Puná and Tumbez was of necessity the subject of ticklish consideration, for we scarcely wished to confound our ultimate purpose by untoward partisanship in Indian trivialities. We certainly did not want to flout the proffers of amity from the mighty king and Inca, Atahualpa, who was by no means as ill-disposed to us as we had imagined. In any event into the midst of our council of state Felipillo brought the news that twelve Puná chieftains were meeting near-by the sacred stones of Pachacamac in order to lay plans for ambushing both the Spaniards and the men of Tumbez so that our irksome presence might be expunged once and for all.

Scarcely had we received these advices than the Captain-General gave the order, To horse, and we galloped full tilt to the sacred grove. We succeeded in cornering ten of these chieftains, only two managing to get away. To our brisk questioning they said that they were concerned only with the problem of adding to their depleted store of food by going on a fishing expedition. It had never occurred to them to betray us, they said. It was hard to believe these representations, for we saw at once that our cross had disappeared. Actually they had taken the cross and thrown it into the sea. A careful search revealed no sign of its whereabouts. There was not one among us who believed that the wind had been strong enough to bear such a heavy object some score yards through the air. When chieftains lie about these matters, we argued, it seemed probable they were lying also about their intention to ambush us.

And yet, in spite of the weight of adverse circumstancial evidence, the Captain-General hesitated to pass final judgment. Finally it was his brother, the handsome Don Gonzalo, who conceived of a Solomonian decision. He suggested that the chieftains be given over to the judgment of the men of Tumbez. Their traditional enmity would guarantee insight into the evils which we suspected lay behind their protestations of innocence. If this enmity could find no fault then undoubtedly the chieftains were not guilty, Don Gonzalo reasoned.

Don Francisco stood there weighing the juristic advice. There is no question that it was a moment of great decision. The rain had ceased, but across the sky there still sailed tearful dark clouds, now and then dissolving into tatters through which we could see the full moon looking down upon us with cyclopean candor. Like great black and silver spirit hands, light and shadow sped over the choppy sea, over the dun stone monuments, over the crowns of the high cedars whose branches moaned softly, whispering in mysterious anguish. The shadows moved over the faces of the men, over the defiant faces of the chieftains, sitting bound, over the gleaming faces of the men of Tumbez. The ominous light glittered on our armor, caught palely on the bossed hilts of our swords, and our faces were lost beneath the ponderous casques which we wore.

Don Francisco nodded gently. For a moment he moved into the light and I saw a cruel smile flit across his visage. This little incident sent chills down my spine. In my state of tension it seemed as if the light had but awaited the nod of Pizarro's head to appear, and at his bidding immediately fled in order to conceal the violent purpose which now possessed him.

My reverie was broken when Felipillo with a cry of joy flung himself at Pizarro's feet and covered his hands with kisses. Pizarro drew haughtily back from him. Pizarro's bemused nod had evoked this this primitive gesture.

Better than we the men of Tumbez understood Pizarro's smile. They fell on the Puná, cut their throats with copper knives, smashed their heads between two stones, as we Spaniards crack a nut. The groans of the dying mingled with shouts of joy. All this happened with such speed that I stood there leaden-footed, crippled by horror. The natives were not satisfied merely to kill their enemies. They swarmed over the corpses, striking them, hacking them to bleeding bits. At last they made to carve open the Puná's breasts in order, exactly as Cortés had told, to pluck forth the steaming heart, and would have done this had Don Pedro de Candía not called a halt by flailing them with the flat of his sword, upon which they dispersed howling, like a pack of dogs. Don Pedro told me later that the sight of much blood might have so completely robbed them of their senses that they would turn on us.

Felipillo continued to kneel before Pizarro muttering over and over again *"Muchas gracias, excelencia."* But Pizarro, impatient, balled his fist and struck the kneeling Indian square on the mouth, and said no more. Immediately afterward Pizarro wheeled about and still not uttering a word left the place, we behind, following in silence.

At first Pizarro rode along slowly through the night of moonlight and shadow. Then he came to a dead stop, stood up in his stirrups, turned around and shouted at us, "Forward!" Like hunters we gave our horses their heads and pounded away at such a mad clip, it was a wonder that none of us was thrown. We rode as if the Devil himself were at our heels. Gobbets of foam from Pizarro's horse struck me in the mouth, and I tasted their bitterness. The hoofs of my horse dug up the mossy clots of earth as he pounded along, belly to the ground, a neck's length behind Don Pizarro's mount. Both our horses ran like those magic steeds which, so they say, the Devil rides at night with the speed of thought over the countryside. Pizarro and I soon left our companions behind. The uncertain light shone on the reed roofs when we heard someone blowing a great horn which sounded like a wounded bull, a monster Minotaur. And as background to this ghastly trumpeting there was a hollow roll of drums, faster and faster.

A few moments later and it seemed that all was lost. We were surrounded by dark-bodied Indians. They wore feathers in their hair, their faces were painted red and yellow, blood-red, and as yellow as the moon. In a fearful sustained descant they howled at us. The doors of Hell had opened and a thousand demons had spewed out into the night. Here and there among them was some Spaniard from our company, bewildered by the sudden onrush.

An arrow broke against my breastplate, its stone point shattered. In the midst of this wild confusion I brought my horse to such a precipitous halt that he reared back and sat on his hindquarters, snorting and raging at the bit. I drew forth my father's sword, cut down at a shadowy feathered head.

Frenero appeared beside me out of nowhere. He laughed foolishly, a free, easy laugh. I remember thinking in a flash how strange it was that anyone could laugh in such circumstances, amid the howlings, drum beats and blasts on the great shell horn. But my Frenero was one of those men who will be unable to suppress a delighted laugh on the Day of Judgment. So long as something was going on, he was pleased.

Frenero, as usual, had his drum slung over his shoulder. In derision and defiance he began to play on it, a mighty, clear roll powerful enough to shatter one's ears. Its exciting, blood-curdling clarity was in great contrast to the choked sound of the wooden Indian drums.

On hearing the challenge of the drum more and more Spaniards wormed their way, ripping this way and that, to my side. I saw Juan the thin, vainly trying to blow his little hunting horn, which he could not do, so breathless was he. Diego de Vargas suddenly stood near me, his eyes turning in his head with lunatic delight. I saw Bernal, the one-eyed Bernal, pick up a dead Indian, throw him onto his shoulder, look around calmly and then heave the body into a knot of grimacing Puná, tumbling them to the ground. Sancho appeared last, dragging the little ass Pia with him. The animal was screaming with pain, for an arrow had struck deep into her gray flank. Only Alonso the splendid was missing. His brother Juan shouted for him, shouted and shouted again. But it was obviously impossible to attract his attention in such a terrific clamor.

And then, as suddenly as they had broken loose, the Indians disappeared, simply melted into the night. The horns fell silent, and the wooden drums. We Spaniards were left alone. Don Francisco made good use of this unexpected respite to assemble his men in a long line. Holding their lances forward, pressed shoulder to shoulder, they turned their faces toward the entrance to the village. It was at this point that the Puná would fall on us, should they come again, this time—no doubt—with a definite purpose in mind. Step by step our row of lances moved forward, deliberately. The Dominicans had taken their places in the line of attack. The mounted men had collected behind Don Hernando Pizarro, who guarded the right flank of the infantry.

Don Francisco Pizarro on his giant stallion, his sword balanced across his saddle, rode slowly behind the infantry. He was an awesome sight, a massy figure in the night above his gleaming mount. He gave the impression of challenging the whole world to mortal combat.

Whereas before all had been chaos, now there was complete order. Iron rang, horses pawed the ground, all under control. I felt perfect confidence that the man on the white stallion had succeeded in molding the one hundred and fifty men from all walks of life into one Spaniard, one Spanish body prepared to kill. Our steps grew slower and slower. Father Vicente let out a ringing shout, "St. Michael, dragon-killer! Guide us! Help us!" As in a litany, one hundred and fifty throats bellowed, "St. Michael!"

Again a slow, steady advance by the infantry; again the stamping of horses' hoofs. And then, very loud, the voice of my Frenero: "There he is! He's riding with us!" I saw his lance in the moonlight, piercing the drifting clouds. All eyes looked aloft and indeed, there in the heights, among the scudding clouds, we saw the figure of a giant rider, his angelic mantle fluttering far behind him so that he all but covered the moon. In his right hand upraised, he held a glittering white sword, drawn to aid us.

Our confidence then knew no bounds, and Don Francisco Pizarro gave the command to advance in quick time. Over a flat space the living Spanish wall moved forward. We closed with the Indians. They fought packed together, in a struggling mob, which hindered rather than helped them. For the first time I saw how Spaniards conducted themselves in battle. The line of men began to curve, their flanks closed inward like pincers, and like a single axe-blade they cut into the mass of their opponents. Like a phlebotomist's lancet they cut into the quivering pile of flesh. If a Spaniard was wounded, his comrades shoved him into the rear, and closed ranks.

There came a moment when I was filled with both horror and joy, because nothing moves the greatness of the human spirit, the immortality in a man's soul, so much as battle. For over and over again, a thousand times, a man gives himself up, a deliberate sacrifice to an idea. This struck me as we advanced across the little arena like a scythe, cutting and leaving behind us dead men. He who has never been in battle, what does he know!

The Indians, be it said to their credit, fought with courage. But their arrows spent themselves harmlessly on our breastplates, and we halved their spears with our Toledan steel as if they were reeds. But the most important factor in our favor—quite outside the help of St. Michael—was the Spanish formation, which has prevailed on all the battlefields of Europe, in the face of which, though armed as well as we, the Moors, the Italians, and the French have wilted.

Before such an attack neither the most extraordinary valor in the single man nor the greatest weight of numbers can avail. Now I realized how justly the man Iñigo de Loyola had spoken when he had instructed me in the principles of warfare. My heart now sang with joy when I thought how he in realizing militant things had utilized a spiritual attack, and so assured the victory of our Holy Mother the Church against the disorderly heathen mob.

Perhaps all these thoughts did not actually come to me in the heat of battle. For at such exalted moments the tendons of our soul are strained so tight that we can know nothing but immediate goals. Nevertheless, the mind does take in splintered images, which remain unknown to us until later hours when, once again, they unfold before our eyes in slow time.

Our musketeers, seven in number, had their hands full. With incredible alacrity they loaded and fired their weapons in the time it takes to say a Hail Mary. Without even bothering to aim at any particular object, they shot into the press of Indians. Even if they had not struck home, the violent explosion and the belching fire from the guns' bell-mouths would have had an excellent effect. Now, as the Indians gave way under the pressure of our organized attack, Don Hernando Pizarro, standing up in his stirrups, bellowed out the signal for the mounted men to charge. "On, for God and Castile!"

Slantwise, over across from the right flank, we galloped directly in among the thick of the Indians. A hail of arrows and spears rang against our breastplates; they no more stopped us than a shower of rain and our swords mercilessly cleaved downward on feathered pates. Our iron-shod horses trampled wildly over the fallen and put the finishing touches on the wounded. The horses were crazed with the ear-splitting noise and the pain of the arrow wounds. We would not let them shy to right or left, but held the bits iron-hard in their mouths, so that in their anguish they had no choice but to force their way forward, tearing across the fallen bodies of the Indians. If the mass of men became too great to plow through, they beat down a path with their fore-feet, and those who clung to our stirrups and to the horses' manes, we killed by the sword.

If it had not been for the horses there is no doubt that our attack would have failed, however carefully conceived, for the Indians were much more terrified by the animals than by their riders, as were the Romans by the elephants of Pyrrhus and Hannibal.

And so victory was achieved just as pale streams of the rising sun began to illumine the peaks of the mainland. The field was laden with the dead and dying. The Indians had carried off the lightly wounded into the grove of Pachacamac, where the great body of them had retreated. We had conquered the Indians, but to our great regret we saw that we had not annihilated them. Our victory was no Cannae, no Aquae Sextiae, we soon learned to our sorrow. The Puná, who for centuries had fought with the kings of the South Country, were much too accustomed to reversals in battle to give way to a single defeat, however terrible. They were not like the Cimbrians who grappled with Marius and his legions. These wild people entertained no thoughts of suicide, but changed their strategy, avoiding all further pitched combat. In the ensuing days, we lost many men by sudden ambush.

Again, we Spaniards too had suffered many casualties. Five had died on the battlefield, and many more were seriously wounded, among the latter the leader of our cavalry, Don Hernando Pizarro. Curiously, both of his calves had been partly torn away by spear wounds, and he had had to be carried off by his long-faced brothers, his horse led behind. Don Hernando, however, bore up well, managed to smile grimly, and said, "It was good sport while it lasted."

All of us had wounds of some degree. I had myself received a cut in the buttocks, so that I was waddling about cod-bound like Mephisto. But my heart was gay, for I had proved myself a knight, and Don Francisco himself had sprung down from his pale stallion and kissed me on both cheeks, a kiss that at the moment pleased me more than a buss from softer lips.

Don Francisco went from man to man, and there was not one but who received a friendly word or comradely embrace. He examined everyone's wounds, regarding them gravely as if he were a doctor. With him came a number of Indian women who rubbed our wounds with a reddish, good-smelling salve, made out of the resin of a tree. At first this made the raw flesh burn, but gradually soreness disappeared and we were comforted. There was not one among us, in consequence, who suffered from cramps or fevers, and the worst gashes healed very quickly after this Indian treatment.

Among the unwounded was my Alonso. Smiling somewhat uncertainly he said, "What a battle!"

His brother Juan, whose neck had been sliced open, said to him, "Where were you all the time? I didn't see you when we lined up at first, nor did I see you when we started to fight."

"No?" said Alonso, affecting amazement. "Why, I was standing right next to you. Don't you remember, I poked you in the ribs with the haft of my lance?"

"Is that so? To tell the truth, I don't remember anything like that at the time," said Diego, breaking into the dialogue. "I was on the other side of Juan. I didn't see you."

"Good God in Heaven!" shrieked Alonzo. "If you really want to know the truth, I was invisible. That's the way the saints protect those who believe in the Immaculate Conception. Isn't it wonderful? If that Dominican we met back there in the jungle could have seen it happen, he'd have chirped a different tune."

"Coward," said Juan, and shook his brother by the collar. "You've trampled our family honor in the dust. While we were risking our lives you were skulking in the huts feeling Indian women's legs. You're a blot on the escutcheon of the Miracle Players' Guild. You horse thief!" He shook him with increasing vigor. "So you're the first-born, are you? I'll shake it out of you, you loathesome hulk! From this day on I, Juan, am the head of the family. How nice you look, you splendid fat man! But are you splendid, you rosy apple? No, for you are eaten up with worms. A self-respecting hog would turn his snout away from a maggoty apple like you. You're eaten up with cowardice, my fine fat brother. Outside, ah, what a lovely sight you are. But within, you stink!"

"Woe is me!" said Alonso. His face flushed red. "Behold how the faithful suffer martyrdom. The evil frolic at their expense."

"Silence," said Juan, his voice thrilling with command. "I've had enough of that pap. Clean my sword. When you get through, fix me up a little soup, a pleasant little *cocido*. I feel a bit hungry. When I've relaxed, I think I'll eat."

He threw his sword at Alonso's feet, and it struck him a resounding thwack on the instep. Alonso stood with his mouth open, his eyes popping. The corners of his mouth drooped and his habitually indignant eyes filled with tears. He looked first to the right, then to the left. Then, with infinite reluctance, his glance averted, he stooped and picked up the sword. With the stained weapon trailing along the ground, he walked away toward the huts where the Indian women and children stood watching him.

We now buried our dead, with the Dominicans assuring us that their souls would ride into Paradise in the company of martial archangels. In the ensuing days we missed them greatly, but if the truth be known, we did not long mourn their loss, for in a sense their fate was better than our own, so we soon thought, when we began to feel the nag of Indian reprisal.

Several days after the battle, as we all lay still exhausted in the dirty Indian huts, our stomachs clamoring for food no longer proffered by our erstwhile hosts, early in the morning we were startled by the sound of a cannon shot. Full-tilt we all ran down to the beach. Some of us did not even bother to put on our clothes and armor. I remember how Don Pedro de Candía stood there in a very long and very dirty nightshirt which some months before had been white but which now dangled about his skinny legs in strips. On his enormous melon head was perched a limp nightcap.

Out in the bay were two caravels, hove to side by side. We cheered wildly when we made out the shield on the sails, for it was the lion of Castile. "From Panama!" cried Don Francisco Pizarro. "Friends from Panama!" He ordered his brother Don Hernando carried on a litter down to the shore to let him, too, see the gladdening sight. He himself helped carry the heavy burden. Passionately Don Francisco pressed his brother's hand. Gonzalo offered him a beaker of water. Juan and Pedro wiped the sweat from his forehead. Then, Martín de Alcántara propped up the wounded man the better for him to see.

As we all stood watching, Don Hernando, plucking up heart and wishing to respond to this solicitude, turned to me. "How are you this morning, my friend? I hope the ships are bringing us another one of your noble stock. Don Hernando Cortés was right. We cannot do without men of noble blood. They decide the issue. But just the same—" he tried to laugh—"I hope that no more than one comes. If we divide up the booty much more than we must now, the lot of us will land in the debtor's prison of Don Pedro de Los Ríos."

The other Pizarros listened to this pronouncement with gravity, nodding their heads, as if they had just heard a latter-day parable. To one another they murmured, "He knows what he's saying. How true! How true!"

We saw the puff of a second cannon at the bow of the larger ship. Soon the heavy crack came over the glassy waters of the bay, and echoed again and again from the mountain walls on the mainland. The continued echo multiplied the single explosion into an impressive cannonade, and this made us very proud to be Spaniards, authors of such tremendous displays of force. We answered the ship's signal with musket shots. Soon we saw a man aloft, scarcely larger than an ant at such great distance, waving to us from the masthead. A boat was lowered. With unfaltering strokes of the oars it crept toward us, and it was not long before we could make out the leader standing in the stern, pointing at us. Scarcely had the boat scraped bottom on the beach before he climbed over the thwarts and leaped ashore.

He proved to be a tall young man with brown hair and a meticulously barbered beard. Over his shoulders was draped a black cape, held together at the throat by a golden chain. As he jumped down from the boat his cape whirled to one side and I saw that he wore the Order of the Golden Fleece, a little lambskin hammered out of gold.

Don Hernando also must have seen the impressive ornament, for he commanded his brothers to lift him up from the litter in order that he might receive the stranger standing on his feet. But when the newcomer saw the difficulties the brothers were having raising the oldest Pizarro upright, he rushed quickly to his side, begged them not to move him, bent low and begged him to stay where he was on his litter. He expressed his sadness at seeing his excellency so badly wounded, and ventured to say that he hoped his excellency would soon be whole again.

Don Hernando beamed at this attention, and on his side expressed the hope that the stranger had had a good journey. This exchange of small courtesies in such completely strange and majestic surroundings was almost ludicrous. It was especially ludicrous when one considered that the lot of us were clothed in bloodstained rags, and looked far more like a band of thieves fresh from a fray in the Triana than a company of warriors. The stranger, however, paid no attention to our dress. He behaved with as much politeness as if we were nobles at the court whom he had chanced to bump into on a pleasant spring afternoon. But there was nothing in the graceful bearing and language that smacked of mockery. His sharply cut face, his long cheeks, revealed the aristocrat.

There are certain animals of prey—the black panther, for example—who have so much grace, so much ease and charm of movement that one is inclined to forget their savagery, to overlook the tendons ever ready to spring, the hidden, spare muscles, iron hard. There are predatory animals among men as well as among the cat breed. They are much more dangerous than those men who betray their character in rudely massive bodies, in roaring voices and a readiness for quarrel. This stranger was the panther type. He brought to mind one of those slender little Damascine swords, lightly engraved with arabesques, which look like ornamental daggers but which, properly wielded, are more dangerous than a German broadsword.

Our company, assembled faces thoughtful, took in the compliments and pleasantries of the stranger. Everything he did was Castilian; his preference for excellence of form over excellence of content. He would much prefer the company of a delicate murderer to the company of a blundering saint. In this he was exactly like a woman.

The stranger, who was making such a good impression on the lot of us, now turned to Don Francisco Pizarro and told him that his name was Don Hernando de Soto, and that he had got news of our Coaque successes in Panama. There, he said, the word had got around about our gold and emeralds, and had caused immense excitement. He had collected eighty men and had made a decision to place himself at His Excellency's service, to share, if possible, in the conquest of the South Country.

There was a murmur of approval. The Dominicans loudly praised God and the Holy Virgin Mary mild, for this offer of help came at exactly the right time, just when our provisions had shrunk badly. Our wounded were heartened by the knowledge that someone stood ready to reinforce our waning strength. This was especially true of Don Hernando Pizarro, who that very day began to hobble about the huts on two sticks, making all sorts of plans for the removal over to the port of Tumbez on the mainland. Needless to say, Hernando de Soto's offer was gratefully accepted. It was agreed immediately to turn our backs on the isle of Puná and its superstitious inhabitants and to shift our operations to the golden arena of Tumbez.

But now we were forced to endure a second and even greater disillusionment, which once again cost the lives of many of us. One fair morning we set out over the calm waters of the bay. To transport our party and its stores and weapons we used Indian balsas so-called, that is, rafts supported by bundles of reeds. These are uncertain craft unless one knows exactly how to handle them. Each man on his particular raft was more concerned with keeping upright than with preserving any particular formation in the passage from Puná to the mainland.

And it so happened that at this time the tide was very low, so low that between navigable water and the solid shore there was an area of quicksand and mud interspersed with winding rivulets of sea just barely deep enough to float our balsas. Many of us capsized attempting to negotiate this salty quag, and floundered up to our necks among the crabs. Struggling to get out of this predicament in the hot sun caused some of the company to faint away, weakened as they were, and several of them drowned before anything could be done.

And to make matters worse, while we were floundering about in this treacherous half-land we were set upon by Indians from the mainland. They had gathered on the beach. Wildly they swung their spears and brandished their clubs. Before long, their arrows were flying by our heads, and more than once we had to duck down into the foul water to escape being hit.

All about could be heard the cries of the wounded as they failed to leap quickly enough out of the way of a shower of arrows. From where I was struggling to drag my way forward, pushing the balsa ahead of me, I saw that the raft bearing all the Captain-General's paraphernalia had capsized, and that it was beset by Indians. All appeared lost. Loudly we cried for help, hoping that Hernando de Soto's caravels would hear us.

They were anchored far out in the bay, much too far, it seemed, to hear our cries for succor. But hear they did, and soon they were firing their single cannon. They put out boats, which slowly worked their way toward us, much slower than the tempo of the Indian attack. For the wild men were growing bolder and bolder, and started to risk their own necks by coming into the salty quagmire to get at us. We saw, too, that at last De Soto's men struck the shallow area, and themselves were floundering about up to their necks in sucking, black slime. It was plain for all to see that we stood in imminent danger of being done away with before they could ever reach us.

At this point, Hernando Pizarro began to bellow for someone to help him onto his horse. This was done, though it was hard to see how Pizarro, mounted or not, could ever prevent our doom. But he kept on shouting that his brothers and Pedro de Candía and I should follow his example, and attempt to force our horses to the hard line of the shore.

We did as he commanded. Now we rode to attack, the strangest attack that man ever saw. We flailed our horses until they were crazed with pain. We hammered them between the ears, rammed our heels into their ribs, tore their mouths bloody. Up to their bellies, they strained every nerve, near bursting with effort.

Gradually the muck grew shallower; gradually we were able to lurch along at a heavy trot. We were covered black with the sticky clay. Once, I remember, I fell off my piebald when he plunged over his head into a hole and all but broke his leg. I was saved by Don Hernando Pizarro, who threw me over my trembling beast after it had fought its way out of the deathtrap.

When at last we reached dry land and could gallop as strenuously as the sand permitted, the Indians became frightened and ran away. Indeed, we were a horrible sight, caked with mud from head to foot, both horses and men. Our animals were really beyond control, mad with eagerness to feel terra firma underneath their hoofs. Once they got up on the beach there was no holding them in. Bleeding, muddy and covered with lather about the head, they plunged forward toward the screaming natives. We lopped off the heads of several Indians with the greatest ease. It reminded me of the cockfights in Seville, when the feathered heads roll into the sand and lie still, gathering flies in less time than it takes to say a Hail Mary, Full of Grace. Later we threw the headless bodies into the muck and were overcome with laughter at the sight, probably because we were so overstrained.

Once away from the beach, and on hard ground that did not give way under the horses' hoofs, we killed Indians by the droves. Not since the days of Granada had my father's sword drawn so much blood. Down the runnels on both sides of the weapon, the blood dripped steadily, demonstrating the usefulness of the design better than anything I had ever idly imagined. Those Indians who threw themselves on their faces before us we let live, for we were too far gone to risk climbing down from our horses.

We rode always after the biggest knots of Indians, and pointed to them with our swords for one anothers' benefit, like women picking berries who greedily reach for the thickest clumps of fruit, ignoring the scantier patches.

Gonzalo Pizarro especially had sport that morning. He would rein in his horse and trot slowly behind the laboring Indians as they ran to get away. Then, after a time, he would speed up, and one after the other hack them down, shouting the meanwhile a loud cry of thanks to the Mother of God.

All this happened on a sort of peninsula sticking out into the mucky flats. In the midst of this wild chase, with my blood singing in my ears from the superhuman exertions, I saw that the Captain-General and Hernando de Soto were approaching. With them came the foot troops. In a brilliant maneuver, sacrificing immediate reprisal, we cut off the remainder of the Indians at the point where the peninsula joined the wooded part of the mainland. Relentlessly we drove the survivors toward what they saw was sure death. In a fit of panic many of them simply threw their weapons away and began to crawl on their hands and knees, as ill-bred dogs do when they are in for a thrashing.

But Don Francisco gave a loud command to cease the slaughter. He shouted to us, as we rounded up the Indians, that the men of Tumbez had already been sufficiently punished for their cruel ambush. Against our will we let our swords drop, and probably would never have done this had we not been worn out with the great expenditure of wind and muscle.

Don Francisco now had the alcalde of Tumbez brought before him, for this man had been captured. We heaped endless reproaches on his head through the interpreter, and over and again reminded him that his people had betrayed their friends the Spaniards. The alcalde refused to answer, but stood by sullenly, his head hanging, awaiting death. And now, to my astonishment, Don Francisco had the man's bound hands loosened. Later, so he said, he had decided after the experience with the Puná that it was perhaps better to practice grace than justice. In any case, whatever may have been his diplomatic theory, there is no doubt that he took into account the fact that the alcalde was a subject of the mighty king, Atahualpa, and that it was a good idea to handle him softly until he had found out precisely how the land lay. He never forgot that his forces, at the very outset, were already numerically inadequate for the enormous task at hand.

It was late afternoon and the sun was casting long shadows when we finally drew into the city of Tumbez. It proved to be one of the greatest disappointments of my whole life. After all our sufferings there was not the slightest trace of those fairyland qualities Don Pedro de Candía had so eloquently described. No golden palaces or temples shimmered in the dying light of day. There was no maidens' laughter to greet us; there were no wreaths of flowers and jewels strewn in our path. Dumb, mute and dirty, Tumbez lay before our eyes—lifeless alleys, burnt black walls of lime, fire-seared wooden beams. And no one was to be seen. Here and there we made out a cowering old man, looking at us out of the corner of his eye. Our steps rang hollow in the empty streets. Our heads drooped with disappointment.

We entered the wide low buildings constructed of huge blocks of stone. They were windowless, and there were no doors blocking the entrances. These entrances were trapezoidal in shape, like the face of a truncated pyramid. These cyclopean structures also were deathly still, deserted. There was nothing in them except bats which might have been the departed inhabitants of Tumbez, mysteriously transformed, for all we knew. Nothing but musty twilight and soft-winged birds brushing our faces, and no hard gold, nothing to weigh in our palms.

These larger structures—temples, monasteries, or whatever they may have been—for the most part were roofless, robbed of coverings which, I suspect, in the beginning had consisted of nothing more than wooden beams laid over with bundles of reeds, and now were only charred wood, ready to crack at the touch of a hand.

But Don Pedro de Candía swore a thousand solemn oaths, endangering both his own and his ancestors' status in eternity, that when he had last seen them, these temples had been covered with silver tiles and the walls with gold leaf. He showed us the niches, dust-filled and covered with spider webs, in which had been placed the many lovely works of native art.

But the soldiers laughed in contempt, crawling with disappointment. Under their breath they called Don Francisco Pizarro and Don Pedro de Candía the two biggest liars ever born of woman. So great was the chagrin of some of them that they hurled their weapons to the ground in speechless anger. Some even threatened to do away with the leaders, and the Pizarro brothers had no small difficulty restoring order, for the men were still hot with blood-letting. And I, tired to death from so much strain, moved from one to the other, begging them to have a little patience. I had no end of trouble with Frenero and Bernal. These two had all but decided to make good what they called a betrayal with some knife play, in the Potro style, for a good man—as they say—had been done in by a thorough bastard.

Don Francisco Pizarro himself, however, seemed completely untouched by the uproar. He apparently did not share in the common disappointment. As quiet as stone, he sat on his big roan stallion and gave his brothers orders to use the stone structures as billets. He then turned to Don Hernando de Soto and asked him to bring provisions from his ships at once, and to ration out food and wine among the soldiers.

This was done. Soon fires were lighted, and all of us sat around eating and drinking. The wine, the good bread and the fires' warmth chased away the men's evil spirits. Before long they were making jokes, and were able to laugh, bitterly to be sure, over their nagging disillusionments. The gall drained from their brains in a few hours. Such is man. And, indeed, their current situation for all practical purposes would have been but little different if we had found gold. As they ate their supper, of course, they could have gambled for high stakes instead of worthless baubles, and the lucky winner could have congratulated himself on the immense luxury—hypothetical to be sure—which he carried about in his pouch. Yet the greatest charm of gold is scarcely more than imaginary. It whips the imagination, the possession of gold, and to the mind conjures paradise, even though the realization of this imagined paradise multiplies a man's care ten-thousandfold.

I have thought at times that things are a little different with the Flemings. So far as they go, they heap up gold because they are afraid the day will come when they will lack bread and clothes to cover their fat backs. Yet I prefer not to dwell upon these cowards who have no trust in God, or in their own strength and dignity. Here I wish to speak only of my own comrades, with whom gold served merely to tickle them to the pleasures of chance, and the imagining of an earthly paradise.

In fact, the ultimate possession of this gold, they soon began to figure, was merely postponed, its delights removed but a few more steps forward into the misty future. Gradually, as they grew heavy with sleep, they could count off even greater treasures, the gold and precious stones that would fall into their hands the next time, or perhaps the wonders that would have been theirs had Tumbez been all that Don Pedro de Candía had promised. And so the premature destruction of Tumbez at the bottom was a godsend for our undertaking, since it whetted the men's appetence and indurated it. This appetence is an inner fire, an interior, all-consuming conflagration, a sickness, a flux that is worse among the rich than among the poor.

Don Francisco Pizarro, sitting morosely by the fire with his brothers, seemed to feel the general disappointment only after his soldiers had all but forgotten it in the general relaxation. Only slowly shaking off his dejection, he finally had the Indian alcalde brought before him and inquired why the city had been destroyed. At the same time, he attempted to find out what had become of the two Spaniards he had left behind in the city on his first visit to become versed in the language and customs. The haggard Indian was unwilling to let anything out. He said nothing at all for some time, and when he did talk it was only in monosyllables. He answered reluctantly, like a child, after Felipillo had described to him the frightful tortures to which we Spaniards would subject him if he persisted in holding his tongue.

Even then what we forced out of him piecemeal was contradictory. First he said that Tumbez had been sacked in revenge by the sun-god. The sun-god had sent down a great pest on the city after the two

Spaniards had tampered with two of the god's virgins. Then he said that the Indians of Puná had besieged the city, taken it and set it on fire from all four sides. But this we knew to be untrue, for we surely would have heard about any such undertaking, living as we had been among the Indians. Beyond that it seemed that the Punás, for all their ferocity, could hardly have conquered a city like Tumbez. So far as the supposed plague went, we failed to understand how that could have caused roof timbers to burn and temples to be despoiled of all their treasures. The story concerning the two Spaniards was equally hard to believe, and all that we could credit was the news of their death. The reason for their murder remained a mystery. Once the Indian said they had been killed on the battlefield fighting against the Puná people; again he reiterated his fabrication that they had succumbed to the pest. Finally the Indian gave us a third and more likely reason, that after the rape, as he called it, they had been done away with on orders from the priests of the sun-god.

Pizarro was deeply irritated. Raising his hand he gave the Indian permission to be off. With catlike motions, the alcalde worked his way backward, suddenly wheeled and was lost in the stone maze of the city. The three leaders of the expedition stared silently into the fire. Then Don Francisco turned quietly to Don Hernando de Soto and asked, "What do you make of it, sir?"

De Soto did not reply at first. I began to think that he had not even heard the question, so long did he blink into the fire. He might have been seeing in the sullenly glowing coals the salamander that will tell man his future if it can be caught. Despite his youth, Don Hernando's face was lined and severe. Over his features there hovered a curious sadness, the kind of sadness one imagines might veil the face of a Pan forced to live among men. At last he turned to Don Francisco and searched his face. The old soldier, confused, lowered his eyes.

Although Pizarro had expressed no opinion whatsoever, and on the contrary had specifically asked De Soto to give his, the dreamy young man said, "Your Excellency is a good judge of men. There are only two powers this Indian feared more than he feared us. One is the power of the daemons. The other is the kingly power of the Inca, who sits over there in the mountains. Atahualpa plundered the city of Tumbez. Our two men were killed on his order. And now Atahualpa is waiting for us in order to wipe us out. There are only two ways to escape this fate, so far as can be seen."

"And these two ways? What are they?" asked Pizarro.

"To get out of the South Country. That's one," replied de Soto.

"And the other?"

"To get within range of Atahualpa, to fasten onto him, and take his life before he knows what is up."

"Yes, yes," said Pizarro. Full of agitation, he jumped to his feet. "Who told you such things, Don Hernando? That was my own thought. That's just the way I would have chosen."

"So much the better, then. We both know where we stand, no?" said Don Hernando, laughing outright. "But the question now is whether that band of dissatisfied ruffians you've collected are up to the task. If I'm not very much mistaken, it's going to be no merry Maypole dance climbing up those mountains."

"I'm leaving this place tomorrow morning at dawn," said Don Francisco Pizarro slowly. "I'll sift them down seven times over, until there's nothing but a handful left. But we'll still get there. A Pizarro never counts his strength in numbers."

"Very good," echoed De Soto.

"A Pizarro never turns back," the leader went on softly. "A thousand times I've staked my neck. I can do it again. And if I live, and live I will, I can do it still once more and once more again, until my mouth fills up to the back of my teeth with dirt."

"Yes, a Pizarro never turns back . . ." It was Don Hernando Pizarro, starting out of a sound slumber on hearing the familiar refrain.

On the next day we took leave of Tumbez and marched south over a broad highway paved with thin, flat stones. The march was not particularly difficult. Both sides of the road were planted with willow trees, so that much of the time we moved along in shadow that protected us from the lively heat of the day. Along the road from time to time we came on stone houses or fortresses which looked something like toll-houses or little country inns in Spain. But all of these were empty and forsaken. We marched through villages where the Indians came out to greet us holding green branches before them. And yet we could not help but remark that most of these were women and children, and that seldom were any younger men to be seen.

We learned that all men of military age had been summoned to the army of the Inca, who was immured in the city of Caxamalca. Piecing together the Indians' stories we calculated that Atahualpa must have a huge army supporting him, ranging in numbers from fifty to a hundred thousand men. This information very naturally did not give us much assurance. When night came, we found shelter in a kind of caravansary. The cacique of the place offered us food for ourselves and our horses.

The next day, the character of the landscape altered radically. The little checkerboard fields disappeared, and the trees along the highway became much smaller, a different variety altogether from willows. We began to wander, always following the same road, through a stony waste. It was like traveling over an old Roman road in the homeland. There were still the small stone buildings, always spaced the same distance apart. But now the going was hard. The sun burned on our backs, and in the afternoon a wind from the sea blew great clouds of gritty dust in our faces. In places the way was half blocked by shifting sand dunes.

At this point, some of the party began to lose patience. Their complaints were loud, and they demanded that we turn back toward Tumbez. They prophesied that we would all come to a bitter end if we continued on to the south. To pacify them, Don Hernando de Soto had a party of mounted men ride on ahead, himself leading them, to find how far it was before the desert country ended.

In the meantime, the Captain-General had the men gather before him, and drew a paper from beneath his breastplate, saying that the alcalde of Tumbez had given it to him. It was the last message from the two Spaniards, he told us, the two whom long, long months ago he had left behind in the city of Tumbez, the two who had died of the pest. Our men listened sullenly to this unlikely tale. Nevertheless, they listened as Pizarro had Master Pérez, the scribe, read it off. It ran as follows: "To whatever hands may first find this, whoever first sets foot in this land, be it known that here there is more gold and silver than there is iron in Biscaya. This is the gospel truth." The paper was signed "Reginaldo, the Unhappy," and the signature was followed by three crosses, as if in this subscript the dead man had wished to create some sort of memorial for himself.

The men, however, were not much moved by what they heard. Many refused absolutely to be duped into thinking once more of the illusory gold. Others felt that even if there was gold, there was scarcely any reasonable chance of getting it, since it was guarded by at least fifty thousand men. Some openly expressed doubts of the paper's authenticity for they professed to see a falsified version of Master Pérez' handwriting in the script.

However, when Don Hernando de Soto and his party returned much earlier than anyone had expected, to bring us the news that only a few miles distant there was a beautiful, well-watered valley which the Indians called Tangarará, spirits rose at once. We all pulled our weary bones together and, in truth, after another hour's march actually entered into a valley. The road fell away steeply and before us lay a lush country, dotted with groves of trees at the boundaries of fine fields.

At first sight I was struck with the resemblance of Tangarará to the Duero valley near Tordesilla. Of course here there was nothing more than little villages, no castles or church towers. But I thought at once that in this valley life could be very good, and that the Valley of Tangarará must have been foreordained by God to harbor a fine Spanish city. My sentiments were shared by many in the company, and there was much talk of going no farther but of settling down on the spot to build homes instead of bothering to our sorrow with the Inca's gold.

Even though Don Francisco Pizarro could not for one moment lose sight of his goal, and besides knew perfectly well that prospects of founding a Spanish city in the New World were idle unless the power of the Incas was broken once and for all, nevertheless it was his policy to listen to any sort of advice, wild or sound. And so he decided to take these proposals seriously, quite beyond anything his brother Don Hernando would have countenanced.

Don Francisco saw immediately that building the foundations of a city in the Valley of Tangarará would accrue to his ultimate advantage. In the first place by so doing he could rid himself of the backsliders. In the second place he could establish a post from which communications could be sent, if the worst came, to Panama, asking for help—help that might very well never come, to be sure. The river that ran up the valley seemed wide and deep enough to bear our caravels, or rather the caravels of Don Hernando de Soto. They could serve, in case they were needed, as a fortress and refuge in flight from the Inca.

The third ground for acceding to the domestic sentiment that had seized the company was to make peace with the Dominicans, who were constantly demanding that we stop and build a church, in which the reliquiæ, the images, and the usual implements of the Mass could be put. The Dominicans, too, wanted a point of vantage for their crusade to win souls for the Mother Church. So far their mission had been rather a complete failure. Only occasionally were they able to baptize some old woman or a sickly child, and so never were they able to their satisfaction to snatch the heathen fully from Satan's hands. The officers of the Crown who were with us were eager to have some place in which they could exercise their customary functions.

Then, finally, there must have been hidden in Pizarro's soul a prideful wish to be a founder of a city. Although he had a son of his own flesh, yet he no doubt yearned for a long-lived daughter who would spread the fame of his name after he was dust.

So, some days after our arrival in the Valley of Tangarará we began to build a city. With his own hands Don Francisco laid the cornerstone of the church, which we dedicated to San Miguel for his aid in our war with the Puná. The city itself we named San Miguel, as well, for the Archangel Michael who had not disdained to ride above his servants in the clouds.

Our hands grew calloused and the sweat dripped from our brows as we built the first Spanish town on the great southern continent of the New World. I could linger forever telling how we felled and cut up great trees, how we sawed out and planed boards, dug stone out of the earth, mixed mortar. I could describe how all of us, cavaliers and soldiers both, hammered, sawed and dug. We forced thousands of Indians to work with us, collecting them from the near-by villages. The work was pleasing to them. They seemed to think it a kind of play, and they shouted happily as the saws screamed and the sawdust flew. With their hands raised over their heads they shouted in amazement as they saw us move big beams into place with the aid of levers.

Soon the church was finished. When the Dominicans had arranged the altar with vestments, and put in place an image of the Virgin Mary, when for the first time the candles were lighted, the Indians' delight was endless. They streamed inside and squealed with joy at the splendid sight. The Dominicans lost no time in baptizing dozens of them. The mothers carried their red-skinned brats to Father Vicente who, standing before the awed women in his robes of office, dipped his fingers in the consecrated water and made a wet sign of the cross on the infants' foreheads. The Indian children lay quite still, like little wooden dolls with big black eyes. It looked as if they were fully aware of the solemnity of the transformation they were undergoing.

Those mothers whose children could not be baptized the first day complained bitterly and cried for the magic water. There was so much trouble that, having first secured the permission of the Dominicans, the soldiers got a cask of consecrated water and went about sprinkling it freely over all small people in sight. The mothers, however, were ill content with this substitute, and stormed up to Father Vicente, demanding that he perform the ritual properly. So great was the press that they threw the holy man to the floor from his own altar.

His pleasure at this overwhelming enthusiasm was great and he forgave the women the bodily affront. He kept mumbling to himself as I, along with others, rushed to his rescue, that Tertullian assuredly had been right when he said that man's soul by nature is Christian. For the great African saint was most beloved of Father Vicente de Valverde, unfortunately not in his gentler aspects alone. He was convinced—it is Father Vicente I am speaking of—that one of the greatest joys of the blessed was to watch the death of the damned. In this he was quite like his Afric Tertullian, who so eloquently expressed the same lively opinion. Father Vicente never grew tired of reading tales of rack and whip, of fire and ice, which awaited the damned upon their demise. When Father Vicente from the pulpit recounted horrors of his own conception, he outdid Dante's description of Hell, and made the chills course up and down his hearers' spines.

On the other hand I was struck again and again with his kindness toward the Indians, and his eagerness for self-sacrifice in their behalf. How such sentiments could flourish side by side in the same soul with such love of violence was hard to comprehend. He was even unafraid of the Pizarros when it came to protecting his Indian charges, and at times he would address the leaders as if they were stray dogs in the street.

This paradox often appears among men of the cloth, I have observed. The idea that possesses them is the mightiest of all ideas, and their campaign to turn the hearts of men is so vast in scope, that all else beside seems petty, even the worst of fleshly tortures. I have heard that Saint Bernard of Clairvaux, San Domingo de Guzmán, yes, even Savonarola himself whom some consider to be a saint, were men of this sort. They were men ready to obliterate themselves a thousand times in order to save the soul of a beggar child, and ready, too, to tear the limbs from a thousand ignorant men and women in order to keep, as they saw it, the common faith undefiled.

But time presses, and I can tarry no longer with notations on the colonization of the cities of San Miguel, Trujillo and the Ciudad de los Reyes. I wish to say, however, that I consider them to be the finest sprigs of myrtle in the crown of fame which our Captain-General now wears. For, through them, all that we later gained we held onto. A new home was prepared for tens of thousands. Today every child in the streets of Spain, every beggar and vagabond knows that the land of Pau is the most beautiful and the richest possession of the Crown in the New World.

Although my pen is adrip with words of praise for these new cities, I will limit myself to saying that we worked a half-year before the city hall was erected. Then the day came when our Captain-General again set out on the road, after placing the city under the protection of Don Antonio Navarro. Fifty soldiers were left behind to garrison our stronghold. Of my party I left Alonso the splendid behind, for it was clear after his conduct in the Puná affray that he would be of little use in combating the far greater dangers we now looked forward to.

We proceeded forward over a broad, quiet highway which the Indians called Piura. Along the way were primeval woods, immensely tall trees, and sometimes we had to skirt sandy spots where the sand had drifted over the road. This time we were not discouraged by occasional stretches of difficult going, for we knew that soon we would strike into a watered, fruitful countryside where we could find nourishment and friendly welcome among the caravansaries of the King Atahualpa.

In this coastal land it rained but very seldom. At night, to be sure, the chill wind coming in off the sea brought fog, and it grew uncomfortably cold. Yet wherever fresh water touched the earth it was incredibly fertile. Everywhere possible the Indians had built canals, dams, water wheels and stone aqueducts to spend the life-giving element as wisely as possible. The land looked in places like a Moorish garden.

The aqueducts I speak of are found also in Spain, though most of them are in such a state of complete disrepair that they could never be used. When I was a small boy my good Sancho once told me that these gray walls of masonry were put up by the Devil, and that the common people call them devil-walls. I told Master Agrippa this, and he pulled my hair. "You little dunce. Those walls are viaducts and were built by the Romans to bring water down from the mountains to the cities. In those days the Spaniards were as stupid as oxen, and knew nothing of such tricks. If you ever went to Italy, into the Campagna, you would see miles of viaducts carrying the cool water of the Apennines."

We saw as we penetrated deeper and deeper into the country that everywhere there were signs of a strict order, almost inhuman, far more severe I am sure than anything of Roman pattern. A command, given by a village chief, no matter how insignificant, was carried out immediately to the letter. All this was utterly different from at home in Spain where it is as much as man's life is worth to give a harsh command, where the first sign of order arouses resentment, where the authorities can reckon only on one sure thing, that their orders will never be carried out as they schemed. Of course, as we proved in the battle with the Punás, there is such a thing as order among the Spaniards, an order that cannot be broken since it is voluntarily entered into by free men.

This much stricter Indian model, since it depends on the will-lessness of its puppet members, who never think for themselves and who long ago lost any sense of independence, is much more easily cracked. The lack of independent thinking showed itself plainly in their soft, fine faces, which were as alike one to the other as so many eggs in a basket.

True, it is harder to distinguish the individual among strange peoples, I have discovered, for their personal peculiarities are expressed in ways so foreign they escape the newcomer's notice. Nevertheless we could still observe that there was greater diversity of bearing among the unconquered people of Puná than among these subjects of the Inca.

It was difficult for us not to treat them with abrupt contempt, to lord it over them and make them our slaves, to box their ears at will and give them a solid kick in the buttocks if the mood happened to suggest this crotchet. They were much kinder, much more polite than the people of Puná. But that made no difference. They invited the heavy Spanish hand. It is pleasing to the vanity to belabor a donkey, if not a lion!

Our Captain-General took great pains that we should not wreak any irreparable injuries on the Indians. He permitted no gross injustices or cruelties. He feared that the experiences we had so hazardously endured at Puná and Tumbez would be needlessly repeated, that the rumor of our vile behavior would reach the ear of the Inca before we could get to him. On the whole we bore ourselves well enough, just as if we were marching through Spain. We plundered no cities and made no attempt to find gold, however much our fingers itched to touch it. In every village, nevertheless, we stopped in the marketplace, planted the standard of Castile, and had all the inhabitants assemble to swear allegiance to it, as a symbol of our king Don Carlos. At the beginning we took platonic possession of the kingdom of the Incas, and consoled ourselves with prospects of a later more realistic ownership once we had waylaid the great Atahualpa in his distant mountain stronghold.

Although the tractability of the Indians we came on was very encouraging to most of the company, there were still some of our men who clamored to get back to the land of Nicaragua. For the farther south we went, the more populous became the towns and villages, the more imposing the buildings. Oftentimes our little file was surrounded by thousands of Indians, leaping and grimacing, throwing flowers in the path of the horses. The dissatisfied ones conjectured how things would be when the Indians began throwing spears and stone knives instead of flowers. Furthermore, they argued, what was the point in continuing to risk our lives day after day, never knowing when the throng of red heathen would turn on us, if we were not allowed to do a little plundering along the way.

Hearing all these bickerings and grumblings one morning Don Francisco had us assemble before him. He said that he had heard some of us were of a mind to turn back. That suited him well, he told us, for he would like to see San Miguel more strongly garrisoned. He ordered those to step forward who no longer wished to go on with him. There was an uncomfortable silence, and all the men began to eye one another sheepishly. Already our company seemed much too small to most of us for such an ambitious undertaking, and now Don Francisco was proposing to diminish our numbers still further!

Finally, with seeming reluctance, some men did step forward out of the ranks. Don Francisco wished these men luck, and in parting gave them some detailed advice on how to proceed back to San Miguel.

Then once more he turned to those of us who were left and repeated his offer to let them quit now. No one moved this time. He looked us over, his gray slanting eyes ironical. Then, slowly, he made this little speech while the delinquents were still within earshot, "From now on there will be no more talk of going back. The die has now been cast. You have made your choice between fame and safety. You made that choice freely. From now on keep your mouths shut no matter what happens, no matter how hard the going may be. I am fed up with cowards. I hope now to be rid of them. And henceforth any man who proves himself a coward will be cut down by my hand."

This talk of cowardice evoked some dark looks. But most of us were ashamed for our reluctant fellows and felt that Don Francisco had spoken justly. The larger body of soldiers struck their halberds against their steel breastplates, making a martial tumult, and roared into the brilliant morning a long cheer: "Long live our Captain, long live the Adelantado!"

18

THE ANDES

WE SPENT that day resting, and moved on the next. Now we were one hundred and sixty men in strength. Of these, sixty-two were mounted. That was scarcely enough to have made a single company for the great captain Don Gonzalvo de Cordova. But there was a great difference between our company and the undisciplined horde which had left Panama long months before. The vicissitudes of the march, the battle on Puná, the clash on the beach at Tumbez—all had sifted us seven times as the Captain-General put it. What was left was made of steel, in body and heart. There were no sullen faces. All mention of Nicaragua was forgotten. The goal was clear and simple before every man's eyes—the conquest of the South Country. It is true that more than once our glance wandered apprehensively to the east where there towered an endless range of mountain peaks, like a giant wall guiding us along the way. The mystery of the Inca hidden somewhere in the forbidding heights lay ominously on all hearts. We dreamed about the terrors of these unknown steeps. Each man tried to unriddle his own impending death. But no one turned back, nor really wished to. The die was cast indeed.

In good time we arrived at the city of Zaran which lies in the floor of one of the green valleys running in from the coast. At this point our Captain-General dispatched the well-mounted Don Hernando de Soto to reconnoiter and to look for a city by the name of Caxas, which the Indians had talked about. Don Hernando stayed away several days, and we began to wonder whether he had not been ambushed when one afternoon he reappeared, perfectly whole. With him he brought an emissary of the Inca Atahualpa, whom he had met in Caxas. This man was quite different from the coast Indians we had seen, and his imposing and remarkably diplomatic manner occasioned much gloomy speculation about the kind of people we were up against. His noble bearing, however, was disfigured in our eyes by his having the right ear lengthened in the most extraordinary fashion. This "Big Ear," as we called him, reminded me of some kind of night animal, a cat or a bat, with large organs of hearing, enabling him to note the finest sounds.

The Indians—and it sounds not altogether unreasonable—thought that such physical alterations brought about alterations in the soul, arguing like ourselves that every cause has an effect. It is for this reason, as I had occasion to remark, later on, that they make little round holes in the skulls of the mortally sick so that the influence of the sun and the sky can pour unhindered into the brain. The operation, which is done with a bronze knife, makes great demands on the skill of the doctor. One slip of the knife and death or some form of lunacy is sure to follow. The common people, too, who are doomed forever to manual toil like our galley slaves, endure a peculiar kind of treatment at the hands of the Incas. When these helots are still sucklings, and the bone of the brainpan still soft, the Incas have their skulls bound round with bast and woven cloths, in the belief that the brain will have no room to grow to fullness and strength. They hope thereby to keep these people stupid and dull of feeling, to deny them the gift of meditating on their lot, of ever brooding over it to the point of revolt. For the Incas think that the single man means nothing, and the state, the life of the kingdom as a whole, means everything. They do not know that in the heart of the humblest as well as in the heart of the king, there is a spark of godliness which does not bear mutilation. In many ways they pursue this twisting of the human soul for the sake of the state, exactly as we castrate a boar in order to make his flesh softer and of finer flavor, or as we ruin a goose's liver to make it fat and more edible.

To us Spaniards all this seemed an invention of the Devil. Man's misery is bad enough, but not to know that one is miserable to a Spaniard would be the intolerable misery of miseries. We saw that the Inca's emissary traveled on a palanquin carried by four strong men whom he treated like mules. He was surrounded by other servants who read his wishes from his eyes, relieving him of the nuisance of uttering them. Only very seldom did he bother to direct as much as a word to any of his attendants.

However, through Felipillo, our interpreter, he told us many important things that reinforced our decision to drive on to our goal. He told us, for example, that his master the Inca Atahualpa had just conquered the rival brother Huáscar, who was caught in the city of Cuzco. True, he had not directed the siege in person, but through his chieftains Chalicuchima and Quizquiz. Atahualpa himself was attending us in Caxamalca. After receiving us, it was his intention to remove to Cuzco and there to decide the fate of the captured brother now imprisoned after the recent collapse of his army.

This information gave us pause. All along, since the advices we had so cunningly wrung from the Indians of Puná, we had counted on tractable Huáscar as a potential ally, and we had often discussed the possibility of restoring Huáscar's prestige and using him as a façade while we actually exercised his kingly powers. Now this pleasant fancy was at an end. Fate had decided that we would have to reckon with this steely king Atahualpa and not his pliant brother. And yet these chilling premonitions were partially erased by the friendly manner of the Inca's messenger, who was good enough to bring numerous presents for us in the name of Atahualpa, the king. We were very much impressed with the fineness of the stuffs which were woven out of vicuña wool, so soft that it felt like silk. These bolts of cloth were richly ornamented with inwoven figures, and at their outer seams the cunning weaver had run finely drawn threads of silver and gold. We were amazed by two urns, hewn out of a gay mottled stone similar to our marble. But we were most impressed by a gray, coarse, sweetly-smelling powder, that, so we were told, was made out of dried goose meat, and which was used by the nobles of the South Country as a perfume. Similarly, in our land the women use oil of orange blossoms laboriously pressed out by the Moors. This last, I know, is very costly stuff, for I once sent a small flask of it to Doña Isabella.

And now our Captain-General had his gifts brought forward. These did not look comparable to our eyes. As we saw it, it was in truth a shabby exchange. Don Francisco offered the emissary of the Inca some bright glass baubles, a few iron tools, and a red cap made in Flanders. But the Inca official seemed completely satisfied and was more than pleased with the iron implements, a hammer, a knife and a corkscrew. At once he hung them from his belt, and continually fondled them to make sure that they were firmly suspended.

This exchange of gifts was followed by another of politest compliments. Both the Captain-General and the Indian praised the greatness and goodness of their respective masters. Father Vicente de Valverde could not forbear from mixing in this conversation in order to introduce some basic points of the Christian doctrine. The Indian, however, not to be outdone, pointed to the sun. Unfortunately since Christ is invisible and the Holy Ghost is not an easy concept, whereas the sun is preeminently there for everyone and anyone to see and feel glowing on his face, the Indian soon got the upper hand of Father Vicente in this odd competition. All the while the Indian was talking his seeking, lively eyes examined us, measuring our strength in weapons and horses, and trying to estimate what our purpose in coming to his country could be. Whatever conclusions the Indian came to, it appeared they were going to be favorable to Atahualpa. For as time went the emissary waxed more and more good-humored, and his manner grew less formal.

In vain Don Francisco described to him the might of Don Carlos, the invincibility of his armies, his ships, the number of his castles and cities, for all these it was impossible for the Indian to conjure up. At the end of the lengthy interchange the emissary once again pressed his invitation, presented it in such a manner that it was all but a command. We were to appear before Atahualpa as soon as possible. After this summing up of the situation the Inca's representative nodded for his palanquin, and made off, refusing Don Francisco's plea that he stay with us for a while. We all saw that he could not wait to get back to his master and let him know just precisely how weak we were, and to disperse all fear of our being a threat to the realm.

We watched uneasily as the Indian bobbed away, borne at a trot by four muscular red slaves. Our eyes were fastened on the ornamental bunch of feathers adorning the back rest of the litter, and we did not turn our gaze away until feathers, palanquin, emissary and trotting men became nothing more than a moving ball of dust that disappeared into the wall of mountain.

A few days later we reached the city of Motupe. This place looked dull and deserted, for all able-bodied men had been called to arms in the service of Atahualpa. The feeling of loneliness was enhanced by the silent proximity of great naked masses of stone towering all about. The town lay in the one isolated strip of tillable land. At the edge of this waste of rock there were some half-ruined terraced pyramids. All around were strewn great blocks of hewn stone, and among this massive rubble were scattered countless human bones, dark brown and so old that they fell to dust when lifted from the ground. There were shin-bones, the flaring leaves of the human pelvis, ribs, arms, backbones and now and then a skull. The place looked like some ancient battlefield, like the one described by the prophet Ezekiel when he tells how on the Day of Judgment the angels' trumpets blow, all the bones reassemble, and are given new life by God. Hosts lay here in piecemeal decay and dust, more than the Caesars ever brought death to, and waited in the burning sun for the millennium. The bones lay among the ruins of houses and temples, and one could easily picture to himself how here all once was life, laughter, commotion and tears.

I walked about among the ruins with Frenero and Bernal and more than once I stumbled over a skull, or caught my foot in a piece of rotted cloth which easily gave way. All around scampered tiny gray salamanders. Sometimes I could pick them up as they lay, their throats quickly pulsing, on some flat block of stone searing hot in the sun. Diego told me, laughing as he said it, that the pious Greeks had once called salamanders the little playmates of the gods, because they seemed to be drunk with so much sun. Frenero and Bernal were possessed with far less poetical thoughts, however, and I caught them whispering to one another about the gold that might be found in these graves. They had not forgotten what the Puná Indians had said. They kept at me till at last I gave them permission to open a grave, and sample what was hidden within.

With no delay they got to work, while Diego and I sat down and watched them. With much effort they moved away the flat stones barring the way to the graves, and then we saw that the burying place was shaped like a little roofless house. It had several compartments, or rooms, and it was easy to see that the one with clay and copper utensils was supposed to be a kitchen, that another was a bedroom, complete with mats, covers and a broken wooden frame of some sort. In the third and largest room of the grave, which undoubtedly was supposed to be the living room of the dead, were five mummies. The dried bodies were kept in sacks of woven reed. The mummies within the sacks were covered with finespun cloth. Their long, thin, desiccated heads, the cheeks as brown as mahogany, lay pressed against the fleshless knees, as if they were sunk in prayer. This sight moved me deeply, and on the impulse of the moment, I prayed for them, asking for the redemption of their souls.

Frenero and Bernal wasted no time, pulled everything apart in their greedy search. We could see that the dead were a family. One of the bodies must have been that of a full-grown man. At his right side sat a half-grown boy. Another of the strange figures had once been a woman, and at her left there was a young girl. Between father and mother, though pressed closer to the female than the male parent, was a small child. Bernal reached up various objects out of the grave, which we pawed over carefully only to find they were of no use to us. On the man's knee there was a big net, all folded, the lines of which were draped about his neck. Near him were placed hooks, fish-spear and lines. It was clear that during his lifetime the man had been a fisherman, and that after his death he had hoped to fish again in the waters of his Heaven.

I commanded Bernal to put back all the implements he had taken from the grave. I looked down with strange excitement into the yawning pit. I might have been looking into the dim past, seeing Adam and Eve whom my Queen Doña Juana once talked about in her castle in Tordesillas. When Frenero tried to straighten up the dead man's head, a coin fell out of his mouth. Like a flash I remembered that this must be the obol my Master Agrippa had once spoken of, which according to the Greeks is the coin that must be paid to Charon, the gloomy ferryman who transports the dead across the waters of the underworld. It chilled me to think of it.

Bernal handed me a little spindle and a folded pouch which lay in the lap of the dead Indian Eve. I opened the pouch, and some pieces of wood fell out which were cut in the form of knitting needles and spools. I saw that the dead girl had believed she would continue to spin, to weave and knit in the beyond, to make ghostly garments on the Isles of the West. Around her shoulders, under the straight black shining hair, there was a gay neckerchief into which was woven a design of little jumping monkeys. I thought how often during her days on earth, she must have fingered this neckerchief, examining it fondly, and how she had worn it when she made obeisance to her gods, to the demon of the broad sea, Pachacamac, or to the glowing sun.

The young maiden also had colors in her lap, little sticks and containers of a long since dried-out salve as if even among the dead she wished to be beautiful and desired. Right away I thought how I would tell Doña Isabella all about this, and I kept one little hollow bird's bone filled with some red stuff, unquestionably a cosmetic with which the Indian girl had once rouged her lips. Around the head of the little boy there was bound a beautiful yellow band gaily decorated with mussel shells. The little child, in his lap, had a dried parrot, the animal that had once been his playmate. The very last thing that Bernal found was a baby's rattle, made out of two mussel shells carefully bound together with a little stone in between.

Suddenly Frenero let out a cry of joy. In his hand he held a gold bauble in the form of a butterfly, just like thousands of those creatures which at the moment were flitting above the field of the dead or, wings tightly folded and feelers vibrating, were poised on the old gray stones. But before Frenero could give it to me it fell to fine gold dust in his great brown hand, as sensitive and as fragile as the creature itself. I held the little rattle to my tear, and idly made it resound. The sad little sound brought back the forgotten days of my early childhood and filled me with sweet nostalgia. The little rattle evoked fragmentary images, the memory of things once seen, and to me it was a great music, like the music of masters.

The legend of Appuleius came to my mind, the story of that anxiously errant, cruelly buffeted soul which ever sought to find respite from the envy of the gods in the arms of love. I thought of the writing of Heraclitus, that superlatively masculine thinker among so many philosophical women, priest of Diana in Ephesus. It is a writing that befits austere Doric columns and the stony forehead of the sun-god. It says that godhead is a sportive child, a child that sits on the seashore completely abandoned to breathless, joyous play, making shapes out of easily molded sand only to break them. I remembered how, when I had first heard of this intuition, I had thought it a chilling blasphemy. But here, beneath the mighty Andean sun, here at the edge of an open grave that was like a house, here, as I gazed upon long dead carcasses smelling of salt and bird droppings, carcasses with their heads bowed thoughtfully forward to their knees, this intuition seemed instinct with piety. I bent over the grave and, leaning forward as far as I could reach, I dropped the rattle back at the little boy's feet.

Bernal and Frenero were disgruntled. The result of their labors, the little bit of gold dust, was more than unsatisfactory. But I was satisfied, for I felt that I had taken something more important than gold from the grave. Diego stared as if bewitched. He, too, had heard the echo of long still voices, speaking of man's common destiny.

Evening was falling when we wended our way back to lonely Motupe. Behind us was the gigantic field of ruins, knife-edged shapes in the vibrant salty air. It was getting dark, and yet even at some distance from the stones, one could feel and see, not only their nearest face, but their other dimensions, their depth and height and weight. The monstrous silence, the stricken immobility of the city of ruins, I felt to be alive with expectation. This mood found sudden release when before our eyes thousands, yes, tens of thousands of bats rose up over the pyramids like a great host of winged souls.

On the next day we came to a river, that we forded only with the utmost difficulty. Now we were in the foothills of the great Andes, and the stream roared down to the sea in rapids as if overeager to be free of the stony fetters binding it to the heights. Here and there the river fell thunderously making great clouds of iridescent mist, and sprang down and down moss-green, slippery shelves of rock, over which dark pine trees hung, kissing the moiled water. It took us some time before we found a place that we thought navigable. With great toil we made a rough sort of raft. It was very hard to hold the raft against the stream. We stood up to our armpits in the ice-cold water as we worked it along. The horses and mules balked at going into the water. We had to shove them to get them to go in the deep places, where they began to thrash their way along in order to save their lives. By the time this was accomplished we were wet to the skin and glad to huddle about the fire that the Captain-General had had kindled.

Don Hernando de Soto, not bothering to dry himself, set out on a scouting expedition. It was not long before he was back, and with him he brought an Indian he had stumbled across, hiding on the riverbank. The slender Don Hernando de Soto, a whip of a man, drove the Indian before him toward the Captain-General with his naked sword. He suspected that the man was one of Atahualpa's spies. The Indian refused to say anything to Don Francisco's questions. We made him find his tongue in this fashion. Two men took him and before a blazing fire they held the soles of his feet. It was amusing to see the expression on his face when we blew the flame toward him. Scarcely did he feel a good blast of heat before he began to babble. Our amusement, however, did not endure forever. The Indian's revelations staggered us.

"It is true," the Indian said, "that I am a newsbearer for the child of the sun, the Inca. And yet my only commission was to make sure that you were taking the right way to Caxamalca."

This seemed strange to us. The Inca Atahualpa need not have employed such roundabout measures to ensure our safe passage. We saw this at once, of course, and began to press the Indian.

The Indian talked and talked, avoiding our questions in the artful manner of these people. Yet we soon put a stop to this. We took him and roasted his feet until he gave us more certain information. It took our breath away; it left our hearts hammering hard against our ribs.

"As for me," he said, "I know nothing, not I. I do not sit in the council of the Inca. I am only a common man. I only do as I am told. But I can tell you this. Through the army at Caxamalca the rumor is running that the Inca is going to lure you to the mountains, to cut you off from the sea. And when he has done this, he will strike you down and take your horses and your thunder weapons. That is all that I have heard. I know nothing about the details of the plan. But I know that the Inca has countless warriors. In the night their fires make the skies glow. Every day new troops come from Cuzco, so that soon the Inca will have the whole flower and strength of the South Country assembled about him."

We passed a restless night despite the fatigues of the day. Many slept not at all, but passed the time close to the fire, whispering and speculating on what was to come. The thunder of the near-by waterfall, the murmuring and rush of the river, the moaning of the night wind in the pines deepened a profound sensation of hopelessness. Already to retrace our laborious footsteps would be difficult, even impossible, for it was quite within reason that Atahualpa's intention to encircle us had already been carried out. In any case every step forward brought us closer to the final danger.

Don Francisco went from one campfire to the other, trying to hearten the men. We were well armed, he pointed out, and no true Spaniard flinched when it came to an issue. Father Vicente also made a pilgrimage among the campfires, carrying his black cross, and assuring us that God would never forsake us in time of stress. Just as the Archangel Michael had ridden with us against the Indians of Puná, so now the gates of Heaven would open up to save us. It was unthinkable, Father Vicente argued, that the heathen should triumph over the angels, even though they were more numerous than grains of sand on the seashore.

Gradually, as we pressed our lips to the cross he offered us, making vows that we would dedicate part of the golden booty to its spiritual purpose, we picked up heart. The feeling came over us, out of the midst of danger, out of the consciousness that God alone must now decide whether we should live or be annihilated, that we were unconquerable. We were taken by a tremendous fearlessness, a sense of being much larger than we really were. We thought that no matter what happened to us here on earth, things had come to such a pass that beyond any moiety of doubt Heaven would welcome us with open arms. Murderers, thieves, robbers and honorable knights as well were convinced that at least salvation was within their grasp.

The battle fever in our veins was so hot that camp was broken in time for us to be under way with the first gray of dawn. Hardly a bird had begun to sing in the pines when we began to march. Today, looking back, it seems to me as if God himself had spoken to us in that heathen mountain cleft, near the foot of the great waterfall. I only regret that I did not preserve the exaltation of the moment the rest of my life, and live in accordance with it. I wish that the purity of will which invested me then, free from all mundane coarseness, picayune considerations and deceits, had kept on animating my existence. But who is man, to measure himself with the angels while still here on earth! After all, our hearts are but weak vessels of clay. In vain we struggle to hold in them the great breath of the sea-god, or the breath of Christ.

Before us rose up another mountain. It was not lost in blue distance any longer, but towered up nakedly so close that it seemed ready to topple down on top of our heads. The weight of this mountain, felt with the eyes, doubled the leaden weight of destiny in our souls. We fought against it, and in all of us began a struggle to free ourselves of all weight whatsoever, of all physical hindrances, an Icarian travail. The Indian messengers and guides whom we took with us from Motupe led us over a paved road, but one very much narrower than the coastal highway. Our column was strung out as far as it would go while we tramped on in single file.

Beneath the steep walls of rock, or stuck on their sides like swallows' nests, I saw terraces cut with infinite labor into the living stone and covered with transported earth to raise a small patch of edible things. Most of them were planted with Indian maize. They often covered the whole side of a mountain, at least until the mountainside became a vertical cliff reaching up, crag on snowy crag, into a hard blue sky. Countless generations must have hacked at the adamantine surface of the mountain to achieve this monumental result. I confess that these garden terraces filled me with more awe than had the pyramid ruins and broken temples built in forgotten times by the people of Chimu. On the terraces we saw men hard at work with crude farmers' implements. From a distance the laborers in the narrow strips of field could not be distinguished from Cordovan peasants. We heard through the clear air the singsong of the women, a child's peal of laughter. And there was the clanking of our steel weapons, the ringing of the horses' hoofs on stone. It is these terraces which give the great range its name—the Andes. I have also heard, however, that they are called after the copper of which there are so many rich veins, and which the Indians have mined since time immemorial. For the Indian word for copper is *anta*.

It was so bright and the atmosphere was so clear that looking over our shoulders we could see the whole coastal plain spread out to the sea in a checkerboard of fields, woods, desert patches and little villages. Only the weakness of our human sight prevented us from seeing the actual line of breakers where the sea met the shore. Although the sun was so bright our eyes hurt and began to run water, all the time the sky over us became a darker and darker blue. Some thought we were moving into a terrible storm, so blue-black was the vault of heaven. It was the color of the sky itself, however, and not cloud. It changed from a light blue to cobalt and finally into violet.

But at this stage we had little time to look upward. Our attention was claimed by the path itself, which narrowed down continually. It began to wind about jutting rocks, described dizzy curves. It was like a road built to be traversed only by gods, who had no fear of the silent abysses threatening him who made the smallest slip.

Sometimes the prospect was so terrifying that the men let out moans of wonder. Bottomless canyons, sheer-sided, opened up in front of us as if carved out of the mountains with a clean stroke of a hammer. It seemed impossible to get through such places. Men and horses pressed hard against the raw rock, trembling and unable to move either forward or backward, dizzy and sick with the mere thought of the monstrous, cloudy depths not two feet away, ready to swallow them up. Only the mules clambered serenely on, placing one foot carefully ahead of the other.

The Indian guides ran back and forth, skipping over the loose rock fragments like goats, quite unconcerned with the height. They saved the day for us. Willingly they carried our heavy pieces of armor for us, leaving us free to pick our way over the slippery path. Some of us they led by the hand over the narrowest and most dangerous spots, where much of the road had broken away from the cliff.

Once we experienced exactly how this breaking off could happen. There was a sudden thundering, grinding and rushing noise far above our heads. The Indians shouted a warning, and all of us—men, horses and mules—shoved ourselves hard under the shelter of the cliff. Past us flew huge stones, caroming off one another, falling to pieces in mid-flight down into the abyss. Accompanying these gigantic missiles was a hail of little stones and gravelly dust. Trees came flying through the clear air, the dirt and stone loosening from the roots in mid-passage. The crashing and reverberation sounded strangely like rude laughter. The chills went up and down my back. For a moment I was sure that some mountain demon had tried to waylay us. But the Indians simply squatted quietly until the tumult had ceased and then rose to finish their work. In short, they thought no more of this ghastly performance than would a Spaniard of a heavy rainstorm.

The world of plants we had by this time left behind us. Only now and then were there stunted, twisted fir trees clinging to a split in the stone face of the mountains. As evening overtook us we wound our way over a natural stone bridge traversing shadowy depths so shattering to look down upon that I all but fainted with giddiness. After this passage over the canyon, which had been hollowed out by eons of tumbling water, the way quickly widened. Our Indians urged us to hasten so as to negotiate the pass before nightfall hemmed us in completely.

But night had already fallen when, high above us at a curve of the road, there rose the walls of a fortress. It was easy to see that a handful of determined men could prevent any number of invaders from moving along the highway beneath. They did not even need military weapons to do this, but merely to roll stones on top of us, carrying all of us into eternity.

We began to think that the end had arrived. There was every reason to believe that the way back to the coast was by now cut off for good. We had traversed many places where the work of one man could easily render the path impassable. Cold with apprehension and the bitter mountain chill, we watched the soundless, catlike movements of the Indians as they flirted with death at the brinks of the canyons. We realized how utterly helpless we were. Our heavy armor hindered us on such terrain. We were out of wind, our hearts hammered with the height, we could not use our horses on such splintered stony ground as this, and in the dark our arquebuses—the few that there were—would be useless.

Perhaps merely for the sake of action the Captain-General divided us up into small groups. He commanded me and my men to storm the fortress. This we attempted to do, though storming is a charitable way of putting it. Breathing heavily, our swords getting in the way every minute, we climbed up the sloping face of the cliff. Every minute I expected to hear the swish of Indian arrows, and to feel them pinning my belly to my backbone. And when I was not entertaining such unpleasant thoughts, I was wondering how soon it would be before I slipped and tumbled down into the rocky depths, carrying the rest of the party with me.

But there was no attack. We reached the steps cut into the sheer wall above the slope without any alarms. There was no sound at all. Only the deeply silent Andean night. I could not understand it. I pictured an Indian scheme to slaughter us in unimaginable ways. But in vain I tapped my way along the walls; in vain I strained my eyes. There was no one in the fortress, neither friend nor foe.

Here we spent the night. We kindled a fire, using wood we had brought along for that purpose. But the fire was much too small to give warmth to such a large company of men. They pressed close to it, standing up one behind the other to take turns at absorbing the blessed heat, to thrust out their hands to the flame over the shoulders of the man in front. It was icy cold. The sky over us was as black as black satin, and in it were stuck like golden nails stars so immense that a Spaniard who has not seen them could not believe them possible. We wrapped ourselves in our cloaks and lay down together in a mass. Our teeth chattered as the chill of the stone crept into our bones, and it was hours before we could go to sleep. I know it was long after midnight before I managed to sleep. Even then it was only a half-sleep in which I was aware of the unrelenting stone beneath me, of the frost in my limbs.

During the night I woke up. Next to me my good Sancho groaned aloud in a dream. Over me were the enormous stars. I raised myself half up. I looked about me.

Everyone was asleep, stretched out on the rocky floor of the fortress, like so many dead men. Only one tall man, his back turned toward me, stood at the edge of the wall, his crossbow ready, headed into the east. So great was my uneasiness and terror that I was on the point of calling to him when I realized that I was looking at Don Francisco Pizarro. Often during the night of his own accord he would relieve the night watch of his duty, though very naturally he was under no compulsion to do this. But he was one of those men who need almost no sleep at all. Day and night he was troubled with a deep-seated unrest. Under the stony calm of his features was that watchfulness, that unearthly agility and readiness for action, which God grants those destined for a time to rule and open the path for others.

As I studied this silent figure at the edge of the Incan parapet I gradually recovered calm.

That morning when we rose groaning with stiffness we found the water in the skins had been filmed with ice. Our noses blue, we set out on the march through the lonely peaks, through ravines and over passes which were marked by little loosely piled pyramids of stone.

At one point high over us on a ledge where there was a sunny strip of grass, we saw a herd of vicuñas grazing. These animals bear a striking resemblance to the Indian camel. I would say that they look like our sheep, except that they have a long neck curved upward and tall, pointed upright ears. They are strange creatures. From their shoulders hangs down matted wool much prized by the Indians. They stuck out their necks and looked at us with insatiable curiosity. They were like deer, who so often seem torn between fright and a consuming interest in human marauders when surprised in their haunts.

Our Indians told us that all the vicuñas of this Andean range belong to the Inca. Every year he and his nobles hunt the beasts. They are not killed, however, but merely trapped to be robbed of their wool and then freed again. Don Francisco ordered an arquebusier to shoot one of the beasts, but no sooner had he prepared his shot and raised the weapon than the vicuñas were off like a flash. They let out strange cries, wickering sounds and shrill flutings. Wonderfully graceful, they leaped from one ledge to another and were soon out of sight.

About noontime we began to climb up a wide meadow of bare stone. Here there were little animals who sat on the rocks like so many squirrels. They would not let us draw very close to them before they dashed off, piping resentfully. The sun on this stony meadow bore down on us mercilessly. At first we were glad to be warmed through by its rays, but soon it became intolerable, so knife-thin was the air. Many of us were overcome with mountain-sickness. These unfortunates staggered along like drunken men, and had to be supported by the Indians. Their eyes stuck out and became glassy. They vomited ceaselessly, retching when no more would come, as if stricken with seasickness. So bad did they feel that they begged us either to turn back or to run them through with their swords, a service they were too weak to perform for themselves. Their pain was terrible to behold, as if their bellies were being forced up through their gullets.

I myself was spared any serious attack of this mountain ailment. However, my lips began to bleed, and red ran from my nose in a steady stream. Some evil mountain spirit might well have given me a ringing blow on the snout, it appeared. Even the horses began to suffer and their quivering nostrils struggled for air. Only Indians and mules moved with the same slow indifference through the stony waste.

We had at last to remove our breastplates, so hot did they become, hotter than we had ever experienced them in the swamps of Panama. Our eyes burned like fire. Every forward step was an ordeal, a great journey. But our Captain-General forced us on. Don Hernando cursed the company for its slowness as we wound our way along at a snail's pace. But suddenly, in the very midst of his cursing, the breath in his throat failed him, his voice was a gurgle and his eyes began to pop from the injudicious effort of shouting. Two Indians had to be assigned to support him.

When the sun was sinking behind our backs we saw two birds come down from the peaks, which were still glistening unbearably bright. These two giant birds were such as the eyes of man never beheld before, except perhaps Sinbad's in the Arab tale. Slowly, their wings carelessly flapping, they swooped down low to inspect our company. We shouted at them and prepared to defend ourselves, for it looked as if they were going to try to carry one of us away. But they swept by heavily, really far above our heads, into the sun, indifferent. The Indians called them condors. They told us, frequently interrupting themselves to beg pardon of the condors' spirit, that these birds often swoop off with the young of vicuñas and llamas, and that sometimes they are even bold enough to attack shepherds, seeking to tear out their eyes.

When the sun plummeted out of sight behind the peaks, the cold became intense. The sweat of the march froze stiff in our garments, making them as hard to the touch as wood. We kept on until we reached another one of the fortresses identical with the one in which we had passed the night before. We were infinitely glad to have this simple shelter, and in the fullness of our hearts we sang a *Te Deum Laudamus*. The Indians told us, too, that the last pass was not far distant from this fortress. And so we picked up hope, despite the iron cold.

The next day the march became less difficult. For even though there was a repetition of the great heat and incredibly piercing light of the previous day's journey, yet somehow we were less afflicted by the sickness of the mountain heights. Our faces by now were burned black. Some had lost a layer of skin, and the underlayer was a blackish pink, very evil-looking. We were now wandering over a highly elevated plateau, a generally flat surface quite barren of vegetation. This region reminded me of the sierras at home, except that here everything was much larger, stronger, much more overwhelming. It was like marching through space that served as a courtyard to the halls of eternity, or one might have imagined he were slipping and sliding over the very roof of the world.

Occasionally in this supernal world we hit upon lakes with water so clear and so perfectly reflecting the walls of rock encircling them that the eyes were put to it to distinguish appearance from hard reality. Then we would come to the base of the snowy peaks themselves, thrusting up all jagged and riven and tortured whiteness, high, high above us until the heart and the bowels ached with the sight of so much immensity. When the sun failed, the white peaks threw great long bluish shadows, fingers pointed at us in implacable admonition. Indeed, it is hard to describe the effect of this landscape on our souls, the soundlessness, the ineffable silence, the unearthly extent of view no matter in which direction we looked. The prologue to eternity is hard for man's tender being to support. We longed mightily for villages, fields, for the narrow spheres of everyday man. We craved to be out of this titanic waste, this strewn work of first Creation made only for the habitation of God and His angels.

And I, though so young, actually felt like an old man who all his life has grubbed among the writings of the wise to piece out the final answers of life, and who now lets the last parchment fall from his hands, seeing that the unknowable must always remain unknowable, that the horizon ever slips farther away however much we struggle forward. Like such a sad old man I cried for smallness, for that which is familiar, beloved, childlike and close, for girls' chattering and laughter, the smell of herds in the stall, for narrow rooms and little things. The unanswerable, mute interrogation of this mountain land, the unheard ringing cold, gripped my heart.

For two days more we threaded our way along the saw-toothed range. On the second day we saw before us the most amazing clouds bundled together, all colors, a color that was almost music. Soon the whole sky and the rocky landscape was emerald green, as green as sea water. This green gave way to a rosy-red sheen, then violet, a color of renunciation which colored our armor and faces in the most melancholy tones, so that we looked like crusaders in a painting.

The Indians were not at all touched by the beauty of these clouds. On the contrary, they urged us to make as much haste as we could. Their anxiety was well-grounded. Soon it began to snow. A few gusts of wind, and the mountains were shut in by the falling snow. We moved through a whitish gloom that melted on our faces. Our steps were muffled and there were several narrow escapes when members of the party became separated from the column. But suddenly the snow shower stopped, quite as suddenly as it had begun, and then the sun painted the pure white covering in the gayest of colors.

The descent from the sierra was also a laborious proceeding. Although the road on the partly sun-protected side was not so steep, it was covered with a light film of ice. It was all we could do to keep our feet at all. From jutting rocks hung long icicles. At times we were taken by the horrible thought that perhaps our guides were leading us on into ever wilder country with the intention of finally abandoning us. This doubt was dispelled when a second emissary of the Inca came to meet us. With him he brought a gift of Indian camels from Atahualpa for our Captain-General.

We looked at these animals with disbelief. The llamas have a beautifully curved neck, thick wool and dark, rather fearful eyes, like the eyes of the Indian women. Their ears are long, placed somewhat forward of where one ordinarily expects ears to be, and stick up very straight. The Indians do not drive or ride them, but lead them along by a sort of halter. Generally they are good-natured patient beasts, and will carry heavy loads slung in panniers over their backs. But when they get ill-tempered, because the load is too heavy or because someone has been maltreating them, they spit at their masters just like the streetboys of Spain. Our men laughed until they nearly burst when they first saw this odd performance. We were much pleased with the Inca's gift, however, for our own beasts were overburdened and so worn out with the journey they could scarcely move forward.

It was on a November afternoon that we had our first sight of the city of Caxamalca. It lay in a fine valley whose lush green was a pleasure to the eye after the monotonous gray of the mountains. The little city was built of closely ranged, cubicular houses, white-walled and shining brightly, for the sun had just come out after a shower. In this intense light the distant city appeared to jump forward suddenly into our field of vision, and then was as suddenly veiled again by billowing showers of fine rain, a glittering pearly mist.

We saw that the town had a three-cornered plaza ringed round by buildings. At the edge of the town, in a little wood, there were long, low white structures brooding peacefully, and looking to us like cloisters. My eyes followed the valley winding away from us at the foot of the range. Through it ran a rather broad river with silver, flat waters. In places the meandering stream was crossed by little falls that shone brighter than the rest of the bright ribbon. Beyond the river the valley began to climb slowly, up into the heights of the middle cordillera whose jagged tops could be seen on the dim horizon, peeping over the intervening mist of secondary heights. The cordillera disappeared from view as we got down into the base of the valley.

The landscape here was idyllic, like one of those places in Tivoli or in the Sabine Mountains of which the Roman poets wrote in sonorous hexameters. This sense of *procul negotiis,* of detachment from the press of life, was strikingly enhanced when in between showers a rainbow began to hover over the shining waters of the river. The bow was not completely formed, just clouds of iridescent mist which seemed undecided whether to float off in fragmentary veils of color or to take shape over the river and town as a perfect arch. After the trials of the march the rainbow to me was an omen of release to come.

I did not suspect that before the headquarters of the Inca hung standards bearing flags into which the very colors of the rainbow had been worked. For it is precisely this natural phenomenon which these people consider to be most propitious for them, a sign of military victory, of successfully prosecuted war. To the men of Tavanta-Suyu the rainbow stood for the triumph of the sun in spite of darkness, and for the splendor of their god-king the Inca, when he rises up against his enemies and overcomes them. All this I had no inkling of. And yet, even as I watched this rainbow, I remember, I was uneasy. For one thing, out of the slope across the valley there arose white clouds of steam, something I could not account for. Diego de Vargas, whom I asked about this strange matter, said that perhaps they were hot springs such as those found on the slopes of the Pyrenees and Alps, where the gouty go to seek a cure.

We were all talking about Caxamalca when a heavy shower of rain began to fall, which turned into hail. We moved forward on the double-quick, soaked through to the skin. The shower did not last long. As on a capricious April day in Spain, the afternoon sun came out to warm our backs. Its slanting, dewy rays illumined a scene that boded ill for the lot of us. On the opposite side of the valley, some distance up the slope, we now saw countless ranks of white, pointed tents, which previously had been invisible because of the lay of the land. We strained our eyes toward this ominous scene, and as we drew closer to the town were able to discern thousands of men moving among the tents. We were faced by a host of Indian warriors, an army comparable in size to that once assembled before Granada by the dead King Don Fernando. We saw that the Indian outpost had not exaggerated Atahualpa's strength.

Our faces grim, we marched into the little city of Caxamalca. And once again we were doomed to disappointment. The place, just as Tumbez had been, was completely empty. Not one Indian came out to meet us or to dispute our entrance. Not one maiden rushed to us with a green bough of welcome in her hand. Not one child did we see. The disillusionment was that much the greater because the little city this time showed no signs of having been disturbed. The narrow streets and the white-walled houses were washed fresh with the rain and shone brilliantly in the sun. When we peered into the dark interiors we could see, neatly arranged just as the owners had left them, the household utensils and simple furniture of the vanished inhabitants. Hanging from hooks on bast cords, I remember, were thick ears of Indian maize. Some magic might have caused this disappearance, as complete as that related in the Arab tale of a ship with sails all set which flies over the water without a single living soul aboard to guide the passage.

The city of Caxamalca looked as much like a city of the dead as the weird burial ground at Motupe. And the worst part of it was that mocking us was the tent encampment of Atahualpa, right before our eyes. The forsaken city must mean some Indian trap, we thought, and could not puzzle it out. On tenterhooks we reconnoitered in the great three-cornered court.

We stopped before a massive building. Our Captain-General saw that this particular house could serve us well as a fort. It had no windows, and only three doors, which opened upward. Over the middle door a coiled snake was cut into the stone, and on that account we Spaniards called the place the "House of the Snake." The structure was made of cyclopean blocks of stone. The blocks were fitted together without mortar to make smooth walls, gently sloping backward. Around the roof there ran a breast-high parapet, and from this eminence there was a view over all the city, to the mountains beyond and the Inca's encampment.

The inside of the house consisted of several large rooms and of many little cell-like chambers. It brought to mind a cloister, with refectory, hall and many monks' cells. The temple, cloister or whatever it may have been, was a labyrinthine, evil retreat. Indeed, long years after as I look back, I am convinced that some inimical destiny invested the basalt floor, reflecting our faces like polished ebony, the dark stairs, and rooms which had never seen daylight. It is hard not to believe that fate had deliberately prepared the place for the purpose it later served. Yes, I would almost say that some invisible taurine monster lived in the building, a gluttonous Minotaur. Though I must admit that I was no second Theseus! No Ariadne came to hand me a ball of thread to guide my path.

19

ATAHUALPA

HOW things were with us that afternoon may easily be imagined. In the triangular plaza the soldiers lighted campfires and suspended blackened kettles over them. Others took care of the animals, a few of which had gone badly lame and needed attention. It was just the usual business of preparing for the night. Commonly at this time of the day, after the march was once again finished, everyone felt in good humor. Some of the men always began to whistle a merry tune and others would join in and sing. The loud voice of Father Reginaldo was much in evidence at this hour, for he was a wonderful taleteller, and not all his tales were fit to be recounted by a cleric.

It was always possible to gauge how the world was treating our company by observing the Dominicans. If the general spirits were carefree and lively, if we had come into something worth-while, as at Coaque, everybody gathered round Father Reginaldo, who came of peasant stock, and who was a worldly man—anyone could tell by looking into his heavy face—despite his holy calling. He could always make the men laugh.

But if the general state of mind was thoughtful, troubled with homesickness, everyone gathered about Father Juan de Vargas. For this monk, too, was a good storyteller, though he spoke very slowly and without Father Reginaldo's robust gusto. Father Juan knew every little village in the whole kingdom of Spain. He had been to Italy and Germany also, for his order had often commissioned him to act as messenger. He had wiped the dust of half of Europe from his shoes, and in his memory lived images of Seville, Toledo, Valladolid, Cologne, Augsburg, Rome and other great cities.

Besides these great centers of population he knew countless small cities, villages, crossroads, countrysides and cloisters which he could pull out of his hat, it might be said, like a magician. He had something interesting to tell about each place. In one it was the learned men, the nobles, the burghers or the Jews that he had come across. In another it was a battle, an execution that he had seen. In some other village he had given a woman or child a flask of wine, a piece of cheese or a loaf of bread to still her hunger.

Although Father Juan de Vargas' treasure chest was gradually exhausted, until at last every member of the company was intimately acquainted with his experiences, nobody minded that, and we would all patiently sit and listen once again to a story grown dog-eared with use. It was just the same as thumbing through a well-beloved book, this listening to Father Juan. In fact, now and then someone in our company would take exception to what Father Juan was saying, correcting him in some detail or other. These corrections he unfailingly accepted in good grace, and unfailingly his hearers were delighted and satisfied.

But if things were going really badly, as on this day, if we were on the verge of battle, or had suffered grievous misfortune, then Father Vicente de Valverde was the man of the hour. Father Vicente told nothing. Indeed, it was hard to get him to read a chapter out of the *Lives of the Saints*. He was silent and inexperienced in the world. Before coming with us he had scarcely ever left the narrow circle of the cloister. But it would never have occurred to him to leave his serenely withdrawn existence for such a life of turmoil as ours had not his Prior recommended him to our King Don Carlos as a serious, brave and steadfast priest who would be a good confessor for Don Francisco Pizarro.

The order once given, this simple man had taken a grip on his wanderer's staff with the same good grace in which he had dedicated himself to the small affairs of the monastery. Without great expectations and with no pride in adventure, he had casually embarked with us on our voyage toward the farthest Indies. And yet, simply because he anticipated no more than vicissitudes, misery and perhaps a martyr's death, nothing could feaze him. Now that he had been commanded to work for the Indians—a command which to him came directly from God through his superior officer—he knew no other goal. Again and again he overcame great trials, the while patiently, blindly holding onto his Bible, his breviary and his simple black cross. With these feeble weapons in his hand, he crossed seas, mountains, deserts, primeval forests and blooming meadows alike, oblivious to all change, set on spreading the teachings of Christ.

He regarded the company as men dedicated to the work of God like himself. In accordance with this idea he nurtured our spirits with Masses, prayers, songs and constant genuflection in outlandishly inappropriate places. And whenever there was fear, or need or suffering, then Father Vicente de Valverde became the rock of Moses out of which courage flowed without cease. For he never doubted for a moment that our company stood under the special protection of the angels who, since the beginning of time, had made possible what no man could seriously undertake even in his boldest moments.

So now in this trying hour every eye stole toward the monk who sat as if he were in a cloister orchard. Don Hernando de Soto was the first to go up to him, accompanied by several of his caballeros, and ask for his blessing. This aroused everyone's curiosity, for heretofore there had been a decided coolness, even downright dislike at times, between the two men. When Don Hernando, the knight of knights, bent his knee before Father Vicente, we all knew there must be some special reason. At once the rumor spread that Don Hernando was going to propose some unusual course of action to the Captain-General.

For me this rumor was soon translated into staggering fact. De Soto, after consulting with Pizarro, came over and asked me to accompany him in seeking an audience with the Inca.

Before the city there was a marshy meadow which we traversed at a rapid trot. We came to the banks of the river that I had seen from the heights. To our left was a narrow wooden bridge, but we preferred to swim our horses across or let them wade if they could, in order to test the difficulty of the ford should retreat be cut off at the bridge. To our relief we found that the water at no point was deeper than our stirrups.

Soon we began to pass isolated groups of Indian warriors who regarded us with hostile curiosity as we flew by them at a smart clip. Suddenly a horn blew clear and wild behind us and, wheeling, we saw that the Captain-General had sent twenty riders led by his brother Don Hernando Pizarro to accompany us. They were a stirring sight as they galloped headlong to catch up with us. These twenty were fewer than we secretly hoped for, but at least they represented some attempt to show the Inca what the power of Spain meant to those who dared oppose it. Looked at coldly, this trifling display of strength might well do more to injure our cause than to help it. But we did not think of that, and turned our eyes straight ahead and away from the endless ranks of red-skinned fighters on every side.

As we got deeper into the encampment we saw that many of the warriors were busy around the tents. Their lances, leaned against each other, were neatly stacked up in what I had been told was the Swiss style. I remarked this, and remembered, privately, that the Swiss are reputed to be the best foot soldiers in Europe. We would have been overwhelmed in this sea of red flesh had we not had our horses. They aroused much more curiosity and awe than we did. I could very well understand that. What astonishment there must have been in the camp of the Greeks when down from the wooden mountain slopes, long-maned and round of beard, came trotting the Centaurs, their bodies all alather. We must have caused similar consternation, with our white faces—browned now by the mountain sun, to be sure—with our armor and our prancing horses.

Indian runners led us without dismounting into the presence of the Inca himself. He sat in a sort of garden house, bedded on soft cushions, his legs drawn under him like a Turkish sultan. Clothed in white, lovely women and young girls stood behind him. Around him stood his chieftains and courtiers, if such they could be called, splendidly dressed, all of them. He however wore a simple red robe. But we had no trouble recognizing him. It was not only the fillet with the fringe hanging over his brows. It was the nobility of his bearing, the calm self-possession so different from the fawning solicitude of his underlings.

And beyond that, as I have noticed in so many men of great deeds, there was a terrible coldness in the face of this king. It was a face hewn out of red porphyry, the face of a young man perhaps thirty years old, a face that has seen far, far too much. The soft, easy contempt which comes from much knowledge of men's ways was in the lineaments, that contempt for humanity which must ensue if there is no belief in Christ, immortality and the high purpose of the soul. He did not look at us directly, but appeared to be lost in thought as he stared at the ground. Not a single word did he utter to relieve us of a constraint holding us rigid on our horses, which pawed the ground in front of him.

At last Don Hernando Pizarro rode up close, and informed him that he and his brother, the Captain-General Don Francisco Pizarro, were like all of us subjects of a great King from the other side of the sea. Don Hernando spoke in measured tones. He said that Don Francisco, on the other side of the sea had heard about Atahualpa's victories, and that he and his men had come to render the Inca homage and to bring him the salvation of Christ. He ended with the wish that Atahualpa on his part would pay us Spaniards a visit.

Don Hernando's words were translated by Felipillo. But there was no answer. The whole assembly appeared to be transfixed, as in the fairy princess' castle when the witch spoke the magic words of banishment. Some of the women stood on tiptoe the better to see over the broad shoulders of the courtiers. But even they said nothing, quite different from the women of the court in Spain, who will whisper excitedly even when the King is present. For some time, a small eternity, we waited, simply staring at the Indian leader. At last one of the men standing at the Inca's side said, "That is good."

The words were meaningless. Don Hernando Pizarro began to talk some more, laboriously and much louder, as if he were addressing a deaf man. Yet he was polite, and excused himself repeatedly, as if in the presence of Don Carlos himself. He said in conclusion that he would like to have an answer from the lips of Atahualpa himself, some word that he could carry back to the Captain-General.

A faint smile came over Atahualpa's face, as if he had heard for the first time. But the smile immediately vanished when he began to speak. Felipillo translated his speech, which he delivered curtly. "Today," he said, "I am fasting, but tomorrow this will have finished. Then I will come with my warriors. Until that time you can stay in the big houses in the square. But keep away from the houses of the people. Tomorrow I shall give more commands."

As he spoke, Atahualpa measured us slowly. His eyes came to rest on Don Hernando de Soto. De Soto's horse, an expensive beast, was a full-blooded Arabian. He was pure black with a white marking on his face. De Soto sat as light as a feather in the saddle, his right hand quietly poised on his hip. The spirited animal bit at the metal in his mouth, tossed his head and pranced unceasingly. But De Soto with no trouble at all held him in, using only the left hand, and seemingly paying no attention to the horse's gyrations. Horse and rider were the image of controlled strength. Together they looked quite different from the gigantic Don Hernando Pizarro on his tall roan, and from me, a beardless youth, on my piebald.

When De Soto saw that Atahualpa was looking at him—and at his horse—he correctly interpreted the Inca's unspoken wish. He nodded and eased up on the bit. The horse began to pace in a style which is like the Spanish gait, lifting the hoofs up daintily, the head turned sidewise, but with so much spirit that the procedure was free of the painful gravity often seen in such exhibitions. An excited whisper came from the Indians, and the women leaned still farther forward on tiptoe in order not to miss a thing. Atahualpa's face came to life. Pleasure and interest were written on it, and for the first time the features lost their casual pride and bored irritability. He showed the reluctant excitement that children show at the sight of weapons—fear, delight and simple, engrossing curiosity. From where I stood I could see that the Inca's eyes were marred by little red veins. They were choleric, bloodshot eyes. I was struck by the sudden, absorbed change, as if symbol of majesty had by some magic become naïve, vulnerable man. From that moment on, having seen this side of the Inca's nature, I always inclined to take his side in the grievously violent events which shortly ensued.

De Soto now put his animal through other paces for the Inca's delectation, and I was amazed how easily the sensitive horse shifted from left to right in full gallop. I had never seen De Soto show off his riding skill before for of course there was no occasion for any such maneuvers on the march. Finally he rode off some distance, wheeled about, and came up to the Inca at full gallop, the horse's hoofs all but striking the belly. Then, drawing in the reins, he brought his mount up short. The foam from the horse's mouth flew off and flecked the Inca's red robe. Don Hernando de Soto bowed deeply from the saddle, letting his open gloved hand sweep down in obeisance to the Indian king in the fashion of a winner in a knightly tournament of older times. Not a word did the Inca say. Just once did he cast a swift glance out of his bloodshot eyes at two of his warriors who had recoiled from the galloping horse as it loomed up on them. I learned later what this single glance meant. Both soldiers were immediately hanged for cowards, their bodies sliced open, and the bowels removed, so that they resembled slaughtered oxen as they hung from the Indian gibbet, their throats stretched out of shape.

The Inca made a careless, scarcely perceptible gesture. Two women crept toward us, carrying in both hands ceremonial beakers of gold. One of these white-clad girls stopped before my horse. She was hardly more than a child. Her skin was light bronze. Silver bracelets tinkled softly on her arms. I could not take my eyes from the tender wrists, the great black eyes and the soft oval of the face. In my own language I thanked her for the gift, and told her—Spanish fashion—that the wine would taste a thousand times better since it came from her hands. It never occurred to me that this ritual was pointless since she could not understand a single word of what I was saying, any more than she could understand the murmur of a brook or the sound of the wind in the treetops. And yet, curiously enough, she apparently did catch the sense of what I was saying. For do not all young men say the same things to girls? In any case, she dropped her eyes, and a deep blush darkened her face.

As this happened, I became aware that someone was watching the little drama. It was the Inca, Atahualpa, observing me carefully, and not inimically, so I felt. Whether his approval was caused by my person, by my courtesy toward the girl, or by my horse I could not tell. Or whether all three of these contributed to his mood. In confusion I raised the beaker to my lips. It was filled with chicha, a foamy, cooling drink which the Peruvian Indians make from crushed corn fermented, just as the Flemings make their heavy beer from hops and malt mash. Still unsure of myself, I returned the empty beaker to the maiden, who moved backward as lightly as a fawn and vanished into the crowd.

Don Hernando Pizarro drank too, and after this formality we left the presence of the Indian king, bowing our way out, uttering many polite phrases that no one understood. Slowly we rode back to Caxamalca, letting the Indians see that they did not bother us a single jot however great their numbers might be. But our thoughts were not so self-assured. The Inca Atahualpa undoubtedly was a proud man and a worthy enemy. The men of our little party spoke of the strangely bloodshot eyes, and in conversation Don Hernando de Soto compared him to Don Cesare Borgia, the natural son of His Holiness Pope Alessandro, the sixth of his name, who, so he said, had identical eyes.

I listened to all this with only half my mind. I was busy thinking of the slender arms and the black eyes of the Indian girl who had favored me with the draught of chicha. I thought of how she had blushed and that I had acted like a bumpkin right under the eyes of the Indian Borgia. I imagined a long story in the manner of those in love, and spun it out as busy as a silkworm. I remember how I thought the fifteen-year-old girl must be the Inca's sister. Following Don Hernando de Soto's cue, I made her into another Doña Lucrezia Borgia, of whom I had heard so much whispered in the house of Don Garcilaso. In my daydream once again this Indian Lucrezia reached me a foaming golden beaker while her brother out of his bloody eyes watched thoughtfully.

Each of us in his own mood, we reached the House of the Snake in the triangular plaza. The ones who had remained behind came rushing out to ask a thousand questions.

The sun had already set when we all gathered for a council of war—the men on guard excepted—on the roof of the building. In the western sky there was a light reflection illumining the greenish tumbled clouds of the mountain country. Hail was still in the air. We could see it gathering in the tattered clouds clinging to the distant peaks just before night closed in. Our faces were the color of sulphur in the ominous light as Don Francisco Pizarro commenced to bare his plans to us.

I could not help thinking in my fevered mind, as Pizarro began his discourse, that great events in the history of mankind are always preceded by awesome catastrophes in nature. The ancients always maintained that before mighty battles the earth trembles and thunder rocks the walls, as if the battle were already in progress in the heavens and in the earth beneath, as if the deeds of men were after all but a timid epilogue to a battle of demonic powers that has forced partisanship on fragile mortals treading the earth. But the somber yellow light soon gave way to blackness. A few stars were out, and about them the sky was a deep blue.

All the time that he talked, Don Francisco Pizarro stood in thick shadow, so that he was a full voice disembodied. His cavaliers confronted him in a half-circle, and behind them crowded all the common soldiers. Everyone hung on his words, scarcely daring to breathe, quickly choking back a cough if it gathered in his throat. Not one of us but knew that the hour of decision had come at last, inevitably, as surely as the hours of a clock creep forward, as the stars roll through the heavens, as time itself.

Our Captain-General himself felt this hour of fate now reaching its zenith. For this fate, which carries all of us with it whirling along on the chariot of time, was instinct in Don Francisco Pizarro. He felt it in the very marrow of his bones. The voice of destiny rang in his ears where it might whisper in ours. It spoke to him as the Sybilline oracles spoke to the devotees, and to no one else. And we were the supernumeraries, the ones carried along in the rush, robbed of any personal capacity for decision. For his part he was free, in his element. For him it was his hour of release, of that irrevocable steely giving up of the self which Antonio Cardinal de Guevara has called the most exalted time of a man's life. I, for my small part, was distinctly aware that I was abandoning my freedom, and I thought, He, too, is losing his, this Pizarro, the swineherd. So I thought, in my greenness. I felt as if all his past deeds, his thoughts and plans, his whole life had caught him up as an avalanche, gathering speed, sweeps an unlucky traveler along with it down a mountainside. All during the discussion I was depressed, filled with dread, not dread of pain or death, but of something undefinable. I know now what I did not know then. Only my heart by intuition perceived what was happening, this renunciation of my will to the grandiose destiny of Don Francisco Pizarro. The monstrous will power of this wild Spaniard had chained us all to him.

Today I often have a vision, perhaps a dream—for I often dream. And in this vision I see, fastened to the triumphal car of Pizarro, two women, as in those pictures which artists paint for kings and princes. One of these women looks like my Queen, Doña Juana. She wears a black shawl over her forehead, half covering the sad eyes. And the other woman is an Indian princess—a princess like the Laanta whom I shall soon tell about—with dark eyes downcast, a tender, supple figure clothed in white. For me these women in the little vision stand for Spain and the Indies, for my homeland and the land of the future. On and on the triumphal car drags these two, while behind them, straggling, disappearing into the distance, marches a murmuring throng, chained men and women, weeping children, a pitiful segment of humanity.

Don Francisco, the breeder of history, stood up straight, his back to the parapet; his hands leaned on the stones, like Antaeus gripping the earth, sucking strength from it.

"There is only one way, just one," he said quietly. "We must go this way, or we shall die, I and all of you. There is no choice." He fell silent, and let these words sink in until we were taut with expectation.

"This Indian king, the Inca Atahualpa, is a traitor," said Pizarro. "He has betrayed his relatives and his brothers. He has put them to death. Not the smallest of his subjects can really consider himself safe from his caprice. He is a heathen. He prays to the sun. In his harem he has a hundred concubines, like a Turk, his own brother in heathenish disbelief. God curse them both, I say. God curse him, this Inca! May he rot standing up. What can we expect from such a man? What can Spaniards expect, trapped in this little city? Nothing. Nothing at all but death. Behind us, in front of us and on all sides are mountains, waste land and the empty sea. And beyond this the armed power of the Inca."

He thrust out his hand to the east where countless fires were glowing and shadowy figures darted back and forth, pigmy-size at such a distance.

Again the silence grew oppressive as each one of us meditated in his fashion on the hopelessness of the situation. Then Pizarro with his gloved hand struck his breastplate a ringing blow. "Now is the time to speak up! Now is the time to say that I am the guilty one. That I have led you into this impasse."

But no one said a word of reproof.

"Yes, it is true, I am the guilty one. I, Francisco Pizarro, I have led you here. And I have not done it out of poor judgment. I have done it deliberately, scheming every inch. I knew that every step we moved from Tumbez, every step we took through the mountains, would lead us to this final point. Now, on my initiative, we must all face the crisis. But there is a way out, my friends. Tomorrow at this time all the riches of this land will be in your hands."

His voice rose powerfully as he said this. A cry of astonished incredulity went through the company. I, myself, thought that at last this gray man had gone mad. He let all of us share in this wonder, and then continued, "Did not Don Hernando Cortés burn his ships behind him? I have no ships to burn. But there are walls of stone between us and home. No escape for us! Not one of you can escape so long as the Inca has control of his armies. And so, what does that mean? It means the Inca must die or do as we say! For weeks the Inca's warriors have crept into the passes behind us. They are watching at the swamps, in the narrow places. The fortresses are now peopled with Indian soldiers, ready to fall on us.

"No going back. And above all, not for me. For not once in my life have I ever flinched. Now I am not afraid. It is the happiest moment of my life. The blood is singing in my veins. I may die, but I shall have shot a pretty bolt before that happens. Yes, the Inca must die or bow his neck to my will.

"There is a way out, if the angels stay on our side. And they will, so I believe with all my heart. God has never forsaken his obedient servants in their time of need. We are fighting for him, for him and the Blessed Virgin and her beloved Son against the heathen. What good are these masses of men? What do they mean as they stand now? Nothing, nothing until they are under the whip of sanctity! A whip which we shall wield with Spanish hands and wrists. What do such numbers mean? Nothing! The very size of the army shall prove its undoing.

"This is my plan. It is a plan that I have dreamed of for years. It will work. Tomorrow this Inca, when he comes to us, must be seized. He thinks he is coming here to deliver orders, so he says. His eyes shall be opened, for he is dealing with Spaniards. In his whole life he has never felt the weight of a Spaniard's sword. He has known nothing but slaves. Shall you lick his spit? Or I, Francisco Pizarro? When the signal is given, we shall come to grips with him, make him a prisoner of Spaniards."

Pizarro now laughed wildly. His laughter caught on, and soon all of us were roaring with laughter, bursting our sides at the wonderful riposte we were about to deliver. It was unnatural, devilish, the sensation of power, of invincibility, that was in us.

"My little plan," Pizarro said, "depends entirely on sudden execution. Not one slip must happen, or we are done for. Every man must carry out orders, and at the same time act on his own initiative. We must be as sudden as a mountain storm. There can be no thought of quarter. This is no time for milksop reflections and holding back. The swords must slice those red bodies to ribbons. Otherwise we shall die, and die slowly. Cut down anyone who stands in your way. Do it in the name of the Father, the Son and the Holy Ghost. But no one must harm the Inca unless the very worst comes. He must be kept whole at all costs. So long as he is safe in our hands, we too shall be as safe as if we rested in the arms of Jesus."

"And now, whoever is against my plan must speak up before it is too late. In this we must all be one. If anyone can improve on what I have had to say, out with it."

Don Hernando de Soto strode to the fore. "We can't do this," he said. "It is betraying a host. Atahualpa has done nothing to us. He has given us wine, has he not? He has been friendly enough. I am against this plan. I fail to see how such evil seeds can ever bear good fruit."

And Juan Pizarro shouted, "Yes, by God, it is treachery!"

Don Hernando Pizarro stroked his long beard and looked gravely at his youngest brother. Gonzalo said, "I don't see any treachery in it. It's war. All's fair in war."

"But we are not at war," objected Pedro Pizarro.

"I don't know much about these matters," said Don Francisco amicably, talking to Don Hernando de Soto, "but it strikes me that we should all like to hear what Father Vicente has to say."

Don Hernando nodded agreement slowly, then shrugged his shoulders contemptuously.

Father Vicente said, "Between Christians and heathens there is always war. God himself has cast the gage. It is not necessary that mere men should trouble their heads over any such decisions. It has already been done for us. The Cid himself, the flower of Spanish knighthood, fell without mercy on the kingdom of the Moors. Charlemagne did not hesitate to raise his sword against the Caliph of Cordova, who had done nothing to injure him. In these matters all knightly argument is utterly pointless. Are you forgetting that this heathen Atahualpa is living in sin with many wives, that he is flouting the holy sacrament of marriage before our very eyes? He is doing this in sheer perverse blasphemy, like a Flemish anabaptist. Why does he not content himself with a stallful of whores, like a Christian prince, if his flesh burns? Weakness of the flesh is quite different from obstinacy in the very teeth of God's commands. To go to bed with a pretty girl is in itself no negation of the sacrament."

Some of the soldiers began to laugh at this involved argument, but Father Vicente silenced them, and his voice grew hard. "Furthermore," he continued, "according to the very laws of this land Atahualpa is not the rightful king. He is no more than a usurper. This, too, is a serious breach. For the Apostle Paul has said, Obey the law. And our Lord Jesus Christ has said, Give unto Caesar that which is Caesar's. On all these grounds I see Atahualpa as standing condemned. To me our Captain-General's plan is inspired by God himself to meet God's ends without spilling too much precious Christian blood."

It was now Don Pedro de Candía who had his turn. He wore his richly golden armor and his eyes were sad. "But suppose," he said, "just suppose that the Indians fight back when we try to take their king. Or usurper, as he may be. Supposing that they get the upper hand with sheer numbers. Supposing they take us all prisoners, that they make martyrs of us, burn us up, put us on the rack, dig out our eyes, wrap us in nets and cut off our balls? What then, Don Francisco? They do such things, as we all know. Can we stand it, this possibility? I can, if the test comes. I can even stand being castrated. It nearly happened to me once, and it's no joke, so I'm wondering how the rest of you can face the issue. They say, A man who courts danger dies. I'm not speaking out of cowardice. But to be gelded . . . that is not easy to bear."

"I've thought of all that, my dear friend," said Don Francisco Pizarro. "You must believe me that no one will raise his sword against us so long as Atahualpa is alive. These Indians know only one thing, and that is to obey. It is impossible for any one of them to learn to command overnight! There are people of small spirit, like the Moors, like the Arabs. All these people, what do they count for? They are red puppets who dance when someone, some Atahualpa or other, pulls the strings. It is true that if we were dealing with free men our situation would not be so easy. That's true enough, but if that were the case over the door to this house they would have carved two, or three, or four snakes instead of one. This people who face us have only one head. This head is Atahualpa.

"Do you remember the night that Don Hernando Cortés talked about the people of Tenochtitlan in my brother's house? Did he not compare them to bees in a hive? I have not forgotten what he said. Not I. His words are seared in my brain, whatever you people may think.

"I have watched. I have kept my eyes open. Every time that Felipillo talked to the alcalde of some Indian town, every time that he passed words with the overseers of the caravansaries, the Inca's emissaries, the shepherds, the porters, yes, even the peasants in the fields, I have listened. And one thing I saw every time. I saw that every man had sold his freedom for security, for some position or other, for bread and a certain future, however small it might be.

"I admit that I was impressed. I was impressed, to be sure, by the wisdom, the foresight, the greatness of these Indian schemings. Perhaps nowhere else on earth are there such roads. Who else but ourselves has even seen fortresses hewn out of living stone, bridges swinging in the air, aqueducts and all the rest of the Inca's accomplishments?

"But at the same time I saw something else. This is something that makes all the difference in the world. The security these red-skinned people have does not stem from God, nor does it stem from the soul. It is a security engineered by the Devil. The greater the works of these people, the more miserable the men who create them. Don Hernando Cortés spoke the truth but not the whole truth. In my opinion he overestimated the worth of an Indian. Is there, consider, a single suffering beggar on the streets of Spain, a single leper with flesh hanging in strips, who would change his lot with an Indian? What do you think! I never saw a Spaniard who would exchange his freedom for a piece of bread and a roof over his head. That is impossible, whatever may come. We all understand that. And as for me I would rather have for brother a common murderer, a street thief, the hardest ridden man in Castile, why, even a pot-gutted merchant, than one of these Indians, even the best of them."

All of us murmured agreement to this, for all that Don Francisco Pizarro said was as plain to see as the noses on our faces. Our Captain-General had only put into words what every one of us felt in his heart.

"If I think of these things, it is impossible for me to be afraid of these Indians even if they are as thick as flies. A lion would not shrink before a herd of ten thousand sheep, or a hundred thousand, when he lurks behind them to strike down his evening meal. But there is no point in starting a war to death. It would net us nothing at all to kill them all off. There is an easier way, I tell you. We can wage a little war, over in a minute, like pulling a tooth. Tomorrow night, if we act with courage, this whole kingdom will be in our hands, to the glory of God, to the honor of Spain and of our King Don Carlos. See! The booty is immense. The land is rotten with gold. There are whole mines of it to be dug out at our leisure. Why, the humblest among you will have more slaves than the Duke of Béjar has peasants working in his fields."

There was no resisting this speech. There were loud cries of relief. Friends put their arms about each other, and struck each other happily on the back. The riches about to become our own glistened madly in front of our eyes. The wild voices, a great roar, rang through the night over the empty city.

Now Don Francisco raised his hand in admonition, cautioning us to silence. "Easy, my friends, easy," he said. "Talk is cheap. The work has to be carried out before we can pat ourselves on the back. First we have to bell this wether. Or as Cortés puts it, capture the queen bee. We've got to do it smoothly, so that all the workers hardly know the difference until it's too late to do anything about it. Quiet, now! Tomorrow morning we'll make ready. I'll share out the rest of the wine. We'll be in a good mood for the day's work."

Not one of us had a good night's sleep. On the stone floor we tossed and rolled, impatient for the day to come. And indeed hardly had the eastern sky grayed before cockcrow ere the trumpets blew, summoning us to duty. We assembled in the triangular plaza. Pizarro inspected the ranks, making little jokes, warning us not to do this, telling us to be sure to do that. With infinite care he tried the tautness of the crossbows. He wet his fingers to try the edges of our swords, which were razor-sharp. And he could find nothing at fault. Not a man but was prepared to do all in his power. And more than that. Not a man but was aware that his life depended on the excellence of his weapons and the hardiness with which he used them. Pizarro examined the horses, felt their hoofs and fetlocks, ran his hands over their hides. Once a thought struck him, and he had us fasten upon our saddles and bridles the little bright bells we had brought along as trinkets for the Indians.

He divided the mounted men into two detachments. One of these he placed under his brother's, Don Hernando's, command. The other he put under the command of Don Hernando de Soto. These two detachments he placed to the right and the left of the House of the Snake in the open place. They were to wait for his signal and then hem in Atahualpa's bodyguard. And hidden in the houses along the two sides of the triangle leading to the point of exit were the foot soldiers, whose duty it was to cut off any counter-attack by the Indians not immediately attached to the person of Atahualpa. Don Pedro de Candía was put in charge of the two cannon—which vainly enough we called "our artillery"!—set up on the roof of the House of the Snake. These commanded the narrow entrance by which any Indian reinforcements would have to enter the city. He was given extremely explicit orders to avoid directing his fire down into the plaza under any circumstances, in order to obviate any possible risk of hitting his own men.

After our Captain-General had inspected everything and everyone to his satisfaction, Mass was celebrated by Father Vicente de Valverde. Our weapons clattering, our spurs all a-tinkle, we fell on our knees and gravely sang, *Exsurge, Domine, et judica causam tuam.* Sang it, that is, as best we could, many of us not understanding a word of what we said. But what we meant in our hymn was this, Rise, God, to defend Thy cause. Because we rallied Him thus, perhaps, God poured immense courage into our hearts, glad to see men of His own heart. Our spirits, fevered and wearied from the sleepless night, became calm and fresh as a spring morning.

Thus we refreshed our souls, the most important thing for men about to enter into battle. Then we refreshed our bodies. We filled our bellies with meat, bread and freshly roasted Indian corn. This we washed down with red wine. After this ritual was over and done with, satisfied and without a quiver, every one of us the same, we took our places. I stayed with Gonzalo Pizarro, with Master Pérez, my Sancho and the three Dominicans, the lot of us surrounding the Captain-General. This entourage made as if they were about to greet the Inca in the middle of the plaza.

It was well that we had eaten and stiffened our spines for a good part of the day elapsed before the Inca finally appeared. The Captain-General's face grew gray with waiting. I could see this, so close was I to him. But he did not falter. It was only that his face looked old and weary with so much waiting. The uneasy soldiers could not keep their eyes from the entrance to the plaza through which the Inca was to come, and persisted toward the end in ducking out their heads for a fleeting glimpse. At last one of the lookouts informed us that the Indians were now a mile and a half or so from the little town. Don Francisco gave orders that I was to ride out and greet the Inca, telling him that supper was awaiting his pleasure.

I gave my piebald my heel, and trotted on the fateful errand, not too fast, nor too slow. I rode alone, for the Captain-General at this critical moment was taking no chances on being betrayed by our frightened interpreter Felipillo. When I drew up before the Inca, I saw that he remembered me. I had some difficulty making myself understood. I knew some words of the Indian language, which is called Quichua, but in all the excitement what I knew slipped my mind, and I had to rely for the most part on sign language. The Inca hesitated, so it seemed to me, and looked carefully into my face. At last he nodded slightly, still keeping his eyes fixed on me. Then, as I was bowing preparatory to taking leave, he moved suddenly forward and, reaching up to where I sat on my horse, let his beautiful hand rest on the hilt of my sword. He caressed it exactly as a man caresses a women's leg underneath the knee. I believe I have already said that I inherited this sword from my father.

Facing the Inca, aware of his appraising look, of the fine hand that caressed the hilt of my sword, I became thoughtful. Of a sudden it horrified me to think that this sword, instead of bringing me lasting honor, might bring me lasting shame. The same sword, I told myself, that had once made its edge felt among the Moors before Granada in the service of our great Queen Doña Isabella, was now to be turned against a trusting king come to share an evening meal with the Captain-General in our camp.

But with harsh clarity the necessity of the situation also stood out in my mind. I saw that no matter what my belated feelings might be, the sword must be so used. Yet I could not stomach my mission. I saw that Pizarro's star, even though I had irrevocably committed myself to it, was an evil one. Better, perhaps, I thought, if the Inca's land had remained forever undiscovered between the two great seas! The New World looked to me like a magic garden, a gigantic garden replete with topless mountains, black forests and immense plateaus, in which demons, strange customs, gold and bronze-skinned women must ever bewitch Spanish mankind.

With the Inca, indeed, were some women, brought this far and then sent back. Among them was the girl who had offered me the drink of chicha. She was watching me, I saw. Moving about the Indian chief, I held in my horse with a great deal of ceremony, and saw that she watched me with fear, expectation and hope. She looked at me on the horse as if I were a half-god. This wrenched my heart, for I knew that by no standard did I merit this exalted consideration. I had to look the other way, for I liked this girl and I was afraid that she would read the betrayal in my eyes. In confusion I dug my spurs into the piebald who, astonished at this uncalled-for treatment, reared up, took the bit in his teeth and made off wildly in the direction of Caxamalca. It was all I could do to get him under control.

Back in the market place I informed the Captain-General about all that had taken place. His drawn face relaxed. He took off his helmet and wiped the sweat from his forehead. In his moment of intense anxiety he had looked like an old man. Now, magically, his features changed, and once again he seemed forty years old. It was plain to see that his great exploit was what lent him energy and youth enough to carry on so arduously. This was the Pizarro style. Don Hernando once remarked to me that he and his brothers were not among those fops who gave up the ghost around fifty years of age, excusing themselves with a weak heart or an ailing lung. No such childish nonsense for them, he said. We all take it for granted, he informed me, that we'll live to be a hundred even if we have to suck the marrow out of our own bones to do it. Providing that the hangman of the Indians doesn't nip us off first, he added grimly.

There was another long wait, then we heard thin music coming from a distance. And there were thin, high-pitched songs sung out of key, but in an exciting rhythm. It was like the singing of spirits from Hell. Involuntarily some of the men gripped their swords, and were reprimanded by the Captain-General. Shortly after this, the first Indians came into the market place. There were hundreds of them, carrying brooms made of bundled reeds and grasses. Singing all the time, they swept the plaza clean.

Following them were hundreds of men with baskets of flowers which they strewed on the paving stones. A sweet perfume crept about among the houses, and flecks of red, blue and yellow covered the dull gray stone so that it became bright as a stained-glass window.

After these flower bearers, thousands crowded into the square. The men were all dressed in white robes covered with red checkers. The Indians chanted steadily. Now and then they would burst into a little hopping dance. Some of them leaped up into the air, seized by an inexplicable ecstasy. They were the court fools, dancers and singers of the Inca, it appeared.

In the wake of this group came long ranks of Indians who carried axes made of copper and silver in their uplifted right hands, bringing to mind the lictors of ancient Rome. Of course, they had no fasces, and the axes were hardly more than toys. I was astonished to see that not one of the Inca's subjects was armed. Even the *orejones,* the lop-ears, who wore trailing robes of azure blue, carried no other badge of office than little staves decorated with gay tufts of feathers.

This entire company, which must have numbered ten thousand people, marched in perfect order, the rows straight as a rod. Every man put his right foot forward in time with the fellow next to him. They were like so many puppets, just as our Captain-General had said. When the plaza was filled, the columns parted to allow the entrance of the Inca's palanquin. Slowly the conveyance moved toward us, borne so carefully that it scarcely swayed. The litter was decorated with gold leaf which in the late afternoon sun shone like fire. The inside was upholstered with bright feathers. Against the cushions leaned the king, wearing the same simple red garment and the fillet about his head with tassels over his brows that we had seen the night before. The same bloodshot eyes stared in the rather handsome face, but they looked far more severely at us than they had before.

The singers now stopped their chanting. A great silence fell over the throng. The odd-shaped houses, the immense, brightly garbed crowd, were unreal. And facing the Indians was our little group pressed close about the dun form of our Captain-General. And now it happened that at the most important moment of his life, Don Francisco Pizarro's voice stuck in his throat. He stood with his mouth half open, the face muscles moving helplessly under the straggly beard.

This taut silence was broken by the sharp voice of Atahualpa, cutting it as clearly as a knife. Rapidly Felipillo translated his words, "Where are the strangers?" he inquired.

Don Francisco Pizarro still did not have himself in hand. But with instant decision Father Vicente de Valverde stepped forward. He held out his small black cross to the Inca. In the other hand he clutched his tattered Bible, bound in pigskin. Atahualpa was amazed at this gesture. His eyes widened with displeasure. Father Vicente was not in the slightest dismayed. The pomp surrounding the Inca meant nothing at all, absolutely nothing, to him. Calmly he addressed the Indian king.

"My son," he began, "we have come to this land to save you and all these thousands of Indians from a terrible fate. We have come to offer you the teachings of Christ. And now let me give you the essence of this belief of ours . . ."

Forthwith he began a rapid disquisition on the meaning of Christianity. He spoke of the Trinity, and described the mystery over which so many good men have cracked their brains. Felipillo tried the best he could to translate the monk's words. It was plain he was having a hard time of it. The sweat stood out on his brow. But Father Vicente paid no heed to the enormity of his undertaking. On and on he went, describing the whole history of the world, beginning with Creation and continuing on through the fall, the banishment from Paradise, not missing a single great event until the advent of the Saviour of mankind. Then, with passion he told of Christ's sufferings on the cross.

As he listened, the Inca's eyes widened with displeasure. His brown hand closed on the side of the litter. Undeterred, Father Vicente droned on ceremoniously.

"It shocked me to learn," he said loudly, "that you have laid waste cities which did not even belong to you. You have martyred people who did you no wrong at all, outside of preferring to remain loyal to their own king. Beyond all this I hear you are leading a riotous life with many young women. And yet there is no need for you to despair. God is omnipotent. He has love enough and to spare for the greatest sinners. God is nearest to those like you who have fallen lowest. I counsel you to take to heart at once the gracious teachings of our Lord Jesus Christ. You must bend your head to the Emperor, the bearer of the secular sword. Once you have made obeisance to him as a true vassal he will treat you kindly."

Atahualpa struck the edge of the palanquin with his fist. His body was rigid, the bloodshot eyes ablaze. Felipillo turned pale and stuttered with anxiety as he translated the Inca's reply.

"Who are you, you black creature?" the Inca said evenly. "Who are you to talk to me this way? Don't you know I am descended from the sun? Don't you know I rule a great part of the earth? I rule to the very edge of the boundless forest where the great rivers begin. Are you unaware that not a bird on the bough may sing unless I so wish it?

"Your emperor may be great. But I have never heard of him. The Inca can never bow his neck before strangers. Since my forefathers came down from the holy lake, Titicaca, many arts, order and a peaceful life have been bestowed on the people. Before we came they lived in the mountain clefts like beasts. The blessings of the sun have come to earth through me and my line. Today men go smoothly through life. There are no riddles to puzzle them, no difficulties. Life for the people of Tavanta-Suyu consists of work, and not too much work, of frequent songs and dances. Death comes softly to them.

"I am no more interested in your god than in your emperor. You say that he is invisible. If that is true, how do you know there is such a god at all? You say that he is both three and one at the same time. That seems completely ridiculous to me. Fools dribble out such nonsense.

"But just look up there, over the roofs. See who is sinking behind the mountain peaks. It is the sun. See! It is my god, red as fire. My god gives men food and animals. My god brings out green shoots from the earth, ripens the ears of maize, makes the green-silver mountain meadows, lets the llamas have spicy mountain grass for their soft mouths. The sun-god gives warmth, and this warmth causes the waters to rise high above the earth in great mist clouds. The clouds spill over in sweet rain and nourish the earth. The rain melts the blue ice in the mountains. The streams thunder down into the valleys where we catch them in canals and water our fields. Then we have corn, sweet potatoes, cotton, sugarcane, to fill our bellies and clothe our backs. Not only that. The sun-god gives spiritual nourishment. I cannot stop marveling at his beauty, in the gray dawn, high in the heavens at midday, or now when he is sinking to rest in the Isles of the Dead so that the departed may enjoy his blessings. Great sun-god! The one god! Soon the evening star will step forth through the azure door of heaven, the youth with the long locks, and look long after the sun-god, as I even do myself."

Atahualpa lifted up both arms, his palms widespread in supplication to the setting sun. The houses were now throwing long shadows over the motley crowd in the market place. Involuntarily I, too, looked at the sun; involuntarily I thought how much goodness the Indian's god had bestowed on me. I thought how the sun had caressed my face as a mere infant, how the olives and grapes in Sancho's little garden had ripened beneath its rays when we were poor and had nothing to live on but the produce of our few acres. Oh, happy time, I thought.

Atahualpa let his arms fall. His voice was milder when he spoke this time.

"No, my friend, my god is not invisible like yours. Even at midnight the pure-hearted can feel his certain coming. Irresistibly he will come. Soon there is a light rustling in the trees. The first scattered voices of the birds let us know that he is mounting the steep mountain passes from the forest. Soon the hour comes when a blue twilight covers the earth, and light wakens men asleep in their huts. This god is not threefold, but one. And he is there, for all to see. Everything you have told me about god is strange to me, unreal, far-fetched. Your argument to me sounds like the twisted reasoning of a madman. It is all like the tales foolish women gabble to children to put them to sleep. Where did you learn all your stories, you dark man? What makes this Jesus Christ of yours such a great god? How did your emperor ever get the idea that he would rule the world, this world which we descendants of the sun rule in deed?"

It was now Father Vicente's turn to show anger. He raised up his thick little Bible and waved it at the Indian king.

"Here is the Book of Books," he shouted. "Here are all the wisdom, all the revelations of God, the unfolding of the dimmest past and the dimmest future. Here it is written for all to see, set down by the prophets, the seers, the apostles and holy men to whom God has spoken in quiet room and on high mountain, in deserts and in cities. Our God has appeared as a great light, greater than the sun, as a burning thorn bush, far more terrifying than lightning.

"And I say to your face, you blasphemous dog, that what to your stupid mind is invisible is greater than any visible thing, greater even than the sun which gives light and life to the earth. For on the second day of Creation God put the sun in the heavens. It is the work of His invisible hands. It is He who has given it command to proceed on a daily course, never faltering. All things visible, you heathen dolt, flow out of the unseen. In the unseen the visible has its beginning, its home, and its grave. That is why the sun disappears from sight during the night.

"And even on this earth we men are bound to the unseen with fine threads. Who is not so bound must perish, as you will perish. Beyond the boundary of boundaries flows the water of life. Who does not believe in God is like a tree without a crown of foliage, a tree without leaves. The soft winds do not touch such a man, and water does not come to him sweetly singing. The lightning will splinter the dry trunk, and the raging wind will snap off the rotten limbs and topple trunk and bough.

"Do you see Eternal Love, Inca? Do you see joy or sadness? Is truth a quadrangle or a straight line only? Have you a pair of scales to weigh good and evil? Do you not see that at the bottom men are moved only by the unseen, the godliness in life? Even you yourself would consider the sun no more than a hot red ball if you had not the godly power in your heart to make it an image of life. But I can tell you deeper things than lie in your heathen poetry. I can show you the naked truth. This Book is my sacred sign."

With reluctance Atahualpa took the Bible in his slender hand. Idly he thumbed through the pages. The black letters meant nothing to him at all. One more mystery, one more incomprehensible thing, like our horses, our beards, our cannon. But the Book seemed to strike him as the most monstrous of all our peculiarities. And indeed it was the most formidable weapon we had, far greater than gunpowder, containing enough explosive power to smash all the Indies into fragments.

As the Inca pondered the little pigskin volume, it was easy to read his uneasy thoughts. Clearly he was feeling the compulsion of God's sacred mystery that lived in the pages of Father Vicente's Bible. He was aware of the fluent strength dammed up in the little magic symbols, symbols which have torn mankind from the breast of Mother Earth and directed its struggle toward God. All the struggle felt by man is contained in the holy pages that have been read and reread a thousand times.

This alien struggle was sensed by the Inca. He glimpsed Christianity. And to him it appeared impious and ugly, a profound blasphemy of earth and sun, a black magic shot through with a crawling host of lepers, blind men, cripples, beggars, whores and cheats, all overshadowed by a black crucifix. He sensed the power of that cross on which God himself was hanged that man might live. Atahualpa, with the faultless insight of the simple man who often senses what we cleverer ones cannot know, however hard we strive for the vision, saw through all the brooding pageant of Christianity.

Suddenly, in a tremendous passion, he took the book and flung it to the ground, where it lay like a stricken bird, the wings outspread.

"Reckoning," said Atahualpa deeply. "I will have reckoning, you on the gray beast. You will pay me for the cities you have plundered. You will pay for the people you have killed and the women you have raped and the provisions you have stolen. I shall not move from this place until I have seen justice done, until every one of you white strangers has paid for his arrogance."

The Inca's words, directed to Pizarro, were not heard by Father

Vicente. He rushed to pick up the Bible, picked it from the dust and kissed it. Then, like a madman, he threw himself on the Captain-General, who sat stony and silent on his horse. He shook his scabbard and shouted, "What are you waiting for? Do you see what the red beast did to the Bible? Can't you see that more and more of these heathen dogs are crowding into the plaza? What are you waiting for? I give you absolution! I give all of you absolution! Fight for God!"

Slowly, as if in a dream, Pizarro turned his head and looked down on the Dominican's tonsure, as if in its ridiculous baldness he saw the solution to all his troubles. Slowly he drew a white cloth from his belt, turned heavily in the saddle and waved it three times. At this critical moment Don Francisco looked like a man who has been stunned by a heavy blow.

A cannon shot roared. The shattering echo bounced from house to house, and rang against the mountain walls. Thereupon a great change came over Don Francisco Pizarro. Life and strength came back to him, like water flowing when the sluice gates have been drawn up. In a startling move he whipped out his sword and raised it on high.

"Santiago! Attack!"

The mighty roan under him reared, found his bearings, plunged forward like a horse in the Apocalypse. The Indians let out a shriek of terror. Father Vicente tumbled sidewise, the crucifix held tightly in his right hand as if, like Moses in the battle of the Amalekites, he were making sure of the help of Heaven. Before me, plunging forward, I saw the great haunches of the roan, the muscles bunched with effort. Out of the doorways, from all sides, the Spanish riders forced their way. The foot soldiers, jabbing with their lances, rammed forward steadily into the panicky crowd. Repeatedly the two cannon in Don Pedro de Candía's charge, rumbled violently, belching fire.

I found my father's sword naked in my hand, and set to the bloody task, following Pizarro. The unarmed Indians clung to my saddle and stirrups, and to the mane of my horse. In terror the animal reared, reached his head round, and bit his tormenters. And over and over I brought my sword down, cleaving heads, clearing a free space about me. Don Francisco was forcing his way toward the Inca's litter, and I pressed along behind him. I cut into heads, hands, shinbones and soft parts, aware of the varying toughness of the flesh into which I struck. A piece of torn cloth became entangled with my scabbard, and before it slipped to the ground, it was sopping with blood. An elderly lop-ear, the skin over his cheekbones as dark as a mummy's, tried to sink his worn teeth into the calf of my leg. I caught him in the belly with an upthrust of my sword, and out fell his purplish guts, while his mouth opened and the whites of his eyes shone in the twilight. He sank to the ground.

The crush was terrible. All the time I was afraid that the Indians would lift up my horse and me bodily and topple both of us to the paving stones. Don Hernando de Soto's riders reached the center of the arena. Now and then two or more Spaniards would slash into the same Indian, allowing another near by miraculously to escape. At times we fought so close together that we almost did ourselves injury. We shouted to one another to make room. Once a musket was discharged directly behind me. I felt the bullet rush by my leg, grazing the skin. The sound was deafening, and for a moment I was stunned.

In the very midst of this fearful blood bath a quiet voice, not to be ignored, spoke to my innermost mind. While I struck down the Indians like Ajax slaughtering sheep, the sweat bathing my body, I tried to unravel a paradox, like a man in a fever who cannot rid himself of a consuming thought.

I kept thinking of Master Agrippa and asking myself why I really had learned Latin. Whoever has been in battle will bear witness that a man at such times is obsessed with errant cerebration. It is as if the mind, temporarily freed from its usual round, simply cannot stop, but goes on and on like a windmill without grain to grind, nothing but the two stones working.

I recall today that I saw many little things very closely—a stone running dark with blood; an Indian holding his entrails in with two hands, his face surprised; a hand with clenched fingers lying on the pavement; an ornamental bronze axe. All these unimportant things nested themselves securely in my brain and remain there to this day.

Slowly we worked around the Inca's litter which swayed on the bearers' shoulders like a ship in a storm. The Inca himself sat immobile, his eyes madly staring at the chaos in which he was engulfed. In places the dead had heaped up into waves, and always fresh bodies rushed up to become impaled on our swords and lances. It was the suicide of a whole people about the golden litter of their emperor. We scarcely had to do more than hold our weapons braced and, shouting, the frenzied Indians swarmed against the cutting edges in their eagerness to get near the Inca. Some of the Spaniards were strangely affected by this blind devotion. I saw the tears rolling down the face of Diego de Vargas, even as he rammed in his sword furiously.

Several times a litter bearer was hewn down, but every time another Indian rushed to take his place. To us, unused to these strange faces and accustomed to thinking of them as all alike, it appeared as if the slaughtered men had been miraculously endowed with second souls.

Frenero and Bernal handled their lances like lunatics, like two berserkers who have been led to the battlefield in chains and released only when the conflict has reached concert pitch. Frenero's helmet had fallen off and his thick red hair was disheveled like the ruff of a predatory beast. Bernal's one eye glared with unaccountable malice, and sometimes he neighed a horrible laugh. To my horror I saw he was thrashing his way ever closer to the Inca. And I heard Don Francisco shout, "Don't touch him! Keep your hands off the Inca, you red bastard!"

But it was too late. Just as I put out a hand to steady it, the cushioned barrow began to tip and the Inca slid to the ground. He would have perished beneath Frenero's lance if Don Francisco Pizarro had not by more than human effort forced his way between them. Even at that, he was unable to prevent the knife-sharp lance point from slithering along the edge of his protecting sword and into his own flesh. The blood flowed in a river, dripped from the ends of his fingers.

And so it happened on this memorable day that Don Francisco Pizarro was the only Spaniard to suffer a wound. Many of us, to be sure, were bruised and scratched, but there was not one deep wound among the lot of us. This was amazing, considering the lunging horses and the sheer press of the crowd. God himself dictated the fall of the Inca's kingdom, as Father Vicente later had occasion to observe.

As the Inca tumbled off his perch, Don Hernando de Soto and I caught him in our arms. A soldier called Miguel Estete tore off the fillet round his head, the one with the fringe I have mentioned before. But Don Hernando kicked the soldier aside, and together we hoisted the half-fainting king onto my horse. Slowly we thrust our way out of the crush, toward the House of the Snake. There we gave him over to the keeping of a strong guard.

The fall and imprisonment of their Inca created consternation in the Indian throng. A moan of despair arose in the plaza. Then, without warning, the crowd broke, fled like a flock of birds, unaccountably. But even to escape many of them had to die, for there were twenty Spaniards with lances barring the way at the point of the triangle. Unafraid they stood and met the crazed mob. Row after row of Indians broke on the twenty points of steel, like so many waves on a breakwater. Masses ran wildly about the plaza, sometimes catching up in their midst a rider too tired to kill any more, or an arquebusier, his crossbow held over his head as if he were fording a stream.

A senseless terror had possessed the Inca's subjects. Now they thought only of saving their own lives. Foolishly they ran into friend and foe alike, blind with fear. And so it was in the world of the ancients when Pan let his voice ring out into midday stillness, making the herds gallop off beside themselves with terror, the laughter of the cloven-footed god echoing in their ears.

Now the Indians threw themselves against a wall which shut off one point in the market place. The stone barrier, built without mortar, trembled and gave way. As the stones fell, many of the Indians were mortally injured. We Spaniards watched, our mouths agape, weapons trailing idly. It was a spectacle of pure madness, and in all men's breasts madness evokes anxiety and awe. This is because the man who watches sees naked before his eyes the chaotic elements of his own soul, hidden in us all, and yet more compulsive than the overt reason that operates in everyday life. Through the wide breach the Indians stumbled and fled, their robes in bloody tatters. The unwounded ones scrambled quickly over the rough blocks of stones, and the injured crept painfully, unheeding, leaving patches of skin on the rude surface.

And now we took off our helmets, sank to our knees, and thanked God for his infinite mercy.

The massacre had lasted scarcely an hour, and the sun was still hanging red over the roof tops, as if it had drunk up the puddles of blood in the plaza, as if awaiting to bear the souls of the dead to the Isles of the West. Thousands of dead bodies lay on the stones, and over them came the stillness of twilight, pure and indifferent. A chill wind from the mountains began to flutter against our blood-soiled faces. It was easy to see where the Inca's litter had been held up. Here the pile of dead was thickest, a tangle of corpses. There was a heavy sweet smell of dead flesh in the place, and the little wind carried it about, into the houses and into the House of the Snake.

It was pitch-dark when we finally sat down to that evening meal to which our Captain-General had invited the Inca. We sat at a long improvised table in the front hall of the House of the Snake. The pitch torches burned quietly and shone in a glitter on the Inca's golden bowl. The men's faces were furrowed with weariness, the eyes red-rimmed and large in the sockets. Atahualpa, the king, sat at the right hand of Don Francisco Pizarro, at the far end of the table. The Pizarros and the cavaliers sat on both sides, I among them, and the three Dominicans were at the far end. Father Vicente broke bread, blessed it, and sat down again.

We all ate, with indifferent appetite, and drank the sour red wine. I was able to swallow only a small piece of bread. The Captain-General, too, I noticed, scarcely touched the food set before him. But the Inca ate everything, apparently with relish. To all appearances the death of his entourage and his own imprisonment no longer stirred him in the least. After a time Don Francisco Pizarro turned to the Inca, and said, "You are not to think that the Spaniards are a bloodthirsty people, whatever may have happened today. We . . ." He stopped lamely, and the interpreter repeated the words before anything could be done to mend them.

"It was a neat piece of treachery," said the Inca, indifferently.

"That's true," Pizarro told him. "But we used it only when we had no other choice. Really we dislike to draw blood. It's true we fight our enemies any way we can, and think of nothing but beating them. But our friends we treat with honor and kindness. You must put your trust in me and my friends."

"All this has nothing to do with me," said the Inca.

As we talked, huge, hawklike birds settled down on the corpses in the market place. Greedily they flapped from body to body, quarreling over soft tidbits, their throaty voices cracking. The guards tried to frighten them off with stones but they flew off only to return when the coast was clear. It was a good thing that darkness obscured the scene. We could hear soft ripping sounds as they dug into their meal. All the time their numbers increased. Their wings rustling heavily, they settled down to the loathsome feast. Soon the whole plaza was alive with the curious birds, shining, their red tongues flashing in the torchlight.

"That's bad. I hate that business," said Pizarro, who had got up to look out the door, then returned to the table.

There was silence as fruits were brought in. Atahualpa picked up a pear-shaped tropic fruit, broke it open and drew in the aromatic odor of the flesh. We could smell the flowerlike perfume. With no change in his expression he answered Don Francisco, "That is the god of war."

20

THE RANSOM

FROM that day, Atahualpa the Inca lived with us Spaniards in the House of the Snake, where he and his court occupied a whole series of rooms. Within the wing that he occupied, Peruvian style, there was a kind of courtyard, something like our own Spanish courtyards. In the middle of this open space there was a fountain. Climbing vines bearing bright flowers hid the rude masonry. It was in this courtyard that the Inca preferred to be, with his courtiers and concubines. Don Francisco had not heeded Father Vicente's wishes, and had given permission for the women to be with their lord. Among the women, who behaved themselves with great modesty and served the Inca hand and foot, was the same Indian girl who had once proffered me the bowl of chicha. I had found out that her name was Laanta and that she came from a noble family in Quito. I also discovered she was one of the Inca's relatives.

Here sat Atahualpa, hours on end, motionless, leaning back in thick cushions, just as we had first seen him in his pleasure house among the warriors. Seen thus, he still had all the majesty of a man who rules over a mighty kingdom. The oldest and most trusted of his retainers approached him half creeping, their heads bent to the floor. It was part of this ritual that the servants always put some small burden on their left shoulders, perhaps a little stone, to indicate their humility before so much greatness. The Spaniards guarding the Inca kept out of sight in the corridor outside the wing. But the simplest soldier was quite aware of the gravity of his task, and understood that the fate of the whole company depended on his watchfulness.

For all that we could tell, the Inca was not entertaining thoughts of flight, although it was difficult, in fact impossible, for most of us to read any sort of emotion in his impassive features. He bore himself without a trace of restraint toward us Spaniards. It was hard to believe that he even remembered the terrible slaughter in the market place and the fact that he was imprisoned. No one went into his quarters uninvited, and whenever we approached him on invitation, we took off our helmets and bowed our heads. The prisoner was soon a favorite with the soldiers because of his genuinely royal generosity. Any one of them would run to do his bidding. Only the greatest wish—the favor of freedom—was denied him.

The Inca liked to see us pay attention to him, and his still face sometimes showed signs of amusement when a Spaniard entered the courtyard. Don Hernando Pizarro, Don Hernando de Soto and I were his favorites. This was because all three of us knew about court formalities, and perhaps in the case of the last two of us, because we were of different origins than most of the men in the expedition. Hernando Pizarro's massive dignity could scarcely be missed by any foreigner, however alien in customs and blood. The Inca soon began to regard him as the true leader of the company, and ceased to pay any attention at all to his brother Don Francisco. In fact in time the Indian king treated the Captain-General with open contempt. This contempt became especially noticeable after the Inca had discovered that Pizarro could not read.

The Inca took delight in talking about traditions and ways of making things. Nothing struck him more than our letters and the books which rows and rows of them made up. He often said that these black signs were the root of our superiority. He took pleasure in fingering through the leaves of the Bible, and often spent hours idly musing over the open pages. He asked me to show him the word "God," and to our amazement he was soon able to pick it out of the text for himself. When he did this he noted that the word was repeated over and over, almost on every page of the book. As he saw it, the whole book was nothing but an attempt to make our invisible God visible. This interpretation unsettled me. But in time I saw the Inca had merely made a good shot in the dark, as any naïve man is liable to do. At least he asked me to etch the name, the main word, on his thumbnail, since it was the key to unlock the meaning the whole book contained. I carried out his wish, and he was deeply pleased.

"Now I too carry God with me," he said. "I will see now whether they can read me as well as they can read the book."

He showed his thumb to Hernando Pizarro and to De Soto, and he was satisfied when both cavaliers repeated the wonderful word without a moment's hesitation. Then he turned to the guards. He was surprised to see that many of them shook their heads and in embarrassment admitted that they could not read. Again he turned to me for an explanation, and I had to tell him that these men were of poor circumstances and had never mastered the art. He listened earnestly to my story and admitted that also in his kingdom not everyone had been initiated into the mysteries of the sun and heaven, only the nobles and the priests.

From this day on he used the name inscribed on his thumbnail as a sort of touchstone to determine the status of us Spaniards. Our Captain-General had to submit to the test, and in confusion once let it out that he did not know what the letters meant. The Inca, his bloody eyes strained wide, smiled at him in triumph. Though he treated his guards no differently after he had ferreted out their weakness, from the day when he had tripped up the Captain-General he always looked at him in remote derision. He even went so far as to make fun of "the Old One" for the benefit of those about him. He, too, had learned to call Pizarro "the Old One." All this must have put the Captain-General somewhat out of joint, but he went on as if he had noticed nothing. As a matter of fact, many of the words which I caught on to, since I soon took pains to get a working knowledge of the Quichua language, quite escaped Don Francisco Pizarro. In vain I tried to remedy this unfortunate situation, which obviously might breed trouble, by explaining to the Inca the military genius and the fantastic durability of our leader. It made no difference. For the Inca, Pizarro was an inferior man, who ruled only through lies and cheating.

It became my custom each morning to have an audience with Atahualpa, just as at any king's levee, to inquire about his health and spirits. He was consistently friendly with me. Indeed, after a time I saw that he was impatient for me to appear. Whenever my military duties hindered me from coming at the usual time, at first he would be very curt and plainly disgruntled, in the familiar manner of great nobles and fine ladies if their wishes are not interpreted on the spot, without explanation. This did not annoy me; rather it touched me to think that the destiny of this absolute monarch had become so clouded and petty through our machinations. I always tried my best to honor his position by appearing at the proper time. This became possible when Pizarro relieved me of all morning obligations for the express purpose of humoring the Inca.

Our position at that time was anything but secure. The Inca's principal army was far to the south, in the neighborhood of Cuzco, and might set out to crush us at any moment, undeterred by the superstitions which now demoralized the Indians about us. If this army ever laid siege to us—it was more than a hundred thousand strong—the outcome was foreordained. We had to depend entirely on the graciousness of our prisoner to prevent any such disturbing turn of events.

Already Pizarro had dispatched messengers to San Miguel bearing orders that all the men there forming the garrison should immediately march to Caxamalca to reinforce our inadequate numbers. As yet we had had no news of them, and could not even know whether the messengers had even reached their goal. For out of the north, too, rumors were floating in that another host was bearing down on us from the direction of Quito. We fell to thinking that we were trapped like rabbits in a hole, with hunters on all sides of us. In time murmuring began. Some of our men began to voice the opinion that now was the time to about-face, and to take the Inca with us as hostage until we had united all our forces and were able to look to more ambitious undertakings.

The Inca had often watched the guards throwing the dice. This sport fascinated him quite as much as the printed words in the book. Into the excited cries of the players, the mutual threats, the strained faces, the passionate absorption he read a wonderful mystery. He thought that the dice had been a prime factor in aiding us to arrive at our present position of mastery over him. This interpretation also amazed me, after I had pondered it. For are we Spaniards not great gamblers? And if we were not, would not the Indies still lie undiscovered between two oceans?

Atahualpa immediately caught onto the simple rules of play. Sometimes he and I would sit for a whole hour casting the dice. When the little cubes rolled, the Inca's Indians and the women of his court became terribly excited. They came nearer forgetting the presence of the half-god who had been their ruler than at any other time. Whenever the Inca threw three sixes they clapped their hands and let out shrieks of delight, and they wailed aloud, their hands raised to heaven, when he could do no better than three ones.

I, too, felt the lure of the game, and I would wager some bauble, perhaps a bright piece of cloth or a glass pearl, against an ornament of the king's. Whenever the Inca won, carelessly he would hold the trinket in his hand and smile at it, then immediately hand it over to one of his attendants. I saw, of course, that I must do the same though it was hardly to my liking, for many of the Inca's trifles were made of pure gold. And so I gave all my winnings to the women. Because of this the audience was divided into parties. The men stood behind the Inca and the women behind me, the latter bursting with eagerness for me to win so that they might have one of the Inca's fine ornaments.

Later, when the game of chance proved boring, I introduced the Inca to the intricacies of chess. Don Hernando de Soto brought out a beautiful black-and-white board. The men were made of ivory by Moorish craftsmen. The finely carved knights, bishops and pawns made a great impression; the king and queen were regarded with awe. In the rooks the Inca quickly saw a resemblance to his own forts. He mastered the much more difficult rules of this game with ease. Soon it was a familiar sight to see him leaning in concentration over the board, his fingertip pressed into his upper lip, a gay turban wound around his head. Since I am only a moderately good player, it was not long before the Inca began to get the upper hand. Nothing convinced me more that he was a clever, foresighted man, for no fool can play chess. His play was daring, full of sudden assaults and surprises, into which I often stumbled headlong. The speed with which he became my master in chess gave me no little cause for uneasiness. I remembered only too well how many military leaders had been great chess players, for example, our Don Gonzalvo, many of the Italian *condottieri* and above all the Arabian caliphs.

It happened one day that I had won a rather fine trinket from the Inca, and this I offered to the girl Laanta. She looked questioningly at her master, and he nodded quiet assent. I should have completely forgotten the whole incident had not I one day caught my man Bernal gripping Laanta by the arm, trying to tear the little piece of gold from her hands. When he saw me, Bernal let the girl go and she ran off in a flash. But for once in my life, if never again, my temper was up. I shouted bitter reproaches at Bernal for thus endangering the lives of the lot of us, and ended by tearing off my leather glove and smacking his face with it, first one side and then the other. I really did not do this out of need to vent my own spleen, but because I had learned that this was the only way for me to deal with the likes of Bernal and Frenero. I know that if anyone else had dared to treat either of these cut-throats in so summary a fashion he would have found a knife in his ribs. Even the Captain-General would not have been so foolhardy. But it was a need of their natures to give loyalty to someone, and this someone was I. They treated me with amazing deference and love, and would as soon have thought of turning on me as on the Virgin Mary—much less, in fact, come to think of it. Whenever I struck them, which was seldom, they merely shrugged their shoulders and walked off abashed.

When shortly after this incident I appeared before the Inca, he received me with unusual cordiality. It was plain to see that something was on his mind. Behind the stony features I felt a keen excitement that he was controlling only with effort. And as the seaman reads portents of the storm in the seagull's flight, even when the waters are as smooth as a mirror, I read a crisis in the uneasy whispering of the women, the quick glances among the courtiers. Secretly I armed myself with calm phrases to meet the Inca's anger, whatever cause it might have. I became tense with expectation when all the attendants, men and women both, silently withdrew to leave me alone with Atahualpa. The splash of the fountain grew loud in the courtyard.

Atahualpa's silence endured for a long time. I, too, held my tongue. I cursed Bernal's stupidity.

Without warning he raised his head and looked at me squarely. I could see the little red veins netting the whites of his eyes, which lent such a startling cast to his gaze. He smiled, almost apologetically, I thought, and then placed his right hand on my shoulder.

"My Chasca," he began—he called me by the Indian word for "young man with golden hair"—"you saved my life the day you carried me off on your horse's back."

"Not altogether," I objected quietly, hoping not to ruffle him, yet determined not to yield. "It was Don Francisco Pizarro who protected you from the men. He was wounded in the arm doing it. Do you remember?"

"Oh, the Old One," he said. "Some day I'll make him a present. You must keep reminding me of it"—he made a movement as if throwing a bone to a dog. "Let us not talk about him. It is to you I want to talk. I trust you. You are different from him. When you were a boy you studied the stars in the sky."

"That is not altogether true," I said. "I merely listened to what my Master Agrippa taught me."

"Perhaps," agreed the Inca. "But whoever has observed the movements of the stars knows something about the workings of the universe, that world in which treachery, ambush and slyness have no part. We have a city high in the mountains. It is where the rivers come down and rush off into the forests in the east. There the priests teach our best youths about the course of the sun, the phases of the moon, the movements of the stars. You see, it is necessary to have such experienced men in ruling a great kingdom like mine. They are useful not only in determining the time for sowing, for ripening and harvesting, for telling when the ice will melt in the clefts. It is not only that. They are needed to set the times for feast and sacrifices for all those duties prescribed by the sun-god. They are not trained to serve man alone. Now, such men as these will judge earthly things differently from other men, will they not?"

"Yes, I understand," I told him. "For these people who have a superior view of things, who see the world in its relation to eternity, we have the same use."

"So, then, listen, my Chasca," the Inca continued with greater animation, "consider how you and I may meet together in eternity." He pointed at the sun, looking at it unblinking. "Why should you and I lie to each other and practice deceits? What can you and I do against the will of the stars? Nothing, nothing at all. This the Old One does not know. But when his turn comes he will find out the truth you and I have known for a long time. My priests tell me that his life is closely bound up with my own. And now, I command you to tell me the truth. If this you cannot do for fear of injuring your friends, then say nothing, and we'll let it pass. Are you agreed?"

"I am," I told him.

"Now"—he bent forward close to me—"tell me why Spaniards love gold so much."

"Gold!" I said.

"Yes, gold," the Inca went on. "Isn't it true that they stripped all the gold off my pleasure house at the baths? Haven't they even made off with my gold plate, pitcher and goblets? Isn't it true they even took gold from the dead men in the market place? And today didn't one of your men try to take the necklace from Laanta, not because it is beautiful, but because it is made of gold? Don't the guards almost go out of their minds whenever I give them something made of it? Isn't all I say true? Or am I mistaken?"

"It is true," I told him.

"What is it, then, about gold that makes them want it so much? It isn't belief in the power of the sun-god that makes them worship the metal. Is it because it is beautiful and shines? But surely young girls, flowers and butterflies are far prettier to look at. Doesn't polished silver shine just as much?"

"There are other reasons," I told him.

"Tell me what they are," he ordered impatiently.

"A man can buy anything with gold," I explained.

"Anything!" He drew back in astonishment.

"Almost anything." I corrected myself hastily, alarmed by his astonishment, which struck me as strange. "But it is true that gold can buy anything that is made by man. Man's labor, services, obedience can be purchased with gold."

"Go on, tell me more, my lord," he said breathlessly. "This is the most curious thing I have ever heard of. I think I may soon be able to understand you Spaniards."

"There is really not much more to tell," I said. "Our princes make round coins out of the gold, and on them they print their image. The gold can buy this or that much depending on its weight and purity. In Spain for a little gold a man can buy bread and wine; for a little more, clothes, shoes, armor and a horse. The person with a lot of gold can build castles, estates, own flocks of Merino sheep, have wild beasts on his land to hunt. And he can buy favors and offices, last of all. When he has very great quantities of the metal he can buy himself services, foot soldiers and riders. He can bring armies together, send ships over the sea, and so become a master, a noble, perhaps a duke, even a king like you. He can buy peoples' souls. There are men who lend gold. And for the use of this gold, others must pay back what they have borrowed and more besides."

"But the gold that was lent is just as good when it is returned!" the Inca cried. "Is it not?"

"Yes, you are right," I said, "but that is what Spaniards do. For you see, the gold that is lent gets work done for him who borrows. It is just like a horse that has been lent to plow, or a slave to dig. This service the gold performs must be returned. And so gold makes gold, as the peasant people say."

"Why, the gold has little ones among you Spaniards, like the llamas in the mountains?" The Inca stared at me in disbelief.

"You are right again," I said, smiling at the Inca, who in his amazement looked like a child. "And sometimes—when there is war, for instance—gold becomes scarce. Then its services cost dear. It is like this today in Spain. Right now it is easy enough for a lender to double his gold."

The Inca held his face in his hands. "Stop," he said. "I beg you, stop. My head is going round. Tell me, what do people do when they haven't any gold at all?"

"It is bad with them," I replied. "There is nothing they can do except find someone who has gold and offer their services."

"You mean, they become slaves?"

"Yes, slaves," I assured him, though I had never thought of it exactly in that direct fashion before. "Of course, there are some without gold who get themselves weapons, and then they rob those who have it."

"That is the brave thing to do," the Inca said.

"And still others," I went on, "travel over the sea to the Indies and try to find gold for themselves, and to conquer . . ."

"Conquer!" exclaimed Atahualpa. "Is that why you came to my kingdom?"

"I . . ." I could only stammer.

"You? I don't know whether you came to find gold. I shall find out. But the Old One came on that account, I know, and the man in the golden armor, and the brothers of the Old One. All of them came for gold. So did your man with the red hair and all the rest. You people are not children of light, but children of gold. Are you, too, a slave, Chasca?"

"I am like my comrades," I told him. "My house is poor. My lands are so small that hardly one olive tree can grow on them. I had great trouble getting a horse and armor for this expedition. As it is I couldn't have got them but for the favor of another conquistador. Yes, I need gold."

"That may very well be, Chasca," the Inca said. "But you are betraying yourself. Something is wrong. It is not the same with you. You are looking for something else. And so is Don Hernando de Soto, and the huge brother of the Old One. For that reason I can understand you three. Your faces are different, you walk in a different way and you sit differently on your horse. If I were free I would take you three with me and make you viceroys.

"You are like the chieftains of my blessed father, Huayna Capác, who has now gone with the sun. You are like the men I grew up with, like the ones who conquered Quito. You are like the men who went down to the great stream that runs through the endless forest, where live the fighting women who use bows and poisoned arrows and roast the heads of the slain over the fire.

"Life for you is an unending adventure. Every morning the sun brings you new life out of the depths of the night, because you have open hearts. You are good people, even when you are wicked. Gold, whether you are greedy for it or not, will run through your hands like sand. It does not touch you, any more than water touches the flesh beneath a swan's feathers.

"But in those other men gold has crept in under their skins. It will kill them. I am beginning to understand the magic you see in the metal. Now I understand why my forefathers, the priests of my house, made laws which say that the people of Tavanta-Suyu shall possess no gold. For here, in my kingdom the Inca gives to all who are in need. The Inca shares out the earth, which can never be owned by any one man. He gives his people houses, work, women and feast days. Nobody steals, for nobody needs to steal. With us gold is nothing more than a shining metal. We use it in fine works which please the eye. It has been like this for centuries in the house of the Inca. Gold lies heaped up in the temples."

All this Atahualpa told me with great pride. It was now, for the first time, that it dawned on me that the Indians had no gold in the form of coins, and that all the metal was in the possession of the supreme king.

On the afternoon of the same day it happened that our Captain-General visited the Inca in his private quarters. At this time Atahualpa offered Don Francisco Pizarro that enormous sum of gold as ransom which has aroused the wonder and envy of the whole world, and which they speak of in whispers even today in the Spanish homeland. Never before had any man seen so much of the precious metal piled in a heap as we were about to see. The riches of Croesus, all the gold of Ophir, the treasure of the Queen of Sheba could have been collected in this one room. For the Inca proposed to fill a room in his palace nine feet high with gold, providing we should let him go free. The Captain-General and the rest of us at first thought it impossible that any one man could have so much. Don Francisco summoned all the caballeros together and told us what the Inca had said. We talked with one another, fever in our veins. Don Pedro de Candía advised the Captain-General to accede to Atahualpa's offer.

"But can I give him freedom?" the Captain-General asked, swaying back and forth in his decision.

"Freedom! Give him anything. For that amount of gold I'd give anything," was Gonzalo Pizarro's reply.

"Can gold buy honor?" asked Don Hernando de Soto.

"What has honor got to do with it?" said Gonzalo. "It's simply a question of getting our hands on some gold before their priests hide it away in the temples! Honor's got nothing to do with it at all."

"I quite understand how you feel about honor," said De Soto. "I'm not talking about you and your kind. I am speaking for myself, of course."

"More of that sarcasm and we'll see your fine blood!" shouted Gonzalo. He put his hand on his dagger.

"Shut your mouth," interposed his brother, Don Hernando Pizarro. He shoved him to one side. "When there's any question of honor to be settled for the Pizarros, I'll do it. I am the oldest. Anyway, why get worked up over nothing?"

"Then do something about it!" said Gonzalo. He was white as chalk with anger. "Do something about it, or I'll do it myself. You don't seem to care if a down-at-the-heels noble treats your brother like a dog!"

"I do care! I say I do care!" bellowed Don Hernando. He spoke so loudly the shivers ran up my spine. I could see the veins begin to stand out on his forehead. "The smallest drop of my blood I prize more than all the heathen gold in the world. I would still prize it if it were as watery as the blood in your own veins."

"Hernando is right," said the Captain-General. "You must ask his pardon and let him be, Gonzalo."

"Yes, yes, of course. I expected that," shrieked Gonzalo. He plucked out his dagger and threw it on the ground. "I cannot even express an opinion. If I do you all berate me as if I were a boy."

"Measure your language, then," said Pedro Pizarro.

"Yes, but the gold—what about it?" cut in Don Pedro de Candía. "That beautiful metal. Let's stick to the point. We lose more time with this quarreling among Pizarros than with any other one thing, Captain-General."

"What? Whose mouth is running over!" It was Don Hernando Pizarro. His face was grim. He stood like a stone statue over a grave.

Don Francisco looked absently at his brother, shrugged his shoulders, and sighed. He cleared his throat like a judge, and said, "The question remains the same. None of you has helped to unriddle it at all. Can we let the Inca go, keeping our side of the bargain? He has asked for a written guarantee, put on paper by Master Pérez. It's very strange. All of a sudden he seems to have as much respect for the written word as a notary. I'll admit I'm stuck. On the one hand we can't very well let the gold go. On the other it seems folly to me to let the Inca go free. Impossible, even. For even supposing he lets us go—his army will have a leader again. The kingdom will have an Inca. The people will be welded together and begin to act. There will be commotion and war. It will mean that we have lost the South Country, for Don Carlos and for ourselves."

The cavaliers looked at each other in silence. Don Hernando was like a deaf mute as he stared at the ground. And now Father Vicente stepped forward. "It is absolutely necessary that we have the gold," he said firmly. "That is, if the Inca really does command so much wealth. In the first place, if we don't take it the biggest part of the metal will be used to ornament heathen temples. That would be an intolerable blasphemy. As crusaders in the service of Christ we would never stand for that. In the second place we must have gold to attract men from Panama, New Spain and Castile to this South Country. Our crusade can never be successful, it's plain to see, unless we have reinforcements. Without gold we can never colonize the land. Getting this gold will not be something done for our personal advantage. We must do it for God."

Everyone nodded in thoughtful acquiescence.

"So far as the Inca's side of the compact is concerned," the priest went on to say, "so far as our obligations to him go, giving him his freedom, and so on, that cannot be avoided. We can't get out of it as Christians, cavaliers and soldiers with honor."

Many nodded again; others spoke against the proposition in whispers, hissing softly to one side.

"I say," Father Vicente added carefully, "we can't get out of our part of the bargain. Our names will be written down on the document. On the other hand, the future is always uncertain. Many months will pass before the gold is collected in this house."

"What Father Vicente says is true," Don Francisco cut in brusquely. "The Inca himself admits that it will take a good three months. It's a long way to Cuzco, nearly six hundred miles over the mountains. They'll have to freight the metal by llama train. It will be a slow process. Again, it will take a long time to collect the gold at the mines, or wherever they intend to get it. Some of it, the Inca tells me, will have to be taken from walls and roofs. But still I don't see how time is going to make it any easier for us, Father Vicente?"

Don Francisco Pizarro was very gentle and reasonable as he asked this.

"Things will work themselves out in time," the priest said shortly, unwilling to commit himself. "Many things can turn up in the interim. I hope to win over the Indian chiefs to our belief, for example. You can readily imagine that a people in their new-found zeal would not be unwilling to listen to words of caution from their father confessor!"

Some of the men laughed at this, upon which Father Vicente said, "I quite fail to see anything amusing. What is there to laugh at in the Sacrament? Or in the anxiety of a Christian soul confronting its judge? I only wish that a few of these persons standing before me now would show a little zeal and concern for their own souls. There is nothing jolly in the prospect of being boiled in oil after death, in my opinion, at least! But, let that go. What I'm counting on a good deal is the Inca's liking for some of our cavaliers. Perhaps they can influence him for his good and our own. Isn't that so, Don Hernando de Soto? Isn't that so, Don Pedro?" He looked at me, and like the slender Don Hernando I bowed my head in agreement, although unlike him I did not smile bitterly.

"To tell the truth I'm not a statesman, not by any manner of means," said Father Vicente. "I can't waste my time on temporal matters. But my fingers itch to get at the task of converting the Indians. Think of it, thousands of them! Millions, perhaps. There are some of you who never seem to think when you're throwing dice with the Inca and paying court to the Indian women that we have another Inca, a man by the name of Huáscar. It's he who is the rightful ruler of this country. Have you ever thought of it? Of course, he's rotting away at the moment in the prison of his half-brother—who is our prisoner. This Huáscar is doubly imprisoned, so to speak. But just one word from us and there would again be two kings in one kingdom, two rulers. And as I see, Huáscar isn't going to embrace Atahualpa fondly. Am I making myself clear? Was it not the Emperor Tiberius who said: *'Divide et impera'?* He was a wondrous sinner, Tiberius. But his head was hard as crystal. Divide, my dear sirs, and rule."

Don Francisco now spoke up. "You do us an injustice, Father Vicente!" he said. "Or me, at least. I had not forgotten Huáscar!"

"Then act, Captain-General. Stop chewing your fingernails and act," the priest advised tartly. His face darkened, and the eyes impaled Pizarro. "Three months is a reprieve long enough to convert Huáscar and set him on the throne of his fathers in Cuzco. And then—and then, if all fails, we have another way." Father Vicente drew back his lips from his teeth.

"What is this way?" asked the Captain-General softly.

All of us were taut with silence. We looked at the ground, and some of us looked at each other.

"Atahualpa is only a man of flesh and blood. Let us not forget that," said Father Vicente.

At this, Don Hernando Pizarro stepped forward. He raised his huge fist, and the monk shrank back before him. He looked like a stone colossus placed before a sepulcher of the ancients thousands of years ago.

"I tell you this, you man of God," he said slowly. "Anyone who lays a hand on our prisoner will have his head twisted from his body. And I'll do it if it's my own brother. I'll tear off his head and throw it in his face."

"You turn my words out of shape, my son," said Father Vicente. He actually edged forward, his hands on his breast, now commanding himself. "But you must admit that Atahualpa could die."

"I admit nothing," said Don Hernando violently. "I repeat, I admit nothing. A Pizarro does not have to admit this and that, like two philosophers making water behind a tree. I know what you're driving at, monk. But we Pizarros—I—I am a fighting man! None of us is really anything else. You know that. Even Gonzalo at the bottom is a man of honor. We are not thieves. And still less are we murderers. I do not allow a hairless schemer like you to lead us by the nose. Is that clear to you?"

Father Vicente turned gray as ashes at this. His underjaw dropped. He got himself in hand. "At least respect my office, Don Hernando," he said. "At least have some consideration for the frock I wear."

"It is not your duty as a man of God to counsel murder," said Don Hernando coldly. "Act your part."

"Then you stand responsible to our King," the monk shrilled wrathfully. "I am here on Don Carlos' orders. In my person you are slandering the Church and the King."

"I'm not afraid of the King," said Don Hernando. "I'll take my chances with him. Don Carlos has no more honor than I. When one of his servants crosses me without cause, or crosses my brothers, I shall cut his throat, whoever he may be. And right now you can thank the cloth you wear for the breath in your own throat."

"But, brother," said the Captain-General, "Father Vicente means well. He spoke for everybody's good, not for himself. What has he to get out of it, one way or the other?"

"That's a lie," said Don Hernando. "I'm fed up with talking."

"Are you for making the compact, then?" Don Francisco added quickly.

"Yes, I am for it," said the brother. "And I am also for something else. I am for everybody making up his mind that he is under obligation. We get gold. The Inca gets his freedom. When the gold comes, no one must forget that he is on his honor to fill his part of the agreement. I want to say this so everyone can hear my words. I'd rather see the house of Pizarro dissolve on a dung heap than to buy gold with shame."

"Then everyone is willing?" Don Francisco looked around from man to man.

"Good enough! Let it go at that!" There was general agreement.

Now Don Hernando Pizarro walked up to the monk and said, "I regret losing my temper, father. I recognize that you are a pious man.

I was really less angry with you than with my brother." He bowed low, then straightened up.

Father Vicente smiled thinly. With some hesitation he took the proffered hand and said shortly, "All right, then, my son."

And so this important conference was concluded in peace. Not one of us, as we moved away laughing and talking, had any intimation that the heated discussion was only the prologue to a far more serious event, in which the judged was innocent, the judges guilty.

That same evening the compact was worked out by Master Pérez. When our Captain-General was handing over the paper to the Inca, it occurred to him that the document declared that so much gold should be given over to the Spaniards, but not exactly to whom. The Inca answered that all the gold should go to the Captain-General, to his brothers and cavaliers, and to his soldiery. In order to be completely sure, the Captain-General asked the Inca whether the Spaniards in San Miguel or Panama were supposed to share in it. Atahualpa said to this that these strangers, so far away from Caxamalca, had nothing to do with it. This decision the Captain-General ordered inserted in the compact. Apparently it was nothing more than a formality, but as it later turned out the simple clause had great meaning, for it decided the fate of the Inca, of the Pizarros, and of the mighty kingdom of Peru.

There is hardly any time left, in recounting these great events, to go into personal matters. When we are caught in the midstream of history we cease to be persons in our own right, with a will and purpose peculiar to ourselves alone. Our thoughts are the thoughts of the time; our deeds are no longer personally willed. Indeed, even our feelings do not belong to us altogether, but are shared by many men on the same course, shoved forward by the identical harsh hand. And yet it is always dangerous to lose sight of oneself.

During these days when we were waiting for the gold I was living with my faithful Sancho in one room of the labyrinthine House of the Snake. In the room there was always half-light, since there was no window but a little square in one corner of the ceiling. I fell into the lazy habit of lying half awake on my bed in the morning while Sancho was busy taking care of the horse, or engaged in other duties that he had taken on himself. It pleased me to daydream about my experiences, about the men whom I was with. The twilight of the room was excellently suited for this occupation. The heavy stone walls were another magic circle like the one Master Agrippa used to draw on the floor when he undertook some particularly important task.

Anyone who has lived with many men for a long time will understand how I felt. The sight of the same faces, the sound of the same words and phrases, the almost identical events of the day that every soldier knows make up his round, the dry monotony, lacking all feminine caprice and brightness, in time becomes a grievous burden. A powerful hunger for change arises, a need for deeper, fresher thoughts. However, when this is impossible the man can do only one thing, and that is discourse with himself. The soul of man is a deep spring, the bottom of which has never been plumbed. It is a spring whose murmurings can become audible only in loneliness.

At times as I lay on my pallet merely thinking away the morning hours, loath to get up to meet the humdrum world, I would fall asleep. It was easy enough, watching the golden shaft of light streaming in through the little square opening, a shaft of dancing motes. On this particular morning which I want to tell about for my own reasons, in order to know myself better, if the truth must be said, I was dreaming a most absurd dream. In spite of its humor it had a quality of bitterness.

I dreamed that I had put on Don Francisco Pizarro's helmet instead of my own. This helmet was much too big for me, as indeed it would have been in reality. And yet despite its too large size, the helmet pressed against my temples. It was apparent that it could be both too large and too tight at the same time. In the dream I struggled to understand this peculiarity, why the helmet should fit so tightly and be so tremendously heavy. Then I remarked that it was made out of pure gold, though at the same time I knew that Pizarro's actual helmet was made out of gray iron, for he hated any sort of show. That is, he hated any show for himself, but did not mind it in his brothers and his comrades, perhaps looking at it as a reflection of his own power.

The weight of the helmet was so oppressive that it pushed my head forward like a tired flower on a stem. When I tried to straighten up I found my shoulders bowed like a caryatid's, and my knees buckled. In vain I tried to remove the dreadful object. It sat on my shoulders as if it had grown fast to them.

In this miserable condition I suddenly heard a soft voice singing in the Indian language. Opening my eyes I saw a girl standing before my pallet. I rubbed my eyes, thinking that I was still lost in the dream. But I was really half awake, and shortly realized that someone had put a gay Indian blanket over me, a blanket decorated with half-fanciful, half-realistically threatening bird-creatures with widespread wings, clutching claws and rounded eyes. The girl was holding a corner of the blanket in her hand as she sang:

"Over the earth I go, I go,
And far-off places seek.
On wide wings I go, I go
Over highest mountain peak."

I lay back in confusion, no doubt looking the zany I felt myself, and stared goggle-eyed at the singer. It was Laanta, the Indian girl who had once reached me the golden bowl of chicha.

"Who is going over the earth?" I asked stupidly.

At the sound of my voice she started, let the corner of the blanket fall from her hand like a thief caught in the act and looked at me anxiously. "It is the wind that goes," she explained timidly.

"What is it about?" I asked her.

She pointed to the blanket. "That is a picture of the wind," she said. Then I remembered how we had taken the cover from the royal storehouse at Caxamalca where thousands of them were piled up. I looked at the birds on the blanket, then at her.

"The wind," she informed me, "blows before the sun comes up. He rustles through the leaves like a messenger, letting them know. We all hear his voice before the rain comes. The wind guides souls over the great ocean, to the Islands. He leads the dead to the living, so that we can see our forebears with our own eyes."

"Where did you learn all that?" I asked her, for it sounded as if she were repeating something from memory.

"I learned it in the House of the Sun," she said. She looked at me gravely out of two dark eyes, eyes as dark as hidden pools in a wood never trodden by man.

"Did they teach you to come unbidden into young men's bedrooms?" I asked, trying to find some composure in sarcasm.

She raised the flat of her hands and turned away, as if I had threatened to strike her. Then she said, still candid and without a trace of guile or coquetry, "They taught us that the will of the sun-god is the highest will on earth. They told us that duty without questioning is the highest service a girl can perform."

"Duty—what do you mean," I said, rising on my elbow. "Do you mean to say that the Inca sent you to me?"

"The Inca sent me," she said.

"Well, what does he mean?" I persisted. "What is he driving at? Does he want to find out something?"

"I don't know. He didn't say anything. He doesn't want to find out anything." She was bewildered by my suspicion.

"But why should he send you unless he wants something?"

"I don't know. He wants nothing." She smiled uncertainly, and observed my confusion with childish curiosity.

"He didn't say a word about what he wanted?"

"He said, 'Go to Chasca, the man with the yellow hair, the one the strangers call Don Pedro.' "

"Well, that was meant for me, certainly," I said.

And then a sudden change came over the Indian girl. The smiles vanished from her lips. She looked down at the floor, completely crushed. "Laanta is sad," she complained.

"But why?" I asked in amazement.

"Chasca wants to send me away," she said. Tears began to roll down her cheeks, while she stared straight ahead in stubborn misery.

I looked at her, unable to believe my eyes. That she might want to stay with me of her own accord had never occurred to me. Secretly I had concluded that feminine curiosity had attracted her to my chamber, and that getting the Inca's consent in the form of a command was nothing more than a roundabout device. Now, of course, I saw clearly that she was speaking the truth. And the truth disconcerted me. "It's out of the question," I said firmly. I imagined Doña Isabella's face if she ever saw me with this Indian creature hanging on my arm. Why, even my Sancho would look at us with bitter condemnation in his eyes. Diego would understand, but then he was only too tolerant. It was altogether impossible.

"How did the Inca ever happen to think of presenting me with a girl?" I inquired inanely.

Her weeping stopped as suddenly as it had begun. "I don't know," she said, and shrugged her fine shoulders. They were a smooth bronze under the white robe. "But everybody is talking about the great service that Chasca has done the Inca the time he talked to him about gold and what it means to the strangers."

"But sweet loving Jesus!" I shouted. "Nobody gives away his sister, his ward, just for a half-hour's conversation. Politeness has its limits, after all!"

I jumped out of bed, wrapped in the Indian blanket with the bird design, and began to walk up and down in the room. The girl watched me with great interest. Her sadness had entirely disappeared, and she seemed very much amused, either by the gross vulgarity of my insistence on form, or by my lack of clothing. I suppose my naked legs projected below the hem of the blanket, and that I must have resembled a stork wandering over a pavement.

"Impossible, quite impossible!" I repeated over and over again, trying to be as much of a hidalgo as my limited experience would permit. I thought again of Isabella, of the sweetness of our parting, and in my foolishness I thought I could stay true to her by repeating, "Impossible!" In my heart, very naturally, I felt that nothing was impossible. I felt both in my heart and in lower regions of the carcass. When I looked at Laanta everything about her pleased me. I liked the beautiful lines of her shoulders and legs, her small feet quietly crossed in red sandals, the ivory toenails, the half-developed hips of the fifteen-year-old, the slender throat and the high cheekbones of the oval Indian face. Her hair was blue-black and straight, and this, too, was delightful to my eyes. And it was not long before my reason began to contribute wise words to my inclination. I thought never would I dare return such a lovely gift to the Inca. It would be the height of ingratitude.

I finally stood rooted to the spot, and said lamely, "Good enough. You can stay."

The girl gave a cry of delight, like a pleased child. She got to her feet, came over to me and put her hands on my shoulders. Her bracelets tinkled, just as they had when she offered me the drink from the golden bowl. But this time she offered me her mouth. Her head bent slightly backward. I held the back of her head in my left hand. I could feel the fine skull under my fingers as I kissed her. The pressure of her lips against mine, like the steady, deep pressure of a torrent, filled me with a dark peace, the like of which I had never known before, and have never known since. I breathed in the aromatic perfume of her hair, the pungent, strange smell of her body, which was like spices. I was lost in a purple twilight. I felt that I was holding all the Indies in my arms.

For the first time I began to understand the mystery of thundering surf on the rocky cliffs of the coast, the silence of the primeval forests, the snowy peaks of the cordillera. Not until this sweet creature kissed me did the earth of the South Country make itself known to me. For it is the strange, mute power of love that makes articulate the strength and purity of the growing corn, the sound of wind in the grass, the murmuring of the stream, the deep thunder of the distant avalanche.

When this slender-waisted Indian girl was nestled in my arms, when her hands lay in utter trust on my shoulders, for the first time I felt like a true conquistador. Everything that had occurred hitherto, the struggle and pain, the killing, the scheming, was no more than a troubled prologue to the long-awaited consummation. And yet within the apple, as there must be, was a maggot. I felt from the very first kiss that this must be a dream, that the kisses were an already withered premonition of coming things, that they were their own death.

I kept Laanta with me. She lived with me in my room. This occasioned very little comment. Not one of us Spaniards was without a woman of some sort or other. In fact, my friends were pleased. Up to now they had been a little bit put out with what they called my prudery, and they had taken great pains to twit me about my puckered virginity. Now they let me know they considered me a man among men, ready for the next step of acquiring the pox. They took great pains to clap me on the shoulder, to caress my buttocks and make the customary masculine gestures associated with the rite of initiation into fornicatory mysteries.

Don Hernando de Soto complimented me on my excellent taste, and I accepted his flattery in embarrassment, trying to smile it off. Gonzalo Pizarro could not refrain from remarking that still waters always run deep. Only my old Sancho, just as I had expected, looked at me with incredulity. His notions of conduct were rather literal, in the rural retainer style, so I did not complain. I explained to him—I admit in a fit of cowardice—that Laanta was the Inca's gift, and that being such it was impossible to return her in her former state of virtue.

Of course there would be nothing unusual to the soldiery who, debased by the protracted leisure of their situation in Caxamalca, were getting out of hand, taking whatever woman tickled their fancy. And their fancy was not hard to tickle, since they were idle and living like fighting cocks. It should be added that the Indian women did not behave in such fashion as to necessitate their rape. Any dark corner was good enough for them to tumble into and spread wide their legs for Spanish explorations. Besides, sheer curiosity made us Spaniards desirable objects. How we compared in spirit with the Indian men I have never heard, for the women spoke no invidious comparisons.

Everything was quite different with the girl Laanta. This very moment I can see her standing before me. I can see her quick body, the swaying hips and the little breasts. I can see her hurrying to me through the alleyways of Caxamalca, after going out into the gardens for vegetables or fruit or flowers. She always wore a bright Indian robe wrapped tightly about her, so that she had to take small steps. Ten paces or so behind her went Frenero. In comparison with this svelte child-woman, he looked like a pock-marked monster, a horror from some other more brutal world. She was like Psyche followed by a beast of prey. But many a Spaniard who had it on the tip of his tongue to pass a tentative jest on Laanta felt the words die on his lips after one look at the lurking Frenero. Of all men in the company he was perhaps feared the most, for murder was graven and furrowed into his features. The light eyes had no soul in them, except what little I had lent them by my curious mastery and his curious devotion.

Sometimes Bernal took over Frenero's task of acting as Laanta's bodyguard, and his knife demanded almost equal respect. He lacked Frenero's maniacal strength, but he was suddenly and mortally vicious.

On occasion this little parade became amusing. Out of sheer exuberance the forgetful Laanta would burst into a run. She was quick as a deer. Her black hair would fly out behind her. Then Frenero would be forced to race after her. In his anxiety to keep her in sight, he would often knock to the ground someone she had darted around, and then he would stop and curse, whether the collision had been caused by a Spaniard or an Indian.

But there was such a thing as overdoing this. Frenero, to whom all Indians including Laanta meant no more than the dogs of the Potro, might very well have twisted her neck in a moment of rage, however much he might regret it later on my behalf. Laanta could never be warned, however. Sometimes when she mocked Frenero's clumsy motions, darting about the floor and over my pallet, I was profoundly concerned. This I could never make clear to her. Yet again, sometimes when the two came back from the gardens outside the city walls, Frenero would be loaded with fruit and flowers, and on his flaming pate would be perched a wreath of bright posies. Indeed, he looked like an antique Pan, his eyes sticking out, his brutal face in wonderful contrast to the delicate flowers. And perhaps I was wrong. Perhaps he would not have wrung Laanta's neck however much she teased him in her innocence. For even lions and tigers quite eager to rend grown-up people can be led by children, so the legend has it.

Laanta was really a child, both in body and years. And yet in the child was a wood-sprite, a fey spirit that hovered teasingly over all that was ordered, planned and made carefully by man. This part of Laanta was like the early morning mist over the water, something cabalistic, not to be captured, like the voice of nature itself. It was a spirit pensive without thought, melancholy without pain, joyous without measurable cause. Really, when I first saw her in the half-world of the dream, she was like a sprite suddenly risen from the very wellspring of my soul, a sprite such as those seen by wanderers at twilight flashing purely among the still reeds along the shore.

Laanta filled me with awe and a kind of trepidation. All that I had learned, all that was ordered and human as I knew it, meant nothing to her. She was a Peruvian. I was a Spaniard. Perhaps that sums it up. What did I know about the miracles of sun and moon! My miracles were the miracles of our Holy Mother the Roman Catholic Church. How could I know, besides, the laws and manners of Peru, which bore not the slightest resemblance to our own? How could I find my way in a land without our markets, muleteers and all the rest? And Laanta was the essence of this land, the pure breath, the hidden inmost part. It may be that another Indian would have seen in her just another desirable virgin. But to me, I say once again, she was the Indies itself.

After Laanta had been with me for some time she began to call me, in her language, "Father." This naturally threw me off balance, as anyone can well understand. At that time I was hardly turned twenty-three, and scarcely felt qualified to play the part of parent, as well as lover, to a half-grown daughter with breasts like ripe pears. But it must be understood, in explanation, that among the Indians all older people may be called "Father" out of respect. Above all they revere the older people, their fathers, grandfathers, and forebears, these Indians. I did not understand this for some time. I believed that Laanta merely felt I was too old for her. At first this idea injured my vanity, but then I entered into what I conceived to be the proper spirit of the play, and parodied carrying out my paternal duties. Among other things I began to instruct her in the eternal truths of our Christian beliefs, for I had a genuine horror of losing her into hellfire after her death.

But no sooner did I try to do this than I arrived at the odd position of the hen who has hatched a brood of ducklings. No sooner did Laanta learn the holy story of our Lord's life on earth than she swam away with it into the treacherous waters of heathendom. She intermingled sacred matters with the most frightful, heretical nonsense. Squatting crosslegged on my bed, her eyes as big as saucers, she called our Lord the firstborn of the sun-god and the earth. I let out a protest, and crossed myself. I looked around, fearful that Father Vicente was hiding in the dark corner, ready to chastise the sinner. With heat I banned further blasphemies, and did it so forcefully that it made Laanta cry. She sobbed bitterly, and said that she had meant well. That mollified me.

It is easy to imagine my terror when in a trice she had made Maria Magdalena Christ's love, and ventured the opinion that Maria of Bethany, sister of the holy Lazarus, was another and somewhat tiresome mistress. This made me despair completely. I pulled her over to the image of the Virgin Mary that my Sancho had stuck up on the wall. I made her fall to her knees, and together for a long time we prayed, so that our Beloved Lady might bring light to this poor Indian soul. Laanta prayed enthusiastically, and called the Virgin Mary the "Mother of the Corn." I let this go without further criticism, for the Virgin in the image wore robes that were decorated with golden ears of wheat.

And so we kneeled there, I often looking sidewise at her dark head. I could see the light skin where the blue-black hair was parted, and this moved my heart. Laanta was passionate in her prayer. She called the Virgin "my sweet mother of God," "my golden treasure among the stars," "queen of the flowers." Hot and cold shudders of apprehension coursed up and down my back. I was hard put to it to say whether this was blasphemy or fervent praise. But I assumed that our Blessed Virgin knew better than I what was in Laanta's heart. For it is common knowledge that the Virgin pays but little attention to the words on our lips, preferring to look within the soul. Many a time, I do not doubt, the Virgin has heard highest praise in what the mob might hear as blasphemy, and mortal sin in the choicest encomiums.

Laanta, kneeling there under the image, became tremendously excited. To my amazement she repeated to the Virgin the very stories she had heard from me. She whispered hoarsely, "Do not forget, sweetest, how your Son at the wedding changed water into chicha with his lovely hands. How they all laughed when the bride put the golden horn to her lips! How proud you were! How glad the earth was! Let your Son come again, to walk on the earth. Let Him come over the sea to Laanta. Let Him wear His red robe, like a king, the robe they did not cut up, the one they gambled for like the strange people now in my country, when He was on the cross. Tell Him to help me to learn. Tell Him I will try to understand and to do as He bids. Tell Him Laanta is not very clever. Have Him make my father kind and good to me. Have Him come sit with Chasca and his friends as He sat with His friends at the table."

21

THE COMING STORM

IT IS high time that I turned from personal affairs to the consideration of matters concerning the whole company. Caravans of llamas, porters and slaves soon began to arive at Caxamalca laden with burdens of gold and silver. Scarcely a day passed that at least a few solitary messengers did not come staggering in with a load on their backs. They came from the hot coastal regions, from the mountain fastnesses of the east, even from Quito, far, far to the north. Little by little, the room began to fill; slowly the pool of gold crept up the walls, like water behind a dam. Master Pérez and the other secretaries in his charge were very busy inscribing in the account books the amount of each consignment.

The Inca Atahualpa himself kept an inventory with the help of the many-colored woolen threads knotted at intervals like a ship's sounding line, which the Indians call the "quipu." His fine, nervous hands fluttered ceaselessly as he watched the day of his freedom draw closer and closer. I never could learn to decipher the principles of counting with the quipu, although the Quichua language seemed to be very simple for me and it was not long before I was almost as fluent in it as a native.

We saw that the Inca was keeping his word, and that in a few weeks the compact would be fulfilled. But this did not give us, cavaliers or soldiers, the satisfaction one might have thought. The men now came to believe that this mass of gold multiplying daily before their eyes was only a fraction of the booty awaiting them in Cuzco. They reasoned according to the dubious maxim that where much comes from, there a great deal more must be. They considered themselves already duped by Atahualpa, and began saying that he was deliberately delaying the delivery of the gold in order to hide infinitely larger quantities of it in the mountains. The House of the Snake was troubled by ceaseless gossip and rumor. There were bitter words and sometimes open quarreling. At times half the company of cavaliers would not be speaking to the other half. The soldiers followed their masters' example, and were alarmingly ready to exchange threatening glances. The unity so painfully forged by Don Francisco Pizarro seemed to be rapidly dissolving under the baneful influence of the ever growing wealth. We were in imminent danger once again of becoming a loose aggregate of adventurers, merely waiting to be paid off our due before disappearing to all points of the compass.

The most unfortunate aspect of this demoralization was the behavior of the men toward the Indians. Every soldier had many Indian servants. He himself never so much as lifted his hand, but hung around, complaining loudly, arguing, threatening, viciously scolding, administering blows to the head and the behind, and generally playing the highborn noble, even though in Spain it would have been difficult for him to peer over the cobbles of the gutter.

I have often observed that soft talk about the goodness of the lower people is so much nonsense. They are good and kind so long as they are afraid of treading on their betters' toes. But there has never been a tyrant so brutal and thick between the ears as the man of the mass when given power and freed of his habitual shackles.

These men, who up to their joining the Pizarros had never possessed a rag to wipe their noses, who had earned their living through arduous toil, showed not the slightest respect for property created by the Indians. Everything that fell into their grimy fists they handled as if it were worthless. Often, in Caxamalca, when I saw some of our rabble misusing the possessions of the Inca and his subjects, I thought how my good Teresa had scoured a common earthen pot, how she had polished the big spoon until it shone like silver, how she strewed white sand over the floors and how she made good use of every last morsel of bread or meat. These common soldiers soiled and beloused the costly blankets spun from the silken vicuña hair. Tapestries which had hung in the Inca's rooms they flung into the filth of the streets, filth largely of their own making. They were always invading the royal magazine to pull out new blankets, only to render them dirty in hardly the time it takes to tell, textiles which any fool could see had taken Indian women years to weave. They treated the dishes and cutlery of the Indians in the same fashion.

One day I surprised a gang of them deliberately smashing piece after piece of crockery against a stone wall. Among the pottery that was wasted under their hands was some from the coast with artistic ornaments worked into the surface. Many of these pieces were hundreds of years old, curious jugs and vases, and had been carried up into the mountains only with the greatest expenditure of energy. On them were worked the animals of the country—sea lions, llamas, frogs, crabs, condors—all very naturally and effectively portrayed. There were also pictures of life among men, peopled with many figures, images of battles, dances, of men plucking out hairs from their chins, of deceased warriors and kings. I felt as I would if I saw barbarians taking Cellini's work and melting it down for sport.

But it was the hate of the mob that spoiled it all, the mob that cannot, being doomed to anonymity, bear to contemplate what has come to fruition and completeness. The beautiful to them is like a cry of contempt, and their ears, coarse though they may be, do not fail to hearken to this derision. They will have their revenge, even though it nets them nothing. I have heard that Frundberg's lancers acted similarly in Rome, and fed their campfires with the priceless manuscripts of the ancients.

Our men behaved in the same way when it came to using the Indians' stores. Not a vagabond who in Spain considered himself lucky to have a handful of bread, and favored of the gods when he had a taste of mutton, but now demanded as part of his daily diet the tenderest part of a llama shank, or a fattened fish from the Inca's ponds. Every day a hundred and fifty llamas were driven into the market place and slaughtered. The breeding mothers were not spared, and no one paid the slightest attention to the possibility that the herds might eventually be all killed off. Even the Indians, who had no minds of their own, were eager to get into the spirit of the game, and amid the bleating and scurrying hacked away with fantastic delight. The herdsmen, standing in the background wrapped in their blankets, their skins black with the sun, their black hair tightly braided, watched with baleful eyes as they saw their charges ruthlessly done away with. But they said nothing. Like all the Indians, they let it pass. These herdsmen, I used to think, were a warning, a warning of what might happen to us Spaniards up on the flowery mountain meadows.

Some of the soldiers developed an epicure's taste for certain parts of the llama carcass. One wanted a brain, another a tongue, a third the sweetbreads. The rest of the flesh they would wantonly discard. These Spanish soldiers behaved like Lucullus. I am sure if they had thought of it they would have asked for larks' tongues.

From time immemorial this harsh mountain land had been able to support its large population—large, that is, when the barrenness of the land is weighed in the scales—only by frugal distribution of its products. Everything edible had been dutifully piled up and shared out, making the most of the slender gain from the little strips of irrigated land. Only on feast days did the Indians ever taste meat.

But now every day it became the custom for the Indians to crowd into the market place to pick up the leavings. When the Spaniards had had their fill, the Indians fell on the llama meat like vultures, and squabbled over who should get the choicest bits. It did not take long for the triangular market place to be cleared of all vestiges of the daily sacrifice. The Indians would actually get down on their knees and lap clean the puddles of warm blood.

Great crowds of Indians had collected around Caxamalca. Day after day they streamed in, bringing wives, children and all their household goods. They had abandoned their work in the fields, on the roads, in the mines, at the loom, to sit day and night before the House of the Snake where they knew their Inca was incarcerated. But not once did he show himself to them, and so they had to content themselves with staring at us Spaniards and our horses. At first their numbers caused us no little apprehension, but in time we came to realize that they meant us no harm, and were only too glad to perform services for us with no hope of perquisite other than what, like Lazarus, they could pick up from our table.

However, our Captain-General became concerned about the chances of our all getting the pox. Beyond that, the mob was eating up everything in the great valley, like a herd of locusts that has settled down on a cornfield. Pizarro made representations about this to the Inca who, the following morning, had the city cleared, so that it was as empty as when we first arrived. In the distance, on the mountain trails, we could see the stragglers disappearing obediently, a pathetic line of ants.

The monotony, the silence, the empty faces, the incredible willingness to serve that distinguished these people, had something unnatural about it. Even their sheeplike pliancy lay heavily on our spirits. Secretly we would all have been glad once again to see red men like those at Puná, however much more difficult to handle. We could not imagine how such a great kingdom as Peru could have been built up by such a spineless lot. And it was not long before rumors were flying that a great army of Caribs was coming down from Quito to unite with the Inca's armies from Cuzco under the leadership of the chief Quizquiz to release Atahualpa. Day and night a ceaseless watch was kept by the posts on the roof, but all they could see, strain their eyes as they might, was the lonely range of mountains.

Hot summer came creeping into the valley. At night crickets chirped a shrill song in the sere grass, so that the black night trembled like a harpstring. This music, which went on night and day never ceasing, and the hot, clear, cloudless days contributed greatly to our uneasiness. We became increasingly irritable. In spite of the physical comfort in which we were passing the period of waiting, we all looked forward to the time when our backs would be turned on the valley.

It was a time of endless waiting, filled with a vague anxiety that had no real object to pin it down. At the bottom we all felt reasonably sure that the Carib and Indian armies were but inventions of our fancy. To some degree with intention, we duped ourselves with such imagined threats, in order to avoid facing something far worse, a consequence that approached us softly and surely.

Step by step this horrid ghost began to take shape, until its evil alternatives were planted squarely before our gaze. What the Great Inquisitor, Don Antonio Cardinal de Guevara, had described to me—he was a man who knew his fellow men!—the final decision which sooner or later all of us must face, the greatness of man and his inevitable responsibility that comes with God's gift of freedom, that moved closer to us, until it was as close as a brother. And when it came we were all hurled into a damnable state of not-being, because we listened not to our consciences, but to the whisperings of worldly reason, of greed and the burning lust for power.

It began when our Captain-General decided to have the Inca Huáscar, Atahualpa's half-brother, brought before him. The place where he was imprisoned was a mountain fortress only about a hundred miles away from Caxamalca. Don Francisco Pizarro made up his mind that the time had come when he must begin playing the one Inca against the other. Gonzalo Pizarro ventured the opinion that perhaps it would be possible to extract an equally large ransom from Huáscar as the price of his freedom and restoration to the throne of Cuzco. Then Atahualpa, of course, would be sent back to his originally inherited kingdom of Quito.

Nobody found anything to complain of in these purely political plans. The Captain-General eagerly set about interpreting the will of the great Huayna Capac. Only one was against the plan. Atahualpa himself objected vigorously. He trembled with rage when he first heard of what was being hatched under his nose, and for some days he prohibited Don Hernando de Soto and me from coming near him. On the other hand there was a constant coming and going of Indian porters and messengers in the Inca's quarters. It was easy enough to see, we thought, that he was garrisoning his roadside fortresses and spreading the alarm among his peasants, should he need protection.

Nevertheless negotiations with Huáscar were spun out to their desired conclusion. Gonzalo Pizarro finally told me, laughing with pleasure, that Huáscar of his own accord had promised twice as much gold as the Inca for his ransom. Through his go-between, Huáscar told us that he alone knew where the greatest treasure in Cuzco lay, for he had grown up there, it was his home, he was the rightful heir, and so on. Furthermore, he added, Atahualpa was nothing but a half-wild barbarian, and no child of the sun. Only through treachery and exploitation of the aging Huayna Capac's addled wits had he been able to wrest the power from Huáscar.

It was not long before the soldiery heard about the prospect of more gold. There was uncontrollable excitement. Everyone wanted Huáscar brought immediately to Caxamalca, the quicker to seal the bargain. In the midst of this uproar we heard the crushing news. Huáscar was dead. His guards had drowned him in a river while he was taking his bath. So the story went. It was like a cannon ball ripping through a tent, this annihilating reversal of all our plans.

The disappointment was terrific. The men shrieked for revenge and for golden retribution to the full, just as if this Huáscar, whom not one of us had ever seen, was our closest friend and patron. Many of the men even went so far as to pretend to shed tears. Others were numb with chagrin, as if they had already felt the gold weighing down their pockets. Don Francisco Pizarro and many of the cavaliers at first simply refused to believe the report. They hastened to the Inca. As ever, he received them with calm and courtesy. The Captain-General was so worked up that he completely forgot his acquired manners and behaved like the swineherd he had been. It was the only time I ever saw him lose his self-control. Without bothering to pause at the door to bend his head, without so much as a greeting, he rushed up to Atahualpa, and shouted, "Is it true, you Indian cow, that Huáscar is murdered!"

Felipillo, who always ran after the Captain-General like a little dog, rapidly translated, not sparing any of the tone. But Atahualpa merely said, "Huáscar is dead."

Pizarro now lost his temper so badly that the breath failed him. He threatened to strike the Inca with his clenched fist, and cursed him in gutter Spanish that of course the Indian king could not understand. The Inca, with incredible calm, once again told Pizarro, "Huáscar is dead. He drowned in the Andamarca River. He was careless."

Atahualpa's icy reserve served only to increase Pizarro's wrath. He sensed that he had been outwitted by a better player than himself, that he had been checkmated. The sudden collapse of his political plans completely robbed him of his reason. He spewed out frightful epithets, openly called the Inca a whoreson, a scabby dog, a eunuch, in the fashion of the lower orders of Spain when they are angry.

I heard all this with my own ears, for unwittingly I had stumbled in on the scene while making my customary morning visit. Felipillo, currying favor in coward fashion, began to translate the words. I took him by the throat and threw him out of the room. Pizarro looked at me out of eyes narrowed with intense dislike, and my hand fell to the hilt of my sword. But at that moment our Captain-General caught sudden sight of Don Hernando de Soto standing just inside the door. De Soto was leaning forward, one hand against the lintel. His eyebrows were drawn up high in mockery, and the corners of his mouth were fixed in a hard smile.

"What is going on here!" Pizarro shouted. "I am the master here."

Attracted by the commotion Don Hernando Pizarro had by this time arrived.

"That is enough, brother," he said, and laid his hand on the Captain-General's shoulder.

"Take your hand off me!" roared Don Francisco and shook his brother's hand away.

"I said enough, enough!" bellowed Hernando, and took a new grip. He shoved the brother against the wall, and forced him out through the door, away from the presence of the Inca. Juan Pizarro followed them out, his eyes starting with horror.

"It is mutiny," the Captain-General whispered hoarsely, his eyes blazing, but his shoulder still in the iron grip of Hernando. "You will kill me, will you? You will strike me down like a hog in the pen? We shall see, we shall see who will win. My brothers . . . Almagro . . . the nobles . . ." He put his hands to his face.

"Enough, enough," said Don Hernando quietly, trying to pacify his distraught younger brother, Juan.

Almost out of the corridor, still burning once more to face the Inca, his Spaniard's blood at fever pitch, the Captain-General tore himself loose from Hernando's grasp, and raised his fists in the air.

"The murderer will not escape justice," he screamed. "He will not get off. I never forget. . . ."

He would have said more, but his brother roughly shoved him out of the Inca's quarters entirely. The Inca was watching all this down the length of the corridor. He was silent, his arms over his breast, folded tightly. He began to shudder, as if with the ague, so great was his disgust. This made Don Hernando de Soto laugh without sound. Quickly he stopped, and said thoughtfully, "He never forgets, the gray Pizarro. . . ."

In this way were sown the seeds of implacable hatred between the Inca and the Captain-General. Almost all the men thought and felt exactly like Don Francisco. Everyone suspected that Atahualpa was the true murderer of Huáscar and so of all our dancing hopes. I vacillated between this and that opinion. It was impossible to read guilt or innocence in the Inca's impassive features. I saw it was quite possible that the situation had forced the Inca to take drastic action. And again the guards, thinking to do well, might have performed the deed out of consideration for their master.

The Indian king's destiny flowed on and on into the final dark canyon. All men's lives are like the flow of streams, impelled or retarded by this or that small event. Small happenings in themselves are of little consequence. It is their total mass and their combined pressure that drives us on without redress.

Often when folk talk about the destiny of men and of peoples, they speculate on what might have happened, on how things would have been if this or that had come to pass. If Caesar, so they prate wisely, had not gone that evil March morning into the Senate, had followed his wife's urgent advice, he would never have been murdered. If the man Judas had never sat among the twelve at the table, then our Lord would not have been betrayed and crucified.

But to me such disquisitions have always seemed childish. Caesar would not have been Caesar if he had listened to the advice of women and beggars. Our Lord would not have been the Man of God if he had not prepared a place for a wicked man at his table. For it is easy to see that there was a different and deeper relation between Jesus Christ and Judas than between Him and the rest of the Apostles. It is notable that Judas was the only one to follow his Master immediately into death, and with him to be taken from the earth. Just as Caesar had courage, and despite all danger to his person did what he had set out to do, so too our Lord had a love for evil-doers and fished most eagerly in troubled waters.

In short, what we call fate is nothing more than character, spread out through space and time. What we call chance is a point which least of all merits the name. Here the soul stands out naked in the glaring light of day, showing what sinews support it unseen in less critical times. And so the fate of man is long predetermined, even though he is not denied the freedom of choice—a choice which will always be made in character.

Always, at all times, as Master Agrippa taught me and as I have good opportunity to discover is true on my own account, necessity, God himself, intervenes in the erratic wanderings of the stars. And intervenes, too, in all manner of freedom. Few have the strength to listen to the dictates of the higher power. By no means is necessity always sweet and mild. On the contrary, for the most part it is revolting, crushing and not to be borne. What fate demands of us always appears, it seems, to be opposed to our good, and more often than not outrages all that men have learned to prize in conduct.

The events which led to our final decision I shall outline without going into detail, since so they were, and could not have been anything else.

First of all there was that vulgar, vengeful and corrupt creature, our Indian interpreter Felipillo. This loathsome being, through his intercourse with us whites in Panama, had learned only too well to assume all our greeds and overweening responsibilities. This is usually what happens to weak, evilly disposed men when they find themselves among strangers. Felipillo outdid any soldier in his dicing, cursing, drinking and whoring. His own kind, the Indians, he treated far worse than did any Spaniard, no doubt because he felt that he really belonged with them and was their betrayer. He had a besetting hatred for anything that was fine and beautiful. He persecuted the *orejones,* the Indian nobility, and attacked Indian virgins whenever he could get his hands on them. His special hatred was directed toward the Inca, and this hatred he could not dissemble.

I will admit that more than once I was tempted to slice his head from his body, and perhaps would have done this but for my experience with the law in Panama, and my knowledge that without Felipillo we would have suffered the lack of a man who knew Indian ways and Indian tongues. Sometimes I imagined with horror that in this miserable man the whole race of Peruvians, all the generations of obedient slaves, was crying out for revenge. In some way or other Felipillo had smelled our freedom, without understanding it and its grim responsibilities. And in this respect, I must continue in all fairness, many a Spaniard has an equally poor notion of the meaning of freedom. Felipillo had grasped the simple concept of rights, but had failed to counterweigh this revelation with the more subtle concept of duty.

One day Felipillo caught one of the Inca's handmaids in the bath and raped her. The Inca demanded that he be executed without delay. He reminded us that according to the law of Peru, for this misdeed not only the culprit but the culprit's whole family should be massacred, and his house leveled to the earth. But in this case, the Inca said, he would be satisfied if Felipillo should die a particularly difficult death. He requested that the Captain-General give the interpreter over to his own torturers who, he assured us quietly, were masters at the art.

When Felipillo heard about this he rushed to the Captain-General, sprawled on the ground, and kissed his feet. He begged him not to give him over to the Indians. The Inca's maid, he swore up and down, had given herself willingly, in fact had demanded that he copulate with her after threatening to wreak bodily harm on him if he did not comply. This, naturally, was a ridiculous lie.

The Captain-General listened to the commotion with a dark face.

Then he had the guard take the rapist into the market place and give him a frightful whipping that tore the flesh from his back. An ox-whip was used for this purpose, and when they were through with him Felipillo was a sight of horror. The interpreter, repudiated on all sides, crept away dripping blood. And, indeed, all that prevented Pizarro from acceding to the Inca's demands was, as I have pointed out before, that an interpreter's services were indispensable on our journeyings.

From this day on Felipillo often mistranslated the Inca's words and read into them a threatening content which was not really there. He also took unflagging pains to spread false rumors among the soldiers, which he purported to have overheard in the Inca's rooms. Although the soldiers were quite aware that Felipillo was a liar, they lent him a willing ear, because they were eager for the final division of the gold, and long since had become sick of their stay in Caxamalca. Even the more reasonable among them shook their heads doubtfully, for they argued that where there is so much smoke surely there must be some fire.

About this time the Captain-General sent two men to Cuzco on the Inca's own request. Their mission was to bring back news of how the stripping of gold from roof and wall in that city was progressing, so that the Inca would no longer have to make explanations about the slowness of collecting the ransom. These consummately unreliable scouts actually did convince themselves of the multiple difficulties of the undertaking. But at the same time they brought back swollen descriptions of the splendor of Cuzco. They talked just as men of their small souls would be expected to talk, exaggerating all they had seen and heard in order to share in the artificial perfection of the dream. Everything they came in contact with was the largest, the most powerful and the most numerous that anyone had ever heard of.

These lurid tales only served to prod the common longing to have a look at Cuzco. And the hatred of the Inca, which had become serious after Huáscar's death, was afforded a more reasonable basis, for now only the ransom was holding us all back. Felipillo, of course, spread it about that Atahualpa was the hindrance separating us from home.

Our prisoner's status was still further endangered by the arrival from San Miguel of Diego de Almagro, the old comrade in arms and partner of our Captain-General, with no less than a hundred and fifty foot soldiers and fifty mounted men. There was great joy among us Spaniards that afternoon when we heard the trumpets blowing far off in the mountains, and saw the glitter of Spanish harness. The little army wound its way down through the foothills like a shiny snake. Everyone, including the Inca's numerous Indian attendants, rushed out with welcoming shouts to greet the newcomers. The Captain-General and his old friend embraced. It was apparently a very moving spectacle, although many of us knew perfectly well that at the bottom the two distrusted, even hated each other. For in Toledo the Captain-General had been heaped with titles, honor and emoluments, whereas his comrade had come away empty-handed. But at the moment all these differences of advantage appeared to be forgotten. The booty in Caxamalca and the as yet unrealized treasures of Cuzco seemed to be great enough for all to have a share, and to satisfy two leaders even more exacting than Pizarro and Almagro.

We were all glad that we were now strong enough to risk the southward journey over the mountains to Cuzco. Only one dissented from the general opinion. This was Don Hernando Pizarro. In Diego de Almagro, a man with a choleric, red-veined visage, he saw a betrayer, one of those good-for-nothing adventurer acquaintances of his brother's dating back to their salad days. Hernando felt that now he was merely clinging to the Captain-General like a bloodsucker in order to share undeserved successes.

However, Don Hernando Pizarro's notion was incorrect. The short, thickset Almagro had risked his neck to carry out the Captain-General's plans. And legally considered, by compact made in Panama, he had a right to one third of all gold, land and slaves falling into Pizarro's hands. There is nothing man likes better to forget than these galling obligations, which always seem to stem from times one can scarcely recall. It is discouraging to have an old friend drop in just when the festivities and a new day are about to begin.

Again, Don Hernando knew about Almagro and his services only through the meager accounts his brother gave him. Don Francisco Pizarro was not one to present his debts in a glowing light. Don Hernando, beyond this, had an instinctive dislike of what he called the bumptious, overweening shapelessness of Almagro. He was nothing but an up-and-coming peasant, Hernando thought, so he often let me know. And in the inmost chamber of his heart Don Hernando firmly believed that the kingdom of Peru was to belong to the Pizarros and to no one else. He thought it belonged to them in the same sense that their armor and horses belonged to them.

I believe now that he even dreamed of controlling the new-found land apart from Spain, or at least bound to the mother country by the loosest tie. Already in his family he envisioned another royal line like the Hapsburgs, the Valois, the Tudors.

The Inca was to play a great role in these plans. For through his person, ruling as a puppet king, Don Hernando thought gradually to come into full power. He wanted to use Atahualpa exactly as the Carolingians had used the effete Merovingians in their climb up the great ladder. In his dreams the enormous nobleman had come almost to love the Inca, and stood between him and the uniformly inimical Spaniards like a massive wall. The slightest impoliteness of address, the smallest negligence visited on the helpless Inca was punished with a hand of iron. He, too, at the time of the rape of the virgin, had demanded the immediate death of Felipillo. The interpreter had shrunk away from him with his water running down the inside of his leg in fear, like a frightened dog. And this is easily understood, for Don Hernando could have torn his neck from his shoulders, and scarcely have breathed hard afterward.

Some weeks after Almagro's arrival the Captain-General with his own hands divided out the ransom gold. The entire sum had not been met, but the jealousy and envy of Pizarro's soldiers, who were afraid they were going to be done out of their full share by Almagro's men, could be stilled only by this direct sop. Rumors of Indian uprising, of large armies on the march toward Caxamalca, also hastened this fateful decision. The Indian goldsmiths had now melted down gold and silver into little bars. Only some few especially fine works of art had been preserved intact as presents for Don Carlos and Doña Isabella, the rulers of Spain, and as gifts and mementos for the cavaliers.

One bright morning Pizarro's whole company lined up in the triangular market place. Behind them stood Almagro's men and a huge crowd of Indians. When the ingots were carried out of the House of the Snake, a shudder of amazement and delight passed through the feverish onlookers. Almagro's men were gray with disappointment at not being able to have their part in this wonderful dispensation of earthly wealth. But the agreement between Almagro, Don Francisco and Father Hernando de Luque very definitely had a clause in it which obviated any such possibility. In their simple fashion the Indians clapped their hands and squealed with pleasure, until Don Pedro de Candía commanded them to silence in a menacing voice. For as he saw it, and he was indubitably right, the division of the gold was a weighty matter, and not one to occasion a festive spirit.

A deep, almost religious quiet gripped the men in the plaza as the Captain-General strode forward, faced them, and prayed to God that he might be given the power of justice in administering the task at hand. Our Dominicans also prayed long and hard, their eyes straining upward. The heap of gold sparkled, shone and ran with little streams of light in the clear mountain sun, as if for the last time the demons of Peru were at work in it before it disappeared forever into our pockets. With great circumstance, quite as much as if he were celebrating Mass, Don Francisco now measured out the first share, which was the King's.

Then it was his own turn. Fifty-seven thousand gold pesos, over two thousand silver marks, he took for his share. Then, thirty-one thousand gold pesos and over two thousand marks for his brother, Don Hernando Pizarro. The rest of the Pizarros, the cavaliers, the riders, the foot soldiers, the hangers-on—no one was forgotten. The gold pesos and the silver marks ran out of Fortuna's cornucopia. An enormous deluge of riches poured down over our heads, over all of us. My eyes popping, I looked at my comrades to see how they were taking it. There was Diego de Vargas, the poet, and his hands were trembling. Frenero, his hair tousled even on this day of days, one-eyed Bernal and my Sancho. And they trembled, all of them. They were bewitched, touched by a magic wand. For here in their hands was ringing, hard, heavy, lovely gold. Their faces changed as they got their portions, grew harder, more serious, more concerned. They were almost like strangers.

And then I heard my own name called out. Don Francisco Pizarro, his voice hoarse as always, spoke my name, and intoned, "Seven thousand, seven hundred and forty gold pesos, seven hundred and twenty-four silver marks."

I, too, began to tremble violently. Castles with bastions, towers and gardens, broad fields, meadows filled with herds of cattle and sheep, peasants and fine-livered servants—all these delights danced before my eyes. All of it was mine. At one stroke I had become the richest man in Cordova.

And yet, looking back, I was not so delighted, really, as I had expected. There was a weight on my breast, an undefinable sense of guilt. I had the strange feeling that I had lived through the whole affair long ago. I knew that as I took my spoils I should bow my head in acceptance, and forthwith determined not to do it. I remembered once before—where was it?—I had bowed my head. I was trapped, choked by a finely woven mesh of gold. And then I did remember, as suddenly as the lightning flash illumines the night, the dream I had had as a child. I remembered the sensations when gold poured over me onto the covers of my bed so that I all but smothered. I thought of the pretentious vow that I had made to Doña Isabella, when I told her I would conquer Satan.

Fearfully, in confusion, I looked at Don Francisco, saw the tall, gray form, the straggled beard, the hard face, tired somewhat from the strain of parceling out the booty. As I looked at him I could not for the life of me see in him what I so fearfully sought, the Satanic being of the dream. All that I saw was another one among the many who have made Spain the most powerful nation in the world. And beyond that I saw a man who was close to me by virtue of common experience.

As I stared at him foolishly, for a moment he seemed old and almost helpless. Then visibly his energy returned, the energy of his mission and his leadership, the strength of his will to meet the greatness of his physical task—and the sixty-two-year-old became a powerful man of forty. How pleased I was with this metamorphosis, which seemed intended for my private reassurance—though of course it was not in any sense.

I watched him bend forward, a light smile on his lips. He pulled an object out of the Indian baubles, held it aloft, and said, "The golden ear of Indian corn with the silver silk I give to our young cavalryman, Don Pedro de Cordova, in recognition of his services at Puná, when he and my brother drove the savages to Hell."

There were murmurs of envy and pleasure at the sight of such a pretty ornament. I heard shouts, and knew that they expected me to say something appropriate in acceptance.

I moved forward, took the golden ear of corn carefully in both hands. I was immensely taken with the gift, actually far more taken with it than with the more valuable gold and silver ingots. Forcing the words out I said, "I thank you, my Captain-General."

"No thanks are necessary," he said with military curtness. "Service is service. You have earned it."

With my present in my hands I went back to the ranks. Many hands reached out to wish me luck. The cavaliers all were impressed by the precious gift. I shall never forget how Sancho looked. He had his hand on the hilt of his sword, vanity and pride tightening his simple physiognomy, as if on this day he had been dubbed a knight by the King himself.

And so the gold was divided up. The Inca Atahualpa now demanded that the Captain-General fulfill his part of the bargain and let him have his freedom. More than once he sent Don Hernando Pizarro, Don Hernando de Soto and even me to see Don Francisco and remind him of his written word. We three became openly known as proponents of the Inca.

Don Hernando Pizarro was amazingly persistent in heaping reproaches on his brother's obdurate head. He told him in the most savage fashion, threatening reprisal, that he had broken his promise, that henceforth he could not regard him as a true Pizarro. In vain the Captain-General painted for him in minute detail our hopelessly cramped position. It did no good for Don Francisco to remind him of the rumored armies, and of the innumerable dangers and almost certain loss of carefully earned booty that would ensue once the Inca was free to plan revenge as best suited him. "A word given is a word given," Don Hernando would roar rebelliously. "The man who breaks his word is not fit to draw breath."

"But we can't let him go. It would be impossible—suicide," the leader would remonstrate.

"That is just the time when the honorable man keeps his word—when it is impossible," Don Hernando would retort with violent contempt. "I say there is no other way. The Inca will thank the Pizarros all his life. We can become great through him."

"And Don Carlos? And the Council of the Indies? What shall we tell them?"

"Don Carlos has no right to demand treachery of the Pizarros. And those doddering, slack-jawed scriveners in Seville have still less cause. What's up with you, brother? You're like an old maid in a village of gossipers! What do you care what this one or that one thinks? Who are they? Let them rot. A word is a word. And we have given it."

"I have heard you say that before, brother," Pizarro would answer.

"I shall keep on saying it, now, tomorrow, and until the end of my days," Hernando would roar. "I, I am a man of honor."

At this Don Francisco would become beet-red. "Good," he would say. "I tell you this much. I'll do as you want, brother. I will give the Inca a document, which I'll sign myself, showing that he has filled all his responsibilities in the contract. And in a few days—perhaps a few weeks—when things begin to look a little clearer, he'll be a free man."

"I don't like that," was Hernando's objection. "I don't like matters to be put off that way. What's the need of it? Don't forget it's a question of the Pizarro honor." Then he would pause, having come to the end of his rope, and add, "Well, if it's only a matter of a few days."

And of course the rumors grew thicker, the situation more impossible, and Felipillo wasted no opportunity to warn the Captain-General of the Inca's plans for revenge. Don Francisco more than once tried to get his brother to see his side, but he was always summarily repulsed. There were bitter quarrels between Don Hernando and Diego de Almagro, for the latter was all for putting an end once and for good to the Inca dilemma. "Sweet Virgin Mary, Mother Mild!" he would say, his red face as big as the setting sun. "So many Indians have fallen. Why not one more? It's all a part of war and conquest. Personally I don't have any bone to pick with Atahualpa. But why not?"

From that time on Don Hernando to his face called the leader of our reinforcements the "Little Clod," a name which stuck. Differences all but reached a point where blood would have been let, and then Don Francisco hit upon a characteristic idea. He decided to send his brother to Spain as an emissary and so be rid of him for good. He was filled up to his back teeth with admonition. At first Don Hernando hesitated, but finally gave in. The temptation was too great to be resisted, to be there first. He saw the triumphs, the honors, the receptions at court. He departed before the Inca's fate had been decided in fact. But one thing he did do. He commissioned Don Hernando de Soto in the course of long conversations to carry on his cause while he was gone. He also earnestly commanded me and his youngest brother to do all within our power for the imprisoned Indian king.

"If you fail to do this," he said ominously, "an ineradicable shame will beset Spain, the Pizarro family, all of us. We will have to turn our faces away from honorable people, and go out in the night like bats.

And as for that Little Clod, Almagro, kill him before he kills you. We Pizarros will lose everything we have if it comes to an uprising and war between the Indian cities. The Inca must live. So long as he is there, you are safe. Be kingly with him, and keep your word. If he falls, you all will fall. And you will fall far lower than he."

At the time his words seemed somewhat strained to me. But now I see that he was speaking to us out of seventy years of care and strife. Don Hernando was like this. He was almost intolerably proud and arrogant, often cruel, surly and easily aroused to wrath. But he was a tower of strength in battle and in the council chamber, a faultless comrade in danger. I still see this giant man, quite unbent by age, his back disappearing from view as he clattered away on his tall horse after he had stooped to embrace first his brothers, then Don Hernando de Soto and myself. I recall how each of the Pizarros zealously offered him some little service. One of them held his horse, another fixed his stirrups, a third tested the cinch of his saddle, and even the Captain-General set his brother's mantle aright when it became snarled in the seat of the saddle. Then Don Hernando Pizarro rode away to the head of his column, followed by a long line of Indians and heavily laden llamas, and the armed men chosen to accompany him to San Miguel.

That same night I was waked out of a sound sleep by Sancho. My little room was soon filled with Indians. Among them was Laanta, wringing her hands, weeping. Horrified, I asked her what had happened.

Sancho reached me my clothes and said, "The Inca wants to see you."

"Now? In the middle of the night?"

Sancho shrugged his shoulders. "He is a prince. What does he care what time it is, day or night? . . ."

"What is it, Laanta?" I asked the girl.

"Chasca must come," the weeping girl told me. "Chasca reads the stars, for he has talked with the old priest."

"That is so much foolishness," I said uneasily. The night felt different from when I had gone to bed. Some new power was abroad. I could feel it in my bones, and it made me shudder. "Virgin Mary," I whispered, and kissed my cross, "stand by me."

Half-dressed I stumbled out of the room, and following me trailed the excited Indians, moaning and groaning. Up and down I ran through the long corridors until out of breath I reached the Inca's quarters. One of the guards at the door was my Frenero.

"What's going on, Frenero?" I asked.

"They're all crazy, master," he said. "The Devil has got into them."

The Inca was not in his bedchamber, I discovered. He was up on the roof. I went out into the starlight. Atahualpa was poised motionless, his head hanging. I made out that he could hardly keep intact the calm that had covered his features since childhood. Unable to say a word at first he took my arm and led me to the balustrade. Then he pointed with a slender, sinewy arm into the eastern sky. High over the dim mass of the mountains among the constellations was a comet. The enormous powdery tail swept far across the heavens. I saw whole masses of stars fall in a glittering shower, as if disturbed in their courses by the errant body rushing through their midst.

"Do you see the star, Chasca?" the Inca asked tonelessly.

"Yes, I see it," I told him.

"Do you know what kind of star that is?" he asked.

"That is a comet," I assured him. "They come every so often."

"That is the death star," he said with finality. "When my father, Huayna Capac, laid himself down to die, that same star appeared in the heavens early in the morning. The priests came to me and bade me make all preparations at once for the funeral, for he was going to die, they said, even though he still lived and breathed. They were right. On the seventh day after the star came into the sky he was dead. Seven days from now, Chasca, I am a dead man. There is no one who can help me now. The heavens themselves have willed my destruction, and have dispatched a messenger to warn me. I am all alone, and I am afraid. My priests say that I will go to the sun. But I do not want to go to the sun. I would rather stay here on earth. I would like to see my children grow up. The voices that call us all to book are whispering in my ears and I am sad. I am sad to go, to leave my body, my name, my women and the earth."

He put his hands to his face. At fitting distance his attendants squatted on the roof, groaning softly. Above us the heavens were dark despite the busy multitude of stars. A chill breath of mountain air brushed our cheeks and foreheads.

"You strangers! You don't fear death," the Inca murmured. He took his hands from his face and again looked at the comet.

My eyes fell on the silver cross that I had kissed only a moment before. It shone against my breast. Holding the cross I moved close to the Inca. "We are all afraid, and yet there is nothing to fear." I pressed the cross in his palm.

He took it, and he looked at it a long time. "Tell me, Chasca," he said. "Is it true what that man in the black clothes said, that your God came down to earth, that they killed him, that he rose and went to Heaven? Is it true?"

"Yes, it is all true," I assured him.

"Isn't it true that the gates of Hell yawned before Him, and that He took with Him the great hosts of dead long ago?"

I nodded acquiescence.

"And it's true that everyone who believes in Him will rise from the grave? My priests say the same thing about us who pray to the sun. But I am afraid, whereas you Spaniards do not seem to fear anything. Yet perhaps we all are afraid when death comes near."

"We doubt . . . we have no trust," I murmured uncertainly.

"No belief?" The Inca was so close to me that his breath touched my cheek.

"No," I said, now speaking to myself. "Sometimes we doubt. We believe in gold, not in God."

22

THE TRIAL

WHEN I started to rise from my pallet the next morning I felt miserable—as if the whole world were dirty and revolting, and above all I myself. I tumbled back on the bed and lay partly clothed under the covers. My Sancho came into the room. Wildly my brain began to work, and refused to follow my will. Images from the past whirled drunkenly through my head. When I closed my eyes I saw the Grand Inquisitor with his wooden crucifix in his hand. I saw Doña Juana kneeling in front of the image of the Mater Dolorosa, the Governor of Panama in his bath and Rodrigo the devil on his deathbed. All these remembered people talked and whispered conspiratorially to one another; they pointed at me and they laughed loudly. The Cardinal was the worst of them all. All of a sudden he tried to throttle me, and shouted, "I do this to you as you would do to me."

In misery I forced open my eyes, and saw Sancho standing beside me. "Water, water!" I croaked hoarsely. "I'm dry; I'm on fire."

The nightmare forms once again crowded in on me; they lifted me, and wanted to carry me away. I defended myself furiously, for they were now trying to drown me. I began to shriek aloud.

"Don Pedro," said Diego de Vargas, close to my ear, "try to calm yourself. Straighten yourself out in the bed. You'll never be able to sleep that way. You're all cramped up like a mummy."

But I would not listen, and struck him heavily on the chest. I shouted for Frenero and Bernal. The sight of my two strange monsters comforted me. "Sit beside me, Frenero," I said, "sit beside the bed. Sit down at the foot of the bed, Bernal. If anybody comes, especially the Cardinal, throw him out."

"I will," Frenero promised. Then he lifted me up, and they all smoothed out the bedclothes. Sancho put a beaker of water to my lips and all trembling I drank deeply. The water ran wonderfully cool down my parched throat.

"Do you remember the old clay jug, Sancho," I asked wearily, "the one in the olive garden? There used to be blades of grass in the water. That was Spanish water."

"I remember," said Sancho, "but now you have to sleep, Don Pedro, and stop talking."

"No, I don't want to sleep; I can't," I mumbled. But in the same moment my eyes closed. It was terribly hot, and then of a sudden my forehead was cool, as if a wind from the sierra was blowing over it. My fancies became less horrible, but still unfriendly. Doña Isabella appeared with gold net over her black hair and wanted to make me eat sweet figs from Sidonia. Doña Sobeya, the teller of tales, swam into view, and with her, huge and white, the King of the Spirits. Learned men sat about in the fevered dream, among rolls of parchment, these covered with illegible Arabic writing. There was Master Agrippa's spirit from the alchemistic kitchen, and all about pestles, mortars, flasks and alembics. Master Agrippa said, "Today the experiment must succeed. We'll make the philosopher's stone; we'll make God." But Abu Amru argued and quarreled with him, and said, "We aren't trying to make God, we're trying to make gold." "That's only one step in the process," Master Agrippa replied sharply. "We aren't novices any more in this business." And at last they began to pull each other's hair.

Then Abu Amru struck a scroll with a delicate fist, his long silver beard shook, and he cried, "Fire, that is the true element of elements!" And Master Agrippa shouted, "Come closer, you ass, you stupid little Spaniard." Now there I stood, as I must have looked as a child, lustily working the bellows. At the same time I saw myself at the bellows I also spied a little person—it was also I—no bigger than a finger, hiding behind an alembic.

In a pipsqueak of a voice I shouted, "Why don't you go on making the element of elements and leave me alone? It's terribly hot here."

"No back talk, my son," said Master Agrippa to this objection. "You wouldn't understand, to be sure, but the element of elements is in you, inside you. Don't you have any faith in us? Don't you believe in alchemy? Why do you act like a dirty little mouse?" "The sisters will do away with him," Abu Amru threatened. And Master Agrippa took the flask, contemptuously hurled it against the wall. It splintered into a thousand fragments. This frightened me so much that I woke up.

At the foot of the bed stood Bernal. He looked at me out of his one eye as if he had been watching the goings-on in Master Agrippa's laboratorium and did not like at all what he had seen. Beside me was Father Vicente. He said, "You have a high fever, my son. Look out for the damp cloths. Don't brush them off. When you feel a little better, I'll draw a little of your blood."

I nodded fearfully, remembering the dead actor. "The sisters," I mumbled, "those terrible . . . the big hammer . . ."

"What is he talking about?" asked Frenero.

"He's making it up," said Father Vicente. "He's talking nonsense. Change the cloths more often. Give him as much water as he can drink."

I went to sleep again, and once again woke up with a start, this time to find Laanta standing beside my pallet. "The Inca sends you this," she said, and offered me some gray powder on a leaf. I swallowed it. It was intolerably bitter, bitter as gall, and I had to drink more than a beaker of water to get rid of the taste. Then I lay back quietly and stared at the ceiling. A feeling of utter comfort and relaxation possessed me. I felt myself become as light as air. The heat ran from my limbs, and I was cool as on any day. This sensation was followed by one of immense fatigue, of an intense desire for sleep and forgetfulness. Night seemed to enfold me on all sides. It seemed as if a grove of firs had suddenly sprung up around my bed. My sleep was deep, quiet, and untroubled by dreams.

When I woke up four and twenty hours later, the fever was gone. But I was so weak that every movement cost me an inordinate expenditure of strength. Again Laanta handed me a powder, again telling me that the Inca had sent it. This powder was also bitter. Its taste, however, not altogether unpleasant, was bitter and spicy at the same time. I later found out it was made from the powdered dried leaves of the coca plant. This plant is held sacred by the Indians, just as the old Spanish peasants consider the grapevine sacred. The Indian priests chew these leaves, then prophesy and give counsel in their induced ecstasy.

The powder of the coca plant brought me pleasant fantasies and daydreams. At the same time it refreshed me wonderfully, and soon I was well on the way to convalescence. Diego and Laanta were almost always with me while I lay abed and gradually regained my strength. Laanta kept me amused with endless Indian legends and fairy stories. She was almost another Sobeya in this respect, but what she told was not wise, logical and instructive, but completely bizarre. And sometimes the stories were revoltingly cruel. Demons were busy in the legends, plaguing mankind. Ghostly animals waylaid the llama herdsmen. Giants made of ice reached up high into the sky, higher than the mountain peaks.

Laanta told me about the world as it was before Creation, about the sacred lake in the mountains, about the islands where Pachacamac tarried when the moon fell out of the sky and the seas overflowed on the earth. She told about the sun door of Tiahuanaco, hewn out of a single monstrous stone, and how Pachacamac stands there, black and stony, a bundle of condor-headed lightnings in one stone hand. His powerful head, almost cubical in shape, is crowned by rays of light, while twenty-four small demons and demons' attendants zealously wait on him, with their men-and-condor faces ever turned in his direction.

Diego and I listened to the girl with incredulity cramping our faces. But as she got into the spirit of the game, her voice became a singsong, a monotonous, endless chanting, that sounded like the sobbing rush of the sea breaking on the shore. Often we did not understand what she was saying, for she was no longer speaking the everyday Quichua language, the one with which I was fairly conversant. The content of her songs, so far as I could make it out, was very odd. It appears that this demon Pachacamac sheds great tears of pity for all human beings. When these tears fall on the earth as rain, then plants bloom and flourish, bearing fruit from which man and beast can live. And so we all live through the compassion of the god.

We asked Laanta why Pachacamac pitied mankind and felt sympathy for the inhabitants of the earth. She sat very still in the corner of the room, and meditated. Then she sang another song, which I recall went something in this manner:

"Pachacamac has compassion, and his heart is full of sadness because men die. The moon vanishes and goes out and then once again grows round. But men never return once they are dead. Once men were made of stone, and lasted as long as the rocks. These stone men built the great houses, stone gates, towers and fortresses that once were seen in our land and still exist in some places. Their strength was beyond belief, they could not be tired out and their span of life was interminable. And since they were made out of stone their hearts too were of red stone. Because of this they were hard, proud and relentless with one another. In their hardness and endurance they worshiped neither the gods nor the great mother Mamapacha.

"At last Pachacamac grew wroth over this and threw the moon down on the earth, split the heavens which are made out of blue quartz, and commanded the waters of the sea to rise, until only Aconcagua and Chimborazo rose above the turbid flood. Then there was nothing to see but the corpses of mankind lying about like great blocks of stone. Only the condor continued to live. He is a bird from the times before the flood. When he moved his wings after the waters had receded, seeds fell out of his wings. These grew into a plant blessed by Pachacamac, the coca plant, which gives the priests forgetfulness, strength and mild dreams, and brings them joy.

"Pachacamac went to the place that today we call Tiahuanaco, and from there created another world. He formed the giant fir trees, the tender grass on the mountain meadows, the sweet cane and the cotton plant. He formed the bodies of animals and made the herds of llama and of vicuña. He made the parrots, the hummingbirds and the butterflies. These are all the thoughts of Pachacamac, created by himself, for he is not like mankind, who do not think things into life.

"And when the world was once again bright green with plants, and alive with beasts Pachacamac's heart was heavy with sorrow. For more than anything else he wanted a creature who would marvel at his handiwork, who would be thankful to him and make him offerings. He was afraid to create men again, for he did not forget their hardness and impiety. And so Pachacamac went to the great mother. They took council together, and Pachacamac expressed his fears. Mamapacha advised thus. She said, 'Let us make man mortal. Have death standing behind him night and day, during the day at his work and when he feasts, and at night beside his bed. This will make him pliable and easy to handle. Then men will honor and fear you. They will also be sorry for each other, since they share this common fate, and will treat each other with solicitude. There will be a great brotherhood of death among mankind.'

"Thereupon Mamapacha formed the body of man from lime, and Pachacamac breathed into the form. The great clot of lime opened its eyes and lived. It is because the life of man is only a breath, a little sigh of air, that he declines so quickly, and is gone in less time than it takes to utter the words.

"When men began to live and be active there was death, always with them. It was not long before Pachacamac began to feel a great compassion for these men so grievously afflicted. The dying cried out to him, and the suffering begged for his succor. Pachacamac saw that even in the idle play of the suckling, in the sleep of the virgin, in the passionate embrace of lovers there was the seed of death. This shook him, and he said, 'Men are like me. They have the gift of knowledge. For it is my breath that stirs within them. I shall give them succor.'

"And Pachacamac thereupon called the condor and ordered him to carry the water of life to the earth. When Mamapacha saw the condor coming with his precious burden, she became very angry. She cursed the irresolution of the great god. She turned herself into a fat goose. When the condor saw her he forgot his load, plummeted down to earth with his talons outstretched, eager to get her. So, through the cunning of the great mother, even today men remain mortal and must always die. Out of the watered earth a shoot came, a shoot of corn, the staff of life on which Pachacamac's red children have always lived and still live today.

"Pachacamac continued to shed endless tears of pity for mankind. He spoke with the young sun, and said, 'Go now over the earth, command day and night, and rule mankind, you fiery one. For I can help them no more.'

"Then the sun said, 'So be it, old man. And now since I, too, cannot give men the water of life because the earth holds it in her earthy hands, I shall give them the second best. I shall give them my son, Manco Capac and my daughter, Mama Oello. I will send them into the south, and with my shining hands point out to them the navel of the world, which shall be called Cuzco. There they shall found the kingdom of the four corners of the world. With wisdom they shall partition the acres of land and protect the flocks of llamas. There shall be no beggars, nor shall there be hungry people, or those who lust for power and possessions. Everything shall belong to everybody. No one shall own the smallest scrap of earth for himself alone.

" 'I shall instruct them in the laws of the sun. They will even do good deeds to the savages, who live in the forests and wastelands like wild animals. I shall instruct them in a thousand arts, in building dams, in trapping water, in increasing the herds, in melting copper, in working gold, in weaving cloth, in the art of writing in knots, in dances and songs, which last shall honor you and me. And even if men do die and their lives are short, yet shall they say that their lives are beautiful, without plague, hunger, hate, war and misery in the villages. They shall praise me for everything, for the splendid order they enjoy, the firmly placed, the unchangeable. They shall praise me and my children, the Incas. I will shelter and protect them, hold my hands over them, ward off cold, hunger, war, and war among brothers so long as they stick fast to my law, from now until the farthest future imaginable.'

"So spoke the sun and kept his word. Ever more powerful became the kingdom of the sun children, from the limits of the sea to the primeval forests. And then—so the priests whisper—Huayna Capac, the ruler, broke the law of the sun, setting two Incas on the throne out of sheer love. Since that day unrest, war, murder and theft have come into the kingdom of the four corners of the world. Already Huáscar is dead. Today in the skies stands the fiery messenger who asks for the soul of Atahualpa."

Laanta's song ran in that fashion, though I have transformed it into ordinary language to the best of my memory. Often it would become unintelligible as she lost herself in it. Animals spoke to one another and even plants had words to say. At times her chant was like the murmur of waves and the rushing of wind through a wood. The heresy of her song terrified us. But at the same time we were attracted by, and often recognized a similarity in it to Christian history, except that in Laanta's version the old ideas were distorted, as if seen in a curved mirror. It was as if Laanta sought for the truth, felt it dimly, as a plant in deep shade seeks the sun with its pale leaves.

The other cavaliers often paid me visits, inquired after my health and told me the latest gossip. But they could not abide long with me. Anxiety and uneasiness were rife in the House of the Snake. Prone on my bed in the depths of the night I used to hear my comrades pacing back and forth through the corridors, nervously talking together. Frenero, Bernal and Juan the thin also came less often to see me because, so I was informed by Diego, the Captain-General had doubled all watches. Since we had become rich through the Inca's treasure we all seemed infinitely more concerned over our lives and safety.

Rumors of an Indian uprising grew apace, and prospects appeared to be more and more threatening. Even during the night the horses stood ready saddled and armor in place. The men slept fully clothed and armed. The whisper was going the rounds that the enemy might appear any moment. This suspense was almost impossible to endure. The soldiers during the day slumped about with grim faces, red-eyed and drawn from lack of sleep, irritable and deeply dissatisfied with their lot. No one ventured any more outside the city proper.

Then I heard that the Captain-General had talked with Atahualpa in order to find out what basis there was to all the rumor. The Inca had smiled coldly, and said that the kingdom was at peace, that nowhere within miles and miles of Caxamalca was there an armed Indian. He himself had commanded his armies to withdraw and to lay down their weapons. It was unthinkable, he said, that even one of his subjects would so far forget himself as to break the command of the Inca.

The Captain-General continued to express his doubts, and then the Inca, crying out in despair, wanted to know how was it possible that the strangers could fear him. Was he not completely helpless in their power? Did he not know that he would be the first sacrifice, should there be an uprising? Still unsatisfied and unconvinced the Captain-General left Atahualpa.

The rumors refused to die down. To this day I really do not know where they came from. I am hard put to it to say whether they were lies cut from whole cloth by the vengeful Felipillo, or whether they were generated by the fear and idleness that had us Spaniards in a mortal sweat. We knew perfectly well that we had made the Indians suffer all that flesh could stand. We had humiliated them, pressed their faces in the dirt. We felt that a day of reckoning must come, a day of uprising and battle.

Alas, we read too much scope into the mute Indians, long-suffering creatures who had been enslaved for years, unable to think and feel for themselves, and much, much less able to act. We understood we were not dealing with men like us, but with a lower order of beings, yet we thought that in their hearts must still be some glimmer of pride and the need for recognition. In this we were wrong. These Indians had long ceased to be men.

And now it happened that the persistent rumors began to take definite shape. For us it was almost a relief. Nothing is harder to bear than what cannot be grasped and dealt with, however unprofitably. The fantasies of fear are always far worse than the most grievous reality. And yet the concrete news that was now bruited about the House of the Snake was terrible enough to think upon. The story went that in Guamachucho, not a hundred miles distant from Caxamalca, there was an army of thirty thousand Caribs, waiting their chance to fall on us.

The mere thought aroused terrible apprehension. This tribe is more cruel than all others, much more wild and skilled in battle. What the inhabitants of Triana and Potro are to the Spaniards, so are the Caribs to the Indians. They murder for the pleasure of it, out of pure love of it. They do not till the fields, weave or make pottery. Indeed, it is only with reluctance that they hunt and fish. They have only one talent, and that is war. In that they are masters. They do not quail before the most numerous enemy. Our horses, cannons and armor mean nothing to them. They shoot from ambush with long poisoned arrows, and bend back their enormous bows by sitting on the ground and bracing them against their feet. Their only objection to the Spaniards is that their flesh is too salty and hardly edible. They are cannibals, and in the time of the great Admiral almost every year they would attack Hispaniola and other islands in order to get for themselves a loathsome mess of human flesh. These Caribs are very ugly, small and treacherous. Their bellies are as fat as drums, and their legs are bowed.

Excitement in the House of the Snake now reached its zenith. Wild protests against the Inca's conduct rose on every side. For it seemed to be the very abyss of Indian cunning so to egg on the Caribs against us. Many openly expressed the common fear that we Spaniards would come to an unchristian end in the boiling pots of disgusting man-eaters. Even the Captain-General, who was as nearly fearless as any soldier I ever saw, seemed to be impressed by the reputation of the Caribs. No doubt during his long stay on the Islands and on the Terra Firma he had heard many tales of their deeds. The Caribs were the only real evil in the Indian paradise. In any case, the clamor became so great that the Captain-General felt himself constrained to put the Inca in chains and to keep all his attendants away from him. Atahualpa at last found himself in the most pitiable stage of imprisonment instead of enjoying his promised freedom.

Only one man among all the Spaniards kept his head and ventured to reprove the Captain-General for his unconscionably bad treatment of

Atahualpa. This was Don Hernando de Soto. It was he who pointed out that not once on the march, neither along the coast nor in the South Country, had we ever come across a single Carib. So far as he knew these people were only on the East Coast and in the deepest recesses of the continent. He laughed down the frightened ones as thickheads, who were ready, he said, to credit any old wives' tale that came to their ears. He said that no Spaniard up to this time had seen an army of any kind, Carib or whatever they might be. De Soto's contempt evoked a wave of resentment. Nothing is more difficult to let ride than scorn for one's fears, and the imputation that they spring out of a soft head.

Despite this anger, everyone had to admit that Don Hernando de Soto was justified in his argument. Not one among us had seen a hostile Indian. When the coin of general rumor was weighed, it was found that not one of the Indian messengers had seen an enemy face to face. Every man, Indian or Spaniard, had heard this or that from someone else, the second had heard it from a third, and so on. In the end alarm was lost in mist. The only indubitably real element in the touchy situation was the fear of the Spaniards themselves, a fear without object. That and a dark, insistent belief that the danger threatened from Guamachucho.

To combat the specter De Soto offered to make a trip to the city accompanied by some riders, and there to find out for himself how much basis there was to the wild stories. The Captain-General agreed. He even pressed Don Hernando to leave immediately on his reconnoitering, and said he would be only too glad to be convinced of the Inca's innocence.

All these matters came to me like muffled sounds, sounds heard at a a great distance. My sickness had narrowed my world to what was within the four small walls of my chamber. The rancorous world of daily affairs was shut out. Laanta told me wondrous stories. When she had no more to tell, Diego was there, to talk with me about my plans for the future. My convalescence gave me new confidence. I saw my life stretching out to fulfillment, without serious flaw. I was at the goal of all my wishes, so it seemed to me in those days. Soon I would go home to Cordova, to settle down in Spain and to lead Doña Isabella into a beautiful home. The old dream had become reality. With the Pizarros I had achieved the conquest of a kingdom so boldly assumed in childhood. Riches and fame had become mine. Little did I see then that my being was hanging by the finest hair, ready to drop into an abyss from which there was no return. Little did I know how seriously in jeopardy were my knighthood, my honor and my love.

And yet it was not that this abyss yawned under me without warning. I had had premonition enough in dream and sign. Yes, today when I look back over my whole life, everywhere I see paths to catastrophe. The signposts were clear enough then, had I had eyes to read them. But it is only these latter days that I have learned to read such things, only after I have wrestled mightily with myself. The miracle play of rich and poor I had seen as a boy was no more than a chance conversation overheard, a pretty simile, having no real bearing on me, the man. The uprising in the cities passed by without my turning as much as a hair. Master Agrippa told me about the *quinta essentia,* the element of elements. The terzinas of Dante moved my ear, the words of the Great Inquisitor, Loyola's plans, Doña Juana's penetrating thoughts. I saw the monks wandering restlessly, armed only with a stave, all over the Isthmus of Panama, over the Terra Firma to Hispaniola, to ease men's pains. I saw the market place of Caxamalca dyed red with Indians' blood. I saw the vultures fly down to gorge themselves, and I saw the evil Mass of sharing out the gold.

All this I saw, heard and felt. But among all these signs I erred like a blind man, like an illiterate, like a Pizarro. Nothing forced its way through my iron-hard skull, because there nestled only one all-consuming thought: I, and I again, and yet once again. I, a Cordovan of noble blood however poor at birth, a distant relative of the Sforzas, a friend of Cortés, a conquistador. I, in the end a rich man.

One morning—I believe it was the day that Don Hernando de Soto left for Guamachucho—Diego de Vargas came to me. He was very much excited. "Don Pedro," he said, "I don't know what's going to become of the Inca."

"Are they letting him go finally?" I inquired.

"I'm afraid. . . ."

"Afraid? What is it? Speak up, Diego," I said. "Are they going to keep on holding him in the House of the Snake?"

"It isn't a question of letting him go. That can't be done in the circumstances. I'm worried about the Inca's life. I'm afraid while Don Hernando is away they'll kill him."

"Why, that's impossible!" I said. "The Captain-General would never allow that. Juan Pizarro wouldn't stand for it either, nor would Pedro. After all, we aren't a band of murderers."

"No," admitted Diego. "We are worse than that. We'll cloak our deeds in self-righteousness. The murder will be blamed on the murdered. They'll say he deserved it for betraying us. If you remember, Pedro, I studied the law a little in Salamanca. I have a hazy recollection how such things are explained away."

"I don't understand you, Diego," I said.

"The Pizarros and that filthy Almagro have started a suit against the Inca. Master Pérez, helped out by Father Vicente and Gonzalo Pizarro, made out the indictment. And now Don Francisco Pizarro and Diego Almagro are sitting as judges."

"As judges!" I said. "As real judges?"

"Not exactly as real judges," said Diego. "Ordinarily there's some pretense of bringing justice to light in a process at law. In this case the whole point is to hide the truth. I don't know whether they'll dare run everything according to form. By rights the Inca ought to have someone to defend him."

"He will have someone to defend him!" I shouted, and rose to my feet, reaching for my clothes. "He will have counsel to carry on his defense."

"For the sweet love of God!" cried Diego. "What are you doing? You can't get mixed up in this affair. You aren't strong enough. What do you know about the way these matters are run!"

"No, I won't do it," I told him. "You will. You must defend him."

"I! You must be out of your head," said Diego. "That's madness. I belong to the Germania. I'm a highwayman. Can I be counsel for a king? You're talking like a wild man. Shall we make the goat into a gardener perhaps?"

"Why not! Twist it any way you want," I insisted. "Forget what happened in the past, all the seedy side. There are saints who were robbers in their youth."

"Yes, that's quite true," said Diego, "but I don't happen to be of that saintly stripe. Besides, I've forgotten everything I ever knew about the law. I can't remember any more about it than I can about the tales my mother used to tell to put me to sleep. I'll only make a fool of myself, and of you in the bargain. And perhaps I'll put a seal on the Inca's death warrant. I have neither enough inclination nor talent."

"The time has now come, Diego," I reminded him, "when you can pay back your reckoning for the injustice done Abu Amru and Doña Sobeya. Where there was injustice, there shall be justice."

"I don't see any relation between the two cases," Diego objected.

"I see where they meet in a thousand places!" I said. "Nothing stands by itself in the world. Justice itself is all clouded in our time. In Spain Abu Amru was struck down by it, Doña Sobeya and a hundred thousand more. Moors, Christians and Jews have been robbed of their property and lives, driven out of their homes. Right here in the Indies there have been orgies of violence. Now they are reaching out their hands for the Inca's head. And you must do your best to stop it."

"I'm afraid it will be the end of me," said Diego bitterly. He looked at me with despair on his face. "But if you want . . . after all, I'm your friend, and I came here with you. . . ."

"That isn't the way to look at it, Diego," I insisted. "You must be convinced that the opportunity is one that will never come again. You must realize that you do have the talents for the task. The time has come to sow the seeds of justice. It is an opportunity that cannot be missed. It is far more important than the life of the Inca alone. It is more important than the life of any one of us that justice be done, right now, in this new land."

"We shall try then," said Diego. "But, sweet Virgin Mary, Mother Mild, I feel my powers are too limited. I wish I hadn't been thinking so much about women when I was listening to the doctors expounding the *Jus Romanum* back in Salamanca. Why have I always strayed through the tavern door? Why is it, pray tell me, that I always preferred to feel a fine girl's buttocks, stroking them down like a lion's tail, instead of employing my fingers more busily turning the pages of the *corpus juris utriusque?*"

"Come on now," I said. "That's enough wind. You can do it all right." I pulled him along. His hands were clammy, and the sweat stood out of his forehead. All the while he mumbled self-reproaches at allowing himself thus to be gulled.

We arrived at the main room of the House of the Snake where the trial was to be held. Don Francisco Pizarro and Don Diego de Almagro sat beside each other on the high podium. Before them, a few steps lower down, was a long table lighted from above by a shaft of light. Both the Captains—or judges—were hidden in shadow. Around the table, turned toward the judges, sat our Dominicans and Don Pedro de Candía, Master Pérez, Gonzalo Pizarro and Master Riquelme, the Crown treasurer attached to the expedition, who had come along from San Miguel with Almagro. Farther back, by themselves, sat several cavaliers. I thought I recognized Juan and Pedro Pizarro among them. On the table was a gay Indian blanket, and on this cover was a lone object, the only piece of evidence, it seemed, the dog-eared Bible bound in pigskin that belonged to Father Vicente.

The strong column of light streaming in through the ceiling illuminated the faces of the men around the table in every detail, showed every fold and wart as in a Flemish painting. Only the judges were really obscured. Their faces were white blurs framed by their beards, and the rest of their bodies were hidden from view.

Gonzalo Pizarro wore a splendid doublet made of gold brocade that contrasted beautifully with his blue-black hair. He looked so handsome that he would have taken any woman's breath away. He seemed to be in charge of affairs at the table. He was just taking a document from the hands of Master Pérez when his glance fell on Diego and me. He got up, surprised, and said, "Welcome to the proceedings, Don Pedro. I'm glad to see you're able to stand on two feet again. But are you sure you want to watch this boring business when you're really not well yet? I purposely neglected telling you anything about what was going on."

"I'm healthy enough for this," I told him. "It's a question of the company's welfare, isn't it?"

"As you want," said Gonzalo drily. "Give Don Pedro a place at the table, will you? Just as you want. Only, I thought . . ."

"Thank you all the same, Gonzalo," I explained. "I brought my friend, Master Diego de Vargas, to take my place at the table. He will act as counsel for the king."

"The Inca's acts speak for themselves. There is no need for a defense counsel," Gonzalo said harshly, and looked up at the judges for support.

"Then if there is no need for a defense, there is no need for a prosecution," I answered with equal stubbornness. "In fact, in that case the whole trial is useless. But you have assigned a prosecutor, have you not?"

"Master Riquelme is the prosecutor," said Gonzalo coldly. "Master

Pérez will be his assistant. But Master Diego cannot be made a defense counsel. He knows nothing about Spanish law."

"I have studied the law in Salamanca," said Diego. "I have often served as a notary, drawing up wills, contracts and other legal documents."

"But you have never served as a counsel," objected Gonzalo.

"Was Master Riquelme ever a prosecutor before?" inquired Diego. "Was Don Diego de Almagro ever a judge?"

"Master Riquelme is the Crown treasurer," said Gonzalo. "Don Diego de Almagro is the alcalde of Tumbez."

"And I am Don Pedro de Cordova's secretary," said Diego. "Beyond that I am a bachelor of the seven humanities."

"You may be," said Gonzalo, "but you won't have much chance to be clever today." He threw the paper onto the table. "Well, never mind. If you want to, take your place. You can be the defense counsel. Are you aware of what the indictment contains?"

"No, I am not," said Diego. "And the first thing I beg is that the court will postpone the trial so that I can consult with my client about its contents. It looks rather voluminous to me."

"Why, man, that's impossible," said Gonzalo, his temper rising all the while. "The lives of nearly five hundred Spaniards depend on the speedy outcome of this trial. This isn't any pleading about a will or a bill owed for forty-five years. You can't spin this business out making jokes a rod long. This is a matter of life and death."

"The weightier the issue, the more reason for measured consideration," said Diego.

"There can't be any postponement," said Almagro out of the shadows. "The court refuses to allow it."

"Is it impossible to postpone the trial because then Don Hernando de Soto will be back from Guamachucho?" inquired Diego.

There was a mutter of anger in the room. Diego Almagro got up and shouted, "The court forbids that kind of language. Keep to the subject, or keep your mouth closed."

"We are not prejudiced," said the Captain-General.

"I take the question back," said Diego. "I'll substitute a new one. How does it happen that this court dares to sit in judgment over a sovereign? A king may be judged only by those of his own rank. In this case it would have to be Don Carlos, or the Inca's own chieftains, perhaps."

"That's so much lawyers' gabble," commented Diego de Almagro. "We'll never get anywhere at this rate."

"I beseech the court to take the Inca Atahualpa to Spain," interposed Diego de Vargas, "so that he may stand trial before Don Carlos, or before a court appointed by the Crown."

"We are all appointed by Don Carlos as it is. We have commissions to prove it," said Almagro.

"You have commissions to humiliate and murder kings?" asked Diego.

There was a great uproar after this. I heard cries of "Throw the bastard out," "Put him in chains," "Kill the interfering dog." And so on. Diego smiled palely. He was now caught up by his purpose, like an actor on the stage.

The Captain-General pounded for order. "Quiet, quiet," he shouted. "I warn you, Master Diego, either measure your words more carefully and pay more attention to the dignity of this court, or you will find yourself in trouble. I have already told you once. We are not prejudiced, and all that we want is justice to be done. If you persist in insulting those of us assembled here, I shall be forced to have you thrown out of the room."

"I regret the harshness of my address," said Diego. "But I beg to state for consideration that I do not consider this court in order and properly authorized by law."

"That view cannot be accepted," shouted Master Riquelme.

But the Captain-General nodded his head. "Write down his objections; take them down," he said. And so Master Pérez did this.

The indictment of Atahualpa was then read aloud, and I shall not attempt to repeat it in detail for it was four pages long. The four most serious accusations:

Ad primum: The accused was a heathen follower of gods and demons, and followed heretical customs, insofar as he kept concubines, calling them his wives.

Ad secundum: The accused had violated the royal decree of Tavanta-Suyu; with treachery and force he had persecuted the royal party, and finally caused Huáscar to lose his life by drowning.

Ad tertium: He had used his illegally acquired royal power to disperse gold and other riches of the land among his relatives, followers and other creatures unworthy of such perquisites, to the detriment of the commonalty and of the royal treasury of Castile.

Ad quartum: He had planned uprisings and war against the Spanish crusaders, and had gone so far as to collect great hosts of Caribs in the neighborhood of Guamachucho.

Now the prosecutor, Riquelme, began to tell the most revolting tales of the Inca's heathen practices. He mentioned numerous human sacrifices, and went on at length about the immoral behavior of the accused in *puncto feminae.* This was a bad example to his people and to the Spanish soldiery, the prosecutor declared. At this Father Vicente nodded vigorously in approval.

Then Diego said, "We know less than nothing about the gods and demons of this land. All that we know is that the accused according to his own lights honors the sun as a benevolent power and as one of his ancestors. This to be sure is a grievous error. But it is the common superstition of the land. We should have to wipe the whole population of the country off the face of the earth if doing this is a crime. But that would be impossible. Neither the Inca nor his subjects had ever heard before of the true religion. They never had a chance, and should not be judged on the score of belief until given full opportunity to mend their ways."

At this point Father Vicente broke in. He said sharply, "I have been talking to the Inca for more than six months about the true belief. He listens to me and understands what I say. But he absolutely refuses to change his beliefs and to be baptized. He prefers to remain up to his neck in the muck of heresy."

"Six months is no time at all in such matters," said Diego to this. "It took the saints centuries before the greater part of the Roman people under Emperor Constantine embraced the only true faith. Even after that there was Julian the Apostate, who would certainly have uprooted Christianity if it had not been foreordained to endure forever. And if the saints, men of purity and insight, had to work centuries to achieve their ends, and this among an enlightened people, then our Dominicans, for all their zeal, cannot expect to arrive at the same results in six months of working among simple barbarians. Such impatience, however intelligible it may be, however much it may spring from zeal, nevertheless to the layman's eyes borders on blasphemy. The greatest truth in the world is not to be inculcated in a few days.

"And so far as the concubinage of the Inca is concerned, I hold that to be of no relevancy. Consider the Patriarch Abraham, who had two wives, Sarah and Hagar. Think of Jacob, who entered into marriage with both Leah and Rachel and other lesser wives as well, wives in common law. I beg to draw your attention to the woman of Samaria who spoke to our Lord. She had once had five men. Since all these men and women are considered to be pleasing in the sight of God, I fail to see any mortal sin in the conjugal excess of the Inca. Furthermore, his wives are not come to him through his lusts. They are part of the royal establishment, his servants. His father, Huayna Capac, and his brother, Huáscar, both of these also had many wives."

The Captain-General bent forward. "But you admit, counsel for the defense," he said, "that the Inca Atahualpa is a heathen and that he has married many wives?"

"That I do admit," answered Diego reluctantly. He looked steadily at the Captain-General. Riquelme, the prosecutor, tittered at the exchange.

And now for a long time there ensued an argument over whether Atahualpa was a real king or only an usurper. This was very hard to decide. The principal difficulty depended on the fact that no one had ever learned anything about Huayna Capac's will except through hearsay. Diego lost no time in pointing this out, and also in bringing to the court's attention that hearsay also had it that Huáscar was the one who had really begun the war, who had assumed the initiative. He had occupied a part of Quito, the inheritance of Atahualpa.

The argument lasted so long that at last the Captain-General interposed and advised the prosecutor and the counsel for the defense that the court would quash this particular part of the charges. Diego turned to me and smiled. He had won an important point. It was his first score.

Riquelme saw the two of us exchange looks and he shouted, "But we shall never drop the charge of fratricide!"

"Then prove the charge," said Diego.

"No, prove the Inca's innocence," said Riquelme. "That's your task, to prove he's innocent."

"Gladly," replied Diego. "I'll be glad to accommodate the court. At the time of Huáscar's death, the Inca was our prisoner. Huáscar died a hundred miles away from Caxamalca. No matter how sleepy our guards may be, I doubt that Atahualpa could have made a two-hundred-mile round trip and his absence not have been noted."

Some of the cavaliers laughed at this sally. I took heart, for it is always good when a man's argument can tickle the sense of humor against odds.

Riquelme cut in violently. "I didn't say that Atahualpa killed his brother with his own hand. I say that he instigated the murder. It was he who hatched and directed the scheme."

"Then why don't you express yourself more precisely, my honored colleague?" said Diego.

There was more laughter at this, and Don Francisco called for order.

"Pray, tell me what makes you think that the Inca planned the murder?" inquired Diego politely.

"The death of Huáscar was to his advantage," said Riquelme.

"So that he could have himself accused of murder and risk his life before this court, perhaps?" asked Diego.

"I mean to say it happened just at the time when the Captain-General was beginning negotiations with Huáscar," continued Riquelme, very softly.

"But that proves nothing," retorted Diego.

"It is a clear indication of intent," declared Riquelme.

"All that it is, is evidence that a wish for Huáscar's death might have arisen in Atahualpa's mind. But it is not evidence that such a wish actually did arise. And it is still less evidence that any such wish was ever carried out," said Diego.

"Then who else would have wanted to kill him?" asked Riquelme, his voice edged with sarcasm and anger.

"I am not by any means convinced that Huáscar actually was murdered," said Diego. "He might quite as well have been the victim of an unfortunate accident."

The Captain-General now rose. "So you believe the Inca when he says that Huáscar was careless? You believe it was an accident! Speak up."

"The explanation is at least as good as Master Riquelme's circumstantial evidence," said Diego, giving way.

"I want to know whether you believe it," insisted Pizarro.

"It isn't my task to express my opinions and my beliefs," retorted Diego, somewhat lamely. "I am defending the Inca, no more. I maintain that what has been offered is not evidence, but the flimsiest of hearsay. There is nothing that inclines to establish the Inca's guilt beyond exception."

"We're bogging down again," objected Diego Almagro. "Nothing but lawyers' hairsplittings!"

Again the Captain-General turned to Diego. "You will admit," he said, "that there is a possibility the Inca had his brother Huáscar murdered?"

"There is such a possibility, of course," Diego said.

"You admit further, do you not," Pizarro insisted, "that this possibility develops into a probability when the circumstances, the time and so on are taken into consideration?"

"The probability is not very great," Diego said. "The Inca surely must have said to himself that he must suffer the Spaniards' revenge when unable to defend himself. He could better have waited until his hands were untied to even scores. And besides, men are never judged on mere probabilities."

"It's enough for me, Master Diego, that you have admitted the possibility and the probability of the deed," said the Captain-General quickly. "Put down Master Diego's statement on the record, Master Pérez. Leave the judging to us, if you please."

Diego sought my eyes, and shrugged his shoulders very lightly. He had lost this score, and lost badly. But he made one more sally. "I still hold," he said loudly, "that this court is not fitted to judge the differences of two pretenders to the crown of Tavanta-Suyu. It is quite possible that Huáscar received the customary punishment of the land for his attempt at usurpation."

The audience began to whisper busily.

Now the third point in the charge was arrived at. The two lawyers took up the matter of the Inca's supposed wasteful expenditures. Master Riquelme spent a great deal of wind on this issue attempting to prove how unworthy subjects had received enormous benefits in land and gold.

"As a sovereign," Diego retorted, "the Inca had a right to give away land and gold at his will, and to whom he wanted. He has also paid us Spaniards vast amounts of gold. If we refuse to recognize his right to dispense his wealth, then of course we must return what we have received."

"Sweet Lord Jesus asleep in the manger!" roared Almagro. "Whoever heard of such a stupid thing? Since when have we Spaniards troubled our heads about the prerogatives of infidels and Indians? What do we care about the law of a heathen land when it comes to doing something to lift still higher the crown of Castile?"

"If you do not admit the possibility of justice," Diego said harshly, "then you are wasting your time trying to punish an apparent crime, as in this instance."

"The man is talking like a fool," shouted Almagro. "He makes my head go round. He is trying to make us all dance to his tune like a pack of idiots."

"That's right," chorused the audience. "He's merely trying to make sport of the judges."

The Captain-General pulled Almagro by the sleeve and forced him back to the bench. He was very angry with everybody at this point.

"I say that the court will cast out this section of the charge," the Captain-General said. "But not because I am moved by the argument of the counsel for the defense. The whole question is closely related to the point of whether Atahualpa was the lawful king. If he were, then he would have certain right to dispose of his goods and benefits as he chose."

"And that is that," echoed Diego.

I was amazed at the Captain-General. Outside of Diego he appeared to be the only man in this curious court who was able to think with any logic at all. Yet at the same time this frightened me. I saw that it boded ill for the Inca, far more so than the simple impatience of Almagro.

Now the supposed uprising planned by Atahualpa became the subject of discussion. Master Riquelme named off the great armies which were reputedly assembled ready to fall on us. He could not prevent himself from portraying the horrible fate that was in store for us when we fell into the hands of the Caribs.

"But all that is so much imagining," objected Diego. "It is the fancy of frightened men that is at work. We haven't the slightest piece of evidence that any enemy is marching toward Caxamalca. And even if that were the case, it would still have to be demonstrated that the Inca had a hand in it."

"In that you differ with the Captain-General," said Riquelme. "Don Francisco Pizarro has doubled the watch; he has sent out men to reconnoiter; he has ordered that the horses be kept constantly saddled and in readiness for battle."

"Foresight is the mother of wisdom," agreed Diego. "But Don Francisco's general precautions against danger are no proof in themselves that this peril actually exists. On the contrary! The mere fact that the Captain-General has sent out a party to reconnoiter is demonstration that at the bottom he doubts these rumors, that he is merely looking for visual proof. Otherwise would he risk some of his best men?"

Master Riquelme was checkmated. He lifted up his thin shoulders, and looked at the Captain-General, seeking help. There was a painful silence in the room. It appeared as if this most important part of the indictment had proved untenable.

Slowly the Captain-General rose and said, "You must admit, Master Diego, that the Inca is the focus, the middle point, the inmost center of all possible revolt?"

"Yes, yes," shouted Gonzalo in relief, seeing which way the wind was blowing. "You've got to admit that!"

"But I do not and cannot admit it," said Diego boldly. "I maintain that the Inca is the very center of peace and order in this land. It is my belief, quite opposite, that we tarry here in safety in Caxamalca only by virtue of his person. Were it not for his hand, that he has yet to raise against us, we should not be here at all. The Inca's death is the worst luck that could possibly befall us. That is what I believe in my heart. I do not agree with this hypothesis, Captain-General. And others besides me have felt the same way. For example, Don Hernando, your own brother."

"I can vouch for that," I said, unable any longer to hold my tongue.

The Captain-General was taken aback at this unexpected resistance.

"Don Hernando Pizarro is not among us," said Almagro, coming to Pizarro's rescue. "When he left the most serious developments were not so much as suspected."

"But nothing of importance has happened since he left," interposed Diego. "I beg the gathering to consider the advice of the man who is not here. A single word from a nobleman is of more weight than a tumult of rumor from the mob."

"That is going too far," said Almagro. "I demand that this man be taken from the room. He has insulted me."

"Calm yourself," said Don Francisco Pizarro to the infuriated Almagro. He did not look at him, but simply waved him to his seat with a hand held backward. "My brother Hernando is very dear to me. I respect his every word. Since Master Diego has brought his words to my attention, things begin to look a little different. I think we shall adjourn this court."

"What!" shouted Almagro, unable to contain himself. "And what about the thirty thousand Caribs?"

"Yes, what about them?" said Master Riquelme.

"The thirty thousand Caribs are part of a fairy tale!" shouted Diego de Vargas.

"This run-down scholiast is ridiculing me," said Almagro.

"Wait until Don Hernando de Soto comes back," said Diego, "and then you will see right enough that the Caribs are nothing but the blue mist that hangs over the mountains."

"The court can no longer continue," said Don Francisco coldly. "Everything depends on the news that Don Hernando de Soto brings back with him. When he comes back we'll take up where we left off."

"Just a minute," roared Almagro. "What about your promise that we would soon leave for Cuzco? What about me? How am I going to be repaid for my trouble? How can we go to Cuzco while Atahualpa is still alive? You're a rich man, Francisco. You've had your share. You've got fifty-seven thousand gold pesos. But I, your old friend, have got exactly nothing. I'm poor. Cuzco is my only hope in the world. And the gold in the temples . . ."

"Think of Don Carlos," pursued Master Riquelme. "Think of what he will say! The day will come when the King of Spain will demand reckoning for your having caused him to lose so much land and gold. This Inca cannot live."

"And what about God? What about Him?" shrieked Father Vicente. He got up and leaned forward at the table. "It has been clearly demonstrated that Atahualpa is a miserable heretic, and we all know that he leads a filthy life with his women. Even his own defender admits he may have taken his brother's life. How do you think it will be if you have to face God after letting these vile sins continue?"

"I shall judge when Don Hernando de Soto has returned," said Pizarro flatly.

"The punishment of heretics and sinners against the dictates of our Holy Mother the Roman Catholic Church cannot be delayed!" screamed the priest. "Spiritual works must not be pursued in such a lackadaisical fashion, no matter how one goes about worldly matters. Thousands and thousands of benighted souls can be destroyed by this heretic in a single hour if he gets loose, and so perish forever. You would not endure a leper among your friends and comrades. Much less should you endure the heretic in our midst."

"What can I do?" said the Captain-General. "No matter which course I take—postponement or judgment—it will be bad."

"Think only of your honor," cried Juan Pizarro, who had moved up to the table so that his young face was limned in the light streaming in from above.

"Is it a part of honor to forget one's friends?" said Diego Almagro.

"Nobody has honor unless he serves the King and Castile," added Riquelme.

"Outside the pale of the Church there is no honor," said Father Vicente.

"You are like a swarm of gnats," said the Captain-General. "What is the just way out?"

"There is no way out," said Father Vicente in triumph. "There is only a choice between good and evil. You must make this choice now, today."

And now Don Francisco chanced to turn toward me. "You have said nothing all this time," he declared. "Why don't you lend your voice to this tumult? Everyone else is advising me, why not you, my young friend? You had a great teacher. When you were a boy you sat among knights at the table. What do you say?"

"It appears you have made your own decision," I told him. "The charges have crumbled into so much dust."

Thereupon Gonzalo Pizarro got up to have his say. He was very impressive in his gold brocade doublet. From his girdle hung a dagger in a golden sheath. "We are all one, and must be," he said pleasantly. "Why should we turn and rend each other? Actually, none of us is worrying about honor or shame, about justice or injustice. It doesn't make a jot of difference whether Atahualpa is a heretic or a saint. It is simply this. What are we going to get out of it? What is our advantage and our power?"

"Well said," shouted Almagro.

"Then the whole trial is a monstrous lie," I said with equal vehemence.

"Justice and injustice are only devices, excuses," said Gonzalo. "We all are aware of that. When the rich judge the poor for reaching their hands toward their property in order to eat and live, is that then justice? Where does it lie, this justice? All of us are men, rich and poor, mighty and humble. By rights we should all be poor, weak and humble, as our Lord Jesus Christ would have it. Riches, power and superior position are all injustices of one sort or another. And too long have they lain a leaden weight on the Pizarro family.

"Must I remind you, brothers, how men have looked down on us? Must I call to your attention that we have starved like mangy dogs? Have you forgotten, Francisco, that your ten years of service in the Indies was rewarded by a strip of swamp fit for nothing but to breed mosquitoes? Now we have opportunity within our hands, right before us. Shall we act like cringing animals and prick up our ears at the cry of justice? We must act in good style. We must bear ourselves like rich men, like the soldiers and noblemen that we are. Let go these hollow words about honor, justice, sin and the like. They mean nothing except among slaves. Let us do what we must do."

"Bravo, bravo!" roared Almagro. "Gonzalo has spoken what was on the tip of my tongue."

"Only Atahualpa stands in our way," said Gonzalo. "Only he separates us from the riches of Cuzco. On that account he is guilty of a crime against us Pizarros and our friends. He would be still guilty no matter if a thousand charges collapsed. The fact remains he is unjust to the Pizarros. Therefore he must die."

"I will have no part in this murder!" I shouted. I turned to leave the room, overcome with emotion.

"Not so quickly, my young friend," said Gonzalo. He smiled quietly. "You made an agreement with us. You signed your name. You got your share of the gold. You must also take a share of the unpleasant duties of our expedition."

"What are you talking about?" I said, seething with anger now. "Did I not take my share of battle? Did I not ride out as a messenger and risk my neck more than any of you? Have you faced any more danger than I?"

"Nobody knows that better than I do," agreed Gonzalo. "Nobody holds you in greater esteem than I, Don Pedro. But this is one more danger, and this added danger must be shared. For it is quite possible that at the moment you are of more value to the expedition than you were at Puná or Tumbez. Many a man dares to face an enemy in mortal combat. It is much harder to face the evil whispers of the mob, to run the risk of a bad reputation."

"Do you mean to imply I am afraid, Gonzalo?" I asked. I could feel myself getting dizzy with wrath.

"I didn't say that," admitted Gonzalo. He shrugged his shoulders.

"It is against all spiritual and human justice," I said. "It is a shame, a travesty of honor—this trial. I shall have no part in it. Not if I die for it!"

"What do you mean?" shouted Gonzalo bitterly. "You talk like a fool. Where did you, personally, get the right to invade this country? What right had you to slaughter the Indians in the plaza? What right have you to hold the Indians' gold? Every step you took with us, and did not once question the justice of it? Now you fall back! What's wrong with you? You are talking like a child."

"Gonzalo!" said the Captain-General. "Watch what you are saying."

I hung my head and accepted the denunciation without a word. I felt that I was beyond injury. "The right to conquer this land is found in the words of our Lord," I said weakly. "Christ said, Go into all lands and baptize them. And likewise it was permissible to take up arms when Atahualpa threw the Bible on the ground...."

"Don't be a long-eared ass," said Gonzalo. "Are you making it up as you go along? And what about the gold? Have you an excuse for that, too?"

"Forget about the gold," said the Captain-General. "It has nothing to do with what we're talking about."

"Don Pedro is right," said Father Vicente. "The justification for our deeds comes directly from God. Only one point is left unfulfilled. He will never be satisfied so long as Atahualpa lives and the demons' temple of the sun stands in Cuzco. And Gonzalo is right, too. The

Lord said, You will be hated by all the world because of my name. But who endures to the end, he will be saved. We must submit to the appearance of injustice and we must put up with dishonor and whisperings. The Kingdom of God will shine forth that much brighter in the end."

My head was on my chest. Never before had I felt so confused and utterly bereft. In vain I tried to find objections to Father Vicente's cunning arguments. Then suddenly Doña Isabella's parting words came to my mind—"Pedro, the Cardinal wants you as his conscience." It came to me with such force that I started, and involuntarily turned half-around as if I had heard it over my shoulder. I looked closely at the Captain-General, trying to see him with new eyes. He was standing in the half-darkness talking busily with Diego Almagro. He had little resemblance to the Cardinal, to Antonio de Guevara. He would never understand such a train of thought. I felt there was only one thing for me to do, give back my share of gold on the spot. And it was both greed and the fear of being laughed at that finally prevented me from taking this drastic action.

That is one of the worst threats to virtue, being laughed at. Wickedness and lies seem so natural, so inevitable, have such an apparent correspondence with reality that more often than not goodness seems to be allied with stupidity. The truth as often as not looks for all the world like an extravagant exception to what counts and holds good among men. Truth really is not of this world. It comes naked from heaven. It arouses as much ribaldry and astonishment as would a naked savage parading in the market place of a Spanish city. And yet, a little thought makes it clear that there is nothing laughable in the naked human body, which was formed by God. Much less ridiculous is the naked spirit and truth among men, when stripped of prejudice and superficialities.

But when the moment of decision came for me I failed, I was mute, and I did nothing.

The Captain-General and Diego Almagro now returned to the council, diverting further attention from me. In his hand the leader had the itemized indictment against the Inca. We were all standing at attention. Pizarro began to speak.

"We judges find the accused, the Inca Atahualpa, guilty of the following crimes. He is a heretic and a follower of demons. He has entered into marriage with more than one wife. Furthermore, he is a fratricide. He has acted treasonably toward Don Carlos, whose vassal he is, insofar as he has assembled thirty thousand Caribs at Guamachucho against me, the emissary of the Crown."

The Captain-General fell silent. The indictment slipped from his hands to the table.

Diego Almagro, close by the Captain-General, said, "We judges find the Inca Atahualpa guilty of all these crimes. We sentence him to death. Since he is a heretic, he shall be led this night into the market place of Caxamalca, and there consumed by flame."

My legs began to turn to water, and I had trouble holding myself upright. Diego de Vargas took my arm. He whispered, "We did all that was possible. It simply did not suffice." Then he turned to the men assembled around the table, and said in a clear voice that was unmistakable, "For the last time I protest that this trial was illegal."

But no one paid the slightest attention to him. The papers were quickly collected. Father Vicente took his Bible and his crucifix. Nobody looked very long at anyone else. Soon the room was empty.

Two hours after sunset the horns were blown in the triangular plaza of Caxamalca. Once more we lined up in ranks, as we had when the gold was partitioned among us. Every fifth man held a flaming torch in his hand. The faggots burned fitfully, crackling noisily in the puffy breeze. A heavy pall of gray smoke hovered above us, and when it parted we could see the immense stars of the southern sky. On the same place where the gold had been parceled out now stood a heavy stake, in front of which bundles of wood and dried grasses had been piled.

The Inca was led out of the House of the Snake. He walked slowly, heavily. His feet were chained together. At his right walked Father Vicente, Bible in hand, the crucifix about his neck. At the Inca's left walked the Captain-General. They reached the middle of the plaza. We stood stiff and silent, all under the same spell. We could all plainly hear the Inca's chains clanking on the stones, and the snapping of the torches.

Father Vicente talked rapidly to the Inca, but he seemed not to be heard. Atahualpa's face was turned away. He was grim and stubborn. He was the Indian warrior, inured to administering and enduring cruelties both. He looked at the stake, the piles of dry wood. There was cold contempt on his face. He looked around, and in his own language said plainly, "Is Chasca here?"

"I am here," I said, and went up to him.

He looked at me closely, laid his hand on my shoulder. "It is all true," he said. "The star did not lie."

My heart was sick as I peered into the Indian face. I thought how these fine features, the slender body would all be ashes in less than an hour. The eyes would never glisten and command again, the voice never speak. The horror of the murder pressed down on me like a hill. Had not Laanta told how Mamapacha had made men mortal in order that they might have cause to love each other? My mind raced, trying to think of some escape. There was none, I saw. A mysterious will had ordained it.

"Chasca," said Atahualpa, "my kingdom is gone. My people are dispersed. My warriors are not by my side. Everything has come to an end. Even the sun has turned his face away."

"But it is night," I whispered to him.

"Yes, it is night," he said; "the hour of the invisible god has come." He removed his hand from my shoulder and pointed to the stake.

"I am afraid to fall into the hands of your god," he went on to say quietly. "He is the powerful one, I see that. I am going to die, Chasca. Then the great mountains will be gone; they will vanish as the dew vanishes in the morning. The sun will go out, the moon and all the stars. There will be no more earth, and no more sea. There will be no more children playing, no more girls' laughter, no more clatter among the people and the roar of battle. All that, everything, will be gone and past. And my own body, that too will be gone. It will disappear and the wind will blow its ashes away. And then soon I shall see the unseen face of your god. Already I have an idea how terrible he will be. I see him like a cliff rising out of the mists. I have dreamed about him."

"Master," I said, "there is still time left. Accept our faith and allow yourself to be baptized."

This last word I spoke in Spanish, for I had not invented any Quichua equivalent to describe the Sacrament. Father Vicente caught on to what I was saying. He whispered loudly to me, "If he lets himself be baptized, he need not submit to the ordeal of death at the stake. I'll see it's made easier for him."

I told the Inca what the priest had said to me.

"But what does it really matter how a man dies?" the Inca inquired ironically.

"But now you believe in the unseen god, do you not?" I persisted.

"Yes, my gods have forsaken me," he agreed slowly. "The kingdom of the sun has collapsed, and with it the sun. Pachacamac has turned his face away. Even Mamapacha, the earth, is cold and indifferent. Tell them, Chasca, that I want to be baptized."

The Inca's announcement evoked great excitement among the cavaliers and soldiers. The Dominicans hastened to get out wax candles and light them. They had long since made preparations for this event. They brought baptismal water in an old silver vase. Father Vicente drew on priest's vestments over his monk's robe. Almagro talked wildly to the Captain-General who listened and now and then shook his head. "But we have no choice," I heard Almagro say, his voice rising in pitch. "It's absolutely a necessity . . . unavoidable. There's still the treason charge, even if he does become a Christian."

"I can find no fault with him now," the Captain-General whispered back hoarsely.

Thereupon Riquelme, the Crown treasurer, mixed himself into the council, and said, "Anyone who protects a man accused of high treason is suspect of the same crime. Don Carlos will demand severe reckoning of you and your family if you change your verdict."

The Captain-General looked at Riquelme, and deliberately spat at the ground before his feet. He looked blackly at Almagro and said, "Let it go, then. Let it go."

It was the night of the twenty-ninth day of August in the year of our Lord fifteen hundred and thirty-three, the night after the feast of John the Baptist. On that night the name of the Inca, Atahualpa, king of Tavanta-Suyu, was changed to Juan de Atahualpa. Diego de Vargas and I stood by as his godfathers, while the men undid the chains binding his feet. We kneeled down and folded our hands as Father Vicente sprinkled his head with the blessed water.

Father Vicente opened his leather-bound Bible, and read out of the chapter of Luke about John the Baptist, how he was reared in the wilderness on the other side of the Jordan, and how he nourished himself with grasshoppers and wild honey.

The words came to me from a great distance. I did not understand their sense. The voices of those who call in the wilderness are always understood only when it is too late, it seems. The story seemed an irrelevant tale out of times irrevocably past; it seemed bizarre, almost laughable, when I feebly tried to imagine the actual hairy, unwashed saint. But I must have had some intimation of the inner meaning of the story, and the words must have made some impression on me. For even to this day, without ever having read them since, I can repeat the story word for word without faltering.

And so the words came out of Father Vicente's mouth, and he, I am sure, was no more aware than I of what he was saying. He intoned loudly, ". . . whose fan is in his hand, and he will purge his floor, and will gather the wheat into his house; but the chaff he will burn up with unquenchable fire that cannot be put out. . . ."

The Dominican let the little Bible sink to arm's length. He then raised his right hand, and said, "The Holy Mother, the Roman Catholic Church, absolves you, Juan de Atahualpa, of all heresy, and receives her beloved child into her bosom. All sins that ye have ever committed are now absolved. . . ."

"What is he saying?" muttered Almagro hoarsely. "Did you hear what he just said?"

Father Vicente turned and measured the Captain contemptuously. "From the standpoint of the Church," he said, "Juan de Atahualpa is as innocent as a babe in the cradle. That is the Sacrament. That is what it means."

"But what about treason . . . he murdered his brother," said Diego Almagro.

"That is no concern of mine," retorted Father Vicente, "for secular justice is outside my province. It is none of my affair what you others do."

"It must be done. We cannot draw back now." It was Almagro again. "My God! Everything will be the same as ever!"

The men in the plaza were silent. The houses and the men alike were motionless, breathless, like figures painted on a board. Only the sound of the faggots was audible.

And now Diego Almagro screwed up his courage, and shouted in his high voice, "Juan de Atahualpa is condemned to die by the garrote. The executioner will do his duty."

I stood near Atahualpa as if rooted to the spot. My limbs were solid lumps of lead, and the sweat trickled down my forehead. Three dark figures moved quickly to the center of the market place. They threw aside their cloaks, and among them I recognized Miguel Estete. With practiced movements they pushed the Inca back up against the stake. Then Miguel Estete cast a length of fine rope about the Inca's throat, and twisted it tight with a little stick.

"My children," cried the Inca, "Chasca, my children . . ." Only these words and then all sound died in his throat. For a moment there was a violent gurgling and groaning. Blood spurted out of the beautiful nose. The body died slowly, in heavy cramps that came regularly, as they come to a woman in travail. At last there was no more sound.

The strangler stepped back, eased off a few turns on the stick, and let the body hang thus from the stake. It seemed as if the Inca were staring at the ground with enormously bulging eyes.

Miguel Estete turned to the Captain-General. "The task is finished, my lord," he said. He rolled down his sleeves over hairy forearms.

The Captain-General made no reply. He stood erect, very tall, gray and stony. Tears rolled down his cheeks. I looked closer. It was really so. The Captain-General was weeping. It was terrifying to see, for not a muscle in his face had changed. He did not appear to be aware even that he was weeping, as if something in him he had never suspected was weeping for him. The old man, the conquistador, the founder of cities, was weeping like the rock in the fairy tale.

He observed the corpse at last and commanded that the trumpets be blown.

The horns blew. According to the old custom they blew, half merrily.

Then the soldiers were dismissed, and they all returned to their quarters. A good meal was all prepared, and the beakers that had belonged to the Inca passed from mouth to mouth, filled with foaming chicha. Among the company there arose a spirit of gladness, of joy, almost. It was infectious. The men began to make little jokes and laugh. Now that the Inca was dead, all the fears dissolved, and we were free. The decision had been made, and it worked a miracle. In the distance, far on the other side of the mountains, golden Cuzco beckoned. The way was free to the temples of gold, to all the treasure, to new women. The way was free once more.

After a time I returned to the plaza in the company of Diego de Vargas. Two soldiers had been posted as a guard of honor for the dead king. They were talking in the manner of soldiers, philosophizing about the world.

"It's a shame, if you stop to think of it," one of them declared, "taking any man's life. Especially when you think that it's all a man has, just one life."

"You're right, friend," agreed the other. He was chewing on a crust of bread to ward off the chill of the night and keep himself occupied. "When I was a boy I used to run off to see every hanging and burning. But now I wouldn't walk around the corner to see the best of hangings. I'm tired of executions—there are too many of them; they're becoming too much of a good thing. Besides, when I think how I'm going to rattle on my deathbed just like that Indian bastard. . . ."

I looked at the dead man. He was still sagged down in the same position, his head on his chest. I felt sure that his neck was stretching, that very soon his forehead would be touching his toes. I had to look away. Then I saw that we Spaniards were not alone with the Inca in the market place. All around, before the houses, against the walls, in corners and doorways, crouched countless Indians. They hardly stirred, did not utter a word to one another, just sat and looked. They were as quiet as a thousand cats stalking a mouse. I wondered whether it was curiosity or love for the dead man that had brought them back to the city. Was it wordless grief or hatred for us that was heavy in their hearts?

Diego and I relieved the guards and kept watch the night through. We loosened the thong about the Inca's neck. We laid the body on a pile of Indian blankets. But we were too late, really, for *rigor mortis* had already set in, and the Inca lay so drawn together that his corpse was like an old man's. The silent crouching multitude did not stir.

At last the sun rose. It was a mighty red sun that rolled up out of the mountains in the east. The first rays colored the old buildings a tender coral pink. The clouds were suddenly dappled a wondrously sweet green, and the cover of the dead man was gilded wondrously, a warm, rich color, the kind of tawny brown that I have so often admired in the paintings of the Flemings.

And when this happened it was the signal for a tremendous groan of pain from the Indians assembled in the market place. It was a long wailing. The hair on my flesh stood up in terror. The people had turned their faces to the sun. They were staring into the fiery ball and crying out in anguish at their loss. What had been formless in their souls during the long night now took shape. The faces of men and women, young and old, were now apparent, and in all of them I saw an immense sorrow, which seemed to be much less sorrow for the death of the Inca than for the sun itself. There was nothing wild or barbaric in these bronze faces. The black eyes were not filled with anger, but with submission. Their song's rhythm was gentle, almost imperceptible. It was like feeling great waves from a distance, the waves of a storm sensed at first only through a gentle heaving of the ship. It is strange indeed, should you not know it, to be on a glassy sea, heaving slowly up and down, and then to sense this steady rise and fall, as the mast suddenly groans a little, and the sails puff out only to sink back languidly.

The Indians had thrown their heads far back. They held the palms of their hands up to the sun, as if awaiting a gift. Their chant became louder and louder. Now and then one among them would let out a terrible cry, and soon groups of them would shrill out their song at the sun. After which the throng would echo the words. The broad rhythm, at first hardly well defined enough for the ear to catch, now was powerfully accented, as sure as the beat of a heavy drum. The sound entered into their feet, their hands, their whole bodies at last, and they began to writhe, as devoid of will as kelp in the sea when the waves break over the rocks. Their movements became unnatural, jerky, rigidly shaped, like a man with the falling sickness. An invisible gale of passion was blowing over them, forcing them into incredible postures.

I watched with Diego. I was fascinated by the spectacle. For the first time I saw the power of the demons who had forsaken the Inca. I did not doubt for a moment that it was Pachacamac who hovered over the scene, and even to this day I do not doubt it. It was the great demon who had possession of their bodies and their souls. This sight filled me with great fear. I kissed the silver cross, Doña Isabella's parting gift, and in a whisper I tried to pray. But my words were jumbled and I could not think. The unseen god was a vapor, far away, now that the night had given way to the day. The insatiable sun rose higher in the heavens, ever more present, an undeniable being, a mighty flame that seared the eyes to gaze upon. Pachacamac had come. In terror I watched. My legs were knocking together and my male parts were weak. Diego, too, was under the same spell as I. His hands trembled; his feet moved uneasily, half in time with the mighty dirge.

"We are bewitched, Diego," I whispered into his ear. "The demons have come."

"Now it's beyond human understanding," he said. "I am afraid of losing my wits. It is hard to believe. But let us see what happens."

"Yes, let us wait," I whispered.

The words the Indians were singing sounded like the verses of a litany of the Church. Soon I was able to distinguish single words and, as they were endlessly repeated, I grasped their sense. They went something like this in our language:

"Behold, my heart grieves bitterly
To think our sweet span of life
Should end so soon,
For now I see the realm is doomed
And the rule of Tavanta-Suyu will end.
Behold, I go into the open and weep
Since this land is doomed
To bend down and be wiped out.

"Splendid once was your name
And your might gripped the earth!
And yet you were cast aside like a feather,
And like an emerald you broke apart,
Before your eyes, you, your breath,
Have been lost in the abyss.

"Grief and anguish cry out in my heart,
When I think of your death, Atahualpa!
Do you still see me, I would know,
From afar in the land of the dead? Do you hear
When I sing the song of what I feel?"

They now expressed their terrible suffering by reaching up with their hands. Loudly they wept at the sun. The women pulled their hair out by the roots.

"I want to give you eternal happiness and peace;
I want to assuage your fearful pain
And to smother all pain in my song.
But where shall I find you? How reach you?
How can my spirit meet with yours as one?
Is the dead ear beyond my song's compass?
Is my song chained forever to this earth?"

Once in a while a man or woman would separate from the crowd. Turning slowly, in great fatigue, the arms held widespread as if trying to fly, the one possessed would move out into the market place. I could see that they meant no harm, they had no desire to rob us Spaniards of our baptized Inca. Slowly turning, I say, they approached the Inca, and looked into his face. One man, I recall, chanted wildly:

> "The cliffs are sounding,
> The cliffs are sounding,
> The mountains are singing with stony mouth!"

And then a woman, her blue-black hair all disheveled and fallen about her face, cried out in utter loss:

> "Pachacamac! Take pity on us.
> The earth is empty.
> The waters have dried up.
> We are hungry. Our tongues are dry.
> Have pity on us."

Another man fell as if dead, face down on the ground. He remained there, outstretched and motionless. The woman continued to turn, dancing slowly and lightly. Her smooth bronze arms writhed like snakes. Then, awaking from my dream, I realized it was Laanta I was looking at. It flashed in my mind to rush to her, take her into my room and bring her back to her senses. I would have done this, had not just then horns blared. Out of the House of the Snake came the cavaliers and the soldiers in a ceremonial procession.

Some of the Indians who were not so ecstatically taken crept up to Laanta, gently took her by the arm, and pushed her away from the corpse. Ever turning, even as she moved away, Laanta disappeared into the swaying crowd. She was robbed of her reason and seemed quite unaware of where she was.

With the appearance of the Spaniards the Indians' song died down, and became a low moaning as they saw the Inca's body moved onto a bier. The Spaniards covered him with costly robes. On his forehead they laid his crown, the kingly borla, which Miguel Estete had once stolen and now Pizarro had made him restore for the occasion. Four cavaliers supported the litter with the cramped body of the king on it, and slowly followed in the footsteps of the Dominicans. Behind walked Don Francisco Pizarro and Diego de Almagro. Next came the remaining nobles of our company, all of them in their long black cloaks and wearing black hats with the wide brim pulled down over their eyes, Spanish style, to indicate that they were mourning the dead. And in the rear were the soldiers, in full armor, their halberds and lances over their shoulders.

We then marched with the body to that house in Caxamalca which shortly after our arrival we had dedicated to San Francisco de Assisi, the name-saint of our Captain-General, and which later became a cloister richly endowed with Indian wealth.

Here the Mass of the dead was sung.

After the Sacrament had been given, and we had risen up from the stone flags, the crowd that had assembled outside was allowed to enter the chapel. They flowed in like a great spate of water when the sluice has been opened. Although in everyday life they were all mortally afraid of us Spaniards, at this moment they brushed by us heedlessly, bumping us out of the way, intent only on being with their dead Inca. The throng was so great that I thought the walls would burst. They fell on their knees before the litter on which Atahualpa lay. They pounded themselves senseless, banging their foreheads against the huge stones of the floor. They pressed their mouths to the coverings over the dead man. But no one touched the body itself.

So great was their grief that we were afraid. Nothing seemed more natural to us than that they in their loss should turn on us like maddened beasts, for we were the agents of all their ill. But I, who understood a good deal of what they were saying in their songs, realized that they were paying no attention to us at all. They seemed to consider us mere tools in the hands of some fate greater than all of us together, Indians and Spaniards.

Among the Indians I saw a man who was called Chacama. He was very old and had to use a staff to get along. I knew from Laanta that this Indian with a face so wrinkled that he looked more like a little old woman than a man had often counseled the Inca during his imprisonment. Occasionally I had come across him in the corridors of the House of the Snake, whereupon he would brush by me murmuring a muffled greeting. After all these visits Atahualpa, I remarked, was severely depressed.

This man Chacama stood at the head of the barrow in the chapel. The candles at the altar were extinguished. He laid the forefinger of his right hand on Atahualpa's forehead, between the tassels of the borla. It was quiet now in the chapel. Chacama began to sing slowly:

"The splendor has fled from Tavanta-Suyu.
Already the stars in heaven
Are assembling against us."

At this there were outcries of pain, and the women over and over shrieked, Aye, aye, aye. Chacama, keeping his finger on the dead man's forehead, uttered these words, just as if he were pronouncing a spell:

"He who bears the burden of care for the quipu,
He plains loud as decline begins.
But the faithful, they make themselves ready
To follow the dead, to the Island of Twilight
In the Western Sea...."

We Spaniards stared at the proceedings, wondering what was coming next. Suddenly a woman worked her way hurriedly to the bier, kneeled down, and plunged a copper knife into her breast. The blood pumped out over the covers, and ran down the naked dead arm lying outside, with the relaxed hand limp at the edge of the litter. Other women, and then men, moved toward the Inca. They too thrust knives into their own flesh.

"Captain-General!" shouted Father Vicente. "Clear the church! Clear the church! They're killing themselves! They're sacrificing themselves to demons."

"Clear them out! Get them outside!" ordered the Captain-General before the priest's words were really out of his mouth.

Halberd and lance were turned against the half-naked red bodies. Slowly, step by step, they retreated to the outdoors. The kneeling human offerings had toppled over, and were lying in a dark lake of blood.

"What a monstrous sin!" said Father Juan in horror.

Father Vicente raced to the altar and again lighted the candles. The face of the Man on the cross, crowned with thorns, peered down sidewise at the pool of blood and the crumpled bodies, a tender smile on His lips.

I left the church. I was completely crushed by the gruesome spectacle of the Indians' grief and worn out as well from the long night watch. I sat down on my pallet and looked dully at the floor. Will I always have to share the sufferings of others, of whole peoples? I thought. Is it not possible to be alone? Shall I never have time to think, to find my bearings the better to meet new shocks? Then I heard Frenero shouting to me. "Master! Master!" he said, beside himself.

"What is it?" I said, frightened out of my wits.

"Master . . . the girl . . ."

"What girl . . . what do you mean?" And then I saw. Frenero had Laanta in his arms. Her head hung down helplessly, like a flower from a broken stem. Her legs dangled limply over Frenero's red arms.

"What have you done, man?" I said, weakness showering through me. "Didn't I tell you to let her alone? I shall cut out your heart, you red son of a cow."

"No, no, I didn't touch her. I didn't do anything to her," Frenero protested, as he laid her on my bed. "I lost her in the crowd. I went looking for her. I found her in the Inca's garden. When she saw me she began to run. I could tell something was the matter. She wasn't fooling this time. I'm a good runner. I'd have caught her. But she ran up onto a high rock. I begged her not to do it. I even got down on my knees. I never did that before, master, for anybody. Then she began to laugh. It made me have goose flesh. Then she jumped. She fell on her head. I don't know . . . why she did it. I couldn't . . ."

"Never mind, Frenero," I said. "Watch out you don't move her. She's warm yet. Maybe she is just knocked senseless. Bring damp cloths . . ."

Frenero rushed out and got some wet rags, which we laid on her head. We washed her face clean, and bared a terrible gash, with white bone showing through. My stomach turned over in misery to look at it. Her eyes were closed, when I looked away from the wound seeking comfort in the rest of her face, and the lashes brushed the pockets over the high cheekbones. With her eyes thus shut, she looked like a queen, rather severe, as if through her lids she were observing critically our attempts to restore her to life.

The sight of the tenderly modeled face broke my control. "Come back, come, come to me," I adjured her. But she did not move. I kissed her face, but under my kisses the warmth faded from the flesh and the shuttered gaze grew even more disapproving. I brushed the blue-black hair with the palm of my hand, and I saw the light bronze part, the clean skull. "She is only a little girl," I said to Frenero, who stood watching. The fine skin over the skull seemed somehow defenseless, childlike, to me. It cramped my heart to look at it. My hands wandered over the slim, rounded shoulders, and found them cold.

"It is too late, master," Frenero said evenly.

"Atahualpa has taken back his gift," I said.

Two days after all this distressing change Don Hernando de Soto came back with his tidings of what was going on in Cuzco and Guamachucho. The latter city and its satellite villages were quite free of enemy soldiers. There was not a Carib in sight. The Inca had never intended any sort of betrayal. There was no doubting Don Hernando's word. He was grim, drawn, keyed up to trouble, his eyes blazing in his head.

The Captain-General began to pace, to walk in circles. "Didn't I say it right along?" he said. "Didn't I tell you over and over? I never believed these rumors."

"Then why did you have him executed?" asked Don Hernando vaguely. It was plain his thoughts were far ahead of his words. He was pale and he stood with his legs spread apart, his feet planted squarely on the floor.

"I tell you, I always maintained he was all right," said the Captain-General. "It was Father Vicente and Master Riquelme and Diego de Almagro who wanted him to die." He smiled coldly, absently, just talking for his own sake, and for De Soto's sake.

"That's not true," said Father Vicente, rising to the bait—though of course he did it deliberately, as part of the game. "I absolved him of his heresy. Everyone can vouch for that."

"But you did it only at the last minute, when it was much too late," the Captain-General reminded him.

"It was not too late," said Father Vicente. "Juan de Atahualpa was alive. The Church is not responsible for his death."

"And it's the same with me," Master Riquelme cut in. "How was I to know that all these stories were so many foolish lies? I'm an officer of the Crown. What do I know about Caribs and uprisings? There were enough officers, real soldiers, to take care of those matters. What about Gonzalo Pizarro! Pedro de Candía! And both the captains! It was their duty to straighten out any such confusions."

"Very good," said Diego de Almagro. "Only you should have complained a little louder. You admit then you are nothing but a dribbling fool."

"You are insulting the Crown. You're slandering the name of Don Carlos when you talk like that," said Riquelme, half pretending, half feeling offense. "I shall write to Seville all about it."

"You will write?" asked Almagro. "What zeal you show, my dear Riquelme. Are you sure you are going to write? That would be difficult, wouldn't it, for me and the rest, I mean? But write away. Wear down the point of your pen into a shovel, for all of me. And, incidentally, why are you here with us, anyway? You are of no use. Are you spying on us, perhaps?"

"A spy. Spying . . . !" Riquelme looked into one hard face after the other. He lowered his head, backed away a few steps, and gathering speed left the room.

"Why, you miserable bastard!" Diego de Almagro shouted after him, following up his advantage. "You mother-tupping spy, you sucker on cows' udders, you drippings of drunken love on a feast day, you coward! I'll make you shorter by the length of a head!" Almagro's red face was purple with wrath. And then he roared on. "I admit it! It was I who condemned the Inca to death. But I did it after Don Francisco Pizarro had found him guilty on three counts. Of course, I had him garroted, even after he had been absolved of heresy. But what of it? What could I do? Who stood back of me? Who lifted his voice? Not a single cowardly soul! I wanted the Inca to die. And die he did, and so it stands. We shall all have our day. And that is that."

"It was you, do not forget," said the Captain-General, now slightly amused, "who first suggested the trial."

"Let us cease this recrimination," said Almagro, no longer in the spirit of the game. "I'm sated with taking the blame for shortcomings. Do you think you Pizarros can lord it over the whole world? Do you think you can pass off your crimes? Shall I load my shoulders with your pack of sin? Not I! I refuse, do you hear me, I refuse! Mark my words, all of you. I mean you, Don Francisco, and you, Gonzalo. You planned the murder. You kept coming to me, the both of you, whimpering about how the Inca stood in the way no matter where you turned. How shall we ever get to Cuzco, you kept saying; how will we ever get our hands on the rest of the gold? No doubt about it. And there were a thousand other complaints always ringing in my ears. You wanted me to play the alley bravo. And so I did, lapping up your vomit for you, for the Pizarros. This much I say. The Pizarros will stop at nothing for gold."

"Another word, and I'll cut you down," said the Captain-General calmly. "Enough is enough. There will now be order and respect. We begin anew. I say this as a command. Anyone who disobeys will have a chance to see who is master of this company."

There was silence. Pizarro had bared his teeth. His eyes were starting from his head, and his hand was on his sword. Almagro stared at him as a bird stares at a snake. The soldiers were drawing around, drawn by the loud voices. They whispered among themselves. Pizarro looked significantly in their direction. The quarrel came to a sudden end. Don Hernando de Soto had listened without saying a word. He shrugged his shoulders and left the room when the soldiers had gone.

The Inca was buried in the graveyard of the Cloister of San Francisco. The Inca's maiden, Laanta, we buried in the Inca's garden, under a little fir tree that grew slantwise out of the bank.

23

HOMECOMING

WHEN Atahualpa was dead and buried we got ourselves ready to move from Caxamalca to Cuzco to see with our own two eyes the navel of the Indian world. It was soon apparent that with the death of the Inca the kingdom of Tavanta-Suyu had lost its binding force. News of uprising and battles came from all directions. One village was fighting the other. At night we saw the flames of burning fires. On the march during the day we often passed through blackened ruins. Skeletons picked clean by the vultures lay in the fields. The Indians themselves plundered the royal storehouses. Metal and precious stones had vanished beyond recall. It looked as if the kingdom of Tavanta-Suyu, like the men and women at the bier, like Laanta, was deliberately committing suicide before our eyes. Instead of the orderly state we had first trod there was now an Indian chaos.

We marched over the great highway running from Quito to Cuzco. Once again we clambered over icy mountain passes, and when we came to the liana bridges swinging over dizzy heights we had to make tedious detours, for they would not support our cannon and horses. It was a slow journey. We ran into many small bands of hostile Indians who always fled when we made demonstrations of force.

Our soldiers, having found no more gold and now forced to endure unremitting trials, became evil-tempered. They treated the Indians with abominable cruelty. They persecuted them with fire and sword in order to press from them knowledge of hidden treasures. But they learned nothing. Worst off were our bearers, who were lashed on day after day until they dropped, to be replaced by others impressed for the purpose of doing our heavy work.

The crusade developed into a straggling caravan of misery which barely crawled its way to Cuzco. A few days' march from the city we encountered our first real resistance. Don Hernando de Soto came very close to being sacrificed to the fury of the natives. They came rushing down out of the mountainside and attacked the van of our company, the riders led by De Soto. The Spaniards were barely able to take refuge on the far side of a mountain stream. Many a cavalier had his head cloven to the chin by the broad Indian battle-axes, and many a horse died an equally unpleasant death. The Captain-General saved the day by dispatching Diego de Almagro with the rest of the riders to De Soto's aid, and so managed to preserve a segment of the mounted scouts.

We reached Cuzco one November evening, camped outside the city, and paraded in the next morning. The very narrow streets between the stone walls of the houses reminded me a little of the Moorish city of Cordova, except that here the houses were much lower, and built Peruvian fashion out of large stone blocks laid one on top of the other without the use of mortar.

The Captain-General led us into the big square while the crowd gaped and shouted. There we encamped. At first we did not dare to billet in the houses and the palace for fear of being overpowered. Our apprehension was groundless, it proved, for the populace, over two hundred thousand souls, received us with open arms. It appeared they considered us to be avengers of the Inca Huáscar who had once been their master. Atahualpa had never set foot in this city.

I shall not go into a description of the city itself, which has been so excellently reported on the whole by Cieza de Leon and Ondegardo and many others. I say, however, that these first two men are quite just in their tale of the extent of the city and its population, of the splendor of its palaces and temples. However, their stories of gold and precious stones were utterly false. The Indians had spirited away a good portion of all movable objects of any value, and now these were nowhere to be found.

The Captain-General had given orders not to plunder the city, but his authority failed in the face of the Spaniards' rapacious greed. It was not long before they were roaming at will through the royal storehouses and magazines. The next step was to ravage private homes of all valuable material. Often they would torture the owner of the house to find the gold they firmly believed he had hidden.

If the Cuzco Indians had been warlike and possessed of common courage they could easily have assaulted and overcome us when we were dispersed in house and public building. But such a course never entered their heads. They feasted continuously. Their singing and dancing kept up day and night, as if they were quite unaware that the kingdom was seething with disorder, and that we were robbing them of all we could lay our hands on. They seemed to want to get every moment of joy possible out of life before it was too late. They did not pay attention even to the executions and torturing of their fellows. The anguished cries of Indians whose feet our Spaniards were expertly searing with flame to make them talk intermingled with the shrieks of the dancers. The lives of these people of Cuzco were one endless crazed song. One feast followed the other. The drunken clamor was so loud the Spaniards could not sleep nights.

A few days after our entrance into the city, Manco Capac, a brother of Huáscar, was crowned Inca with great ceremony. The Captain-General hoped to control the kingdom by working through the young man. He was bitterly deceived. Behind the youth's smooth forehead there teemed thoughts of revenge, of rebellion and war, the very scheme which we had falsely attributed to the Inca Atahualpa.

We got our richest booty from the Coricancha, the great Peruvian temple of the sun. This Coricancha has been differently modeled since then, and consecrated as the Church of Santo Domingo. But the walls, made of gigantic blocks which so astonished us when we first laid eyes on them, still remain. The Coricancha was then and still is the most impressive building on the southern continent of the New World. Seen from the outside it was something of a disappointment, for the roof was made of nothing but straw, like an enormous peasant's hut. But this rude covering, which brought to mind the buildings of early Rome, served only to heighten the contrast found in the interior.

Inside all was richness and splendor. Especially rich was the western wall, so placed as to catch on its golden surface the first rays of the sun admitted through an aperture cut into the opposite wall. Golden friezes ran about the interior, and in niches were placed images of plants and animals sacred to the sun. Among these the most striking was a llama of solid gold. I am certain today that the golden ear of corn that the Captain-General had presented me in Caxamalca must originally have come from this temple of the sun, for we saw that many of the niches were empty. The gold on the wall had been partially torn away, and no doubt this ornament had already found its way into our hands as part of the Inca's ransom.

In the long, corridorlike vestibule of the temple on both sides sat the mummies of dead kings and queens of Tavanta-Suyu. The men were on the right side, the women on the left, in long rows, staring straight ahead. This assembly of the dead, leaning slightly forward on their golden chairs as if whispering to one another, made the hair rise on my head. They appeared to be discussing the present fate of the kingdom. They were whispering of experiences in the world beyond the grave, moving thin, leathery lips. They were talking about ways to hold the kingdom together with their withered hands and their withered words of wisdom.

All these mummy kings were clothed in gay though faded garments into which were woven big-eyed soul-birds with human faces. The heavy material fell down all about their feet, in wooden folds, over their narrow thighs and knees. Down over their bowed foreheads hung the reddish tassels of the royal fillet which all but hid the parchment-lidded sunken eyes. They all looked alike, absolutely dominated by the race in them, as like to one another as so many eggs in a basket. Their faces were at once harsh, simple and yielding. The brown skin was stretched tight over high cheekbones. The women's faces had lost all femininity, their sex erased by death.

Just as in the unborn child, all curled, pale and wormlike, one looks in vain for the spiritual, lifelike quality of the living face, so too in these faces all trace of humanity had long since vanished. The form of the face was there, but all content was gone, all meaning. Nothing but herbs and guano preserved the remains, supporting a mockery of immortality. The leather skin covered nothing but a still more contemptible litter of dried bones and dirty strings of sinew. The bellies were caved in, robbed of the full soft parts underneath, and the basket of ribs covered neither heart nor lungs. The oldest, at the beginning of the line, were amazingly small. They sat like dwarfs in their tattered robes, little huddled skeletons plastered with strips of foul brown skin sprinkled with occasional hairs.

It was not the greatness and splendor of a royal line that were here placed on show, not the immortality of man and woman who had believed themselves children of the sun. It was the triumph of death that was on exhibition, over king and queen as well as over slave.

And yet here and there, among the stinking garments, on the wrinkled neck, on finger and wrist, glittered gold. At first the soldiers contemplated the dead bodies with fear and reluctance. It did not take them long, however, to screw up their courage and strip the ring from the finger, the necklace from the withered throat. They fell on the mummies, plundering them, sparing neither king nor queen. If a bracelet could not be worked off easily, off they twisted the dry bone, and found a way. At first they did this out of necessity, in the end to make merry. Laughing and shouting they tore off the bandages around each head, and threw dried hairy scalps at each other in sport. The low vestibule was filled with dust, the dust of human decay, and it made them cough wildly. The soldiers got completely out of control, as if nothing in the world had ever amused them so deeply as this game of mocking and desecrating the dead monarchs. They took off their helmets and tried them on kings, asking how they looked. "Was it not side-splitting!"

During all this fantastic tumult the Indians knelt on the floor and mumbled their prayers. Some put their hands up to their faces so as not to see. And yet some of them followed us, consumed with curiosity, their black eyes as big as saucers. Gradually one Indian after the other began to imitate the soldiers, and mixed awkwardly in the game. Even they spat into the eyes of kings and laughed, showing their teeth. They helped the soldiers carry out the golden chairs, tipping the dead to one side, grinding them carelessly underfoot.

The Captain-General was greatly disturbed when he got word of this desecration. He became pale with wrath, assembled the soldiery and lectured them fiercely.

"Have I not given orders not to plunder?" he roared. "Haven't I told you all to keep out of the sacred places? Is this the way you obey orders? Are you blind to the fact that a man from these people has been chosen by me to be crowned king? Do you realize that our well-being, our lives now depend on the favor of this man? You sons of decayed dogs, you would rob the grave of San Fernando in Seville if you had half a chance!"

The soldiers grumbled and mumbled to one another. "Didn't he do the same with the living Inca? At least the kings we touched didn't feel anything. Now he sits on his high horse and insults us." Only a few among the whole lot were ashamed.

On the next day what was left of the mummies in the vestibule of Coricancha vanished. It was said that Manco Capac had ordered the dead to be hidden away where we could not get at them.

And a few weeks later the gold was as ceremoniously divided in the market place of Cuzco as the ransom at Caxamalca. The treasure was not so great as we had anticipated. Nevertheless each rider received six thousand gold pesos de oro, and each foot soldier one half of this sum. I became twelve thousand pesos de oro richer than I had been before. The silver, textiles and other works of art apportioned to me added another four thousand pesos.

As his share of the booty Juan the thin got an image of the sun from the Coricancha, which was made cunningly of heavy gold. He gambled it away that same night, and the next morning woke up the same poor wretch that he had always been in Spain.

With the fall and occupation of the navel of the world, and the investiture of a puppet king, it appeared that all the land was now in our control, and the Captain-General began to look around for a suitable place from which to rule. Cuzco was too far away from the rest of the kingdom, in his opinion, and too high up in the mountains. He found what he considered to be the best site in the valley through which flowed the River Rimac. It was not far from the sea, and the earth flourished there. On the sixth of January the founding ceremonies took place. The place was christened after the three holy kings who on this same day brought to the Christ Child asleep in the cradle presents of incense, myrrh and gold. Our soldiers found the name Ciudad de los Reyes too long, and got into the habit of calling the city simply Lima, after the Indian name for the place.

Twelve days later the big square and the main streets were laid out, much bigger in all dimensions than any counterparts in Spain. For Don Francisco Pizarro wanted to make his city the capital of the New World, the queen of the Southern Ocean, the most beautiful city ever seen by man. Great crowds of Indians transported the wood and stone, and the broad space teemed with dark bodies at work. So the same thing happened in the Ciudad de los Reyes as must once have happened in the Egypt of the Pharaohs when the pyramids were built. The sixty-five-year-old Pizarro built himself a monument. But it was no dead, pointed mass of stone in the desert. It was a city of palaces and cathedrals, alive with thousands of people busy living out their lives, crossed with palm-lined promenades, lightened with fine plazas in the midst of which fountains played.

A great change came over the Captain-General when he stood protected from the sun by his broad-brimmed hat among the workmen and examined the master-builder's plans.

"I shall prove to be the envy of all Panama; I shall surpass them all," he once told me. "I see the day coming when my city, the city of Pizarro, will be ranked as one of the wonders of the world. It will surpass the Moorish cities, it will be better than Seville or Bagdad. That is the way I shall have it when I am through."

Then he bent over the plans, and these he really could read. He read them better than the master-builder himself. Already in his mind's eye he saw the city spread out, many-towered, white, complete. It was bizarre to hear him say, "Over there in the shadow of the cathedral there shall be a plaza lined with palms. I'll have a fountain there. Perhaps a monument." And at that time there was no cathedral, much less its shadow.

Something childlike slowly crept into Pizarro's features. The conqueror had all but laid aside his armor. He was like one of those Italian princes who after a whole lifetime of labor and violence at last have built for themselves an enchanted palace in which they collect wondrous works of art. But Pizarro really was greater than any of these. He did not think of erecting a splendid dwelling for himself. He thought only of the future, of the business and activity which would support hundreds of thousands of productive people as yet still but seed.

The canals, bridges, streets and the deepening of the Rimac occupied him almost as much as the plans for palace and cathedral. He talked of his plans as if he were now an Inca, bitten by the ambition to do great works for the commonweal. He dreamed great dreams, and immediately set about putting these dreams into three measurable dimensions. He was intent on his labors even during the night. Even then he found no rest but stalked about wrapped in his mantle observing his Lima *in posse*. He improved everything according to his lights. Nothing was good or fine enough for him. If he had had his way, the Cathedral of Lima would have been larger than the mosque of Cordova; it would have had far more columns, and its tracery of stone would have had the perfection of Venetian glass and Flemish petit point.

He complained bitterly about the lack of skilled workmen. He told me he would pay them more than they would ever get from Don Carlos if he could find some way of transporting them to Peru. If Pizarro could have had his way Titian, whose art is so beloved of Don Carlos, would have painted the cathedral's altar piece, and Benvenuto would have been commissioned to make many smooth pieces of bronze for him.

Pizarro was so taken with the construction of the new city that he forgot everything else. We heard rumors that Don Pedro de Alvarado, onetime colleague of Don Hernando Cortés, and the conquistador of Guatemala, had taken Quito and plundered it. Although this province really belonged to the kingdom of Peru, the Captain-General merely ignored rumor, and turned again to his plans. Everything was quite different from other years. Formerly Pizarro would have not waited an hour to strike out against the interloper and teach him his place.

The news came that Diego de Almagro on his expedition to Chile had discovered nothing more than salt deserts and forests of fir. He had found no gold, and had lost over half his men through hunger, sickness and savage Indians. Pizarro heard all this, turned back to his plans, and said, "If I only knew where to find some blue-veined marble in this country!"

A different and more importunate kind of news now began to filter into the Ciudad de los Reyes. The Inca had left the throne and vanished. Diego de Almagro was on the march against Cuzco. The whole kingdom was in an uproar. In one place it was the threat of an Indian uprising; in another war between two Spanish captains. Don Francisco at last paid attention. For a long time he paced up and down lost in thought. Then he said, "My brothers will take care of these matters and restore order."

The rich silver mines and the countless gold pans of the country poured metal into Lima. Textiles, golden statues and other works of art, painted earthen pots of strange shape, came down to us from the mountains. In the storehouses the products of the land, fine woods, llama and vicuña wool, cotton and dyed materials piled up. It was not long before a whole shipload was ready to be dispatched as a gift to Don Carlos.

In the division of the lands an extensive holding on the bank of the River Rimac fell to my lot. I got rich copper mines in the mountains, too, and a host of Indian slaves, over ten thousand of them. These repartimientos, the parceling out of Indian labor, seemed necessary to the Captain-General in order to make full use of the wealth of the country.

"Instead of being the Inca's slaves, now they are slaves of Castile," he said. "If no one were here to force them to work, they would do no more than was barely necessary to hold their bodies and souls together. The land then would become worthless, and we should be cheated out of the fruits of conquest. Besides, when we do this we give them the advantage of intercourse with Christians."

Everyone agreed with his notions. The only one to object was Father Juan. He said, "The Incas were heathens, and because of that considered their subjects to be slaves. This slavery is not allowed us Christians. For our Lord has commanded, Love one another. He taught that we must treat the most humble as our brothers."

"I know," said Don Francisco. "But everything in good time. First the Indians must be proselytized. Then they will be set free when they are good Christians."

Father Juan advanced many more exceptions. He pointed out that the Indians' work under the Incas had been broken by a great many feast days, in order to give them time to rest and to do as they willed. He said that there was a great danger that the Spanish lords would treat their Indians with cruelty, not thinking of their souls at all. He reminded Pizarro of a certain edict promulgated by our deceased Queen Isabella, forbidding any slavery in India, and mentioned, too, that the Popes of that time had spoken out against the mistreatment and forced labor of the natives in the newly discovered lands.

Father Vicente and the other Dominicans lent their support to Father Juan, but to no avail. The Captain-General, in measured argument, demonstrated beyond doubt how the future welfare of the land depended on Indian labor, and ventured to say that under such circumstances even Jesus Christ himself would have no objection. For was it not all really to make His Name more glorious?

The plans were all-important; the work increased ten fold. In the great rush of activity the admonitions of Father Juan were completely overlooked, finally ignored. The pious discourses of the clerics were laughed down as impractical, even by men of the cloth. But very soon the iniquities of this arrangement became clear for all of us to see.

From day to day the torture and execution of intractable Indians increased. On the coast these practices were still relatively infrequent. There the Spaniards feared the heavy hand of Don Francisco Pizarro. But deeper in the country the slaveholders often treated their slaves far worse than dogs, and certainly considered them of less intrinsic value.

The mortality in the mines became tremendous. In the day of the Incas men worked only six months at a stretch at this dangerous and unhealthful labor. Now they worked till they dropped. Often they were forced into the bowels of the earth chained together. Flogged on by Indian overseers the red-skinned men worked in eternal darkness. When they died at their labors, which was common occurrence, the corpses were carried to the surface and given to the dogs to eat. Another and another unfortunate would be forced to replace the dead, and the cries of women and children were fearful to hear. They had to be driven away with whips. Many Indians condemned to this doom preferred to kill themselves. And so it became the practice to chain them together whenever possible to prevent such unprofitable contingencies. And if they finally did succeed in committing suicide, their wives were executed to pay for the crime.

We heard stories about this gross cruelty. Indian caciques appeared before the Captain-General, and were supported in their testimony by the monks. Then, exactly like Don Pedro de los Ríos of Panama, Pizarro would shrug his shoulders and say, "What do you want of me? What can I do? The Crown is always asking for gold and for more gold. The Council of the Indies is greedy for whole fleets of ships laden with silver. If I should put an end to the repartimientos, there would be no more treasure from Peru. There would be an uprising, if we let go our hold now, against me and my brothers. For the men who were once my soldiers now think themselves lords. They feel entitled to some favors. I say they deserve them."

In this fashion was the strong-willed Pizarro shackled by the prejudices of his own past and indeed by fate itself, quite as much as the Indians in the mines. But in the night his conscience may well have been deeply bitten. It is not unreasonable to conjecture that his preoccupation with the building of Lima was in part an escape from the nameless miseries he had visited on Peru.

Even in those early days I felt the intimations of doubt. I felt myself rushing along the same evil path as the Pizarros; I had only too much in common with them, pride and shortsightedness. True, I did side with the Dominicans in the struggle to impress Pizarro with the horrors of the Indians' lot. Yet I did this, come to think of it, in a hypocritically interested way. It never occurred to me to free my own Indians. And, as always when one takes a half-hearted course, I soon observed that I was pleasing neither the Dominicans nor the slaveholders. I had tried to sit down between two stools, as the people say.

At that time I did not realize that in moral decisions there are no half measures, although it was plainly enough written down in the New Testament. For our Lord has said, Let your speech be yea, yea: no, no: and that which is over and above these is of evil. It is an old experience among men that we cannot make the slightest concessions to evil. Reach out as much as a fingertip, and the whole arm is gone.

All these simple homilies are clear and self-evident enough to me today. But not then in Peru, before my spirit had been chastised. Then it did not even occur to me that I was evading a decision. I did not realize that the decision I was so briskly dodging was the same one all along, the same one that had been posed before my eyes ever since Antonio Cardinal de Guevara had torn the veil from them.

The circumstances were always different. One time it was the fate of Abu Amru at the hands of the Inquisition. Another the life or death of Atahualpa. Now it was the well-being of millions of Indians. But the question was always the same. It was the question that God always puts before mankind, always in varying situations, a question that must have an irrevocable yes or no.

It is not the circumstances which make the decision so important, although in my own case the life of a king and a whole people hung in balance. It is the moral decision itself that is the serious thing. It is so easy for me to imagine how on account of a small injustice the whole world might well end in chaos. For it is God alone, His will and sense of justice at work in us, which gives living content to the society of men, to the Church and the State. It is this fragment of godhead within us which makes life among men possible. Without it we should be so many beasts of prey, and would all soon perish in a terrible struggle of everyone against everyone else.

I felt this question of good or evil coming over me like a sickness. Whatever inward heaven I may have had turned black. Heavy dark billows of cloud rolled over the landscape of my soul. The whole world was melancholy and evil. I was like a man who looks through dark glasses on a rainy day. In me there was a breathlessness, a damp, oppressive sultriness, the first lightnings before the heavy drops of rain begin to fall.

My comrades and the Dominicans began to treat me differently, so it seemed. I imagined that their conversations died on their lips when I approached, that they whispered about me in corners. Yet I knew that it was not they. It was I who had changed. I went about oppressed, and at times in order to relieve the tension in my bosom, I permitted the grossest indignities in my dealings with the Indians. I loaded my faithful Sancho with bitterest reproaches for the slightest negligence, and, with my own fist, I would smite Indians in the face for as much as brushing my sleeve. And when I did this I was filled with horrible memories of the Spanish slave driver in Panama, whom I had killed for the very excesses to which I now was myself committed.

I thought of the words of the great monk, the wanderer, whom I had met at night in the forest. I was overcome by a great longing to see him again, and to talk to him. The confusion in my heart I blamed entirely upon the influence of this strange new world, on its mysterious magic powers. So I reasoned. I refused to prize out the real reason, which resided in me myself, in my moral impotence.

It may be understandable then how welcome a change it was when the Captain-General ordered me to return to Spain, in charge of recently collected treasures and objects of art. I prepared myself for the journey, never doubting for a single moment that but a few months separated me from the conjugal delights of life with Doña Isabella. I was a rich man. I had even fulfilled her every thoughtless childish wish. A kingdom was conquered, a gigantic kingdom, much larger, stranger and more fraught with wonder than anything a small girl's imagination could possibly conjure.

When I got on board ship, the good wishes of the Captain-General and Father Vicente echoing in my ears, for a time I felt gratefully free of all dissatisfaction. Diego de Vargas and Sancho accompanied me. We talked all night long on the poop deck, speculating on our reception in the homeland. Diego de Vargas had now the means to allow Doña Sobeya to come to Lisbon. From there it was his plan to bring her back to Lima, where, he believed, they could live a life of peace, far from the argus-eyed cut-throats of the Holy Inquisition.

The full moon hung white over the sea. The black broad waves were rimmed with silver. Behind us the helmsman stood silent at his task. The compass cast a pale light about us. Now and then we heard the thunder of the breakers at the base of the mountains, and the sea lions roared like hoarse dogs, the sound echoing back to us from the black cliffs now spilled over with silver. When about midnight the moon rose to its zenith, to the starboard we could see outlined the jagged ridge of the coastal range. Silently the ship drove along by the endless wall of Tavanta-Suyu's highlands.

Never were earth and sea so endless as during these nights. We were sailing through the stars, through a gentle universe borne on soft waves of ether. Spontaneously we began to talk about the shape of the earth. We talked about the Cape of Storms discovered by Bartolomé Diaz. We talked about Magellan who in the middle of the Southern Ocean found the Islas de Los Ladrones, and of Sebastian del Cano who, after the murder of his admiral, still unafraid sailed farther into the west, and on his ship *Mão Victoria* reached the island of Timor whence he wended his way homeward to San Lúcar and so, for the first time circumnavigated the globe. I remember how we talked about this brave man's coat-of-arms, fashioned in the shape of a globe, beneath inscribed, *"Primus circumdedisti me."*

"Yes, the first one ever to encompass me," cried Diego, "ever to measure my girth." He spread his arms out as if he would stretch them over the southern and western oceans both. We went on to talk about the great ball of earth which is the world, how it ever whirls, misted by white clouds, moving along like a misty choir of angels. And our thoughts swept on, reaching up to the fixed stars. Where, indeed, was the end of the world? We tried this and we tried that, and we had to admit that we must think of the universe as both limited and limitless.

"It is like God," said I, "of whom the Cardinal de Cusa remarked, that human understanding can as little comprehend Him as a quadrangle can ever cover a circle."

We talked about the insignificance of man, his lack of insight, his puniness when considered against the immensity of the astral universe. We ruminated on his greatness, on his insignificant fragile being, vulnerable to the whim of every storm, who yet has the courage to face all difficulties and to impose his reason upon the stars, the heavens, and the seas. Sancho listened helplessly to all our majestic wanderings. The helmsman stared at the compass, glanced up at the stars, and held the great timber with a firm hand. The bow of our vessel cut into the eye of the north; the waves seethed and hissed as we plowed steadily on. I thought how often man, too, on his journey through life, stands in the need of a compass, of a needle to show him the right way, of a good helmsman and a strong hand. For without these advantages he will be the sport of every wind and wave, and at last be thrown onto the jagged rocks, there to be lost in the smother of surf, a helpless, ignominious wreck.

In these long conversations I completely forgot myself.

I was given a delightful reception in Panama. Don Pedro de los Ríos entertained me at one feast after the other. I then traversed the Isthmus and in Nombre de Dios for the first time I took charge of my own ship. I spent a vast amount outfitting, manning and provisioning it. At that time it was almost impossible to find enough seamen either in Panama or in Nombre de Dios, for they deserted as fast as they set foot on shore—to seek their fortune in Peru, Guatemala, Venezuela and the Pearl Coast.

When the Azores were safely behind me, and I neared Spain, my excitement was so great I could no longer sleep, and, to the astonishment of the ship's crew, I once even crawled up to the masthead, thinking to catch the first glimpse of the homeland. Three days from Cadiz, we were attacked by an English pirate, who thought that he was dealing with an unarmed merchant vessel. But he soon discovered his error when he closed with us. The grapples were thrown, the ships locked, there was a bloody battle on the forehead, and we took two men prisoners, whom we hanged from the yardarms. The rest retreated to their vessel, cut loose the grapples, and made off.

As soon as my affairs in Seville had been put in order I took the shortest road to Cordova. It struck me for the first time when I was received by the Council of the Indies that their greeting was tinged with more than a little chill politeness. The special presents for the Crown that the Governor of New Castile in the Ciudad de los Reyes had entrusted to my care were graciously accepted and aroused much wonder. But no one troubled to inquire about my journey, or about the health of the Governor or my other friends. I had the feeling that they all wanted to leave me to my own devices as soon as possible. But in my joy at soon seeing Doña Isabella again, I scarcely noticed these slights. Only on the journey to Cordova over the rough road in a heavy springless carriage did it dawn on me that for some reason or other we conquistadors might have incurred the displeasure of the Court. And yet that seemed peculiar to me, for within a few years' space we had shipped to the Court several hundred thousand gold pesos, not to mention countless works of art, rich coverlets and tapestries. Beyond all this in the same years we had conquered for the Crown an immense territory, as least ten times as great as all Castile.

Of course, I did not overlook the fact that in his heart of hearts Don Carlos is a cold man. In him there is something moribund, which may well spring from his unhappy childhood. But on this very account I hardly thought he would ever act against his own interest. And his interest certainly lay on our side. We had won him a greater kingdom than Don Hernando Cortés, the Marquis of Oaxaca. Yet even Don Carlos had aged, and the constant unrest in Germany and Italy must be weighing heavily on his mind. I considered it quite possible, too, that in his jealousy the Governor of Panama, Don Pedro de los Ríos, had spoken unfavorably of us to the Council. For what was his miserable puddle of swamp, quaking with fevered miasma, compared with the glory of the Ciudad de los Reyes, of resplendent Cuzco, of the mighty fortress of Quito!

But the troubled premonitions that came to me in the solitude of the night journey I suppressed quickly whenever I thought of Doña Isabella. I dreamed of her, how she would sit in her garden, there under the chestnut trees that bower the fountain. She and her small brother Miguel and Doña Catarina, her duenna. And the three of them would hear all my story. Doña Catarina would sit with her mouth wide open, but in a while she would go to sleep according to her habit, and we would send off little Miguel to fetch a shawl or a glass of wine from the house. Then for the first time, I would speak freely. Even now, in the swaying carriage, I felt I would speak with power, although I had never attended the Escuela de Artes in Salamanca. But why an Escuela de Artes, when the heart itself spoke? For the heart creates its own eloquence from intimate sources, not from the dull, dead waters of wisdom scummed green with time. And at the end I would bend my knee, as I did once before to Doña Juana, and I would give her the golden ear of Indian corn.

Lost in these quick dreams I reached Cordova. I hardly bothered to take time to wash my face and hands, to beat the dust from my clothes. I presented myself in the house of Don Garcilaso de Gómez, and was told that the master was absent on a journey to Italy. That affected my spirits very little. I really did not care so much to see Don Garcilaso. I longed to see Doña Isabella herself, and tried to overcome the reluctance of the house steward with a few pesos.

A long time passed while I sat in the cool darkness of the hall. My heart was hammering in my throat. I thought I heard several persons talking excitedly in the rooms of the upper floor. And then a side door suddenly opened; a dark-haired handsome boy stood before me. I recognized him immediately as Miguel, who in my stupidity I had imagined still a small child. I had quite forgotten that time had not stood still in Spain during my absence. Miguel looked at me, and tears sprang into his eyes. He rushed to me, embraced me, kissed me on both cheeks. I was rather astonished at the excess of his welcome and good-humoredly tried to free myself from his embrace. I wanted to say something, but with a warning gesture he laid the palm of his hand flat across my mouth.

"Quiet, quiet, Don Pedro," he whispered, "nobody must hear us. We can't talk together here."

"In the name of the Holy Virgin Mary," I cried, "what has happened? What's going on?"

"I beg you by all the saints, be still, Don Pedro. You don't know my father!"

"But he's in Italy."

"No, he's not."

"Then the servant lied to me."

"Be still, I beg you, Don Pedro. But before you go I want you to hear that I, for one, don't believe a thing. No, you couldn't be up to such a cowardly act . . . even if they poured all the riches of Scheherazade in your lap. . . ."

"What act? What are you talking about?" I said in a burst of anger. "Are you talking about the English pirates that I hanged from the yards of my vessel?"

"It has nothing to do with me, Don Pedro," he whispered hoarsely. "And this isn't the place to set matters aright." He drew back from me, gazing at me big-eyed, fearful and yet tenderly. He opened the door behind him.

I stretched out both arms. "Come back, Miguel," I said. "Listen, I have brought something for you."

"I don't want it," he stammered in confusion. "I don't want anything to do with that treasure."

"Are you afraid of gold, Miguel?" I cried, and showed him my outthrust right hand on which I wore a heavy gold ring sparkling with an emerald.

"It's sticky with blood," he said, and banged shut the door.

I stood there dismayed. Slowly it came to me what the trouble was. But where is there gold that is not smeared with blood? I thought bitterly. If there is such, it rests deep in the bowels of the mountainside. Gold and blood, they are close kin. Mankind has soiled everything with blood. The bigger a thing is, the more blood of men it has soaked up. Has not our most sacred Church been washed in blood, more even than the pyramids of Tenochtitlan which Don Hernando Cortés stormed in triumph to the brazen cry of war trumpets?

The steps creaked heavily and I saw the large person of Doña Catarina descending with laborious care. She held her double chin formidably high. She stopped at the foot of the stairs and regarded me as if I were a leper. The sound of our breathing was raucous in the room.

"Don Pedro," she said at last, "I cannot bid you welcome. It would have been better for you to stay over there with those miserable heathen. Or if both you and your gold ship had been swallowed up by the sea, your soul would now be in Purgatory and at least you would have some prospect of finding an easier lot on Judgment Day. But as things stand now, I'm very much afraid you're going to remain an unregenerate sinner for the rest of your days."

"Doña Catarina," I said curtly, "what are you talking about?"

She sighed heavily, raised her eyebrows, began to sniff. To my amazement I saw that tears were trickling down her fat cheeks. "I am so disappointed, Don Pedro," she sobbed, "so bitterly disappointed!" With this her tears coursed more freely. Suddenly she moved quickly over to me and struck me on the hand, as one punishes a child who has lifted some forbidden object. "It doesn't matter so far as I'm concerned," she said, sniffing loudly and wiping her eyes with the backs of her large hands, "but the poor child, Doña Isabella, she has cried her eyes out on account of you."

"What!" I said, and wavered between pleasure and fear.

"What!" she mimicked me. "Doña Isabella and I prayed for you every night. Hardly a week went by that Doña Isabella did not light a thick candle for you under the image of the Virgin Mary. Everything in the house hinged on Don Pedro, on Cotopaxi, Caxamalca and a thousand other such matters that your name brought to mind. And what thanks did Don Pedro give me for curbing my tongue a thousand times? He throttled a Christian king bound to the stake, after having stripped him of his goods like a bandit from the Sierra. . . ."

"Just a minute!" I shouted, now genuinely aroused to anger. "Hold on. I have a name to defend, Doña Catarina. If you weren't a woman . . ."

"That's right, Don Pedro," she sobbed. "Take it out on a poor old woman like me. You did the same with the women of New Castile. It will be nothing new."

"What do you know about New Castile?" I asked, beside myself.

"More than you would like me to know," she mumbled stubbornly.

"It's an old precept of justice," I said, trying as best I could to get myself under control, "it's an ancient custom, to give the accused a hearing before he is condemned. *'Audiatur et altera pars,'* said Emperor Justinian, and he was a just man."

"I don't know anything about your *'audiatur'* and *'altera,'* and I'm not acquainted with any Emperor Justinian . . . they must have lived before my time. But I want to tell you one thing, Don Pedro, and that isn't two. Judgment has already been passed on you and your fine companions. You can talk till you're black in the face, if you want to. But you can't talk away facts. And as an old friend who still likes you a little, I have this much to say to you: Give away all your gold to the poor, and become a barefoot monk as soon as you can. Go begging from door to door, from village to village, take care of the sick and the lepers, sleep with the swine and eat their fodder out of the trough. Perhaps God and His beloved hosts above the clouds will have some consideration for you and give you a little conscience. Doña Isabella and I will keep on praying for you all the time. I am sure that Doña Isabella's prayers are not without some influence in Heaven. So far as my own go . . ."

I was fed up with her righteous gabble. In one decisive rush I shoved her to one side and raced up the stairs. But I was unable to reach Doña Isabella. On the uppermost step Don Garcilaso suddenly faced me, a sword in his hand. The veins on his aged temples stood out like cords, and his heavy unfashionable white beard seemed to bristle with fury.

"Is this the hospitality of the house of Gómez?" I shouted. "I carry no weapons when I visit the homes of friends."

"The King of Tavanta-Suyu also carried no weapons. He trusted you cowards. What was his reward? He did not come to the hidalgos, to the Knights of Castile. No. He came to the offal of mankind, to the sweepings from the gutters of Seville, Cadiz and Trujillo. And of Cordova, worse still. He came to swineherds, beggars, pimps and thieves. Get out of my sight, coward."

The room turned red before my eyes, and I clamped my teeth. But he was an old man.

Then I bent my head and said, "Don Garcilaso de Gómez, you have taken my honor. Finish the rebuke; take my life!"

"Who is talking of honor?" said Don Garcilaso, more quietly. "It is not I who have taken your honor from you. You yourself cast it away. For you should have defended the life of the King of Tavanta-Suyu to the last drop of your blood."

"I did what I could," I answered, too evenly.

"If that were true you would never have walked into this house a living man," he said. "Never could the gold of betrayal have touched your hands."

When he spoke of gold I felt a terrible pang in my heart. I thought of my long years of poverty, of the years of hunger, of homesickness, of fever—all that the gold had cost me. The gold was mine.

"I took my just share, and no more," I murmured, more to myself than to him.

"Just share?" said Don Garcilaso. "Since when has a knight's just share of stolen gold been measured?"

"Don Carlos himself made the contract with Don Francisco," I said. "Don Carlos himself received the gold with his own hands."

"Don't talk to me about Don Carlos," said Don Garcilaso, his hands trembling. "How should he know the way this gold was won?"

"And our holy mother the Church herself took a share in the gold," I added. "Her representatives were there on the spot."

"What kind of representatives were they?" he retorted in a rage. "A couple of miserable Dominicans, not good enough to say Mass to fish in a pond."

"That may be," I replied, and got to my feet. "But I must see Doña Isabella myself. All this concerns her alone."

With an alacrity that I had not believed possible in such an old man, Don Garcilaso again drew his sword, prepared to thrust. My life at that moment hung on a thread.

That this thread was not cut through I have Doña Isabella to thank. Without warning she appeared in the upper hallway. She was more lovely than ever. Trembling and weak, I stared at her. She wore a long robe of black silk and a shawl of bright brocade over her shoulders. The black, rather slanting eyes flashed in her face. Her white cheeks were faintly hollowed, and this gave her an aspect of suffering. The moment she appeared Don Garcilaso lowered his sword. I bowed deeply.

"Don Pedro," she said, and in her voice was a metallic ring, that peculiar tone which had always fascinated me and even now sent a sweet shudder through my body, "I should be most deeply grateful if you spared my father a deathblow."

I looked at her. She made no effort to conceal her profound contempt. On her breast hung a thin silver chain, my parting gift to her. The sight of this chain emboldened me to say, "I shall leave this house forever, if Doña Isabella commands. But I cannot believe that one judges and casts out a friend merely on hearsay because of a deed that he has had no chance to explain."

"I waive all excuses," she said arrogantly. "Answer me one question: Is a part of the gold really in your possession?"

"Yes," I replied, "it is. That is true." I rummaged in the heavy pouch at my belt, drew forth the golden ear of corn, and held it up. The slanting sunlight coming through a small window struck the Indian smith's little ornament. The gold shone, and the glitter seemed to come from within the gold itself.

"What's that?" said Doña Isabella. I watched her closely, and saw on her face an expression of pleasure, curiosity and yet disgust. Yes, in her eyes there was a faint trace of greed, a flicker of that same insatiate hunger I had seen flame so often in the eyes of my crude comrades-in-arms.

"That is the young corn, Doña Isabella," I replied and pointed at the shining symbol. "They see it as the greatest gift of the sun to his children, mankind. Because of that they put an image of the corn in their temples, one made of gold. . . ."

"Enough," intervened Don Garcilaso ominously. "You have heard, my child, that Don Pedro admits his wealth stems from betrayal."

"I had no part at all in the betrayal," I retorted.

"But you don't reject your share in the booty?" cried Doña Isabella.

"In the booty?" I shot back. "Where do the gold and possessions of the greatest Spanish families come from? Is it not all the spoils of war, land and treasure taken from the Moors . . . or the Jews? Did not our holy mother the Church take Allah's mosques and dedicate them to the Holy Trinity? Did not the house of Gómez take the houses, lands, olive gardens, fishponds and fields of a man called Abdur el Kadr? Why should I, a conquistador with a charter given me by the Crown of Castile, refuse to take the gold doled out to me according to the measure of my leader, the Governor of New Castile?"

Doña Isabella's face grew dark. She belongs to that breed of women not uncommonly found in our country whose countenance in pain, sorrow or anger grows more beautiful. The unfathomable dark, the mystery ordinarily hidden in modesty then seems freely to command the face. When she began to speak the metallic ring in her voice sharpened.

"Don Pedro," she said, "when we love a man, we do not love him because he is like others, but because we feel that he stands for something different and better. We feel that his being is his own, no one else's. And this being in some strange way completes our own."

Doña Isabella halted, reddened and lamely continued, "I know that in the general opinion you have a certain right to your gold and your treasure and the golden ear of corn. I know, too, that you have suffered a great deal to get these riches. Storms, shipwreck on the sea, for aught I know, hunger and thirst, fever and homesickness. If it were anyone else I should face him without criticism and say, Poor fellow! To get this gold he has endured everything, risked his life perhaps a hundred times. But what good will all this gold do him, when the Lord calls him, the Lord who says, There, where your treasure is, must your heart be also? . . ."

"Doña Isabella," I said gently, "don't ever forget what it was like for me as a child. Many a time Sancho and I didn't have even a crust of bread. Our clothes were so shabby they were really made of nothing but rags and patches sewn together."

"And yet," flung back Doña Isabella, her eyes fiery, no longer lost in the distance, "that poor boy was a thousand times better than the rich man, the worthy, who stands before me now. Can you have forgotten Master Agrippa so completely? Don't you remember coming to me one day and telling me how he sat in his room in the cold, shivering over his Latin manuscripts? How he smiled at your remonstrances when you found his cupboard empty and his mantle torn? He opened the Vulgate, which always lay on his desk, opened it and read, Be not solicitous for your life, what you shall eat, nor for your body, what you shall put on. Is not the life more than the meat, and the body more than the raiment? . . . Do not be afraid——! But you, Don Pedro, you have been afraid! Your fear was so profound that you looked death in the face a thousand times to get gold in your hands. Yes, your fear was even greater than that. It grew into monstrous proportions. You helped to kill a man who placed his trust in you."

"No," I cried. "You are wrong, Doña Isabella. I did not do it. . . ."

"You talk as casuistically as a jurist of the Crown," she retorted, harsh with contempt. "I'm not contending that you strangled him with your own hands, that you held the cord yourself. And yet you are more to blame than the torturer. He did only what you and your kind ordered him to do. But you knew what you were doing when you smirched the arms of Castile with this unspeakable shame. . . ."

"You forget I was a young man, without any experience in the affairs of state and of war. . . ."

"You knew what was right and what was wrong. It is possible that your friends didn't know, coarsened as they were by endless wars and expeditions. You and the servants of the Church, you are the guilty ones."

I felt all was lost. The old Don, his sword hanging athwart his legs, watched me thoughtfully. I imagined that in his gaze there was hidden a certain scornful pity. That nettled me beyond reason. Too long had I been accustomed to play the unfettered master over thousands, a being to whom the mob all but fell on their knees in prayer. A wave of bitterness engulfed me, took away the breath in my throat. I said nothing, in silence watched with mazed intensity the motes of dust dancing like a silver shower in the sunlight that streamed through the little window. To me they seemed like so many worlds that rise and sink and impinge crazily upon each other. Clearly I sensed that my life had lost all meaning, that before me yawned a frightful emptiness. In that moment, I truly believe, I doubted reality, God himself. In anguish I raised my eyes. I saw that she was observing me with breathless anxiety, as if she awaited a decision of the utmost finality. Her proudly chiseled mouth was slightly parted.

"No," I said, "no, that can never be." I was listening to my own alien words. Yes, I hearkened with a certain curiosity to what I myself had to say. "I did everything, everything possible. But the gold is mine. It belongs to me as does my heart, my soul. I needn't justify myself. Neither before youths nor old women, before girls nor old men. It is mine."

"Then keep your gold," she said, "and lose your life."

"And I shall keep my life, too," I retorted, in triumph. "I shall go to the Court of Don Carlos, whether I have to travel as far as Brussels or Palermo. I shall remind Don Carlos that it is we, our kind, who have conquered the world, who have poured teeming cities into his lap. For him we subdued the whole round earth. The sun never sets in his kingdom, thanks to us. And now the brave ones, the stay-at-homes, begin to whine, and say we did not do right. . . ."

Her head bent low, she turned away and left us. I felt an intolerable remorse. Fumbling in the pouch at my belt I dropped out of sight the golden ear of corn, which all the time I had been holding in my hand.

"Go," said Don Garcilaso, courteously. "I beg you, leave."

I turned my back and slowly walked down the stairs. Down below Doña Catarina cowered against the pillars and sobbed. I passed her by, and went out of the house.

24

VOICES OF THE NIGHT

AS I walked away through the streets the white walls of the houses faced me, alien and hostile. It was spring, and the alleys of the city were alive with people. Water venders with their donkeys pressed by me, crying their wares aloud. Men and women of the servant class hastened along, busy on their errands. The throng of buyers and sellers among the tent-stalls haggled noisily. How senseless all this seemed, a mad ado about nothing at all.

I betook myself to an inn, and for a long time sat on the hard bench of the narrow room and stared at the whitewashed wall. Whenever I tried to compose the future it was always gold that filled my thoughts. Finally I pulled myself together, ordered some writing paper, quill and ink, and busied myself with working out the plan of a house and the expenses of its household. Thus I became as busy as the teeming crowd in the streets, and when I lifted my eyes from the paper I saw only too clearly that all my zeal was pointless, a whirligig in empty space.

On the third day I threw my quill into the corner, and bought a house. I was not very happy in that house. I had envisioned my future in Spain as something quite different indeed. And yet I had almost everything. I was swathed about with the loyalty of Sancho and the clumsy kindness of Teresa. Often friends from across the sea sought me out, and together we talked and planned the hours away. But the nights, the summer nights when the moon rose over the Sierras and the fountains in the courtyard would begin to murmur to each other. Such nights were not good. The void that they brought stood between me and my activities of waking day. It was like deep water alive with swimming things. And I would have the feeling that people knew just how it was with me, and said nothing out of kindness, politeness or shame. Many a time my good Sancho looked after me sadly. I could feel his glance on my back.

Often I would wake up in the night, and could not get to sleep again. Then I would sit by the window, and look through the iron latticework out over the courtyard. The walls of the house shone white in the light of the moon, snow-white like the peaks of the Cordilleras, and threw deep black shadows on the tiles, and it was dark in the corners, and so quiet in the night. Clearly I would hear the soft creakings in the house timbers, and sometimes I imagined Sancho was snoring down below.

Outside the fountains splashed. They were talking and whispering to each other these enchanted summer nights, and now and then their voices rose, as if they had something especially important to tell. So, too, my heart murmured to itself. I often felt as if this heart of mine did not belong to me, Don Pedro de Cordova; as if I, a trespasser, were merely overhearing its soft, endless discourse like a trembling thief at the keyhole of a closed door.

There was good reason for my wakeful nights. It was not the light of the moon which, streaming through the lattice of my window, made silver arabesques on my bedcover. It was not the voice of the fountain which softly drummed at my temples like the seething rise and fall of my pulse. It had nothing to do with this world. It came from afar, from so wonderfully far away, and yet was closer to me than I am myself. It stood at the end of the world and called my name, Pedro, Pedro. Yes, Pedro, it called, gently, urgently, fraught with warning yet kindly, fraught with sorrow. And it called to me as if from a world to which ours is but the rude shell. This voice could not be missed, soft though it was. Because it was the voice of a spirit. . . . I know that it must have been the voice of a benign spirit. In spite of this it filled me with anxiety, if not with fear. And it was really not the voice itself which troubled me. I know it is hard to describe, and I write down this admission really for my own benefit and none other.

It is ridiculous, but I really believe that men were different once. Since the great Admiral sailed westward and discovered Hispaniola something new has come into the world. I often think that he must have sailed over the end of the world in his caravel *Santa Maria,* as if he had splintered to bits with the sharp bow of his vessel the crystal ball of Heaven that had so long protected us. I, myself, was another person before that land rose up on the blue horizon firm above the restless hillocks of the sea. The old house is destroyed, and it will be a long time before a new one is built.

During these sleepless nights there was no doubt in my mind where my dreams of knighthood and greatness had led me. I saw that I was a man who could not keep his vow, that I had been a robber and, what is worse, a murderer. Even though my own hands had not applied the strangler's noose, I had allowed it to happen. At the critical moment I had lacked the spirit to step forward and intercede for the Inca. In vain I sought to find excuses, to reason away my cowardice. I tried to console myself by building up beyond fact my act of assigning a defender to the Inca for the trial. But that was not enough, and I knew it, and I must surely have known it at the time. It was just so much lip service to my notions of honor. My reasonableness and coldness throughout the whole trial and execution shocked me as I looked back. I was ashamed; my self-esteem was nothing at all. I saw with acid clearness that tolerance and fearful weighing of both sides of the case can cause as much misery to mankind as active evil. I was a coward; I had turned away. And for this I loathed myself beyond telling.

There is nothing more despicable than spiritual cowardice. These days I so very often thought of Saint Peter, how boldly enough he had lopped off the ear of the soldier Malchus, but how later, in the house of the high priest, when recognized by the maid of Galilee, he had renounced his origins, himself and his God, whereat the soldier laughed to himself, warming his cold hands at the fire. And so I, too. I had crossed the sea bravely enough; I had traversed difficult mountains, and stood up to my adversaries in battle. But in fearful, cowardly fashion, in great fear of appearing ridiculous and different from my fellows, I had betrayed my conscience and had countenanced the murder of a man who trusted me, who had treated me with kindness and love.

For hours I would sit at the latticed window, watching the moon shine on the city roofs, whispering to myself. I could never ultimately have altered his fate, I kept telling myself; the very stars themselves had decreed his end. But on the other hand Saint Peter could not have prevented the crucifixion of our Lord, and yet after this had happened he put his hands to his face and cried bitterly, the Gospel tells us. He was unable to console himself with the idea that all was foreordained. No more was I.

Night after night I wandered through my rooms, always repeating the same sentence to myself: Something must happen soon. But nothing did happen. Nothing at all. And I knew in my heart that nothing could happen until I myself instituted it. I pictured to myself what I should do. But everything that I conceived as retribution had the same flaw—it involved making a laughing stock of myself. If, for instance, I should give away all my gold to the poor and to the hospitals, even if I should take the vows and become a mendicant monk making a pilgrimage to Jerusalem, as Don Iñigo de Loyola had done, on the surface the people would praise me and say how wonderful a man he is. But underneath their breath they would whisper, "What a fool! He does not know how to take care of himself. He is witless."

Or, worse still, they would interpret my actions as a sign of a bad conscience, that is, see through my scheming. Which would be beyond endurance—to be seen through by the mob. I might present myself before the Council of the Indies, or petition for audience with the King, in order to denounce the plundering and murdering of the Inca. But I saw that was pointless, for it was plain that both the Council and the King were interested in nothing beyond pressing more metal from the new-found lands, and that they had little or no interest in the welfare of their myriad new subjects.

Beyond that, such a denunciation would be a betrayal of the Captain-General and all my comrades, not excepting anyone. No doubt the Council would answer me somewhat like this, "Yes, we know that everything wasn't rosy and delightful in the Indies. We know the course of conquest without being told. But in any case this huge territory has just come into our hands. It is too early to pass opinion on what we shall make out of it. Perhaps centuries will pass before we can bestow an ordered regime on these Indians. Until that happens you must expect a little brusqueness, my son. Adventure is natural in a colonial situation. It is deplorable, perhaps, but justified."

And then among themselves the same old men would say, "Oh yes, first you make sure of your wealth and then you set up a boresome hue and cry about your own friends' rudeness. And they the very friends who made it possible for you to become the richest man in Cordova!"

No matter which way I turned, I was caught on the horns of a dilemma. I was unable to move without injuring someone or other, and at the same time I was much too miserable to sit quiet and let bygones be bygones. Like everyone in such circumstances I did the worst possible thing, that is, I did nothing at all. I lacked the impetus, the ordinary courage, to forget my self-conceived importance and plunge into spiritual battle.

Really I never gave a thought to the Indies and the Indians for their own sake. I considered this beautiful land and all the people native to it only so far as they affected my small self, my pride, my knighthood and my noble origins. And my conscience, of course! I was not interested in the Indians' suffering, in their senseless decimation. That was not what my melancholy hinged on, but on Pedro de Cordova, who in the councils of the Pizarros and the Almagros had kept his mouth clamped shut, risking not so much as a hair of his head. I was not interested in saving the Indians, but myself.

However, today I can say that this frustration was the beginning of positive action, that is, my alliance with the best and greatest man I have ever met. Today this man is reckoned almost with the Apostles, and at the same time hated and scorned so deeply that his life is endangered.

For while I was writing in indecision a profound change overtook Spain, a change which directly affected the newly conquered lands. Bent over my sorrows I heard little about what was going on, but my cool reception in Seville was one clear indication of the coming storm. I could not understand why I was not welcomed by Don Carlos, and I was hurt. I did not so much as become the recipient of a testimonial. All that came was a letter from Don Guilelmo van Male, the trusted chamberlain of the King, informing me that His Majesty had received the Indian works from Tavanta-Suyu sent him in my name, that the King thanked me for them, and that in recognition of my knowledge of the Southern Ocean and the islands, and on account of services rendered to the Crown on the island of Puná and the mainland, by royal command I had been made Lord Admiral of the Southern Ocean. Somewhat later I received the official scroll going with this title, and I hastened to send back my thanks.

After that I heard no more from the Court. My name appeared to be completely forgotten. All that I got in the way of honors was an empty title. Of course I had always heard that the House of Hapsburg was rather chary with dispensing words of gratitude.

But the worst blow, the one I dislike even to write about, was that I had been so thoroughly repudiated by Doña Isabella. At first I could not believe it. I assured myself that during my long absence she had half forgotten me, that she was in love with another man, no doubt one of Don Carlos' courtiers. Indulging this reasoning I would laugh sarcastically to myself over the fickleness of womankind. Sometimes I declaimed lengthy diatribes. On the other hand, when I remembered how she had talked to me as we were parting, how as children we had vowed always to love each other, I was equally convinced that my fancy was running away with me. It was merely one more attempt to avoid the guilt hounding my every hour.

In this period there came to me a most curious dream which showed me clearly how much I was at odds with the world.

One night I dreamed I was on Montserrat. I was standing in a great hall, waiting, my heart anxious. Noiselessly the tall doors opened, and in walked a throng of knights. They wore long white mantles, white helmets, through which their eyes showed darkly. Four of them carried a bier on their shoulders. On it was a monstrance. This bier was like Atahualpa's litter, and was decorated with bright feathers and gold. I wondered how such an object had ever found its way to Catalonia. Under the silver filigree of the monstrance there was a grail. I looked at the vessel and saw that it was beginning to glow like some precious jewel deep in the mountainside. The glow did not last long, but it was so intense that it paled the lamps in the room, as stars pale when the sun rises. The light was so intolerably strong that my eyes could not bear to look at it, and I had to raise my cloak to cover my eyes. The white knights whispered among themselves, and I saw they were discussing me. Then I saw what they were talking about. My heart had begun to bleed. There was a red spot on my doublet.

"He is the murderer," said the knights. Avoiding their eyes I stole from the room. They appeared not to notice my departure. I saw they did this out of consideration for my shame.

"He is a coward," I heard them say.

I stood alone in the night on the high mountain. Damp mists were all around me. Out of the depths rose a frightful clanging and clamor. There were human voices, like the voices that had moaned at the death of Atahualpa.

In the dream I struggled tremendously to throw off the fetters of sleep. I tried to move my legs, my body, but I was like stone. Finally I did manage to sit up, and then I was awake. Trembling, sick, and running sweat, I got up from bed and staggered over to the window. The morn was graying, just as in the dream. It was a fresh, sweet morning. The wind was tossing the column of water from the fountain to one side, so that it wet the tiles.

Forehead in hand I thought a long time about the depths of the human soul, where ghosts live, where demons rise up in sleep and flutter like bats through our lives. I saw, trying to calm myself, that the soul of man also reaches up to the very throne of God, beyond the vault of heaven. I remembered that after all I had seen the Holy Grail. At the window I knelt down, and prayed long and fervently.

And it was while I was at prayer that I at last realized why my knighthood had fallen to shards in the stormy reality of the Pizarros. I realized, with the power of revelation, that I had always taken pride and pleasure in the superficialities of knighthood, in good swords and armor, in spirited horses, brave companions and loyal servants, in adventure and trials of all sort. The true kernel and meaning of knighthood I learned for the first time in that morning prayer. This was the Holy Grail and the Bleeding Heart. The dream revealed this to me.

It was at this time I got to know Manuel in the market place. A little brown-haired, brown-skinned boy, terribly dirty, tugged at my clothes. I looked down at him, and saw his torn shirt, his naked legs and feet filmed over with white dust. "I don't know you," I said, preoccupied, and reached without thinking to give him a coin.

He stared at the maravedi, spat on it, and thrust it out of sight. Without a trace of discomposure he said, "You don't know me, but I know you, and don't think I'm just after your maravedi."

Miserable little ingrate, I thought, but then it occurred to me that once I was just such a ragged waif.

"Yes," he went on, and gracefully drew himself into a swagger with his right foot moved forward, the while eyeing me with sharp urchin's eyes. "You're Don Pedro de Cordova, the Lord Admiral of the South Sea. I'm an orphan, and people call me Manuel. But some day I'm going to India and who knows, perhaps I shall discover for myself a greater kingdom than you did."

"God grant you luck," I said, with disproportionate irony. The word orphan rang in my ears. On the spur of the moment, I cannot say why, I made a decision to take him into my service. "Do you know where I live?" I asked him.

"Who is there that doesn't know?" he replied boldly. "The whole city moves around your white house."

"Very well, then," I said smiling. "Go ahead of me, as becomes a page."

Manuel let out a cry, then stared at me in suspicion. "You're not joking, are you, Don Pedro?" he inquired.

"I never joke," I told him.

As if shot from an arquebus Manuel ran five steps ahead. With his head high he walked before me. Later I saw him cowering in the doorway of my house, gnawing on a melon rind. In the evening I heard his piercing screams, the sound of splashing water and the scrubbing sound of a brush. Then I knew that Teresa was polishing the future viceroy for the first step in his career. Poor Manuel, it did not take you long to learn that titles, honors, riches are bought with infinite vexation!

This orphan child whom I took into my house was close to me. I got into the habit of talking to him, and let him sleep nights at my door in order to have his company. It was at this period that I stood on the verge of the most uncomfortable, the most humiliating and yet the most inevitable acquaintance life can bring us—acquaintance with myself. Most men very carefully avoid such a harsh experience. Rather do they throw themselves into adventures, into affairs, concupiscence and social intercourse. They even prefer war and mortal danger rather than to face themselves.

But how contemptible is the man who knows everything, yet who does not know himself, who has something to say about everything—the Church, politics, his fellow men—and yet wastes not a thought on the state of his own soul. In the world such people are called sound men, since most of them are ever restlessly active. All their business, their force, their prying into the affairs of others, their rushing over the face of the earth are really nothing but blasphemy, a sure sign of their consuming fear.

Today I consider it one of the luckiest turns of my life that so young I plunged into loneliness. But at the time I was ill pleased with my desert, my land beyond the Jordan. It was peopled with ghosts great and small, with evil memories, fearsome expectations, with melancholy and bad dreams. The dead were lively in this loneliness, as if they were most at home with me, my dead.

There was the Inca Atahualpa, standing on the roof, pointing up at the comet. There was Laanta, sitting as she had so many times on the edge of my bed, only now her face had become cold to me. She reproved me, even though she said not a word out loud, merely contemplating me in silence. The Spanish soldier was there, the one I had killed, arm in arm with the headless Indian. Abu Amru, the tortured one, lifted himself up from his deathbed in the Palace of the Inquisition and looked at me through heavy, suffering lids. Rodrigo the devil walked soundlessly through my room, and frightened me more than he had when I was a boy, for now there was not a trace of irony in his features. Often the Queen, Doña Juana, would sit among the dream figures, nodding to herself in her dark room under the guttering candles, mumbling about her lost paradise. And in the background was a great crowd of anonymous ones, as after the execution of Atahualpa, weeping and groaning. In my nightmares I had trouble telling whether they were Indians or Spaniards. Even in sleep in time I saw that it made no difference, that it was a chorus of the damned, of harried souls. Persistently they shadowed me in sleep and troubled my rest.

When I awoke I would open the door and look into the corridor for Manuel. He would be asleep, his mouth half open, his brown legs hugged up to his breast almost like a babe unborn, gestating anew in the womb of the great mother night. Neither demons nor dead bothered him. I envied him. I saw the innocent sleep of childhood in his face; I saw how it obliterated all the small thoughts and cares of the boy, like a soft coverlet shutting out the cold. Sometimes I would disturb him with the candlelight I held in my hand. Then he would turn on the other side, his open hand sprawled carelessly on the floor. He would sigh with deep satisfaction and sleep on, deeply, without a tremor. This spectacle was no consolation to me. I observed that there still was such a thing as sleep. And I hoped only that I too would enjoy the most perfect anodyne before daylight grayed the sky.

In the end matters became so bad that I was afraid to go to sleep. I know this sounds ridiculous and overdrawn. There I sat, a conquistador, a Lord Admiral, a soldier, dead-tired before the trembling candles' flame, and yet afraid to go to sleep, like a little child. Often I would mutter to myself over and over, like the village idiot, always the same words "conquest" and "conquistador." Once I had thought that these words summed up all life's meaning. Now they were leaden on my tongue, loathsome. Then I would recall the Arab saying I had heard so many years ago, *"Lha ghilab ilah Allah,"* that is, "No one conquers but God."

It was always so terribly still in the room. I got into the habit of thumbing through my Vulgate. Sometimes I would read. In time the secret sense of the priceless verses grew clear to me. They were illumined, took on a more than earthly brilliance and aptitude. I remembered that my Master had once said to me something about the second sense of the word of God, which remains closed to us so long as we remain in self.

This sense came to have a strangely intimate connection with me and my destiny. The Book came to life, as if I were forming the words painfully for the first time, as if the Book were speaking directly to me in exalted tones that rang like bells on a bright morning. All that I read seemed to admonish, to threaten me, even when the verses were full of splendor. "And God saw the light, that it was good: and He divided the light from the darkness." How often have I read this sentence! How obvious, how irrevocable, was the first day of Creation! ". . . and the evening and the morning were the first day." The beginning of the world, of order, of harmony, of the mighty torrent of time and history!

But now I saw things differently. Like the cut of a sword the word divided light from darkness. Like enormous storm clouds the darkness balled itself together in the depths, according to command. Keen-rayed the light came forth and spread out into an infinite, luminous blue. That was not awesome. But it was awesome that I should be standing between light and darkness. I was drawn down to the depths, and lifted up to the heights. And I could not decide. I was disrupting the ordained harmony, the order of day, encouraging the return of chaos, the universe of mists, of twilight, of indecision neither light nor dark, neither good nor evil, indifferent, godless, wandering.

"And to the angel of the church of the Laodicea write: I know thy words, that thou art neither cold nor hot. I would thou wert either cold or hot.

"So then because thou art lukewarm, and neither cold nor hot, I will begin to vomit thee out of my mouth!"

These words horrified me. My forehead was damp with sweat; my hands trembled helplessly. The angry voice of the seer of Patmos was in my room. The words were inhuman, fanatic, spoken by another Father Vicente de Valverde. There can be no half measures in the face of God. Even evil is nearer and more beloved of Him than appeasement.

"Because thou sayest: I am rich, and made wealthy, and have need of nothing; and knowest not, that thou art wretched, and miserable, and poor, and blind and naked. I counsel thee to buy of me gold tried in the fire and purified. . . ."

What did that mean? Where is this gold? Where is it to be found?

I wracked my tormented brain. And in the end I knew what the gold was, but did not want it. I feared God and His seers, patriarchs, prophets and warriors. I feared His words and His revelations, the face of His holy ones, just as fool's gold fears the Lydian stone knowing that its false glitter will have to give way before such hardness. I banged shut the Bible, snapped to the copper clasps, and put the volume in the farthest corner of my chest, after which I locked the lid fast. I treated the Book as if it were gunpowder ready to blow my house, my possessions and me with them off the face of the earth.

But emotion seethed within even after the Book had sunk from sight. I felt like a murderer who has hidden his victim's clothes or some damning piece of evidence. I eyed the chest with mistrust. It was old and made of oak. The bolt was of heavy, dark iron, and the lock weighed many pounds. Then I became aware of the folly of the whole proceeding. I sat at the table, buried my head in my hands, and groaned, "Holy Virgin Mary, I must be losing my senses!"

I made up my mind to find some kind of diversion. Since I could not sleep I would read something gay, something worldly and bright. I opened up the *Decameron* of Giovanni Boccaccio. He seemed to be just the right one to release me from my doubts and self-inflicted tortures.

I read.

"Here begins the book called *Decameron,* dedicated to Prince Galeotto, containing within it a hundred tales told in ten days by seven young ladies and three young men.

"PROEMIUM

"It is a friendly thing to have compassion for the suffering. . . ."

"There it is again," I mumbled, disappointed. But I read on, for the morning was far away. I read and read but the words were oddly incoherent. They formed neither ideas nor images. Black letters, signs without sense. It was very still. I heard the worms ticking in the ancient chest. One by one the candles began to flicker out. I snuffed them all with a weary hand.

The room changed. Table and chairs were old-fashioned, very heavily constructed. The air was heavy, thick, lying heavily on my breast. The door opened noiselessly and a man walked in. I stared at him, for he was completely hooded. Only his eyes could be seen gleaming out through narrow slits cut into his white cowl. He stood before me, looking at me inquisitively. There was a certain contempt in his manner, and yet the eyes told me he was ready to flee.

"Who are you?" I asked wearily.

"I am the doctor," he said, and from the folds of his white garments he drew out fine knives, lancets and forceps.

"But I am not sick," I told him.

"That is what they all say," he said, and made a brusque gesture with his white-gloved hand. "But I don't trouble my head about that. I let blood; I purge, cut and burn. That is my medium. That is my pleasure."

"What is the matter with me, then?" I inquired.

"That is good, indeed!" he laughed, and his eyes gleamed brightly. "He talks just as if he didn't know himself! Haven't you read that the pest is in Florence? The great, black woman with the whip in her hand? She is come from Asia, on the Venetians' ships. She has crept along the trade routes, with the wagons, the drivers, to Bergamo, Padua, Ferrara and Pisa. And now she has arrived in Florence.

"The pest came on your caravels, it came in with your gold, your treasures and slaves. O you crusaders, you spreaders of the Gospel! You murderers, torturers, thieves and rapists! You fine fellows! You knights of cowardice, you destroyers of innocence, you vipers in paradise! How you lord it over women and sucklings! Didn't you kill Laanta, an Indian girl? Didn't you strangle Atahualpa?"

"No, I did not!" I shouted. "Never! I wouldn't do that."

"No, you didn't, come to think of it. You didn't have the bowels for a man's job, my son. Anyway, Lord Admirals don't get mixed up in such nasty affairs," he said. "You were neither hot, nor were you cold. Lukewarm, that's you. He will spit you out of his mouth, the Old Man. You don't know this Old Man, I suspect. He's a very rigorous hidalgo, you can count on that. He likes to see how far the blade will bend. He hasn't much use for the timid. It's the same way with the weak and sickly ones. He's a great man, is the Old Man, harder to get to see than your Duke of Béjar. It's a different matter with me, of course. I'm just an ordinary fellow. But He sits up there with His seraphim and cherubim and holds court. I have to do all the dirty work. For example, I have to deal with you and your kind. I have to play the doctor with you, and get you up on your feet and waste my time with a hundred and one nasty jobs. Of course, one thing is true—I earn plenty of good yellow gold doing it."

"You're not a doctor," I said. "You're the Devil."

"Nonsense," he said nasally. "Not at all, not at all. You foul little lumps of people think that the whole machinery of Hell grinds away for your personal benefit. What an idea! Newly kindled fires, all the monster frying pans newly scoured, the tongs polished and sharpened. Just for you! If I were the Devil, which God forbid, I wouldn't be here moralizing with you, my child. I'd take you by the back of your noble neck and hustle you off without further ado to where you belong. But as I say I'm only a trifle in the scheme of things. My income is relatively small. I get myself a stipend by wasting an hour gossiping with my patients. Then I set to work picking open their boils with my lancets. . . ."

"I don't believe it," I groaned. "The learned men say that the Devil is a logician and is always moralizing. . . ."

"That's a bore," said the man behind his cowl. "There's nothing I hate more than explaining myself to other people. I'm of far too little consequence for that, I tell you. Now, if for example I were Asmodeus, or Moloch, Belial, Dagon or Thammuz, then it would be worth the trouble to go on talking about myself."

"You are dissembling," I said. "You are the Devil. I know you no matter what you have on."

"I am the doctor," the man said. "I can't heal you, any more than your own doctors can, but at least I'll uncap these sores so that we can see what's under the damp crust. I'll lay them open so that the flames can strike home and get at the hidden core. For I always come to the judges who condemn the innocent and let the guilty walk away free. I come to the priests who have revenge and vanity in their hearts even as they are mouthing words about God. I come to hot young girls who open their legs to ease the itch between them. I come to merchants who give false measure, to the landowner who misuses his peasants, to superstitious monks, to the self-righteous haunter of Masses, to the scribes who write lies, to apothecaries who mix poisons, to tyrannical princes, to bold experimenters with the supernatural, the metaphysical. The list is endless, my friend, for the world, the times themselves, are sick, and are nearly dissolved in pus. The sweat drips down the collar of my shirt, so fast do I hasten from one to the other. And you! You call me a devil. Is that polite?" He pretended to sob bitterly into the arm of his robe.

"You said yourself that you can't heal," I said irritably.

"I've been denied that privilege by the Old One," the spirit said. "It isn't my fault. Everything that is good, healthy, strong, constructive, he keeps to himself. It's a shame. All that I got was a little knife. He's a very jealous Old Man, take my word. But enough of talking. Time flies. Now, don't be afraid. It's very painful, and it doesn't heal very quickly. But it has to be done."

With that he took out a long fine lancet so swiftly my eye could scarcely follow him. Before I could stop him he pulled open my shirt and buried the lancet in my breast, just over my heart. I groaned in pain. The cut was deep. My heart bled.

I snatched the book on the table and hurled it into his face. It went right through him and hit the wall, doing him not the slightest harm. "Is that what you do to me, you foul dog?" he said to me.

"Holy Virgin Mary," I shouted, "protect me!" I touched the little silver cross and held it up to him. Then he grew larger before my eyes and filled the room from floor to ceiling. But at the same time his lineaments grew vaguer, and the lines of his cowl vanished.

"I'll see you again," he said ironically, his voice coming out of vagueness. He departed, laughing, and the laughter rang powerful and hollow as if heard from out of a great well.

I was alone, petrified with horror, at my table. One candle that I had failed to snuff burned just as it had before, so that the whole occurrence could not have taken more than a few seconds. Perhaps not even so much as a second, or even a fraction of a second, had passed. Perhaps no time at all since I had stopped reading. I was beyond telling. I held the little silver cross tightly pressed between my fingers. I slipped from the chair to my knees, pressed my head against the table edge, and cried heavily, bitterly, like a child.

When I awoke the next morning the sun was already high in the sky and Sancho had come into the room. He told me that a student was in the vestibule, bringing with him an important message for me.

I was completely exhausted and pale as wax, but I nodded assent to Sancho's query whether he should usher the man in. He proved to be a thin young fellow in seedy black clothes. He stumbled toward me awkwardly over the heavy carpet, chafed together his bony hands, and said deferentially, "I have a letter for Your Excellency, which my Master told me I must deliver in person. Forgive my disturbing you, Your Excellency."

I let out a cry of pleasure, for at once I knew whence the letter came. I tore it from his hand, and broke the seal. I was not mistaken. It was from him.

"Salve, my friend," it began, "my old pupil.

"Come as soon as possible to the good city of Valladolid. Here you will find me at the court of Don Felipe, the Infante. Hasten on the wings of Mercurius. For it is a matter of millions of lives, perhaps the future of the world. Therefore make haste.

"Give my messenger something to eat. He is young, and he has a tremendous appetite, like all students. The rest I will tell you privately. I embrace you.

"Thus writes Master Agrippa of Nettesheim, by far the greatest philosopher of this ailing epoch, to Don Pedro de Cordova, the Lord Admiral and the noble Castilian."

"The horses, Sancho!" I shouted. "My clothes! Tell Manuel to get ready. Tell Teresa to get us something to eat before we leave. Hurry, hurry!"

My eyes came back to the student, who was cautiously rubbing his hands, exactly as when he entered the room. "Give the man a cold chicken, some white bread, some fruit, some sweets. Give him anything he wants. Give him a flagon of wine, Malaga wine."

"What! A whole flagon!" said Sancho. "Why, he'll get drunk. I thought perhaps we could get him to do a little doctoring for the peasants. He'll never be able . . ."

"A thousand thanks," the student broke in hastily. "When my imagination is warmed up with the wine I can put on as pretty a plaster as you ever saw. I'm better than old Galen himself after a little Malaga."

I had to laugh at this. It was good to laugh.

25

LAS CASAS

AFTER a quick and uneventful journey I arrived at Valladolid with my page Manuel. I found Master Agrippa in one of the numerous guesthouses connected with the palace. His hair was snow-white, his face deeply furrowed, and he was bent over a staff. But in his eyes there burned the familiar proud fire. I imagined that he was even livelier and more active than he had ever been when he devoted all his time to the study of alchemy.

Overwhelmed with emotion I rushed up to him, took his hand and kissed it. I thought I could taste the salty chemicals on the back of the old hand. I felt: Now I am home again, now things are right once more. There was the same familiar feeling of awe, of respect. I was so moved I could scarcely speak, and had to move my lips vainly, for no words came out.

"Come now," said Master Agrippa roughly, pulling his hand away. "Enough of this sentimental nonsense." He put his hand on my shoulder. It felt light and thin. He looked into my eyes and said, "You were always my favorite student, even if you did speak the worst Latin that ever crossed man's lips. Yes, you are the same. I can see. You're still hunting the *lapis philosophorum*. Look at the folds under your eyes, for a young man, and the hollow cheeks! That must mean sleepless nights. I can tell. You don't look like a rich man, God be praised for that. As long as there isn't any complacency. Or pride in money. Never forget where you came from. What was sacred in youth should be sacred in manhood. Anyone who laughs about the dreams of childhood is laughing at his own corruption. I thought I could picture how you would be, without even setting eyes on you. I knew what you'd be like even long ago when you couldn't read or write, when you used to ask me foolish questions about the Scripture, about the sympathy of things! Do you remember all that?"

"My Master, my father," I said, "I remember it all as if it were yesterday. And right at this moment, at this good moment when I see you again, I feel I have been seeking the element of elements all the time I have been away. On that account I went over the sea. On that account there has been a murder, and neglect and sin and sleepless nights. Where is this element of elements? Tell me, where is it? I must know."

"The time has come for you to discover this element. The times are ripe for it to be found again. A greater master than I has come. I do not like to admit it, for where on this earth would one expect to find a greater one than me? But he really is my superior. You shall be his colleague, this magician of magicians."

"Who is he?" I asked, amazed. "Who knows more than you do!"

"It is not a matter of alchemy," Agrippa retorted sharply. He made a rude gesture with his hand, as if he were slamming shut the furnace door, sweeping into fragments the delicate glass retorts, knocking aside the thick books. "I have traveled the stormy sea of ideas longer than you ever tossed on the Southern Ocean. I've sat at my desk longer than any Pizarro ever bestrode a horse. I have investigated everything—the growth of metals, the path of the stars, the mysteries of hermetic books, the poisonous plants, the second sense of revelation. In short, everything. I can measure myself against the old masters, and force them to the wall. I am like Momus, who let no one get off without mockery; I am like Hercules, who persecuted monsters; like Pluto, the king of the underworld, I rage against shadows and dark places. I laugh at everything like Democritus. Like Heraclitus everything fills me with sadness. Knowing nothing like Pyrrho, omniscient like Aristotle, scorning all like Socrates. All that am I, my son."

He spread out his broad, aging hands, and began to declaim:

"Scorned and prized,
Knowing and ignorant,
Laughing and weeping,
Persecuted and mocking—
It is I, Agrippa,
A philosopher, a demon,
A hero, a god,
The microcosmos."

He was seemingly beside himself, and momentarily the horrible thought struck me that he was out of his mind with old age. He interpreted my expression, and then impatiently nodded at me to sit down.

"My wandering in error has come to an end," he said, no longer on fire with passion. "I investigated everything and forgot to investigate myself. You conquered, and forgot yourself. We are alike, the father and the son. I am knowledge; you are the deed. What more can knowledge do than raise the deed out of the cradle and shape it for the future? There are two tasks in this world, my son. One of these tasks comes from ourselves. This we both have fulfilled. The other comes from God. The hour for the second fulfillment is at hand. You in Peru, I at my books. The other comes from God, I say. The hour is here."

Master Agrippa wiped the beads from his forehead. His long white hair hung down on his shoulders. He put his hand on mine and looked at me. "I have trodden false paths. So have we all," he told me. "I thought that the element of elements must be material, perhaps related to gold. Now I know it is spiritual, that it is of the nature of love, a love that has intimations of the future. It is a love which will shape the future. Everything else is meaningless without it. Everything that men have thought will only be so much dung in the street without it. Knowledge without love is worse than ignorance. Action without love is madness, so much crazy motion through time and space.

"Most certainly this is true. For a long time I refused to believe it. For at the bottom, of course, I am a learned man. I take pride in my books, experiments and apparatus. Just as you take pride in your conquests, horses and men.

"Then I sat down to write a final work, my testament, on the vanity and uselessness of all human knowledge. I wrote it down, word for word, without hate or ambition. I pierced with every bit of power I had into the wasp's nest of nonsense. It was a herculean task. And I can honestly say I have killed the Nemean lion with a club, the Lernaean snake with fire, the great Erymanthian boar I have felled to the ground, and pressed down Antaeus with my elbows. I have shot the Stymphalian bird out of the air, and led the hell-hound Cerberus about by the collar, like a lady's lapdog. I have embarked on a holy war against the sciences. All the pedants, scholiasts and polyhistors are ready to flay me alive. They call me 'Podagra.' The dialecticians shoot their syllogistic arrows into my hide. The coprophagous doctors empty their patients' pittle on my old head. The gold-makers would like to shove me into their furnaces...."

Master Agrippa laughed loudly. And I laughed with him, for he was talking wildly now like old times. But when he heard me laugh in sympathy, he became very angry.

"There's nothing to grin about, my friend," he said. "This question of the sciences is a grave matter. The overbearing tone! Everybody will and will know what is true. And everyone thinks that his own crooked thoughts are the last word of wisdom. Look at Luther. He says that good works count for nothing. All that matters is belief! Belief makes the Christian, he contends. Then Karlstadt roars, Down with paintings, statues, for they are the signs of heathendom. Then the Inquisition comes along and whispers, Let us burn all Jews and Moors, for in the first place that is good, and in the second we can confiscate all their property. Then the Sevillians shout, The Indians aren't people!

"Everybody is bellowing out his prejudice and blaspheming the others. The Church is tottering like a rickety old barn. The state can never continue to exist where there is so much strife and dissension. Soon it will be an oligarchy, and end in a tyranny. Some demagogue will come along who will speak for all of them at once, and play the diapason. Others will follow him, honor him, pray to him like another Baal. He will be an Antichrist. I see it coming. For they are all unwashed, sick, empty, stinking, perishing for the need of the positive and healthy. Nothing pleases them better than spiritual emptiness, violence and vulgarity. The king of the masses, Antichrist, revolt, war, hunger and the pest—all these will come together. The four riders of the Apocalypse on their ghostly steeds!

"That is why I'm writing my book. Because I see it all coming. I want my book to be a dike holding back the flood. I can hear the far off rumble of the waters now. There is nothing good on this earth outside of good will, my son. There is no truth outside the word of God. That is the way, the norm, the goal."

He paused for a moment, sighed heavily, and then took up his discourse. Now and then he plucked my sleeve to emphasize a point.

"Probate spiritus, utrum ex Deo sint," he said slowly. "Prove men's souls, to see if they have godliness. That is the criterion which alone can separate the false from the true. There is no other proof. The secular

sciences scorn the word of God, because the word of God is clear and intelligible even to the most stupid. There are no decorative arguments, no graceful sentences. There is no erudition at all. 'I am the resurrection and the life'—what is there to explain, to improve on in that! But they will interpret it. They will comment, explain, add glossaries, syllogize. And always they seek to pervert the naked truth to serve vanity. Yes, they endure the word of God only because it serves as a platter on which they can pile high their steaming excrement. They imagine their privy cleverness is eternal wisdom!

"Soon it will go so far that they'll be doubting the existence of their own souls. They will hold that immortality is a lie. Yes, that will be the next step. You can imagine the despair that will grip the souls of men when this happens. Death will be staring them in the face every minute, for death is the wages of sin. In their deep despair they will martyr one another. They will kill and torment one another. They will rend one another like thirst and hunger-crazed shipwrecked seamen washed up on a hot desert isle. They will try to arrange things on earth so as to get along without God. They will try to build a state greater than God, another tower of Babylon.

"But God will confuse their tongues and their ideas, as once happened in Babel. New wars will break out like great forest fires. And even if they do build this new kingdom, what then? Is not the kingdom of Antichrist Hell? Won't these befogged creatures at last cry out in an ultimate misery, writing with despair, their hearts bleeding? For even in them, hidden deep, is the immortal godhead which is their gift and heritage. They still have in them the given freedom, the power, indeed the necessity, of making private decisions, of choosing. All this they will have repudiated. By so doing they will think to get more comfort, a more secure life. Like herds of animals!

"Thou, O God! Do not give men peace and security! Give them danger, doubt, misery, hunger, sickness and death! But leave them the priceless pearl, freedom of soul, inner belief in Thee! Do with them as Thou once did with Thy chosen people. For to be one with Thee is eternal suffering—and eternal joy. And, Thou, O God, if Thou wilt listen to my voice, wipe from the face of the earth these stupidly proud, empty, know-all, overweening arch-heretics. Smite them down! Wipe the slate clean!"

Master Agrippa brushed back his long white hair from the huge forehead. He glared at me, and said sharply, "Do you know what I'm talking about?"

"Yes, Master," I said. "I understand you. In a sense you are talking about me." Once again I was the small boy at the feet of my teacher. It made me warm with pleasure to listen to him.

"You were always slow to grasp things," he said gloomily. But he smiled thinly just afterward, almost against his will and better judgment. "I'll admit that when you did understand something it stuck fast. I prize that quality. That's far better than catching on like a flash only to lose it not ten minutes later. You are thorough and rigid in character. Therefore your life must be rigid in character, all of a piece. It isn't suited for you to jump about like a dancer on his toes."

"You are right," I told him.

"Right! Of course, of course I'm right," he said rudely. "Don't interrupt me so often. Don't try to do all the talking. I stand before you like the great prophet Isaiah talking to the Chaldean philosophers and wise men. He said, if you recall, *'Sapienta tua et scienta tua haec decepit te. . . .* Thy wisdom, and thy knowledge, this hath deceived thee.'

"That doesn't apply to you nearly so much as it does to me. And along with me all the magisters, baccalaureates, doctors and professors. All the poor little candles and stable lanterns that serve these dark days instead of the sun. True, *luci a non lucendo!* How wonderfully, with what loving detail, we have analyzed every miserable flyspeck! How joyfully we have waded about knee-deep in enormous lakes of filth, laughing when we tumbled in over our heads, splashing like children in a pool, lapping up the revolting excrement while God turned his head away! Smeared, smeared, smeared with muck and lies until we are veritable stinking blackamoors of knowledge. Small wonder that the world retches at the spectacle, and flees us, hand over mouth. It is enough to turn the stomach of a self-respecting hog. No wonder that the world is out of hand. For truth today is really no more than a personal thing.

"The people can't be blamed if they think their stupidities and wickedness are the shining light of excellence. Don't they accord one to one with the swollen, thoughtless lies trumpeted from every podium? For it seems no matter how evil, how stupid, how utterly invented the idea is, there will always be someone to champion it, to take it lovingly to heart. It's all a question of repeating the nonsense over and over again until it has been learned by heart. A little time and any man, it appears, can grow an impressive pair of asses' ears.

"But enough of that. I've been talking about myself long enough as it is. Nevertheless what goes for me goes for you as well. I don't know how you behaved yourself in Peru. But I can readily see after one look at you that everything hasn't been completely rosy."

"No, it hasn't been rosy," I stammered. "I'd like to tell you . . ." But Master Agrippa cut me off with a wave of his hand.

"I don't want to listen to any confessions," he said. "I hate people who are always concerned about their own souls and naught else. I'm tired of giving suck to them. Has mother's little lamb hurt himself? Is he unhappy, the cunning little lambkins dear? I puke on such people. They arouse in me a gigantic, rending pain in the ass. Has little lambkins a green stool today instead of brown, the poor tiny-toed sweetling? That's what passes for loving-kindness!

"But to hell with that loathsome drool! We have other fish to fry besides half-grown herrings. A man's soul must be manly. If a man feels querulous, if he gets wrapped up in himself and can't sleep nights for bad dreams, let him get himself a large pail of spring water and soak his head in it. Go out to work with the peasants in the heat of the day. Sleep will come, I warrant that! Freeze honestly, sweat honestly and don't look for a nipple to hang onto. That sort of business leads only to more tenderness, to more self-pity."

"That is all very well," I said. "I can easily understand that and believe. But supposing one can't sleep nights because of pangs of conscience. What then? Suppose it is a question of deeds irrevocably committed?"

"In that case," said Master Agrippa observing me narrowly, "a man must pay up. He must give measure for measure, like an honest merchant. He must pay for his guilt, and even the score. Beyond that he must hope for God, for the opportunity that will surely be given him to atone. Oh yes, I've heard the stories about the death of Atahualpa, about the slaughter of the Indians, about burning up innocent people. I've heard all the rumors about broken compacts and stolen treasure. You need not look at me so fearfully, my son. I couldn't help but hear all about it. There's very little else talked about at the Court."

"Master Agrippa," I said, "when will I be a free man again? When can I walk about with my head up? As I used to when I was with you?"

"Tomorrow, my son," he replied.

"Tomorrow!" I took him by the sleeve. "That can't be possible. I'll still see the sun rise. I'll still be probing my soul. Only now it will be in Valladolid instead of in Cordova!"

Master Agrippa put his hands on my shoulders and looked into my eyes. Anxiously I met his glance, which had something bewitching in it, something that reassured me.

"You are a knight," he said slowly. "Not only that, you are my pupil. I depend on you absolutely. Tomorrow you shall go out and ride for the poor, the suffering, the persecuted and the plundered like a Christian. What you did was no worse than what I did. I forgot God, bent over my books. You forgot God, in conquest. Don't you know that a man should dip his quill in ink with a prayer in his heart, with a dutiful spirit? Don't you know, too, that you may draw your sword only when fulfilling your duty toward Him who is the Knight of Knights? Remember what He once said, I am come not to bring peace, but the sword. War, then, in the name of Christ! War against unbelievers! I with my quill, you with your sword. True knighthood should no more vanish from the earth than true wisdom.

"But do not imagine that by unbelievers I mean the red, brown and black men of the New World. I don't refer to the Indians, to the Negroes and the Moors. Not them. I mean the infidels in our very midst. First we must clear our own house. I mean the good Catholics who pray to the gods of gold, force, betrayal and cruelty, whose bellies are as big as casks with wickedness.

"You needn't look at me that way! Are you still a round-eyed boy? I could stuff you up to the ears with knowledge, as a cook stuffs a goose. I could take a funnel and pour into you all human wisdom from the words of the Egyptians to the superficialities of our humanists. You still look at me like a boy looking at an elephant's tail? Oh, the fools, the ignorant, the children and the chattering women! God bless them! *'Surgunt indocti et rapiunt coelos et nos cum scientia nostra mergimur in infernum,'* said Saint Augustine. The ignorant puff themselves up and pull heaven down to themselves and we men of knowledge take the Devil's path. By Bacchus, I feel the urge to sing the praises of foolishness, in tune with my colleague Erasmus!" He paused suddenly, cupped one hand behind his ear. "What's that? Do you hear someone coming? It must be he. I hope he doesn't knock anything over. That monk is so big! He smashes everything he lays his hands on!"

The door did creak open. It was all bewildering. Filling the opening was the huge figure of a Dominican. His shoulders were round and broad, his body heavy, and his big round head, encircled by a wreath of gray curls, hung forward so as not to strike the top of the doorframe. In his hand he held a heavy gnarled stick, which with a couple of knife cuts he had taken from a tree and peeled down for his use. He looked like Saint Christopher, who once carried the Christ Child over the flood. His large gray eyes smiled, and in a thunderous voice he said, "Are the potions I'm to send to Hispaniola ready, honored Master? Have you got the salves and herbs ready for me today?"

"Patience, patience," said Master Agrippa, smiling in open admiration.

The Dominican sat down without further ceremony, the chair groaning under him. My mouth fell open. I realized who it was. I went over and shook his hand.

"The little conquistador," he said mildly, and pressed my hand in return. "It was on the Isthmus. I remember. In a burned-out Indian village. I remember. We talked for a while. It was at night. I remember."

"Then you two know each other?" asked Master Agrippa. He seemed to be a little disappointed.

"We know each other one way. And in another we do not," the Dominican said. "We met as two wanderers on the Isthmus. We talked for an hour. Then each of us went his way."

"You don't know who he is then?" inquired Master Agrippa eagerly of me.

"I don't!"

"That is Father Bartolomé de las Casas," said Master Agrippa. "He is the pride of Spain, the true conquistador of the Indies, the colonizer...."

"The scourge of Spain, the whip, the lash," said the monk. "That's more like it. The slave of the Indies. The most hated Dominican who ever trod the earth of the New World...."

He said this smiling at first, then his face changed. It was the most curious expression I had ever seen come over a man's face. His cheeks grew a little hollow, and his face appeared longer. His eyes stared hard at me. It was a terrifying gaze, impossible to bear. The lids dropped over his eyes and he bowed his head in momentary submission. Then his face became round and full as it had been before.

"An honor, a distinction!" interposed Master Agrippa. "It is an honor, father, to be hated by the mob."

"I cannot say I find it so," said the monk humorously. "I should much rather have them be fond of me. For at the bottom I like them."

"Why, that's impossible!" said Master Agrippa. "I believe this giant of a cleric even likes the insects that sting him, the vipers of the jungle, the jaguars."

"My fondness of them is limited, but it is there," the monk admitted. "They are beautiful, you see. I believe I once explained it to this young man here. I like to pick up pretty snakes. They have lovely eyes and such delicate tongues. I have always wanted to stroke a leopard, to feel the hide and the muscles. . . . Of course . . ." He laughed at his own fancy.

"He is mad, out of his head," said Master Agrippa. "Don't listen to him. Or you'll be as lunatic as he. He handles human leopards—you conquistadors, for example—in a way that's far from stroking! He lays to with a seven-thonged whip until their hides are in ribbons!"

"Yes, that is true," the monk said. "That's a different story, Master Agrippa. They are the animals that I shall slay. I expect no quarter from these beasts. And I give none. So long as I can lift my hand they shall feel its weight." He raised a huge fist over his head, clenched so tight the knuckles whitened. He lowered the fist slowly, and said, "Well, enough. I'd like to keep on talking with you and your friend, Master, but my time is limited. His Majesty the King arrives in Valladolid today. He is going to see me and His Eminence the Cardinal the first thing tomorrow morning. I have to get my argument straightened out. . . . Things have come to a head."

"I understand," said Master Agrippa. "You will have to look through your notes."

"No, I'm not preparing that way," the monk said, and got up to go.

"Wait a minute," Master Agrippa shouted after him. "Just a minute, father. I've forgotten the most important thing. I want you to meet my friend and pupil—and my patron—Don Pedro de Cordova, the Lord Admiral of the Southern Ocean, one of the Peruvian conquistadors. Tomorrow morning he'll stand by your stand and help argue the cause of freedom."

"What!" The monk stared at me. "On my side!"

"Yes, on your side," said Master Agrippa boldly. "He is a knight. He is ready to ride forth for Christ."

"That would be a great help," the monk said quietly. "To have at least one backing me. But is he ready to take the consequences? Does he know what he's letting himself in for?"

"I am ready, Father Bartolomé," I said.

"I will see you there in that case," he said simply. He hesitated, then took me by the hand and pulled me along with him. "Perhaps you had better come with me now."

I looked at Master Agrippa. He was smiling grimly, his disheveled white hair hanging down to his hawk nose.

"Don't be afraid," he said sarcastically. "He will hammer the *aurum potabile* out of your soul, my son. He will renew you with an elixir you never dreamed existed. My work with you is finished. I give you to him. He is a better magician than I. He is also a better man."

"Master!" I said.

"Go on, go on," he said. "The time of torment is over. Your mortification has run its course. What magic and science could do for you has been done. Now only the deed remains, and your free will."

"But Master!" I cried, and once again tried to pull myself away from the iron grip. For somehow I felt that this time our leave-taking was for ever.

"Go, my son," he said roughly. And then the monk let me free. Master Agrippa rose onto his tiptoes and made a commanding gesture in the direction of the door. "Go and battle with the hounds who yap at the heels of Christ!"

I followed in the wake of the broad-backed monk.

Early the next morning a court attendant led us through the high white corridor of the palace. He walked on ahead of us like a sable ghost, his feet in dark silken shoes. The sun caught on the curve of his ornamental dagger, and his shadow wandered palely along the white walls. It was a warm September day. In the soundless white building it smelled strongly of lime, almost like a grave, a choking smell. Only the heavy tread of Father Bartolomé made the situation real.

The ghostly chamberlain now opened a heavy oaken door in the middle of which was a carving of a unicorn rampant. The chamberlain turned his dry, lifeless face to me and said pedantically, "His Majesty likes this unicorn room the best of all for giving audiences. It's cool, but not damp."

I nodded, ill at ease. Father Bartolomé said, "That's fine. It suits me." He spoke in his natural deep voice that filled the space. The chamberlain was horrified. An echo came from somewhere in the depths of the castle, ". . . suits me."

I saw now why this narrow, long room was called the unicorn room. On the walls were wonderful, richly colored tapestries from Tournay or Bruges, showing a hunt for unicorns. The room was filled with a pleasant, greenish twilight. It was easy enough to imagine that one was in the depths of some forest glen. It was cool here, as outdoors in the shade of a great oak tree.

This illusion was strengthened by the bucolic landscapes portrayed on the tapestries. Beasts of the forest looked out from the walls—hares, does, foxes, pheasants and quail. Wood flowers nodded in the tender grass, the shy violet, the little starflower and the bold golden dandelion. Through this idyllic scene rode brave knights on horseback, dressed in splendor, accompanied by beautiful ladies on white palfreys. With them were green-clad squires wearing horns over their shoulders, spear or crossbow in their strong brown hands. All about them were hounds giving voice, snuffing at the ground for the curious prey. They were Dalmatians, gaily checkered black and white.

In the greenish half-light of the room all this was so astonishingly real that the sight rooted me to the spot. I looked toward the end of the room, and there I saw on the end wall the image of the unicorn himself, peacefully grazing, his grayish head sunk into the meadow grasses. From out of a thicket little birds with their beaks agape gazed down at him, as if singing the praises of so wonderful a beast.

Under this final tapestry, three steps up from the floor, was a seat covered with red damask. In the chair back was carved still another unicorn. There was an odor of spicy wax, something commonly noticeable in princes' rooms when they are seldom used and yet constantly kept polished and cleaned by a swarm of servants.

"That is Doctor Juan Ginez de Sepúlveda de Salamanca," said Father Bartolomé in a lower voice, and prodded me in the ribs. I was surprised to see that on both sides of the wall under the tapestries six chairs were placed, and that some of these were already occupied. The man that Father Bartolomé drew my attention to was busy with some papers a secretary had handed to him. The doctor had a pointed beard, very long and brown. Once his eyes darted over to us, taking us in. His face was very thin. He turned back at once to his papers.

"What is he?" I asked.

"He is a famous lawyer of Salamanca," said Father Bartolomé in my ear. "He has just written a thick book. It's called *'De justis causis belli apud Indios.'* About the justness of the war against the Indians, or something of the sort. I haven't read it. It's too rich fare for me. He's the one who will defend the legality of our Spanish cut-throats, our conquistadors. He's not such a bad man. He's married and his wife has borne him twelve children. Think of it! But when he starts writing he works himself up into an awful lather. He strikes out at the Indians as if they were personally responsible for his having to scribble for a living big enough to support that tremendous brood he has so assiduously spawned."

"What does that other one do," I whispered, "that one over there with the thick black hair and the big lips?"

"That is Don Alonso de Molina," said Father Bartolomé quite loudly. "He is a friend of Alvarado's. A pretty specimen, I must say. He has plenty of influence here at Court. His mother was a lady-in-waiting in the Empress' entourage. They say he'll be the future governor of Hispaniola. . . ."

Father Bartolomé sighed, and talked very softly. "I've had a great deal of trouble with that man. As with Don Pedro de Alvarado. He has run wild on the Pearl Coast. He knows India like the back of his hand. He has been everywhere. And everywhere he went he sowed the seeds of trouble. The son of a cow ruined my colony! He got the Indians to revolt, and made me into a laughing stock. The Council of the Indies most certainly had him come here to give me another setback. All they know about India, you realize, is from hearsay. They've never been there. It would be foolhardy for them to venture any opinions without someone from the spot to support them. But they will talk. Don't forget that!"

I stared at Alonso de Molina, and he saw me doing it. I thought he looked something like Gonzalo Pizarro, an ugly Gonzalo with Negro's lips. He answered my stare with a mocking sneer, and turned deliberately away.

The door opened and two cardinals walked in. My legs almost gave way when I saw that one of them was the Grand Inquisitor, Don Antonio Cardinal de Guevara. He did not appear to have grown a day older. His eyes were just as dark and lively as when I had seen him in the Inquisition's fortress in Triana. His brows were black and bushy. Next to him was Cardinal Loaysa, the Emperor's confessor, and now president of the Council of the Indies in Seville. He was a tall, white-haired man, and walked rather bent forward. He constantly brushed his hand over his forehead, as if brushing away flies. He looked care-worn and nervous. When he saw Father Bartolomé he began to smile. He nodded, greeted him warmly and passed a few friendly words with him. Cardinal Guevara also stopped and greeted the monk. He was going to talk, bethought himself, and moved on to a chair, preceded by the chamberlain, who carefully dusted off imaginary motes of dust before letting him sit down. The Grand Inquisitor closely inspected the room. His glance rested for a while on the unicorn. Then he examined Sepúlveda, the secretary and Don Alonso de Molina. All of them had risen when he entered. At last his eyes came to me. In a minute I knew he had recognized me though he gave me no sign.

At this very moment, at the appointed hour on the very dot—I heard the bell in the palace chapel ring—Don Carlos came in through a side door followed by his privy councilor van Male. The King was a complete Hapsburger. His nose sprang heavily out of his face, his upper lip was almost nothing, the brows were highly arched, and small, deep-set eyes looked out in coldly quizzical disappointment at the world. From his mother's side he had a certain fineness of hand and foot, and her bell-like clarity of voice. These characteristics of Doña Juana were startling in him. They seemed to stand in complete opposition to the rest of his being. The voice, hands and feet were somehow youthful, fresh and eager. But the face was tired, a mask of inner fatigue. And in the face, too, were the petty cares of a thrifty housewife or the look of a penny-pinching master of many drays, which went strangely with the luxury of the room.

Don Carlos was not what one would expect an emperor to be, a ruler of the earth. He was as little like Charlemagne as Pizarro like Roland. Through and through, it was plain to see, he was a man of the counting room, a merchant, a man to draw up contracts. And yet this man was the grandson of Maximiliano, who has been called the last of the knights. He was the grandson of Charles the Bold. And he was the son of a visionary.

I had no time to meditate on the chagrin I felt at this first sight of the ruler of all Spain. Everyone hurriedly took a seat. A chamberlain moved to the middle of the room, bowed his right knee, and said, "Does it please Your Majesty to give audience to the messengers from across the sea?"

The Emperor nodded. He threw back his ermine-trimmed tippet, which he wore over his doublet even on this warm day. The door was forced open. A large white mastiff rushed in, made directly for Don Carlos, went up to him and began to lick his hand.

"Couche-toi, biche!" said the Emperor. The dog flung herself heavily to the floor in front of the damask throne. She laid her big head, the ears pricked up straight, on the first step of the podium, as near to her master's feet as she could get. The Emperor shrugged his shoulders, and said to Cardinal Loaysa, *"Toujours la même!"* . . . excusing the animal.

This trifling incident changed the atmosphere of the room. It was as if the great white bitch had brought a feeling of loyalty and animal spontaneity into a world of dry numbers and dry laws, a world smothered in moribund ceremony and angularity. This was doubly noticeable when the Emperor, forgetting himself, spoke in the language of his childhood, a language that for a time he had carefully avoided using in Castile, remembering only too well the revolt of the Comunidades.

Cardinal Loaysa was the first to rise. He said slowly, "Your Majesty, fifty years nearly have passed since the Admiral, under Queen Doña Isabella, now at rest in the arms of Christ, discovered the Western World. This discovery proved to be greater than the Admiral himself ever imagined it might be, or his learned friend Toscanelli, or any other of the savants of the times. The earth has stretched out to incredible distances before our eyes. And now, through the bravery and endurance of our captains and conquistadors we know of an enormous territory, so large that all Spain and its European satellite states could be swallowed up in it without leaving a mark. The huge land stretches from pole to pole and almost covers half of the world. It is made up of two enormous islands connected by a small Isthmus. Near this Isthmus are the wonderful islands of Hispaniola, Cuba, Jamaica and hundreds of other smaller ones. Among them is San Salvador, the one which Don Cristóbal Colón discovered October of the year 1492 by the grace of God.

"According to ancient custom we Spaniards call this double continent India, the West India. We know, of course, that actually it has no connection with the real India, with the Cathay and Cipangu of Marco Polo and the Portuguese. It has nothing to do with Asia. It is a new part of the world, self-contained. The Italian and German cosmographers call it America, after the learned seafarer, Amerigo Vespucci, though it is my opinion that it should be called Columbia after its true discoverer.

"I repeat all these well-known facts, Your Majesty, in order to get at the reason why we have gathered here. This great land is Your Majesty's most important possession. Already we have taken hold on the previously mentioned islands in the Caribbean Sea. We have occupied and begun to colonize the Isthmus of Panama, the most strategic part of the New World. We have spread out to the north as far as the peninsula of Florida, and south to Peru and Chile. Ruling this gigantic kingdom daily becomes a more arduous task. Everywhere there are primeval forests, endless savannas, high mountains, wide deserts in which the emissaries of the Crown are lost like single grains of sand on a beach. I doubt that the territory will be settled before centuries have passed. Therefore it seems fitting to the Council of the Indies that certain regulations and laws bearing on the indigenes of these lands should be formulated.

"You realize, Your Majesty, that this great land was not empty of people. It is populated by great numbers of red-skinned men, particularly the islands. And also on the mainland, where the great cities of Tlascala, Tenochtitlan and Quito were found.

"When the Spaniards first arrived they thought they could prevail by sheer force of arms. And so the first fifty years of Spanish rule in India is a chronicle of robbery, war and wild adventure. The Council of the Indies now feels the time has come for Your Majesty to call a halt to such practices. There is a real danger that the redskins will be entirely exterminated. A statesman like Your Majesty scarcely need be advised that when a land is depopulated it loses the greater part of its value.

"Beyond that, I am certain that Your Majesty in considering this question will not limit himself to pecuniary judgments. For these

Indians are the free vassals of Your Majesty, just as free presumably as the men of Castile, Aragon and Flanders. Her Exalted Majesty, the Queen Doña Isabella, expressly declared the Indies free in her testament, with none of the red-skinned subject to anyone but the Crown itself. On her deathbed she admonished her consort, Don Fernando, her daughter Doña Juana and her son-in-law Don Felipe, the royal parents of Your Majesty, always to protect the Indians from assaults on their freedom. This sacred charge now rests with Your Majesty."

Don Carlos watched the Cardinal closely, impatiently stroking the fur collar of his tippet. The big white bitch lay quietly at his feet, her eyes empty and large.

"The Church, too," the Cardinal went on, "at that same time became concerned about the future of the Indies. Two popes have expressed themselves on the matter of the Indians' spiritual and corporeal welfare. I shall pass by the edict of His Holiness Alexander the Sixth, and rest on the words of His Holiness Paul the Third who now occupies the Throne of Saint Peter. In his bull called *Sublimis Deus* His Holiness has forbidden all forced labor among the Indians and all forms of slavery because these forms are contrary to the dignity of the human soul."

"I don't quite understand all this," said Don Carlos. "On this subject the State and the Church are in agreement. What is the difficulty? I see no differences to discuss."

"In your long experience as a sovereign, Your Majesty," the Cardinal said, "it must not have escaped you that not all your subjects are worthy creatures who bow to the dictates of the State."

"God knows that is true!" said Don Carlos. "It didn't take me long to find that out."

"In the Indies it has become law by custom, so to speak, a law not recognized by the Crown," the Cardinal went on to say, "that Indians be impressed for labor. To further this end the Indians are divided among the Spaniards, according to an arrangement that is called the repartimiento."

"Why do they do that?" said Don Carlos naïvely and at the same time with some irritation.

"It is the general opinion," the Cardinal explained with equal naïveté, "that this institution is necessary in order to exploit the riches of the new lands. In any case, it has come to a pitch where the Council of the Indies dares not decide without giving Your Majesty an opportunity to express his opinion. On that account we have brought before the throne Doctor Juan Ginez de Sepúlveda of Salamanca, one of the greatest doctors of law in Spain, in fact in all Europe. Your Majesty is not unaware . . ."

The doctor got up, placed himself before the throne and bowed deeply, all but bending double. The Emperor nodded pleasantly and said, "It will be a pleasure to hear such a learned man." At this the doctor's ears reddened. Once again he bowed, this time nearly losing his balance.

"Furthermore," said the Cardinal, "we have brought Father Bartolomé de las Casas. . . ."

"What!" The Emperor's nervous hands left his fur collar and clamped down on the arm rests of the throne. "Our Las Casas is here! By the Holy Virgin, there he is! Come here, Father Bartolomé. Let me have a look at you. . . ."

Father Bartolomé hoisted himself to his feet and strode forward almost up to the throne. Briefly he inclined his enormous torso, straightened up, and waited for the Emperor to speak.

"It's you all right!" said the Emperor. His face beamed palely. "Good God, just look at him! He's even bigger than he was! Look at him, van Male! He hasn't grown a day older than when we last saw him. . . ." Obediently the privy councilor bent forward, inspected Father Bartolomé's face, and smiled at him. The dog looked up expectantly. "Let's see," the Emperor said, "it's a long time, isn't it! It was at the Diet of Worms before the entrance into Antwerp. It was, let me see, yes, in Coruña. . . ."

"It was at the time Your Majesty became sovereign," said Las Casas. "I remember the young King, how he expressed his loathing of slavery and the cut-throats who enslave. . . ."

"I was young, Las Casas, I was very young," said the Emperor, sighing. "And it's a way you have, Father, of dragging your hearers along with you, *nolens volens,* all in the one sack. . . . I didn't know the world, Las Casas. . . ."

"It is not important to know the world, Your Majesty," Las Casas corrected the Emperor in his powerful voice. "So long as you know your own heart, that is enough. This the young King knew. . . ."

"Now, just a minute, Las Casas," said the Emperor mistrustfully, "you haven't come here to start lecturing, have you? Yes, van Male, this man can give more advice than you ever dreamed of." The Emperor laughed softly, and shook his head.

Las Casas again bowed, and returned to his place. At a nod from Cardinal Loaysa, Doctor Sepúlveda again stepped forward and began to speak.

"Your Majesty, in humility and reverence I stand before my Imperial master and King. It is only with profound hesitation that I presume to express my opinions, however clear-cut they may be, before Your Majesty. As a simple subject I would hold my tongue forever if it had not been that in these latter days there have appeared certain fanatics, preaching monks and run-down captains who threaten the safety of Your Majesty's possessions in the Indies. They explain their actions by quoting outmoded laws, orders in council, testaments and bulls. They contend that the war against the Indians is opposed to all godly and human justice. They say that the forced services of the Indians is a crime against humanity so-called. *Quo usque tandem!* I can hear Cicero crying out against these untimely Catalines. How far will you go! *Abutere patientia nostra!* How long will you misuse our patience!

"Your Majesty, my tongue grows as thick as a felled bullock's, my teeth chatter like a man stricken with the ague, when I think how these criminals will never be content with their protests, wranglings and deeds of violence until the ships of Spain come back with empty holds to Cadiz or Palos. They will never be satisfied until we cry out, *Sic transit gloria Indiae!*

"But this emotion I shall choke down. I shall limit myself to a cold, ordered argument fitting for a doctor *juris utriusque*. Otherwise the cares of my homeland would exalt my tongue and give me the wings of Pegasus!

"But enough of that. However passionate the soul, it must be controlled before Your Majesty. . . ."

The Emperor turned his head slightly away, and carefully covered a yawn.

"It is my contention, Your Majesty," the lawyer went on to say, "that the institution of the repartimiento and the war against the Indians are shining examples of both secular and divine law. In the first place, God, the Master, has created men and peoples in unequal stature. There is not the slightest doubt that the Indians are an inferior people, doomed to slavery, and that on the other hand the Spaniards are a ruling people, born to command. It is not only the right, it is moreover the duty of Spain to rule the Indians, to force them to work, and to kill them should they presume to question the superiority of us Spaniards. This is the *lex naturae,* which decrees that the stronger is always in the right.

"In the second place Spanish culture is infinitely superior to the Indian culture. It is as superior as a Spanish cathedral is to an Indian temple. The better among men always has the right to impose his will on the inferior. This is also true among different races. For the needs of the better must of necessity be superior to the needs of the inferior, even if the inferior refuse to recognize this distinction. Do not the burghers and the peasants complain incessantly about the taxes, the perquisites, the duties which flow into the coffers of the Crown! And why? Because their stupid eyes are blind to the wars, the castles, the splendor of the Court which must be supported for the eternal honor and glory of Spain. Where would we be if anyone paid the slightest attention to this quibbling? Perhaps we would have a state of peace and stagnation. All the generals, the military advisors, the captains and the soldiers would be without employment. Spain would be overpopulated. All strategic talent would go for naught. It would be a frightful state of affairs, anyone can see.

"Now, how much less can Your Majesty pay the remotest attention to the complaints of Indians and their spokesmen! Here it is a much simpler case. Because of their sins the Indians must be punished. Among these sins I count heathenism, human sacrifice, cannibalism, concubinage, indecent dress, painting the face and other parts of the body, the use of a poisonous plant called tobacco. And beyond all these a boundless laziness. All day long these heathen rock back and forth in their hammocks, letting their wives do the work in the fields. They flout the word of God, Who said, Thou shalt eat thy bread in the sweat of thy brow. In short, they behave as if they were still in paradise, which of course is rather out of the question considering their condition of sin.

"Again, these Indians have a rude and contrary nature. They are virtually mules in human form. They would often rather be killed than go into the fields and mines of the Spaniards, there to do an honest day's work like anybody else. They ignore their duty shamefully, and should be punished.

"Again, it is necessary that they serve, because in constant intercourse with Spaniards, by living in the Spanish colonies they can enjoy the proximity of men who live in the religion of Christ, the Redeemer. They can learn and be turned from their errant practices.

"And my last point is this, that the Indians kill, maim and torture one another. They are constantly fighting among themselves, behaving like the wild beasts they are. It is God's blessing that the Spaniards have come to reduce them to order and civilized behavior. Did not the great Admiral for this very purpose build the first colony, the Fort of La Navidad from the ruins of his shipwrecked *Santa Maria?* And did not these Indians shout in jubilation when they heard that the Admiral was going to protect them with his cannon against their mortal enemies, the Caribs?

"But I have already labored the point and tried Your Majesty's patience. I won't dwell on any more points, though there would be no difficulty in elaborating the subject. So far as the outmoded laws, orders in council and bulls are concerned, they are rooted in theories which take no cognizance of the facts of the world. The repartimientos and the peonage of the Indians are the fruit of practice.

"It is quite true, I admit, that these institutions contain certain elements of harshness. I am only too glad to hear that the revered fathers of Santo Domingo are probing into the particulars of the situation in order to bring to light unnecessary impositions, and to have them mitigated.

"But it is quite another matter when some of them brazenly suggest that the whole institution be discarded, or presume to think that this abolition will redound to the pecuniary and spiritual advantage of Spain and the Crown. They leave out of account the disastrous effect this would have, not only on Spain and the Crown, but on the thousands and thousands of loyal subjects who have dedicated their lives to the new found lands. It would mean, in brief, losing all the Indies. Hispaniola, Cuba, New Spain, New Castile, Guatemala, Venezuela would revert back to the jungle. They would be overgrown, and all Spanish blood and labor would have been expended for absolutely nothing. The Spaniards in the New World would grow poor and die of hunger. For what can nourish them, if not the labor of the Indians? The caravels would rot in the harbors, and great parts of the population of Spain who are now supported by the products of the colonies would lose work and daily bread.

"Therefore I adjure Your Majesty to believe that in this world the stern course is always the best. The hesitant ruler in the end always finds himself deserted by his subjects. The people always hang close to a man capable of harshness and violence if this method is not carried too far. For India there can be only one course of action. The repartimientos, which have become legalized by custom, must cease to be merely prescriptive and be affirmed by a law of the State. The Crown should recognize slavery and it should be made a formal practice, by the Council. This must be done for the honor of God, of Your Majesty and of Spain, for the edification of the Indians and for the welfare of the world!"

"That is blasphemous!" It was Father Bartolomé. All the while the lawyer had been talking he had squirmed wildly in his seat. He could stand it no longer, and now jumped to his feet. "That is the most stupid, the most cowardly and heartless thing I have ever heard any man say!"

"Sit down, Las Casas," said Cardinal Loaysa. "You will have your opportunity later to speak out what you have to say."

He threw Las Casas a warning glance. The monk sank back in his chair. Doctor Sepúlveda bowed deeply, his right hand pressed over his heart. But the Emperor paid no attention to Sepúlveda. Anxiously, almost fearfully he stared at Las Casas. Indeed, the voice had been so powerful that it struck into the room like a clap of thunder, enough to make a man's hair rise on his head.

"Just a moment, Your Eminence," the Emperor interposed. "Let Las Casas speak now. He looks like a black cloud. I'd rather get it over with at the beginning, if you don't mind. I'd rather have the worst tooth pulled at the beginning, to tell the truth."

The monk did not content himself with standing up before his appointed chair. He walked out into the middle of the room, and proceeded almost up to the Emperor's throne, near the dog. He bowed slowly, then began to talk.

"My King, I know only one reason for freeing the Indians and immediately banning the whole practice of slavery. This ground should suffice for Your Majesty. It is God's command that the poor, the humble and the ignorant shall not be tormented and used. That they shall be taken in as brothers, that they shall be helped and taught. Such is God's command.

"It is on account of this command that I entered into the Order of Santo Domingo. It is why I boarded a ship and crossed the sea to the

Indies, where I have spent many, many years, as you know. There I have cared for the sick, and comforted the suffering and taught those who knew nothing of Christ. For our Lord has said, Go into all lands and baptize the heathen.

"I must tell Your Majesty that never have I carried a weapon in my hands. Seldom have I run into danger. And as for food, I have never troubled my head about such trivial matters. I am a man at peace with myself, Your Majesty. For wherever I go on the islands or on the mainland, my children, the Indians, come to me. Without my asking them, they lead me through the forests. They carry me over the rivers in their canoes, and over the bays and wide estuaries of the New World. They bring me maize, fruits, fowl and fish to eat, and they prepare a campfire for me. And when I talk to them they listen to me thoughtfully. When I take my leave of their poor huts, the whole village follows after me, men, women and children—they follow me, for hours on end, until I am deep in the forest. Everyone wants to carry my bundles, my pouch. When I take final leave of them they beg me to return as soon as I can.

"So Your Majesty can see that my life in the forest is a happy one, and that I should be glad to stay there forever. All that has driven me back across the sea is the cruelty of my compatriots. I must tell Your Majesty about this. It is a fearful thorn that God has plunged into my flesh. It is called Spain.

"It is not the Indians, Your Majesty. Not at all. It is the Spaniards. The case is clear. Because of these Spaniards, my own brothers, I sometimes cannot sleep at ease beside the fire. On their account I am always wandering over the sea. And on their account I am here in Your Majesty's council chamber, where very obviously I do not belong. It is strange for me to stand among cardinals, doctors of law, statesmen, councilors and captains. I am a monk. No more and no less. And whatever cleverness I once learned in my youth, Your Majesty, that has all long since been forgotten. I am monstrously ignorant and prejudiced.

"I care about only two things. One is the welfare of my children, the Indians. And the other, Your Majesty, is the soul of my homeland, Spain. About laws, strategy, the forms of administration, colonial politics and sovereignty I know nothing at all. It is my conscience and not my knowledge which permits me to take my place in this council.

"But however ignorant I may be, I know some matters of which I can inform Your Majesty. I can throw an altogether different light on what goes on across the sea. Yes, I can do that. And first of all, I declare that every word, every phrase that this Doctor Sepúlveda has uttered stinks of corruption, and is a lie which I shall ram down his cowardly throat. . . ."

He balled his fist and directed it at the lawyer, who crept back in his seat. Cardinal Loaysa raised his hand in admonition.

"Yes," Las Casas continued, "while I listened to the word-spinning of this curious man I began to wonder whether he was not confusing the Indians with the inhabitants of the moon, if such there be. The fool! What can he know about them? What can he know except at second and third and fourth remove? Old wives' tales—that is all he knows. He knows what the criminal conquistadors and superstitious seamen spread about. He had the temerity to quote the Admiral, this man who has never felt the deck of a ship underfoot, who has never risked his neck beyond lifting five books instead of four!

"I think that the Admiral can bear good witness for the Indians, not against them. It is well known that he was a very keen observer. He saw clearly whatever he came in contact with. He never mingled invention with reality like our doctor of laws, whatever his excuse might be, weakness of body or a simple lack of courage. And I have heard from the mouth of the Admiral himself when I talked with him in Seville, and also from my father, who accompanied the Admiral on his second journey, what our first discoverer thought about the Indians. In his ship's log, which I have taken the pains to read, I have read, 'So kindly, so pliant, so peaceful are these people, that I swear there is no better nation in the world. They love their neighbors like themselves. Their mode of address is friendly and mild and is always marked by a smile. And although it is quite true that they go naked, nevertheless their morals are decent and certainly not unworthy of praise.'

"Is that not a fine piece of evidence, Your Majesty? And a single look at the landscape which the Admiral described in such poetic language is enough to make one believe that indeed it was a garden of Eden when white men first trod its shores. Don Cristóbal has said that the air was like balsam and soft, as on a lovely May day in Andalusia, that it was rich with the perfume of a thousand aromatic smells. 'So powerful was the birds' song that sorrow tugs at my heart when I think I must leave this land,' he wrote. 'The flocks of gaily colored parrots darken the sun at times, and in the smooth ponds there are rosy-white flamingos, and thousands of other birds, large and small, whose names I do not know. The trees grow tall,' he said; 'they make a broad shadow and bear curious edible fruits. The ground is covered with plants of all sorts, and it is my belief that they could be used for medicinal tinctures and brews, and on this I meditate day and night. When night comes, other birds and beasts awaken and give throat to their song, which fills the night like the strings of a wonderful viola. There the stars are much bigger, the moonlight is clearer and so is the sky, and the sea is bluer than the most beautiful mountain lake of Europe.'

"But, Your Majesty, the Admiral was talking only about the islands. What would he have said if he had seen the green savannas, where the grass grows as high as a man's head? What would he have written if he had seen the mountains, rising luminously into the sky, and the broad streams teeming with fish, the thundering waterfalls, the endless dark forests, the mighty hill-lands stretching on forever like a carpet of virginal breasts, the canyons cut deep into the ground, so deep that it is easy to believe that the rivers of Hell run through them? For this archipelago in the Caribbean Sea is but a minor sample, a prologue to the heavenly chorus of the Tierra Firma.

"But what am I saying? Does this land need me to praise it? The melodies of the birds praise the land, and the rush of the winds through the forests. The thunder of the waterfalls is a deep hymn of avowal. The winds sing over the immense sea of grass, of grass silver and green under a bright heaven across which white balls of cloud float majestically.

"What is the voice of man, always stammering words, helpless, labored words, in comparison with the song of the earth? What are man's works, hammered together, in comparison to the effortlessly rising peaks, the quick waters, the sheer wall of cliff? What are man's works when placed beside the veins in an insect's wing, the color in a bird's feathers, or even beside the bits of crystal in a rock? What do all these inventions amount to, rootless, prefigured, unenduring, incapable of reproducing themselves?

"The tapestries here in this room, the work of the greatest masters—what do they amount to? Imagined flowers, trees, beasts and men—how can they be set alongside the real thing? How pale and awkward are they when measured to the works of the Master of Masters, the greatest Weaver and Builder of all!

"Your Majesty, remember that the Indians are also a work of God. As such they are no more nor any less than the King himself, than the cardinals and all the rest of the people in this room. It is God who puts the mountain goat on the rocky heights, the fish in the water, the bird in the air. It is He who gives you, the King, his crown, the red robes to the Cardinals, and to me my staff. He has given the Indians nothing more than a loincloth, a childish pleasure in laughter, dancing and lively colors, and then has set them down in paradise. Who dares say these Indians may not be more pleasing in the sight of Lord God, naked as they are, than we in our fine dress? For the Lord has said, Let the little children come unto me, for theirs is the kingdom of Heaven.

"And they are, besides, unusually slender-boned and delicate, much more sensitive of body even than the sons of Spanish princes. They are not suited for unremitting labor. God has made them thus.

"When the Admiral's ship was wrecked on Hispaniola the cacique Guacanagari helped him in many ways. He gave him food to eat and sheltered him. The ship was unloaded and taken apart without as much as a single nail being stolen. Indeed, this Indian was so disturbed by his guest's misfortune that he shed tears of pity, and in the end it was the Admiral who had to console him, not the other way around.

"But this attitude is not true only of the superior men among the Indians. The common folk are just the same. Greed, beggary, thieving are vices unknown to them. They simply are not given to white men's practices. I have never seen them let another Indian or even a Spaniard go hungry so long as they had a mouthful of corn to share. They are grateful for the smallest present. They are more pleased with a little bell such as those we Spaniards wear on huntsmen's caps than would be a Spaniard if some one handed him a piece of gold. Yes, they even rejoice over the gift of a rusty nail.

"And their hearts are open to God and His Holy Church. They gladly come to Mass and try to sing our hymns and chorals, even though they may have scarcely heard the words once before. I often think that they must have been waiting for the Gospel, as if they had had intimations of it. They have followed the teachings of Christ before anyone told me His name. They were Christians in practice even before we came to baptize them, not even knowing it."

At this point the heavy-lipped Don Alonso de Molina cleared his throat heavily behind his hand, and looked impatiently at Cardinal

Loaysa. The Cardinal gave him a sign of approval, and he began to speak, even as he was springing to his feet. He talked with irony in his tone, and yet very respectfully.

"Your Majesty, the image Father Bartolomé paints of the Indians," he said, "is both sympathetic and beautiful. One could go on listening to his poetic descriptions for hours on end. They bring to mind the bucolic verses of Virgil. But unfortunately, they are only the fancies of a very imaginative man. They lack correspondence with reality. It is quite possible that the Admiral had such experiences with the Indians. It is my private opinion that in the heat of his success he saw everything as wonderful and perfect, though that is neither here nor there. And if what he says was once true, I am here to declare that since his days the redskins have suffered drastic change. They are so lazy that they stink. They are suspicious, sullen, greedy for gold and do not hesitate to commit theft and murder. Secretly they still pray to their demons. They do not even draw the line at suicide, and have all sorts of mysterious poisonous plants to effect that purpose. They run off into the mountains and forests and there behave like degenerates. Sometimes they try to wage war against us.

"So far as the Indians of the mainland are concerned, all we have to do to see them in the typical light is to recall the teocallis of Tenochtitlan, those black priests with obsidian knives, and the thousands of torn-out hearts. There is nothing paradisaical about these aborigines, I can say that much. Father Bartolomé assuredly errs when he tries to represent them as gentle creatures. The same is true of the Incas of Peru. Think of their pitiless civil wars, their tyrannical enslavement of thousands upon thousands of people. And what about the Caribs? Is it not true that they use bows and poisoned arrows, that they eat human flesh? The Carib stakes at which martyrs have died don't quite fit into this idyllic picture the good father paints. At least, not as I see it!" He snorted with vicious contempt.

"All this is distortion!" Father las Casas cried out. "The teocallis were made up out of whole cloth by the murderous conquistador of Tenochtitlan to cover up his own crimes. And there are no Caribs. They are like the black men we Spaniards used to fear as children. They are the fruit of a bad conscience."

"But father!" expostulated Don Alonso. "How can you gainsay the evidence of thousands? The teocallis have been seen! Many Spaniards have come to a bitter end on them. And what I have said about Peru, the civil war and tyranny, has been reported by officers of the Crown more often than not opposed to Pizarro. Why, even the Indians complain about the Caribs!"

"Indeed, it is hard to doubt that these things exist," murmured the King, turning to van Male, who nodded his head in response. "However fantastic it may seem, it surely does go on—the practice of cannibalism and so forth. Only a madman could invent such notions, and not all Spaniards are that!"

Las Casas looked around uneasily. His eyes sought mine. I sat there as if struck by a bolt of lightning. I knew that everything Molina said was true. I had heard it all out of the mouth of Don Hernando Cortés, who surely had not lied. And I had seen things with my own eyes.

I did not understand how reality looks different to men of great will power. At first I forgot that such beings crush all ideas that oppose their own, that it is precisely this blind part of their being which is the foundation of their success. I should have known these simple facts, for I had seen Pizarro often enough, and he was just such a man. Indeed, at this moment the mighty monk looked strikingly like the tall, gray conqueror himself. They were both conquistadors, men possessed, driven by a sense of destiny far greater than themselves. At moments the inner stream of force, the soundlessly thundering strength of the animus within them, obliterated all personal characteristics. Sentiment dried up in their faces, and they became Spain itself, proud, infinitely stubborn, brave without limit, half crazed in their prejudice. They looked like wandering knights, their lances thrust in the direction of some envisioned eternity, riding on oblivious to all else. And of all conquistadors I had ever seen at that moment the monk looked the most formidable.

"Your words stink, Molina, and they lie," he roared. His voice made the pale King turn even paler, and all the men in the room shrank back. He raised his fist as if he were going to fell Don Alonso to the floor, and he stretched forward his bull neck. "You lie, you cow. And what if they were true? Who in the name of God cares about a man like you! What if you say the whole Mexican plateau is covered with teocallis, and what if it is true, which it is not? What if the skulls are piled up into mountains? What difference does it make if the corpses hang up in Carib villages like oxen in a butcher shop waiting to be carved? What do I care, you liar? I have never seen any such thing. I don't believe it. I—you understand!—I shall never believe it!

"But supposing it were true. What would it all amount to in comparison with the cruelty and greed of Spain? With the infinite, studied corruption? The red men of the mainland have never heard the word of God. They have never been privileged to partake of the Gospel's teachings. Not so the men of Spain. The Indians have never heard of the saints, of the miracles of Christ and His Apostles; they know nothing about the martyred saints! Not so the creatures of Spain!

"What are they doing, these Christians who were baptized as infants, who have worn holes in their shoes running to Mass, who have mouthed the name of God since they were old enough to talk? These Spaniards! Have they taught the Indians? Have they attempted to persuade them to be different? Have they shown them how a Christian behaves, and why it is good to be one?

"Murder and destruction are their watchword. Theft and the infliction of misery are the Mass they sing. Gold is their god! Gold, gold, gold! Fire and sword are their Gospel. They have acted worse than the Arabs, worse than the Vandals and the Tartars. Their slaughtering is so terrible that the blind can see it, the deaf hear the cries of the dying. The dumb cry out in agony with it.

"And the people of the future will ask, How was it? How did it ever happen? Who was the king who permitted such monstrosities to occur? Don Carlos was the man, they will say. Don Carlos has permitted the scourge of Antichrist to rage. But I, a monk, know that Don Carlos would strike down these greedy murderers if he really knew the things that were happening across the sea. If he were not surrounded by lying sycophants who breathe soft stories into his ears, then he would see. I know that he longs for the truth. And I am here to tell him.

"Fifty years ago there were two million people alive on Hispaniola. Today there are scarcely five hundred suffering creatures left. Where have they gone? Have they all flown away to some other place? No, they have been slaughtered like cattle, torn apart and burned at the stake. See, Your Majesty, how God's scales sink deeper away from the Spanish side. Eternal damnation threatens, Your Majesty! The whole Spanish people are in danger. I cannot stand by with my hands folded and watch this happen. I shall always cry out about this terror, and complain from every corner!

"Where shall I begin, and where shall I end? It is hard to know, so dense is the chronicle with horror. I have seen children torn from the breasts of Indian mothers and their soft skulls smashed against cliffs and trees. I have seen screaming infants tossed into the fire for sport. I have seen hundreds of men imprisoned in three small houses—men, women and children, people who had done the Spaniards no harm at all, who, on the contrary, only a short time before had gone much out of their way to be kind to them. And what did the Spaniards do to these people in the houses? The Spaniards set the houses on fire and burned the contents to a mass of char. I saw one Indian, Your Majesty, whose hands had been cut off, tied together, and thrown over his back for a joke. And then they told him, Go let your people know what kind of folk they are dealing with."

The Emperor turned his face away in disgust, and had to fight with himself to keep his self-control. Cardinal Loaysa crossed himself rapidly several times.

"Day after day thousands of Indians die of hunger, not only because the Spaniards rob them of their stores," the monk shouted, the foam white at the corners of his mouth, his face contracted. "No, it is more than that. What the Spaniards do not want to eat, they destroy, deliberately burn up. Thousands of Indians die of overwork. And these are considered lucky by their Indian fellows, for the Spaniards have long since turned the Carib paradise into a hell from which death is a desperately sought-for release. Without the slightest qualm they tear away women from their children, men from their families, and then it goes worse with them than if they were pigs in a sty.

"When the beast Alvarado—he is one of the worst of the lot—came to Quito he had hundreds of Indians slowly roasted over fires, after he had strung them up by the hands to timbers. This he did because the gold he had expected to get proved to be vapor. When night came the cries of the dying disturbed his slumber, and he ordered that those still remaining alive should be summarily killed. But his inferiors, worse even than their noble master, prodded the unfortunates and amused themselves by watching the cramped writhings of the dying bodies."

"That cannot be true," said the Emperor. He was pale as wax. His crooked Hapsburg beak hung out wildly from his pinched face.

"All this is exaggeration," said Don Alonso. "Soldiers are always rough. They say that when Rome was sacked . . ."

Doctor Sepúlveda pulled Don Alonso by the sleeve, and he said no more. Sepúlveda turned his eyes in the direction of the Emperor, and Don Alonso followed his glance.

"What right had these men to execute as much as one man?" Las Casas bellowed. "What right, I ask you! What about this cut-throat of a Pizarro, who has neither faith nor honor? Didn't he slaughter hundreds without the slightest need? Didn't he have Atahualpa throttled after he had betrayed him and stolen everything he had? And he did that in the name of the King, in the name of the Holy Roman Catholic Church!"

"These are the exigencies of war," shouted Don Alonso.

"No," I said.

I found myself on my feet, carried away by the heat of the monk's discourse, and ready to help him. "There was no necessity at all. The Inca was well disposed to us. He was killed against all reason and justice. He was betrayed after we had his gold. In the end he was sentenced to die by a mock court."

Upon hearing this new voice, all the company fell deathly still and began to stare at me, who had been entirely forgotten. The Emperor looked at me narrowly.

"How do you know all these things, young man?" he inquired.

The room began to sway before my eyes. But I forced myself to go on. I kept my eyes fixed on the unicorn.

"Your Majesty, I was there. I was one of the murderers who played at justice. I took part in the murder."

"What! How was that?" said the Emperor. "How is it you are condemning yourself?"

"It has dawned on me," I said, "that Father Bartolomé is right, that justice must come to the Indies. For this land is now a running sore in the body of your kingdom, Your Majesty, and in the body of mankind. Countless thousands will lose all belief in the possibility of meaning and goodness in life, thousands will perish, if something is not done very soon."

Don Alonso de Molina stared at me in contempt and dislike. The Great Inquisitor, Antonio Cardinal de Guevara, watched me closely out of glittering black eyes, like a doctor observing a sick man who has been struck with a disease that may soon become a plague. The Emperor was uneasy, angry. He gnawed at his long lower lip.

"All this has been purposely thrust on my shoulders," he said, almost petulantly. "First it was the revolt of the city of Castile, then this foul monk Luther, then traitors among the nobles. Then next it was Rome itself, standing on the side of my enemies, with the King of France. Even my own city, Ghent, turned on me like a mad dog. They did the same to my grandfather. And now this India, from which I expected to hear nothing but good . . ."

He sighed bitterly, then added like a child, "And to think there it is thousands of miles across the sea! What a Sisyphus of a man I am, trying to bring order into the whole world! And always, no matter what course I take, whether I punish the Lutherans or come to a purely tactical peace with them, whether I conquer Rome for Christianity or forget all about it, whether I have Spain cleared of heresy by the Inquisition or try to curb the Anabaptists in my Flemish cities, it is always the same—hate, curses, and more curses, always at me.

"Is it possible, Las Casas, to be just on this earth? Tell me. You are a man of God."

"Your Majesty," said Las Casas, "so long as you stand foursquare with your conscience it is of no importance what the people say."

"That is true," said the Emperor, turning to van Male for confirmation. "I fear that all the monk says is true enough." Then, turning back to Las Casas, he added, "You can go on now, Las Casas."

"It gives me no pleasure," said Las Casas, "to load Your Majesty with new cares. I would gladly hold my tongue if it were not a matter of shame on the honor of Castile, if it did not concern the fate of an immense portion of the earth's surface. And if it had nothing to do with God's commands, which no man dare shirk.

"These people say, if I understand rightly, that the exploitation of the Indians is necessary on political and military grounds, and to make money. Although these excuses can never hold in the light of God's word, I say they are false even on these purely secular grounds. War can only destroy substance and men. No land can live for long on robbery. Slaves are the most dangerous of all subjects. They can be watched, tortured, put into irons, their tongues and ears cut off, but so long as a heart beats within their breasts they will long for freedom. Why? Because God Himself has put this longing in them, because he created men free. Therefore a proponent of slavery is not only a monster, he is also a fool. For he is undertaking to change something over which he has as little power as over the course of the stars.

"But if the Indians were free, they would willingly work with the Spaniards, as they have done a thousand times since the days of the Admiral, as I personally have had occasion to see. Great areas of land would be turned into fruitful fields. Everywhere would stretch out plantings of Indian maize, cotton and cane. There would be gardens of palm trees, orchards of tropical fruit, and great beds of healing herbs and roots. More metal would come out of the earth, and the herds of llama and vicuña would increase amazingly. The cost of administering the colonies would be reduced. For not only does war cost thousands of men's bodies, it costs also plenty of gold, which in the last analysis must come out of the coffers of the Crown after being put there by the people.

"Men, men are the greatest possession of all. For wherever they are, nothing is impossible, there is no swamp that cannot be drained nor waste that cannot be turned into fields. Where there are no men, useful land becomes overrun with brush and is useless henceforth. And the Spaniards have treated these men, the most precious part of the land, exactly as they treated storehouses, fields, villages, llamas. They have acted badly, if Your Majesty but observes his interests closely. They have been dishonest servants of the Crown, thoughtless of its welfare.

"I say and swear that it is true, more than thirty million Indians have already been wiped off the face of the earth by these servants of the Crown. That is as large as the whole population of Spain, as much of mankind as inhabits all Castile, Catalonia, Estremadura, Andalusia and Leon, taking into account all the cities, villages and estates. What would Your Majesty say if that happened here in his European kingdom of Spain? What if Valladolid, Toledo, Burgos, Cordova and Seville became empty heaps of ruins, inhabited only by rats? What if all the vineyards, the orchards, the fields of grain, the herds of sheep were destroyed? What would Your Majesty say if all the cattle of Spain were made corpses that filled the air with a penetrating odor of decaying flesh that no one could possibly eat! What if all Spain were transformed into a desert, stony and of no use to man, like the land of Gomorrah which God struck down because of its sins?

"Would he appraise all this in terms of military and political necessity? Rather not! He would summon his knights, and put on armor himself! With fire and sword he would seek out the evildoers and run them into the ground. The crows would have enough to eat for months when he and his knights were avenged for the horrors visited on Spain. All the gallows would be lined with thieves and murderers strung up for the very last time.

"And is it really any different with India because it is a few thousand miles across the sea? No, it is exactly the same, the very same. I say that the day will come when India will be a greater possession, a more beautiful jewel in the crown of Spain and in the crown of mankind than this proud Spain itself, or of Flanders, or of any other of Your Majesty's lands. The day will come when no man would presume to compare the worth of Spain with that of India. What, they will say, this Spain, where is it, really? Is it somewhere in Europe, near that pond they call the Mediterranean Sea? No. When I am long dead, I should like to think to myself, This Spain, my fatherland, is small. It is rough, shot through with barren uplands. Its rivers are trickles in comparison with the rivers of the New Spain. Its population is no greater than the population of one of the New Spain's cities.

"But once this old Spain sent out its best over the waters, and converted the Indians, and taught them to be great. It brought to fruition what the Indians began in times so far distant the mind aches to think of it. In a time of chaos, I will think, of unbelief, of mobs and of storms threatening the foundations of the Church, the children of Spain crossed the sea in a great crusade, carrying the gift of justice with them, and raised a mighty monument to God.

"Spain was the last knight, I shall think. Therefore, however small Spain may be, it is nevertheless great, a wellspring of strength. For the true greatness does not come from endless spaces, from giant mountains, broad rivers and countless masses of humanity. It comes from the infinity, the heights, the endurance, the breadth and the mildness of spirit within us. That is how my thoughts might run.

"But shall I really be able to say this, Your Majesty, when I am long dead? Shall my dead eyes have nothing but scenes of cruelty and terror to dwell on? Shall I have to cry out in pity for the hosts of silent dead all about? Shall I say, These Spanish knights knew no self-control when they encountered the helpless, ignorant Indians, and so slaughtered them all to a man? Shall I say, They wagered pieces of gold to see who would have the chance to strike off an Indian's head with the sword? Shall I have that to remember when I dwell on the Christianity of Spain?

Shall I say—and the dead will hear me, while God Himself turns His ears to my words—shall I say that the Spaniards on their expeditions often took the dead flesh of Indians with them, often enough the flesh of women and children, to feed their dogs? Shall I say that one of these monsters told an Indian, 'You, I'm not going to kill you today . . . just give me your arm for my dogs . . . that will do'? Shall I say that about Spain?"

The Emperor sprang to his feet, and with him the dog, startled, baring her teeth.

"Cardinal de Guevara," he shouted, turning to the Grand Inquisitor for the first time, "I demand that you make this Dominican hold his tongue. He is blaspheming God, Spain, the Crown, me. Nothing is sacred to him. I will listen to him no longer . . ."

The Grand Inquisitor rose and pointed his thin, red-gloved hand at Las Casas, saying nothing.

"I will not keep silent," Las Casas roared on. "The world will hear that I have had no part in this crime; and if my King, whose office it is to hear my complaint, even if Your Eminence too turns his head away from me, turns against me, still I shall not hold my tongue. I take my stand on the bull of His Holiness, of the Pope, in which he speaks of the God-given worth of the human soul, which has been created to look on the face of God. And if I am cast out, then I shall set every press in Spain to working. I shall plaster the walls with my words. I shall hand out pamphlets on every corner. If I am put in prison I shall write on the walls of my cell, and cry out my beliefs into the jailers' ears. And even if I am killed, I shall find no rest in the grave. I shall come back to earth. I am a free man, a Spaniard. No one can rob me of my freedom of speech when I am convinced of the truth and justice of what I say. . . ."

"Las Casas," interrupted the Cardinal, "remember that you have spoken vows before the altar to obey your superiors. I am your superior and I order you to be silent. Do you want to spread unrest, chaos, religious war and dissension within the Church, like that thrice-damned Luther of Wittenberg?"

"I am speaking for the truth, for the Gospel," said Las Casas, hoarse with passion.

"Everyone thinks he is doing that," said the Cardinal sharply. "But where has that led? His Majesty the Emperor is well disposed toward you. And so am I. We have shown this a hundred and one times, I am sure. We have put up with your attacks, your harshness and libels. We did this because behind it all we believed there was a pure heart. We have protected you from the conquistadors. The Emperor has made you the Protector-General of the Indies. He has helped you out of his privy purse and supported you because he likes you. But there are limits to everything, Las Casas. This wild talk, this anger with Spain and with the regime of His Majesty, does you little credit. I shall not tolerate having all Spain plunged into blood and revolt just because a fanatic monk cannot curb his tongue."

The Emperor fell back into his chair and there slumped. The big dog stretched out again on the floor and kept her eyes on the enormous figure of the monk.

Las Casas breathed deeply, as if he were sobbing. Then he said, "I did not want to insult my King. Nor Your Eminence. If it sounded that way, it was only because I am a rough, simple man who has been traveling much in wild country. It was not done deliberately."

"Deliberately!" said the Grand Inquisitor. "It looks as if you had lost all sense of propriety. At the moment we are concerned whether the Indians will be free, or the property of the Spanish colonists. And you, Las Casas, have let your temper get the better of you. You have done nothing but shriek out recriminations, and recount horrors in the most revolting fashion. Do you think for a moment that His Majesty, or I, or anyone else in this room, approves of these things?"

"No," said Las Casas, "I don't believe that. If I did, I should have never gone to the trouble of telling you about them."

"What!" said the Cardinal.

"I believe," Las Casas said, "that when His Majesty has seen the evil results of slavery, when they have been described completely for his benefit, he will erase the practice from the Indies. For slavery is the root of all misery. Not only does it injure the Indians themselves, it also makes beasts and slaves, which is even worse, out of Christian Spaniards. Even the most superior among those who command slaves is only a slave himself. He can never be a free man. The disobedience of God's command will multiply the misery to such an extent that in time the authors of it will themselves be consumed. For the Indians at the worst will lose only their bodies. But the Spaniards will lose their souls."

"How curious it is," the Grand Inquisitor said, "that it never occurred to a man of your experience that the majority of men are nothing more than slaves and do not want to be otherwise. They would lick the ground to be ordered about; they want command, authority and protection. Nothing do they want less than freedom! It is security, peace, and relief from the tedious business of thought that they look for!"

"You are right," Las Casas said slowly. "I have known many such men. They want to live smooth lives, apart from their fellows, as if they were traveling alone down a royal highroad. But as for them, I have ignored them. They are beneath my attention. They had better not get in my way, or I should crush them like flies."

The Grand Inquisitor stared at Las Casas with curiosity in his face. His darting, heavy black eyes fastened on the monk.

"On the whole, Las Casas," he said, smiling coldly, "you are a man of my own kidney. But you do not coin your gold. You waste your energies, my dear father. You do not dwell on differences, and measure them. Everything flows out of you like water out of a fountain, blessings and curses, sadness and joy, the truth and downright fancy. Have you never heard of *caritas,* of Christian love? Have you never heard that the weak, the innocent and the inexperienced, the children of the world, shall be protected from harshness?"

"What!" shouted Las Casas. "You say that to me! *Caritas* is my life. I have never thought or lived anything else! You know that as well as I."

"And yet you would cast these innocents naked into freedom," the Grand Inquisitor went on steadily. "You would hurl them into the maelstrom of the world just to have your way. You want the Indians—your children, as you call them—to know what it is to be free. Whether they will hunger, thirst and have no shelter after this concerns you not at all. You are like a father raven who forces the young ones from the nest."

"Out of the nest of slavery?" said Las Casas. "Yes, that is exactly what I want to do."

"I am not talking about slavery, as you well know," said the Great Inquisitor. "I don't want any more outbursts from you. I am talking about a gentle, piously conceived, kindly compulsion. I am talking about the division of the Indians among the planters, providing that they remain under the strict protection of the Church and the Crown.

In this fashion their children will be sure of bread and of work when they are old enough. At the same time they would receive spiritual instruction. They would be given feast days off. In short, everything, everything they could wish for—within bounds, of course. And that they must work, that is also one of God's commands, even as Doctor Sepúlveda remarked."

"Everything?" said Father Las Casas, dazed. "Really everything? They would have care? And help? That would be splendid, something hardly to be expected . . . but I . . ."

"Well," said de Guevara, "but what? What is the trouble now?"

"I implore you, Your Eminence," said Las Casas, "do not try to probe into me. It will do no good. No . . ." He shouted loudly, so that the room rang with his heavy voice. "No, I will not do it. I will not sell the Gospel for bread and shelter and peace. I do not want school, cathedrals and towns if they have to be bought with freedom. They are a lie. I will not have them on such terms."

"And yet they will come," said the Grand Inquisitor, his voice rising in answer. "They will come whatever you may think, you mule. For it lies in the nature of man, in his humility, in his longing for safety, in his fear of life."

"I believe in men," said Las Casas. "I believe in their worth and their immortality."

"You do!" said the Cardinal sarcastically. "You believe in all of them, do you? Do you believe in men who feed their dogs with human flesh, who murder and roast them over fires? Do you believe in them, Las Casas?"

"Yes, even in them," said the monk. "I even believe in Pedro de Alvarado, in the Pizarros, in all the conquistadors who have dyed red the earth of the Indies. I know that at the bottom they are men like all the rest. Somewhere in them burns the spark of God. I believe in them even as I call them beasts. I believe that for their crimes they suffer grievous torments which are as bad as the fiery deaths of the Indians. I know that when Pedro de Alvarado died a hard death, the doctor asked him where was his greatest pain, and he replied, 'In my soul, doctor.' That is convincing enough for me. I believe that even these men were cast in the mold of freedom at the start."

"There is nothing to be done with you, Las Casas," said the Grand Inquisitor. "You are really as innocent as a child in the ways of the world. You are shot through with contradictions. I believe you yourself do not really know exactly what it is you want! First you love Spain; then you flay it to the ground. At one time you indict the evildoers so that our hair stands up on our heads; and the next minute you are condoning them, as if they were saintly converts, like Maria of Egypt. First you want to protect the Indians; then you want to let them return stripped to the forests. What is it you really want, Las Casas?"

"I want freedom," said Las Casas. "Nothing more than freedom."

The Grand Inquisitor shrugged his shoulders. "Freedom, Las Casas, is nothing but an empty word," he murmured, half to himself. "It is nothing more than a gift from Pandora's box. It is not designed for ordinary men." Then he looked at the Emperor, and added, "I have formed my opinion, Your Majesty. Indeed, I had formed it before I came into this room, and nothing has happened which makes me believe I should modify it in any way."

"Kindly tell me what this opinion is, Your Eminence," said the Emperor, bowing slightly.

"The repartimientos," the Grand Inquisitor said thoughtfully, "shall be all over the Indies and the mainland, in all the New World. But they shall exist henceforth under strict civil and religious supervision. There shall be laws for the protection of the Indians, their fields, herds and all their possessions. There shall be the most severe punishments meted out to the Spanish thieves, murderers and rapists who disturb the order imposed by the Crown and by the Church. Work shall be limited to a certain number of days a week. Immediately work shall start on the construction of hospitals, schools and churches. And much else that can be planned in detail by the Council for the Indies far better than by me."

"I thank Your Eminence," said the Emperor. "That is a clear, intelligible decision. And you, Cardinal Loaysa? I see that you have something on your mind?" He bowed in the direction of the spiritual president of the Council of the Indies.

Loaysa reddened at the courtesy. "I regret that I must disagree with my colleague," he said softly. "I agree completely with the opinion of the Father Bartolomé. There will never be peace and order in India unless the evil of slavery is torn out by the roots. I am for an absolute ban on all forced labor in any form, and for the manumission of the Indians wherever they are now enslaved."

"See!" said the Emperor, wearily. "Has Your Eminence followed all this discourse carefully? What laws do you want, then?"

"I want no more laws," Loaysa replied. "I wish only that the present laws, which are based on the testament of Queen Doña Isabella and on the bull *Sublimis Deus* of His Holiness Pope Paul the Third, be adhered to. If necessary they should be enforced with the sword. I want everyone who does not obey them to be branded as traitor to the State and God, and forthwith to meet his proper fate.

"Ultimate revolt, Your Majesty, is on the other side, on the side of the so-called prescriptive law, which is but another word for lawlessness, as I see it. The time has come for states and colonies to develop out of conquest, and possessions of the Crown out of what is held by brute force. Just as other lands ruled by the Crown are kept in place by hard and fast laws holding for all, so too must these be if the New World is to grow into greatness. Conquistadors, robber chieftains, swineherds and all the rest are not fit to further this task, it is plain to see. Personal will must come to an end. The epoch of discovery and occupation is over. Colonization begins henceforth. It cannot be done through robbery and plundering. It must be accomplished through the labor of millions of free men who can participate in the fruit of their labors. From the yield of the soil, the riches of the forest, and the treasures under the earth they can find something for themselves and for the Crown as well.

"I consider Your Majesty fortunate that it is he who can initiate these healing works. I consider it to be a good sign that our great Catholic Queen Doña Isabella has already set down the rules and laws for Your Majesty to take up and carry out to the letter, thereby reducing the chaos of the Indies to order such as obtains in the other possessions of the Crown."

"Your proposal is sound, too," said the Emperor. "But it is hard for me to understand why two such well-informed men of long experience should interpret the same situation so differently. You two cardinals agree on only one point. You both want to see an end to lawlessness." The Emperor paused. His eyes sought Las Casas.

"Las Casas, you troublemaker," he said, smiling, "you've forced your way in again and doomed me to many sleepless nights. It's what you always bring me, isn't it! I'll make up my mind very soon. But I have to think it over, Las Casas. Do you follow me? I'm not the young man of Coruña you used to know, who would bull his way through every obstacle. There's no more little Carlos, ready to sign his name to every paper stuck under his nose. I'm old, old, Las Casas. I'm almost as old as the Grand Inquisitor."

"May God guide my King's thoughts!" said Las Casas.

"So be it, so be it, Las Casas," said the Emperor and got up. "I thank all of you for your counsel and your loyalty." He dismissed us with an inclination of his head. We left the unicorn room.

I saw the Emperor turn to his privy councilor, van Male. Shivering he drew the ermine tippet closer around his shoulders. His face was tired and sunken, almost suffering. The big white bitch rose, stretched herself slowly and looked at her master.

26

THE RED ROSE

WHEN I left the cool twilight of the unicorn room for the white-walled, sunny corridor, I went to a window and looked out, trying to array my thoughts. I did not see the garden, the fountain and the trees, or whatever it was that met my eye. I was shaken by the discourse of Father las Casas. The monk had boldly uncovered a hidden, dangerous growth, I felt. He had cut directly into it, into this sickness which was sapping the life of both India and Spain. It was the same sore that had made me into a miserable, persecuted man.

Now I felt a wonderful sensation of relief. At the same time I reddened with shame to think how little I had been able to support Father las Casas. I was troubled with doubts about the decision of Don Carlos. It was common knowledge that the King, like all old statesmen, avoided clearly defined decisions as he did the plague. Everyone knew he preferred to leave matters hanging fire, until irrevocable circumstances forced the issue. And Don Carlos was old, despite his mere forty-two years. He was resigned and disillusioned, overburdened with the great task of patching together the declining world of the Church and the Holy Roman Empire and so bringing unity again to life in Europe. It was a task for a Titan, for such a man as Charlemagne or the Saxon king, Otto. But Don Carlos? What could this son of Doña Juana do among so many hard, brutal men, men teeming with vigor and purpose? What could he do, with the blue veins close to the surface of the skin, and gout in his feet? He doubted himself and he doubted those about him.

And the times, were they not destined to change? Had not the Church split under the hammer blows of the monk of Wittenberg when he nailed his thesis to the cathedral door? Had not the closed, strict, three-dimensional world of the Florentine turned into a chaos of alternatives and doubts where anything might happen? Had not the crystalline Heaven of pious centuries been smashed into countless fragments, and did not a new concept yawn, barren infinities?

No matter in which direction one looked the universals by which men had lived since the decline of Rome—the dogma of the Church, the law of states—were collapsing like houses built on sand. Everywhere there were new things, new particulars, until at last the incidental had risen up to triumph. The trivial, or what had begun as trivial, became outlined, it took on features, and then stared men down boldly and contemptuously, taking revenge for long years of confinement. *Res ante universalia!* That was it. Things clamored for their rights, four-cornered, hard, earthy things. They ignored the grand concepts, dismissing them as empty imaginings and dreams.

It was like this everywhere—in the savant's study as he pried into the nature of matter; in the painter's atelier, where now a wart on the model's nose meant more than an angel's wing; in the council chamber, where the guilds fought the patricians for more money, better pay, higher prices and other material advantages. It was a terrific debacle, taking in everything, from Heaven down to the smallest village. Nations had evolved from kingdoms. Out of nations had come independent duchies and free cities. In the cities themselves the population had split up into rich and poor, great and humble, Lutheran and Catholic. In the end only one thing remained: the individual, the single person and his private world.

But this person, I saw, was by no means a sound, durable final segment of division. For all the once-banished ideas now came to assault the man standing alone with inner law. The ideas writhed in his mind, filling him with melancholy, doubt, visiting dreams and madness on him. Death has become fearful, I thought. The dance of death imagined by the painter depicts this for all to see. God and immortality, even the existence of the soul, have become dubious.

And now where shall man turn, if he can no longer turn to God? Shall he heap up gold? Shall he do deeds of violence and so impose his will on others playing God in the little? Shall he chase after fame in posterity? Shall he devote himself to a life of sensual self-indulgence? Shall he steal, betray, wound and murder in order to possess many articles and have sway over the world? Shall he wander into the garden of Epicurus? Shall he choose the harsh, stiff, frozen insensitivity of the Stoa?

No. Who looks deeper sees well enough that all such people are only more doubters, men of despair. They may plant flowers and water the grass! They may utter words of wisdom like the slave Epictetus or the Emperor Marcus Aurelius, and take everything in their stride. Nevertheless, they despair! They are nothing but cowards. Is not the criminal the true man in a world without God, the man who hates all evasion, all half-happiness, all empty show?

Such is our world, I thought, standing at the window after listening to the words of the mighty of Spain. Perhaps it is not so completely bad as I envision it, I told myself, but the seeds of destruction have been planted. In time they will spring up like weeds, choking out all that I believed as a child. If only Don Carlos would listen to the monk Las Casas! For this monk, however rudely he may express himself, however coarse his great body, carries in his hand the idea of ideas, the cornerstone on which the world can be built, the one universal. If only Don Carlos is not driven into the ground with the confusion of political and economic cares, blinded by the clever shortsightedness of his professional councilors!

Suddenly I started from this reverie. Someone was standing behind me. It was Don Alonso de Molina, examining me with irony dry on his cold face. He stepped very close to me, so close I could feel his breath on my cheek.

"You are a cheat of the commonest sort," he said to me. "You have informed on your comrades to the Emperor. They were not there to protect themselves."

"You know nothing about such matters," I replied. "There is nothing you can say that can touch me."

"Why don't you say right out, you milksop, you don't think I'm much of a Christian?" he said icily. "You abase yourself like a mendicant monk in his filthy rags before his prior. I will tell you what's the matter with you. You are not a caballero. You are no more a knight than a cow is. I have heard stories about you. I have heard that judging from your childhood you belong in the Potro rather than before a king."

His thick negroid lips were pouted out with anger, and his eyes blazed as he pursued his insults. But curiously enough I was not moved.

All that he said seemed far away. I was preoccupied with thoughts of Las Casas and of the great decision. And the more indifferent I was to him, the greater Molina's anger.

"You are a coward," said Molina to me.

"You may think so," I told him. "But if you do you are a fool. Your gabble moves me as much as an ass's braying."

I moved to go, and he caught me by the arm. "I challenge you to duel!" he said hotly.

I took his hand off my sleeve, and shrugged my shoulders.

"You cannot deny me," he said. "I am just as much a noble as you. You have insulted me . . ."

"So be it, then," I said, "if that's the way you want it."

"No, it will not be that at all," another voice behind us spoke up. "I shall not tolerate it."

We turned quickly. Framed in the door of the unicorn room was the King Don Carlos. Behind him stood van Male, his privy councilor.

"What does this mean, Don Alonso?" the Emperor said. "Are you injuring a guest in my house? Have you never heard of the King's peace? Where are your manners, Don Alonso? Have you lost your respect for the Crown?"

Don Alonso dropped his eyes, and his lips compressed with wrath.

"Your Majesty," I said, bowing, "Don Alonso believes that I have betrayed my comrades . . ."

"Betrayed them!" said the King. He walked up to us. "In my council chamber the truth must be spoken. There is no point in thinking about this or that one's advantage. When you come before me, personal scruples must be laid aside. But outside of that, I am astonished, Don Alonso. Are you not aware that this was a secret meeting? Don't you know that all you have heard must be struck from your memory? Do you intend, perhaps, to use your knowledge for your own predatory ends, Don Alonso? You ride over the Crown's rule of sanctuary and fall on my guest like a thief in the street! Before my eyes! You dare to do it! I have half a mind to ban you from the Court and from Castile. You have insulted Don Pedro. You must ask his pardon."

Suddenly Don Carlos lowered his head in thought. His huge, crooked nose sank lower, his square-cut beard almost disappeared into his robe. He looked up at us coldly. "Van Male," he said, "this is what I've been waiting for."

"I don't understand Your Majesty," said van Male, eyeing us both severely.

"The decision, van Male," whispered Don Carlos. "The sign I was telling you about . . ."

"I still don't understand," the privy councilor said.

Don Carlos turned to me. "Is it true?" he said. "Have I understood you correctly? You are for the freeing of the Indians? And the enforcement of the law as it stands? The testament of the Queen?"

"Yes, Your Majesty," I said. "That is what I want."

"And you, Don Alonso," the Emperor asked, "you are for the repartimientos, are you not, for forced labor in the Indies? You are for dividing up the red men among the Spaniards?"

"Yes, Your Majesty," said Molina, "I consider it to be dictated by necessity."

"I cannot tolerate a duel, sirs," Don Carlos said. "Such bloody devices can never arise from anything that is said or done in my house or in my council chamber! For a duel is civil war in miniature, as I see it. But since your differences can scarcely be settled by law, and since the honor of both of you is involved, I choose the only possible, knightly solution. I propose that early tomorrow morning you shall meet in the Plaza Mayor, and there under the eyes of the King break three lances. Then we shall see. . . ."

The Emperor turned to van Male. He could not hold back a little smile of triumph.

"Oh, I understand!" said van Male.

And I also understood. I saw that Don Alonso too had caught the larger meaning of the tourney that the King proposed. He offered me his hand, and said, "I beg your pardon for my outburst. I take it back. I regret that my temper got the better of me. We will break the lances for an idea, then, not for ourselves."

"That will be right," I said.

"I am satisfied," said Don Carlos. "We have all understood each other, then." His face was younger, he took off his heavy mantle and handed it to a servant who lurked in the background. "Come, van Male," he went on pleasantly. "We have had enough of State affairs for one day. The sun is shining. Let us go into the garden."

He took his leave with a gracious wave of the hand. His doublet and his hose were made of yellow silk. In the slits were inserted strips of carmine-colored silk. He walked away, leaning lightly on van

Male's arm, rather dragging his right foot. That was because of the gout, which he had inherited from his grandfather, the Emperor Maximiliano, along with the rule of a hundred countries.

On the next morning I stood in one of the leafy arcades of the Plaza Mayor that had been fitted out as an armory. My page Manuel stood on a stool. The sweat ran down his face from the effort of binding over my shoulders the heavy jousting harness. I had never thought a man could carry so much iron on his back. The light field armor of Don Sandoval was nothing in comparison with this old-fashioned armor from the King's armory. I felt imprisoned like a beetle in its shell. It was almost impossible to breathe with such a weight heavy on my chest. Manuel shouted, "You're ready, my lord," and reached me, having to use both hands, the Augsburg helmet decorated with gay ostrich feathers.

At the very moment I was finished several men came into the arcade to see how things were going with me, and to inspect my armor. With them, I recall, a messenger came, who handed Manuel something. But he was soon forgotten in the crush. The noblemen who had come to give me a hand tried the leather straps and buckles of the harness. They girdled me so tightly that my breath left my body. Then they placed the helmet on my head and hooked it fast. When this was done I felt all alone. I heard laughter and excited comment from a great distance. My horse was led forward. It took a great deal of effort to climb into the saddle. My arm almost crushed Manuel as he helped me up.

I took the reins in my iron fingers, which screeched metallically in the joints when I bent them, and headed my horse out into the square. The sun was very bright. From behind the iron grating of my visor I saw that the middle of the square had been strewn with sand. It looked as if the crowd expected a bullfight rather than a tourney. It occurred to me that today I was going to be both picador and bull, and at this I smiled to myself behind the slits in the helmet. I told myself vacantly that everything would be all right if the *chulos* didn't drag me off by the heels. Indeed, at this final moment I was not dwelling at all on the idea of victory. I hoped only that I would stand up squarely to the first lance, and so comport myself like a man.

At the windows all around the space, on the roofs and on balconies there were people ready to watch the show, among them many finely dressed men and women. All round the periphery of the square a boisterous crowd had gathered. Everyone was talking loudly. Some were laughing, others had long faces, prepared for the worst. And others betrayed nothing in their expressions. There was a humming sound beneath the broken voices, like the sound of a great swarm of bees. Some of the people had brought out barrels and were sitting or standing on them, chewing bread to make up for the breakfast that the tourney had interrupted. With them they had brought flasks of wine, protected in our old Spanish style with wickerwork. But the ladies above on the balconies were offered wine out of shining beakers. There is no doubt that Spain has plenty of gold these days, I thought. Their faces were red with morning joy and the excitement of the joust, and they laughed when the men talked gallantly to them.

But there I was alone, sweating powerfully, getting weaker in the knees every moment. I forgot the real meaning of the tourney, and felt like a man who is paid to make sport for others, a jester or something of the sort. All that I need now, I thought, is a few bells on my helmet. The helmet was very heavy. It was pressing in on my brain. I sat slumped on my horse, hidden behind a lattice. I envied the most bedraggled beggar in the crowd, and would have sold my birthright at the moment to be out of the suffocating armor.

There was a great fanfare of trumpets. The sound chilled me, and I began to tremble violently, at the same time hoping that the trembling would not show in the lance. My horse danced, and in the struggle to get him under control and ready for the charge, I forgot the crowd. As in a dream I saw Don Carlos come out of a balcony of a house in the center of the square, followed by his van Male and by a blond, thinnish young man that I later discovered was the Infante Don Felipe.

The young prince, who sometime will be King of Spain as Don Felipe, the second of this name, providing that God holds together body and soul for him, was never such a devotee of the joust as his father had been at his age. Even at that age this youth found it more pleasurable to carry the cross in processions, to walk behind the reliquiae or to attend an *auto da fé*. On the other hand in common with the masculine ancestors of his line he had an enormous predilection for women. His long, disillusioned features now were bitten with a half-embarrassed delight as he sidled close to a full-bosomed tittering blonde who, as could be discerned even from the distance where I was, unquestionably had already seen about all there was to see. But it was all like a flashing dream.

When the Emperor appeared a respectful hush fell over the crowd. But in this silence I sensed the same fearful expectation I had once felt pulsing in the Court of the Oranges at the time of the miracle play. When the herald gave the signal I rode forward to the King's balcony. From the other side of the square another mounted figure came out, similarly obscured in a costume of iron. The heralds called out our names, our titles and ranks. Don Carlos got to his feet, and bent toward us. Even the scrawny Infante leaned forward the better to see such an unusual sight. We could scarcely move, so heavily encased were we in the unaccustomed armor.

I looked up at the tapestry, decorated with the royal coat-of-arms, which hung from the balustrade of the balcony. My heart almost stopped. Not far from the Emperor, holding on tightly to the railing, was a young lady. Her hair was very dark and combed back from her forehead. She wore a golden net of fine mesh, the kind that the Venetians alone can make. I saw her watching me. She looked at my armor, strained toward me anxiously. She seemed to be seeking something. I looked at Don Alonso and noted that on his right shoulder he had attached a fine glove made of silver thread.

Then, from far away, I heard the Emperor's voice, "My lords Don Alonso and Don Pedro, ride the best you can for victory. No matter who wins or who loses, bear yourselves like Spanish knights."

The two pages took the horses' bridles and led them back to the sanded place. The trumpets blared into the breathless square. It was like suddenly spreading the space with a great scarlet cloth. The barrier was lifted, and I dug my heels into the horse's ribs. He plunged forward onto the sand. My mount seemed to gain momentum through the sheer weight of my armor. I met my opponent like a stone from a catapult. The contact almost knocked me out of my senses. I saw lights. I heard the saddle girth and the stirrup straps crack with the strain. But Don Alonso's lance slithered off my left shoulder after striking me a blow that almost unseated me. My lance also struck home. I saw Don Alonso's horse rear, almost topple backward. The shaft in my hands splintered as if it had been struck by a bolt of lightning. I heard the shouts of the crowd. Olé! . . . olé! . . . olé! . . . they roared I began to feel confidence, almost to enjoy the game.

Behind the barrier another lance was handed to me. Many advisers had gathered at the barrier, and all of them proffered me counsel at once.

"Aim for the chest!" one old don persisted in telling me. "Try to strike him on the heart." "No, don't think of it," said another *aficionado*. "Catch him at the pommel of the saddle, let the lance get underneath, then pry up. That's far gayer. It has humor, that style." "Humor!" shrieked the older man. "What do you upstarts know about style? I say the knightly style . . ." And a third said, "Keep your head down, Don Pedro. I know Don Alonso. He'll try to rip your head off if he gets the chance."

We came together again, and I thought I was finished. The lance caught me at the forehead, just over the visor. Blood streamed out of my nose and mouth till I choked on it. There was nowhere to spit the blood, and I felt sick. I needed to vomit, but had no space. In the saddle I swayed like a drunken man, and had to hold onto the pommel to keep from collapsing to the ground. My own lance appeared to have struck Don Alonso on the breast, but this time the impact had not been so great, for the horse was not lifted backward.

"I'm done for," I thought. "Back to Cordova!"

I walked my horse to the barrier, hanging on, my head down. The many seconds unhooked the helmet, rubbed my face with vinegar to stop the bleeding and bring me to with the smart, and let me vomit. "He looks bad," I heard one say, "he looks very bad." "He got him on the head," another one said, his voice high with excitement. Manuel came running up to me, and said, breathlessly, "Here's the rose."

"What rose? What are you talking about?" I asked.

"A lady sent it to you," he said. "I forgot it at first. You ought to wear it." He danced with nervousness.

"Who was it?"

"I think she said she was Doña Beatrice. . . ."

"Beatrice!" I looked at the rose. There were fine gold threads wound around its stem.

"Get out of here," one of the men said, "get out of here with your roses! This is no time for sentiments, little cow."

I laughed crazily, and someone said, "Well, the poor devil still has a laugh in him!" The thoughtful don who had recommended aiming at the heart said doubtfully, "All these Cordovans have thick skulls. Maybe he's all right after all."

"Put the little rose on my shoulder," I said to one of them, my voice thick with the blood trickling into my throat.

"Roses aren't going to do you much good, my friend," remarked the man who had plumped for a humorous style. "If that lance ever catches your square head again, all the roses you'll need will be the kind they strew over graves!"

"Never mind too much practical advice," the old man interposed. "Let him do as he wants. It's the knightly thing to do, isn't it? It's the heart that counts, not the head."

"A heart!" they all took up the cry. "He has a heart this time!"

"Aim for the heart," squealed the old don. "Try it once again. Right at the heart. It will unseat him as sure as God fashioned green pears for boys to chew on."

They fastened down the helmet. I could smell my own sticky blood, and my mouth was sour. Once again we rode forward, into the scarlet echo of the trumpets. I gave my horse both spurs, and he strained madly to get into a gallop. I held myself to one side in the saddle, leaning to the left. For the third time my lance struck Don Alonso's breast, this time solidly. And this time I was lucky enough to have his thrust slide harmlessly past me. My lance did not break. I found I was holding it against empty air.

A mad cry went up in the square. The women began to wave from the balconies. They threw flowers and kerchiefs into the sand. I turned my horse in a daze. I saw Don Alonso sprawled on the sand. His horse was several yards away, his sides heaving, the saddle almost twisted from his back. Don Alonso struggled to get up. His armor was too heavy, and he rolled over. The horse ambled off, back to the barrier, while the crowd shrieked and laughed.

Carefully I descended from the saddle and helped Don Alonso to his feet.

"The show is over," he said, hardly able to speak. "I have broken some ribs."

"Well, my nose is smashed," I said, thinking childishly to console him. "It was pure luck, of course. If we had tried another time it probably would have been your turn."

The pages took off our helmets, and we staggered over beneath the Emperor's balcony. "That was a good joust," said Don Carlos. "Thank you very much for it. You have forgotten nothing while you were across the sea, my lords."

My eyes searched the party on the King's balcony. The Infante was talking to Doña Isabella. I half heard, half read his lips. He was saying, "How did the rider from Cordova get your rose?"

Don Carlos leaned over to van Male. "I would really like to try my own hand the next time anything like this happens." He laughed slily, expectantly.

"Your Majesty!" objected van Male, rising to the bait. "That's simply out of the question. You know what the doctors . . ."

"Yes, yes, of course, the doctors. I could die of hunger and thirst if they had their way," the Emperor said. "But . . . perhaps we can break a lance over the table, van Male. How will that be?"

Don Alonso prodded me. We both turned and went back to the arcade that had been set up as an armory. There I found Sancho waiting for me. I was surprised, for I had thought he was safely at home in Cordova.

"Master!" Sancho shouted. "The courier from Seville . . ."

"From Seville?" I said. "Has something happened? . . ."

"Yes, Pizarro is dead."

"How did it happen," I said, refusing to believe, wiping my face. "It's probably just another story."

"He was murdered!"

"Murdered! Good sweet Virgin Mary!" I said. "That's surely only another lie. What is it, the Indians?"

"No, the Spaniards killed him," said Sancho, grave and pleased to be the bearer of such portentous tidings. "It was the men from Chile, Almagro's men. It was a man called Rada, and Almagro's son."

"You're sure about that!"

"Yes, my lord," said Sancho. "The news comes from Father Vicente de Valverde himself. The King must know about it by this time. The news is spreading like wildfire. They're all talking about it, even in the villages."

"Tell me, how did it happen? Exactly," I said.

"Well, my lord, this is the way I heard it," began Sancho. "It seems that the Captain-General was sitting with his brother Martín de Alcántara and some more people at the table. The traitors fell on Pizarro and killed him with daggers. Martín de Alcántara tried to protect himself and the Captain-General. Pizarro killed one man. Then someone stuck a dagger in his neck. He began to die. His throat filled with blood. Then he said, 'Jesus, save . . .' and that was all he could say. He put his finger in the blood and made a cross on the floor. Then he kissed the cross. While he was lying there someone struck him on the back of the head with a sword, and he died."

"I can imagine it!" I said. "Pizarro dead! How could I ever think that he would die in his bed?"

"They took everything out of his palace," Sancho went on. "They stole all his gold and silver. Everyone in the streets began to shout, 'The tyrant is dead!' But the burghers and the soldiers were not happy over what had happened. At first the traitors wanted to mutilate the body. They wanted to hang it in the square, like a murderer's. Then they thought better of doing that and allowed it to be taken in secret to the cathedral by some servants. They buried it in a corner, Pizarro's body. . . ."

And with it, I thought, they buried all his dreams of mastery, of riches and might. They buried the dreams, a bloody cross, and a despairing cry in a shallow grave, smelling of lime. I saw the conquistador before me that night when the smoky light of the torches burned in the little fort of a church in Trujillo. Where have you ridden now, gray old man on a horse? I thought. Where have you gone, you brave, curious, benighted man? I knelt down and prayed. I was still in my ceremonial armor, with the red rose on my shoulder, and for this I was glad afterward. Sancho and Manuel knelt down with me. Later I gave orders that Masses he held in the Cathedral of Cordova for the murdered man. Father Juan conducted them, under the same hoof-shaped arch I had known as a boy.

Some days later I was called to the Court by a messenger. I found our King in a small, rather mean house in the neighborhood of the old Cloister of Santa Maria la Antigua. In this house the Infante Felipe had been born. Don Carlos did not like to be in his huge palaces and fortified castles when he was with his family. He preferred small surroundings, preferably near a church. Often these dwellings were connected with the place of worship by a secret passageway.

Don Carlos sat in a comfortable leather chair placed before a mighty oaken writing table. The table was covered with papers and books laid open. An inkwell, different sized quills and a box of sand were there, very evidently having just been used. Don Carlos wore a simple robe of black fustian, the kind that savants like best to wear. Even though it was a warm autumn day, next to his chair was a little open stove, into which from time to time as the flame needed replenishing van Male dropped pieces of charcoal.

"Sit down," said Don Carlos, pointing to a chair opposite him at the table; "sit down, if you please, my lord. At home I am not the Emperor. There is no need for dealing with me as such. In the unicorn room, as you no doubt noticed, it was another story. Here I am just one of the many thousands of Don Carloses in Spain. Here I look over my accounts like any burgher, and they give me many a bad hour. Did you know that van Male had written a book? *Chevalier Delibéré* it's called. A good book. I'm translating it into Spanish. A very, very good book. I'm fond of it."

Don Carlos fell silent. Through the latticed window of the room I saw into a small, empty, sun-drenched square. Tufts of grass grew up among the flagstones. In the cloister garden, beyond the square, two white-robed monks were busying themselves among the plants, bent almost double. A noonday hush was on the place. From the distance I could hear the cry of a water vendor, *"Quién quiere agua, agua, agua, quién quiere agua?"* Monotonously the cry was repeated, and came drifting in between the white-walled houses, through the lattice over the window. Again and again the water vendor plained his question, dragging the words out like a mourning dove, *"Agua helada fresquita, como la nieve, agua helada fresquita, quién quiere agua?"*

"Ah yes," said Don Carlos, "cool as snow, cool as snow. You might think he was trying to sell the water of life, and no one there to buy it. Everyone taking a siesta, of course, snoring away, forgetting the water of life. Poor water vendor! Poor friend of man!

"This morning Father Bartolomé de las Casas was here. I almost bowled him over when I told him that I would make him Bishop of Cuzco if he would take over the task of being spiritual lord of the New World. No one can fathom this Las Casas. He said he preferred to keep on as a monk, to go wandering around as he always has done. He said people would consider him ambitious if he took such a position. They would no longer trust him, he insisted.

"How ridiculous! As if their trust mattered so long as he has mine! He has it, of course, and he will have it as long as I draw breath through my nostrils. And after me comes my son.

"This Las Casas, I feel, will live to be a very old man. I have never seen a healthier man. The big body is filled with an idea. The idea is

Christ Himself, Christ the Master, living in His servant, Las Casas. Isn't that wonderful! The man is great, whether he is in a castle, a church or an Indian village. He is always the same. I fail to see that he has changed one jot in the past quarter century.

"Agua helada fresquita! Always the same cry, the same voice, the same thirst to fill. Yet most of them snore away and barely turn their heads to listen, the best of them. The years roll on. Blood, misery, poverty, hate and greed. It's like a dream, a puppet show. Wars, alliances, treaties, pacts of peace, they come and go. The history of the world is mostly the history of fools. I am so tired...."

He turned as was his habit to van Male, and pulled down the corners of his mouth in mockery.

"Tired of being a master of puppets, van Male, tired to death. Wars are nothing but the suicide of the people, and we make treaties only to delay for the time when we can best break them. There is nothing without God, Las Casas says. And he is right. Chaos, Babel, a nightmare. Without God life is but a slow dying. The art of dying well. Shall we stop there, van Male? Without God even pity is an outrage, so much salt in the wounds.

"Well, I've made Las Casas Bishop of Chiapas. I told him he had to be bishop of something or other. I wouldn't tolerate any holding back. But what is this Chiapas? A fever swamp, a handful of Indian huts, a miserable final place to die in. It is ridiculous, of course, to have a bishop in such a place. But that's where he wants to be. That means shortly I shall have to dig into my pockets. But curiously, Van Male, for once I won't mind. It's about the only money I've let out of my hands without feeling a twinge. You know what my Flemish blood does, don't you? I'll enjoy doing it as much as when I bought Felipe his first toys...."

Don Carlos had put his hands behind his head, and leaned back comfortably in the chair.

"As for you, Don Pedro," he said, "I've called you here to thank you once again. Not only as Emperor, but simply as a Spaniard and a father...."

"A father? ..."

"The Plaza Mayor of Valladolid plays an important part in my family," the Emperor said. "There my forebear, San Fernando, King of Leon, was crowned King of Castile, and so laid the groundwork for inducting Cordova and Seville into the Crown. There Don Fernando and Doña Isabella were married, and with this Aragon and Castile united. There I rode in my first Spanish tourney. There the people shouted and made merry when the Infante Felipe was born, after the heralds had summoned them for the news. I regard this Square with a certain superstition. I confess it. It's hard to believe it, when you look at the place during the weekday, when the merchants are selling their wares. But for me everything that goes on there seems to have a special meaning for my family. And for the welfare of Spain.

"From the start I wanted to see Las Casas' argument win out. But there are always so many practical considerations, more than you can readily imagine unless you carry them in your head...."

Don Carlos observed me sadly, his face long.

"I myself am not a free man. I can't decide the same way you would buckle on your sword. I'm in the middle. They're all around me, pushing and pulling. I have to play the spider, the old spider! What a way to live, is it not, van Male? When I fasten a thread here and loosen one there I have to think about the balance of the whole. If I draw in India too close, then Spain and the Low Countries will be endangered. There will be new cause for uprisings of princes and heretics.

"And then for a long time I have thought that perhaps unbeknownst to him the ideas of this Las Casas were strikingly similar to those of that other monk, the monk of Wittenberg. It is my misfortune, you see, to observe all sides. I have had to fight for years with Luther to preserve the unity of the Roman tradition in Europe. These peasant minds will never understand. I have been afraid that my Las Casas would disturb the effectiveness of the Spanish Inquisition, that he would stir up Flanders. For however much truth he speaks, he is a creature of revolt, an iconoclast. He stands on the word of God. That alone is enough to brand him a rebel. But then, he also believes absolutely in bulls and testaments, which Luther does not. That is the difference. He has a kind of balance. Yes, that is it...."

He paused and thought for a time.

"The decision was made in a knightly fashion. I am satisfied now. I am glad that once I could use my own enemies' weapons to hold them in check. I am happy that it happened in the Plaza Mayor, in the presence of the Infante. My son shall be the most Spanish of Spanish kings, it is my hope, free from the Imperial burden. I trust that the pity of Las

Casas and the honor of knighthood both shall live on in the kingdom. . . . And I enjoyed the joust! My God! I was not bad at it myself when I was young!

"And now, Don Pedro, I want you to make known your desires. Something I can do to help you. In this affair of Peru you have done me a great service. Perhaps later I shall ask you to perform greater services. What is it then? Speak up."

"I thank Your Majesty," I said. "I have no wish beyond preserving Your Majesty's trust."

"That's no wish," he said sharply; "that's only the usual polite answer. What is it you want? Something definite."

Something definite? I thought. What can it be he wants me to say? I could decide on nothing. I had land, and more than enough gold to live on. There was something else that I wanted. But this lay beyond his power. Then I made up my mind.

"Come now, what is it?" he persisted.

"I should like . . . if it please Your Majesty . . . I should like to see my Queen again . . . Doña Juana. . . ."

"My mother!" Don Carlos was startled. "What do you mean? My mother is sick. She never sees anyone. She doesn't want to see anyone. How did you happen to think of that?"

"The Queen once gave me a task to perform," I said. "Today it is done, I believe. But that isn't the real reason. I honor Doña Juana. It would be my pleasure to see her again. My own mother died . . . when . . ."

"Yes, yes, of course," the Emperor interrupted. He leaned over the table, and plucked my sleeve. "You can do it, I suppose. You must be reasonable, that's all. You can see her best at evening about sundown. That is the hour when she talks if she talks at all. But if she doesn't want to say anything, I adjure you not to bother her. You can stay only a few minutes. My mother is sick. The smallest disturbance upsets her. Maybe she will recognize you. That would be good for her. . . ."

He thought for a moment. "Perhaps you had better take a young lady with you. She is always quieter when a young woman is there, too. Only don't take a blonde with you. You know . . ." He smiled wryly.

"A young lady?" I asked, taken aback.

"Why not? Surely you must have a dozen. Don't all young men have that many? Why don't you take that girl who gave you the flower? It was very touching, was it not!" The King smiled at van Male, and began to laugh soundlessly.

"Oh yes, the rose," I stammered.

"Isn't she called Doña Isabella de Gómez, or something of the sort?" said Don Carlos. "Why, her father is my corregidor in Cordova. You know that yourself. You have good taste, my son."

Don Carlos reached for a piece of paper and wrote rapidly, strewed it with sand, and folded it with a practiced hand. "Take this," he said. "It's something to make you known in Tordesillas. In a time, perhaps some months—I can't say about that—anyway, I intend, I have my mind set on sending a viceroy to Peru. It isn't enough to have the laws there. Someone will have to enforce them. There must be men there to impress my will on the land. Someone to carry out the plans of the Council for the Indies. I cannot stand these captains much longer. I am fed up with their willfulness. They were necessary. But they have had their day. I don't know whom I will send. I am thinking it over. Maybe Don Pedro de la Gasca. This, of course, is in confidence. I don't know yet. Order in the Indies depends on enforcement of Spanish law. In any case, when I do send a man, I would like you to go with him. You know the land and the people. I trust you."

"I thank Your Majesty for this honor," I said thinly, hardly hearing my own voice. "I shall be glad to do whatever I can. I should be glad to go back. I like the country."

"So much the better, then," he said drily. "So much the better. It will be a work of love, will it not! You are like one of these *caballeros determinados* van Male describes in his book. You can make up your mind. I rather envy you, that is plain enough to see. Everything is so simple when the goal is within sight, as clear as crystal. Just a moment. I forgot something. In a few days the Infante is holding a hunt near Tordesillas. You are invited. Doña Isabella, this young lady I was talking about, will be there. You can arrange with her then to go with you to see my mother."

I took my leave of Don Carlos, thanking him, and carrying away the assurance that soon he would call me again to discuss the matter of going to Peru with the viceroy. Van Male led me down the steps, and then I stood alone in the square. The city of white houses now lay quiet in the heat of midday. It was very still. The water-carrier was still calling in the distance, but far away now, too far to hear his words.

The monks had given up their gardening, and the two of them sat like white statues on the steps of the cloister colonnade.

Behind me the door closed heavily. I heard van Male carefully turning the key in the heavy lock. I stepped out into the blinding light. It was almost as clear, it seemed to my unaccustomed eyes, as the mountains of Tavanta-Suyu. But in the air there was a breath of coolness hidden, a sign of the autumn now closing in.

I had walked a few steps, deep in thought, when I saw a man huddled back in the third or fourth entry away from the house of Don Carlos. Something about him sent a chill up my spine. He had his hat low over his face. He watched me with mingled curiosity and malice. For a moment I thought he must be a spy, perhaps in the pay of France, or of one of the German princes. Was he stationed there to watch all the comings and goings of visitors to the house of Don Carlos? But I saw that if this were true the man was no ordinary spy. His mantle was of the finest material. And his manner, on closer inspection, was not that of a man of such base calling. Perhaps he is a watchman in the pay of the Emperor, perhaps he is a cavalier, I thought, someone whom the marshal of the Court himself has posted to preserve the safety of the King.

Then I heard the man say, "Don Pedro, just a minute. I want to talk to you...."

I stopped at the sound of the voice, half remembering it. The man took off his hat. I saw gray hair, a gray pointed beard, now partly silvered, and brown eyes, lifeless brown eyes. I knew who it was.

"Don Hernando!" I cried out. "Don Hernando Cortés! Am I right? What a pleasure to see you again!" I hastened up to him.

"Not so loud," he warned me. "I don't want to be seen. And much less recognized. I was just standing here . . . you see, there's no telling when I shall be asked for an audience. My enemies, they are working against me! . . ." His handshake was limp, his eyes mistrustful. "You were just in to see the King, weren't you? Did he get my petition? Does he favor my plans?"

"We didn't talk about that," I said.

"You didn't!" He very evidently did not believe me. "Then why were you there? You must have had some reason. You can't deny that . . ."

"Of course I had a reason," I told him, astonished at this abrupt behavior. "We were talking about the new government in Peru!"

"So that's it," he said, and burst out laughing. "So my fine cousins, the Pizarros, are going to get their kick in the ass. Are they going to rob them of their money before Francisco's corpse is cold in the grave? I understand. If any man understands Don Carlos, it is I. He envies all men the smallest title of honor or riches. Now, I suppose, he's preparing to send his own men to Peru, just as he did to Mexico. We have to do the dirty work. And then the lickspittles get the benefit of our risk. He has us by the short hairs, that gouty bastard."

"But Don Carlos is working for the best of everyone concerned," I said, very much nettled.

"That's what you think, my son," said Cortés. "That's where you're whistling into the wind on a very dark night. He is doing what is best for himself! I know him. My kind are now *personae non gratae.* He has treated us in the style of the Italian princes, the way they treat their murderers, you know. And after we have done our part, then out we go, square on our backs. He avoids us as if we were a stench under that nose of his."

"I am surprised to hear you talk this way about the King," I said harshly. "Didn't he give you titles? Didn't you get lands out of it, and mines?"

"But what do I care about lands and mines?" shouted Cortés, forgetting himself. "I am a conquistador, not a money grubber. What has anyone done yet about Cipangu and Cathay? Mexico was just a beginning. He wants me to become a nice tame old soldier, sitting on my land raising hens and counting up the eggs. For the sweet love of God! I am a man of war, not a farmer. Perhaps you don't understand how this Don Carlos is envious of me! He's afraid to have another Alexander the Great on his hands. Somebody who would remove him from the face of the earth simply by spitting in his face. He ruins my plans, he has destroyed my life, he evades me as I if were rotten with the pest. I have to stand here in this hole in the wall like a leper."

"But Don Hernando," I said anxiously, "it isn't quite like that. There are other grounds . . . the Portuguese . . ."

"Oh yes, other grounds," he laughed again. "Did you ever happen to hear, for instance, that he wanted my Aztec jewel for his wife? That I almost had to lay the stone at their feet? And that jewel, my friend, was intended for my own wife, who is just as good, even better, than the Queen herself. For her forebears were kings of Navarre. They, my son, were great when Castile still lay under the Moorish yoke. And my wife should have been a queen in her own right. She should have been Queen of Mexico, queen of a land before which Castile should crawl on hands and knees, a land that I, Don Hernando Cortés, conquered with my will and brain.

"But they have betrayed me. They've cut my throat and smiled at me, the dogs! What will become of my sons? They are fit to sit on a throne. Far more than that narrow-gutted abortion of a Felipe, that piss-pants, that pot full of gall who will rule Spain if he doesn't die—happily for all of us! What did Don Carlos ever do? Tell me! Can you? He inherited his possessions, he married into them, got them through women, the thin-blooded rat. All of it, lands, provinces, castles and the whole miserable list. But one thing he didn't get. That was the blue stone of Montezuma. He didn't get that. It will never hang round the Queen's bony neck. The sea swallowed it up before Tunis. I had to swim ashore with my boy when we foundered, and I lost it. Castile will never get that. Greed or no greed! It's on the bottom of the sea. And there it will lie till Doomsday."

I grew more concerned as the outburst threatened to overbalance Cortés. His eyes were blazing, staring, fastened on his one intolerable grievance. He was a sick man, I could plainly observe.

"Don Hernando," I said, trying to turn the subject, "you have probably forgotten I owe you five hundred florins."

"Five hundred florins!" He was surprised.

"For that pearl," I reminded him. "Don't you remember the pearl? You gave it to me. Don't you remember telling me to get my hair cut and ride a horse instead of an ass?"

"A horse! Yes, I remember. It was when I urged you to join Pizarro."

"And you gave me your son Sandoval's armor. Don't you remember that?"

His eyes filled with tears. "Sandoval? Yes, poor Sandoval. I remember," he said. He turned his face away, ashamed of such quick show of feeling. "I can't forget him, not Sandoval. He died in my arms. He was just coming into his own. The Franciscans buried him under the pines. I remember the wind from the sea, how it sounded in the trees. Pedro, why is it that we all do not die at the right time? Why shouldn't I have been the one instead of him? And now what is left for me but to wade up to my ears in humiliation? How fine it would be, really, to lie in the garden at La Rábida near the sea. Never to plan any more, to know nothing, feel nothing, never to suffer again. Never to feel life again, the endless sotted foolishness."

He looked away, fingering his thoughts. Then he went on to say, "The pearl? Yes, I know. It made you into a conquistador, didn't it? And it brought you plenty of misery, I'll guarantee! But what's the difference? You probably would have succeeded without it, to be honest about it. I've got enough money. What do I want with it all!"

He hesitated, and looked at me closely. "The best things cannot be bought, Pedro. . . . I have enough of it. I'm no merchant. But if you want to pay me back for the pearl . . . I'm really only joking, of course, but . . . you could do me a great service . . ."

"I'll gladly do it," I said, "gladly."

"It's not so easy for me to admit it," he went on, "but there's no doubt that from now on you'll be seeing far more of Don Carlos than I ever shall. You might mention my name. Not too boldly, of course. You needn't put yourself out particularly. Just by chance. You might do it as if you were talking about an old friend. You can be deprecatory. I don't mind that! But don't say anything about my plans. That would put him on his guard. At the bottom I don't completely despise Don Carlos. Not at the bottom, my friend. After all, once he did give me my chance. I can even stand the Infante . . . if I have to. He's pious enough, I suppose. We can let it go at that. Do you think you could do it? What do you say? It would cost you nothing, and might help. . . ."

"I'll certainly do it," I said. "It's small enough thanks for what you have done for me."

"That's kind of you," he said.

"I should like you to come visit me at my home in Cordova," I told him quietly. "We could talk about old times. We might go hunting."

"Yes, later on, later on," he whispered. "Right now I have to stay right here in Valladolid. Every moment is precious. I feel that everything is coming to a head . . . maybe today . . . tomorrow . . . soon. Don't be offended. I've already talked with van Male. . . ." He looked uneasily in the direction of the King's house, as if he expected a sign, a wave of a handkerchief, or something equally cabalistic, to summon him into the quiet place.

I now left, feeling that he was glad to be rid of me. At the other end of the square I looked over my shoulder. He had wrapped himself closer in his mantle, this hero of my youth, and was still looking carefully up at the windows of the house where the King was safely immured from his eyes.

The Infante's hunting party took place on a fine autumn day, one of the last good days of the year. The smell of ripe fruit, the aromatic smell of much ripeness was in the air. The morning was cool. The dew glistened on the bright leaves, yellow and red, and the gauzy mist webs hung from bough to bough. A fall haze hung over the woods and fields. Already in the vineyards hundreds of hands were busy plucking the swollen bunches of grapes hanging voluptuously like great purple breasts under the cool leaves.

The Infante was greeted with gay shouts as he rode up to take his place at the head of a procession of knights and ladies. Many a greeting was shouted at us, and many a peasant maid leaving the grapes strained up on her toes to see the wonderful people from the other world. I wondered what these broad-hipped lasses thought of the thin heir to the Crown of Castile as he bounced along on his sorrel, smiling painfully and inclining his head in acknowledgement of the plaudits.

We met heavy, creaking, two-wheeled wagons on the white highway. Their unequal wheels tipped and sagged under the rich burden of grapes. Many a rider dipped into the pile and took a bunch to cool his mouth with the sweet juice, chill yet with the morning. Old peasant wives marched steadily along, the huge baskets of grapes poised on their heads, or slung over their shoulders on a yoke. They stood with downcast eyes, murmuring blessings for Doña Juana's grandson, the pride of Castile. He would reach now and then into a pouch of silver coins and drop one or two into the horny, brown palms lifted up to him, all trembling with eagerness and age and unaccountable pleasure.

"God bless you, little one," the peasant women screamed at the Infante. "God keep you ever from harm." If he had not been up on a horse they would have surrounded him and smothered him with kisses. There was a crowd in every little village out to greet us—children, dogs and goats all bunched together, staring round-eyed. I thought how once I had been in just such a crowd, how dirty my legs had been, and how stained my mouth with the juice of the grape. Except that I had never seen the Infante of Spain ride by!

There were young men and women in the village squares, round-faced, with powerful legs pressing the grapes in the wooden tubs. The women had their skirts tied high around their waists, and when they bent over we could see their white thighs and buttocks. They sang as they danced on the mash, their faces hot and streaming sweat, as if they were singing a song to Pan, praising the fruitfulness of the earth. There was great excitement. Their legs were spattered purple with the juice, like blood.

"A good wine year!" the Infante called to them.

And the young men, pausing at their work, shouted back, "A good hunt to you, Don Felipe!"

The peasant girls tittered loudly, dropped their eyes, looked again, and shouted, "A good time in bed to you, Don Felipe!"

We all laughed at this, though some of the ladies pretended to look displeased, while others laughed overmuch. But the Infante turned readily in his saddle and shrieked at the girls, "The same to you, my sweets, and many of them!"

We left the villages behind us. The road grew lonely, and the wood shut us in. Over us, against the blue sky, was the heavy tracery of the oak trees. The air was sweet with the smell of sunburned heath, of pine and of the fall of the year. In a woodland meadow the hunting party set up its headquarters. Like magic a brilliantly colored tent was pitched, and into this the ladies disappeared to dress themselves for the hunt. At a great table pewter mugs of wine were passed around. The men drank greedily, athirst from the long ride. They told rough jokes and dirty stories, which might not have sounded fitting in a house, but here in the woods seemed appropriate enough.

"When a man goes on the hunt," said the Duke of Béjar, "it's just the same as making love. After it's all over with it's hard to understand what made it seem so stirring at the time. At the moment it's the wish of all wishes. Then an hour later—what is it? A dead deer or just another woman like all the rest!"

Everybody thought this very much to the point and laughed. A haggard man, putting down his mug and wiping his mouth, said, "And the hunt has another relation with love."

"How is that?" everyone asked.

"Well," the haggard man said, "it's like this. In the hunt, there isn't much point in all the rushing around and getting covered with sweat.

All a man does is to get heated up. Then he catches a cold. On the other hand, a cool-nerved poacher with his gin is the one who bags the game. It's the same way with a woman. Why get all excited? By the time you have her in your arms, you are so weary and bored that it's about like tupping a sack of meal."

"To the first arrow!" cried the Infante, in the best of humor. "To the first arrow from Saint Hubert's quiver, and to Love's first arrow!"

"To the first arrow!" they all echoed, and drank.

By this time the women were coming out of the tent, their faces freshened, pretty in their green hunting costumes. I saw Doña Isabella. She looked like Artemis, very tall, slender and cool as the woods themselves.

The hounds were tugging at their leashes. They rolled belly up on the greensward, delighted to be out of doors and ready for the chase on such a fine day. Their tongues were hanging out with joy, and they lapped every face for yards around that they could find to lap. Then the horns were blown, to assemble us for the chase. I held back, my crossbow dangling from my shoulder.

"Master," my page Manuel inquired, "aren't you going along with the rest of them?"

"Go along with the Infante," I said. "You'll have a chance to see how a king hunts."

"I'd like to," said Manuel.

"Go on, go on, get out," I said impatiently, for I had business on my mind that brooked no interference, however well meant.

"And you?"

"Sweet Holy Virgin Mary Mild, get out," I said sharply. "Don't bother your head about me. Don't worry at all. If I'm not in on the kill, that will be all right. I think I'll take a ride around. Go on, now."

He turned and wandered off, moving faster and faster. I could hear him crashing through the bushes.

I was alone. I could hear a woodpecker hammering away, and that was all. Good God, I thought, the bird might be perched on my shoulder, the ill-mannered beast, and laughed at the thought. The drumming stopped. And then the sound began again, mocking me, and my loneliness bore in upon me, and I was desolately sure in that moment that it would never be assuaged.

All the beauty of the forest around me made my pulsing pain the keener. How full of golden color was the weft of life, how subtle the weaver! Through the boughs came the yellow light of the sun, dancing like a million gnats, elfin gay. There were the dark lacy ferns in the low coolness, in the shadows the toadstools so cold and bizarrely fashioned, the yellow tears oozing from the pines. The tall, sharp grasses waved in the open dell, and over them moths fluttered, uncertain, fearful of the evening chill. The hares, startled by my wandering, hopped away crazily, fragile yet eager things, turning their white rumps to me, not knowing how easy it would be for me to strike them down. Over all this was an endless pale blue autumn sky. And I beneath—a man. A man with sinews any knife could slice through, with soft blue veins ready to gush to any blade tip, with a heart already set bleeding by the hand of a girl.

I raised my face to the flaky sunbeams and groaned aloud, like a mourning hound. For I knew that I should never find her. She despised me still; she would avoid me, flee from me. What stupidity, what softness had led me out here roaming, hopeful as a schoolboy? I might as well have gone with the others.

I was standing beside a little brook. There was a plashing, a silvery tinkling and murmuring that half drugged the senses, and I listened, praying that it would wholly drug mine. Above there were rough red pine branches, all jags and masses of small dark spears. The earth was covered with the springy needles and pine cones. In the brook there were gray stones, and at the edge of these purled the water, now liquid green, now silver and black.

The shrill, raucous voice of a jay reawoke me to my unhappiness. Loudly complaining, he hopped from limb to limb. I started off heavily over the carpet of packed needles, making my way unheeding through the trees. I lowered my head to pass under a bough that barred my way. And then I saw her, as I stooped low. She stood and looked at me, a wood sprite in her green costume. She began to run. Not away from me, but toward me! I ran too, and we went violently into each other's arms. I covered her face with kisses, and her lips were warm with the sun and her racing blood, and tasted of the aromatic ferns.

"It's you . . . it's you . . ." she gasped. "Oh, Pedro, I knew that I should find you!"

"I've found you in the woods," I said, and repeated this many times, like a fool.

"I've wanted you—I came looking for you. . . ."

"Don't cry," I said, "don't cry," and wondered whether I were admonishing her or myself.

"Oh, Pedro, you haven't changed, have you?"

"No! No! I love you, my little heart. I always have. Ever since the first night we met."

She laughed softly, tearfully. "In the Court of the Oranges. It was summer. I had red shoes on. Oh, I loved you then, too."

"Darling red shoes," I said deliriously; and clamped my lips hard over hers. She strained her lithe body back to look at me again.

"Oh, Pedro, *swear* it, swear you love me! Because you did hate me then."

"Then?" I mumbled.

"When you came back from the Indies. When I was so horrible to you. Oh, but if you'd only known . . . my terrible dreams. You, you my sweet and gentle Pedro . . . with poor Indians hanging dead on your sword. . . ."

I sank my head down against the tender bones of her shoulder.

"It's all true. How can you forgive me now?"

"Because I know now. I knew, I knew myself, even before Master Agrippa wrote me."

"Master Agrippa?" I jerked my head up in surprise.

"He wrote to tell me how you were suffering. How muddled you were. How your very soul was in torment on earth, and how you wanted to make amends now and help the Indians to be free."

"It's true, Isabella. I do."

"Then you will. You have helped; you helped Father Bartolomé plead for them before Don Carlos, and you'll go back to Peru some day and work to bring the poor creatures peace."

"I am going back, Isabella," I told her, "Don Carlos is sending me along with the viceroy as soon as one is chosen."

The jay was screaming at us furiously. A pine needle floated down on a sun shaft and lay on Isabella's dark hair, a tiny sliver of light. "I'll go with you," she whispered.

"Of course!" I cried, for now it seemed that it could never have been any other way. All this had been settled the day she had worn the red shoes. "We'll sail very soon. But first, first we must go together to see the Queen. Today. Right now."

"The Queen?" she echoed, astonished.

"Yes, poor Doña Juana, our Queen Mother. I have an appointment already made, and now you must come too."

She snuggled against me, half fretting. "But she's so strange, poor thing. She lives in such a dark house..."

"It will grow sunlit with you there."

Her mouth brushed my neck, my chest, sweetly hungry. "I'll go with you, Pedro darling. Because from now on I'm always going wherever you go."

But there was still something of which I had to make sure. Half fearfully I fumbled in my pouch and drew forth the golden ear of corn. I could feel the blood course to my temples as I held out to the girl I loved that gleaming symbol of my hateful conquest.

"Isabella . . . I always meant this for you," I told her.

She stared at it in a sort of bemused wonderment. Then she reached for it slowly and gazed at it, lying in her little moist palm, for what seemed to me an eon during which the rest of my life hung by a thread as fine as her silken hair. Her hand lifted then and she kissed that golden ear and turned her eyes up to mine, luminous with understanding. Her lips awaited mine, and to mine they were still cold from their last strange kiss, but they warmed quickly with the surge of our young blood.

Presently we walked back to the tent, our arms still tight around each other, and parted reluctantly to get on our horses. Knees touching, we rode along slowly between the pines, toward Tordesillas. Sometimes we talked happily, sometimes we jogged in silence, snugly warm and close in our thoughts, and it seemed I could not take my eyes from the beloved and lovely face at my side. The shadows glided over her cheeks, and every now and then I would lean and kiss her, as gently and carefully as I could, forcing myself to draw away lest my roughness should hurt her. She seemed disappointed and impatient each time I drew away. The afternoon sun, as it sank, turned red and the woods were drenched in its fiery glow.

"It goes crimson like that into the river Rimac," I said.

"Rimac? How odd that sounds, darling, that funny name. And yet it's rather pleasant too, isn't it? Nicer than the Guadalquivir."

"Juan the thin is waiting there for me. And his brother Alonso will come over from San Miguel. They're the ones who really brought us together, you know, in the square, in the miracle play."

"The actors? The poor fellow and the splendid one? Of course I remember them."

"And Frenero and Bernal will come."

"I'm afraid of them," she said, "but I'll like them because you do."

"And Diego de Vargas."

"The poet!"

"And Sobeya."

"Is she coming? Oh, I don't like that a bit."

"You don't? Why not?"

"I suspect she's beautiful."

"She has dark eyes like yours."

"Does she love you?"

"Of course not. She loves Diego. She's more like my sister and she'll be yours too."

We rode along, both lost in our warm thoughts, or so I believed until Isabella gave a great fierce sigh.

"Oh, I hate it," she said. "I just hate it."

"Hate what?" I demanded in amazement.

"That there should be so many other women in the world. Even in Peru. On the Rimac, even."

I blinked and then chuckled at her. "You're foolish."

"Am I?" She was looking at me in a quizzical way. "Do you remember when I hit you with a stone, when I stamped on your toes and bit your mouth? You were certainly very foolish then. You didn't know how to treat me. And you still don't. You're still foolish. Foolish as a soft-brain. Oh yes, I mean it. You don't know how to act at all to a woman who's crazy about you. Do I have to tell you? You should treat me like a hussy. Yes, a hussy! For all women have hussies' hearts. Didn't you know?"

"Don't talk like that," I said, flushing. But I could feel my blood pulsing faster. She stared at me, and I felt the redly sunlit woods engulf me, and what took place in that moment in our locked gazes I shall never be able to recount.

But I saw the blood drain from her face and then rush back again, flooding into her black hair. "The conqueror!" she called wildly in a strange, rich voice, and gave her horse the spur.

We arrived at the Alcazar and made known our purpose. I drew forth the letter Don Carlos had given me. A guard led us into a room with a high vaulted ceiling, very white. He told us to sit down on the stone bench. Without a word we did as we were told. The room was cold. Somewhere we could hear the quiet drip of water, water that no doubt had gathered on a damp wall.

The guard returned and now led us through a long, round-ceilinged corridor, upstairs and down. At last we found ourselves on a wide balcony that gave out on the river. I recognized it as the balcony on which I had first seen the Queen, years ago.

The Queen sat on a chair with a carved backrest. She was dressed in black. Under the seam of her long dress the tips of her shoes peeped forth. Her hair was snow-white, and she held her delicate head slightly drooping, as if she were dreaming. The slender white hands rested lightly on the arms of the chair.

Some older men and women stood behind her, also dressed in black. Their dress was of old-fashioned cut, of the time of the great Queen Doña Isabella. The ladies wore pointed mantillas and in their hands the men held black birettas.

"Don Pedro de Cordova, Your Majesty," said the guard, "and Doña Isabella de Gómez, with a letter of introduction from His Majesty the King."

She made a slight movement of her hand as we advanced within five paces of the chair and bent down on our right knees. She appeared not to notice us. For a long time all was silence. The men and women stood stiffly, and we kneeled like painted supplicants before an image.

"What is it you have in your hand, my daughter?" the Queen asked suddenly, breaking the difficult silence. Her voice was as pure as a church bell, and the dark eyes in the old face were passionately alive and youthful, like a sixteen-year-old girl's.

"That is an ear of corn, Your Majesty," said Isabella. "It is a golden ear of corn."

"Where did you find it?" the Queen asked, bending forward to inspect it.

"It comes from India, Your Majesty," said Isabella.

"From India!" the Queen said. Her slender body stiffened. "Are there such things . . . in India?"

"It was in the Temple of the Sun, Your Majesty."

"The Sun? Of course. Ears of corn do need the sun, don't they? And the earth and rain. How big the sun must be in India. Give me the thing, my daughter."

Isabella moved closer, hesitating, and handed the ear of corn to the Queen. The last rays of the sun streamed into the balcony and sparkled on the fine kernels.

"How lovely it is!" said the Quen, "How it shines! What wonderful kernels! What is it, though, what is it? I see all sorts of pictures. Every kernel is like a mirror. I see mountains towering on mountains. Still, white heights. Endless blue skies. I see the white foam of the waves breaking on the gray cliffs, rising up in great billows. And endless fields, fields of corn. The land! The land! That is the new Earth, promised by God. It is the new Heaven, which arches over it. The giant double island in the sea! I can see the Indians with their feathered crowns, just as they stood before my forebears' throne. I see men in harness, monks, peasants, a confusion of people. But what is that? . . ."

The Queen put her white hand against her cheek.

"There are great bridges over the rivers, cities are growing towers like white pyramids. I see fields, meadows, orchards where once there was dark forest, where the savannas stretched as far as the eye can range. What a hammering of iron and stone! What a crush of caravels in the harbors! . . . or am I dreaming?"

The Queen's eyes were dilated with wonder at her own wild fancies, as if she were looking over the land as darkness crept out of the mountain clefts, the swamps, the forests.

"Holy Virgin Mary, protect the coming generations, the grandchildren and the great-grandchildren as you have done in my day! . . ."

The Queen folded her hands over the golden ear of corn.

"Protect them when I am no longer here in Tordesillas. Let them not forsake you, even when fate calls, as it has in my day."

The white hands sank. She kept the ear of corn folded between them, and bent down her head with the white hair. Her narrow shoulders shook softly. The oldish, black-gowned men and women became uncomfortable and whispered to each other behind their hands. One of the men walked up to me soundlessly on the tips of his toes, and said, "The Queen is tired."

"Yes," said the Queen. "I am tired. I am very, very tired." But her voice betrayed no fatigue. It was clear as crystal, as it always had been. The whites of her eyes shimmered in the twilight like mother-of-pearl.

"Come nearer to me," she said; "come nearer, for it's getting dark already."

We kneeled down before her.

"Is that your wife, son of the Admiral?" asked the Queen.

"Yes," I said.

"Is that your man, my daughter?"

"That is my man."

"And the ear of corn," whispered the Queen, so that nobody but we two could hear her, "the golden ear belongs to both of you. Here, take it back and take good care of it. Keep it in your house. Show it to your children. I love both of you very much. But go now. . . . For the night is coming. And the night is mine."

Doña Juana stretched out her right hand. Isabella kissed it. Then I pressed my lips to the slender fingers. I could feel with my lips the cool ring on the Queen's middle finger, the two engraved lions, the lions rampant of Castile.

We stood hand in hand before the Alcazar. The heavy door crashed softly to behind us, gently creaking. We said nothing. The bats swooped over our heads, gray thin shadows. On the horizon there was a glow of reflected light from the sun that had set some time ago. High up in the sky was Hesperus. Lights began to appear in the windows, to slant out.

Children were still playing at the river edge, the last play before going to bed. A candle was being passed around the circle, from hand to hand. I knew the game. In the middle there was a blindfolded child. It was his task to find the candle.

The children's shrill voices came to us through the clear air, out of the cool wave of the night. There was laughter, shouted childish happiness. Then they became earnest, lost in the play. There was a lilting question, and a gay answer.

Is the little light here?
No, it's there, over there.
Is the little light here?
Might be there, anywhere.

Have you got the light?
Just think a bit faster!
Come tell, where's the light!

And then all joined in chorus, shouting in singsong:

It's in God, in the Master!

THE END